The Geoffrey Hartman Reader

The Geoffrey Hartman Reader

Edited by

GEOFFREY HARTMAN AND DANIEL T. O'HARA

Edinburgh University Press

© Geoffrey Hartman (extracts/readings), 2004
© Geoffrey Hartman and Daniel T. O'Hara (editorial selection and arrangement), 2004
© Daniel T. O'Hara (Introduction), 2004

Edinburgh University Press Ltd
22 George Square, Edinburgh

Typeset in Bembo
by Hewer Text Ltd, Edinburgh, and
printed and bound in Great Britain by
The Cromwell Press, Trowbridge, Wilts

A CIP record for this book is available from the British Library

ISBN 0 7486 2016 8 (hardback)
ISBN 0 7486 2017 6 (paperback)

The right of Geoffrey Hartman
to be identified as author of this work
has been asserted in accordance with
the Copyright, Designs and Patents Act 1988.

Contents

Authors' Acknowledgments

Geoffrey Hartman wishes to thank Daniel Feldman for his assistance, and unfailing courtesy working under pressure. Patricia Dallai of Yale's Koerner Center gave benevolent advice on technical matters. Jackie Jones, who suggested this volume, has been a steady help. Daniel O'Hara also wishes to thank Gina Masucci MacKenzie, his research assistant, student, and friend, with whom he had invaluable discussions about the issues raised by Geoffrey Hartman's work.

Publisher's Acknowledgments

Grateful acknowledgment is made to the following sources for permission to reproduce material previously published elsewhere. Every effort has been made to trace the copyright holders, but if any have been inadvertently overlooked, the publisher will be pleased to make the necessary arrangements at the first opportunity.

Eleanor Cook (ed.), *Centre and Labyrinth: Essays in Honour of Northrop Frye* (Toronto: University of Toronto Press, 1983), pp. 213–22, 225–26. Reprinted with permission.

Geoffrey Hartman, *The Longest Shadow: In the Aftermath of the Holocaust* (New York: Palgrave, 2002), pp. 82–116, 125–8. © Geoffrey Hartman. Reprinted with permission of Palgrave Macmillan.

Geoffrey Hartman, *Scars of the Spirit: The Struggle against Inauthenticity*, (New York: Palgrave, 2002), pp. 67–84, 119–35. © Geoffrey Hartman. Reprinted with permission of Palgrave Macmillan.

Geoffrey Hartman, *The Unremarkable Wordsworth* (Minnesota: University of Minnesota Press, 1987), pp. 129–52. © 1987 by the University of Minnesota.

Geoffrey Hartman, *Criticism in the Wilderness: The Study of Literature Today* (Yale: Yale University Press, 1980, 1982), pp. 42–52, 95–101, 115–33, 199–204, 284–7. © 1980 by Yale University.

Geoffrey Hartman, 'Midrash as Law and Literature', *Journal of Religion*, 1994. 1994 by The University of Chicago. All rights reserved.

Reprinted by permission of the publishers from *Minor Prophecies: The Literary Essay in the Culture Wars* by Geoffrey Hartman, Cambridge, MA: Harvard University Press, © 1991 by Geoffrey Hartman. All rights reserved.

© 1989 from *The Future of Literary Theory* edited by Ralph Cohen, pp. 86–95. Reproduced by permission of Routledge/Taylor & Francis Books, Inc.

Geoffrey H. Hartman, *Saving the Text: Literature, Derrida, Philosophy*, pp. 100–9, 111–17, 123–38. © 1981 Geoffrey Hartman. Reprinted with permission of The Johns Hopkins University Press.

Geoffrey Hartman, *The Fateful Question of Culture* (Columbia: Columbia University Press, 1997), pp. 26–42 and 67–99. © Columbia University Press, 1997.

Geoffrey Hartman, *Easy Pieces* (Columbia: Columbia University Press, 1986), pp. 126–31 and 137–54. © Columbia University Press.

The first page of *Glas* (Paris: Galilé, 1974) is reproduced with the kind permission of Jacques Derrida.

Note on the Text

Typos and infelicitous phrasing in the original articles have been quietly corrected. Occasional words or redundancies, up to a sentence, have been left out. Any large omission is indicated by the conventional omission signs. In all other respects the essays or notes have not been altered or updated.

The Culture of Vision
Daniel T. O'Hara

Geoffrey Hartman published *The Unmediated Vision*, his first book, in 1954. It was and remains a prescient text. Through a series of studies of modern poetry, it argues that the dream of avant garde writers from the Romantics to Valéry and beyond has been to create a literary language in which the mind and its object coincide without mediation of any kind. The rejection of mediation, for the radical modernist, is a challenge to face realities without prejudice or the armature of tradition. (See 'The New Perseus' in this collection). As Hegel, however, demonstrated in a famous passage in *The Phenomenology of Spirit* (1807), any use of language, no matter how original and imaginative, involves an inescapable temporal mediation. Belatedness defines the human condition.

When I say the word 'now' to designate the present moment, for example, the moment intended by my designation is already gone. No amount of creative invention of the human mind can overcome such in-built temporal mediation. The object any word of mine may intend is already fleeing into the past and so is not the same object I originally intended. Not only has it changed, but so, perhaps, have I. The paradoxes and puzzlements of quantum physics have now made Hegel's point a commonplace of popularizations of modern science. And doubtless both Zeno and Heraclitus are somewhere smiling at this ironic development.

The drive for unmediated vision and its consequent inevitable failures may be said to define (or at least circumscribe roughly) what we mean by 'modernity.' From Descartes's (and later philosophy's) attempt to reach an Archimedean point resistant to the most corrosive doubt ('I think, I represent, I will, I desire . . . therefore I am'), to the political, social, and religious projects that aim at breaking definitively with the past and with human temporality so as to begin absolutely anew, *ab ovo*, no matter at what cost in material, cultural, and human destruction: all these projects disclose the drive to achieve unmediated vision. This vision would be a point of origin from which we could begin, as it were, the cosmos over again and so make it possible to resituate the condition of the clean slate, a pure innocence distributed equally to all. 'All God's children got wings!'

Although Hartman's book dealt with European literature, America, surely, is still the Protestant sanctuary of this dream of exceptional innocence. As Nietzsche and Freud in their different ways have analyzed, the consciously modern resents its inherent belatedness and runs the risk of destroying the present in the interests of a future which would restore the situation of being as if at the creation. The global reach of the American empire, with its mythic status as the Virgin Land, offers another testimony of this utopian illusion. 'Romanticism and Anti-Self-Consciousness,' in Hartman's *Reader*, though not an analysis of political adventures, describes how the literary imagination tries to overcome corrosive doubt and self-critical impasse, drawing a new immediacy of conviction and feeling out of the increasing and competing mediations, choices, alternatives, of contemporary life.

In short, Hartman in his first book intuited the essence of modernity, and identified it correctly with romanticism, which is the culture of modernity par excellence: the culture of secular vision.

Wordsworth's Poetry, 1787–1814 (1964) is Hartman's next major work. (A book on André Malraux, an interesting, brief study on a once important modern figure, is written during the years intervening and published in 1960). *Wordsworth's Poetry* is the last of the four major achievements in literary study of the immediate post-war period, the other three being Erich Auerbach's *Mimesis* (1946; 1953 in English translation), M. H. Abram's *The Mirror and the Lamp* (1954), and Northrop Frye's *Anatomy of Criticism* (1957). It is not until the boom time of high theory in the 1970s that literary study will again produce such ambitious, exciting, and well-executed texts.

The argument of Hartman's study, to which the excerpt 'Wordworth's Magic Mountains' cannot do full justice, defines the already distinctively modern dilemma of romantic poet or artist. Wordsworth is representative of those swept up by 'the spirit of the age' – the French Revolution. He is captured by the vision of natural man freed of the sophisticated and mal-forming constraints of traditional society. The excesses of such revolutionary liberation, as well as Britain's 'betrayal' of its own ideal of liberty, eventually appall Wordsworth and make him give up moral questions in despair, his imagination rudderless in the intense inane of bloody abstractions derived from Rousseau, Godwin, and other Enlightenment philosophers.

What to do with a self-consciousness roused to apocalyptic pitch is the question that Wordsworth, as Hartman reads him, wrestles with in his greatest poetry. (Although the political turmoil, and fears about a run-away Industrial Revolution, do this to Wordsworth, he is also wary of other forms of enthusiasm, new or old.) His response is to rebind the imagination to nature (the nonhuman environment) in a reciprocal relationship of love and respect, and to envisage a new *translatio*, the transmission of that ethos into an era of city life and industrialization.

Wordsworth literally becomes the priest as well as prophet of Nature. The English countryside is experienced as a dynamic influence, fostering the soul that loves her aspects of beauty but also, when necessary, of fear, even terror.

The 'spots of time' episodes from *The Prelude* trace this education of the would-be self-sufficient and apocalyptic spirit, in which Nature's both gentle and fearful guardianship disciplines the mind to recognize its own often wild and unconscious role in what it experiences. In Wordsworth's developmental scheme, Nature, like a permissive mother, allows the child and the man to err, so that he may later learn the limits of his mind: the limits both of the integrity of the objects resisting him and of the blind and empty strength of that mind itself. It is as if Milton's Eve, as first seen by Satan – so startling to him and so all-absorbing that he almost relents of his resentful plan – has been transformed by Wordsworth into his Nature-Muse-Mother. 'Romance and Modernity: Keats's "Ode to Psyche" ' also addresses such belated myth-making, together with the startling lushness, even womanliness (as perceived by his contemporaries) of that poet's style compared to Wordsworth's.

Wordsworth's Poetry marked the completion of a critical redefinition of romanticism and its relevance for the modern temper against the background of T. S. Eliot's apparently tough-minded poetic strictures and such tracts as Cleanth Brooks's *Modern Poetry and the Tradition* (1939), which in effect elided the great Romantics in its claim for seventeenth-century continuities. The studies of romanticism and modernity that followed – by Harold Bloom and Paul de Man, to cite just two major examples – conform to the scope and substance of the argument of Hartman's magisterial study. Of course, neither Bloom nor de Man chose to follow Hartman in his espousal of the Wordsworthian *Bildung*. (As we know, they chose a darker, antithetical, even what to some appears as antinomian perspective.) Many others, however, do follow Hartman's Wordsworthian vision, to one degree or other; and Hartman himself, in his later works, on the damage to human hope inflicted by the Holocaust, or what the title of his 1997 book calls 'the fateful question of culture,' follows his own lead. (See in this *Reader* 'The Question of Our Speech.') For him, the Wordsworthian vision of Nature's role in the growth of the mind authorizes a liberal sense of culture anticipating Arnold and Freud, and later the unforgettably destroyed German-Jewish intellectuals and their people, of which Hartman speaks so eloquently in his introduction to this *Reader* ('Life and Learning'), and with whom he might have perished too if not for good fortune. Though the largest number of the victims were Jews from Eastern Europe, whose culture was quite different, the intensity of their learning tradition was similar. 'Midrash as Law and Literature,' reprinted here, is Hartman's effort as a contemporary Jewish intellectual to value their kind of fidelity to Scripture, their older and venerable 'saving of the text.'

Beyond Formalism (1970), *The Fate of Reading* (1975), and *Akiba's Children* (a 1978 collection of poetry) mark a transition in Hartman's career. Something is being said good-bye to in them, and what is being hailed as coming is uncertain and disconcerting. The poetry volume clearly says good-bye to Hartman's aspiration to be a poet, yet not to an ambition that would convert criticism into a more creative act, and to bring the intensity of the religious commentary tradition back into play. The many reviews on contemporary poets he wrote during the late fifties and the sixties (unfortunately not represented here) were attempts to circumscribe Hartman's own contemporary poetics, and the poems in *Akiba's Children* are artful but rather tentative results of experimenting with a higher style, derived from romanticism but also leaning on biblical and midrashic sources. 'Purification and Danger in American Poetry,' from his later *Criticism in the Wilderness* (1980), is exemplary in capturing the heroic form of unmediated vision taken by American poetry from Emily Dickinson on, as it seeks its independence despite the burden of tradition.

Beyond Formalism highlights the change in Hartman's work and in the profession of literary study at the time. Hartman's argument is that despite all attempts to go beyond it, formalism of some kind will always be with us. The political and revolutionary pressures of the period, as well as the exhaustion of the New Critical model of reading, opened the American academy both to calls for more relevant criticism and teaching and to more systematic theoretical engagements with literature as a social institution.

Hartman's point in these essays, however, was not just negative and reactive. It was the plea for an enlarged criticism that would include theory and social relevance, without throwing out the lessons of early philological and critical achievements. 'Ghostlier Demarcations: The Sweet Science of Northrop Frye' (not included here) is the central essay of the theory section of *Beyond Formalism*. Once again, the essay serves as a cautionary tale, but never harsh nor severe. The first piece in that collection, moreover, 'Structuralism: The Anglo-American Adventure,' suggests that Frye's work represents a mode of 'Structuralism' *avant la lettre*, an Anglo-American or home-made brand. Here is Hartman's summary judgment of Frye's legacy:

> I recall ruefully Aristotle's remark that unity of plot does not consist in unity of the hero. The plot was criticism; the hero, Frye – and in case my reflections have been too picaresque, I would like to end with a firm and even didactic estimate of Frye's importance to contemporary criticism. The more we read in him the more we understand how essential the romance tradition is, both in itself and in its modern afterlife. Poetry is inconceivable without it; even Shakespearean drama and the vast majority of novels conform to a romance poetics, or are significantly clarified by it. Frye's permanent achievement is as a theorist whose recognitions favor romance rather than tragedy; had he no more than rescued for us the spiritual form of William Blake and then the spiritual form of romance, it would have been sufficient. (*BF*, 39–40)[*]

Frye's achievement, despite his synoptic and encyclopedic intention, is limited, provincial even. It is in the confrontation with tragedy and with the terror beyond tragedy that we see this. While Frye honors the Romantics and moves beyond formalism in challenging with his romance-based theory narrow aesthetic notions of the unity of individual works of art, he swerves toward recapturing that unity by a totalizing conception of the world of art itself.

Like Structuralism, then, Frye's work reifies a system, in his case 'the verbal universe,' with its hierarchy of elements (from the level of the letter to that of the comprehensive vision of biblical poet or cosmic philosopher). In any particular literary instance, the system in the guise of one or more of its elements, may fleetingly appear and then has to be retrospectively constructed as a totality from this instance and many other recollected and analogized ones. Structuralism, before or after the letter, Anglo-American or French, is thus potentially the totalizing revenge of the belated mind in relation to a universe, verbal or otherwise, that perpetually escapes its conceptual and experiential grasp. The theoretical equivalent of political totalitarianism is certainly too harsh a judgment on structuralist tendencies, but the gaps between these equally radical responses to the modern dilemmas of human temporality are as uncomfortably within range of each other as 'Radical Art and Radical Analysis' and 'The Sacred Jungle,' excerpts from Hartman's *Criticism in the Wilderness*, intimate. In some of these pages Kenneth Burke helps to counterpoint Frye.

The Fate of Reading (1976), Hartman's next collection, anticipates *Criticism in the Wilderness* in which he calls for a more creative view of the critical act, indeed in which he suggests that criticism could become Matthew Arnold's modern literature of imaginative reason. A courageous collection of essays, *The Fate of Reading* attempts to develop a capacious and flexible poetics that would avoid the pitfalls of Frye and Structuralism, even as it serves a synoptic and systematic intention. (See 'Christopher Smart's "Magnificat".') The strategy Hartman follows is to emphasize that critics have their own style, which at best is integral to their vision. Hartman then performs a difficult balancing act in terms of his own critical performance. By taking the essay in its original sense as a trial run, by using aphorism and epigram, by deliberately and ironically playing with critical modes, he hoped to offer an entire vision but preserve it from the temptations of totality. (The later essays, 'Literary Commentary as Literature' and 'The Critical Essay between Theory and Tradition,' develop these insights.)

By opening the critical canon to the works of popular culture in 'Literature High and Low: The Case of the Mystery Story' and 'Hitchcock's North by Northwest,' both included in the collection of 1976, Hartman would also keep the totality permeable and open, flexible and non-coercive. Although receiving harsh criticism at the time, *The Fate of Reading*, even more than *Beyond Formalism*, is a major theoretical accomplishment and an example we could still learn from today. 'Evening Star and Evening Land' is an excellent place to start.

As I have commented at length elsewhere on *Criticism in the Wilderness* (1980) and *Saving the Text* (1981), I won't reproduce those arguments here. I will comment, however, on the general project of 'psychoaesthetics' announced in

The Fate of Reading and developed further in these books, especially in Hartman's readings of Shakespeare and Smart. (That project of 'psychoaesthethics' is also memorably expressed in *Saving the Text*'s 'Words and Wounds,' about which more in a moment.)

For Hartman, the Wordsworthian faith in the power of poetry remains paramount despite Freud or Lacan's psychoanalytic pessimism about the discontents of civilization or the perverse jouissance of the death drive. 'Psychoaesthetics' is the name Hartman gives to this Wordsworthian and indeed Romantic project, a project he sees more generally operative in human culture. To put it in the terms of our initial formulation, then, the only mode of mediation that could be satisfying, that could soothe the savage beast of belated resentment and the urge for unmediated vision, is that of poetry or art itself, the main secular source of the drive's inspiration, paradoxically enough. Although first collected in *Easy Pieces* (1985), 'The Interpreter's Freud,' a beautifully realized essay that uses Wordsworth to illuminate Freud, as well as the other, more usual way around, best captures the spirit of Hartman's position on psychoaesthetics.

A 'kakangelic' Freud, according to Hartman, demystifies all ecstatic emotions, all unrealistic, self-deceiving dreams, in his attempts to heal our soul-sicknesses. Hartman, however, interpreting Wordsworth, argues as follows:

> In all his most interesting work, [Wordsworth] describes a developmental impasse centering on eudemonic sensations experienced in early childhood and associated with nature. Whether beautiful or frightening, they sustain and nourish him as intimations of immortality; and . . . he shows the strength and usurpation of those ecstatic memories as they threaten the maturing poet who must respect their drive. If there is a death wish in the . . . poems, it is insinuated by nature itself and asks lover or growing child not to give up earlier yearnings – to die rather than become an ordinary mortal. (*ACJ*, 219)

What Freud shies from as pathology, namely the 'oceanic feeling' in its many dreamy but also seductive political modalities, Hartman respects as an 'ordinary and incurable' emotion that must find through literary language its nuanced expression. 'The dream peculiar to Freud, as interpreter and scientist, a dream which survives all self-analysis, is of a purified language that remains uncontaminated by its materials, that neither fulfills nor represses an all-too-human truth' (*ACJ*, 222). Hartman's psychoaesthetics submits such a dream itself – and, indeed, every 'purity perplex' – to demystification by accepting the romantic literary vision of the curative, but not ultimately curing, power of 'messy' artistic mediation. Some of Hartman's recent thoughts on Goethe, as we shall see, revisit these views.

The role French theory plays in Hartman's career lies precisely in this post-structuralist point about there not being any meta-level uncontaminated by the particulars. ('The Use and Abuse of Structural Analysis' demonstrates the significance of this position.) Derrida, Lacan, and the rest provide Hartman with sophisticated and highly elaborated positions supporting his essentially romantic argument for openness, non-coercion, the imaginative resources of language, and 'the productive force of close reading.' Here is Hartman from 'Words and Wounds' in *Saving the Text* (a book that includes a path-breaking study of Derrida's *Glas*), as he writes somewhat lyrically in support both of his counter-vision and Gertrude Stein's experimental prose: 'In the beginning was the Word, and the Word was the loving repeating being, the ticking of the watchful heart, the soft namings of a maternal voice'. (*ACJ*, 246).

Hartman's latest thinking, collected in *The Unremarkable Wordsworth* (1987), *Minor Prophecies: The Literary Essay in the Culture Wars* (1991), *The Longest Shadow: In the Aftermath of the Holocaust* (1996), *The Fateful Question of Culture* (1997), and *Scars of the Spirit: The Struggle Against Inauthenticity* (2002), often focuses on the potential intersection between literary or artistic expression and trauma theory. As he observes in 'On Traumatic Knowledge and Literary Studies,' an essay from *New Literary History* (part of which is printed here as 'Reading, Trauma, Pedagogy'), his own interest in the relevance of psychoanalysis to literary studies has not centered directly on trauma. Instead he prefers to talk of psychoaesthetics and representation-compulsion. But, he continues, he does share

> with trauma studies a concern for the absences or intermittences in speech (or conscious knowledge); for the obliquity or residual muteness of "flowers of speech" and other euphemic modes; for the uncanny role of accidents; for the "ghosting" of the subject; for the connection of voice with identity (the appeal of cryptonymy, punning and specular names); for interpretation as a feast not a fast; and for literature as a testimonial act that transmits knowledge in a form that is not scientific and does not coincide with either a totally realistic (as if that were possible) or analytic form of representation.

Hartman wonders, in short, whether the vision and practice of a *translatio studii* is possible not only without an imperium, particularly the modern American empire, but also in the absence of hope in a therapeutic effect. Can there be a healing culture of vision, traveling from one civilization to another, which could satisfy safely rather than exacerbate self-destructively the repetitive human drive for reversing time and exacting an apocalyptic vengeance for the shame of belatedness? Can the romantic dream, more savvy and critically aware than Arnold and T. S. Eliot acknowledge, still serve as an antidote to the modern quest for absolute enlightenment – or to the ancient one for spiritual domination (a major theme of Hartman's *Scars of the Spirit*)? Art, in that case, would not only compete with religion but also with politics as a religion.

Hartman is thus reviving a view of education as aesthetic education, the refinement of our powers of perception and response which would not be a sell-out, no shameful collaboration with the powers that be of any kind, and yet could mediate the drive for unmediated vision, and function as a cure of the ground for human grievance against time and the 'it was,' as Nietzsche puts it in the 'Redemption' chapter of *Thus Spoke Zarathustra*. The selections in the *Reader* from Hartman's more recent work discuss the prospects of aesthetic education as an imaginative *Bildung*. (Here is why, I believe, Goethe has begun to preoccupy Hartman as an artist and figure, for Goethe is perhaps the finest modern exemplar of aesthetic education as a *Bildung*, although the most explicit formulation of the theory belongs to Schiller.)

My own choice of a modern critical exemplar for aesthetic education is, not surprisingly, Hartman himself. In his person and critical persona alike he represents, and has represented repeatedly for half a century, this view of a liberal education with the appreciation of art at its center, and forming among those schooled by its fostering discipline an enlarged and enlarging culture of vision.

This culture of vision is not much appreciated these days. Discounted as too genteel or elitist, it is viewed as a vestige of the past in which liberation was narrowly construed and the test of merit often used as a screen for prejudice and exclusion. However this may have been in particular cases, overall the culture of vision, admittedly a Romantic Enlightenment dream, has made possible Hartman and many other exemplary thinkers. And I believe its best impulses are democratic and demotic ones, and this culture of vision can be renewed and still perform its therapeutic and empowering functions. However, just the professional obstacles to the realization of my belief are today considerable, to say the least.

Recently, when chairing my department's search for a romanticist, I discovered precisely how out of fashion the culture of vision is. When in a preliminary phone interview the one person out of the hundred or so candidates who had written on 'The Big Six' (the canonical romantic poets: Blake, Wordsworth, Coleridge, Byron, Shelley, and Keats) apologized for having done so in his earlier work and quickly mentioned he was now working exclusively on the once popular and now rediscovered women romantic writers, I knew that the original culture of vision was history. Unfortunately, this loss has not been replaced with any coherent and compelling definition of romanticism. As a result, the field is being swallowed up from either end, as it were: being absorbed into 'the long eighteenth century' or 'the long nineteenth century.' As new historicist and cultural studies approaches to romanticism have opened up (itself a desirable development), they have not offered any alternative theory of romanticism that would encompass canonical and non-canonical yet still somehow recognizably romantic writers. What sense is there in calling Charlotte Smith's sonnets and Byron's *Don Juan* romantic texts? Or put another way: if thanks to Hartman and his generation of critics we now see dialectical and complex intertextual affiliations among 'the Big Six' (where once we hardly did), precisely in their secular visionary culture as a viable therapy for the apocalyptic drive, what if anything as substantial connects them with each other now and with the multitudes of once popular, long neglected, and recently revivified 'minor' romantics?

This is where I think Hartman's latest work, particularly that on Goethe, can be fruitfully developed by contemporary critics. In 'Who Needs Goethe?' (from *Scars of the Spirit*, but not reprinted here), Hartman underscored the central issue:

> I doubt Goethe ever settled within himself the issue of the therapeutic effect of words: when therapeutic are they so because disinterested – able to raise us up like the scientist's contemplation of nature or the craftsman's absorption in the "Geschick" of his material task, beyond guilt and innocence? The theme Goethe shared with Wordsworth, how internal injury or psychic trauma might be overcome, and how the poetic or scientific mode of thought might strengthen personal growth, has not lost its relevance at the present time. (*SS*, 173)

As Hartman also formulates it, 'the therapeutic action of art on its creator, on readers, on society itself' (*SS*, 171) is an issue that Goethe's very artistry of classical control usually leads us not to see as a question in Goethe's own case. However, 'the more Goethe's artistry is in control, the more aware we are of a contrary, less conscious factor that leads him, by immersion in the messiness of human emotion beyond equanimity' (*SS*, 171). Yet for all of Goethe's double-mindedness, his Apollonian and Dionysian tendencies (to borrow Nietzsche's formula), Hartman concludes that Goethe 'retained a trust that language can heal as well as wound, and that he depicts what we have learned to recognize as unconscious forces' (*SS*, 172) in ways that reflect a belief in aesthetic education.

One interesting and useful reflection Hartman makes in this recent essay arises out of his recognition, prompted by a forgotten study of Goethe by Croce. Often highly digressive parts of Goethe's texts, especially in his fictional prose, are (as Croce puts it) like little 'living organisms' set in an encompassing 'mechanical' structure. Goethe achieves epic effects for the romantic modern age with near-labyrinthine asides that are lightly (if not completely) fitted into a formal assemblage that, while superficially whole, functions nonetheless ironically – unlike Frye's structuralist totality – as if that Goethean whole were a monumental fragment (*SS*, 173). The hallmark of romantic modernity, canonical or otherwise, resides in this paradoxical, self-conscious, aesthetic conjuncture that Hartman, reviving Croce's insight, has exemplified via Goethe.

I would suggest, in conclusion, that in speaking of Goethe's aesthetic practice Hartman is disclosing as well his own procedures. Often his style, from the level of the word and sentence, to that of the essay, chapter, section, or entire book, as well as from book to book over the course of his long career, reads like a critical embodiment of romantic modernity's aesthetics. Each part of a Hartman essay expresses a reflective critical attention that tends to disperse associatively, possibly even labyrinthine-like, the argument or plot for any would-be coercive whole.

Yet Hartman deploys the conventional genres of modern critical prose – textual analysis, scholarly overview and side-view, aphoristic aperçus, even punning analogies – to preserve and raise up the entire wealth of critical judgments in an artifice that itself points the moral of all human artifice: its naturally incomplete and so necessarily ludic status. This chastened yet relaxed sense of totality, which also resists via its always impeccable scholarship a mere aesthetic impressionism, escapes system of any sort, remaining at once critical and creative. As *Scars of the Spirit* and its excerpts in this *Reader* demonstrate, Hartman continues to adapt his critical vision to our tele-media age, addressing with imagination and exceptional understanding questions of mediation raised by our memoir, reality-TV, and video culture. His thoughtful work with the Holocaust Video Archive at Yale University has prepared him for this development.

As an example of Hartman's characteristic style of genial irony, I will cite the first two paragraphs of the 'Interpretation as Preposterous' section from 'The Interpreter: A Self-Analysis,' the opening essay of *The Fate of Reading* (not included in this collection, but quoted in the 'Coda'):

> Belatedness seems at first a modern kind of feeling. It helps to inspire, certainly, the Battle of the Ancients and Moderns that follows on the Revival of Antiquity. Most Renaissance writers are quite lighthearted vis-à-vis the Classics: they steal or adapt to their heart's content. But some are grave and burdened like Gabriel Harvey, who complains of Spenser's *Faerie Queene* that it is "hobgoblin run away with the crown from Apollo." This hobgoblin, as Classicists know, is the infant Hermes who is no sooner born than he challenges Apollo by stealing his cattle, brazening this out by sheer denial, and inventing the lyre from a tortoise shell. The Hermes-myth of the mighty imp counters an author's sense of being preempted by Classical authority. Yet Apollo is not always a heavy father. He is also "golden Apollo," a "rich-hair'd youth of morn" who shakes his dewy locks as if the accumulated riches of antiquity will disperse through him into the effulgence of a new literary day. The success of the Renaissance in opening the storehouse of Antiquity and converting its treasure into native coin produces an embarrassment of riches for the poets that follow, many of whom admire, intensely if ambivalently, native Originals in addition to Classical patriarchs. (*FR*, 15)

It may be that since World War II and the Holocaust the culture of the West has been revealed as always complicit in the sin and guilt of one would-be empire after another, with the consequence that we have suffered the total destitution of all symbolic institutions. Nonetheless, with the example of the essays and excerpts collected here, we not only recall what once certainly was the best self of the culture of vision, but also, perhaps, what could come again – with a significant difference, naturally.

★ The following abbreviations are used: *BF, Beyond Formalism*; *ACJ, A Critic's Journey*; *SS, Scars of the Spirit*; *FR, The Fate of Reading*.

Autobiographical Introduction: 'Life and Learning'*

My giving the Haskins Lecture on 'A Life of Learning' to this distinguished assembly surely involves a case of mistaken identity – and my complicity in it. I cannot claim to be among the scholars, the polymaths of yesteryear or today. When I recall the teachers from whom I learnt the most, René Wellek, Henri Peyre, Erich Auerbach, Judah Goldin, or when I look over the list of your past lecturers, I find myself echoing Matthew Arnold at the monastery of the Grande Chartreuse: 'And what am I that I am here?'

Scholars in the humanities are often seen as containers of idle or obsolete learning. The press we get is pretty bad, even among those who know us best. George Eliot's Casaubon is at least faintly sympathetic, because the author had been in love, or thought she was, with scholarly types like Herbert Spencer. In *Uncle Vanya*, however, Chekhov's Professor is a parasite; and not much more can be said for the mandarins Fritz Ringer portrays in his famous book on the German professoriate. The picture darkens with Max Weinreich's *Hitler's Professors*, which details the opportunism of these guardians of culture (not all in the humanities) and their willingness to be ideologically seduced. Talking of seduction, Professor Unrat of *Blue Angel* fame comes to mind. Today, of course, being involved with a chorus girl or model is reserved for true master builders, like Donald Trump.

I am grateful, therefore, that there is an occasion like this, and, despite my opening gambit, that your choice has fallen on a professional amateur. My story, moreover, may not be untypical of a displaced European, immensely glad to be in America, yet unwilling to let go, to melt down, diverse cultural elements, though they have made it impossible for him to concentrate on one, all-subsuming topic – except culture itself.

Yet, without claiming to be a world-citizen, or that this ideal can still be maintained, I have not felt homeless or in exile – perhaps because literature got hold of me so early, as well as a Wordsworthian sense of place that seemed natural rather than national, Biblical rather than parochial. Sky, fields, pools, sheltering trees, the basic benevolence of the English countryside in which I lived as a refugee, surrounded me. When Auerbach wrote, after the war, 'the earth itself must now be the scholar's home, it can no longer be the nation,' it struck a chord, because my wish for roots was free of a particular national ideology.

I do not recall a voice out of the clouds, saying: Hartman, you are a literary scholar, put all other interests behind you. Nor was I brought up in an intellectually demanding household. A subtle contagion, however, may have come from an awareness that my maternal grandfather, a rabbi and teacher of religion in Frankfurt, who died when I was a year old, had received his doctorate. (His thesis on Midrash, I found out eventually, was influenced by the 'Wissenschaft des Judentums,' the famous nineteenth-century movement aiming to conduct the study of Jewish religion on a secular and scientific basis.) Yet, while I certainly wanted to do well in school, there was always some other influence at work. My curiosity for all kinds of learning mingled with a mystical feeling for the simple fact that I was alive. 'I made no vows,' Wordsworth writes about his dedication to poetry, 'but vows were . . . made for me.'

In addition to being plagued by hyper-vigilance, and a not always healthy empathy for every living thing, including the down-and-out, there was, early on, a faith in art, especially in a therapeutic story-telling that served me well as a counselor in summer camps, comforting the very young children I had to oversee. The notion of books about books, moreover, meant nothing to me until I entered graduate school and took seminars from René Wellek. There, suddenly, only secondary literature existed; and gradually, perversely, I came to enjoy it as a great vocabulary builder. For in those days I was still a collector of words as of stamps, a potential poet rather than a budding scholar, and lived in a sort of mild, monkish ecstasy of reading everything and trying to square it with my delight in phenomena as such. 'Hunting mice is his delight,' a ninth-century Irish scholar wrote of his cat Pangur Bán, 'Hunting words I sit all night.'[1]

Entering the precincts of a life of learning was a compromise. I wanted to be a poet, or to respond to what Wordsworth called 'The incumbent mystery of sense and soul.' I did publish *Akiba's Children*, a small book of verse – but at close to fifty this was a gesture of defeat as much as of defiance. Its title indicated the nature of my compromise: I had funneled my energies into the act of interpretation, and therefore chose Akiba, perhaps the most influential founder of rabbinic exegesis, as nominal father figure. In receding moments of poetic mania I was determined to convert what learning I had into verse. Reviewing contemporary poetry in the late 1950s, I had already protested the prevalent orthodoxy: an aggressively colloquial and demotic speech. With more lofty and erudite models in mind, I thought I could renew a lost high style, if only through parody and pastiche.

There was another competing interest. Indeed, had I the talent, I would have become a painter, not a writer. Alas, as Miss Taffy, our redoubtable Aylesbury Grammar School teacher, made me realize, when she obliged me to spend futile hours drawing an egg or Fido's doghouse, I was hopeless at that kind of imitation. Later my shameful lack of eye-hand coordination was solaced by an ardent affair with photography. I still have snapshots taken with a five dollar Brownie that sported the simplest of mechanisms (no timer, no lens, just a pinhole). If you gauged light and distance perfectly, it yielded surprisingly good pictures. Nothing intervened between you and visual reality: the eyes had to think, fast; and I still enjoy looking at these stolen images of Kabbalistic figures in Sefad (probably just bearded old men), and raggedy children playing amid the ruins of Berlin or the slums of Naples. After my early displacements, I was comforted by a vital and invariant sense of place that merged figure and ground.

The other way of assuaging visual desire was writing about it. My first attempt at theory, in *The Unmediated Vision*, argued that poetry, especially in the modern period from Wordsworth to Valéry, pitted the other senses, primarily the ear, against the eye by a compensatory dialectic. 'Pure Representation,' the chapter tracing how symbolic process undoes visual dominance, subverts 'O dark, dark, dark, amid the blaze of noon,' the blinded Samson's cry in Milton's poem. The verse is made to express my own anguish: at excess of sight, of seeing without understanding, and feeling the guilt of a voyeur for not giving back, through some sort of recreative mimesis, the sheer, early delight of sense-experience. 'Why was the sight,' we also read in Milton, 'to such a tender ball as the eye confined?' I remember discovering, near the beginning of my studies, the theological idea of a glorious, raised, and restituted body, every part of it clairvoyant.

Recently the National Gallery in Washington exhibited Vermeer's *The Art of Painting*, on loan from Vienna's Kunsthistorisches Museum. I was struck by the way ambition and the desire for fame, symbolized by a trumpet and a very thick book held by a young woman dressed up as Clio, contrast with the casualness of her pose, and the fact that the painter does not regard us boldly but sits, elegantly accoutered, with his back to the viewer. His model seems distracted by a thought or perhaps the printed sheet on a nearby table: her downcast eyes are almost closed; nor are the eyes of a perhaps eyeless mask on the same table visible.

If the art emblematized by this canvas alludes to a conventional hierarchy placing history painting at the top, it does so transformatively. The painter's brush, tracing Clio's leafy crown, is more like pastoral's 'oaten reed' than the 'trumpets stern' representing epic endeavors. A wonderful sense of interior space takes over, fostered by genre painting and furthered by a drawn curtain that reveals the scene; we understand that value does not reside in the particular and always partially staged subject-matter but in the inwardness brought to it by the artist. Attention is focused on the painter's care, as he begins his work by recreating the bluish-green leaves. So aesthetic experience, while distinctly this-worldly, occupies a continuum between the pleasures of a perception 'washed in the cleanliness of a remotest heaven/That has expelled us and our images,' to quote Wallace Stevens,[2] and the mimetic accuracy of pictures like Vermeer's.

The downcast eyes, then, might be a contrapuntal allusion to the upcast, ecstatic eyes in religious painting.

Perhaps I turned to writing about reading because I was deprived in younger days of the simultaneously sensuous and intellectual shock great paintings give. Living in a small English village from the age of nine till sixteen, I never had the opportunity of visiting gallery or museum, while well-known poets and essayists, and, through extracurricular reading, novelists like Tolstoi and Virginia Woolf (her *Between the Acts* affected me deeply by its precarious continuity, its cross-cutting, and montage-like notations), were available in cheap, Penguin editions. Once settled in the States, I did visit the Museum of Modern Art in New York, but more for its old movies than paintings.

It was not till my Fulbright year, at twenty-two, that I discovered art through the great museums of Paris and the sculptures of such cathedrals as Autun and Vezelay; and it was not till drafted into the army, some three years later, that, during my furloughs, the even intenser experience of Venice, Florence, Rome, and Ravenna made me desperate again. But it was too late to fall in love with this or that artist, this or that style: I was, and have remained, in a promiscuous daze.

Whether the anti-iconic tradition of Judaism also worked on me to favor the literary over the visual arts, I leave aside. But I did sense an order within the disorder or anthologic flow of early rabbinic readings. Bialik, the first great poet writing in modern Hebrew, remarked that the Talmud's intricate architecture was Judaism's equivalent to a vast gothic cathedral. Certainly, the elongated stone presences of cathedral statuary, biblical figures fixed in their testimonial function, have not ceased to admonish me. The hero, Emerson said, is one who is immovably centered. But I still do not know my center amid the perplexing variety of perspectives yielded by the interpreter's art.

From early on I tried to discover a distinctive logic in each literary work, an exact formal principle that would illuminate its action and so justify its rich difficulty or seeming obscurity. I was impelled to advocate, at the same time, the indeterminacy of literary commentary, or, as Coleridge described Descartes's cogito, its self-determined indetermination. For the problem on the level of theory was that no one had seriously tried to take the historical mass of interpretations that surrounded each work and figure out their convergence or a subsuming kind of truth. Instead, each critic-interpreter jousts selectively with that variorum, claiming to find this or that error, or an overlooked feature in the text.

Given this epistemic difficulty, I was inclined, like Paul de Man, to emphasize the structure of critical reflection itself, and came to feel that it should have a momentum of its own. But here I ran up against contemporary practice, which stressed almost exclusively the explanatory and evaluative function of criticism. Interested in the essay as an insubordinate rather than serviceable genre, and attracted to the more demanding, philosophically based, discourse of Sartre and Blanchot, I wanted to make my interventions both learned and ludic. One hears of passionate pianists who play as if 'attacking the instrument.' That is what I did to critical prose, seeking to develop an intenser style.

It seemed to me, in those tumultuous late sixties and seventies, that literary criticism was limited by a conversational and journalistic mode that had been an English achievement almost three centuries before, and whose strength was kept up by many nineteenth-century critics, and in our time by such public intellectuals as Edmund Wilson, George Orwell, and Lionel Trilling. Reflective and reportorial in balanced measure, it was still modeled on the familiar essay, as was the opening column in *The New Yorker* (now superseded) that usually began, 'A friend writes . . .' The same amiable correspondent had addressed letters to 'Mr. Spectator' (often their actual author) in the eighteenth-century periodical of that name.

The friendship style suggested an embryonic form of democratic ethos, at least in the domain of letters, an ideal equality of writers and readers. Therefore, despite sharp judgements and discriminations, it downplayed the stress of genius, evading the burden – the anxiety of influence, as my colleague Harold Bloom has named it – that affects not just artists but also their audience.

I cannot claim that the sounds I drew from my prose found a welcoming echo. Its punning, its freight of inner quotations, and a type of reading that stuck close to the text, while introducing French theory together with its German sources, was denounced as an offence to good literary manners, or as mandarin, navel-gazing, unduly competitive with, rather than serving, art. Even as nihilistic rather than humanistic: not perhaps deliberately so but, if anything could be worse, blindly so.

What, me, a tenured radical? It is true I was having fun; such essays as 'The Interpreter: A Self-Analysis' or 'Adam on the Grass with Balsamum' (the latter partly inspired by Midrash) filled the boundary-crosser with an exuberance he cannot today recapture. *Mitsingen* (singing along) was not *verboten*. This was also the time when I celebrated Derrida's *Glas* as realizing the Romantic dream of a philosophic work of art and initiating a Thousand and One Nights of interpretive pizzazz. Denis Donoghue, usually a tolerant spirit, wondered aloud whether Hartman's students were writing dithyrambs instead of dissertations.

Yet I never proposed my 'afflicted' style as a model. Its protest was directed against the dominance of a conformist critical prose, useful and educative but hardly an everlasting norm. Not everything should have to be cast in the plain style of book review or teaching. Why cannot literary commentators have the kingdom of their own style, like the artist, like the idiosyncratic Spenser who uttered the rebellious phrase I am adapting? Had I known what would develop in the years to come, I might not have been quite so passionate about the inventive character of technical terms, the illuminations of grand theory, and the virtue of a self-conscious response that claimed an integrity of its own, independent of the work of art that provoked it. However, I would still have advocated a pluralism of styles.

A growing interest in both Jewish and Christian exegesis also played its role. When I started teaching in 1955, Yale College still had policies that restricted the number of Jewish students; and without Judaic studies or any openly Jewish teachers with tenure in the humanities except a very secular philosopher, Paul Weiss, my reading in the tradition was bound to be self-guided. Here and there I did smuggle a poem by Judah Halevi or a Biblical source into my classes. Yet if those years of my first appointment were very lean indeed, the personal study I embarked on, helped by a summer of Talmud at the Jewish Theological Seminary and a semester in Israel, felt liberating.

I was struck by the daring of a multitude of midrashic interpreters, who, secure in their faith, unpacked even the least promising passages of Scripture in a now homely, now mystical and even transgressive way, and anchored everything in the text by puns that modified – or played with – the root meaning of the Hebrew words. This procedure was not just an ingenious exercise of interpretive freedom vis-à-vis an authoritative text; it implied that the Hebrew Bible had originated in a divine voice, now petrified lava, yet bearing traces of its powerful, multivocal source. Contemporary Biblical scholarship may attribute this linguistic richness or contamination to the syncretism of oral traditions, but the great rabbinic readers sound out Scripture by a *participation exégètique* that makes its voices their voice.

A different pleasure came from the personalism of Augustine, whose *Confessions* are interspersed with Scripture verses by which he addresses God in God's own words, or as if these words had been intended for him, so he could give them back fleshed out by his own experience. In general I came to think that, while it was salutary for literary criticism to separate from theological exegesis, it had impoverished itself by rejecting so large a tradition of textual response.

I was also impressed, as I have mentioned, by the intensity of Continental modes of literary-critical thought, and tried to mediate between its major figures and the emerging strength of an American cultural criticism still far less radical than its own literature.[3] On the Continent, studies of Hölderlin and Rousseau, of Poe, Baudelaire, Mallarmé and Rilke, of Rabelais, Nietzsche, Kafka, and Joyce, challenged not only received ideas on the unity of the work of art but many aspects of western thought itself. Derrida, at the same time, who for a decade found a home in Yale's Comparative Literature Department, expanded the concept of textuality to the point where nothing could be demarcated as 'hors d'œuvre' and escape the literary-critical eye. It was uncanny to feel hierarchic boundaries waver until the commentary entered the text – not literally, of course, but in the sense that the over-objectified work became a reflection on its own status, its stability as an object of cognition. The well-wrought urn contained mortal ashes.

Freud's interpretive and speculative vigor had already anticipated this notion of commentary. His recording of dreams did not produce an object with definitive boundaries. To stabilize the dream and make it interpretable, his analyses were sometimes as astonishing in their linguistic and associative flow as the dream-work itself. The commentary entered the text once more, even created a new kind of textuality in the form of the written dream. Saul Lieberman, among the most learned Talmud scholars of our time, confirmed that Midrash, or, to be precise, the freer kind called aggadic Midrash, might have been inspired by ancient methods of dream interpretation. Still, I was shocked when Bill Wimsatt, a senior colleague at Yale allied with the New Criticism, and whose graduate seminar on the history of poetics was legendary, denounced Harold Bloom and me as 'battering the [literary] object.'

If I was guilty of battery, it was only vis-à-vis a tendency to fabricate pseudo-historical narratives of literary or critical progress. Reacting in *The Unmediated Vision* to the attempt by the New Critics to bypass many Romantic and nineteenth-century poets, I had myself succumbed to a fabrication. The book's concept of modernity simply displaced the chronological caesura defining literary modernism from the early seventeenth to the end of the eighteenth century. Gradually, through my association with Paul de Man, I questioned period terms, especially claims made for 'the modern.'

Only a portion, in any case, of the iceberg of interpretations is visible in the contemporary, secular era. The greater part, linked to religious sermons, law-finding, and mystical brooding, remains neglected or deliberately ignored by the predominance of an unreflective Enlightenment paradigm. Art itself, moreover, once it had become free-standing, or separated as an object of study from its religious matrix – a feat that had once required Aristotle's brilliant surgery – art itself resists being historicized. 'Toward Literary History,' the final essay in *Beyond Formalism*, suggested that it was questionable to see literature as the reflex of a highly determined social or political milieu. One had to respect art's *imaginaire*, its projection of a counter-reality, which might include a vision of history but could also create a new distance between words and things. Here Blanchot counted for more than did Sartre.

Over twenty years passed before I was able to relate poetry to politics in a consequent manner. *The Fateful Question of Culture* proposed that if Wordsworth's *imaginaire*, his attempt to envision a modern culture that would not break with a rural sensibility, had taken hold in Continental Europe, the pernicious political exploitation of the gulf between urban and rural, burgher and peasant, might have been avoided.[4] I had previously tried to bring cultural and literary history together by formal constants like the *genius loci*, a persistent superstition that linked inspiration to specific place and time, at best encouraging the revival of vernacular poetry and at worst literary nationalisms. But the history planned on the basis of that figure and the permutations of a geopolitical 'Westering,' a counter-sunwise progress of poetry and liberty, never came about.

A defeat, again; yet even had I succeeded, art's minute particulars would have retained their own way of extruding, of hogging attention. Hermeneutic startlement never dies down. John Crowe Ransom got it right when he said that literature has logical structure and irrelevant texture. A devilish detail is part of art's economy, of a sign-system that produces large effects through micro-material means.

I am both attracted and repelled, therefore, by contemporary overkill, the hallmark of an affluent society that is at once wasteful and caught up in the dream of total restitution. Historicism is only the beginning of this dream. The latest image of restitution actually revives the idea of a clairvoyant body. Robert Taylor, one of the Internet pioneers, evokes a technological phantasm. We could soon be wearing, he predicts, 'an unobtrusive device that will record in full color and sound everything that you see or point your head at, or, depending on how many of them you have, everything that's around you. And share it. Every waking and sleeping moment in your life will be recorded. And you will be able to store and retrieve it and do what you will with it.'[5]

It would seem to me that we already have world enough, though not time enough, and that the passage from 'you will be able to store and retrieve it' to 'and do what you will with it' is far more questionable than that easy, consequential 'and' suggests. Taylor elides the moral problem of the use to which knowledge will be put, especially in an age of information technology. For what is lacking and difficult to increase is *studium*, the capacity to think and interpret, which discovers the curvature of space or of expression, and accepts that, if 'all's oblique,' we can never coincide entirely with ourselves, or a presumed identity.

In this technological era, knowledge is fate once more, is the daimon, and the vital issue becomes how we can turn it into ethos or character rather than into more knowledge, more obsession, more consumerism, more spectatorship. A life of learning has little moral weight unless it communicates the life in learning. Two of my guiding spirits in this respect are Goethe and Thoreau. 'Every observant glance into the world,' Goethe said in his *Farbenlehre*, his treatise on colors, 'has theory in it.' And the scientist in Thoreau looks at knowledge acquisition with what can only be called ecological tenderness: 'heaven to me consists in a complete communion with the otter nature.' 'Do not tread on the heels of your experience,' he also admonishes himself. 'Be impressed without making a minute of it. Poetry puts an interval between the impression and the expression – waits till the seed germinates naturally.'

So I come, as you knew I would, to the relation of art and learning. 'Poetry,' according to Wordsworth, 'is the breath and finer spirit of all knowledge.' Like Goethe and Thoreau he refused to see art and science as enemies. What kind of knowledge is art? And, what kind of learning can we bring to art to illuminate it? Is there today only a hyper-professional field called literary studies, or can we hope for a culture of criticism, despite augmenting burdens of knowledge, including an ever-expanding curriculum? How far are culture and erudition conciliable? The pressure of contextual historical information, as well as the enormous dilation of secondary literature, is potentially disabling rather than inspiring, and may produce a greater divide than ever between scholarly article and performative essay.

B.C., that is, Before Cyberspace, the fear was that a Hegelian increase in self-consciousness would corrode creativity. In the 1950s, with the New Criticism firmly established, there were finicky debates on whether an artist's mind should be so fine that no idea could violate it. For T. S. Eliot, Henry James was the great example of such chastity.[6] Eliot's notorious thesis on a dissociation of sensibility from thought in early modernity expresses the same worry. By the time of the Romantics, anti-self-consciousness theories were not uncommon and expected art to save what John Stuart Mill called, in reference to Wordsworth, a 'culture of the feelings.'

My interest in the Romantics was strengthened by a happy accident. While first-year instructors at Yale, Harold Bloom and I were assigned adjoining offices in a basement of Yale's Old Campus. He was finishing the thesis that became *Shelley's Mythmaking*. It made use of Martin Buber's 'I–Thou' concept of relationship, also deployed, somewhat differently, in *The Unmediated Vision*. A lasting friendship was formed in those dingy surroundings. We both knew that the Romantic poets were underestimated, although Frederic Pottle, Yale's senior Romanticist, kept the flame alive in his cool, scientific way, while Wellek fought a rear-guard action against Lovejoy's challenge that Romanticism as a period-term was unsustainable. Through Bloom I developed an interest in Blake's revisionary theology and large-scale antinomian deceptions, as well as in Northrop Frye's fertile critical machine, a blend of Blake, Yeats and Spengler.

What I valued most in the Romantics was that their art surmounted its own anxiety about the recession of art. Could the imagination, always at odds with the world, always seeking autonomy or a world of its own, and now often held to be useless by the scientific spirit of progress, and the utilitarianism of a soon rampant Industrial Revolution – could the imagination still bond with either art or earth, and so avoid solipsism or apocalypticism?

Wordsworth's nature poetry always implicitly bids farewell to nature: 'And o, ye fountains, meadows, hills and groves,/Forebode not any severing of our loves!' He describes how the imaginative power was lost or went underground, how it sporadically reared up in its unconditioned strength ('like an unfathered vapor'), and is eventually reconnected through nature poetry to nature, to its rural, everyday habitat. I responded to Wordsworth's early experience of a beauty that had terror in it, his awe at what transpired in the mind of man, the ecological fears besetting him, and the way each poem turns into a haruspication of his era's imaginative health. In short, I hoped to squelch the prejudice that met me at the threshold of my studies: the Romantics were, somehow, great poets, but became children when they tried to think.[7] Or adolescents:

> If you think 'twas philosophy that this did,
> I can't help thinking puberty assisted.
> (Byron, *Don Juan*)

The prejudice extended to the charge that they could not compete with writers who struggled tough-mindedly to gain or revise a unified world-picture. Blake compared to Dante was a bricoleur; Wordsworth's religion was sentimental and diluted. Matthew Arnold, the source of the judgment that the Romantics 'did not know enough,' had targeted mainly the English society in which they lived.[8] But the anti-Romantics, by what my *Criticism in the Wilderness* described as a simplification of the Arnoldian concordat between creative and critical, at once exaggerated Arnold's critique and subordinated the importance he placed on the diffusive, cultural powers of the critical spirit. Unlike Arnold, moreover, they refused to see that a new theology was taking hold: a theology of the poets. They feared the very thing he reluctantly accepted as a Romantic legacy: that what would remain of religion was its imaginative truth. One nineteenth-century wit reported dreaming of a new Anglicanism, with nine articles of faith and thirty-nine muses.

On another front the New Critics were more perceptive. They understood that the weakening of established religion was anointing politics rather than art as the new religion. The critical spirit, however, was powerless to counteract this tendency through its own force alone. Without the support of a long-standing, ingrained world of belief or custom, it could not make criticism into a culture.

There is some affinity between Eliot and Nietzsche on this one point. The latter's sharpest barbs are reserved for what he sarcastically names 'Gelehrtenkultur,' egg-head culture. It is marked by an abuse of 'Historie,' the kind of learning that dries up life, and to which Goethe's Faust gives such memorable expression in the drama's long opening kvetch. 'The tree of knowledge is not that of life,' as Byron's Manfred says more concisely.

Yet the learning to which Nietzsche objected was not a magical or virtuoso quest, it was distinctly modern: the pride of nineteenth-century German scholars whose research was destroying a Eurocentric universal history. Myths of emancipation, cultural progress and national destiny were challenged by historicism's resurrection of the dead, as Michelet described the new, secular science. Historians now revived victims together with victors, and produced a positivistic nightmare of endless, mostly anonymous suffering. For Nietzsche this B.C. information explosion had the potential of reinstating a sterile pity, or another slave revolt, that would result in the opposite of historical redemption. The outcome would surely be a relativism sapping conviction and playing into the hands of a reactionary nationalistic fervor. Carl Schorske, always interested in how culture and politics interact, reveals in his Haskins Lecture how astonished he was to discover that some of the most nationalistic German historians in the Weimar Republic and under the Nazis 'justified their doctrinaire nationalism by an explicit philosophical relativism.'[9]

Even today the cultural issue with the greatest political fallout is a form of cosmopolitanism, a globalization that provokes an unintended crisis. When world-wide perspectives are felt to endanger rather than benefit local attachments, to result in identity loss or even a scepticism without borders, theories of the organic community return, and even a nationalism that invests metaphors of blood, soil and roots with nostalgia. The growing complexity of a modern economic system with its multiplying intermediaries or bureaucratic machines does not help matters. A new passion for simplicity, immediacy, and inspired action arises.

Though the revival of learning, moreover, produced a remarkable succession of vernacular writers in Europe, this very richness often sparked the feeling that there could be no second such growth. Modern Romanticism confronts this canonical double burden of the Ancients augmented by native classics, as well as a bewildering diversity of gods and myths in our 'légende des siècles.' Given so much knowledge, and later, with the culture industry, pseudo-knowledge, can the creative still create itself, as Keats declared it must? Blake's phrase 'organized innocence' already suggests that, despite the triumph of the mother tongue, the creative must undergo a process of intellectual mediation and emerge as a powerful second immediacy.

I have not talked, so far, about the field of Comparative Literature, or my experience as a teacher. Probably because I dislike short-term polemics and cannot see very far into the future. To list the critical movements I have known would mean to indulge in mock-epic enumeration.

At Queens College (CUNY) and then at Yale I was so immersed in what I used to consider an unmediated response to literature that even the New Criticism, fast becoming the reigning orthodoxy, did not affect my work except to strengthen a salutary myopia, that of close reading. Having barely escaped deadly persecution, moreover, I shied away from any attempt to politicize art.

Continental literature, and a basic knowledge of both the Classics and the Hebrew Bible, accompanied my focus on English and American poetry. I saw that interpretation would always depend on a text-milieu. If that text-milieu is narrow or impoverished, interpretation too will suffer. I had no hesitation helping to found a Literature Major at Yale that kept canonical works in the curriculum but added detective stories, movies and popular fiction generally. The comparison would stimulate rather than suspend the question of literary value.

I enjoy lecturing but prefer seminars because of the chance of hearing unexpected ideas as well as responding in such a way that the random, Brownian motion of participatory comments eventually settles into a more focused pattern. (Distance learning will never duplicate *this* experience.) My teachers at Yale contributed to an open weave of mind. They were so diverse that they would have balanced each other out even had they been more doctrinaire. Almost all in Comparative Literature were émigrés, cosmopolitan by necessity. They did not need, or even want, disciples. (In the English Department, however, a stricter, more evangelical atmosphere prevailed.) Indeed, to get their attention one had often to break through a detachment that today might be resented.[10]

Where we relied on the teacher's erudition or enthusiasm, and even forgave poor teaching if one could learn something from the texts presented, today the balance of responsibility has shifted. We are so wary of authority, even when as provisional as in the classroom, that everything tends to be viewed in terms of power-relations. Teachers, therefore, who are less than charismatic cannot escape the pressure to be overly tender in their remarks.[11]

You would be right to infer from my observations that I believe recent changes in literary studies belong to social history as much as to the history of criticism. I am quite aware, moreover, that change often creeps up on us and endangers even exceptionally dynamic institutions like the North American university. The increasing reliance on student and part-time teaching is a case in point. It has altered our perception that the academic community's 'fellowship,' beginning with graduate study, is something special. When most decisions are made by a centralized administration, it is no wonder that, especially in a time of job scarcity and distorted salary differences, students in the humanities feel they are employees rather than fellows of the faculty training them. Unionization becomes, then, a tempting outcome as well as satisfying the need for community.

We are idealistic when we depict the university as a place of community. For it cannot escape worldly tensions. This holds for the faculty as well. The more distinguished the faculty, the more collegiality may suffer. It was a lack of collegiality – a lack that also jeopardized interdisciplinary work – that led me to organize a group for 'Psychoanalysis in the Humanities' and to press for a Humanities Center at Yale. My activities on behalf of Judaic Studies, however, were aimed less at redressing a communal or interdisciplinary need than achieving intellectual equity for a learning-tradition – and a reading-practice indistinguishable from it – as old as Rome and Athens. 'Hebrew,' Franz Rosenzweig remarked, 'knowing no word for "reading" that does not mean "learning" as well, has given this, the secret of all literature, away.'[12] Whereas Yale in the 1970s could field five Professors of Pagan studies (a.k.a. the Classics) and a similar number on the Christian side of Religious studies, it allowed the equivalent of one professor for the entire history and literature of Judaism.[13]

I come in this way to a final reflection. As I understood better the vitality of German-Jewish thought before the destruction, I began to fantasize what my life would have been had the Holocaust not occurred.[14] I would surely have stayed in Germany and studied directly with many whom I admired: Buber, Cassirer, Panofsky, Adorno, Benjamin, Fromm, Simon, Glatzer, Heschel, Arendt. Though I met Arendt and Heschel (also Scholem[15]) in one academic circuit or another, they were already books in exile, rather than part of the original dream-team. My grieving for German-Jewish culture was mainly, in truth, for myself – for having been separated from the life of an imagined community.

It was not an abstract duty of memory, then, but a growing sense of the value of what had been lost that gradually turned me toward the Holocaust. My wife, Renée, though a child survivor of Bergen-Belsen, never insisted on that focus; in fact, she sternly advised me against becoming too deeply absorbed. And when I helped to establish Yale's Video Archive for Holocaust Testimonies, I had no inkling that it would lead to scholarly involvement. Indeed, to write about the Holocaust professionally, to do more than honor the witnesses by becoming a secondary witness through the archive project, seemed exploitative. It raised for me the question of what motivates apparently disinterested scholarship. Are we not attracted, like writers of fiction, to the heart of darkness; do we not consume the trauma of others? Or is facing a greater pain than ours the way we manage our own, often desperate awareness of an encompassing social suffering?

I graduated from putting together mission statements that raised funds for the archive, to essays on what I had learned from the survivors, and finally to a consideration, both pedagogical and ethical, of what style of discourse, what always questionable decorum, might do justice to the 'study' of trauma and the 'teaching' of catastrophic events. I became aware, at the same time, of a continuity between this and certain of my previous concerns. I had long tried to understand the relation between words and psychic wounds, and in *Saving the Text* had put forward a thesis about how we become word-sensitive and cure by words the wound words have made.

Occasional participation, moreover, in survivor interviews, though these were not structured as a dialogue but as a way to free the speech of persons who had undergone terrible things, made me more aware of the act of listening, its enabling potential.[16] As for Wordsworth, did not his memory-work respond to both infantile and adult trauma? He describes the lasting impact of early, sometimes ecstatic, fears, and a later, very deep sense of treachery, of psychic wounding, when Britain goes to war against France and the French revolution betrays itself.

The Holocaust experience is monstrous, unnatural; and a comparison with more common developmental traumas is odious. But the issue of how 'internal injury' (the phrase is Wordsworth's own) is overcome, or, specifically, whether man-made disasters like the Holocaust can be worked through by the victimized individual or collective – that question of a possible integration or reconciliation is crucial for today's cultural memory, not only in Germany, South Africa, or the Middle East, but also in this country.

Scholars are, or should be, intellectual witnesses. Hence they too are at risk: our academic hygiene, which often sanitizes art, will not shield us from secondary traumatization when state sponsored, or tolerated, hate crimes are studied. I am still learning how not to turn away from such ethical and emotional demand.

Notes

* The Charles Haskins annual lecture in 2000 sponsored by the American Council of Learned Societies
1. Robin Flower, *The Irish Tradition* (New York: Oxford University Press, 1973), 25. I recall strolling about during a conference in Columbus, Ohio, with René Wellek. He still wanted to know about *everything*, even why certain streets were named this or that. By that time my positivistic hunger for all kinds of knowledge had faded. But into the early twenties some emptiness made me devour new words, from English as from other languages.
2. 'Notes toward a Supreme Fiction.'
3. An exception: Kenneth Burke's demystifying yet not reductive studies of literary form, his 'Thinking of the Body,' 'symbolic action,' and sociological poetics generally.
4. It was only while writing *The Fateful Question* that I read Marc Bloch's *Feudal Society*. I have mentioned teachers who strengthened my sense of scholarship but I have left out the tonic of great books such as – to name only a few more – Jane Harrison's *Themis*, Van Gennep's *Rites of Passage*, Klibansky, Panofsky and Saxl's *Saturn and Melancholy*, Lovejoy's *Great Chain of Being*, Theodor Gaster's *Thespis*, Huizinga's *Homo Ludens*, Halbwach's *Collective Memory*, Scholem's *Major Trends in Jewish Mysticism*, and E. R. Curtius's *European Literature and the Latin Middle Ages*. All except the last three were somewhat offside to my direct interests yet had in common a respect for historical/anthropological research without sacrificing an intense vein of speculation.
5. *The New York Times*, December 20, 1999, C38.
6. Eliot gave further expression to his concern with over-consciousness in 'From Poe to Valéry.' The French poet is chosen precisely because he understood that

Leonardo da Vinci's achievement in reconciling theory, science, and painting could no longer be attained.

7. With respect to Wordsworth nothing could be further from the truth, though he was never a formal thinker in the way Coleridge was. It is amazing that the poetic spirit survived in so self-conscious a person; that the natural man, as Coleridge says about his own dejected self, was not stolen away by abstract thought. Shelley's interest in science is well known; and Keats's 'Beauty is Truth . . .' only serves to assuage the 'fever' of empathy, of an aspiration to know – to enter imaginatively – the life of other modes of being, that came close to 'annihilating' personal identity. As for Blake, his theology fictions are systematic vehicles of abundant satiric as well as inventive energy.

8. 'In England of the first quarter of this century there was neither a national glow of life and thought, such as we had in the age of Elizabeth, nor yet a culture and a force of learning and criticism such as were found in Germany. Therefore the creative power wanted, for success in the highest sense, materials and a basis; a thorough interpretation of the world was necessarily denied to it.' From 'The Function of Criticism at the Present Time' (1864).

9. *The Life of Learning*, ed. Douglas Greenberg and Stanley N. Katz (New York: Oxford University Press, 1994), 59–60.

10. Henri Peyre, though, was a godsend: always personal, witty, encouraging.

11. Two vignettes concerning then and now. What did I learn from a kind-hearted French professor at Queens except his liking for certain lines of poetry which he punctuated, memorably, by smacking his lips? That is one reminiscence. The other comes from my stint as Director of the School of Criticism and Theory, where at one time even seating arrangements were challenged. It was claimed that a certain room with a raised platform (or was it raised seats?) was too 'authoritarian.' A committee had to be appointed to look into the situation. In case I leave the wrong impression, let me add that the intellectual and communal excitement generated by the School, which is still teaching innovative perspectives to younger faculty from this country and abroad, soon dispelled these initial, nervously symbolic, concerns.

12. *On Jewish Learning*, ed. Nahum Glatzer (New York: Schocken, 1965), 216.

13. This contains an exaggeration: the Near-Eastern as well as Judeo-Christian overlap was recognized. The Hebrew Bible in its canonical formation was taught by two distinguished professors from, originally, the Divinity School, while there were slots for Northwest Semitic and Babylonian culture.

14. The 'covenant' of the Jews with German culture and its religion of *Bildung* has been amply documented; also that women played an equal role in fostering this ideal. Martha Wertheimer, who received a doctorate from the University of Frankfurt in 1919 and disappears in the spring of 1942 when deported to the East, writes as follows to a friend in America, despite her precarious situation: 'How impoverished are young people whose mind and soul is not filled with such literary riches [being able to allude in one's letters to Hölderlin's correspondence with Schiller]. You and I can always pronounce an "Open Sesame" that will unlock the gate, not to a magic cave but to a greater and blessed land, which belongs to us and from which no one can expel us.' *In mich ist die große dunkle Ruhe gekommen: Briefe an Siegfried Guggenheim*

in *New York Geschrieben vom 27.5.1939–2.9.1941 in Frankfurt am Main* (Fritz Bauer Institut, Frankfurt am Main 1996), 19. My translation. See also for the general picture, Paul Mendes-Flohr, *German Jews: A Dual Identity* (New Haven: Yale University Press, 1999).

15. Gerhardt Scholem had emigrated to Palestine before the Nazi regime came to power.

16. It also led me to appreciate why Greek and then neoclassical tragedy tended to keep what Aristotle called *to pathos*, scenes of wounding or killing, off-stage ('obscene'), preferring to report on rather than represent terror directly. The stories of the survivors had tremendous immediacy but also a distance – however fragile – that made them bearable.

Part I

The Interpretation of Poetry

Chapter 1

Christopher Smart's 'Magnificat': Toward a Theory of Representation

What is the consummation of perfect freedom? Not to be ashamed of one's self.
                                                                    Nietzsche

For when men get their horns again, they will delight to go uncovered.
                                                                    C. Smart

Theory as Prologue

When we present one person to another, a feeling of formality persists. It may be a residual awe, relating to exceptional presentations (of the child to elders in early or ritual circumstances) or it may be a more general sense of the distance between persons. The latter feeling would still have a psychological component, for the distance between persons is like that between self and other.

What if someone cannot be presented? The sense of distance has been thrown out of balance: either the self feels defective vis-à-vis the other, or the other appears magnified, unapproachable. The someone can be a something: certain subjects may not be introduced into discourse, certain taboos restrict or delimit the kinds of words used.

I introduce the example of words early, because words commonly help to present us.[1] Should we feel that words are defective, or else that we are defective vis-à-vis them (words becoming the other; as is not unusual in poets who have a magnified regard for a great precursor or tradition), then a complex psychic situation arises. It is fair to assume, however, that the distance between self and other is always disturbed, or being disturbed; that there is always some difficulty of self-presentation in us; and that, therefore, we are obliged to fall back on a form of 'representation.'

Representation implies that the subject cannot be adequately 'present' in his own person or substance, so that advocacy is called for. The reason for this 'absence,' compensated for by 'representation,' can be various. In legal or ritual matters, the subject may not be of age or not competent. But even when he is competent, of age, fully presentable, situations arise which produce a fiction of his having to be 'seconded': in presentation at court (and sometimes in courts of law) he does not appear by himself but needs the support of someone already admitted into the superior presence.

The self does not, of course, disappear into its representative, for then the means would defeat the end, which remains self-presentation. Even in visionary poetry, which so clearly sublimes the self into the other, or exalts the other into quasi-supernatural otherness, the self persists in selfhood. Though Charles Lamb is right in remarking that Coleridge's Ancient Mariner 'undergoes such trials as overwhelm and bury all individuality or memory of what he was – like the state of a man in a bad dream, one terrible peculiarity of which is that all consciousness of personality is gone,' the spectral happenings in the poem actually doom the Mariner to survival. He is unable to die, or find release from his experience except in the 'punctual agony' of storytelling.

Whether or not this doom of deathlessness is preferable to nothingness – 'Who would lose,' says Milton's Belial, 'Though full of pain, this intellectual being,/ Those thoughts that wander through Eternity,/ To perish rather, swallow'd up and lost/ In the wide womb of uncreated night . . .' – the self can never be so sublimated, or so objectified, that only its representative is left. Even granted that self desires an absolute escape from self, what would be satisfied by that escape: indeed would anything of self be left to register the satisfaction? To urge questions of this kind is to approach psychoanalysis, but at the same time to link it with speculations on the sublime going back at least to Edmund Burke. These speculations ponder the vertiginous relation between self-loss and self-aggrandizement.

Let me return briefly to Coleridge's poem. Why does the Mariner kill the albatross? A fascinating question; but even the simplest answer, that it was wilfulness, implies a drive on the Mariner's part for self-presence. The killing is a shadow of the Mariner's own casting.[2] What follows his self-determining, self-inaugural act is, paradoxically, the presence of otherness. In seeking to 'emerge,' the self experiences separation anxieties, and these express themselves in motions akin to the defence mechanism of 'beautiful indifference' (noted by Charcot in patients suffering from hysteria) as well as to the terror which may accompany isolation.

At the same time, there is a movement toward atonement (at-one-ment, reconciliation) in Coleridge's poem. 'Representation' cannot be divorced from advocacy. You justify either the self or that which stands greatly against it: perhaps both at once. The situation could be likened to a trial, though not to one resulting in a definite verdict. The trouble with this line of inquiry is that too many metaphors come into play until one begins to move within art's own richness of thematic variation. Yet such metaphors as trial, court, theatre, debut and so on, converge on the idea of a place of heightened demand and intensified consciousness. 'The daemon,' says Yeats, '. . . brings man again and again to the place of choice, heightening temptation that the choice may be as final as possible . . .' Let us consider the nature of this 'place,' imagined or real.

When Christopher Smart writes in *Jubilate Agno*, 'For I pray the Lord Jesus to translate my MAGNIFICAT into verse and represent it,'[3] the pun (magnific-cat), alluding to the 'magnification' of the cat Jeoffrey and of the animal kingdom generally, corroborates what Freud says about wit both submitting to and escaping the censor. To compare a hymn (the Magnificat) associated with the Virgin Mary to the gambols of Jeoffrey is blasphemous – except that the pun remains unexplicit and the poet, in any case, 'gives the glory' to God by asking Christ to make his verses acceptable. Yet the anxiety, I believe, or the pressure resulting in this kind of wit, goes deeper. It is not one outrageously smart comparison which is at stake, but the legitimacy of artistic representation as a whole. The magnific-cat theme expresses, in its marvelous mixture of humility and daring, the artist's sense that he is disturbing the 'holy Sabbath' of creation by his recreation; that he is trespassing on sacred property or stealing an image of it or even exalting himself as a maker – in short, that he is magnifying mankind instead of 'giving the glory' to God. Smart therefore atones the exposed, self-conscious self by 'a-tone-ing' it with the creature. He shows mankind 'pre-senting' before God the animal creation it has exploited. And, in return, he asks that his verse-representation be 'represented' before God by a mediator who enters the first line of his poem as 'Lord, and Lamb.' The opening of *Jubilate Agno* sets the pattern by compounding man and animal into ritual pairs:

> *Let man and beast appear before him, and magnify his name together.*
> *Let Noah and his company approach the throne of Grace, and do homage to the Ark of their Salvation.*
> *Let Abraham present a Ram, and worship the God of his Redemption.*
> *Let Isaac, the Bridegroom, kneel with his Camels, and bless the hope of his pilgrimage.*
>   *(A, 3–6)*

Inspired by Revelation, Smart begins with a judgment scene: it envisages an ark that might survive a second flood. We find ourselves in a place of demand where everything must be 'presented.' The precise nature of the demand is not absolutely clear, and need not be the same in all works of art: perhaps it varies with historical circumstances, and perhaps it is the interpreter's task to make the relation between demand and response (demand and inner capability) perfectly clear. But artistic representation does seem to mediate a demand of this kind: one, moreover, not to be thought of as coming from outside, but rather, or also, from within. Again, whether 'within' means the unconscious, or refers to a self-realizing instinct, may not be possible to determine generally but only in each case.

There is no way of being precise about this without engaging in considered acts of textual interpretation. We have to identify the nature of the challenge met by Smart and the 'place' or 'situation' he is in. It would be inadequate, for instance, to say of his 'representation' of the animal creation that it springs from the same anxiety for the survival of the physical species that, according to Gertrude Levy's *The Gate of Horn* (1948), inspired the Cro-Magnon cave paintings at Lascaux. They may have had an apotropaic function, for they gather the essential traits of the hunted species into totemic sketches that intend to placate the Spirit of the hunted creature and so assure its fertile continuance. The creature is graphically 'represented' by man to a Spirit in order for both human kind and the creature to survive.

Such recreative or reparative magic *is* relevant to Smart's poem; the analogy is too strong, and the theme of generation haunts too many of his verses. Yet it is only a beginning to specific interpretation. For we must add that in Smart the very *medium* of representation – visionary language itself – has become questionable, or subject to a demand which it cannot meet except by being renewed. His recreation of visionary categories is literally a re-creation: the source of vision is not exhausted but still operative through him. That, at least, is the claim he seems to make, or the test he puts himself to. The anxiety for survival has associated itself with an anxiety for language-source, liturgy, and the entire process of representation.

Enthusiasm and Entropy

The fear that visionary language has lost its effectiveness may not be very different from the fear that nature grows old. Such 'depletion anxieties' are linked to the not unrational feeling in us that our appetites – including that for presence – put a demand on the order of things which that order may not be able to satisfy; which, indeed, it may resent and reject.[4] The 'economy' of language use arising from depletion anxiety ranges from such devices of conservation as double-entendre, hermeticism, and classical restraint, to the complementary if opposite ones of revivalist forgery, radical innovation, and homeopathic promiscuity. You can write as sparse a hymn as Addison's famous 'The spatious firmament on high' (1712), which, in spite of its source in Psalm 19, reflects Pascal's fright at the silence of the starry spaces; or you can fill the vacuum with the 'clang expressions' of *Jubilate Agno*, till 'barrenness becomes a thousand things' (Wallace Stevens).

Smart's aberrant verses would have been classified in their time as a product of 'enthusiasm,' and this widespread and loosely knit religious movement was also a kind of counter-entropy. Affecting principally Puritans and Dissenters, it claimed to have uncovered a new source of truth, that of the individual in his privacy, who would know from 'internal' grounds what revelation there was;

but if that was all there was, then we were abandoned to individuality, and prone to the hell of unrelieved, sterile selfhood. The blessing proved to be the curse; the precious was also the accused object. 'My selfhood, Satan, arm'd in Gold' (Blake). The danger in enthusiasm, moreover, was its inevitable closeness to fanaticism, for the enthusiast found it difficult not to impose his 'internal' evidences on others, not to exhibit his 'antitheatrical' truth. He sought out or compelled a like-minded community.[5]

Enthusiasm in literature took many forms: it attacked, for example, the scientific 'Religion of Nature' which affirmed the stability of the cosmos (nature would *not* grow old) at the cost of dehumanizing it and 'untenanting Creation of its God' (Coleridge); and it overrode the pessimism of the neoclassic artist who felt he had come too late in history. The visionary or even the poet was felt to be superfluous in an Age of Reason; but the wish for originality, which enthusiasm abetted, increased in direct proportion to one's distance from the possibility. Yet the dilemma, even for the enthusiasts, was that originality and Original Sin were hard to tell apart.

Smart had to find, therefore, not only a well of visionary English but also an undefiled well. Every attempt to replenish, or imitate directly, the great source-books of secular and religious culture was open to the charge of false testimony – of giving glory to God as a cover for 'representing' one's own passions. Today we have no problem with the first person singular, and fiction is inconceivable without a semblance of self-exposure. Enthusiasm in art has gone public and taken the name of confessionalism. Consequently, it is hard for us to appreciate Pascal's notorious maxim, 'Le moi est haïssable,' and the fact that he was so sensitive to the liaison between egotism and enthusiasm that he condemned even Montaigne:

> The stupid plan he has to depict himself, and this not incidentally and against his better judgment as it may happen to all us mortals, but by design and as a matter of principle. For to say foolish things by chance or weakness is an ordinary fault; but to say them intentionally, that is not tolerable, and moreover his kind of stuff.[6]

Yet Pascal is protesting too much, for the lines of confession (his *Mémorial*) found hemmed in his garments at his death showed how close he was to what his time, and the next century, castigated as enthusiasm:

> The year of grace 1654. Monday 23rd November. Feast of St. Clement, Pope and Martyr, and of others in the martyrology. Eve of Chrysogonous. Martyr and others. From about half past 10 in the evening until half past midnight. Fire. God of Abraham, God of Isaac, God of Jacob, not of philosophers and scholars. Certainty, certainty, heart-felt, joy, peace. God of Jesus Christ. God of Jesus Christ. *My God and your God.* Thy God shall be my God. The world forgotten and everything except God . . . Joy, joy, joy, tears of joy.[7]

Apocalyptic visions, trances, egomania, or what Dr. Johnson was to call, memorably, the 'hunger' and 'dangerous prevalence' of imagination, were the diseases of enthusiasm against which Pascal and others erected their ideal of the 'honnête homme,' with his good sense, moderation, reasonable language. England, after the Puritan Revolution, imported this neoclassical ideal of correcting and improving not only the understanding but also speech itself, since an erroneous or corrupt language encourages intellectual and religious error. Swift's *Proposal for Correcting, Improving and Ascertaining the English Tongue* (1712) denounced the 'Enthusiastick Jargon' of 'Fanatick Times' (the Puritan Revolution and its epigones); and, as Professor Wimsatt has noted in a remarkable essay on the 'laughter' of the Augustans, behind all these calls for decorum there lurked a heightened sense of unreality, which was not dissimilar, perhaps, to experiences of spiritual vastation.[8] The nearness of *flatus* and *afflatus*, of wind and inspiration, the manic-depressive cycle which all these doctors were seeking to cure, kept reasserting itself in epidemics of wit and farfetched conceits, in the incurable prevalence of the mock-heroic mode, in the hysterical style of the sublime ode, and the laughing, biting speech that joins Swift to a late Augustan poet called William Blake.

The wars of religion against enthusiasm are an old story. But why should so irreligious a poet as Keats complain of Wordsworth's *egotistical sublime*? Why is he so defensive with Moneta, denouncing to her 'all mock lyrists, large self-worshipers,/ And careless Hectorers in proud bad verse' (*The Fall of Hyperion*, I, 207–8)? The reason is that he could not give up the sublime. He feared that poetry without enthusiasm was no longer poetry; and he was all the more sensitive to the charge of self-inflation because he knew that to create a sublime mode not based on personal experience was to revert to a vacuous archaism, to that impersonation of impersonality which MacPherson and Chatterton succumbed to. The sublime had to be associated with personal experience: there was no other way. Something drives fiction to that recognition in the two hundred years which comprise *Paradise Lost*, the neoclassical reaction, the emergence of Romanticism, and that renewed valediction to the sublime which fails so gloriously in Browning's 'Childe Roland' and Tennyson's 'Morte d'Arthur.'

Let me add, before returning to Smart, that Freud also treats enthusiasm. He is our latest 'doctor of the sublime,' the twentieth century facing the gods or the pathology of ecstasy. A modern analytics of the sublime must begin with Boileau's remarks on Longinus, study Vico on the way to Burke, Kant, and Schopenhauer, and then admit that Freud is the inheritor of all these in his canny knowledge of the fortress against enthusiasm which polite society, or the soul itself, builds in the soul. Defense mechanisms cannot blossom when there is nothing – no fire or flood – to defend against.

Smart's poetic career is emblematic of the fate of enthusiasm. It divides neatly into two parts. Before 1756 he was 'the ingenious Mr. Smart,' a facile and brilliant practitioner of neoclassic modes of verse. But recovering from a serious fever he began 'confessing God openly' by praying aloud whenever the impulse came. 'I blessed God in St James's Park till I routed all the company' (B 1, 89). He was confined for insanity in 1757–58 and again from 1759 to 63. During his 'illness' he produced two long poems as daring and personal as any the Romantics were to write. The *Song to David* (1763) was dismissed in its time as a 'fine piece of ruins,' while the fragmentary *Jubilate Agno* was not published till 1939. Smart's contemporaries saw him as an excellent versifier misled by religious mania, and though he reverted to such modest tasks as translating Horace and composing hymns for children, he never re-established himself in their eyes.

What is one to do, even today, with verses like 'Let Lapidoth with Percnos the Lord is the builder of the wall of CHINA – REJOICE' (B 1, 97)? The marvelous thing here is not, despite appearances, 'Enthusiasm, Spiritual Opera-tions, and pretences to the Gifts of the Spirit, with the whole train of New Lights, Raptures, Experiences, and the like.'[9] It is the poet's total, consistent, critical rather than crazy, attack on the attenuated religious language of his day. 'Percnos' is a bird of prey, like the Persian 'Roc,' punningly associated with the 'Rock of Israel' in a previous line (B 1, 94), while 'Lapidoth' (Judges 4:4) is linked to 'Percnos-Roc' by an etymological pun which gives the Hebrew name a Latin root that means 'stone' (*lapis, lapidis*). Add the 'Wall of China' as the greatest stonework in the world, and the line as a whole is seen to 'give the glory to the Lord.' It says, in effect, 'Let Rock with Rock, the Lord is the Rock of Rocks, rejoice.'

'In this plenty,' to quote Stevens once more, 'the poem makes meanings of the rock.' Visionary language knows itself as superfluous, redundant; yet its very breaking against the rock reveals a more than gratuitous splendor. The disparity between the sustained base (the unvarying ROCK or REJOICE) and Smart's ever-shifting, eclectic play of fancy, discloses a twofold problem of representa-tion: the traditional one of ineffability, related to the belief that God is 'dark with excessive bright,' or not attainable through mortal speech; and the somewhat rarer view, that the fault lies with language, which has lost yet may regain its representational power. To the crisis which stresses the inattain-ability of the signified, Smart adds the impressively impotent splendor of the signifier.

This is too cold a description, however, of the agony of the signifier. The question is less whether language can represent than whether by doing so it seconds or comforts the creature. Representation, I have argued, contains the idea of advocacy; and in Christian theology it is Christ who pre-eminently acts as comforter and advocate. To rejoice in the 'Lord, and the Lamb' is to rejoice in the hope that the Judge (Lord) will turn out to be the Comforter (Lamb).

Yet the premise of that comfort, hidden away for the most part in the 'Songs of Innocence' of Smart's time – in children's poetry or catechistical emblem books – was that the creation (*res creatae*, Romans 1:20 and 8:19) would help the tormented or doubting spirit to be instructed. By a proliferation of types, emblems, analogies, and the like, the Christian was encouraged to 'suck Divinity from the flowers of Nature,' in Sir Thomas Browne's words. As long as instruction could be drawn from flower or beast, then 'Man and Earth suffer together' (C, 155) while waiting to be redeemed. Smart's poetry serves to strengthen their bond, even if it is one of suffering. But in doing so, in seeking to 'represent' the creature, the poet discovers that language too is a creature in need of reparation.

For Smart's animated diction is the other side of his feeling for the lost animal spirits of a language 'amerced' of its 'horn' (C, 118–62). His poem, therefore, blends theriomorphic and theomorphic as the animals named by Adam in the first act of divinely instituted speech are now named again, restitutively. Language is the rib taken from Adam's tongue to helpmate his solitude before Eve. And it is interesting that in *Jubilate Agno* Eve does not formally appear. Even Mary's 'Magnificat,' when mentioned in B 1, 43, exalts not the woman and mother but rather language in its creature-naming and creature-presenting function. So close is the bondage of language and the bondage of the creature that both are one for a poet who is their male comforter, their *logos*. His Magnificat consoles what originally was to console Adam, by 'translating' and 'representing' it.

Cat and Bat

By magnifying Jeoffrey, Smart is training the telescope of wit on an ordinary creature instead of on the heavens or a certifiably divine subject. The meditation on the creature (that is, on anything created, which included the heavens) was not uncommon; and a contemporary of Smart's, James Hervey, Methodist Rector of Weston-Favell, had popularized the genre by his *Meditations Among the Tombs* and *Contemplations of the Starry Heavens* (1746–47). Hervey provides his readers with a flattering humiliation of the spirit, a Urizenic (so Blake will call it) calculus of apparent human power and actual limitation. Hervey, in short, is second-rate Sir Thomas Browne and third-rate Book of Job.

I have often been charmed and awed,' he writes, 'at the sight of the nocturnal Heavens; even before I knew how to consider them in their proper circumstances of majesty and beauty. Something like magic, has struck my mind, on a transient and unthinking survey of the aethereal vault, tinged throughout with the purest azure, and decorated with innumerable starry lamps. I have felt, I know not what powerful and aggrandizing impulse; which seemed to snatch me from the low entanglements of vanity, and prompted an ardent sigh for sublimer objects. Methought I heard, even from the silent spheres, a commanding call, to spurn the abject earth, and pant after unseen delights. – Henceforward, I hope to imbibe more copiously this moral emanation of the skies, when, in some such manner as the preceding, they are rationally seen, and the sight is duly improved. The stars, I trust, will teach me as well as shine; and help to dispel, both Nature's gloom, and my intellectual darkness . . .

I gaze, I ponder. I ponder, I gaze; and think ineffable things. – I roll an eye of awe and admiration. Again and again I repeat my ravished views, and can never satiate my immense field, till even Fancy tires upon her wing. I find wonders ever new; wonders more and more amazing. – Yet, after all my present inquiries, what a mere nothing do I know; by all my future searches, how little shall I be able to learn, of those vastly distant suns, and their circling retinue of worlds! Could I pry with Newton's piercing sagacity, or launch into his extensive surveys; even then my apprehensions would be little better, than those dim and scanty images, which the mole, just emerged from her cavern, receives on her feeble optic . . . To fathom the depths of the Divine Essence, or to scan universal Nature with a critical exactness, is an attempt which sets the acutest philosopher very nearly on a level with the ideot.[10]

This is also the period of Robert Blair's *The Grave* (1743) and Edward Young's *Night Thoughts* (1742–45). Smart's meditation on Jeoffrey is surely a criticism of such effusions. It replaces their self-regarding, didactic gloom with real observation, empathy, and a spirit as playful as that of the creature portrayed. The cat is the style; and the style, as a sustained song of innocence, is totally unchary. It leaps; it is prankish; not only in its 'mixture of gravity and waggery,' as when Smart avers 'For the Lord commanded Moses concerning the cats at the departure of the Children of Israel from Egypt,' but also in its semblance of plot.

The opening of the passage shows Jeoffrey at his 'exercises.' These ordinary gambols turn into a ritual calisthenics curiously like the 'Spiritual Exercises' of Ignatius of Loyola. When the poet 'considers' his cat, the word 'considers,' which seems to have the Latin root for 'star' in it, is a technical term from the tradition of the Spiritual Exercises. (Compare 'I have often been charmed and awed at the sight of the nocturnal Heavens; even before I knew how to consider them in their proper circumstances,' and so forth.) Here the term is applied *à rebours* to an uncelestial object; yet Jeoffrey *is* a solar creature, worshipping at 'the first glance of the glory of God in the East' and counteracting the powers of darkness 'by his electrical skin and glaring eyes.' The poet's consideration of Jeoffrey is reinforced when Jeoffrey 'begins to consider himself' (B 2, 703) 'in ten degrees' – 'degrees' are also a term common to the genre of the Spiritual Exercises. In the argument prefaced to Smart's *A Song to David*, stanzas 65–71 constitute 'An exercise upon the senses, and how to subdue them . . . [with] An amplification in five degrees.'

It is not my intent to turn Jeoffry the cat into a Christian soldier marching with Loyola. What the poem conveys is a spreading *consideration* from which nothing will eventually be excluded: Smart opens the covenant so that every creature – 'The cat does not appear in the Bible,' W. F. Stead, Smart's editor, notes drily – or at least the *names* of all created things may enter. 'Let the Levites of the Lord take the Beavers of ye Brook alive into the Ark of the Testimony' (A, 16): the Beavers do not appear in the Bible either, but here they enter alive into an Ark which could have proved as deadly as in Exodus 25:9.

At this moment in time the covenant is merely the rainbow language before us, revived by Smart. But perhaps language is the only covenant. Smart renews the responsive prayer of the psalms and of the liturgy as if to provide the Church with a Book of Common Prayer genuinely 'common.' More and more of creation enters the Ark of Testimony as not only the verses pair ('Let . . . For') but also different orders of creation; and it becomes vain to distinguish in Smart responsive poetry and resurrected wit. Both deal with strange conjunctions, hidden echoes, powerful yokings together, the 'grappling of the words upon one another' (B 2, 632). This principle of 'clapperclaw,' with its residual sexuality, sometimes extends itself into the phonation of single verses, which then seem built, like 'clapperclaw' itself, out of the competing responsiveness of mutual parts.[11] 'Let Ross, house of Ross rejoice with the Great Flabber Dabber Flat Clapping Fish with hands' (D, 11).

Imagine the House of Ahab rejoicing with Moby Dick . . . We hear the voice of the hands, in this applause; indeed the animal body itself grows to be all voice and enters the language. 'For the power of some animal is predominant in every language' (B 2, 627), writes Smart; and he exemplifies this by an outrageous onomatopoeic punning. 'For the pleasantry of a cat at pranks is in the language ten thousand times over./ For JACK UPON PRANCK is in the performance of *peri* together or seperate' (B 2, 630–31). (Read *purr* for *pr* or *per*.) This covenant-language is quite literally the Ark where man and animal pair in amity, and the 'Cherub Cat is a term of the Angel Tiger' (B 2, 725).

All creatures in Smart become flaming creatures, and the Great Chain of Being a Great Chain of Language. To characterize Smart as a late or parodic meditationist is not adequate, therefore. It does not clarify the nature of the demand on him or the burden of his response. 'Gird up thy loins now, like a man, I will demand of thee and answer thou me,' God thunders at Job. And Job is finally persuaded to put his finger on his mouth. James Hervey, and other pseudo-enthusiast worshippers of the whirlwind, put their deflating finger of inflated moralistic prose on our mouths. They make us kiss the rod. But Smart is not put out by Newton, Nature, or Nature's God. He escapes the stupor induced by Natural Religion – by the contemplation of Leviathan, Tiger, or the System of the World. And he does so by answering its 'cunning alphabet' with his own force of language. I will demand of thee and answer thou me, means for

Smart, girding up the loins of language and meeting the challenge of a divine text. The Bible is less a proof text than a shame text; and to escape this shame which affects, pre-eminently, the tongue, he must become David again and restore the Chain of Inspiration. 'Rejoice in God, O ye Tongues . . .' The Great Chain of Being is honored not on account of order and hierarchy but only as it continues to electrify the tongue and represent the creature. In Smart's 'consideration' everything stars; and the elation, or jubilation, of speech seems to sustain a demand put on it by the Book of God or the 'cunning alphabet' of the Book of Nature.

Yet Bethlehem is not far from Bedlam. The madhouses of Smart's time had more than one King David in them, not to mention King Solomons and Queens of Sheba. The pressure on Smart of the divine text or of the need to respond to it by the creation of a New Song, that is, by a language covenant embracing the creature which had fallen with and away from man, heaps this Christopher as thoroughly as Melville's white whale 'heaped' Ahab. When we read Smart's boast, 'I am the Reviver of Adoration amongst English Men,' we do not feel the tension of a pun that mounts up in stanzas 50 and following of the *Song to David*:

> Praise above all – for praise prevails,
> Heap up the measure, load the scales . . .

This is followed by twenty stanzas centering on the repeated word 'adoration.' The method is indeed accumulative, additive, rather than calculating and accounting. Double the 'd' in 'adoration' and the pun becomes visible.

A 'Song to David' means dedicated to, or spoken toward, David, but also *add*ing itself by *ad*oration until measure and scale break and the account is closed. Smart's ad libitum at once acknowledges and destroys the Johnsonian morality of style; the Doctor's reservation, for instance, that 'Sublimity is by aggregation' yet that it is impossible to add to the divine glory:

> The ideas of Christian theology are too simple for eloquence, too sacred for fiction, and too majestick for ornament. To recommend them by tropes and figures is to magnify by a concave mirror the sidereal universe. Omnipotence cannot be exalted; infinity cannot be amplified; perfection cannot be improved.[12]

Smart might have enjoyed William Blake's joshing of Dr. Johnson in *An Island in the Moon*:

'I say this evening we'll all get drunk. I say dash, an Anthem, an Anthem,' said Suction

> Lo the Bat with Leathern Wing
> Winking & blinking
> Winking & blinking

> Winking & blinking
> Like Doctor Johnson

I quote only the more decent part. Compare cat and bat.

A Speckled Language

Our delight in Smart is not a constant thing. Even in controlled sequences, like that on Jeoffrey, where the catalogue (no pun intended) is less chaotic than usual, the poet's exuberance may fall into a near-infantile strain:

> For he rolls upon prank to work it in.
> For having done duty and received blessing he begins to consider himself.
>
> (B 1, 702–3)

'Having done duty' may refer to Jeoffrey's sunrise worship, but it could also be a euphemism, especially when followed by a lengthy description of a cat cleaning itself.

> For first he looks upon his fore-paws to see if they are clean.
> For secondly he kicks up behind to clear away there.
> For thirdly he works it upon stretch with fore paws extended.
>
> (B 2, 705–7)

As every child knows, cleanliness is next to godliness, and Jeoffrey provides an emblematic and charming illustration. Yet since Smart seems more wary of mentioning excrement than of mentioning the devil (B 2, 720ff.), and Jeoffrey's ritual exorcism of dirt is continuous with his 'dutiful' worship of God, the thought may arise as to what is being euphemistically 'pranked' or 'worked in' at the higher level of godliness, benevolence, or jubilant verse-making.

One could try to find that 'foundation on slander' (or 'on the devil') which Smart mentions in B 1, 170. 'The furnace itself shall come up at the last' (B 1, 293) he also writes, alluding to Abraham's fearful vision. Whether at the bottom of it all is a lie or evil or detritus, a redemptive poet like Smart has to extend his embrace to even what is excrementitious. The 'soil' needed to fertilize the soil works on language too. Yet Smart's consciousness that when the deep opens, or the foundation rises up, it is the 'Adversary' who may appear – indeed the sha-dow-thought, perhaps there from the beginning, that the tongues invoked in the very first line of the poem might be used for the opposite of glorification – for slander or blasphemy or accusation – could help explain the *Jubilate*'s ritual or litany-like character, that apotropaic iteration which limits an otherwise eman-cipated verse line. Smart's verses are, as he implies, a 'conjecture' (B 1, 173), a 'cast' of the line or tongue whose outcome is uncertain enough to be the object of a wager like that between God and the Accuser (Satan) in the Book of Job.

The nature of Smart's anxiety about 'slander' may never be clear to us. It may not have been clear to himself. It is an anxiety about the foundation, about origins, about genealogy;[13] and so about the truth issuing from his own tongue:

> Let Ziba rejoice with Glottis whose tongue is wreathed in his throat.
> For I am the seed of the WELCH WOMAN and speak the truth from my heart.
> Let Micah rejoice with the spotted Spider, who counterfeits death to effect his purposes.
> For they lay wagers touching my life. – God be gracious to the winners.
>
> (B 1, 91–92)

Yet Smart's anxiety about 'tongues' may have produced too good a poetic defense mechanism. It is not immediately obvious that the animals here are cited for *their* defence mechanisms. 'Let Abiezer, the Anethothite, rejoice with Phrynos who is the scaled frog. For I am like a frog in the brambles, but the Lord hath put his whole armour upon me' (B 1, 95). Euphemism and benediction feed the perpetual motion machine of Smart's poetry. 'Let' and 'For,' and such punnable morphemes as 'cat' and 'ble' (bull), are linguistic simples, easily combined into phrases and sentences. They support the poet's run-on, combinatory technique, his compulsion to perpetual benevolence.

This may turn, also, by a momentum of its own, into a cat-and-mouse game with language, to see how much life can be eked out before the spirit fails and an adversary consciousness, or melancholia,[14] penetrates:

> For the power of some animal is predominant in every language.
> For the power and spirit of a CAT is in the Greek.
> For the sound of a cat is in the most useful preposition κατεὺχην.
> For the pleasantry of a cat at pranks is in the language ten thousand times over.
> For JACK UPON PRANCK is in the performance of περι together or seperate.
> For Clapperclaw is in the grappling of the words upon one another in all the modes of versification.
> For the sleekness of a Cat is in his αγλαιηφι.
> For the Greek is thrown from heaven and falls upon its feet.
> For the Greek when distracted from the line is sooner restored to rank & rallied into some form than any other.
> For the purring of a Cat is his own τρυζει.
> For his cry is in ουαι which I am sorry for.
> For the Mouse (Mus) prevails in the Latin.
> For Edi-mus, bibi-mus, vivi-mus – ore-mus.
>
> (B 2, 627–39)

In brief, the overdetermination of simples like 'cat' or 'mus' keeps us within a sphere of childlike instruction. Smart's poem, at these points, is not so much a renovated liturgy as a marvelously inflated hornbook: a spiritual grammar rock ('Conjunction Junction, What's your function?') which averts discontinuity or catastrophic thoughts. However serious the content, the form remains propaedeutic; however dangerous Smart's insight, the verse recovers into business ('benevolence') as usual.

Despite Smart's delightful and outrageous wordplay, then, his resourcefulness may be a testing of the source, and his witty, promiscuous conjunctions may point to the fear of being cut off, by his family, or eternally by Satanic accusation. How else are we to understand that long fragment which is but a variation of 'Let X, house of X, rejoice with creature Y'?

> Let Westbrooke, house of Westbrooke rejoice with the Quail of Bengal. God be gracious to the people of Maidstone.
> Let Allcock, house of Allcock rejoice with The King of the Wavows a strange fowl. I pray for the whole University of Cambridge especially Jesus College this blessed day.
> Let Audley, house of Audley rejoice with The Green Crown Bird. The Lord help on with the hymns.
> Let Bloom, house of Bloom rejoice with Hecatompus a fish with an hundred feet.
> Let Beacon, house of Beacon rejoice with Amadavad a fine bird in the East Indies.
> Let Blomer, house of Blomer rejoice with Halimus a Shrub to hedge with. Lord have mercy upon poor labourers this bitter frost Decr. 29 N.S. 1762.
>
> (D, 197–202)

Here the themes of house, foundation, fertility and rejoicing are interlaced with cries for help and mercy. The contiguity of 'Maidstone' and 'Allcock' is a parallel puzzle. 'Without contraries,' Blake wrote, 'no progression,' but what is progressive here except a verse that somehow keeps renewing itself?

I want to explore further the 'wreathed' way in which Smart builds his verse. Take his basic words 'Let' and 'For.' Though they 'generate' sentences, they are really a *stutterance*: a verbal compromise-formation which at once 'lets' (hinders) and forwards his song ('Let Forward, house of Forward rejoice with Immussulus a kind of bird the Lord forward my translation of the psalms this year' D, 220). 'Let' is close to being a primal word with antithetical meanings; and the tension between these meanings – whether identified as control and permissiveness or contraction and expansiveness or chastity and promiscuity – can give an extraordinary twist effect to the verse. Sometimes the contraries are almost too close to be spotted ('*Let For*ward . . .'); sometimes they seem apposites rather than opposites because of their position in the paired pattern of the verse ('Let . . . For . . .'); and sometimes they form a crisscross pattern varying in distance (how far is it from 'Maidstone' to 'Allcock'?).

Smart has left us hints of a poetics of pairing, opposition and distancing:

> For the relations of words are in pairs first.
> For the relations of words are sometimes in oppositions.
> For the relations of words are according to their distances from the pair.
>
> (B 2, 600–602)

It could roughly summarize the actual unfolding of verse sentences in Smart: words are in pairs first, 'Let Jubal rejoice with Caecilia'; this pairing may also introduce a contrast, 'the woman and the slow-worm' (B 1, 43). The contrast may be more pathetic as when 'Let Jorim rejoice with the Roach' is followed by 'God bless my throat & keep me from things stranggled' (B 1, 179). The oppositions Smart mentions can also be that of the 'Let' verse and the 'For' response. Relations of distance, finally, are clearest in a group of iterative or antiphonal verses. In

> Let Jubal rejoice with Caecilia, the woman and the slow-worm praise the name of the Lord.
> For I pray the Lord Jesus to translate my MAGNIFICAT into verse and represent it
>
> (B 1, 43)

the first, relatively easy relation of words (Jubal and Caecilia being well-known patrons of music) becomes progressively more allusive and distant. Caecilia and the worm are linked by an etymological play on the Latin for the slow- or blind-worm (Caecilian, from *caecus*), but it needs more than curious learning to connect woman and worm with Mary's Magnificat through (1) the identification of Jesus as the seed of the woman who bruised the serpent's head (slow-worm/ Caecilia; serpent/ Eve); (2) the idea of 'translation,' that is, transformation, as from low to high, or from one species to another; and (3) the pun on Magnificat which turns the word into a compound (Magnific-cat) and so establishes fully the relation between the 'Let' and 'For' verses through the paired opposition of lowly worm and magnified creature.[15]

To refine this kind of analysis is to come ultimately on the *hendiadys* in covert or open form. Puns are condensed or covert two-in-one structures, while Smart's synthetic compounding of nouns or nounlike words provides a more open form of the hendiadys. Allcock and Maidstone, when interpreted as two-folds, are simply hendiadys; Magnificat is a somewhat more complex instance; Jorim seems atomic until we notice its Hebrew plural ending (creating, once again, uncertainty as to whether a creature is to be thought of as one or more than one); and 'the woman and the slow-worm,' as it emerges from the name 'Caecilia,' is an especially characteristic hendiadys. One begins to suspect every name, in this name-freighted poetry, of being potentially emanative: other parts of speech too seem often like the attributes or derived sounds of some magical noun. Smart composes as if he had a choice between analytic and synthetic language formation, as if he were writing a Hebrew-English or Hebrew-Greek-Latin-English. Something of this is certainly in his mind, since he shares in the pentecostal aim to reconcile Babel into a universal code of worship. But whatever it is he wishes to achieve, the hendiadys is indispensable. There are remarkable moments in which his verses 'reproduce' or 'replicate' by drawing two or even three words out of one, yet remain one-ly:

Let Jorim rejoice with the Roach – God bless my throat & keep me from things
  stranggled.
Let Addi rejoice with the Dace – It is good to angle with meditation.
Let Luke rejoice with the Trout – Blessed be Jesus in Aa, in Dee and in Isis.

(B 1, 179–81)

In the first verse above, Roach, a monosyllable, if read on the analogy of
Jorim, becomes disyllabic, with an aspirated ending (Ro-ach),[16] so that the
'stranggled' is not only thematically sustained by the image of the caught fish but
equally by the throaty sound. In the following verses we see a proper noun,
Addi, breaking up into three components that are sounds or rivers or both: Aa,
Dee, Isis (A-D-I). Strictly speaking, we need only the 'i' of Isis to complete Addi
(itself a pun on the additive process?). But even the -sis may be accounted for if
we read Isis as I-c's, and by a bit of scrabbling involve the second proper noun,
Dace, also composed of the letter-sounds, A, D, and – this time – C. One name
is A,D, plus I; the other A,D, plus C; so that Jesus (that famous fish, almost
rhyming here with Isis, considering the closeness of I and J) comprehends both
names, being blessed in A, in D, and in I, C's.

It is almost impossible to summarize Smart's poetic method. It is not, or not
only, a 'mad, philological vision of reality.'[17] It does not, or not merely, subvert the
referential aspect of words like Isis by deconstructing them as acoustic images or
magical sounds. It is best seen as a sacred poetics driving to astonishing extremes the
principle of antiphony or 'parallelism of members' (Is–is!) discovered by Bishop
Lowth in the Psalms. So, Jorim goes with the Roach and is paralleled by Addi with
the Dace, and even by angle 'with' meditation; while Addi and Dace and Isis can
be shown to be 'members' of Jesus. But how do you fit in Hecatompus with an
hundred feet? 'Why, then, I'le fit you!' And, indeed, there is a mad attempt to
speak with tongues and write with all those feet, to re-member or re-present every
last creature by a 'pairing' that will exclude nothing from the 'Ark' of testimony.

In society the simplest form of representation (in the sense of a normative
presentation of the self) is by one's personal name. Names are a compromise, of
course; for no name is unique; and Smart's use of single names (Abraham, Jorim,
Dace, Hecatompus) makes them ambiguously individual and generic.[18] Names,
moreover, like all proper nouns, are curiously split in their semantic character.
They tend to be both subsemantic (so conventional as to be meaningless,
semantically neutral) and supersemantic (they can be analyzed or pseudoana-
lyzed into richly meaningful parts). The idea of naming, therefore, recapitulates
the drama played out in Smart's verse. Names individualize and socialize: they
are always a kind of two-in-one. 'Christopher Smart' names a single person
whose Christ-bearing (Christopher) wit and wound (Smart) are one like the
'Lord, and the Lamb' (A, 1) are one.

Every individual is *impair*. He sticks out or should stick out. Yet selfhood is both a demand to be met and subject to accusation. Analysis could go from here in many directions: religious, sociological, or what I have called psychoesthetic. Smart invariably connects representability of the self (*by* language, *with* the creature, and *to* God) and the treatment of the impair (also the impaired). He first reduces the impair to an infantile charm or a linguistic simple (cat, mus, the opaque proper noun, and so forth). By this method he both acknowledges and comforts the isolation of each creature. The linguistic simple, at the same time, is given the chance to multiply or replicate, but the match that results also escapes divine assessment. It cannot be judged. Will you frown at 'Rehob' because he 'rejoices with Caucalis Bastard Parsley'? Or at the Wild Cucumber with which 'Nebai' is asked to rejoice (C, 152, 160)? Such matchmakings are beyond good and evil.

It may be useful to summarize the ways of Smart with language because his comforting of creatureliness extends to language – to sounds and words, large and small. He delights in (1) morphemes which can be individualized as words (cat, Dee); (2) words that are reduplicative in structure and remain simples because quasi-reversible (Aa, David, Amadavad, Wavow, Immussulus); (3) self-replicating or redundant phrases which can expand into a whole verse, as in the following (D, 175) inspired by the very idea of 're': 'Let Ready, house of Ready' (redundancy) 'rejoice' (Re . . . Re . . . re . . .) 'with Junco The Reed Sparrow' (Ready . . . Reed); (4) the categorical hendiadys, which brings together, not as in the story of Noah, pairs of the same species but unmatable *res creatae*.

If the ark into which these pairs enter cannot be that of generation, it must be that of regeneration. But does regeneration involve or exclude generation? The new order here invoked, at once linguistic and ontic, coexists ambivalently with an older order which it neither subsumes nor yet suppresses. Smart's poetics of relation never quite turns into a poetics of translation. The name 'Jesus' embraces the name 'Isis' and the result is a speckled language. In the opening scene of the *Jubilate*, when Abraham presents a ram and Jacob his speckled drove, we cannot tell whether sexual generation is being sacrificed or consecrated.

Theory as Epilogue

A swallow is an emancipated owl, and a glorified bat . . . an owl that has been trained by the Graces . . . a bat that loves the morning light.

J. Ruskin, *Love's Meinie*

Let Shephatiah rejoice with the little Owl, which is the wingged Cat.

C. Smart

The newest movement in philosophy, which extends into literary studies, questions the idea of presence. It is said to be an illusion fostered by our tendency to privilege voice over the written word. Voice, for Jacques Derrida, is the egotistical sublime, and our desire for the proper name (*mot propre, nom unique*) a metaphysical comfort. The best voice can do is to become literature; that is, to subvert its referential or representational function by bruising itself on the limits of language.

Derrida moves within a philosophical context of his own, and it is confusing to juxtapose his theory and Smart's poetics. I apologize for this 'perspective by incongruity,' as Kenneth Burke would call it, but I see no better way of suggesting how complex yet empty the concept of representation may become. Even if one acknowledges that Derrida's very aim is to empty this concept, at least of its psychologistic and metaphysical pathos, the 'nature' of representation remains a puzzle.[19]

I have argued that representation supports the ideal of self-presence in its psychic and social aspects. 'Vilest things become themselves in her,' Shakespeare's Enobarbus says of Cleopatra. She is 'beautiful in corruption,' like Smart's 'Eyed Moth' (B 1, 93); and Enobarbus may indeed be playing on the idea of life engendered by Nilotic slime. Yet toward this 'becoming,' this triumph over the shame of creaturely origin, artistic representation also aspires. It may turn out, of course, that representation is all there is, and that we will never experience a self-presence in which we see – and are seen – not as in a glass darkly but face to face. Yet who can decide how ultimate the category of substitution is, and in particular the substitution of representation for presence?

The tropes of literature, or similar kinds of imaginative substitution, could as easily be said to pursue that 'presence' which 'identifies' all creatures, as to defer it. Perhaps it does not matter which, since both pursuit and deferment are endless. That the identifying moment, like a snapshot, is too deathlike or ecstatic; that movement or troping must begin again; that the acute self-consciousness must be transcended by an act of what is commonly called imagination – all this is part of the psychopathology of ordinary life, or of that principle of 'clapperclaw' which 'joyces' language in Shakespeare, Smart, and even in Derrida.

It may be that the theory of representation finds a less problematic exponent in an intermediate figure, more congruous with Smart, and exerting through Proust some influence on French thought. Let me conclude, then, with a note on John Ruskin. His prose may be the best nature poetry in the language. Ruskin also 'represents' the creature, though to his fellow-man rather than God. How sane he appears when placed beside Smart, even if touched by a madness and childishness similar to Smart's. There is probably no better antidote to the *Jubilate Agno* than Ruskin's celebration of robin and swallow in *Love's Meinie*.[20]

These lectures, given by him as Slade Professor of Fine Art before the University of Oxford, are clearly acts of reparation toward robin and swallow and, indeed, all 'lower classes' exploited by the Victorian combination of

Wealth and Science 'That, then, is the utmost which the lords of land, and masters of science, do for us in their watch upon our feathered suppliants One kills them, the other writes classifying epitaphs.' The painters and monks, lumped together by Ruskin, do us no good either: 'They have plucked the wings from birds, to make angels of men, and the claws from birds, to make devils of men.' The emphasis on genetic development in Darwinian science seems equally pernicious to Ruskin, who fears that all such speculation on origins will distract us from the present, from the endangered beauty and aptness of the *living* creature.

But it is not the common creatures alone, the swallows, fissi rostres, or split-beaks, which must be saved. The common words too must be 'represented': English names in their vernacular being, winged expressions which lead Ruskin to reflect on the troubadours, Chaucer and the *Romance of the Rose*. The habitat of the creature is in literature and art as well as in wood and field. Nature and art are both endangered by the deadly Latin of modern anatomical analysis.[21] We should not see the things of this world under the species of a false objectivity, or of its killing nomenclature, but through the medium of their own nature and the *lingua franca et jocundissima* of vernacular perception. Reading *Love's Meinie* I repent me for not being able to 'translate' such words as 'representation.' 'All of you who care for life as well as literature,' Ruskin advises, 'and for spirit, – even the poor souls of birds, – as well as lettering of their classes in books, – you, with all care, should cherish the old Saxon, English and Norman-French names of birds, and ascertain them with the most affectionate research.'

Notes

1. In this discussion I occasionally rely on sections 6 and 7 of 'I. A. Richards and The Dream of Communication' in my *The Fate of Reading* (Chicago, 1975). On self-presence, see also E. Goffman, *The Presentation of the Self in Everyday Life* (New York, 1959); on shame (and embarrassment), O. F. Bollnow, *Die Ehrfurcht* (Frankfurt a/M., 1947), and H. M. Lynd, *On Shame and the Search for Identity* (New York, 1958); and on the relation of theatricality to presence of self, the studies of Jonas A. Barish on 'Antitheatrical Prejudice,' *Critical Quarterly* 8 (1966): 329–48, and *ELH* 36 (1969): 1–29, as well as Lionel Trilling, *Sincerity and Authenticity* (New York, 1972), passim.

2. See Coleridge, 'On Original Sin,' in *Aids to Reflection* (London, 1831): "Where there is no discontinuity there can be no origination, and every appearance of origination in nature is but a shadow of our own casting. It is a reflection from our own will or spirit. Herein, indeed, the will consists. This is the essential character by which Will is opposed to Nature, as spirit, and raised above Nature as self-determining spirit."

3. Fragment B 1, 43. My references throughout are to W. H. Bond's edition of the *Jubilate Agno* (London, 1954).

4. See 'I. A. Richards and the Dream of Communication.' Since the first demands of the child focus on the mother, there may be a tendency later on to imagine a less used up, that is, *male*, source of comfort.

5. Coleridge, a century after Swift, is still deeply worried by enthusiasm, and makes this analysis in the 'Conclusion' to *Aids to Reflection*.

6. 'Le sot project qu'il a de se peindre et cela non pas en passant et contre ses maximes, comme il arrive à tout le monde de faillir, mais par ses propres maximes et par un dessein premier et principal. Car de dire des sottises par hasard et par faiblesse, c'est un mal ordinaire; mais d'en dire par dessein, c'est ce qui n'est pas supportable, et d'en dire de telles que celles-ci.' (Blaise Pascal, *L'Apologie de la religion chrétienne in Oeuvres Complètes*, vol. 3, ed. Fortunat Strowski [Paris, 1931].)

7. I have considerably abridged Pascal's *Mémorial* as found in his *Pensées*, trans. A. J. Krailsheimer (Baltimore, 1964), pp. 309–10.

8. W. K. Wimsatt, Jr., 'The Augustan Mode in English Poetry,' in *Hateful Contraries* (Lexington, KY, 1966), pp. 158–62.

9. Part of Coleridge's attack on Enthusiasm in *Aids to Reflection*.

10. From Hervey's 'Contemplations on the Starry Heavens.'

11. "Clapperclaw" is an archaic verb, meaning to scratch and claw, to attack with tooth and nail. Smart seems to be implying that the words in a poem should be associated as violently and powerfully as cats in a fight claw and bite one another.' (Moira Dearnley, *The Poetry of Christopher Smart* [London, 1969], pp. 163–4). But 'clapperclaw' was also theater-slang for applause (a theme dear to Smart) so that an ambivalent and complex relation is suggested between various drives: the sexual-aggressive, the verbal-expressive, the applause-seeking (theatrical and exhibitionist), and the applause-seeking (antiphonal and divine). For the slang term, see the printer's address to the reader in the first quarto of Shakespeare's *Troilus and Cressida*: '*A never writer to an ever reader. News.* Eternal reader, you have here a new play, never staled with the stage, never clapper-clawed with the palms of the vulgar, and yet passing full of the palm comical.'

12. See his 'Life of Milton' and 'Life of Waller' in *The Lives of the English Poets* (London, 1779–81).

13. Consider how many aspects of this poetry reflect a concern with generation: the Biblical genealogies, from which Smart borrows many names; the generic emphasis of the names themselves; the personal allusions to family; and puns that range from the simple and innocuous to the complex and atrocious. Of the first kind is 'Let Gibeon rejoice with the Puttock, who will shift for himself to the last extremity' (B 1, 81), and of the second, perhaps, 'For the power of the Shears is direct as the life' (B 1, 179). Stead and Bond give a tenuous explanation of this line by referring to ancient methods of divination and so on, but a cruder and more powerful one emerges if 'Shears' is read as 'She-ars.'

14. One reason David fascinated Smart was that this 'cunning player on an harp' drove away 'the evil spirit' from Saul (1 Samuel 16:14–23).

15. See W. M. Merchant, 'Patterns of Reference in Smart's *Jubilate Agno*,' *Harvard*

Library Bulletin 14 (1960), p. 23; and Moira Dearnley, *The Poetry of Christopher Smart,* pp. 156 ff.

16. 'Ro-ach,' in fact, moves close to 'Ru-ach,' Hebrew for breath or spirit. See *Jubilate Agno,* B 2, 626.

17. Dearnley, *The Poetry of Christopher Smart,* p. 164.

18. Even representation by the personal name is not so simple a matter, then. Smart's enumerative evocation of names (taken from obituaries as well as genealogies) is analogous to invoking saints or intermediaries, yet he so expands the roster that representation, while verging on mediation, insists on the *proprium* of each proper noun.

19. I do not know how Derrida would interpret Smart's use of names and proper nouns. Or his ritually insistent, repetitive, affirmations. Would he compare all this with Nietzsche's 'affirmation en jeu' or Heidegger's risky 'espérance'? See his crucial essay on 'La différance' in *Marges de la Philosophie* (Paris, 1972), especially pp. 25–9.

20. Much of Ruskin's work in the 1860s and early 1870s was secretly aimed at weaning young Rose La Touche from a religious enthusiasm (not unlike Smart's, though morbid and distinctly Evangelical in origin) which was to end in her mental derangement, symptoms of which Ruskin also carried within himself. *Love's Meinie* (parts I and II on robin and swallow were published in 1873; part III on the chough in 1881) ministers to a mind diseased by giving glory back to life. It has its private as well as public dimension: Ruskin weaves, for example, the *Roman de la Rose* into his book because it must have seemed an equally troubled yet saner version of the 'Romance' he was experiencing in his own courtship of Rose.

21. The problem of taxonomy is at the center of Michel Foucault's work, which views 'science' and 'madness' as obverse modes of representation. Linnaeus, founder of the Latin terminology to which Ruskin objects, was of Smart's era.

Chapter 2

Evening Star and Evening Land

> to say of the evening star,
> The most ancient light in the most ancient sky
> That it is wholly an inner light, that it shines
> From the sleepy bosom of the real, re-creates,
> Searches a possible for its possibleness.
>
> Wallace Stevens

> The perished patterns murmur
>
> Emily Dickinson

For most readers the charm of Akenside's 'Ode to the Evening Star,' a minor piece of the 1740s,[1] resides in its first stanza, perhaps even in its first two lines:

> To-night retir'd, the queen of heaven
> With young Endymion stays:
> And now to Hesper it is given
> Awhile to rule the vacant sky,
> Till she shall to her lamp supply
> A stream of brighter rays.

The rising of the moon is delayed, in Akenside's version of the myth, because she is dallying with a human lover, the shepherd Endymion; there is something like a divine, erotic slowing of time, familiar from myths associated with Jove or the prevention of dawn; the theme of 'staying' (1.2) leads, moreover, into that of 'supply' (1.5), so that it is tempting to connect the moon's dalliance with her brightened lamp, her refurbished rising. Yet the myth does not flower into the form of an epyllion or little romance: it glimmers above the action like a distant star or constelled image. The poem remains a curious variant on addresses to the Evening Star. Hesper's brief reign suits perhaps the idea of the brief hymn whose prototype the eighteenth century found in a small poem attributed to Bion.[2]

Bion's influence can only be understood through some ideal of classic decorum, of silver mediocrity. His poem approximates the length of an epigram or what was considered as its modern form, the sonnet – and it is a juvenile sonnet Coleridge will hymn to *his* Evening Star in 1790.[3] But in Akenside a tension is felt between the compact form and its narrative elaboration. If his opening stanza is more condensed and suggestive than anything in Bion, the remainder of this poem of 78 lines (compared to Bion's 8) is devious and prolix. Akenside seems to have a problem with 'development' or 'manner of proceeding,' not uncommon in eighteenth-century lyrics, and especially nature poems.

In the Romantic poets the nature lyric is as much about consciousness as about nature. Moreover, it is often about the *development* of consciousness; and this dynamic factor helps poets in the otherwise paradoxical task to plot, or narrate, nature. Akenside's problem may hinge, similarly, on finding a developmental pattern. Not for nature so much as for poetry: how can poetry, at this time in its life, be developed? Does it have a future or only a past? The course of the poem is so stylized that one thinks of the sorrows of the poet rather than of Olympia's mourning lover – the tears are tears of the muses, cultured pearls. The poet's concern seems to be with literary rather than personal continuity, or how the first bears on the second. Hesper is invoked as a link in a symbolic chain leading from loss to acceptance, and strongly suggesting the centrality of poetic sublimation.

New Lamps for Old

In its simple form, patterned on Bion, the Hymn to the Evening Star makes Hesper a surrogate moon, a night-light guiding lover to beloved. But Akenside has 'herald Hesper' (Keats) light the way to loss rather than to the beloved, for the star leads him to a second symbolic agent, the nightingale, which wakes memories of loss under the very moon that is the traditional sign of consummated love or restored presence. Ben Jonson's famous lyric from *Cynthia's Revels* (1601) with the refrain 'Hesperus entreats thy light/Goddess excellently bright' and Milton's 'Now came still Ev'ning on' (*Paradise Lost*, VI. 598–609) follow the straight pattern and so illumine the deviousness of the later ode. Hesperus, in Milton, is to the absence of light as the nightingale is to that of sound: both are 'wakeful' powers that bridge a dark moment and prepare hierarchically for the emergence of the moon as 'Apparent Queen.' Compared to the purity of Jonson's, Milton's, and Bion's sequence, Akenside's lyric is the night-ramble of a gloomy egotist.

The formal problem is made more intriguing by the fact that the first three stanzas of the hymn, though prelusive, are a detachable unit. Close in theme and length to Bion's lyric, they constitute a small hailing that sets the scene (first stanza), invokes the star (second stanza), and rounds the invocation with a vow (third stanza). Their internal structure is equally cohesive. What the moon is to Endymion, Hesper is to be for the poet: both condescend, the one for love-brightness, the other for the poet's sake. This descendentalism exists, however, within a vivid sense of hierarchy. The latinate diction, in fact, and the elaborate, even contrived syntax of lines 9 to 12 sensitize the reader to the whole question of subordination.

> Oh listen to my suppliant song,
> If haply now the vocal sphere
> Can suffer thy delighted ear
> To stoop to mortal sounds

The poem's formal development is closely linked to the tension that surrounds the concept of subordination. If the first three stanzas are contortedly archaic in their evocation of sidereal hierarchy and the last three a moralizing frame aiming at a similar kind of overview, the middle or narrative portion of the ode depicts a reversal of influence. Philomel gradually becomes a star-symbol replacing Hesper, as he the moon. Though we begin in heaven, and stars stoop to conquer, as we approach ritually the magic center or 'green space' of the nightingale (a centering movement we meet often in this type of poem), power flows from earth to heaven. In stanza 7 the nightingale's song 'holds' the moon above the lovers in a repetition of the 'staying' which began the ode, and in stanza 10 the breezes that attend the path of the nightingale's song repeat the star's attendance on Hesper (II. 6–7):

> Hark, how through many a melting note
> She now prolongs her lays:
> How sweetly down the void they float!
> The breeze their magic path attends
> The stars shine out: the forest bends
> The wakeful heifers gaze.

This transfer of power, or reversal of earthly and starry agents, was foreshadowed by syntactical and phonemic stresses in the opening stanzas.[4]

'Far other vows must I prefer . . .' With these words, and still paying formal tribute to Hesper, Akenside deviates from Bion. He converts the Evening Star poem into something psychic and strange, haunted by loss, memory, sublimation, and the influence of poetic song. He leads us to a symmetrical and cunning space:

> See the green space: on either hand
> Inlarg'd it spreads around:
> See, in the midst she takes her stand . . .

both empty and full, natural yet ghostly. That narrow, clearly framed, yet open space is not unlike poetry, especially when based on the classical sense of centering. The very predominance of a prototype, the very fixation on theme or symbol, becomes the poet's way to a wilder symbolic action and an enlarged vision of continuity.

A Phenomenological Thematics

The Evening Star poem is a fickle and minor genre. But its brief span of life, mainly as an eighteenth-century idyllion, belies the interest of a theme that poets occasionally renew and which is constantly merging with the larger question of continuity – personal or historical. The dual name of the star, Hesper (Vesper) and Phosphor (Venus), evening and morning star, and its 'genial' (Venus-y or procreative) aspect make it symbolic of a continuity that persists within apparent loss. The epigram attributed to Plato and rendered by Shelley as

> Thou wert the morning star among the living
>   Ere thy fair light had fled;–
> Now, having died, thou art as Hesperus, giving
> New splendour to the dead[5]

is the very emblem of triumphant sublimation, of identity maintained in the realms of death.

In its broadest literary aspect, the starry theme becomes expressive of the problematics of *poesy*. Is there a true literary-historical continuity, a great chain of great poets, or how much vision (sublime style) can be saved? By 1750 the starry theme was in doubt; and while Blake in his deep and virtuoso way talks once more of poets 'appearing' to him in the 'poetical heavens,' their succession is generally felt to be uncertain. Gray's 'Stanzas to Mr. Bentley' (1752) expresses the sense of his age that poetry is in eclipse.

> But not to one in this benighted age
> Is that diviner inspiration given,
> That burns in Shakespear's or in Milton's page,
> The pomp and prodigality of heav'n.

This 'not to one' may well echo Collins's 'Ode on the Poetical Character,' which assumes that each age has 'one only one' significant poet and that his own age has not even him:

> Heav'n, and Fancy, kindred Pow'rs,
> Have now o'erturned th' inspiring Bow'rs,
> Or curtain'd close such Scene from ev'ry future View.

Despite this cultural pessimism, hope does not die. Blake realized that the poets' loss of confidence was related to a wrong understanding of poetry's high seriousness. The divine makers of the previous era had raised poetry to the skies. Their strength had shown that Poetry and Divinity were 'kindred pow'rs.' But this did not mean poetry could compete with religion on religion's ground – as Milton had 'inimitably' done. To burden it with divinity, to raise it to a sky preempted by the frozen forms of national religion, was to sink it under a weight Dr. Johnson's obstinate bass unwearily reiterated: 'The good and evil of Eternity are too ponderous for the wings of wit. The mind sinks under them in passive helplessness, content with calm belief and humble admiration.' The sidereal universe of religion, as he also said, could not be magnified.

In these circumstances, to bring an angel down could be more important than to raise a mortal to the skies. I will call this harrowing of the skies the descendental theme. So Milton enters Blake's left foot, and was already shown by Collins (in a complex image that goes up and down simultaneously) in the Eden of his own invention, and raising an 'Evening Ear' from its ethereal dews toward a sphery music.[6]

Yet *poesy* is by no means a direct subject of evening star poems. The larger historical pathos is simply part of their aura. We begin, rather, with 'the nightes dread,'[7] a power failure or dangerous interval, a moment when the light goes out. The evening star rises in that space, on that loss; and however strongly it rises there is often the fear of new withdrawal ('Soon, full soon, dost thou withdraw')[8] and the dangerous sense that 'sacred dew' or starry 'influence' no longer prevails. To the descendental theme we can add, therefore, that of the dangerous, *interlunar* moment.

It is remarkable that in Blake's poem on the evening star the moon does not actually rise; but were it to rise it would just be a second star rather than a transcending presence. 'Genius dies with its Possessor, and does not rise again until Another is born.' There is a difference between Blake and Milton on this: Blake thinks of each great poet as a new and equal star.

Indeed, though Hesperus is traditionally the moon's precursor, it can be subversive of that 'laboring' planet. As the most brilliant of the early stars it becomes for the expectant mind a singular mark. It seems absolute in its 'steadfast' (if often brief) presence, and begins to stand for itself rather than for something to come. It expresses a power of feeling that is both solipsistic and unchanging, or so transcendently hopeful as not to be fulfilled by a temporal – chronologically easy – next stage. Its 'intense lamp' does not die into another light: it narrows into itself, or sets unmodified in a kind of *liebestod*.[9]

With this we reach a difficult and subtle motif. As the moon of its own twilight zone, Hesperus tends to personify the threshold and evoke an enchanted spot of time in which a richly ominous signifier is all there is. The star-signifier appears as a sign accompanied by signs, or leading to other symbols rather than to a sign-transcending reality. Since man cannot live by signs alone, the evening star poem rouses our reality-hunger and perplexes the very idea of *development*.

In this it is like love itself, or desire. The star cannot be more than a sign, given the intensity of the desire invoking it. The poem feeds the sign, even fattens it: it wants it to be, if not more than a sign, then more of a sign. Yet the most successful poetry is still, so Shelley knew, 'as darkness to a dying flame.' The symbol remains a threshold; and the idea of development, of a waxing and waning that is also a ripening, a movement beyond mutability, remains moot. Darkness re-enters the progression of interlunar moment, evening star, moon-rise, at any point.

Why then, one might ask, do we need a starry paradigm at all? Could not any pseudo-progression serve? The reason why there is a star-symbolism is clarified by Los's struggle with his Spectre:

> Los reads the Stars of Albion! the Spectre reads the Voids
> Between the Stars; among the Arches of Albion's Tomb
> sublime . . .

Plate 91 of *Jerusalem* shows Los decreating the sublime structures of traditional visionary poetry, which have been, in Blake's interpretation, a 'Tomb sublime,' that is, built upon, or in fearful reaction to, 'the Voids.' Los smites the Spectre, or his ingrained habits of perceiving, until

> all his pyramids were grains
> Of sand & his pillars: dust on the flys wing: & his starry
> Heavens; a moth of gold & silver mocking his anxious grasp.

What is foreseen here, though not attained − for Los remains 'anxious,' trembling before his new-found mortality as previously before phantoms − is a sublimity not based on sublimation. The stars, therefore, remain, but become as mortal (or immortal) as men. They are 'consumed' like erotic desire and reborn out of its satisfaction:

> The stars consumd like a lamp blown out & in their stead behold
> The Expanding Eyes of Man behold the depths of wondrous worlds
> One Earth one sea beneath nor Erring Globes wander but Stars
> Of fire rise up nightly from the Ocean & one Sun
> Each morning like a New born Man issues with songs & Joy[10]

The most interesting Romantic lyrics do not begin in the sky. They begin, nevertheless, with an interlunar moment created by the descendental 'smiting' so powerfully stylized in Blake. There is a downward displacement of the stars which gives the impression of (1) sidereal darkness, and (2) new powers (stars) emerging from below. Poetry itself, at this point in history, is generically associated with this downward displacement of the sky's energies. Our phenomenological thematics, in other words, become poetical.

Let me give two examples of the starry theme no longer in its thematic form, or not purely so. We are, for instance, only subliminally aware on reading

> Tyger Tyger, burning bright,
> In the forests of the night

that what is bing evoked is also a star, and that this 'descendental' constellation, Tyger, presides over the moment after Hesper has set, when 'the lion glares thro' the dun forest.' And while there might seem to be no relation whatsoever between Blake's lyric and Wordsworth's 'Daffodils,' the poet who wanders 'lonely as a cloud/That floats on high o'er vales and hills,' could collide with a star. And that is, more or less, what happens: a moment of withdrawal, of Wordsworthian inwardness, is suddenly filled with the shock of *earthly* stars:

> When all at once I saw a crowd
> A host of golden daffodils . . .

The 'golden' hint of these lines is elaborated by 'Continuous as the stars that shine/And twinkle on the Milky Way,' and the 'flash' of the final stanza.[11]

The interlunar moment merges in Wordsworth with the themes of retirement, reflectiveness, and self-renewal. His flowery shock is the downward obverse of the emotion of the sublime. In other poems, of course, up and down are more dizzyingly related – not only in the great passages from *The Prelude* (Mont Blanc, the Simplon Pass, Snowdon) but also in such evening poems as 'Composed by the Side of Lake Grasmere' where the lake that yields a 'vivid repetition of the stars' leads him into a curious surmise:

> Is it [the lake] a mirror, or the nether Sphere
> Opening to view the abyss in which she feeds
> Her own calm fires?

But not only the content of the surmise interests here. If we try to go beyond thematics to poetics, the surmise becomes significant as a surmise, as part of a larger act of the poetic mind.

Wordsworth: (1) Star and Surmise

The surmise comes from a sonnet composed when 'clouds, lingering yet, extend in solid bars/Through the grey west.' This lingering, a moment of suspense or interregnum, points to the interlunar rising of Hesperus. The brightest stars are already visible, intensified by the 'mirror' of the lake. 'And lo! these waters, steeled/By breezeless air to smoothest polish, yield/A vivid repetition of the stars.' The word 'steeled,' which continues the metaphor 'solid bars,' echoes in the mind as 'stilled' – 'Tranquillity is here' (1. 14). Deeply internal, it repeats the wishful progress of the whole poem from martial to pastoral.

Yet no thematic continuity in Wordsworth is as remarkable as the poet's mind 'in the act of finding/What will suffice.' Stillness, for that mind, is never loss: life should appear within loss, presence within absence. The evening sight is analogous, therefore, to the poet's morning vision of London from Westminster Bridge. The 'lo' (1. 2) and 'list' (1. 11) converge as gestures that skirt a desired epiphany. Yet, even as the mind searches for the sufficient, the twilight nature of the moment is fully respected. The very formality of the sonnet prevents the moment from merging into a next stage – it does not 'die' into light. Time is almost suspended, like the clouds of the opening lines. The poem becomes a little sphere, restless within (since neither cloudland nor the battle-scarred earth suffices) but turning on its own axis, and furnished with its twilight, and tutelary, voice.

The image of clouds as bars already betrays the poet's desire for something firmer than cloud, for a *grounding* of eye or imagination. His descendental movement from sky to earth and even into earth is a movement toward both stillness (peace) and that ground. The more human field he reaches is, however, the Napoleonic battlefield, 'earth's groaning field.' The imagination moves away again, trying the nether sphere just as it had previously stepped among the stars. But the image of 'calm fires' is counter-volcanic, and shows how precarious each speculation ('fancy') is: the middle-ground sought by Wordsworth, the twilight moment he respects, is always about to fade into starlight or fire.[12] To call earth's fires 'calm' (sated) only emphasizes in its very boldness the restless journeying of his imagination toward a fold. So that the surmise ('Is it a mirror, or the nether Sphere . . .') is a restraint on that epiphanic movement, a 'lingering' comparable to that of the clouds. The Wordsworthian imagination remains unpastured: it hungers for calm and finds no shepherd. Except Pan, at the every end, in the form of a piped-in, reedy voice, the opposite of panic.

Wordsworth: (2) Star and Symbol

Before showing the deepest use, or displacement, of the evening star theme in Wordsworth, it is best to double back and consider poems where the theme is more explicitly present. Hesperus appears in two earlier poems, 'Fair Star of Evening, Splendor of the West,' written at Calais in August, 1802, and 'It is No Spirit Which from Heaven Hath Flown,' composed in 1803. Both exhibit that tension between *zoning* (the star seen as inhabiting its own zone separated by nature's or poetry's magic from various continua) and *zooming* (a sympathetic or ecstatic movement of identification) that we found in very subtle form in the Grasmere sonnet. The idea, for instance, of 'the sky/ He hath it to himself – 'tis all his own'[13] so corresponds to Wordsworth's own homing instinct that his appropriation of an image he has helped to create threatens to destroy the separateness essential to it. The poet zooms in on the star as his (and England's) encompassing symbol.

Both poems begin in the feeling of distance or exile. The earlier verses are written from Calais, with the poet looking toward his country during the fragile Peace of Amiens. The idea of an interregnum enters – however discreetly – if the political situation is kept in mind.[14] The star is 'hanging' on the horizon's brink above the dusky spot which is England; and Wordsworth, though he sees the star and his country as a twofold – one being the crown or bosom-jewel of the other-merges them finally into 'one hope, one lot, / One life, one glory.'

The star seems to be a symbol yet participates so nearly in the imaginative essence of 'real' England that symbol and reality converge. Wordsworth knows that his imagination needs a 'star' but he also knows it must be a 'native star.' It should encompass his own, human destiny from birth to setting. There is, on the one hand, a finely graded if descendental transformation of Hesperus from 'Star of Evening' to 'Star of my Country,' and, on the other, an identifying movement which collapses distances and degrades the star into an emblem ('my Country's emblem . . . with laughter on her banners').

Wordsworth's later poem expresses a deeper or more general sense of exile. The distance is not that from Calais to Dover but an undefinable one from 'my natural race'[15] to 'some ground not [presently] mine.' The star has transcended its zone by dominating the sky in broad daylight. It is so simply, so startlingly 'there' that it at once incites and repels descendental or metamorphic myths (lines 1–4). Wordsworth's need for a center or zoom, felt in the previous poem, culminates now in an almost hypnotic moment of enchanted stasis.

There is a further difference between the poems as acts of mind. The lyric of 1803 is more akin to experiences familiar to us from the great *Prelude* passages. Something startles sight by anticipating itself. Though the star is hoped for – indeed, one of hope's emblems – it defeats the perceptual or mythic apparatus prepared for its coming. It is there so naturally that it appears to be already *in its place* (compare line 13), that is, absolute, beyond temporal change. It has become a 'fixed star' to imagination.

The poet, it is true, still talks of it as a sign or 'admonition' (line 5). But then the octave of this lengthened sonnet is clearly a sparring for time – for rebounding from a sublime or unexpected impression. The real 'admonition' is to himself; and Wordsworth adverts to his own mind in the poem's second half, which no longer seeks to render the immediacy of an external image. It turns instead (note the tense change, from present to past) to what 'wrought' within him. With 'O most ambitious star' we reach, in fact, the symmetrical center (9–1–9) of the poem, its exact turning-point. This cry, star-oriented yet reflexive, turns us not from image to meaning – nowhere, and certainly not in Wordsworth, is imaging free of the interpretive consciousness – but from an objectifying mode that subsumes the subjective context, back to subjectivity. While Wordsworth's star-staring (lines 1–8) elides the sense of time, now there is an 'inquest' – an inward questing – into which time returns as time-for-reflection.

The final verses, presented as a 'thought' – an illusion sustained consciously and *in* time – are actually an audacious return to first impressions, and quietly merge the idea of ground and heaven. Their subject is transcendence, but this is depicted as a *stepping*, and compared to the ghostly apparition of the soul in a place (that is, heaven) not its own. Yet Wordsworth preserves, this time, a sense of distance: the soul is not of the place but appropriates it 'strong her strength above.'

Wordsworth: (3) Death of a Star

> Sieh, Sie erstand und schlief
> Rilke

A signal transformation of the evening star theme is found in the Lucy poems. 'Fair as a star when only one / Is shining in the sky' is not, of course, a stingy compliment, but an allusion to Hesper which carries with it the suggestion of brief if intense emergence. Throughout the poems which have Lucy for subject the thought of her death blends curiously with that of her presence: she is a twilight or threshold figure that gleams upon the sight, then disappears. There is, almost simultaneously, emergence and discontinuity. As in Rilke's 'Starker Stern,' and in the later *Sonnets to Orpheus*, an image of setting overtakes that of dawning life:

> tausendfachen Aufgang überholend
> Mit dem reinen Untergang.

Though the erotic connotations are much stronger in Rilke, where Hesper is clearly Venus, in Wordsworth too the lover appears together with love's star. The guiding planet of 'Strange Fits' is the 'evening moon' rather than the evening star, yet it is already 'sinking,' and there occurs a ritual stepping and zoning similar to what guided Akenside's lover to a ghostly center. At the end of the lyric, in a reverse play of a familiar theme, both moon and Lucy enter on an 'interlunar' phase, and it is only then that 'thought' rises. The poem's curious use of both centering and descendental movements links it clearly enough to the idylls of Hesperus.

But Wordsworth's poem is as much about symbol as about star: in a sense, the symbol stars. We have, this time, an act of the mind finding what exceeds. The lover goes out of himself into star or moon: it is a mild case of ecstasy in which the distance between lover and Lucy – that precarious or psychic distance Hesper traditionally lights – is overcome by a deep, 'symbolic' association of her with the moon. Lucy, to use a Renaissance term, is eternized, but unconsciously so. The evening moon not only leads to her but she becomes the moon, love's absorbing center. The narrative progressions of the poem make us feel the slope of things toward her until she is seen as their infinite threshold – and sets. When the moon drops it is as if a fixed had become a falling star; the distance between lover and Lucy is restored; the symbol proves fallible.

This purgation of the star-symbol is perfected in 'A Slumber Did My Spirit Seal.' Here is neither Lucy by name nor the visible image of a star. But she who is described in the first stanza, who rises on the poet's 'slumber,' is immortal as a star. Poet becomes Astrophil. She, however, who is described in the second stanza is ground not sky, yet 'heaven' and 'ground' subtly meet because she has merged with the rolling planet. The descendental theme is so subtly realized that the passage from stanza to stanza, which coincides with that from state to state, is a 'stepping' not accompanied by open shock or disillusion. Because the rise and fall of the star-symbol occurs at a level 'too deep for tears,' there is no such formal cry-ing as: 'If Lucy should be dead!' or 'The difference to me!'

The absence of rhetorical glitter does not mean, of course, absence of structure. It means that Wordsworth has purified *exclamation* even further than in 'Strange Fits' and 'She Dwelt': he has killed the exclamation mark, in fact. Instead of a reversal ($\downarrow$) followed by point (.) to make (!) we have a star turned asterisk:

> How went the Agile Kernel out
> Contusion of the Husk
> Nor Rip, nor wrinkle indicate
> But just an Asterisk.[16]

Stanza 1 implies the star ('The whole of Immortality/Secreted in a star'), stanza 2 star as asterisk, or sign of an absence, Lucy's essence and that of language coincide. If she is part of a galaxy, it is Gutenberg's. Yet absence here has its own presence, so that asterisk balances star. At last a poem without artificial center, a poem which does not overcondense consciousness into symbol and symbol into star.

An Excursus on the Romantic Image

> A voice, a mystery.
> Wordsworth

Wordsworth's revolt against the star-symbol has various reasons: its trivialization in eighteenth-century poetry, a religiously inspired prudence, etc. To conventionalize it we can think of his distrust of personification, which it extends, or of English poetry's recurrent bouts of conscience vis-à-vis pagan myth. Yet we read Wordsworth unconscious much of the time of his place in the history of ideas or the polemical history of style. These histories, recovered, allow us to be articulate about his intentions but they describe his novelty rather than his originality. They remain external to his strong poetic presence.

Curiously strong, considering how little 'glitter,' or conventional texture, his poetry has. Many have suspected, therefore, that his imagery comes from a different loom. They have sought to discover the formula of its secret weave. It is equally inadequate, however – though far more interesting – to describe the diffusion of theme or image in Wordsworth, or the change from parallelistic to chiastic patterns in his metaphors. The only adequate rhetorical analysis is one that views his poems in terms of 'mind in act,' with the very temptation of symbolizing – that is, overcondensing, or turning contiguity (metonymy) into identity (metaphor) – as its subject.

This kind of rhetorical analysis does not deal with rhetoric but with rhetoricity, or word-consciousness. Speech, written or voiced, is only a special field within semiotics, defined as the study of signs in the context of signification generally. A poem may have a direct theme, subject, or reference, but it also contains, modifying these, an indication concerning the power and poverty of symbols. The older kind of rhetorical analysis (with its interest in stylistics or psycho-practical acts) was bound to emphasize the persuasive, quasi-visual figure, or such subliminal voicings as pseudo-morphemes. It can usefully point out, for example, a pun in line 11 of 'It Is No Spirit' (the star 'startles') or the pattern of reversal and transference in 'A Slumber' (the speaker's slumber seems to have become the girl's as he wakes).

In poetry, however, we respond less to images or figures as such than through them to the *image of a voice*. The newer rhetorical analysis is caught up in this highly complex notion. It does not automatically privilege voice over 'dead speech' though it can do so, as when F. R. Leavis attacks Milton. We know, however, that the nostalgia for an 'inviolable voice' is based quite consciously on the fact that such a voice is a fiction. It is always associated with prior loss or violation, as the Philomel myth perfectly expresses.[17] Philomel sings in the interlunar moment, when there is silence – and silence is pleased. Through the 'wakeful descant' of poetry we become conscious of the immensity of the detour leading from absence to presence, or from symbol to symbol rather than to 'the real thing.'

What is Wordsworth's image of a voice? It might be said that he seeks to avoid both 'writing up' (the artifices of declamation, of raising speech to oratory) and 'writing down' (the appearance that verse is mere reflection, the mimesis of a prior event, or speech-event). 'Voicing' is clearly part of the subject of the Lucy poems, and thus an older type of rhetorical reading will not suffice. As we have shown, exclamation is more at issue than declamation. Voice becomes intratextual, in the sense of merging with the text rather than seeking to transcend textuality by 'opening' into an underlying or originative emotion.

As one moves, therefore, from 'Strange Fits' to 'A Slumber,' not only does quoted speech disappear but something happens to the intentionality of signs. In 'Strange Fits' the moon-sign is an omen, that is, it presages something greater (lesser) to come. Voice enters as voice when the omen rides the poet. The relation to voice is even stronger in 'Three Years' where Nature takes over in *proprio sermone* at the very point at which children begin to speak articulately.[18] So that we hear Nature, and never Lucy: her life is tied to Nature's narrative. When Nature has finished speaking Lucy too is 'finished.' Nature's logos ('So Nature spoke, the work was done . . .') betrays. It promises life but produces death. Is the deeper thought here that speech always betrays – even this gentle, if still prophetic, mother-tongue?

The fully internalized speech of 'A Slumber' does not cease to evoke a death, or the thought of a death. A representational element persists. Yet the poet's words neither anticipate a betrayal nor vicariously compensate for it. Their 'pointed' or ominous quality is barely felt. There is no moon, no path, no precipitate symbol. They do not even give voice a chance to emerge as Voice.

We still feel, of course, how close the 'idyll' of the first stanza is to a blind sublimity, and the 'elegy' of the second to a false sublimation. Yet they are shadows of moods only, reached through a purified form. The issue of loss and gain – of psychic balancing – has deepened measurably. If poetry still rises from loss, it has no magical (sublimating) or guilty (proleptic) relation to it. 'A Slumber,' a poem of enlightenment – and of the Enlightenment – removes superstition from poetic speech in a much deeper sense than expelling gaudy phrases and mythic personifications.

The Melodious Plot

Akenside's evening star lights him not to Olympia but from her tomb to Philomel's bower. One might take this as representing symbolically the very process of sublimation. A girl dies, song is born. The myth of Philomel already founded song on sorrow. Voice is intrinsically elegiac, Philomel's bower a melodious bier.

But this would simplify both the myth and Akenside's poem. The myth deals with loss of voice, not only with loss. A mutilated tongue speaks again through the cunning of art. In Akenside, moreover, the theme of voice precedes that of loss: if the 'suppliant song' should fail, there would be no light for the poet. Loss of voice would mean loss of light. The lyrist skirts that darkening of the voice. Philomel is a symbol, primarily, for restored song rather than for restored love.

A 'melodious plot,' consequently, is both the aspired-to center of the poet's quest and the form of its path. The star must 'suffer' the poet's song before it can grant a petition that allows song and loss to merge in the 'green space' of memory. What moves us toward that full yet empty space, that para-paradise, is what we find when we get there: voice, our sense of its power and impotence. A memory-fiction of its starry influence survives together with an awareness of its present absence. This poet's poem helps us understand the forces of nostalgic lyricism Wordsworth overcame.

Voice is the only epiphany in Akenside's ode, but it reverberates in the confines of an operatic set. We hear a frozen music; such phrases as 'the wakeful heifers gaze' are stagy orphisms. Nothing remains of the logos-power of the word, of its mimetic or re-creative virtue. What is evoked is a little moony world far tighter it would seem than that generous intercourse of gods and men suggested by the opening verses. How sterile this templar space when compared to the 'wide quietness' of 'To Psyche' or 'murmurous haunt' of 'To a Nightingale'! It is illumined by gaslight rather than by 'a light in sound.'[19] Voice, or poetry in general, is worshipped only as a fiction, as the fetish of a fiction even.

The tension between prophetic voice and fictive word becomes acute after Milton.[20] Not only is paradise understood to be lost (that is, understood to have been, or now always to be, a fiction) but the great voice seems lost that knew itself as logos: as participating in real influence. The *philomel moment* of English poetry is therefore the postprophetic moment,[21] when the theme of loss merges with that of voice – when, in fact, a 'lost voice' becomes the subject or moving force of poetic song. 'Shall we not hear thee in the storm? In the noise of the mountain stream? When the feeble sons of the wind come forth, and scarcely seen pass over the desert?'[22]

The Ossianic poems overhear these wind-notes that try to swell into a supreme fiction but remain curiously successive and apart, wreaths in the Gaelic night. Macpherson's melic vaporizer turns what light there is into motes of sound. One voice spells another in a supposedly epic chain which remains a composite lyric. The chain has no real continuity because what memories pass over Ossian, as over a wind-harp, are not ghosts of heroes so much as 'sons of song.' Their essence is vocative; their strength a fading power of vociferation. By a typical sublimation they die into song, or rather into the spectral, ominously heightened voice of nature. 'When night comes on the hill; when the loud winds arise, my ghost shall stand in the blast, and mourn the death of my friends. The hunter shall hear from his booth. He shall fear but love my voice!'[23]

This melic undermining of the theme of succession – this substitution of voice for blood – is especially remarkable in the *Songs of Selma*. A hero's life flourishes as briefly there as the evening star, and with strange delight in its setting. The poem begins with Ossian's address to Hesperus: the 'fair-hair'd angel,' as Blake will call it, lifts its 'unshorn head' from the cloud, to observe the scene but a moment, then to depart. 'The waves come with joy around thee: they bathe thy lovely hair. Farewell, thou silent beam!' It goes, as it came, in strength; from this, perhaps, the poet's delight in its setting, and the upswing of the ensuing movement: 'Let the light of Ossian's soul arise!'

That light is memory, matrix of epic art. Ossian's soul lights up with memories of dead friends, the heroes and bards who used to gather annually in Selma. The evening star has led us not to the moon, its bright epiphany, but to memory – these dying voices from the past. We become aware of a reversal and a twofold sequence. The star's 'silent beam' leads to memory by distancing the raging sounds of day ('The murmur of the torrent comes from afar. Roaring waves climb the distant rock'); memory, however, recovers an inconsolable sound. 'Colma left alone on the hill with all her voice of song!'

The interlunar moment now repeats itself as Ossianic lover-hero-bard invokes the silence, or hidden moon, or absent friend.

> Rise, moon! from behind thy clouds. Stars of the night arise! Lead me, some light, to the place, where my love rests . . . But here I must sit alone, by the rock of the mossy stream. The stream and the wind roar aloud. I hear not the voice of my love.

These voices are like ghosts, doomed to wander about ravening and unsatisfied. They cannot center on anything because nothing abides their question. 'Thou dost smile, and depart,' as Ossian says of the evening star. The questioning voice alone, in its manifold, frustrated music of apostrophe, invocation, and exclamation, remains. This voice is heard as if afar, a passion to be memorialized but no longer owned. There is a kind of elegy in space itself, in our distance from the sublime of sound:

> The sons of song are gone to rest. My voice remains, like a blast, that roars, lonely, on a sea-surrounded rock, after the winds are laid. The dark moss whistles there; the distant mariner sees the waving trees![24]

A voice without issue, a poetry without succession, is what meets us in the Ossianic fragments. They reflect the anxiety of English poetry as a whole. Macpherson's forgery is strangely true because the original voice he claimed to discover is so lonely, so discontinuous with the origin it posits. The poetry of this new Homer discloses 'the westwardness of everything.'[25] Deep no longer responds to deep and each hill repeats a lonely sound. The pseudo-psalmodic landscape before us actually spells the end of that 'responsive' poetry Christopher Smart sought to revive at the same historical moment.

Now too the poet's self-image changes radically. He sees himself as an aeolian harp, 'self-sounding in the night.'[26] Macpherson is acclaimed as a Northern Homer, an autochthonous poet springing from the peculiar genius of his region. Or, more sophisticated, poets understand that all origins are forged origins. For Blake they are part of the 'mystery' caricatured in his mock-Eastern style, which multiplies births and creates an extraordinary mélange of genealogical fictions. The impossibility of succession leads to a clearer facing of the burden of originality on all poets, which a return to pseudo-origins evades. Blake's evening star, therefore, rises upon the twilight of English and classicizing poetry with the energy of dawn: it is, already, the morning star:

> Thou fair-hair'd angel of the evening,
> Now, while the sun rests on the mountains, light
> Thy bright torch of love; thy radiant crown
> Put on . . .

Coleridge and the Morning Star

> Tell also of the false Tongue!
> vegetated
> Beneath your land of shadows, of its
> sacrifices and
> Its offerings
>
> Blake

My subject has not been a theme, or even thematics, but poetry – poetry as it impinges on those who seek to continue it. The drama begins, as always, in a darkling moment. There is the shadow of a prior greatness, or the discovery of a distance from a creating source. That shadow is always there, but the manifest voice of achievement from Spenser to Milton had made of England classic ground and put the glory on each successor poet.[27]

The burden of creativity became as ineluctable and heavy as the pack Bunyan's Christian wore. After Milton, poetry joins or even rivals divinity in pressing its claim on the artist. Moreover, as soon as greatness is acknowledged, it raises the question of succession. A theological element enters; a reflection on who is – or could be – worthy to continue the line. In these circumstances literary criticism can take the form of a theologico-poetical examination of the pretender. Is he apostolic? The question need not be imposed from the outside: indeed, it generally comes from within the visionary poet, and leads to self-doubt as easily as self-justification. The poet's struggle with his vocation is not always overt or dramatic; only with Collins, Smart, and the great Romantics does it become religious in intensity and direct their voice. What is at stake is, in fact, the erection of a voice. 'Would to God all the Lord's people were prophets.'[28]

Like drama generally, this one can have two endings: a happy and an unhappy. Keats's poetry is representative of the former. His 'To a Nightingale,' with its finely repeated darkling moment and green space, is a fulfilment of Akenside's 'To the Evening Star.' A belated poet rejoices in the symbols and accoutrements of his tradition. They fill his verses with a presence rarely as frigid as Akenside's. But Coleridge is representative of the sadder ending. He is afflicted by secondariness as by a curse: his relation to writing of all kinds is more embarrassed than that of Keats and more devious than that of Akenside. His imagination sees itself as inherently 'secondary' – not only because it follows great precursors in poetry or philosophy (though that is a factor) but chiefly because of the one precursor, the 'primary Imagination . . . living power and prime agent of all human perception . . . repetition in the finite mind of the eternal act of creation in the infinite I AM.' His religious sensibility, conspiring with a burdened personal situation, makes him feel at a hopeless remove from originality.

That Coleridge was deeply disturbed by the priority of others – and of the Other – is hardly in question. Too much in his life and writings reflects it. It can be argued that he was, in his way, as 'counterfeit' a poet as Macpherson and Chatterton. He had done better, perhaps, to invent new origins, as they did, rather than to be echo and imitate imitations in a perverse sacrifice to divine primacy. His poetry shows to what extent he *shrinks* into creation, like Blake's Urizen.[29]

But we are not engaged here in a biography that would expose the *contre-faisant* to creation Coleridge practiced. The one biographical detail relevant to this study is that he had to contend not only with an inherited sublime that 'counterfeited infinity' (see 'Religious Musings' and 'The Destiny of Nations') but also with 'sounds less deep and loud,' with the new voice of feeling in Wordsworth. The latter meets him at the very threshold of his liberation from sublimity.

Some of his early poems – the 'To the Nightingale' and 'Aeolian Harp' of 1795 in particular – are clearly moving in a Wordsworthian direction, as is Southey in his 'English Eclogues.' But then 'the giant Wordsworth – God bless him' preempts them all. Coleridge soon entails his portion of poetic genius on this contemporary giant. Though 'Frost at Midnight' and 'To the Nightingale' (the latter as revised for *Lyrical Ballads*) repay Wordsworth's influence by leading into 'Tintern Abbey,' such dialogue between the poets (Coleridge's truest 'conversation') lasts but a year. It breaks off when the poets separate in Germany, with Coleridge going off to study at Göttingen. To the priority of Wordsworth, Germany eventually adds that of Kant, Schelling, and the Schlegels in philosophy and criticism.

Of course, such nova as 'Kubla Khan' and 'The Ancient Mariner' may make the question of originality seem a blind alley. It is true, nevertheless, that the 'Ancyent Marinere' was written 'in imitation of the *style* as well as of the spirit of the elder poets' and that the gloss added by Coleridge at a later date antiques the poem even more as well as putting its author at curious remove from his own work. The gloss – that cool, continuous trot – frames a precipitous rime. The burden of originality, in this original poem, is relieved by a (repeated) return to fake eld.

A psychological analysis of the conditions that removed Coleridge's literary impotence is not our concern, however. Enough if we understand how problematic imaginative writing was for him. It was, at once, inherently dependent or secondary, yet virtually primary or participating in the divine 'I AM.' His bravest poems tend to recant themselves. The pattern is obvious in 'The Aeolian Harp,' yet elsewhere too, if more subtly, he worships the whirlwind, or puts a finger on his mouth like Job.

A test-case for this sacrificial or self-counterfeiting movement (when originality was in his reach) is the 'Hymn before Sunrise, in the Vale of Chamouni.' Coleridge falsifies his experience in two ways. He had been on Scafell, not in Chamouny. This transposition to a traditionally sublime spot occurred despite Wordsworth, or perhaps because of him. It is difficult to work out the relation, but Coleridge, in this poem, could have celebrated a native mountain in Wordsworthian style before Wordsworth. (*The Prelude*'s account of Snowdon was unwritten or still in manuscript.) There is also his notorious use of a minor German poetess, Frederike Brun. He quietly incorporates essential lines from her short 'Chamonix beym Sonnenaufgang.' This double shift, from England to France in locality, and from English to German (Klopstockian) verse in features of style and experience, is surely a kind of flight from native origins, or from whatever Wordsworth exemplified.[30]

Even were we to accept the Hymn's egregious sublimity, it would remain a strange production. The style, as Wordsworth charged, is 'mock sublime,' a turgid almost parodistic development of Miltonic hymns to Creation. The impression is that Klopstock has been the model rather than an English visionary. Add to this that the poem turns on the old conceit of making silence speak – that its essential subject is presence or absence of Voice – and you have a signal case of Coleridge speaking with a tongue not his own, or adopting a counterfeit logos. 'Bowed low/ In adoration' he ventriloquizes nature, and sacrifices his genius and the *genius loci* to the tritest forms of sublime ejaculation.

This is not the whole story, however. The poem's first section (to about line 37) bears traces of inward record and a powerful grasp of myth-making. The only conventional thing about it is the desensualizing movement from visible to invisible. This is imposed on a remarkable *situation*. The poem begins with the near-mythic contrast of the 'white' mountain (Blanc) shrouded in black, and the silent mountain rising from a sounding base. We feel the contending elements and approach Manichaeanism. For a moment only – but still for that moment – we understand Abel's cry in 'The Wanderings of Cain': 'The Lord is God of the living only, the dead have another God.'

The Manichaean contrasts disappear into the conventional paradoxes of sublime rhetoric that characterize the later portions of the Hymn. (A 'mighty voice' both calls the torrents 'from night and utter death/ From dark and icy caverns' and stops them 'at once amid their maddest plunge,' reverting them to 'silent cataracts.') What does not disappear is the horror of stasis implicit in the opening moments. 'Hast thou a charm to stay the morning-star . . . ?' Dread of stillness combines with dread of blackness. The mountain, co-herald of the dawn because of its snowy height, seems to be in league with darkness. It is a passing impression; yet that there was this *charm*, this bewitchment of time, is conveyed by a pattern of stills that, as in 'The Ancient Mariner,' can suddenly freeze the image of motion. It is as if time were subject to sudden arrest – to an embolism felt in the poem's development as a whole, which is really a non-development, or a passionate rhetorical goad to make the soul 'rise' together with obstructed dawn.

In *this* darkling and enchanted moment it is morning that almost fails to rise. 'Nightes dread' is now associated with dawn's delay. As a slowing of time it is, moreover, the opposite of erotic;[31] the 'bald awful head,' the 'dread mountain form,' etc., suggest if anything a scene of sacrifice. It is also significant that when the mountain is linked to the morning star a second time (lines 30 ff.), the diction swells distinctly toward the Miltonic and repeats the nightmare resonance of the opening verses. Is the mountain or the poet's soul the true subject of these lines?

> And thou, O silent Mountain, sole and bare
> O blacker than the darkness all the night
> > (original version)

> Thou first and chief, sole sovereign of the Vale!
> O struggling with the darkness all the night
> > (later version)

And who is being contended for in this cosmic battle?

> And visited all night by troops of stars
> Or when they climb the sky or when they sink . . .

This place, then, soul or mountain, is a virtual Prince of Darkness. The visiting 'troops of stars' could be the Satanic 'Stars of Night' (*Paradise Lost*, V. 745) or a sustaining, heavenly host.[32] We are on the verge of a 'wild allegory';[33] but nothing really is clear except that the soul, in trying to 'wake' or 'rise,' meets quasi-demonic forces. 'Rising' gets confused with 'rising up' – perhaps through a montage of the image of the morning star with the myth of Lucifer.

What more can be said? In this deeply religious, or mythopoeic, situation, continuity of self (in time) is threatened, and there is need for a rite, and specifically a rite of passage.[34] The morning star must be freed to continue its rising course: a progress leading toward dawn must be restored. The mountain too must 'rise,' for the sable charm invests it as well. But to free mountain or morning star is tantamount to finding some lost intermediary between darkness and dawn, some symbolic form, at least a voice. The darkness is a darkness of mediations. And in this darkness, even constituting it, is the poet's struggle to extricate a religious rather than demonic mediation. The image of Lucifer as Prince of the Air, Prince of Darkness, has merged with that of the mountain as 'great hierarch' and 'dread ambassador'; yet the image of Lucifer as morning star is also there, and blends with a mountain described as 'Companion of the morning-star at dawn.' The poet's soul, in this hymn, tries to call the one and not the other. 'O which one, is it each one?'[35]

At the end, it is unsure who prevails. The mountain's mediation seems to lift the weight of that 'dark, substantial, black' which oppressed air and soul in the beginning, but the supposed upward lumbering of its voice ('tell thou the silent sky,' etc.) merely differentiates a silence which reaches, as in Pascal, the stars. Coleridge leaves us with a depressing sense of hierarchy, measured by the contrast between his bowed head and the 'bald awful head' of 'stupendous' Blanc. His 'Instructions to a Mountain' would sound ludicrous if they were not despairing. They suggest the opposite of Shelley's 'Thou hast a voice, great Mountain, to repeal/Large codes of fraud and woe,' for they effectively make the mountain into the rock of institutionalized religion, complete with frigidly hieratic spheres. In a sense, then, the debased (Urizenic) Lucifer has triumphed because indistinguishable from the religious code. The true morning star never rises.[36]

Only at one point is there something like a genuine release from the 'ebon mass.' It is not unlike what the mariner feels after the spell begins to break and the albatross falls off; and it involves quiet gazing rather than rhetorical shouting. Struggling against the charm, the poet views the mountain as a wedge that pierces the surrounding blackness. Then, as if recanting, he thinks the blackness away as a 'crystal shrine' which is the mountain's home. Finally he desubstantializes it completely when through rapt gazing Mont Blanc vanishes from consciousness only to reappear blending subliminally – like a 'beguiling melody' – into thought. Several stills, then, or re-visions relax the hold of a spell that almost paralyzed the soul. This spell becomes the 'trance' of prayer and a 'beguiling' thought-music. Its power continues to echo as the stills move quasi-cinematically into the unitive swell of mountain and mind.

The most curious of these still ecstasies[37] in Coleridge is also one of the earliest. A sonnet of 1790 shows the lover absorbed in the evening star:

> On thee full oft with fixed eye I gaze
> Till I, methinks, all spirit seem to grow.

By a sacrificial sleight of mind he then identifies the star with the beloved woman, so that, in effect, gazing is all there is – until his spirit should join hers in the star's 'kindred orb':

> Must she not be, as is thy placid sphere
> Serenely brilliant? Whilst to gaze a while
> Be all my wish 'mid Fancy's high career
> E'en till she quit this scene of earthly toil;
> Then Hope perchance might fondly sigh to join
> Her spirit in thy kindred orb, O Star benign!

I am not convinced of the star's benignity. Anti-erotic, it leads to death not love, or to a life beyond life. Nothing is lost by this sublimation except all. Having is replaced by hoping in a fatal movement that confirms Blake's 'O Sunflower.' Coleridge does not hope to have, he hopes that *then* he may hope. He does not seem to know his life has been stolen – as he knows, at least, in his mountain poem. There he recognizes the charm and tries to break a heliotropic (or melantropic) trance by recovering a sense of his own presence amid the ghostliness. But though he resists the charm it gets the better of him. The desire for sublimation is too strong and his soul passes into 'the mighty Vision' and so 'swells' to heaven. This dilation is sublimation still. The mountain's presence is no more benign than the star's.

'Ghost of a mountain – the forms seizing my Body as I passed & became realities – I, a Ghost, till I had reconquered my substance.' This notebook entry, recorded first in November, 1799, is repeated in September, 1802, at the time, probably, of composing the 'Hymn before Sunrise.' The ghostliness he describes also befell the Ancient Mariner. It takes away the sense of easy personal presence while intensifying the presence of otherness. Emptied of personality he must stand on this very emptiness against impinging surreality. It is his only 'ground' (the question of ground being further subverted by locating the action on a shifty sea). One can understand why the 'coal-ridge' of this massive mountain became a place for Coleridge's struggle to ground the self. A late and beautiful letter recapitulates his whole spiritual history as it impinges on the Hymn:

> from my very childhood I have been accustomed to *abstract* and as it were unrealize whatever of more than common interest my eyes dwelt on; and then by a sort of

transfusion and transmission of my consciousness to identify myself with the Object –
and I have often thought . . . that if ever I should feel once again the genial warmth
and stir of the poetic impulse, and refer to my own experiences, I should venture on a
yet stranger & wilder Allegory than of yore – that I would *allegorize* myself, as a Rock
with it's summit just raised above the surface of some Bay or Strait in the Arctic Sea,
>   While yet the stern and solitary Night
>   Brook'd no alternate Sway -

all around me fixed and firm, methought as my own Substance, and near me lofty
Masses, that might have seemed to 'hold the Moon and Stars in fee' and often in such
wild play with meteoric lights, or with the quiet Shine from above . . . that it was a
pride and a place of Healing to lie, as in an Apostle's Shadow, within the Eclipse and
deep substance-seeming Gloom of 'these dread Ambassadors from Earth to Heaven,
Great Hierarchs'! and tho' obscured yet to think myself obscured by consubstantial
Forms, based in the same Foundation as my own. I grieved not to serve them – yea,
lovingly and with gladsomeness I abased myself in their presence: for they are my
Brothers, I said.[38]

So the Valley of Chamouny is truly a 'Valley of Wonders.' But does the poet
succeed in 'reconquering' his 'substance' there? (How much play with that
grounding word in the above letter!) It is hard to say, from the Hymn, whether
loss of self or loss of voice was more important. Yet writing the Hymn meant
recovering a voice. In the Hymn as in the Rime, release from the curse – that
dread stillness, or paralysis of motion – is obtained by the ability to pray. And
prayer is interpreted in both poems as praise:

>   O happy living things! no tongue
>   Their beauty might declare . . .

The weight of the Albatross (like the air's 'ebon mass') is removed, together with
the stone from the tongue.

Yet voice remains uneasy, both in the Hymn and in the Rime. Praise mutes
itself in the act:

>   O happy living things! no tongue
>   Their beauty might declare:
>   A spring of love gushed from my heart
>   And I blessed them unaware

There is too great a contrast between the compulsive speech of the Mariner and
this first, tongueless moment. The Hymn, similarly, is hardly an 'unaware'
blessing: its one moment of sweet unconsciousness (ll. 17–23) does not
compensate us for the forced sublimity of the rest.

Praise, according to the Psalmist, is a 'sacrifice of thanksgiving.' It substitutes
for, or sublimates, the rite of blood-sacrifice. The Hymn on Mont Blanc is
written against this background of sublimation. The exact pressure put on
Coleridge – the offering demanded of him by the dread form – we shall never

know. Coleridge's 'Sca'fell Letter' shows him as 'overawed,' but there was nothing necessarily mysterious. He felt, that much is certain, a loss of substance, a passivity both shaming and sublime[39] – and he recovers himself, at least in the Hymn, by the will of his voice; more precisely, by the willed imitation of a sublime voice.

I cannot deny that the inferred human situation is more impressive than the Hymn produced by it. But that is because, in Coleridge, poetry remains so closely linked to sublimation. Sublimation always sacrifices to an origin stronger than itself. If it did not cherish or dread this origin – this 'hiding-place' of power – it would not shroud it from sight by displacement or falsification:

> Never mortal saw
> The cradle of the strong one,
> Never mortal heard
> The gathering of his voices;
> The deep-murmured charm . . .[40]

Such 'wildly-silent' scenes[41] are not infrequent in Coleridge. He is often, in fancy, near an origin where a 'great Spirit' with 'plastic sweep' – the wind or voice of the opening of Genesis – moves on the still darkness. But he is, at the same time, so removed from this primal scene that it becomes a 'stilly murmur' which 'tells of silence.' The voice redeeming that silence, or vexed into being by it, can be as cold as the eye of Ancient Mariner or moon. 'Green vales and icy cliffs, all join my Hymn.' Its 'sunny domes' are accompanied by 'caves of ice.' In the end what predominates are the strange soteriological images, the 'secret ministry of frost,' the rock 'in wild play . . . with the quiet Shine from above,' or others calm yet glittering: the 'mild splendor,' for instance, of a 'serenely brilliant' star, which summons the poet at evening to accept his death-in-life.

Afterthought

> The Imagination is always at the end of an era.
> Wallace Stevens

These reflections must finally turn back on themselves. Is their objective really 'objective'? Are we, should we be, aiming at positive literary history? Or have we found a kind of history-writing compatible with its subject-matter: poetry?

The theme of the evening star, as a point of departure, is not objective, but neither is it arbitrary. I have described elsewhere the idea of a westering of the poetical spirit, and the fear of a decline in poetical energy which accompanied it. Others too have put forward a thesis on the belatedness of English poetry.[42] While it is notoriously difficult to explain the birth or rebirth of a symbol, I suspect that, after the Renaissance, the complex evening-consciousness of English poets reached toward the Hesper/Lucifer theme as toward a limit.

What was limited by the theme? The fear of discontinuity, of a break in personal or cultural development; but also a vatic overestimation of poetry that put too great a burden on the artist and made this break more likely. Vaticination remains in evening star poetry, yet is diminished in a special way. Symbol or substitute (Hesper/Philomel in Akenside) tends to become more important than the epiphanic source (the moon). A prophetic background supports a purely symbolic foreground. The aura of the symbol is reduced even as its autonomy is strengthened. It is ironic that, by the time of Stevens, 'the philosophy of symbols' (as Yeats called it) confronts the poet with a new discontinuity: the symbols, or romantic relics, are so attenuated by common use that their ground (sky?) is lost. They become starry junk, and the poem is a device to dump them, to let the moon rise as moon, free of

> the moon and moon
> The yellow moon of words about the nightingale
> In measureless measures . . .[43]

Perhaps it was the masque, with its courtly center and operatic machinery, which first encouraged a translation of prophecy into 'descendental' picture. Ben Jonson's masques, for instance, can be elaborate night-pieces converging on queen-moon or *roi-soleil*. Royal center, epiphanic allegory, and pictorial hinge go together.[44] A star-god or genius of some kind 'descends' to point out his representative on earth, or do obeisance. In *Pleasure Reconciled to Virtue* (1619) the center explicitly descends westward: King James and Prince Charles are linked to the 'bright race of Hesperus,' which delimits their royal aura yet still discloses, epiphanically, an origin. To call James 'the glory of the West' evokes a consciously Hesperian ideology with consequences for later English poetry.[45] In Hesperian verse, the epiphanic figure

> Sitting like a goddess bright
> In the center of her light[46]

diffuses into various, equally mortal or westering, presences:

> The Rainbow comes and goes,
> And lovely is the Rose,
> The Moon doth with delight
> Look round her when the heavens are bare;
> Waters on a starry night
> Are beautiful and fair;
> The sunshine is a glorious birth . . .[47]

From Ben Jonson to Wordsworth, and from masque to ode, is too abrupt a jump. But it illumines an important difference between epochs, bridged in part by our previous, historically oriented sketch: a difference in structure of sensibility or mode of representation. Wordsworth's mind, in the above stanza, loses itself only fractionally in the moon-moment. Its delight in other images is even more restrained: they remain as intransitive as the verbs, and alternate deliberately between sky and earth. Sight is segmented by them; and the serial impression they leave is of Wordsworth counting his blessings or storing them against the dying of all light. He is restrained because he is reflective; he is reflective because he is perplexed at nature's losing its immediacy. But the image of the moon challenges his restraint. With it the verses almost leap from perplexity into vision: the poet too would throw off all shadow, like heaven its clouds.

Yet the visionary personification that rises in him is simply the act of seeing – natural seeing – magnified. A personified moon makes the eyes of man personal again. Sight hovers on the edge of visionariness without passing over: 'when the heavens are bare' is not an apocalyptic notation. Wordsworth's restraint is, as always, a restraint of vision. Though his eye leaps up, he subdues the star-symbol.

The evening star is, typically, like this Rainbow, Rose, Moon. A Hesperian image, it both rouses and chastens the prophetic soul. A fixed yet fugitive sign, its virtue is virtuality. It signals at most a continuation of the line. Through its binominal character, moreover, Hesper/Lucifer points at once beyond and toward itself. Always setting, yet always steadfast, it repeats in small the strange survival of poetry within the lights and shadows of historical circumstance.

Notes

1. This is the accepted date, though it is speculative. The poem first appeared in the posthumous edition of Akenside's *Poems* (1772).
2. See *The Greek Bucolic Poets*, ed. J. M. Edmonds, Loeb Classical Library (New York, 1928), pp. 410–13.
3. See *The Poems of Samuel Taylor Coleridge*, ed. E. H. Coleridge (Oxford, 1962), p. 16. In the 2nd (1797) edition of his *Poems on Various Subjects* Coleridge surmised that 'if the Sonnet were comprized in less than fourteen lines, it would become a serious epigram.'
4. The preposition 'to' in st. 1 foregrounds itself so strongly that, to subordinate it, one is tempted to read it on the pattern of 'tonight' (i.e., proclitically) and so bring it closer to the bonded preposition 'sub' in *supply, suppliant* (a near pun, anticipating the reversal mentioned above) and even *suffer*. Compare the syntax of st. 6; also the 'prefer' of line 19 which makes 'vows' both its direct and indirect object. It draws

attention once more not only to the prepositional but also to the syntactical bonding of one verse-line with another. All this fosters a sense of the discontinuous or precarious path followed by the verses' 'feet.' It is interesting that in Christopher Smart's *Song to David* (1763) the problem of hierarchy, subordination (hypotaxis), and prepositional-syntactical bonding reaches an acute stage.

5. Compare Tennyson, *In Memoriam*, 1ine 21, 'Sweet Hesper-Phosphor, double name . . .'

6. See Blake, *Milton*, and Collins, 'Ode on the Poetical Character.'

7. Spenser, "Epithalamium," line. 290.

8. Blake, 'To the Evening Star.' 'Full soon' could mean both 'very soon' and "soon full" (having reached its ripest or intensest point).

9. Shelley, 'To a Skylark,' lines 21–25. This describes the morning star; Shelley wrote an expressively bad poem to the evening star in 1811 (see *The Complete Works*, ed. T. Hutchinson [London, 1960], p. 870) and uses Plato's verses (cited above) as an epigraph for 'Adonais.' His most famous evocation of Hesperus-Lucifer is in 'The Triumph of Life,' lines 412–20. On the importance to Shelley of the evening-morning star theme, see W. B. Yeats, 'The Philosophy of Shelley's Poetry,' in *Ideas of Good and Evil* (1903). To gain a complete phenomenological thematics it would be necessary, of course, to consider the evening star theme in relation to that of the moon, the night, other stars, birds (nightingale / lark), star flowers, the hymeneal theme (compare Catullus, 'Vesper adest'), etc.

10. See the ending of 'Night the Ninth' in the *Four Zoas*.

11. Like 'golden,' these lines were added in 1815. Compare 'She Was a Phantom of Delight,' whose first stanza is clearly indebted to the evening star motif, and whose rhythm is similar. For a large-scale speculation on sky-earth imagery in 'Daffodils,' see Frederick Garber, *Wordsworth and the Poetry of Encounter* (Urbana, Ill., 1971), pp. 152 ff.

12. For an interpretation of Wordsworth's 'middle-ground' parallel to mine, and to which I am indebted, see Paul de Man, 'Symbolic Landscape in Wordsworth and Yeats,' in *In Defense of Reading*, eds. R. A. Brower and R. Poirier (New York, 1963).

13. 'It Is No Spirit,' lines 7–8.

14. Also perhaps Wordsworth's marital situation. He had gone to France to see Annette Vallon and his daughter prior to marrying Mary (in October 1802). There is also the poet's general sensitivity to 'floating,' or images of suspended animation, or even the word 'hung.'

15. For 'race,' a probable pun, see Psalms 19:5.

16. This and the following quotation are from *The Complete Poems of Emily Dickinson*, ed. T. H. Johnson (Boston, 1960), poems 1135 and 1616. See also Eleanor Wilner, 'The Poetics of Emily Dickinson,' *ELH* 38 (1971): 138–40.

17. Compare T. S. Eliot, *The Waste Land*, II. 97 ff.

18. I am indebted for this insight to Frances Ferguson.

19. Coleridge, 'The Aeolian Harp' (1795), line 28. The line was not in the original published version, but entered the text in 1828.

20. For the role Milton as Voice played in Wordsworth, and the Romantics generally, see Leslie Brisman, *Milton's Poetry of Choice and Its Romantic Heirs* (Ithaca, N. Y., 1973), chap. 5. For 'Voice' after Wordsworth, cf. Thomas Whitaker's 'Voices in the Open' (lecture at the 1970 English Institute) and John Hollander's *Images of Voice* (Cambridge, 1970), as well as his essay 'Wordsworth and the Music of Sound,' in *New Perspectives on Coleridge and Wordsworth*, ed. Geoffrey Hartman (New York, 1972), pp. 41–84.

21. See Angus Fletcher, *The Prophetic Moment* (Chicago, 1971)

22. 'Fingal,' in James Macpherson, *The Poems of Ossian*. Compare the role of voice (the wind's and that of – originally – Lucy Gray) in Coleridge's 'Dejection: An Ode.'

23. Macpherson, *Songs of Selma*.

24. Last lines of *Songs of Selma*.

25. Wallace Stevens, 'Our Stars Come from Ireland,' in *The Auroras of Autumn*.

26. Michael Bruce, 'Lochleven,' in *Poems on Several Occasions* (Edinburgh, 1782).

27. For the general thesis see Harold Bloom, 'Coleridge: The Anxiety of Influence,' in *New Perspectives on Coleridge and Wordsworth*, pp. 247–67; W. J. Bate, *The Burden of the Past and the English Poet* (Cambridge, MA, 1970); and G. H. Hartman, *Beyond Formalism* (New Haven, 1970), pp. 270 ff. and 367 ff.

28. Numbers 11:29, and plate 1 of Blake's *Milton*.

29. Norman Fruman, in chap. 6 of *Coleridge, the Damaged Archangel* (New York, 1971), shows the young poet systematically 'vamping' the mediocre poetry of his time. On this 'substitution of conventionality for originality' and the closeness in Coleridge of 'self-construction' and 'self-annihilation,' see M. G. Cooke, 'Quisque Sui Faber: Coleridge in the *Biographia Literaria*,' *Philological Quarterly* 50 (1971): 208–29.

30. The psychological background is extremely complex: he was deeply identified, by this time, with Wordsworth and indeed the entire Wordsworth 'family,' as the Verse Letter to Sara Hutchinson (later 'Dejection') of the previous April shows. His Scafell experience was also recorded in (prose) letters to Sara. Bowles's 'Coombe Ellen,' and 'Saint Michael's Mount' may have been in his mind, though in a negative way – his letter to Sotheby of September 10, 1802, leads into a mention of the Scafell-Chamouny Hymn via criticisms of Bowles's 'second Volume' (*Poems*, by the Reverend Wm. Lisle Bowles, vol. 2, 1801) which contained these poems.

31. Fruman has interesting remarks on Coleridge's use of "hope" in an implicitly sexual sense (*Coleridge*, pp. 425 ff.). Sara Hutchinson is always in his thought at this time (see note 30 above), and the attempt to 'rise' out of a nightmare moment of trance or passivity could have involved sensual 'Hopes & Fears.'

32. 'Stay' in 'Hast thou a charm to stay the morning star/In his steep course' could be ambiguous and reflect the double image of the mountain-darkness as (1) preventing and (2) supporting the star.

33. See the letter quoted on pp. 70–1 above.

34. See Angus Fletcher on 'liminal anxiety' in Coleridge, ' "Positive Negation": Threshold, Sequence, and Personification in Coleridge,' in *New Perspectives on Coleridge and Wordsworth*, pp. 133–64.

35. G. M. Hopkins 'Carrion Comfort,' line 13.

36. Compare Harold Bloom, *Shelley's Mythmaking* (New Haven, 1959), pp. 15–19.

37. Compare 'To the Nightingale,' lines. 12–14; 'This Lime-Tree Bower My Prison,' lines 38 ff.; and passages mainly from the *Notebooks* which tell how gazing produced a 'phantom-feeling' by abstracting or 'unrealizing' objects. See *The Notebooks of Samuel Taylor Coleridge* ed. Kathleen Coburn (New York, 1961), 2: 2495, 2546; also the letter quoted above, pp. 70–1.

38. *Collected Letters of Samuel Taylor Coleridge*, ed. E. L. Griggs (Oxford, 1956–), 4: 974–75.

39. There seems to have been two Scafell letters, now extant only in Sara Hutchinson's transcript (Griggs, *Collected Letters*, 2: 834–45). The second one (no. 451 in Griggs) begins strangely with Coleridge mentioning his 'criminal' (for a family man) addiction to recklessness when descending mountains, then describing a narrow escape. 'I lay in a state of almost prophetic Trance & Delight–& blessed God aloud, for the powers of Reason & the Will, which remaining no Danger can overpower us! O God, I exclaimed aloud–how calm, how blessed am I now/I know not how to proceed, how to return/but I am calm & fearless & confident/if this Reality were a Dream, if I were asleep, what agonies had I suffered! what screams!–When the Reason & the Will are away, what remains to us but Darkness & Dimness & a bewildering Shame, and Pain that is utterly Lord over us, or fantastic Pleasure.' This experience of mingled fear and exaltation may have something of the conventional 'sublime' in it; but it confirms that there was a trance and a deep moment of wakeful, rather than sleep-bound, passivity. It also suggests that, however exalted the trance, Coleridge feared it could lead (by the 'streamy nature' of consciousness?) into painful sexual thoughts. The only explicit trace, in the Hymn, of this shame at passivity is its formal turn: 'Awake my soul! not only passive praise/Thou owest . . .'

40. 'On a Cataract. Improved from Stolberg' (1799?). Both of the F. L. Stolberg lyrics translated by Coleridge – 'Der Felsenstrom' and 'Bei William Tell's Geburtsstätte' – are about places of origin.

41. The quotations in this paragraph come from 'To the Rev. W. L. Bowles,' 'The Aeolian Harp,' 'Hymn before Sunrise, in the Vale of Chamouni,' and 'Kubla Khan.'

42. That there may be a subjective or pseudohistorical element in the thesis does not disqualify it, unless we erect it into actual history: all art, it can be argued, seen from the point of view of 'imagination,' is a second rather than a first – haunted, that is, by being mere copy re-creation, or afterglow. If poetry since the Renaissance (and at times in the Renaissance) felt itself approaching an evening stage, it could mean that poets judged their work more absolutely: either as coinciding with, or failing, Imagination. For the thesis, see W. J. Bate, *The Burden of the Past and the English Poet*; Harold Bloom, *Yeats* (New York, 1970), and *The Anxiety of Influence: A Theory of Poetry* (New York, 1973); also G. H. Hartman, 'Blake and the Progress of Poesy' and 'Romantic Poetry and the Genius Loci,' in *Beyond Formalism*.

43. Wallace Stevens, 'Autumn Refrain.' Compare 'Man on the Dump.'

44. On the relation between vision and representation in the masque, see Angus Fletcher, *The Transcendental Masque: An Essay on Milton's Comus* (Ithaca, 1972), pp. 8–18.

45. Tudor myth, which exalted Elizabeth as 'that bright Occidental star' (Dedicatory Epistle to the King James Bible) and compared James to 'the radiant Cymbeline/

Which shines in the west' (*Cymbeline*, V.v. 474–77), helped to convert the theme of a *translatio imperii* into that of a *translatio artis*.

46. Milton, 'Arcades,' 11. 18–19. This queen-moon, it may be added, is also a 'western star,' since 'Arcades' is based on the conceit of finding a new Arcady in the West – that is, in England. Keats's 'Endymion' stands to the theme of the moon as Shelley's 'Adonais' to that of the evening star: my essay breaks off before those luxurious revivals.

47. Wordsworth, 'Ode: Intimations of Immortality,' st. 2.

Chapter 3

Wordsworth's Magic Mountains

(1) Mont Blanc

'And men go about to wonder at the heights of the mountains, and the mighty waves of the sea, and the wide sweep of rivers, and the circuit of the ocean, and the revolution of the stars, but themselves they consider not.' Petrarch, opening on the top of Mt. Ventoux his copy of Augustine's *Confessions*, and falling by chance on this passage, is brought back forcefully to self-consciousness: 'I closed the book, angry with myself that I should still be admiring earthly things, who might long ago have learned from even the pagan philosophers that nothing is wonderful but the soul, which, when great itself, finds nothing great outside itself.'[1]

Wordsworth's experience, like Petrarch's or Augustine's, is a conversion: a turning about of the mind as from one belief to its opposite, and a turning *ad se ipsum*. It is linked to the birth of a sharper self-awareness, and accompanied by apocalyptic feelings. By 'apocalyptic' I mean that there is an inner necessity to cast out nature, to extirpate everything apparently external to salvation, everything that might stand between the naked self and God, whatever risk in this to the self.

It is often the 'secret top' of a mountain which turns the individual about. Mountains, according to the general testimony of the imagination, are fallen heroes: they have giants in or below them. Atlas stares mutely out of Mt. Atlas. The Titans groan under Mt. Aetna. 'What can have more the Figure and Mien of a Ruin,' asks Burnet, for whom the hills are noble relics of the Flood, 'than Crags, and Rocks, and Cliffs?'[2] An old world, a former self, is passed over; a new consciousness is born. Wordsworth's mountains also tell of the passing of an order – their own order, for nature there prophesies its doom. An eternal witness amid eternal decay, it reveals the 'Characters of the great Apocalypse.' The poet's earliest sketch of Mt. Blanc condenses in one couplet this monitory and prophetic role:

> Six thousand years amid his lonely bounds
> The voice of Ruin, day and night, resounds.[3]

Many years later, after a further visit to the Alps, ancient myth joins personal intuition to give the idea its most explicit form:

> Where mortal never breathed I dare to sit
> Among the interior Alps, gigantic crew,
> Who triumphed o'er diluvian power! – and yet
> What are they but a wreck and residue,
> Whose only business is to perish? – true
> To which sad course, these wrinkled Sons of Time
> Labour their proper greatness to subdue;
> Speaking of death alone, beneath a clime
> Where life and rapture flow in plenitude sublime.[4]

It is as if the mountains exhibited, on a monster-scale, the Christian virtue of self-abnegation. Yet all concepts of transcendence imply some such necessity. The revolutionary or apocalyptic mind sees a future so different from the past that the transition must involve violence. The Titans, in Keats's *Hyperion*, are weighed down by the mystery as well as the fact of change. In Christian eschatology the new heaven and earth are separated from our familiar world by a second Deluge: the flood of fire and terror described in the Book of Revelation. There is a necessary violation of nature or of a previous state of being. Yet Wordsworth keeps his faith in the possibility of a nonviolent passage from childhood to maturity or even from nature to eternity. He converts nature into a paraclete, *the* paraclete. Perhaps he remembers that, though according to Paul 'we shall be changed,' and in a twinkling, a rape of time, there is the counter-balancing promise that 'All shall survive.'[5] The divine hiatus, the revolutionary severance of new from old, is never total: the previous order, as if nothing could die absolutely, remains latent, waiting to return.

Wordsworth's explicit subject, however, is not cosmic or societal except in implication. His subject is the growth of the mind, and the question of apocalypse arises therefore in a limited though specific way. The special nature of his theme, his focus on the individual mind, is already a sign of a 'general and gregarious advance in human self-consciousness.' Keats says that Wordsworth thinks into the human heart more than Milton does, not because he is the greater poet, but because he is a great poet coming at a late time.[6]

On the matter of apocalypse, there was a bridge between Milton and Wordsworth via the theological concept of the Light of Nature. Wordsworth never refers specifically to it, but we need a joining concept from the area linking nature and personal consciousness. Although I am not primarily concerned with drawing parallels between the two poets, that clarifies Wordsworth's apocalyptic view of how the mind grows. He always, of course, looks at growth from within, and this provides a rather rigid limit to comparison. Wordsworth is still part of the experience he narrates, as many subtle and some startling changes of consciousness reveal; while Milton has divided his subject in advance, and is truly *spectator ab extra*, except where the desire to subsume Classical myth allows his imagination an autonomous vigor. But some episodes are directly comparable, and I propose to bring together Adam's personal story of how he woke to his first thoughts, and beyond them to God (*Paradise Lost*, VIII.253 ff.), and the account, already partially covered, of how nature during the Alpine journey woke in the young poet the sense of his own, separate consciousness. In both episodes the human mind is led from nature to beyond nature.[7]

Milton divides the growth of Adam's mind into clear and easily separated phases. The most significant of these is what is attained by the light of nature and what by supernatural illumination. Adam's apostrophe to the sun,

> Thou Sun, said I, fair Light,
> And thou enlight'n'd Earth, so fresh and gay,
> Ye Hills and Dales, ye Rivers, Woods, and Plains
> And ye that live and move, fair Creatures, tell,
> Tell, if ye saw, how came I thus, how here?
> Not of myself; by some great Maker then,
> In goodness and in power preëminent . . .[8]

shows him instinctively seeking knowledge, recognizing ascending order and reciprocity, recognizing also that there are creatures participating like himself in life and movement. By the light coming from nature, and by the light of nature in him, he then deduces the existence of an invisible Maker:

> For the invisible things of him from the creation of the world are clearly seen, being understood by the things that are made, even his eternal power and Godhead.[9]

So far, and no farther, does natural light extend. There is a Maker, he is pre-eminently good and powerful. Mankind, without further illumination, thirsts for knowledge and is unrequited:

> While thus I call'd, and stray'd I knew not whither,
> From where I first drew Air, and first beheld
> This happy Light, when answer none return'd,
> On a green shady Bank profuse of Flow'rs
> Pensive I sat me down; there gentle sleep
> First found me.[10]

In that sleep, which separates Adam clearly yet gently from his previous state, God dream-walks him to Eden, and natural light begins to be complemented by supernatural revelation.

But if Milton distinguishes categorically between natural and supernatural, he still allows the former a generous domain. That is why a comparison between him and Wordsworth is fruitful. His respect for the mind's natural powers anticipates that of Wordsworth. Supernatural guidance enters as late as possible, and even then is not inevitably overpowering. It cooperates with natural light in a most gentle way, though it must indeed occasionally extinguish that light, as before Eve's birth, when the *tardemah*, the deep sleep of Genesis 2:21, falls on Adam (a somewhat ominous occurrence which foreshadows the first wounding of man and the later wounding of creation by the Fall). Even the *tardemah*, however, is not presented by Milton as total loss of sight, for the 'Cell of Fancy,' the internal sight, survives, and Adam is allowed to see the operation that must at once complete and deplete him.

In fact, each internal as well as external 'generation' of Adam is preceded by a merciful sleep allowing the natural being to persist or even strengthen during the influx of divine power. There is first the 'soundest sleep' from which he wakes into being. He is bathed in a balmy sweat, the birth-dew of existence. That nature willingly cooperates in his birth is shown by the grotesque image of a Sun feeding on the amniotic or generative moisture.[11] This image is, of course, a conceit on evaporation; but the natural view and the visionary exploitation of it coexist and suggest from the outset the more general coexistence (in the unfallen world at least) of natural and supernatural. Instead of waking, more-over, to revelation and in Eden, Adam's reason is allowed to unfold more gradually. Only at its limit, thirsting for what it cannot find, does it call on God, and is answered: 'call'd by thee I come thy Guide.' The supernatural does not intervene before the natural is perfected, and responds rather than intervenes.

When it finally appears it is superbly gentle, a 'soft oppression.' For the sleep by which it comes has its own charitable, paracletic function. Before Adam is allowed to see Eden in actual sight, as before he is allowed to look at Eve, both are anticipated in dream, because the reality is too great to bear without the adumbration of a dream, or because Adam's spirit must be gently raised toward the truth that is to meet him. By these repeated dream-awakenings divine light kindles rather than darkens the natural light in man.

But for a further sleep, and awakening into the darkness of the Fall, Adam's eyes might have been permanently tempered to the divine. Within the limits of sacred story, and the explicit framework of natural and supernatural, Milton approaches Wordsworth's view of a mind led from stage to transcendent stage by a similar monitory gentleness. No rape of the mind is necessary; no wounding of nature or of a previous mode of being. Milton's delicacy, in this matter, is absolute. When Raphael, divine historian, has finished his relation of the first things, Adam is impelled to tell of his own beginning: grateful, excited into reciprocity, desiring to converse longer with the Angel, 'now hear mee relate/My story.' The response of his mind to the Angel has by contagion some of the charm and energy of the Angel's own – Adam is already 'ascending winged.'

But Wordsworth cannot, like Milton, go back to a fixed beginning, to prehistory. 'How shall I seek the origin?' he asks, knowing that the beginning is already the middle (and muddle) of things. Nonetheless, deprived of both first term and last, of *arche* and *eschaton*, he still undertakes to trace the history of his mind. To what end? To justify the faith he has in the possibility of his renovation through daily and natural means, or to settle that wavering faith. Nature restored him un-apocalyptically in the past; it surely can do so again. The restoration he talks of is identical with being renewed as a poet: it is not dryness of heart that plagues him, but the fear that nature is not enough, that his imagination is essentially apocalyptic and must violate the middle world of common things and loves.

The Alpine journey contains three distinct reversals. The structure of each is that a disappointment is followed by a compensation. The imagination does not find, and strays like Adam, and is then seemingly completed. Two of the reversals, though having in them an element of surprise, are not violent; and the third, which is violent, and supplants nature as the poet's muse, still somehow returns to nature. For nature remains in Wordsworth's view the best and gentlest guide in the development surpassing her. It is part of the poet's strength that he faithfully records an experience he did not at the time of writing and still does not control. The greatest event of his journey is not the 'Characters of the great Apocalypse,' or the parallel bewilderment of time and way near Grave-dona (VI.688–726),* but the spectral figure of Imagination cutting him off, fulfilling Nature's prophecy, and revealing the end of his Negative Way.

Besides these reversals there is the tempo of the whole journey. This is often neglected for the striking events that detach themselves only partially from it. Wordsworth generally avoids making his epiphanies into epocha: into decisive turns of personal fate or history. A mythic structure would allow him to do that; Milton even overuses his 'firsts' when it comes to a psychological matter: 'Then Satan first knew pain' (cf. 'there gentle sleep/First found me'). Though Wordsworth must pattern his story and life, he is as apologetic about this as Raphael is for having to relate divine matters in terms intelligible to human sense – whenever possible he assumes a mazy motion which makes *The Prelude* a difficult poem to follow.

The reason for Wordsworth's avoidance of epochal structure is complex and linked probably to his avoidance of myth. For though he is compelled to seek beginnings, the unfolding causes of things, nature itself resists this kind of exactness, as if it diminished her generosities, her power to make anything a new beginning. To excerpt the various epiphanies from Wordsworth's narrative is, in any case, to neglect the pull of the underlying verse that refuses them too great a distinctness of self. Much of the drama is played out on a quietly continuing level; the ordinary events swelling into and absorbing the special insights; the peripeties threatening but finally sustaining the light of nature.

* All *Prelude* references are to the 1850 version, unless otherwise indicated.

The young travelers of Book VI instinctively associate nature with freedom. They believe it has the strength to waken or re-awaken man. By glorious chance their destination is a land where human nature seemed born again on account of revolution (339 ff.). Man is again as open as nature itself:

> once, and more than once,
> Unhoused beneath the evening star we saw
> Dances of liberty, and, in late hours
> Of darkness, dances in the open air
> Deftly prolonged. (369–73)

They are not sidetracked, however, by these public rejoicings. 'We held our way' (350), 'We glided forward with the flowing stream' (377), 'We sailed along' (385), 'We pursued our journey' (416) – various clichés and fillers abundant in the topographical literature of the eighteenth century, including Wordsworth's own earlier work, recover life and literal significance. Nature is their principal guide and even the energy which bears them on:

> Swift Rhone! thou wert the *wings* on which we cut
> A winding passage with majestic ease
> Between thy lofty rocks. (378–80)

Along this southerly route marked out by nature, they are caught up in a crowd of delegates returning home from the 'great spousals' (VI.389, the marriage of the People and the King, or of the Estates and the King, in the Constitution of July 1790) in Paris. Though Wordsworth and his friend are also 'emancipated' (387), they remain among them like 'a lonely pair of strangers' (384). We glimpse here the encounter of two different types of human freedom. The encounter always keeps below the level of allegory: it is accidental and unpredictable as all incidents in *The Prelude*. It has, nevertheless, the force of providence peering through chance, or idea through matter-of-fact.

(2) Snowdon

According to the poet's own declaration, the vision on Snowdon in the last book of *The Prelude* is one of several events vital to the growth of his mind and the recovery of his (poetic) spirits. Its import, daring if taken literally, is that there exists an imagination in nature analogous to that in man. Nature exhibits 'the express/Resemblance of that glorious faculty/That higher minds bear with them as their own.'[12] Wordsworth did take the experience literally, and instead of offering at the end of his poem an eighteenth-century Allegory of Imagination, he presents us with a concrete Act of Imagination. He does not consider what he sees as a projection of his mind on nature. The episode returns him to the faith that 'the forms/Of Nature have a passion in themselves.'[13] Nature is not a universe of death that lives only from or within our life. It has a greatness commensurate to that in man: this greatness, this imagination, is revealed on Snowdon.

It is important to dwell on Wordsworth's belief that Snowdon was Nature's 'naked work/Self-wrought, unaided by the human mind.'[14] His literal animism even makes him say that the vision was given 'to spirits of the night/And three chance human wanderers' – it was, that is to say, no private revelation but one for any man and even for others than man. At a later date nature's unusual *activity*[15] might have disturbed the principle of reciprocity, but at this time in Wordsworth's development (circa 1791–95) it redressed the balance between nature and the self by opposing 'Nature's Self' to 'Reason's naked self.'[16] In his crisis years, as the final books of *The Prelude* recount, Wordsworth had been tempted to divorce head from heart, himself from nature; they are the years in which his belief in an autonomous intellect threatened to cut him off from former sources of strength. Only experiences which could not be laid to the fantasy of an excited mind, but which would indubitably be nature's 'naked work/Self-wrought,' were therefore of power to restore him.

Yet Wordsworth is of the mind's party without knowing it, and Snowdon remains one of the most complexly deceptive episodes in literature. When the poet emerges from the mountain mist (1850 *Prelude* XIV.35) two things force themselves one after the other on his senses. The first is the moon single in the firmament: it seems insulated from the lower sphere on which it gazes sovereignly. The second is the roar of waters rising from that sphere: an event as striking as the moonscape's previous silence. The meditation following the vision (*Prelude* XIV.63 ff.) calls this strange reversal a 'mutual domination,' an 'interchangeable supremacy.' Nature, Wordsworth suggests, forced a shift in his attention from one apparently supreme agent to another, from moon to abyss; a shift which makes him aware of an antiphony between them. The active principle cannot be localized.

One aspect, however, not clarified by the meditation, and which may be the most important, is that the ascent of the voice of the waters does not indicate a true mutation in nature, a genuine Second Act. For the voices, if we examine the vision closely, cannot be sudden except psychologically: that is, in their breakthrough to the poet's mind. If he does not hear the stream of sound, which must have been there all along, it is because his senses were fixed by an obsessively visual image. So strong is the usurpation of sight that it masks the continuous sound, and the re-entry of the latter into consciousness appears like a breakthrough. Though the vision, therefore, is about nature, it is also about the poet's perception of nature, since not heaven and earth but only the poet's mind is turned.[17] The domination of which Wordsworth speaks is exerted first on eye then on ear, with neither given ultimacy but with sight more dangerous because more easily fixating the *flow* of attention.[18]

Thus Wordsworth's greatest visionary sight is based on the simplest kind of psychical error. To us this makes it more solid: such accidental epiphanies, almost a modern staple, and popularized by the contemporary novel, sharpen our sense of self-determination, but also our sense of fatality, since blindness to oneself at this level infers greater – immeasurable – blindnesses further on. Many poems in the *Lyrical Ballads* similarly 'build up greatest things/From least suggestions.' Yet the Snowdon episode is not written with the slightly bemused, almost deprecating tone of a Wordsworth ballad. It approaches a Miltonic sublimity. Wordsworth would have found it difficult, perhaps wrong, to stress at this point the simplicity of his error. And to return the emphasis from the objects to the energy of perception in any explicit way might tempt us to locate the whole drama solely in the human mind, and this would defeat his refusal to over-objectify the locus of perception, as well as his awareness that the *correspondence between eye and ear* is but one crucial revelation given by the experience.

'A Voice to Light gave Being' Wordsworth writes much later in 'On the Power of Sound' (1828). His reference to the Logos is secondary; it re-enforces a personal knowledge. The Alfoxden fragments and the vision on Snowdon intimate that the individuated energies of eye and ear might prove the source of a larger, reciprocal vigor. Snowdon in particular shows an interchange rather than reunification of these senses. The sea lends, as it were, its voices to the moon, and that broods (like the Spirit of God in Genesis or *Paradise Lost*) on a lower sphere from which it had seemed utterly distinct. This potentiality of interchange points to the ethics of metaphor and perhaps of poetry as a whole. In MS W, which is of special importance because it gives the Snowdon episode as originally written for the five-book *Prelude*, Wordsworth comments that higher minds

> from their native selves can deal about
> Like transformation, to one life impart
> The functions of another, shift, create,
> Trafficking with immeasurable thoughts.[19]

Snowdon remains an exceptional episode, not in what it discloses but in the form in which the disclosure reaches Wordsworth. He is careful to point out that the 'circumstance most awful and sublime' (1805 *Prelude* XIII. 76) is not necessary: the imaginative mind may also be roused by least suggestions. It could even be argued that the form of the Snowdon vision and its content are at odds, for nature both thrusts itself on the senses and seeks to liberate imagination from sensory thrall.

Yet Wordsworth has previously made it clear that nature may have to pit the senses against each other to undo their individual tyrannies and achieve 'the great ends of Liberty and Power.' His mind, to be genuinely imaginative and free, must transcend the impressive *object* (moon and abyss) as the focal point of its inspiration. The twofold fixation, therefore, on the visual moon, then on the sounding abyss, does not issue here in a double fixation but in the awareness of continuity and interchange. Snowdon thus foreshadows a modern poetry that relies on a deliberate and liberative synaesthesia, or on non-objective (syntactical) forms. And yet, adhering to common sense and common terms, Wordsworth refuses to start at a point beyond object-consciousness. He dooms himself to stay within the limits of the corporeal understanding and of immediate experience.

This is not a lesser but a greater task than that of modern poetry, for starting at a more primitive point in perception Wordsworth raises himself to the same transcendence of object-consciousness. His respect for the natural contours of an experience and the outlines of objects is never artificially suspended, yet by means of a principle of contrast or reversal that seems to inhere in experience itself, all fixities are resolved. Through contrast everything is made distinct yet nothing is defined into absolute independent singleness.[20] No sphere or event, in the Snowdon vision, has exclusive properties. The moon's light flashing through the mist is paralleled by the voices roaring up; these voices are 'one' (1850 *Prelude* XIV.60) like the moon itself or the radiant silence they pierce; the moon, moreover, in its fixity and solitude, stands symmetrical to the 'fixed, abysmal, gloomy, breathing-place' in the vapor; while the vapor itself is a consummate mimic of properties. Even the senses exchange energies and perhaps functions. Discontinuity yields to communion, and if moon and chasm are apocalyptic spots, dangerously fixed points, the second is more vital and becomes almost immediately a strait between two worlds, a 'breathing-place' and 'thoroughfare.'

We see by this that Snowdon is an omphalos vision and that Wordsworth again turns from apocalypse. He achieves a view of the border between realms of being. The oscillating up-down pattern of attention (counterpointed by the strongly horizontal stretching of the mist 'far as the sight could reach') recalls the original of all such visions for minds nourished by the Bible: 'And he [Jacob] dreamed, and behold a ladder set upon the earth, and the top of it reached to heaven: and behold the angels of God ascending and descending on it.'[21] On Snowdon the ladder descends, as it were, into a nether sphere: the Deep or *Tehom*, which the Bible mentions hesitantly at the beginning of Genesis, reopens as strongly as in the Psalms; and the notion of a 'breathing-place,' seen suddenly as in a dream near where the poet stands, helps to enforce the impression that he has passed into himself, and sees his body's life from the inside, or from the pulse-point of the macrocosm. He stands, in any case, where the sustaining (ascending and descending) circulation between worlds is visible.

This circulation, in the lineaments of a style achieved some years before in experiments at Alfoxden, some of the preceding paragraphs have traced. The only difference between the sublime shadowings on Snowdon and the 'subtle intercourse'[22] Wordsworth describes at Alfoxden is that in the former even the least sensitive man cannot choose but feel, while in the latter nature acts imperceptibly. Which mode seemed the greater miracle to Wordsworth? The 'wondrous influence of power gently used.' It was his rediscovery of the subtle links that join past and present, or restore the alienated heart, which prompted the great thaw of Alfoxden and led into *The Prelude*. That poem begins with a 'gentle breeze' which reappears at the second beginning of *The Prelude*, the story of the poet's restoration:

> Ye gentle breezes lead me forth again
> Soft airs and gladdening sunbeams lead me on
> To the green haunts of chearfulness and peace
> And health and liberty, to pathways roads
> And fields with rural works to open earth
> And the calm bliss of an unbounded sky
> The woods the villages the pleasant farms
> Smoke rising up from tufted trees and brooks
> Muttering among the stones[23]

In this almost unpunctuated variant there is no stop to the breeze of a rhythm running over so many things, joining by simple enumeration and the least effort of grammar one thing and the next. Is this not Sabrina of *Comus* dancing over 'The Cowslip's velvet head / That bends not as I tread'? Snowdon, however, is more naked in its display of powers, more abrupt in its passings from mist to light, moon to abyss. The spirit of that place has a resemblance to Wordsworth's moments of terrible beauty and skirts the Miltonic Sublime. Yet there remains a significant distance between Wordsworth at his most Miltonic and Milton. This distance is worth defining; it touches on Wordsworth's general problem in writing an epic poem, that is, a long poem on the greatest possible subject with a style appropriate to its subject.

(3) Coda

At the beginning of *The Prelude* a poet returns to nature, yet the poem he writes is about the difficulties of that return. He cannot always sustain his quest to link what makes a poet, the energy of imagination, to the energy of nature. In its purity the imagination is 'unfathered' – a self-begotten, potentially apocalyptic force. But poetry, like the world, can only house an imagination which is a borderer, which will not disdain earthly things. Whatever the imagination's source, its end as poetry is the nature all recognize, and still a nature that leads beyond itself.

Snowdon is a magic mountain. It is a place of enchantment and danger as Spenser and many Romantics have pictured. Everything that happens on this mountain is deceptive because everything leads beyond (though not away from) itself. It is easy to overlook the fact that Wordsworth sets out to see the dawn and encounters a rising-up of the powers in darkness. 'Night unto night showeth knowledge.'

Reduced to its simplest structure the experience of the poet on Snowdon shows a doubling of the idea of the inscrutable breaking into revelation. Mist into flash of light, mist into stream of sound – the same element bears two surprises. The Inscrutable, one might say, brings forth Immediacy (the isolate moon) which seeks out – is sustained by – the Inscrutable breaking into Immediacy (the real behind the misty ocean, the evidence of the voices rising up).

This is the perfect instance of the ternary pattern characterizing the chief incidents of Books I, VI, and XIV. It provides a clear case where immediacy acts as a medium, which is as good a description of poetry's effect as any. Poetry leads from pleasure to pleasure; and, enjoying each as it engages the mind, we are surprised by the next. This is what Coleridge may have meant when he renewed an old dictum and said that a poem has both pleasure and truth in it, but that the pleasures of the way are as important as the truth of the destination.[24]

Nature and Poetry matter only as they quicken regeneration. The most enthralling impression should still be a middle-term, thoroughfare to a new birth of power and liberty. The vision acts on the man, leads his senses beyond themselves, from moon to sounding abyss and finally back to his own creative powers. But the clearest sign of a truly creative, self-renewing mind is to build up greatest things from least suggestions. As at the beginning of *The Prelude*, anything may guide, even a 'trackless field.' Wordsworth's rhapsodic opening, muted too soon, does not express faith in nature but rather in the quickening relation of imagination to nature. Nature, however, is real and important enough. Spreading light and life in subtle, not catastrophic ways, it has brought the poet to his present faith that self-renewal is possible without violence of apocalypse.

'Visionary power,' Wordsworth writes at one point, 'Attends the motions of the viewless winds, / Embodied in the mystery words' (*Prelude* V.595–97). The contrast of visionary and viewless is that of greatest things built up from smallest. Only in this respect is Poetry a second Nature. It learns from nature the 'wondrous influence of power gently used' (*Prelude* XII.15). We start with something viewless or inscrutable like the source of the Nile, still given in Wordsworth's day either a natural or supernatural explanation.[25] When Wordsworth comes face to face with his own creative power, with imagination rising 'like an unfathered vapour,' that is, hiding its natural source, he glimpses the supernatural fountains of genius. But in the lines that follow, the hiding that bespeaks mystery and apocalypse opens once more into nature. The imagination hides itself by overflowing as poetry, and is compared to the Nile that overflows its banks and the Egyptian plain. Wordsworth the traveller now alludes to the natural explanation for the rise of the Nile. The energy of imagination enters into a natural cycle though apart from it; while the lines describing his soul as

> Strong in herself and in beatitude
> That hides her, like the mighty flood of Nile
> Poured from her fount of Abyssinian clouds
> To fertilise the whole Egyptian plain . . . (VI.613–16)

renew the connection between the 'waters above and the waters below,'[26] between heaven and earth.

Toward this marriage of heaven and earth the poet proceeds despite apocalypse. He is the matchmaker, his song the spousal verse. His dedication to poetry is a dedication to this myth become sense. An awful power rises from the mind's abyss, disowning nature; another descends fertile from Abyssinian clouds. He seeks his earthly paradise not 'beyond the Indian mount' but in the real Abyss-inia[27] – any mountain-valley where poetry is made.

Notes

1. Letter to Francesco Dionigi de' Roberti, April 26, 1336. The end of the quoted passage is an allusion to Seneca, *Epistles* 8.5.
2. Quoted from *The Sacred Theory of the Earth* (1684–89), in Marjorie Nicolson, *Mountain Gloom and Mountain Glory* (New York, 1959), p. 206. Her chs. 5 and 6 on Burnet are especially relevant to the present theme.
3. *Descriptive Sketches* (1793), lines 692–93.
4. 'Desultory Stanzas,' in *Memorials of a Tour on the Continent, 1820* (published 1822).
5. I Corinthians 15:51–54 and Acts 3:21; cf. *The Poetical Works of William Wordsworth*, ed. E. de Selincourt and H. Darbishire (5 vols., Oxford, 1940–49) (*PW*), 5, 337 ('Home at Grasmere,' line 743).
6. Letter to John Hamilton Reynolds, May 3, 1818. Yet did not Saint Augustine think into the human heart, at an earlier time?
7. Cf. also Keats's *Hyperion*, the quest of Apollo in Bk. III, which is directly under the influence of *Paradise Lost* VIII.253 ff. 'The Imagination may be compared to Adam's dream,' Keats says in a letter (to Benjamin Bailey, November 22, 1817), 'he awoke and found it truth.' Keats was haunted by that Miltonic sequence which incorporates, of course, a structural principle of repetition.

8. *Paradise Lost* VIII.273–79.

9. Romans 1:20, one of the proof-texts for the 'light of nature.'

10. *Paradise Lost* VIII.283–88.

11. Ibid. 253–56.

12. *Prelude* XIV. 88–90.

13. *Prelude* XIII. 290–91.

14. MS W, *Prelude: William Wordsworth, The Prelude*, ed. E. de Selincourt, 2d ed. revised by H. Darbishire [Oxford, 1959], p. 624.

15. Wordsworth emphasizes the activity of nature at the expense of tautology, when he adds 'by putting forth' to 'Exhibited' in *Prelude* (1805) XIII.75. He keeps the phrase, though dangling, in the 1850 version, XIV.79. Unless the phrase is construed as a gerund (shadowed: how? by a putting forth) it takes 'That mutual domination' as object and makes it refer to the way in which imagination (the 'one function' of line 78) is exhibited, rather than to imagination itself, as the passage seems to require: 'One function, above all, of such a mind/Had Nature shadowed there . . ./That mutual domination which she loves/To exert . . .' Or is the *function* both the faculty and the mode whereby it is (self-)exhibited?

16. *Prelude* XI.234 ff.

17. With Wordsworth we remain in the phenomenal world, however surprising a particular revelation may be (cf. *Prelude* I.458–60). But reversal is strongly characteristic of apocalyptic experiences, though here it comes to Wordsworth in a purely natural context.

18. My metaphors of 'flowing' and 'fixity' are justified by the vision (XIV.58 ff.) and the meditation (XIV.73 ff.).

19. *Prelude*, pp. 484–85. On this matter of transformation or transfer, see also the living chiasmus depicted in a related episode of MS W, *Prelude*[2], p. 624, the picture of a horse which is 'A living Statue or a statued Life'; and *Excursion* VII.518 ff., 'faculties, which seem/Extinguished, do not, *therefore*, cease to be./And to the mind among her powers of sense/This transfer is permitted.' The reference is to the sensitivity of ear and touch in a blind man.

20. See Wordsworth's critique of Macpherson's *Ossian*, 'In nature everything is distinct, yet nothing defined into absolute independent singleness.'

21. Genesis 28:12.

22. *Prelude* XII.11.

23. MS Y, *Prelude*, p. 430.

24. *Biographia Literaria*, ch. 14.

25. The source of the Nile was one of the riddles of the world, and its annual overflow one of the wonders. Fantastic theories were propounded which that omnigatherer Coleridge knew well, and which may have found their way into 'Kubla Khan.' In 1770 James Bruce discovered the source of the Nile (in fact only of the Blue Nile) in Abyssinia. A five-volume account of his adventures was published by him in 1790, further versions in 1805 and 1813. The book or reports of it were probably known to Wordsworth (fond of travelogues). Bruce, moreover, was himself following up a tradition which placed the Nile's source in Abyssinia. See J. L. Lowes, *The Road to Xanadu* (Boston and New York, 1927).

26. Cf. Hartman, *The Unmediated Vision*, pp. 29 ff.
27. The appearance in relatively close sequence of abyss (VI.594), Abyssinian (VI.615), and 'a depth/of Abyssinian privacy' (VI.661 f.) makes one suspect a perhaps unconscious association of ideas. The earthly Paradise was sometimes placed in Abyssinia, near the hidden source of the Nile (see Dr. Johnson's *Rasselas*).

Chapter 4

The Use and Abuse of Structural Analysis

There is a Yew-tree, pride of Lorton Vale,
Which to this day stands single, in the midst
Of its own darkness, as it stood of yore:
Not loth to furnish weapons for the bands
5   Of Umfraville or Percy ere they marched
To Scotland's heaths; or those that crossed the sea
And drew their sounding bows at Azincour,
Perhaps at earlier Crecy, or Poictiers.
Of vast circumference and gloom profound
10 This solitary Tree! a living thing
Produced too slowly ever to decay;
Of form and aspect too magnificent
To be destroyed. But worthier still of note
Are those fraternal Four of Borrowdale,
15 Joined in one solemn and capacious grove;
Huge trunks! and each particular trunk a growth
Of intertwisted fibres serpentine
Up-coiling, and inveterately convolved;
Nor uninformed with Phantasy, and looks
20 That threaten the profane; a pillared shade,
Upon whose grassless floor of red-brown hue,
By sheddings from the pining umbrage tinged
Perennially – beneath whose sable roof
Of boughs, as if for festal purpose decked
25 With unrejoicing berries – ghostly Shapes
May meet at noontide; Fear and trembling Hope,
Silence and Foresight; Death the Skeleton
And Time the Shadow; – there to celebrate,
As in a natural temple scattered o'er
30 With altars undisturbed of mossy stone,
United worship; or in mute repose
To lie, and listen to the mountain flood
Murmuring from Glaramara's inmost caves.

1.

Michael Riffaterre's essay on Wordsworth's 'Yew-Trees' is, in substance, the best commentary on that poem yet written and ranks with the best commentaries on any Wordsworth poem.[1] Moreover, in the exposition of a method of analysis, it is an equally impressive act, whose significance for the study of poetry – not only descriptive poetry of Wordsworth's kind – is considerable. My own comment here can only be supplementary to Riffaterre's, but it will try to locate certain limits of the structural-semantic method he employs. I am also interested in the role played by literary history – or assumptions about it – in this kind of analysis.[2]

It is a truism, of course, that no method can guarantee an interpretation. At most it can assure an open, articulate, and transferable kind of analytic procedure. But two specific remarks can be made of all methods or techniques of analysis, including Riffaterre's: (1) They are unable to determine, qua method, what finding is to be emphasized. (2) Methods are backed up by methodizers: there is a person in the machine. Consequently, even where the method successfully disciplines the personal factor, the latter can still make its appearance, as in the choice of the object of analysis: this poem rather than that. Without claiming that Riffaterre's analysis could not yield significant results when applied to other Wordsworth poems, one suspects that 'Yew-Trees' cooperates with the method because there is a harmony between the curious impersonality of this 'descriptive' or 'nature' poem and the desired impersonality of structural-semantic analysis. Yet precisely here, on this matter of what happens to 'person' or 'subject' in the method or in the poem, Riffaterre's analysis proves vulnerable, though far from wrong. Let me begin, however, with a synopsis of his findings.

Riffaterre states that (1) even in 'descriptive' verse the words are not there only to describe real trees and other objects, but are also part of a 'system' with its own grammatical-semantic correlation. He names the belief in the direct signifying function or real reference of words the 'referential fallacy.' (2) This deflection from referentiality is enabled by the fact that the word system can extend beyond the boundary of the sentence to encompass the totality of the poem. Riffaterre elaborates clearly the advantages of this verbo-poetic logic which he defines as 'an ideal model for various chains of . . . associations,' 'an imaginary space in which . . . components are distributed so as to define their reciprocal functions,' 'strings of semantic equivalences.' (3) Because of this reciprocity or equivalence an overdetermination occurs which both founds meanings and eventually deprives the reader of his interpretive freedom (really, promiscuity). All functions 'converge and concur irresistibly toward the one single significance . . .' (4) In this particular poem, the structure of significance starts from a chain in which the *tree* cluster of associations issues in the *ghost* variant, at which point (line 25) meaning is no longer conveyed by richly redundant variations on certain commonplaces. The personifications of lines 25ff. literalize meaning without giving us a symbolic key to it. What is being worshiped by these ghosts? There is something like a riddle here, 'circuitous . . . pointers surrounding a semantic hole'; this indeterminacy culminates in a near-onomatopoeic 'soundscape' which reinforces the theme of mere-listening-to-sound (the second 'action' ascribed to the ghosts [31–33]), and again resists symbolic meaning. 'Far from being a letdown after the symbolic meanings of the first part, the strict literalness of the end is a climax. Its significance lies in the meaninglessness of the sound. Sensation is all – which is exactly what descriptive poetry is about.'

My excerpting of a long and skillful paper cannot do it justice. There is no doubt that Riffaterre achieves one of the highest aims of commentary: local illumination of the words of a text together with the foregrounding of a structure that provides a skeleton key for other poems and situates the object of analysis in generic terms ('descriptive poetry'). The analysis is at once minute in its attention to particulars and theoretically ambitious.

2. 'The Yew-Tree had its Ghost' (*The Prelude*)

A more intuitive approach, guided by the genius of Wordsworth's language, could endorse almost all these findings. Riffaterre's key insight – the imbalance between 'mere sound' and 'the infinity of thought,' or the opposition *water murmuring / dulls the pangs of mortality* – is, as he suggests, central to Wordsworth's aesthetics; even the relatively unsystematic analysis found at the end of my Wordsworth chapter in *The Unmediated Vision* reaches a similar conclusion.[3] It is equally clear, however, that an essential feature of 'Yew-Trees' has been slighted. I allude to the poem's elision of the human intermediary or observer:[4] *elision* being a better word than *absence* because the perceptions obviously issue from a speaking source that is human, though not explicitly localized as such.

The elision begins with the opening phrase, 'There is,' an impersonal notation when compared to, say, 'I know of' or 'I am told of.' The impersonal constructions continue and on occasion strongly animate what is inanimate. It is suggested, for example, that the tree has a kind of will (it is 'Not loth to furnish weapons . . .'); while Wordsworth's image of 'sounding bows' is like an ablauted variant of 'sounding boughs' and creates an echo-metaphor intimating a magical or superstitious persistence of the yew's life – as if the wood retained its original characteristics even in this changed form.

Only at lines 25ff., when the ghost personifications appear, does Riffaterre note the elision: 'The listening subject is normally actualized in the person of the narrator. The difference in "Yew-Trees" is of course that the narrator's thoughts, the ghosts, take his place as listener.' But what is true of the *listening subject* has been true of the *speaking subject* all along. The speaking subject never appears on the scene: of him too we could say that 'the narrator's thoughts, the ghosts, take his place.' The strong device of personification reveals a more inobvious and deeply sustaining figure. From the very beginning we must accept the voice that speaks as, somehow, akin to the Yew-tree itself in ghostly extension or longevity.

Why has no one raised the question of who is speaking here or whose voice it is? At one point Riffaterre says casually: 'The descriptive poem, like most of Wordsworth's texts of this kind, is also a narrative in the first person (implicit here).' This shows the danger of such hypostatized genres as 'descriptive poetry.' It also supports our contention that no method can determine what findings are to be emphasized. Riffaterre chooses not to develop such a strong figurative device as the personifications – and he fails to remark how unusual personification is in Wordsworth,[5] how Wordsworth's literary polemic is against it, and how this very poem evades explicit personification until the strong lines at the end breach the poet's reserve.

That there is a disturbance centering on the concept of personification is not irrelevant to the question of who is speaking, or why no one has raised that question. Speech is assumed to be human, and where it is not so we expect the poet to indicate explicitly that he is personifying, or using a mythological idea. No one has raised the question because of the convention that what is normal does not have to be made obvious. Wordsworth, or someone like him, must be the speaker: if the title does not specify *quercus loquitur*, we assume *poeta loquitur*. Surely it is no tree spirit or personified guardian whose voice is represented here?

Yet the shadow of an indeterminacy remains, and for equally conventional reasons. There is a poetic tradition in which a tree or long-lived though mute object is made to speak: perhaps an oracular oak, perhaps a ruined castle, perhaps a genius loci.[6] (See Appendix.) While no such 'eternity structure' or 'speaking monument' is visibly posited by Wordsworth, the adjacence of such a convention to the elision of the human intermediary in 'Yew-Trees' suggests that the poet has subsumed or refined an archaic genre, and created in its stead a composite 'descriptive' sketch which still expresses feelings or features essential to the older genre. This displacement from mythic into what is often called meditative or descriptive verse is a Wordsworthian characteristic and if explored would tell us something about poetic as well as human time: that is, about the relation of Wordsworth's poetry to archaic forms, whether these involve religious ideas or superstitions, concepts of genre, venerable devices such as personification, or poetic diction generally.

All figuration, Wordsworth held, must be grounded in feeling, in a recoverable emotion that would justify the apparently archaic form and explain its persistence. A purely formal interpretation could link Wordsworth's impersonality here to his interest in the ballad as a 'Relique of Ancient English Poetry.' 'There is a Yew-tree' might be construed as a variant of 'There is a Thorn: It looks so old . . .' Ballad and Yew-tree are homologous: reliques, English, part of the poetry of nature. The poet's respect for local tradition (much of the information in the first dozen lines may come from that source) could also be linked to this interest in ballads. But what feeling allows the form to survive, and creates in 'Yew-Trees' a mutant ballad, 'descriptive' rather than 'lyrical'?

Now Wordsworth is obviously not a Polonius when it comes to genres. Rather, his feeling for the Yew-tree, in its historic actuality or as a totemic figure in literary discourse, revives the truth of that *imaginative transference* which is at the root of opposite yet related devices essential to poetry: impersonation (personification, animistic metaphor), on the one hand, and impersonal constructions eliding narrator or human intermediary on the other. Negation of self is, in both, accompanied by a magnified sense of the other, which leads to mythic, archaic, or spectral symbols. The yews make a ghost of the speaker.

This feeling of ghostliness is, possibly, an imaginative need rather than the direct precipitate of a yew-tree experience: what matters is the poet's inward grounding of an idea of ghostliness that motivates elision of self-reference. The archaic or literary forms subsumed by Wordsworth are the literal spooks of Gothic ballad or tale, as well as the etiolated personifications endemic to poetic diction. In a poet like Collins these urbane and demonic types of ghostly personification blend uneasily. In a poet like Shelley they also blend uneasily. Wordsworth's poetic reflection, however, centers not on figures of speech alone but also on speech as a figure: that is, on the relation between spectral feeling and poetic voice. The 'riddling' quality that Riffaterre attaches to the dramatic intrusion of archaic personification resides in the modality of poetic speech itself – at least from the moment we ask, who is speaking?

Trees do not 'speak' to Wordsworth any more than to us. They are mute, like the gods are mute; yet 'the speaking face of nature' is as understandable a metaphor as 'the still, sad music of humanity.' An act of listening precedes or is constitutive of the naturalized oracular voice we hear in Wordsworth's poem. Although no listener appears till the end of 'Yew-Trees,' he is there all the time, as the poet-medium who 'listens' to nature, to the trees, to local tradition, to his own ominous or sensitive imagination – to 'Nothing that is not there and the nothing that is' (Wallace Stevens).

3.

Riffaterre overlooks the problem of voice or of the poet as intermediary. Is this a simple flaw or is it connected with the 'impersonality' of the structural method? His remark that 'the narrator's thoughts, the ghosts, take his place,' localizes an effect which is all-pervasive, though reaching a telltale climax with the personifications of lines 25ff. The poet's extroverted use of personification is taken too literally and his use of elision not literally enough. It seems like a mistake anyone might make. But it could be motivated by a misleading idea on how poems 'develop': as if the end of a poem must show a thematic or semantic increment over its beginning. This too is a common assumption. What makes the mistake suspicious is that it involves concepts of voice and time, and these precisely are what the structural method cannot handle except (as here) by reducing them to a semantic-thematic drift. Wordsworth's lyric, moreover, conspires with this kind of eternity-structuring because it records how the sense of human time is phantomized by the ancient yews. Their span of years compared to ours leads us into thoughts of eternity.

Riffaterre refers to the experience of phantomization, but in a strange and limiting way. 'The yew is not described in relation to the tree of that name, but as an image of an existence closer to Eternity than ours.' A wedge is driven by such an interpretation between name and thing as surely as in Platonic theories of mimesis. The yews become, in fact, a kind of Idea ('image of an existence closer to Eternity'), and the poem a way of approaching it by an ideal, that is, nonreferential use of words. The authenticity of poetry as a temporal art is diminished by importing an unprogressive (Platonic) or too easily progressive (semantic-thematic) concept of development.

Though the structural approach claims to deal with the representation of reality as a 'verbal construct in which meaning is achieved by reference from words to words, not to things,' it does not guarantee an understanding of words as a temporal medium. The method, moreover, elides the status of poetry as mediation by emphasizing the status of language as a determining – and vis-à-vis the reader – deterministic medium. The subjectivity of both author and reader is reduced by the concept of a 'reading' that 'allows the reader no freedom of choice in the understanding of descriptive details.' All these details, Riffaterre goes on, 'converge and concur irresistibly toward the one single significance, once the sequence has started moving – all function as structural variants of that obsessive, rapidly overwhelming semantic variant.'

Yet do things roll on so roundly and irresistibly here? It might be argued instead that the merging of casual deictic phrasing ('*There* is a Yew-tree') and oracular pronouncement ('There *is* a Yew-tree') creates a peculiarly Wordsworthian tone, hovering between pompous cliché and sublime simplicity. This counterpoint of understatement and overstatement is found even in the general development of the poem, where the initial, understated figure (the impersonal construction) leads into an overstated figure (the strong personifications). The thought ghosts of the poet embody as ghostly shapes. This 'Gothic' reversal, of course, never literally takes place, it merely threatens to take place: the poem evokes a borderline situation where voice is environed by ghostly pressures yet maintains an in-betweenness. The in-between character of the Wordsworthian narrative voice can be interpreted in several, nonexclusive ways: as indicating a tension between mutism and oracular eloquence, or self-depletion (the self phantomized by a sublime experience) and self-redemption (through identification with the sublime), and so forth. Coming closer to Wordsworth's own terms, one could emphasize a split between humanizing and eternizing movements of thought: the poet, haunted by the 'unimaginable touch of Time,' puts himself or a surrogate beyond the 'touch of earthly years.'[7]

If there is no irresistible sequence, there is also no 'starter' or 'system component that triggers the sequence' except the poem's first phrase. But any first-term theory makes one suspicious, and suggests in its begetter a sin against time. 'Thought hath no beginning,' Wordsworth wrote: we are always in the midst, or several beginnings exist among which we must choose. My personal way of linking the poem to a dominant theme or 'overwhelming variant' would be to bring to bear a series of juxtapositions which might (1) encompass the mode of the poem by transforming 'speaking monument' to 'speaking tree' (sounding boughs) and 'conscious (oracular) cave'; and (2) analyze the problematic situation of consciousness itself. Consciousness is problematic in these verses because it is *absent* as a representamen (there is no 'I'), problematic elsewhere in Wordsworth because it is *present* as an embarrassed, garrulous, naive, or egotistical voice.

If the absence of self-reference points to a 'ghostliness' in the self, the presence of strong personification points to a 'ghostliness' in fictional or rhetorical language. The 'riddle' of the poem turns on the relation of imagination to rhetoric, on the one hand, and of imagination to human time and personal identity on the other. The riddle brings the simple content of 'Yew-Trees' as a poem about oracular places once more into view.

Yews are identified with the oracular by their longevity and funerary character. In so subtly eliding the human intermediary, Wordsworth evokes a state of consciousness directed toward a quasi-eternal object and proceeding from a quasi-eternal repose. What is that state, however, if not an imagined kind of death? Where could the speech, which is the poem, come from, if not from a mind that has outlived itself: a posthumous mind that reposes in this funerary bower? By a proleptic act of imagination, then, the poet speaks to us from the grave. He provides us with a speech monument, a funerary inscription, a meditation as exemplary as 'Tintern Abbey' on what may survive.

Foreseeing always runs the danger of death-seeing. Think of Thomas Gray's 'Ode on a Distant Prospect of Eton College' with its ghostly personifications. Wordsworth's poem, like Gray's, recalls the sixth book of *The Aeneid*, which vividly pictures the gates of hell beset by a swarm of evil personifications – and in their midst an opaque elm, its branches full of clinging dreams. 'Yew-Trees' emerges into a more soothing prospect, perhaps even into the 'peace which passeth understanding.'[8] As in Virgil, however, the prophetic threshold is shadowed by a threshold peril: the mind of the poet could disappear into that dark wood of dreams.

4.

It is strange to think of 'Yew-Trees' as a ghostly ballad. Yet voice in Wordsworth is often a 'wandering utterance,'[9] an echo existing before as well as after the poem which gives it a home. What he names the 'ghostly language of the ancient earth'[10] is transmitted not by nature alone but also by 'wandering' stories that attach themselves to this or that place, inciting nature poetry, or 'localized romance.' These stories seem to have an impersonal existence; and we are reminded that literary structuralism gained its inaugural success with Propp's analysis of such wandering legends or ballads.

The anonymous or impersonal status of these narratives suggests that they are, like the yews, a kind of triumph over time. They reveal constants which survive all intermixture and accretion. Narrative is the field of combination which foregrounds, by repetition, these constants; yet in the ballads of Wordsworth narrative is vulnerable, as if voice were more ghostly than any story could show or as if time no longer had time. The wonder-wandering of romance or the temporal spaciousness of storytelling is reduced, even punctured, by an urgency I have elsewhere called apocalyptic, but which generally presents itself as a breaking, undoing, interruption of the narrative line.

There is, virtually, no narrative in 'Yew-Trees.' The question is less what interrupts the narrative than how so static a poem makes time and keeps moving. It is no problem for Riffaterre. His structuralism puts language where the subjectivity or consciousness of the poet might be: words are analyzed into kernel statements and chains of derivation. A poem conjugates itself by sequences of words correlatively grammatical and semantic. So all the details in lines 16 to 18 are said to be 'but a grammatical expansion of the meaning of the word "growth" which is in itself only a generalization of "trunk." '

Riffaterre's phraseology is not beyond question. Why 'expansion' rather than 'repetition'? Is grammar always expansive? Is he insinuating a generous metaphor, which views language as a tree of life, branching out into lollipops of words? I am not so sure that Wordsworth's yews are such a tree of life. The relation of these yews to grammar – to articulate speech or writing – is uncertain. So the very first phrase of the poem has an absoluteness the rest of the sentence qualifies without modifying. Speech seems always about to stop. Every clause or addition, even past the full stop of line 8, is but an appositive to 'There is a Yew-tree.' The same holds true of the second subject phrase – 'those fraternal Four of Borrowdale.' What follows has something of the accretive development of a cult hymn, and more should be said about the cultic stutter of this so-called descriptive poetry. Riffaterre's brilliant observation that 'in the midst of its own darkness' reverses a characteristic representation of epiphany is used only to reveal a sequence culminating in the 'natural temple' theme.

The progression of Wordsworth's poem (noted by Riffaterre) toward a final perspective that alleviates the burden of the mystery is, it seems to me, a halting one, and as precarious as that final perspective itself. To ascribe an auto-motive potential to the language of poetry demystifies it prematurely and fails to weigh the relation of cultic and grammatical.

A cancelled ending[11] fortifies our sense that Wordsworth's description is partially inspired by cultic forms. The duplicitous character of his verbal style – the blending of under- and overstatement – allows a number of double readings: cultic-descriptive, cultic-grammatical, descriptive-grammatical. Because Wordsworth's symbols are underdetermined *topoi* ('kernels' in Riffaterre's phrase), they can be expanded in the way he shows, but they may also be viewed as dream-like and overdetermined *places* (fixations) impeding real consecutiveness and narrative flow. 'There is a Yew-tree' seems as simple and understated an opening as 'There was a Boy,' but it could also be a minimalist's epiphany, or an elegiac anticipation of the disappearance from earth of such natural temples.

A reading that recovers the strange interplay of cultic feeling and modern self-consciousness will also recover the precarious subjectivity of the poet. Consider the phenomenon of centroversion in Wordsworth: how his mind circles and haunts a particular place until released into an emancipatory idea of Nature. The yews, in this light, are *omphaloi*: boundary images, or signs of a liminal situation, a cultic and charged threshold.[12] As we follow the poet's words we are kept moving along a border between natural and supernatural ideas; and there is no guarantee he might not go over the line into a dark and discontinous fantasy.

'Nor uninformed with Phantasy, and looks/That threaten the profane' – he could go over the line right there. His description of the Borrowdale yews does more than evoke a natural temple. 'Phantasy,' hypostatized this way, is already a spooky personification: a kind of snake or guardian monster of the grove. To reduce line 19 to topos or figure diminishes the phenomenality of words. We cannot exclude the possibility that 'the forms/Of Nature have a passion in themselves,'[13] though Wordsworth's hint of that is characteristically defensive ('Nor uninformed . . .').

Yet even the negatives have a quasi–narrative ambiguity. They protract the poem, and cue us to the vulnerability of a thinker who is extending so 'heavy' a thought that it tends to collapse his medium. The verbal shape of 'Uninformed' is especially interesting. *Un / in* presses on the root word *form*, all the more so if the context makes *un* and *um* converge. ('Uninformed' is preceded by *Um*fra-ville, circum*ference, and followed by *um*brage, *un*rejoicing, *un*disturbed.) The impression is subtle: read, for example, 'Nor unformed with Phantasy,' and nearly the same meaning obtains. The *in* and *un* struggle to come together as one intense meaning, while *um* presents itself as a stronger or heavier *un*. The final verse's reduplicative onomatopoeia liquefies this pattern (absorbing the vowel plus *r* effect from the 'Nor . . . o'er . . . or' sequence), as if the convergence of *n* and *m* into some mutist sound *nm*, *nn*, or *mm*, had been overcome, though 'inmost' echoes the danger.

Such verses are 'produced too slowly.' There are several other impediments to easy progression. They are felt more, it is true, in lines 19ff. 'Nor uninformed with Phantasy,' helped by the preceding image of convolution, definitely turns the poem away from efficiently linked commonplaces. Even the latter, however, did not get far from an absolute phrase or concept. Each new phrase in lines 1–18 touches back to 'There is a Yew-tree' through apposition or some lingering, contiguous device of this sort. No strong main verbs join the three sentences making up the entire poem – perhaps two sentences, since line 9 does not really introduce a new subject or verb, so that the period at the end of line 8 is more like a semicolon. Line 9, in fact, could easily have come immediately after line 1 or line 3, so close are we still to the original theme. The impression can arise that Wordsworth would have liked to anticipate and close with the simple exclamation 'This solitary Tree!'

After line 19 dashes multiply, phrases accumulate, and we approach an enumeration that is near-chaotic (near-ecstatic), yet carefully reticulated by an abundance of particles. On the one hand, pillared shade, sable roof, ghostly shapes, Death the Skeleton, natural temple, United worship, etc.; on the other, upon, by, beneath, of, as if, for, with, etc. 'United worship' (31) may not be an adjective-noun phrase, but it could be, so weak are the preceding verbs and so forceful the pull of the noun phrases. Other obstacles to an easy manner of proceeding are such tmetic insertions as 'undisturbed' (30), weak joining words, 'o'er/With' (29–30) followed by 'or in' (31), and the occasional sense that one word is the scrambled echo of another: 'noontide' (26), 'united' (31).

'United' is, in fact, the most intriguing case. Its equivocal syntax has been mentioned; but in sound, too, there is an equivocation. The *un* sequence may lead to a momentary and illusory reading of it as *un-ited*. ('umbrage,' in a previous line, if we are sensitive to the *un/um* morpheme, may split into a punning compound, 'shadow-age,' an undersense supported by the more obvious pun in 'pining.'[14] The reader, of course, resolves the riddle word *un-ited* by the proper, forward movement. But once the word has been slowed or foregrounded in this way, a new, less commonsensical deciphering may suggest itself. It again brings the poem to a halt or condenses it as one riddling phrase. *United* could be read *United*, that is, *Yewnited* (Yewnighted).

5.

> Make not your rosaries of yew-berries
> Keats, *Ode on Melancholy*

Slowing the reader makes him aware that the forms of language, like those of nature, 'have a passion in themselves.' A snake lies coiled within 'Phantasy.' The slowing of reading also makes him aware of time. Like language, time is more than a medium. There seems to be no way to force its growth or to subdue it to the predictable. Time has the erratic motion of a snake coiled up.[15] There is something treacherous in the flow of time or of words that makes Wordsworth exceedingly cautious. Though English is not a jungle, Wordsworth is more in the tropics than Huxley would have us believe.

Wordsworth's 'yewnity,' a dream word disturbing further the not undisturbed realism of the poem, has the dark appeal of its double or compound character. Half-perceived, half-created by the reader, it is a centaur shape guiding him to a new understanding of how words and things, signifier and signified, connect. It suggests the possibility of a strangely mimetic or organic literary form, of a language of nature: here is a kernel out of which, however unconsciously – by vegetable genius – the poem grows. 'Yewnity' suggests a model for analysis imitating the branchings of tree or flower from a deeply nurtured, perhaps covert, point:

> So from the root
> Springs lighter the green stalk, from thence the leaves
> More aery, last the bright consummate flow'r . . .
> . . . flow'rs and thir fruit
> Man's nourishment, by gradual scale sublim'd . . .
> (*Paradise Lost* V.479–83)

Paradigm Lost, something echoes in us. For the yew standing in the midst of its own darkness is the opposite of a heliotrope. A melantropic or nightshade plant, it evokes a persephonic kind of nourishment and the role of darkness in the growth of the mind – especially the poet's mind:

> Vallombre's groves
> Entering, we fed the soul with darkness . . .
>
> I called on Darkness . . .
>
> Visionary power
> Attends the motions of the viewless winds,
> Embodied in the mystery of words:
> There, darkness makes abode, and all the host
> Of shadowy things work endless changes . . . .
>
> There I beheld the emblem of a mind
> That feeds upon infinity, that broods
> Over the dark abyss, intent to hear
> Its voices . . .[16]

At this point the reader becomes uncertain. He is asked to view darkness as an element of growth. But what darkness is meant? That which surrounds Milton, his blind, night labor? Or is it a solitariness bordering on solipsism? Or a visionary dreariness close to psychotic dejection: ghostly, apocalyptic thoughts; some morbid or empathic or self-emptying identification? In short, a counter-Enlightenment sense of what nurtures the inspired or demonic artist?

'Yewnity' evokes a drive for fellowship with essence that could be as draining as a vampire. 'My heart aches, and a drowsy numbness pains/My sense . . .' The sympathetic imagination may darken into 'horrid sympathy.' There could be depletion, loss of self, loss of control. The post-Petrarchan love poem is not the only locus of this ambivalent ecstasy, this absence/presence vacillation. Even Coleridge's perpetual quest to hold the one and the many in the palm of his mind, by such semigreek, semimonstrous wordages as 'Esemplastic' and 'Unitrine,' brings us into the realm of sudden reversals. What if in 'Unitrine' the word-drugged mind suddenly hears 'urine'?

Consider a characteristic observation from Coleridge's *Notebooks*:

> Fancy and Sleep *stream* on; and (instead of outward Forms and Sounds, the Sanctifiers, the Strengtheners!) they connect with them motions of the blood and nerves, and images forced into the mind by the feelings that arise out of the position & state of the Body and its different members . . . Thank Heaven! however/Sleep has never desecrated the images, or supposed Presences, of those I love and revere.[17]

The yews, in this darkness visible, are like Virgil's elm full of a difficult, even obscene shadow life. The poem, however, is by Wordsworth, not Coleridge: why view it, then, through the focus of a quack linguistic compound, 'yewnity'? Or why not stress, as a benightmared Coleridge does, the 'outward Forms and Sounds, the Sanctifiers, the Strengtheners!'?

A reader's responsibility is not easily defined. He must decide how much darkness is to be developed. It is always a matter of 'yewnity' versus 'unity,' whoever wrote the poem. For a 'yewnifying' critic, darkness is of the essence: the persephonic food cannot be separated from the bright cereal. In some interpreters, of course, there are three parts of light to one of darkness, as in the Persephone myth itself. Only one season is given to Hades. Some interpreters are more evangelical still, and reduce the part of darkness to that which allows the light to shine or the grain to die in order to ripen. Others are more willing to be badnewsmen. No one can remove the reader's responsibility entirely: in this, to each his own conscience. But Wordsworth's poem, taken as a model, suggests that the relation between dark and light or heliotropic and melantropic readings, is only precariously 'unificent.' In fact, to deny imagination its darker food, to seek and make it a 'Shape all light,' is to wish imagination away.

Darkness, as I use it here, is a metaphor, though justified not only by 'Yew-Trees' but also by an entire group of poems that have melancholy for their subject. More precisely, their subject is the curious link between melancholy and imagination. The group accompanies the friendship of Wordsworth and Coleridge in the seminal period of 1797–1804. The theme of melancholy was, of course, a topical one, and survives into the 'Despondency Corrected' section of Wordsworth's *The Excursion*. The profiles of poetical character and gloomy egotist seemed to merge; and whatever the cause of the perceived link between them – between imagination and melancholy – Wordsworth thought that Nature might temper and even undo it. The one myth he allowed himself was that Nature could turn the 'self-haunting spirit' outward and make it excursive once more. Yeats said that acquaintance with Chaucer's poetry had redeemed his imagination from abstraction, from a void that was the breeding place of visionary thoughts. So Nature, in Wordsworth, is an antivisionary or anti-self-consciousness principle. One impulse from nature – 'one soft impulse saved from vacancy' – may turn the imaginative mind from sterile self-regard or a fruitless brooding on its own abyss.

Coleridge participated in this myth of Nature and may have helped to elaborate it. Yet he never could internalize those strengthening and steadying 'outward Forms.' 'I may not hope from outward forms to win/The passion and the life, whose fountains are within,' as he wrote in April 1802, in what was to become the 'Dejection Ode.' Where are those fountains in yet another April, that of 1798?

> No cloud, no relique of the sunken day
> Distinguishes the West, no long thin slip
> Of sullen light, no obscure trembling hues.[18]

Life seems as shrunk or sunk as in Donne's 'Nocturnal upon St. Lucy's Day.' Yet the poet sees the night filled with invigorating and sanctifying forms. He clears the nightingale of the melancholy attributed to it by 'penseroso' man. 'In Nature there is nothing melancholy.' The nightingale is set, with moon and star, against the night: it is a wakeful, clear, 'allegro' ('Like tipsy Joy that reels with tossing head') presence. So also, in his own tree poem of 1799, 'This Lime-Tree Bower my Prison,' he looks to those 'outward Forms' for a support accidentally or fatefully denied him. He imagines others enjoying them while he sits darkling.

Wordsworth, interestingly enough, had anticipated his friend in a poem that could have been called 'This Yew-Tree Bower a Prison':

> Nay, Traveller! rest. This lonely Yew-tree stands
> Far from all human dwelling . . .
>   Who he was
> That piled these stones and with the mossy sod
> First covered o'er, and taught this aged Tree
> Now wild, to bend its arms in circling shade,
> I well remember . . .
>   Stranger! these gloomy boughs
> Had charms for him; and here he loved to sit,
> His only visitants a straggling sheep,
> The stone-chat, or the glancing sand-piper . . .
>   and so, lost Man!
> On visionary views would fancy feed,
> Till his eye streamed with tears. In this deep vale
> He died, – this seat his only monument.

Wordsworth's 'Lines Left upon a Seat in a Yew-tree'[19] seems to have been communicated to Coleridge by Charles Lamb, and may have directly inspired 'This Lime-tree Bower.' The anti-melancholy group of poems can be said to begin with it, unless we count Coleridge's early 'To the Nightingale' (1795), superseded by his famous 'conversation poem' of 1798. The relation between the two poets is not a simple one, whether in 1797, when these verses were composed, or in 1803/04 when 'Yew-Trees' may have been conceived, or in 1815 when Coleridge begins the *Biographia Literaria*, partly in reaction to Wordsworth's *Collected Poems*, which printed 'Yew-Trees' for the first time in a section entitled 'Poems of the Imagination.' We don't know how Coleridge read 'Yew-Trees' except for the fact that he cited it in the *Biographia Literaria* (chapter 22) as instancing that 'imaginative power' in which '[Wordsworth] stands nearest of all modern writers to Shakespeare and Milton; and yet in a kind perfectly unborrowed and his own.'

The drive toward unity, then, includes the relation between the two poets. Yet within that drive there is a difference. Wordsworth's yews are certainly outward forms, and set a limit to nightmare. In fact, the power of the Wordsworthian mode, as Coleridge describes it in the *Biographia*, is precisely in its ability to create an aura of the supernatural without distorting the outward, natural forms.[20] Wordsworth does not couple with the dark as Coleridge seems forced to do in his night terrors and poems like 'The Ancient Mariner,' which *stream on.*[21] He goes slowly – too slowly, sometimes; an obverse distortion is then produced which tells us that here, too, time is out of joint. And while Wordsworth's trees remain trees, unmetamorphosed by myth or imagination, they are not purely 'outward Forms,' 'Sanctifiers,' 'Strengtheners.' The four of Borrowdale, which are several-in-one like the poem's phantom personifications, suggest a near-vampiristic pressure of unification. Does that pressure come from an oneiric or theurgic or sexual-organic source? Can we go further still and see in this *yewnity* the 'express resemblance' of the power called Imagination by Wordsworth and the romantics?

6.

It would be hard to think of a more striking symbol for *in eins Bildung*, Coleridge's false etymologizing of *imagination*, or rather of its German equivalent, *Einbildungskraft*. Wordsworth himself, in the Preface to his *Poems in Two Volumes* of 1815, cites with approval Charles Lamb's definition of imagination as that power which 'draws all things to one; which makes things animate or inanimate, beings with their attributes, subjects with their accessaries, take one colour and serve to one effect.' But it is Coleridge who cannot leave the concept or the word alone. Not uncharacteristically, he dissolves the word into strange roots and derivations, as if it had to be resynthesized with the help of German or Greek. 'Eisenoplasy, or esenoplastic Power . . . "Esemplastic. The word is not in Johnson, nor have I met with it elsewhere." Neither have I. I have constructed it myself from the Greek words, εις εν πλαττειν, to shape into one . . .'[22] The natural forms of language, under this pressure of reconstruction, project new and distorted shapes, perhaps oneiric, perhaps metaphysical. It is with words as with things: Coleridge 'streams' beyond their natural form. There is an 'uttermost'[23] quality to his etymological word chains and definitions.

This learned or playful yet always compulsive manipulation of words is linked by Coleridge's *Notebooks* to his quest for unity in all areas of life, including the most personal. His concern with imagination reflects directly his concern with Wordsworth's quality of life and mind. Wishing to be unified – atoned – with the Wordsworth household, he devises magical and quasi-theological emblems that suggest the possibility of his inclusion (see his 1805 notebook entry, reproduced below).[24] The 'one life' he always seeks requires here an 'in eins Bildung' of four-(five)-in one. From such *Notebook* entries it is easier to understand the pressure that made Chapter 13 of the *Biographia*, grandly entitled 'On the Imagination, or Esemplastic Power,' deteriorate into fragments, or why he spars with Wordsworth over 'poetic diction' – in some respects a magical technique rather than a natural language – or why he is so involved in panentheistic notions.[25]

Coleridge, of course, does not overlook the demonic side of this imaginative desire for unity, and especially not in his friend. He wants to be part of Wordsworth's 'yewnity' – of his family tree – yet sees the moral cost. 'There is a dark/Inscrutable workmanship,' Wordsworth writes in his poem on the Growth of a Poet's Mind, 'that reconciles/Discordant elements, makes them cling together/In one society.'[26] This growth into unity could be perceived as that of a selfish weed, absorbing the life around it, and actually creating the darkness it seems to change into life. After his quarrel with Wordsworth, never entirely made up, Coleridge becomes more sharply aware of the shadow side of his friend's character. While working on the *Biographia*, and laboring to differentiate himself from Wordsworth, he confides what he calls a 'Gnostic Whisper' to his 'white-faced Friend' and 'negative Comforter' – that is, his notebook, which has effectively taken the place of his other, now uncomforting friend:

> *In*firmities sunk under, the Conscious Soul mourning and disapproving, are less hindrances than *Antifirmities* – such as *Self*-ness = the εἰδωλον = το ον, ⟨= το εν και πᾶν:⟩ and *separative* instead of being, what it ought to be, at once *distinctive* and yet, at the same moment or rather act, *conjunctive*, ⟨*nay*⟩, *unificent!* I will not refer to 'Αυστράλις; but to a *truly* great GENIUS, 'Αξιόλογος – Were *intellect* only in question, στς would rather groan under his manifold sins & sorrows, all either contained in or symbolized by, ΩΠΜ, than cherish that self-concentration ⟨of Αξ.⟩
>
> Community with nature; + the Eye & Heart intuitive of *all* living yet *One* Life in all; + the modifying Imagination, the true creative, εσενοπλαστικος, ενεργεια; + robur intellectuale – Σεπτεντριονίσμου . . .[27]

William ⎫
Dorothy ⎬ Wordsworth
Mary ⎭

S. T. ⎫
Sara ⎬ Coleridge

⟨O blessed Flock! I the sole scabbed Sheep!
And even me they love, awake, asleep.⟩
W + D + M = W. + STC + SH = Ενοπεντας
⟨Well – and if it be Illusion – yet surely an Illusion, which acts at all times and in all moods and places, awake, asleep; sick, & in health; alone, and in company; in sorrow and in Joy; present or absent; in moments of self-condemnation and self-acquittal; o surely that Illusion is hardly distinguishable, from Truth/*Reality* it assuredly is – and such is the Illusion if Illusion it must be, that I am persuaded, I love W.M.D.S. better than myself, & myself chiefly in them.⟩

Coleridge (like Hazlitt, Keats, and Shelley) is here seeking to come to grips with the extraordinary 'self-ness' of Wordsworth, which seems to contradict the latter's concept of the sympathetic imagination so influential on the younger romantics. The conflict, in emblem form, is that of oak versus yew, of 'robur intellectuale' versus 'yewnity.' It continues a contrast between Milton and Shakespeare, which meant so much to an age seeking to define the 'poetical character.' Shelley added to this Garden of Genius the mimosa or Sensitive Plant; while Keats's notion of negative capability sought to reconcile the empathic or animistic verve of imagination with skeptical robustness.

In 'Yew-Trees' there is an imaginative merging with the trees, yet no literalization of an archaic or superstitious figure. To identify even formally with such a figure – to become the voice of the yews – is to be no more than Coelus' 'region-whisper' in Keats: 'I am but a voice./My life is but the life of winds and tides' (*Hyperion* I, 340). Poetry would regress to the Ovidian mode and lose itself again in 'Fable's dark abyss.' Wordsworth modifies not only the instinctual drive toward unity but even the imaginative drive toward such visionary figures as intimate the possibility of unity or metamorphosis, of a transformation *in allo genere*.

Yet the yews are not merely figures of discourse. They are yews. Wordsworth's scruples concerning figuration, if only that, would make him an even drier puritan of the imagination than he is. Words need saying only because of the things they stand for. If the poet is tempted to identify with the yews to the extent of becoming their voice, it means the trees are threatened.

What threatens them? And how far must a poet identify with them for the threat to be removed? If Wordsworth identifies with them, and they disappear nevertheless, what is left of him or to him? 'And O, ye Fountains, Meadows, Hills, and Groves,/Forbode not any severing of our loves!'[28] We enter a perspective that links the poet to nature. His fate is bound up with that of the yews, a peculiar bond that must still be clarified.

7.

> Thine arms have left thee . . .
> William Cowper, *Yardley Oak*

The image of the yews changes as the poem develops. While the Lorton yew is provident of arms, the Borrowdale grove seems to sustain, if anything, only the 'phantasy.' To say 'sustain' is not totally appropriate, for when the theme of nutriment is actually introduced in lines 24–25 ('festal purpose,' 'unrejoicing berries'), it points to a deadly or sacrificial rather than nurturing sustenance.

Indeed, the 'looks' of the trees are now like arms directed against the 'profane' observer. Though pastoral, these yews are also martial, as if girding us for a warfare not dependent on war – for a spiritual combat associated perhaps with the 'ghostly Shapes' now mentioned.

Milton had sought to revalue the theme of epic warfare by emptying it of what he mocked as 'tilting furniture'; and there is a comparable emptying of ballad or lyric in Wordsworth, who writes without remarkable incidents, plot, or visionary artifice. Having removed self-reference from the poem, he at the end also distances the yews, as if they, too, were so much 'furniture.' A few ghostly abstractions remain, listening to far-away sounds. What sort of warfare is this?

What is being waged is peace rather than war. It is a peace that does not come easily here: the wise passiveness, the mighty heart lying still, the burden of the mystery lightened. A peace too much like death, we murmur. For the implied self-emptying is so great that it threatens to take nature with it. The 'pillared shade,' though better than a temple made of pillars – 'Quam si repostus sub trabe citrea/Fulgeret auro, et Phidiaca manu' – still stands between us and unmediated vision.[29] The threat to the yews as emblems of the nearness of nature to eternity comes from within the very drive for 'yewnity.' Repose from that drive is the peace for which Wordsworth strives. It would mean atonement of the guilt of separation or selfness, and a stilling of his scrupling response to intimations of immortality: whether these come as inner moods or as sounds from a distant source. 'Nay, Traveller! rest.'

Wordsworth's earlier yew-tree poem, perhaps his first mature lyric, begins with that call for repose. But the resting is also an arresting of the mind, as the traveler is halted by a voice 'left' in nature. Rest is not only an idling but also a heightened attention. The unidentified voice, itself an 'impulse saved from vacancy,' inscribes the unmarked object with a moral tale. Though this tale comes, as it were, from nature, and calls for rest, it reveals a dark, unnatural incident.

We are told of a man now dead who committed a kind of self-murder by sinning against the sweet air. He used nature to feed his soul with darkness. The theme of rest mingles ambiguously with that of arrest, death, and judgment, as a proud man is described who could not forgive neglect and turned away from the world with 'rash disdain.' His *contemptus mundi* (48–49) entices us to an equal 'scorn' which Wordsworth warns against (54–55). The poem is, as we have said, the first of those anatomies of melancholy seeking to liberate us from the 'penseroso' spell of the imprisoned self-consciousness. Sitting in judgment on himself and the world, the solitary's feelings for the beauty of nature merely intensify his sense of reclusion. Such impulses as come to Wordsworth daily, or from the 'pure source' evoked at the end of 'Yew-Trees,' fail to release him from his living tomb.

We see why the spiritual and historical complexity of romantic nature poetry is not satisfied by such positive assertions as Riffaterre's 'Sensation is all – which is exactly what descriptive poetry is about.' For sensation is all *and* nothing. How does one value 'one soft impulse saved from vacancy,' or a ghostly mood, or the evening sky's peculiar tint of green: 'And still I gaze – and with how blank an eye!'[30] From Francis Jeffrey to Irving Babbitt, Wordsworth suffered the 'rash disdain' he warned against. His 'labor of the negative' (Hegel) was mistaken for self-inflating bombast or a crude nature worship.

Wordsworth does not subdue thought to sensation, or the meditative to the descriptive mode. His poetic labor undoes sensation as well as thought, or self-consciousness, or the visionary desire for absolutes. It is no accident that his first yew-tree poem opens with a call for rest and that the later lyric ends with a supernatural image of repose. For the negative labor presupposed and in part accomplished by these poems is extreme – even if, historically and socially considered, it may not appear to be labor at all. We are already in an era of industrialization where the work ethic prevails. The image of labor is changing, and the idea of the poetical character is in doubt. What 'character' does one show by 'resting,' by entering the castle or garden of poetic indolence? 'What benefit canst thou do, or all thy tribe,/To the great world? Thou art a dreaming thing,/A fever of thyself . . .'[31] The paradox of 'negative capability' had to be founded.

The historical context emerges now with some clarity. Wordsworth's yew-tree poem was written with a sense of impending doom, so that the very phrase 'There is a Yew-tree' (cf. the Immortality Ode's 'There is a Tree, of many one') sounds like a perpetuation wish rather than a descriptive statement. The equivalent of 'Woodsman, spare that tree' or, perhaps, 'Time, spare that tree,' it expresses the poet's awareness that the age of trees is coming to a close, that the agrarian or agricultural mode of life is threatened by a speeding up of the rhythm of events in the Industrial Revolution and the Napoleonic wars. The year in which the poem may have been composed brings the end of the Peace of Amiens, that illusory moment of repose.[32] 'Nay, Warrior, rest.' Those who might have read the poem then would have understood the quietly topical connection between that moment and Poitier, Crecy, Agincourt. Will the trees survive this storm as well, to shelter or inspire a future generation?

8.

> lente lente currite noctes equi
> Marlowe, *Dr. Faustus*

If the yews make a ghost of the speaker, futurity plays a part in this phantomiza-tion. Wordsworth's prophetic fear is that the trees, despite their longevity, will disappear from the earth, becoming mere figures – archaisms, ghosts – in memory. Yet Wordsworth's resistance to overt prophecy is as strong and complex as our resistance, according to Freud, to the death wish. Perhaps, then, prophecy is a death wish. We think of the drama played out between God and prophet in the Book of Jonah. Wordsworth's 'daring sympathies with power' during even the worst periods of the French Revolution troubled him deeply. The Wordsworthian reticence seems to avoid both death wish and self-fulfilling prophecy. He defers or 'dates on' the doom he feels.

So the inner argument may well be: as the yews go, so goes the world. If the yews are a metonymy for quasi-eternal nature, is that nature still 'life and food/ For future years'? Or are the years to come endangered by a modern ghostliness, an alienation of mind from rural nature in the wake of the industrial and revolutionary mentality? Wordsworth cannot conceive of a mind from which nature has faded, unless it is a mind approaching the Last Judgment. Yet, often enough, time appears to him so accelerated that 'thoughts of more deep seclusion' verge on thoughts of apocalypse. This sense of acceleration and of concomitant ghostliness is clarified by comparing three moments in his biography, each five years or so apart.

In 1793 Wordsworth visits Tintern Abbey for the first time; in 1798 he revisits it and writes the poem; and in 1803/04 he begins 'Yew-Trees.' The poem of 1798 is similar in some respects to that of 1803/04: it shares, for example, the themes of time, repose under a dark tree, and waters 'rolling from their mountain springs/With a soft inland murmur.' The great difference is that in 1798 the persistence of nature in the poet's consciousness yields a hope that sets a limit to phantomization and so allows 'repose.' But when this 'repose' recurs at the end of 'Yew-Trees,' it is close to denoting eternal rest. Fear, hope, silence, and foresight, which were living acts of mind and heart in 'Tintern Abbey,' are now phantoms similar to those surrounding the dead Adonais in Shelley's later elegy.

'Yew-Trees,' in fact, imagines a repose *from* consciousness. But this would elide not only self-reference but also – as 'mute repose' – speech itself. Speech, or effective rhetoric, speech as more than internal work, is questioned. While 'Tintern Abbey' is a complex murmur still in touch with mountain spring or flood, in 'Yew-Trees' it is as if Wordsworth were himself among the ghosts, listening to verses written only five years earlier – and how distant now! The square of the distance, one might say, that 'Tintern Abbey' stood from its own source of five years past: from river, cliff, and haunting cataract experienced in 1793.

'The Cataracts blow their trumpets from the steep;/No more shall grief of mine the season wrong.'[33] Present joy, present time, is being wronged by a grief not fully named, but which involves a fear for the future of nature. A repose is sought from an incumbent sense of duty, as if the burden of delaying the Last

Judgment, when nature shall be no more, had devolved on this poet. 'No more shall grief of mine the season wrong' is the pastoral 'murmur' that replies here to a martial or apocalyptic 'voice.' What the cataracts intimate – whether they support Wordsworth's visionary fear or urge him to leave futurity to God – remains unclear. But they are, like poetry itself, a responsive voice. 'A Voice shall speak, and what will be the Theme?'[34] Voice precedes theme, and may even define the future, that is, the future relation of imagination and nature. We are still in a responsive, rather than mute, universe. Poetry, though divided between seeing and foreseeing, or present and future, harmonizes as best it can words and time in a 'timely utterance.'[35]

9.

By this circuitous route, then, we return to the question of words and the rhetorical aspect of human life. The phenomenological perspective I have restored can be reconciled with a structuralist reading. But it integrates better, I would think, concepts of time, voice, presence, and history with language.

Riffaterre proceeds from a methodological assumption that 'words are all' to the conclusion that in descriptive poetry 'sensation is all.' This is a strange reversal, and suggests that behind some types of structural analysis there lurks a positivism of the word and a nostalgic materialism. Though one can be in sympathy with Riffaterre's debt to historical semantics – which traces back every *Bedeutungswandel* or change of meaning to a substantial idea – one misses the chastening and skeptical attitude toward meaning in Valéry and later semioticians. For them a text or its meaning is a residue, an abandoned series of transformations, an incomplete or frozen metamorphosis. Each interpreter is a new Ovid, translating the text into subtler surfaces until it appears utterly 'devoured by forms' like Valéry's dancer or Shelley's cloud.

The figure of a great and venerable tree, 'Survivor sole, and hardly such' (to quote from Cowper's remarkable 'Yardley Oak,' the nearest analogue to Wordsworth's poem), leads to similarly chastening but also to comforting thoughts. A constancy is pictured amid change, and with power to resist an extreme metamorphosis. The theme is still decay, but 'magnificent decay.'[36] Some ancient science of substance, therefore, might seem more appropriate here than a deconstructive 'annihilating all that's made' to shadowy words. The hylic fiction serves to draw us closer to earth or the material imagination.

Yet we remain, with respect to earth, in a state marked by an unresolved, powerful, yet calm ambivalence: a state Wordsworth called 'wise passiveness' and Keats characterized as 'negative capability.' The danger of these trees becoming mere figures of speech, either because they are about to be destroyed or because they are about to lose their hold on the mind of man – this virtual danger may actually reinforce in the mature poet those early or premature intimations he describes in the Great Ode: 'obstinate questionings/Of sense and outward things,/Fallings from us, vanishings . . .' Though such nature-loss, such skirting of the 'abyss of ideality,' may augur a gain, and though Wordsworth engages in 'Tintern Abbey' and elsewhere with the theme of loss and gain, he will not take an ultimate decision upon himself. On this issue there is vacillation rather than an authoritative resolution by means of visionary or poetic voice. 'Milton! England hath need of thee,' yet Wordsworth refused to be Milton on the matter of nature's ultimate importance to the life of the mind.

He delays, in fact, rather than hastens a decision: he intervenes to the extent of being the first poet to grant nature due process. Greatness and scrupulousness combine to make a difficult poetry hardly recognized as such even today. It is in many ways the most ghostly poetry ever written: one in which speech itself is near to fading out, like echo, or the voice of genius that dies with the tree it inhabits. The oracular voice is muted to become, as in 'Yew-Trees,' words that speak 'of nothing more than what we are,' words that do not tilt the balance against nature. Yet these words may give too much to nature, if they must be, in time to come, and for good or bad, a homeless or disembodied utterance. If nature as we know it must die, or change utterly, then poetry as we know it must die, or change utterly. This extreme calculus of words, and this internal, obstinate questioning of every ghostly or glorious mood, is what all readers feel in Wordsworth, although they may not be happy with it if they expect from poetry a decisive rhetoric or a seductive animation.

Appendix

I. Anonymous, 'An Inscription: Quercus loquitur'
    O YE!
'WHO by retirement to these sacred groves
Impregnate fancy, and on thought divine
Build harmony – If sudden glow your breast
With inspiration, and the rapt'rous song
Bursts from a mind unconscious whence it sprang:
– Know that the sisters of these hallow'd haunts.
Dryad or Hamadryad, tho' no more
From Jove to man prophetick truths they sing;
Are still attendant on the lonely bard,
Who step by step these silent woods among
Wanders contemplative, lifting the soul
From lower cares, by every whisp'ring breeze

Tun'd to poetick mood; and fill the mind
With truths oracular, themselves of old
Deign'd utter from the Dodonean shrine.

From Dodsley, *A Collection of Poems by Several Hands.* 4th ed. (1755).

II. Wordsworth, 'Address From the Spirit of Cockermouth Castle' (1835)

Thou look'st upon me, and dost fondly think,
Poet! that, stricken as both are by years,
We, differing once so much, are now Compeers,
Prepared, when each has stood his time, to sink
Into the dust. Erewhile a sterner link
United us; when thou, in boyish play
Entering my dungeon, didst become a prey
To soul-appalling darkness. Not a blink
Of light was there; – and thus did I, thy Tutor,
Make thy young thoughts acquainted with the grave;
While thou wert chasing the winged butterfly
Through my green courts; or climbing, a bold suitor,
Up to the flowers whose golden progeny
Still round my shattered brow in beauty wave.

Notes

1. 'Interpretation and Descriptive Poetry,' *New Literary History*, 4 (1973), 229–57. All my quotations from Riffaterre are from this essay and will not be footnoted further.
2. For a fuller understanding of Riffaterre, the reader is referred to his *Essais de Stylistique Structurale* (Paris, 1971), and an article focusing on the question of literary history, 'The Stylistic Approach to Literary History,' *New Literary History*, 2 (1970), 39–55. Needless to say, Riffaterre's structuralism is one of many types; but I try to emphasize what he has in common with structural method generally. He stands close, on the one hand, to Leo Spitzer's historically oriented stylistics, and, on the other hand, to the structural semantics of A. J. Greimas. His approach is also important for raising the issue of the 'perceptibility' of structure, or what reading (reader) model we ideally posit when interpreting a text.
3. 'The voices come in a continuous stream, a continuous revelation. Through them rise recognitions of immortality and, simultaneously, a repose in the moral and creative will, since they suggest both the final peace and the final judgment which is God's alone . . . The fundamental relation may be described as one between light and sound, light and revelation.' *The Unmediated Vision* (New Haven, 1954), pp. 42–43.
4. Cf. *The Unmediated Vision*, p. 22, and *Wordsworth's Poetry, 1787–1814* (New Haven,

1964), p. 182. In 'Expostulation and Reply' (1798) the poet affirms explicitly that 'there are Powers/Which of themselves our minds impress.'

5. Mary Moorman is so struck by this 'first sign of a change in Wordsworth's handling of natural themes-the introduction of mythical or allegorical figures into the natural landscape' that she associates 'Yew-Trees' with 'Laodamia' (1814) and Wordsworth's intensified interest in the classics. See *William Wordsworth: The Later Years* (Oxford, 1965), pp. 273–74.

6. See the Appendix for two poems of this kind. Cf. also Cowper's 'Yardley Oak' (1791) for a significant allusion to the oracle tree. On trees in Wordsworth, see Jonathan Wordsworth, *The Music of Humanity* (New York, 1969), pp. 118–20; and on the genius loci concept, my *Beyond Formalism* (New Haven, 1970), pp. 212ff., and 311ff.

7. See Wordsworth's 'Mutability' in *Ecclesiastical Sonnets* (1822) and 'A slumber did my spirit seal' (1800).

8. 1850 *Prelude* XIV, 126–27. The affinity of *Aeneid* VI, 276ff., was pointed out by Moorman, p. 273.

9. 'Ode on the Power of Sound' (1828, 1835). Cf. Hartman, *The Fate of Reading* (Chicago, 1975), pp. 289ff.

10. 1850 *Prelude* II, 309.

11. It begins 'Pass not the [? Place] unvisited–Ye will say/That Mona's Druid Oaks composed a Fane/Less awful than this grove . . .'' Ernest de Selincourt, ed., *The Poetical Works of William Wordsworth* (Oxford, 1952), vol. II, p. 210.

12. Cf. Hartman, *Wordsworth's Poetry*, p. 122.

13. 1850 *Prelude* XIII, 290–91.

14. For 'pining' see the analysis in Brooks and Warren, *Understanding Poetry* 3rd ed. (New York, 1960), p. 276.

15. Cf. the 'Conclusion' to *Ecclesiastical Sonnets*, 'Why sleeps the future.'

16. 1850 *Prelude* VI, 480–81; XIII, 327; V, 595–99; XIV, 71–73.

17. *The Notebooks of S.T. Coleridge*, ed. Kathleen Coburn (New York, 1961), II (Text), Entry 2453.

18. 'The Nightingale. A Conversation Poem.' First published in *Lyrical Ballads* (1798).

19. I have quoted the poem as revised for the second edition (1800) of *Lyrical Ballads*.

20. Cf. James A. W. Heffernan, *Wordsworth's Theory of Poetry* (Ithaca, 1969), pp. 134–35.

21. 'Christabel' is also a night poem but where the obverse danger to streaminess, of not being able to move on (toward dawn or awakening), and so again being a prisoner of the dark, is represented.

22. *Biographia Literaria* (1818), opening of Ch. 10. Cf. also Entry 4244 in the *Notebooks*, III (Text): 'The interpenetration of the absolute opposites (which could not *be*, & yet be absolute *opposites*, if they were not the manifestation of *one*), & the perfecting synthetic Third, = Depth, = Gravitation = Galvanism = Chemical Combination–! And these are all the reflected Image of "I" boundless because I; "I" bounded because of self-intuitive, & self-intuitive because "I"–thence I in itself, & the Not-I or Thing itself–& all restored again to its Unity in the Imagination or Eisenoplasy.'

23. I borrow the pun from Coleridge's *The Destiny of Nations* (1796), line 100.

24. *Notebooks of S.T. Coleridge*, II (Text), Entries 2623f.

25. On that involvement see Thomas McFarland, *Coleridge and the Pantheist Tradition* (Oxford, 1969).

26. 1850 *Prelude* I, 341–44.

27. *Notebooks of S.T. Coleridge*, III (Text), Entry 4243. The date is uncertain but probably ca. 1815. The words kept in Greek, *Australis* and *Axiologus*, refer, respectively, to Southey and Wordsworth. The latter is also alluded to as 'Septentrionismou,' i.e., of the North (cf. South-ey).

28. 'Ode: Intimations of Immortality' (composed 1802–04), stanza 11.

29. Thomas Gray, 'Alcaic Ode' (composed 1741). It became well known and was often translated after Mason published it in 1775.

30. Coleridge, 'Dejection Ode' (1802).

31. Keats, *The Fall of Hyperion*, I, 167–69. The debate goes back, of course, to that between the active and the contemplative life; but with James Thomson's publication of *The Castle of Indolence* (1748), the role of pastoral and (Spenserian) romance enters this debate in a new way. Wordsworth's not entirely happy consciousness concerning 'rest' emerges naively in his poem on 'Gipsies' (1807) and more basically in his Introduction to the *Prelude*, 1 (1850), 1–105.

32. This date is disputed. Wordsworth's Fenwick note assigns the poem to 1803, but Mark Reed, in *Wordsworth: The Chronology of the Middle Years* (Cambridge, MA, 1975), finds no evidence of its composition before Sept. 1804. See his 'General Chronological List,' item 123 and note; also his main 'Chronology,' item 107. It is possible that the Lorton yew verses were composed ca. 1804, and the rest between 1811 and late 1814. Even if a portion of the poem postdates 1803, much depends, as in *The Prelude*, on the poet's self-image, or how he placed himself retrospectively while composing. The 1803 date assigned by Wordsworth may reflect the remembered poetic consciousness of ca. 1803.

33. 'Ode: Intimations of Immortality,' stanza 3. Is there in the sound shape of 'cataracts' a scramble association with 'Characters,' as in 'Characters of the great Apocalypse,' *Prelude* (1850) VI, 638?

34. 'Home at Grasmere' (composed between 1800 and 1806).

35. 'Ode: Intimations of Immortality,' stanza 3. The preceding paragraph should suggest that Wordsworth's emphasis on memory is countervailing rather than regressive: an attempt to save 'contemporaneity' from futuristic fears and philosophies.

36. Cowper, 'Yardley Oak.'

Chapter 5

Romance and Modernity: Keats's 'Ode to Psyche'

The invocation of William Collins's *Ode to Evening* (*OE*)[1] delays its own closure for some twenty lines. It begins, moreover, with an apologetic 'if' and continues with a stuttering equivalent to *O*. 'If aught of oaten stop, or pastoral song,/May hope . . .' The syntax of Keats's *Ode to Psyche* is straightforward in comparison, and the invocation immediate. 'O Goddess! hear these tuneless numbers, wrung . . .' The theme of hearing, of getting to the goddess through her 'modest ear' (*OP*, 2) is stated outright.

This directness is relative, however. The meaning of Keats's lines, like those of Collins's, remains shadowy. Who is the goddess called Psyche? Is she, though specifically named, really different from 'buds, and bells, and stars without a name' (*OP*, 61)? What does it mean to *hear* 'tuneless numbers'? Goddess, Psyche, bowers, flowers, gardener Fancy, schmancy language . . . what is going on? what is being represented?

One can claim, of course, that it is the conventions or *topoi* that matter, and they are clear enough; or that what matters is the general impression left by these tendrils of words. Psyche, for example, can be looked up in Lemprière, Keats's mythological dictionary. 'Tuneless numbers' can be construed as the modesty *topos* of a Collinsian poet-votary, hardly fit to touch the hem of the inspiring vision. Please enjoy these flowers of language: they are not obscure to the initiate, the careful student of this mode. They do not distract the devotee of artifice from what is subtly represented.

From one point of view, then, no problem of meaning exists. All right readers see that Keats's poem brings love insidiously close to what the *Nightingale Ode* calls easeful death: 'I have been half in love with easeful Death/Call'd him soft names in many a mused rhyme' (*ON*, 53). Our sole problem is one of judgment: shall we enjoy these perfumed words, these soft names, or should we purge them as euphemisms – pierce through the flowery poesy till we come to a 'desolation of reality'? Keats himself, from the beginning of his career, tried to go beyond the pleasure principle in language, to leave the realm of 'Flora and old Pan,' or of 'Romance.' Is his 'fine spell of words' an antidote to 'the sable chain/And dumb enchantment' (*Fall of Hyperion*, 9–11) or does it simply affirm the liaison between love poem and death poem?

The convergence of love and death has always perplexed the intellect: we describe rather than understand it. But it has not always seduced the intellect, as in this quasi-classical ode full of art-diction and belated myth-making. While the ode's formulas are direct, and derive from an ecstatic or theophanic tradition, the theme remains oblique, retarded by the ode's very richness of diction. Matthew Arnold considered surfeit of verbal detail as Keats's sweet vice, weakening his poetry's structural design. Yet this kind of conspicuously digressive form has been the hallmark of Romance.

Can we find its reason? A close-up of the ode's first lines is almost more than enough. 'Tuneless numbers,' though a modesty topos, can also be a reminder that lyric poetry is no longer chanted to an accompanying instrument. This introduces a sense of loss, however slight, as Keats creates the purely formal paradox of *hearing* something close to silence. 'Tuneless numbers' may then recall the 'ditties of no tone' of the Grecian Urn. In this context, however, 'tuneless' is not a negative at all but evokes a quieter, more natural poetry than Wordsworth's. Despite Wordsworth's claim to simplicity or naturalness his lyrics continue to be, according to Keats, marred by 'palpable design' or 'ugly clubs' of themes. 'Man should not dispute or assert but whisper results to his neighbour,' Keats wrote to his friend Reynolds in lines that anticipate Thoreau. The ideal, then, is that of 'wide quietness' (*OP*, 58), and it comes remarkably close to the neo-Hellenic sensibility of Winckelmann: grandeur in repose, 'might half slumb'ring on its own right arm' (*Sleep and Poetry*, 237). The ideal poetry remains, like the Grecian Urn, a 'bride of quietness.'

The opening of another ode, 'No, no, go not to Lethe' (*Ode on Melancholy*) shows explicitly a 'lethal' drift that, being resisted, fills out the poem. The drift toward quietness in the *Ode to Psyche* also brings with it a fulsome feature: Keats's art-diction in the form of a 'language of flowers.' Where we now read 'O brightest' (*OP*, 36) there was originally 'O bloomiest.' Psyche's brightness is associated more with Flora than with Apollo: it is not that of Collins's 'Youth of Morn' but of Spenser's Clarion (*Muiopotmos*), an aurelian flower-fly that merges with her bowery realm. A sense of violating that bower is present, of course – if Psyche's offence is not alluded to, the poet is nevertheless anxious not to offend the goddess's 'ear' or 'secret' – but it is far less acute than in Collins. The poet's aspiration toward a liberty or enlightenment like that of the gods is retarded by this language of flowers, the equivalent to Collins's 'honeyed paste of poetic diction . . . the candied coat of the auricula' (Hazlitt). Though Keats disenchants his language of flowers by giving it the hyperbolic force of a soft boomerang, one must first acknowledge its euphemistic quality.

That euphemistic strain is so effective that it would be impossible to find a Mrs Barbauld – who denounced Collins's *Ode on the Poetical Character* as 'neither decent nor luminous' – objecting to what allegory there is. Think how gleefully we ridicule Kenneth Burke when he joyces the 'Beauty is Truth, Truth Beauty' equation in the *Ode on a Grecian Urn* as 'Body is Turd, Turd Body.' Keats's ravishment cannot be ravished this way: 'twould make him a sod to his high requiem. Yet a sense of requiem, of covering up (in flowers, in leaves) a feverish imagination, this surely remains; and Burke's ugly club is only a symptom of analytic impotence.

Deconstruction as an analytic mode means disturbing the poem according to its own fault-lines. It examines how the language of flowers – the euphemistic phrasing – is betrayed by 'flowers of language': figures of speech that insist on their figural status, or the fact that they are rich nothings. This may be called reading against the grain; but we actually remain in the grain of the poem. Yet now the negative appears once more as a substantial and barely containable factor. When to the morphemic negative of 'less' in 'tuneless' we add the pseudo-morphemic 'numb' in 'numbers' – recalling also the closeness of 'numbness' in the first line of the *Nightingale Ode* ('My heart aches, and a drowsy numbness pains / My sense') – then Keats's quietistic lyricism declines toward a deadly slumber evoking the opiates he repeatedly rejects. The chime of 'numbers' and 'numbness' revives a sleeping negativity associating poetry with emptiness rather than fullness – and in the *Nightingale Ode* with a self-emptying brought on by passion.

More exactly, with a state described countless times in the older Petrarchan mode of paradox, where the lover is so drunk with the haunting absence (that is, imagined presence) of the beloved that he feels he has no self within him but only in her. He is ecstatic, too happy in the other's happiness; not envious but overidentifying. Keats's poetry turns around this Other, but who is she, even when explicitly named?

> But who wast thou, O happy, happy, dove?
> His Psyche true!   (*OP*, 23)

Dove, nightingale, winged boy: glimpsed here yet in the *Nightingale Ode* only heard, and in the *Ode on a Grecian Urn* not even heard, though the subject of wild surmises – Keats's perspective recedes into 'silence and slow time' as he attempts a positive identification.

I have not managed to read aright even the first line of our ode; and I now stumble over its last word, 'wrung.' Together with 'enforcement' (in the next line) it heightens the decorum of hesitation that suggests a trespass or a necessary ravishing. Is 'O Goddess! hear' a petition, or is it a manly command? Why does the poet want Psyche to hear her own story: why that closed circuit? One poetic impulse moves toward rousing the goddess, a second toward not rousing her. 'Wrung': the very word is like a bell, but does it signal waking or sleeping, revelation (what must be seen) or requiem (what must be laid to rest)?

The line introduced by 'wrung' is indeed peculiar. 'By sweet enforcement and remembrance dear' places a noun adjective phrase against an adjective noun phrase to create a chiasmus. Flanked by the semantic overlap of 'sweet' and 'dear' this chiasmus reduces the gap in meaning between 'enforcement' and 'remembrance.' They are pushed together not only as words but as meanings. Yet they are far from agreeing with each other – unless both refer to the same thing: poetry. Are they a hendyadis, one idea expressed through two words joined by a conjunction? Hear my poetry, Keats may be saying, a poetry that is forced from me through (an internalized, prior) poetry. By understanding his verses in this way we have not righted or solved anything. On the contrary, we have somewhat increased the scandal of the poem's redundancy, or its oblique and mannered mode.

It is not explicitly stated, but the numbers must be 'wrung' from the poet himself. To remember what he has seen (especially since it was dreamlike), or to speak about it, needs a force applied to a memory that retains memory's inwardness. The poet qualifies this force as 'sweet' and is at pains to make it agree with what is remembered, as if that too had contained something forceful. Yet his euphemistic phrasing veils the identity of what makes the memory forceful. We can best infer it from the experience described in the first stanza, or the Psyche-myth as a whole, and say that these impress Keats so strongly that he must tell what he knows. But a hint remains that memory itself is the 'dear' or 'dire' force. Memory makes both the goddess and the poet hearers: they are reminded of something ravishing, and their response is not unambiguous. There is a resistance involved.

Is Keats being forced by memory into 'remembrance'? And can that memory be particularized, or must we take the Psyche story as its true content? The more we lose ourselves in the words, or the more we ponder their euphemistic and figurative mode, the less the narrative or the thematic content of this poem moves us boldly on. This retardation is characteristic of lyric romances that will not give up myth or story-line. The myth remains forceful, a power; but the myth comes mediated by its own literary aura. The story of Psyche is particularly interesting as a model instance because it is so belated that something in it remains unfulfilled; and Keats, while compelled into remembrance, is also tempted toward a self-forcing: toward a poetry more purely his own, neither derivative nor transumptive, but as 'natural' as 'branched thoughts' (*OP*, 52).

There is an impasse, then. To adapt Keats on Wordsworth: 'We are in a Mist – *We* are now in that state – We feel the "burden of the Mystery".' The readerly dimension is so enriched that we cannot 'read aright' or emerge from that 'mist-Mystery.' It will come as no surprise that on the writerly level a similar impasse is discernible, since the pressure of reading aright affects the poet as well.

For 'remembrance dear' is quite literally the remembrance of a prior text. It echoes, in a softer tone, the opening of Milton's *Lycidas*. Milton says that 'Bitter constraint, and sad occasion dear' prompt his poem. That verse is harsh rather than comforting. But the mnemonic force it exerted on Keats, as well as the counterforce in him – by which he transforms it into a verse of his own – these are, wishfully or not, represented as 'sweet' and 'dear.' Milton, moreover, had himself initiated the topic of force in those opening lines by talking of his poem as an untimely enterprise. His 'forc'd fingers rude' pluck something still unseasoned, not fully mature. He doubts his calling even as he tests it – so Psyche too seems unable to tolerate the unknown, and Keats is unsure of having glimpsed his goddess. The quest for identity, or leaving the state of 'negative capability,' implies a prematurely forceful and perhaps disastrous outcome.

Yet the euphemistic strain is so deep in Keats that he evokes not the force that leads to disaster – Psyche's or the Poet's overreaching wish for clarity and identity – but a *beautiful* truth, in the form of a persuasive consonance between hand and ear, poetic speech and imaginative hearing. 'Wrung/By sweet enforcement and remembrance dear' shadows forth Milton's hand as it traces a prior and classic moment of stylized trepidation. This hand, now Keats's own, does not wish to be as *forcible* as Milton's, only – by finer repetition – as *great*. The pastoral element should remain, despite Keats's empathic (sexual or writerly) impetuousness. The quality of the verse is so tender, so involuted, that it already binds up 'with garlands of her own' (*On the Sonnet*, 14) the very consciousness it would rouse.[2]

So equivocal is this double movement, which tends at once toward a hard-core knowledge and a dreamy consciousness, toward truth and beauty, toward a traumatic caesura and its rhythmic internalization (cf. *To Autumn*'s 'Sometimes whoever seeks abroad may find/Thee . . .'), that when disclosure comes it is in the form of a questioning surmise: 'Surely I dreamt today, or did I see/The winged Psyche with awaken'd eyes?' As a statement, moreover, the surmise is opaque from the point of view of syntax. That the seeing is unsure, all can agree: yet the query not generally put is to whom the 'awaken'd eyes' belong.

They are the poet's surprised eyes, yet in the myth they were Psyche's eyes. She discovers Cupid's identity by looking at him with the torch perhaps alluded to in the ode's penultimate lines – and so loses him. And, hasn't she just made love, and is awakened in that sense? Or, is the poet, who comes upon this primal scene, awakened by being granted a visionary truth? Or, did he see her in dream, and was woken by that seeing, as when the content of a dream startles you awake and you see – a blank, or the very thing you dreamed about? 'The Imagination is like Adam's dream,' wrote Keats, thinking of Adam's first encounter with Eve in *Paradise Lost*, 'He awoke and found it truth.' Dream and truth converge, they cross a temporal gap – as they precisely do not in *La Belle Dame sans Merci* where the unfortunate lover wakes up in a desolate landscape, 'And no birds sing.'

Here Psyche and Cupid are the birds: while the textured music, Keats's branched thoughts, the 'fane' ('feign') of his poem, is their internalized song. Our ears are no more startled into guilty knowledge than our eyes, which remain fragrant rather than flagrant in this milieu (*OP*, 10–15). Such lyricism wins for us a region of 'wide quietness,' of thoughts removed from ocularity, from the look! see!, the I spy or I psy (sigh) kind of verse. The romance mode of poetry is neither a confessional nor an over-conscious 'egotistical sublime.'

But am I, having said this, reading or allegorizing. My remarks suggest that *To Psyche* is an Ode to the Nymphal State, or to some magical post-nymphal recreation of it. 'Organized Innocence' Blake would have called this state, and assigned Psyche's bower to Beulah, the lower Paradise of harmony, where all disagreeables evaporate. Mostly Mozart, and no lovers' quarrels. Yet Paradise proper, according to Blake, has only interludes of peace, being engaged in a Mental Strife that forges, like a blacksmith, fiery not flowery conceptions. This Blakean insight is not entirely out of place. Despite the intricacy of the ode's euphemistic structuring, something naively ecstatic remains that allows us to caricature it. There is an archaic skeleton of oriental fantasies, as in Collins: and that is not wholly absorbed by the evening ear or the textured diction. This skeleton, moreover, is a static one, unlike Blake's metamorphoses, his pop-art inflation of the personification allegory of his time, his reanimation, ludic or ludicrous, of stellar junk. In Keats, the apostrophic sequence of O, O, O, Yes, intimates an erotic fantasy reinforced by such images as 'delicious moan/Upon the midnight hours' and 'Heat of pale-mouthed prophet dreaming.' (What heat did you say?) Byron, too worldly-wise, accused Keats of 'viciously soliciting his own imagination.'

Also true is that in statues of Psyche, like those by Canova, the butterfly emblem, which mythographers claim denotes the immortal soul, is shaped like a delicate sexual organ freely exhibited. It compensates Psyche for not having what Cupid has. Cupid is the 'winged boy'; the butterfly too is winged, but in such a way that a convergence of male and female is adumbrated by the merging, in one shape, of clitoris and penis: the labia appear as embryonic wings, 'lucent fans.'

May it not be, then, that just as Keats does not confine the 'awaken'd eyes' to Psyche or Poet, so his poetry also remains sexually indeterminate or double: a daring, inventive mimicry of feminine feelings, of what Erich Neumann, the Jungian analyst, calls the quest for the feminine, in his commentary on Apuleius' Psyche story? Keats's *Ode* begins with the happy ending, with Psyche and Cupid reunited; and the labours or trials Psyche had to undergo seem now to be the poet's. It is he who has to build her temple, institute her worship. Psyche's labours are, as it were, elided into the diction of this very poem. In building Psyche's fane Keats labours to produce a new kind of poetry: an art-diction that is not only Miltonic-male but also feminine – as if Milton had a sister, or one of his daughters had re-indited him? Though Keats's idiom is far from natural it is in search of naturalization, and its special obliquity is characterized by its unembarrassed use of the language of flowers. This, then, is what Keats undertakes on behalf of Psyche. It is the temple he builds, for our psyche too:

> Yes, I will be thy priest, and build a fane
>   In some untrodden region of my mind,
> Where branchèd thoughts, new grown with pleasant pain,
>   Instead of pines shall murmur in the wind:
> Far, far around shall those dark-clustered trees
>   Fledge the wild-ridged mountains steep by steep;
>
> And in the midst of this wide quietness
> A rosy sanctuary will I dress.
>
> (*OP*, 50–59)

The *Ode to Psyche* is a revision of Collins's Poetical Character. The latter is no longer imaged as a Youth of Morn, however richly mothered and endowed with a halo of hair. The recuperation of the feminine is more thorough and more sensuous. It produces a remarkably bisexual poetic diction, which struck many nineteenth-century readers as too feminine. It also produces a remarkable idea, that of 'Negative Capability,' closely joined to Keats's revised conception of the Poetical Character. In one definition he uses enough sexual innuendo to show what is on his mind. Thinking of Shakespeare and Wordsworth, and finding it hard to bring the two together, he writes:

> the poetical character itself, (I mean that sort of which, if I am anything, I am a Member; that sort distinguished from the wordsworthian or egotistical sublime; which is a thing per se and stands alone) . . . is not itself – it has no self – it is everything and nothing – It has no character . . .

Once we see Keats's ode as a redress of the feminine in the Poetical Character – as the very thing ('vale' and 'veil') Collins sensitively described but could not value in itself – could value only, despite his exaltation of Fancy, as the afterglow of an era of literary creativity – once we understand the *Psyche Ode* in this context, then it becomes a language-event that projects its own historical importance. The mythic figure of Psyche is post-Augustan, as Lemprière's dictionary said; but for Keats this meant more than that her myth came into prominence after the reign of Augustus. His psyche-language modifies the Augustan era in *England*. Psyche does not institute a new mystery (Keats, like Wordsworth, always wished to 'ease the Burden of the Mystery' by a 'widening Speculation'); rather, Psyche disqualifies naive concepts of progress or Enlightenment. No wonder we lose ourselves in the diction and cannot get past the opening lines. The manner of proceeding in this Romance lyric is devious, not obvious.

What are these naive myths of progress or Enlightenment? They have to do with the 'grand march of intellect' or similar beliefs that there was a providential forward movement in history, that the Reformation, for example, produced real benefits and dispelled real sufferings. Keats remained haunted by 'something real' not only in the world generally but also in history; and all his poems attempt a career-leap forward, out of a less real, enchanted or superstitious, stage. The idea of enlightenment, of seeing like a god sees, of Apollonian vision, always hovers before him. 'Though no great minist'ring reason,' he writes in *Sleep and Poetry*,

> sorts
> Out the dark mysteries of human souls
> To clear conceiving: yet there ever rolls
> A vast idea before me, and I glean
> Therefrom my liberty; thence too I've seen
> The end and aim of Poesy.

Yet even as he yields to these projects for the sun, his striving for *positive* knowledge is displaced by a *negative* capability: the 'libido sciendi' or truth-drive, honoured by him with the name of Philosophy, is subdued to a more empathic and chameleon imagination, unconcerned with the maleness or the solidarity of the ego. Relaxed moments of visionariness ensue – I have elsewhere called them moments of surmise – that lead to such darkling passage as 'I cannot see what flowers are at my feet' (*ON*, 41). This non-seeing is always a fragrant-eyed, imaginative fullness and the obverse of the enlightenment depicted in Genesis 3, verses 4–5:

> But the serpent said to the woman, You will not die. For God knows that when you eat of it your eyes will be opened, and you will be like God, knowing good and evil. So . . . she took of its fruit and ate . . . and he ate. Then the eyes of both were opened, and they knew they were naked.

The *Hyperions* too are projects for the sun – for a light/Enlightenment that does not purchase knowledge with loss of power. Yet the sun never rises: something holds Hyperion back and prevents Apollo, his metamorphic double, from moulting into the 'rich-haired Youth of Morn.' In the final lines of *To Psyche* there is the same drag against progress of a possibly traumatic kind. As at the ode's beginning, a sense of threshold replaces that of trespass, and time remains arrested between *one minute past* (that glimpse of Psyche and Cupid) and *one minute before* ('A bright torch, and a casement ope at night,/To let the warm Love in'). Love is about to cross that threshold, yet there is no leap of the imagination ('Already with thee!'), no 'Let the warm Love in.' Only, 'To let the warm Love in.' Instead of an imperative we have an infinitive, a stationing moment as at the end of the *Nightingale Ode*'s seventh stanza: 'Charm'd magic casements opening on the foam/Of perilous seas, in faery lands forlorn.' In *To*

Psyche we do not even reach the perilous event, which the received myth gives as Psyche's lust of the eyes, her use of that torch to discover the identity of her lover. A next, fatal step is omitted, as if lyric were opposed to narrative, which can lead too far, which goes *beyond*, to spoil everything.

Despite the bright torch, then, we remain suspended, we hang there in that 'bright . . . night.' The next step might bring the knowledge which is sorrow: open eyes, separation, exile. Thus Keats, in this counter-enlightenment poem, extends the liminal moment and deepens our sense of negative capability. Apposing the *Nightingale Ode*, we see that the latter too almost ends at casement or threshold. Yet it comes upon a word, 'forlorn' that designates the very state Psyche must indeed traverse. But it is only a *word* that is found, and a word that depicts what is *not* represented in the *Psyche Ode* (except through the anticipatory and richly converted negatives of stanza 3). The echoing turn of 'Forlorn! the very word is like a bell/To toll me back from thee to my sole self!' (rather than soul-self or Psyche?) reinserts the elided motif of death, time, and 'thing per se.' Feigned happiness becomes faint once more.

★   ★   ★

The discourse of poetry, then, what Keats lived as *poesy* and kept questioning, goes past Collins's evening ear and past the nostalgia for a homebred 'eastern voice' or archetypal language of the gods (*Endymion* IV. 1–20). It does and does not go past Psyche as the lost nature – the lost womanly nature – of speech. Keats acts out once more that dream of a common language or illustrious vernacular that has haunted Western literature since Dante. When we call Keats a Romantic, we evoke not a moon-eyed, mawkish attitude, or sentiments to be purged; we evoke, rather, a literary tradition that is deliberately post-Augustan and seeks to draw its inspiration from the developing vernaculars, the *Romance languages*, in order to enrich and illumine each mother-tongue. But once Psyche is found, once the Romance element is redressed, she must be lost again, in accordance with her nature. The losing of psyche to poetry means the discovery not of a new myth or matrona (though adumbrations of these appear, from Collins's Fancy and Eve to Keats's Mnemosyne and Moneta) but a poetic texture that cannot be 'righted.' 'If I am a Poet,' Keats declared in a letter about the Poetical Character from which I have already quoted, 'where is the Wonder that I should say I would right no more?' (He then cancels 'right' and puts 'write' above it.) The structure of Romance, its wonder-wanderings, its 'error,' cannot be separated from that rich impasse which proves to be Keats's strength and limit: losing oneself in the very texture of words that wish to be more than marble, that aspire to be genuinely musaic. Keats does not find a pure mother-tongue, which he perhaps overestimated as 'sweet sooth.' But with him the cult-ode becomes so wayward and inwrought that psyche is indeed like a text.

Notes

1. I use the following abbreviations. For Collins: *OE, Ode to Evening*; *OPC, Ode on the Poetical Character*. For Keats: *OP, Ode to Psyche*; *ON, Ode to a Nightingale*.
2. The late fragment, 'This living hand,' comes close, however, to an arousal of consciousness that is unforgiving, unappeasable, beyond pastoral or euphemistic remedy, despite its conciliatory if still minatory 'I hold it towards you.'

Chapter 6

Purification and Danger in American Poetry

a reply to Greek and Latin with the bare hands . . .
                    – W. C. Williams, *Paterson*

Art is a radical critique of representation, and as such is bound to compete with theology and other, ritual or clinical, modes of purification. 'The pure products of America/go crazy,' William Carlos Williams wrote; and it is necessary to admit from the outset that the word 'pure' has many meanings, some ambiguous, some downright deceptive. Although my theme is purity, and more specifically language purification in American poetry, one could easily write on 'Seven Types of Purity.' Empson's *Seven Types of Ambiguity* was, in fact, a response to doctrines of 'pure poetry' around him.[1] Our new, hypothetical book would start by explaining purity in the strictly rhetorical sense: *sermo purus, Latinitas, katharotes, kathara lexis, Ellenismos.* I am not as learned as I pretend: this comes right out of the magisterial compendium on literary rhetoric by Heinrich Lausberg. It allows me to make the point that a first definition of purity would already involve historical notions: of Latinity and Hellenism, of classical norms in opposition to Oriental or so-called barbaric features of style.

When the vulgar languages, the national vernaculars, developed their own literature, they were surrounded by classicist censors and snobs. The native product was often denounced as foreign, incult, Asiatic. Voltaire found many of Shakespeare's and Dante's expressions 'barbarous.' The decorum of the diction itself was taken to be the meaning. It is a nice irony that in our own time Leavis and Eliot attacked Milton's grand style for the obverse reason: their claim was that Milton, unlike Shakespeare, violated the spirit of the vernacular. How complicated and fertile in its tensions this battle over style could become is suggested by the fact that those suspicions of native developments were often fostering a different kind of rejuvenation, a renaissance of the Classics. Contaminated antiquity was to be purified by being reborn in its pristine *vetustas* and *majestas*; this aim of the Renaissance Humanists competed with the birth of a modern, vernacular literature. The break with Latin as an idealized father tongue, an Adamic yet a learned language, was so traumatic because it came at the very time the mother tongue was being cultivated.

Dante, for example, promoted his native dialect not only in the *Commedia* but also in two prose tracts, the *De Vulgari Eloquentia* and *The Banquet*. The first was written in Latin; they spoke with a cleft tongue in favor of Latin and the vernaculars. Two centuries later, Du Bellay's treatise on the enrichment of French was one of the important Renaissance apologies aiding the rise of the national vernaculars as sophisticated media, but it was not uncritical. There was a recognized need to chasten the vernaculars, to purge them of national or local idiosyncrasy and to make them as elegant as Latin. Against their greening was set a weeding and a pruning: a Latinity to emerge from within.

What I want to emphasize is twofold. It was a poet, Malherbe, who proclaimed, 'I will always defend the purity of the French tongue,' and it was a poet, Mallarmé, who set out once again to 'purify the language of the tribe.' Purity is not a scholarly imposition. It is intrinsic to the care of the language we now speak. A 'lingua franca et jocundissima' is always being challenged by some ideal of purification: the very Latin Stevens here uses against itself, or scientific standards of correctness, or 'debabelization' (C. K. Ogden's word) through an artificially engendered language, a 'Universal Character.' Moreover, the issue of poetic diction – an *English* version of the *French* concern for purity – is not a one-sided but a rich and baffling subject. (Owen Barfield's *Poetic Diction* and Donald Davie's *Purity of Diction in English Verse* are still exemplary in this area.) Good poetic diction is felt to be a language within language that purifies it, restoring original power; bad poetic diction is felt to be artificial rather than natural, a deadening if ornamental set of words and rules. Literary history shows, however, how impossible it is to uphold this distinction between repressive artifice and natural virtue, between conceptions of language that stress an original purity and strength, and those that impose an immaculate 'classical' or (in our time) 'Aryan' ideal.

Any call for purification or repristination is dangerous. For it is always purity having to come to terms with impurity that makes crazy. The situation is familiar; and whatever the motive for purity, language and religion are its major battlegrounds. The language of religion especially; but also the religion of language itself, language as a quasi-religious object when a new vernacular is developing. And American poetry, still striving to break with Anglophile burdens in the 1920s, and more puritanical than it knew, was making the vernacular into a religion.[2]

There is a Nyakyusa saying: 'The dead, if not separated from the living, bring madness on them.' Ritual helps this separation, according to Mary Douglas in her fascinating book, *Purity and Danger*. Literature is ritual in this sense. William Carlos Williams, writing in the 1920s, after the charnel house of the First World War, in which the dead had risen to claim the living, proclaimed that America had to separate itself from 'a civilization of fatigued spirits,' from the defiling if urbane and polished plagiarisms of European culture.[3] Williams can justify even Henry Ford in this light. 'My God, it is too disgusting,' he writes, thinking of

Ford (who said 'History is bunk') as the solution. And he adds: 'Great men of America! O very great men of America please lend me a penny so I won't have to go to the opera.'

He means to '*Lohengrin* in Italian SUNG AT MANHATTAN, – ' that is, to this artificial international culture, this elitist hybrid art totally alien to native America. Instead of supporting opera, let the commercial industrial complex support real works, and pay the artist a tithe to create the new culture, or as he says satirically, to 'capitalize Barnum.' The circus metaphor catches something; for the culture that would emerge had plenty of trained animals and clowns (TV before TV) yet lacked the good old animal guides, Blake's 'Animal Forms of Wisdom.'

For the moment we are still in Williams's grain, looking for a penny to escape the 'Traditionalists of Plagiarism,' who perpetuate their dead culture through the star-spangled absurdity of multinational opera. (In Germany, through the genius of Brecht, a Threepenny Opera does develop.) But are we not also, already, with Allen Ginsberg – thirty years, a generation later? A Ginsberg who is equally broke, though trying to 'make contemporarily real an old style of lyric machinery,' 'W. C. Fields on my left and Jehovah on my right,' crying howly, howly, howly, ready to abandon the false India of America for a true one more holy in its stink:

> America, I've given you all and now I'm nothing.
> America two dollars and twentyseven cents January 17, 1956.
> I can't stand my own mind . . .
> Asia is rising against me,
> I haven't got a chinaman's chance.
> I'd better consider my national resources . . .
> America how can I write a holy litany in your silly mood?
> I will continue like Henry Ford my strophes are as individual as his automobiles more
>   so they're all different sexes.
>
> 'America'

It is my purpose to convey a sense of the impasse that came with the Spring Cleaning that Williams undertook in *Spring and All*, and other works of language purification. The impasse was not unproductive: it patented an American type of sublimity. Since then we have not gotten tired of hearing about the American Sublime; its capaciousness, spaciousness, greatness, newness; its readiness to take on experience and remain sublime. Despite ecological and economic disasters that mock these ideals and bust their adherents, the gold rush of every latest poem recycles the agony, redeems the dirt.

Is the pattern, then, all that different from the familiar one of the old European codgers, of William Butler Yeats, for instance, who embraced the 'desolation of reality' after the circus animals, his illusions and histrionic attitudes, had gone? At the very time Williams is thinking of 'capitalizing' Barnum, Marianne Moore is 'translating' Old World 'Animal Forms of Wisdom' in her own way. Her splendor too is Menagerie. Compulsively we wash our hands of the old culture, of its *opera* (in the sense of masterworks as well as the baleful Wagnerian instance); we denounce it for being sublime junk, an artificial resuscitation of decadent art; we ritually strengthen ourselves for a rejectionist type of verse close to improvisation and prose poetry, but it never refines itself into actual gold. Dirt and pay dirt become one. That puristic turning away from opera, why does it produce so much soap opera? Warmed-over Whitman, confessional poetry? Or why, at best, only golden projects, elaborate scales, played on bluesy piano or jazzed up guitar, all prelude it seems, as we wait for the human story to commence?

Stevens is one of these preludists, a sublime improviser; he too is purging Europe from America, but enjoying and exploiting the thought that it can't be done. The purification, if it is to be, must be more radical than cultural concepts imply. No ideas but in things, was one of Williams's slogans. The idea is that things are cleaner than ideas; and Stevens replies: 'How clean the sun when seen in its idea,/Washed in the remotest cleanliness of a heaven/That has expelled us and our images.' Where would that cleaning, purging, expelling, end? The paradoxes are many. Williams realizes that the affected words are not purer than before. 'I touch the words and they baffle me. I turn them over in my mind and look at them but they mean little that is clean.' The dirt of Europe may have been removed, but now the words are plastered with muck out of the cities. When he does write an exemplary poem, antithetical to his prose, with its involuntary waves still tiding after Whitman ('We have only mass movements like a sea'), when he gives us

> So much depends
> upon
> a red wheel
> barrow
> glazed with rain
> water
> beside the white
> chickens

it is marked less by purity than by neatness and composure.

I slow down to look more closely at this well-known poem. It is a sequence of pauses filled by words. It is as if language had only non-natural sentences, and Williams were seeking a natural sentence: properly rhythmed, punctuated, by the mind pressing against what it perceives. Yet the caesuras here are too sharply, too keenly placed to be only rhythmic pauses. They are deliberate cuts – as deliberate as cutting in the movies or surgery – and place things 'beside' each other, avoiding plot or temporal climax. The cutting edge of the caesuras, moreover, here turned inward, suggests an outward-turned force that excludes or could exclude all but its own presence. There is meaning, there is an object focussed on, but there is also something cleaner than both: the very edge of the pen/knife that cuts or delineates these lines.

> A word is a word most [Williams wrote] when it is separated out by science, treated with acid to remove the smudges, washed, dried and placed right side up on a clean surface . . . It may be used not to smear it again with thinking (the attachments of thought) but in such a way that it will remain scrupulously itself, clean perfect, beside other words in parade. There must be edges.

The cleanliness, however, of Williams's phrasing depends so much on what is edged out that we become more interested in what is not there than in what is. The red wheelbarrow moves us into the forgetfulness of pure perception, but also suggests someone can't stand his own mind; it is as functional a carrier of the cultural surplus or whatever nonplusses clean thinking, like Ford's slick cars and other vehicular gadgets made in America. A wheel is a wheel, however glossy, however intricate: the earth itself is a wheel we forget. Gilded chariots or red wheelbarrows are equally soothers of memory, anti-mnemonic like a pastoral nature that hides its motives. The strength of *pure* poetry resides, then, like all poetry, in the impure elements it cuts out, elides, covers up, negates, represses . . . depends on: and the strength of *impure* poetry in the very idea of purity that makes it go – and go like – crazy.

I am as susceptible as anyone to the dream of a clean-perfect language: one that no longer mixes images and meanings, desire and memory; that cuts off, leanly, the attachments of thought; that does not contaminate life with dead matter, or the new and the old. I would like Williams's wheel to be my will, and to carry me beyond mere instrumentality: I'd like to think of it as at the navel or omphalos of a spontaneously constituted place of affection, not barren like the backyards of hospitals, even if relieved by that red and white. I'd like those contagious colors, in fact, to carry me by unconscious metaphor beyond the suggestion of disease into a world where 'it seems sufficient/to see and hear whatever coming and going is,/losing the self to the victory/Of stones and trees' (A. R. Ammons, 'Gravelly Run'). Even here, of course, one cannot lose the self entirely: a certain glaze meets one's gaze, 'air's glass/jail seals each thing in its entity.' Yet in such a prison one could live happily enough as god's spy or transparent eyeball. No Hegel or Heidegger there to turn a wheelbarrow into a philosophic tool. Best of all, I'd like that wheel to depend, to swing low, and carry me 'up' and 'on,' and make me forget what I am now doing, namely, playing with words that do not stand on themselves but rest on other words. That red wheel, that red barrow, archaic mound of adamic or decomposing flesh, that wheelbarrow left there to cart manure, culture, cadaver, whatever: I want it to compost spiritually, to become words forgotten by words, as nature by nature when Ammons writes: 'the sunlight has never/heard of trees.' *There* is purity: in that 'Nothing that is not there and the nothing that is' (Stevens, 'The Snow Man'). 'Gravelly Run' ends on the run, as it were, and frosty, as befits a self-purifying landscape, or verses that recall the link of nature poetry to epitaph:

> stranger,
> hoist your burdens, get on down the road.

> exposing his gifted quite empty hands
> Geoffrey Hill, 'In Piam Memoriam'

American poetry, then, like that of older vernacular traditions, is enmeshed in the paradoxes of purifying its words, of constituting itself as a Palladium in the city of words. This relativizing conclusion is unsatisfying, however; it says nothing about why poets have become absolute for poetic purity, martyrs to the art like Mallarmé or Emily Dickinson. I want to discuss the latter of these near contemporaries by looking closely at two lyrics written about three years apart. Read in sequence, their quest for purity appears in a revealing and frightening way. We glimpse, as in the early Williams, and originally in Wordsworth, the link between nature poetry and language purification; between questions of representation and purity of diction; and we understand that nature enters not as the pretext for sublime self-projections but as a privative and admonitory force. The language of nature replaces the dead language of classical or poetic diction; but the language of nature proves to be as monumental as what it replaced. It is a voice speaking from landscape as from a grave; a modern classical idiom in the making; a hieratic vernacular inscription. The burden hoisted by the stranger, or the promise to be kept, includes this purification of the vernacular.

Here is the earlier of the lyrics (783):[4]

> The Birds begun at Four o'clock –
> Their period for Dawn –
> A Music numerous as space –
> But neighboring as Noon –

> I could not count their Force –
> Their Voices did expend
> As Brook by Brook bestows itself
> To multiply the Pond.

> Their Witnesses were not –
> Except occasional man –
> In homely industry arrayed –
> To overtake the Morn –

> Nor was it for applause –
> That I could ascertain –
> But independent Ecstasy
> Of Deity and Men –
>
> By Six, the Flood had done –
> No Tumult there had been
> Of Dressing, or Departure –
> And yet the Band was gone –
>
> The Sun engrossed the East –
> The Day controlled the World –
> The Miracle that introduced
> Forgotten, as fulfilled.

There is a plot. Two events, perhaps three, are coordinated, and form a beginning and an end. At four the bird song starts, at six it has stopped. That the sun has risen is the third event, unless contemporaneous with the second. But this plot-like division of time, and these numbers, four, six, are in stylized opposition to the multiplying 'force' or flood of the passing music. There is something uncountable despite the counting, the book-keeping; and it extends to a sun that arrives on the scene with 'engrossing' power.[5]

The temporal sequence, then, is deceptive. 'Their period for dawn' already suggests the birds have their own dawn within a scheme of 'Independent Ecstasy' (stanza 4): their song, neither sanctifying nor theatrical, neither expressly for God nor for Society, cannot be subordinated to an 'end.' Nor is it subordinated to sunrise, since it is said to be 'neighboring as Noon.' The sun is already in the music. When the sun is mentioned in the last stanza, it is depicted as risen: already in place. Its exact position or power in the scheme of things cannot be calculated any more than the 'miracle' – the numerous music – that came and went. The presence of Day is a second 'miracle' that replaces the first so completely that the first is 'Forgotten, as fulfilled.'

The relation between 'forgotten' and 'fulfilled' is the depth-charge of this small poem; but on the surface Dickinson's lyric carries a moral message as clear as its plot. Nature has style, Nature has the right decorum. Its daily miracles are enacted unselfconsciously. Joyful and strong they may be, but never self-regarding. The birds 'expend' their voices, the sun 'engrosses' the world. It is a lavish economy, without inhibition or Puritan restraint. 'Engross' may imply an overbearing result, but from intrinsic power rather than from a striving for effect. As a statement about devotional verse, or religious rhetoric, the lyric is impertinent: do we need, it hints, a mode of worship that is pretentious, inmixing self-regard or the wish for applause? Yet Dickinson's lyric is itself not beyond reproach: though it exalts unselfconsciousness, its 'palpable design' conveys a moral that is witty at best, childish at worst. How *neat* all this is, including her verses! 'No Tumult there had been/Of Dressing, or Departure.' But neatness is not a major virtue. It is a form of cleanliness in a religion that puts cleanliness next to Godliness.

To purify words about God is Dickinson's apparent aim. She can do more, as we shall see: she can purify God of words. Here she plays an old game, and confuses cleanliness with purity. Almost every religion claims to institute the right worship, the right words. Evangelical religion, in particular, is often fanatic about purity of diction. The peculiar and fascinating thing is that in Dickinson's lyrics nature and style are the same, a divine etiquette. Nature teaches art to hide art for the sake of unselfconsciousness. What is described here is not Nature, but *a mode of being present* that at once values and cancels the self. If there is 'imitation of nature' it focuses on how to rise, that is, come to presence, come into *the* Presence.

That sunrise may be sunset, that 'the King/Be witnessed' only 'at' death (465) makes no difference to the poet. For the 'I' is always in a state of mortification: it is both a witness, a selfhood, and purged or transmuted by the act of witnessing. 'The Absolute removed/The Relative away' (765, written circa 1863); the pun on 'Relative' suggests that there may have to be a separation from family as well as from time. What o'clock it is becomes irrelevant, therefore; and when the first-person form is used it expresses incapacity: 'I could not count their Force,' 'Nor was it for applause/That I could ascertain.' The strong, elliptical ending, 'Forgotten, as fulfilled' is as close as one may come to an absolute construction: if it relates to anything it must be the eclipsed 'I.' The apparent referent, of course, is song, 'the miracle that introduced'; but that song is really the poet's, whose presence is elided, 'Forgotten, as fulfilled.'[6]

The more we ponder this lyric, or its pseudo-progression, the more curious it appears. Is the desire to come to or into Presence so strong that it verges on a death wish? Could we read stanza 5 as intimating: May the departure we call death be as orderly! Could we interpret the hiatus between stanzas 5 and 6 – no explicit causal connection joins the vanishing of the birds with the risen sun – as a space death has made or could make? With the last stanza something other than common day seems to be evoked. It is as if the daily event we call sunrise had been quietly displaced by divine day. Do we, after all, reach 'Degreeless Noon' (287) 'Without a Moment's Bell' (286)? Is the natural silence also the preternatural, as the sun's absolute presence obliterates everything else?

Dickinson's ellipses bear study, though they put an interpreter in the uncomfortable position of arguing from silence. This silence becomes typographic in one formal device, baffling, but at least obtrusive. In many poems an idiosyncratic mark – dash, hyphen, or extended point – replaces the period and all other punctuation. It can appear at any juncture, to connect or disconnect, generally to do both at once. It is a caesura or *coupure* more cutting than that of

Williams. It introduces from the beginning the sense of an ending and both extends and suspends it. The semantic value of this quasi-hyphen is zero, but it allows the asyndetic sentences to become an indefinite series of singular and epigrammatic statements. The zero endows them with the value of one, with loneliness or one-liness, as in an amazing poem that begins 'The Loneliness One dare not sound' (777).

Why does this formal mark, this hyphen with zero meaning, have intraverbal force? If we magnify this fly-speck of a mark (and it is always magnified in printed editions) we can surmise the following. Perhaps because it both joins and divides, like a hymen. Perhaps because it is like the line between dates on tombstones. It may be an arbitrary sign or it may be nakedly mimetic. In any case, the decorous proposition that nature is style is radicalized: this elliptical, clipped mark evokes style as nature. That hyphen-hymen persephonates Emily. At every pause, which it institutes, it can remind us of her wish to be a bride of quietness. 'Title divine – is mine!' (1072) But her only title may be her epitaphic lyrics, that sum up a life by brief inscriptions, very much like titles. The briefest inscription would be the letters E. D. and a set of hyphenated dates. The hyphen-hymen matters more than the dates, for what is crucial is the moment of juncture: dawning/dying, a non-violent transition from natural to supernatural, like waking into a dream, nature not being put out but 'Forgotten, as fulfilled.'

We come to Dickinson's later, less readable poem (1084):

> At Half past Three, a single Bird
> Unto a silent Sky
> Propounded but a single term
> Of cautious melody.
>
> At Half past Four, Experiment
> Had subjugated test
> And lo, Her silver Principle
> Supplanted all the rest.
>
> At Half past Seven, Element
> Nor Implement, be seen –
> And Place was where the Presence was
> Circumference between.

How dry and bookish, as if a computer had been given a number of words, and instructed to produce a minimal narrative! Only that narrative remains from the earlier version, though more stark, more outlined; the pathos and the moral play are gone. The sun too is gone, and the personal focus of reference. In this emptied landscape abstractions nest a 'single Bird,' the remnant of a purification whose motive we are trying to find.

Now one-stanza-one-act is the formula; and this new, unlavish economy extends to theme. A single term, a single note, rather than a numerous and multiplying music begins the action; then the bird sings freely; then it has ceased. One, two, three.

The time indicators, which periodize the event, terminating its three parts like a stop watch, heighten the contrary force of the poem's last word. That last word is like the first of each stanza, 'At Half past. . . .' It marks what lies *between* integers.

The between remains: something not whole, not at one. Yet the drive toward at-onement is haltingly continued in this poem, which is paced without auction or augmentation – without pseudo-progression. *Half past* is repeated, and half past is a turning point that does not turn. The first of these poems was written close to the age of thirty-three; the second three years later.

Though 'between' sticks out, is it a middle or a mediation? Other words too stick out, despite their effort to blend. They resemble each other as terms of art, even when their meanings are separable. So 'Experiment,' 'Element,' 'Implement' rhyme obscurely. It is hard, moreover, to hold onto the distinction between 'Place' and 'Presence.' A non-representational quality suffuses everything and counterpoints the temporal markers – we don't even know, for sure, whether morning or evening, sunrise or sunset, is the period, because all mention of light is omitted. We could be listening from the grave.

Not quite: 'silver Principle' contains a hint of light breaking. Yet the paradox remains that light breaks what it should illumine. Something, at the end, is not seen that was seen before. The very words become obscure. What visibles do 'Element' and 'Implement' describe? Does 'Element' refer to sky or bird or the music itself? Since 'Implement' follows, we assign 'Element' to a range of meanings exclusive of 'Bird.' The technique, if we can so designate it, approaches modern devices that Hart Crane called 'as independent of any representational motive as a mathematical equation.'[7] The earlier lyric had as its subject a problematic coming to or into Presence; now it is a coming into absence or indeterminacy.

The only way to resolve the indeterminate meaning of 'Element' and 'Implement' is to remember the earlier lyric and its conclusion: 'Forgotten, as fulfilled.' This suggests that 'Implement' may have its etymological meaning of *implere*, that which fills, and 'Element' could denote either what is filled or the beginning, the first term, in contradistinction to the last. 'Neither beginning nor fulfilment is seen' (at the end), is what the stanza says. The meaning of the two poems is comparable.

If so, how do we interpret the later poem's shift toward verbal abstraction and a non-representational method? Hart Crane thought that between Impressionism and Cubism poetry as well as painting was moving away from religion and toward science. This largish and imprecise speculation does not help too much. For the themes of Dickinson's lyric are neither religion nor science. Words as words have moved to the fore, words that are about to be 'terms' – fixed, as if by rigor mortis. The clock strikes for them too. If they escape that fixity, that transformation of language into *last words*, it is because they still evoke, in their very abstraction, past meanings, referents at once mathematical, musical, chronometric, experimental, teleological, even typological.[8]

The poem, therefore, never progresses; it is still moving, at the end, toward a 'single term.' This term is not found in the dictionary: the dictionary, perhaps, is in search of it. At present, or *at* any moment that can be fixed with the mock precision of 'Half past,' it is merely a cipher, a divine clue. An expected *god-term* (to borrow from Kenneth Burke) supplants all the rest and places what was life and time in a radically displaced position: into a place for which the names Death or Purgatory have been used, though they are not definitive. If we take this 'term' seriously, then time may be transformed at any moment: by a cockcrow that is taps, or a single note that is the trumpet call of the Apocalypse. As you lie down, each bed is a grave. 'The Grave preceded me – ' (784). As you rise up, a bird is the prelude to revelation. The structure of human life, from this phantomizing perspective, is a chiasmus, a crossing over from nothing to all and vice-versa: from life to death, from death to life, absence to presence, and so on. 'Love – is anterior to Life – /Posterior – to Death – /Initial of Creation, and/ The Exponent of Earth – ' (917).

Looking back at both poems, we can spot where that chiasmus rises up and phantomizes as well as founds the terminological work. 'And Place was where the Presence was' is two-faced, since it could be an expression for sheer vacancy or sheer plenitude. Place is the absence of a Presence that had been; *or* Place coincides with Presence. The one meaning does not merely coexist with the other as a type of ambiguity: the one meaning is the other, so that both remain occupying, in the same words, the same place. That is the unsettled and interminable state of affairs which 'Circumference between' seems to fix forever.

Let me conclude by exploring this cryptic phrase. It is again an 'absolute' construction, which we cannot attach to specific meaning or referent. To play a little, we might say that it makes reference circumferential; it so broadens it by abstraction that referentiality itself, or the representational force in words, is simultaneously evoked and revoked. Representation itself is 'between' us and Presence. Or representation is the only Presence we have. 'Myself – the Term between – ' (721).

Whether or not this impasse (founded in the religious sensibility, but removed from institutionalized words that refer us to religion) is the residual meaning, the absoluteness of 'Circumference between' is like a shudder, a cold shower perhaps. Faith and Hope, that rely on 'the evidence of things not seen,' are emergent at this point; yet there is no overt sign of this, and it is hard to imagine what sustenance they could find in such a void. The silent sky has returned, and the landscape is washed out, although we don't know whether by radiance or by darkness. All we can do is explore the impasse by means of those terminating words.

Circumference is a periphery, away from the center, whether the figure thought of is spatial (a circle) or temporal (the earth's circuit around the sun, bringing back the beginning or the whole event just recounted). 'Circumference between' could point to earth (life on earth), or the clock itself in its roundness: that repeated watching and waiting which is a religious duty as well as a symptom of alienated labor. 'Circumference between' could be that displaced place for which the Christian name is Death or Purgatory, and which intrudes 'between' us and God, eternally perhaps. Circumference as that which interposes could be the most abstract cipher of them all, zero, or whatever non-representational figure can hold together, in some imageless image, the juncture of life and death, death and life, self-presence and the divine presence. 'I could not see to see – ' (465). If we ask what 'be seen' at the end, as at the end of this poem, the answer would have to be: nothing, *or* all, *or* their juncture as zero.

The two endings, then, 'Forgotten, as fulfilled' and 'Circumference between' are simply a hyphen-hymen written out, or last words *not* given to the void. They help us to understand why the poetry Dickinson brings forth is so lean. It would not be wrong to ask how she can be a great poet with so small a voice, so unvaried a pattern, so contained a form of experience. Is her desire for purity perhaps the sign of a sensibility easily exhausted, depleted by smallest things that inflate: 'You saturated Sight – ' (640)? Whereas, with many poets, criticism has to confront their overt, figurative excess, with such purifiers of language as Emily Dickinson criticism has to confront an elliptical and chaste mode of expression. The danger is not fatty degeneration but lean degeneration: a powerful, appealing anorexia. She herself called it 'sumptuous Destitution' (1382). Since this is certainly prompted by her interpretation of Puritan scruples about language-art – 'Farewell sweet phrases, lovely metaphors' (George Herbert) – we cannot dismiss the possibility that she so identifies with an askesis forced upon her, that instead of the milk of hope she substitutes the 'White Sustenance – /Despair' (640). Her criticism of Puritan culture, or of the God of the Puritans, would have been to make herself a visible reproach by becoming so invisible, by wasting the substance of poetry with such deliberation and precision, like a saint. Yet not believing in saints or mediations, only her poetry can stand for her: representation, not mediation, is her hope. Her words, always tending toward last words, may be an act of resistance: her literal acceptance of Puritan decorum figures forth the uncompromised life of the words that remain.

> Capacity to terminate
> Is a Specific Grace
> Emily Dickinson (1196)

I am not good at concluding; I would prefer at this point to lose myself in the thought that poetry, like life, goes on, despite this amazing, dangerous quest for purity, manifested in Dickinson's endgame of words. I would prefer to quote John Ashbery, for example, because he is more relaxed, always convalescing it seems, converting what was oracular and blazing into divine chatter:

> Light falls on your shoulders, as is its way,
> And the process of purification continues happily.
> 'Evening in the Country'

The burden of light, in Dickinson, despite her attempt to maintain decorum, seems heavier. Like Mallarmé, she is a crucial poet, a dangerous purifier, the offspring of a greater Apollo. In the German tradition, Hölderlin, Rilke, and Celan have a similar relation to a purity more radical than what went under the name of Classicism. These poets are so intense – Shelley is another – they place so great a burden on the shoulders of poetry, that language breaks with itself. Mallarmé said he wanted to take back from music what belonged to poetry; that is one way of describing a break with representation more complete than conventional or classical form allowed. That form is but a second nature, a cleansing and not a purification. A more radical Classicism had to be discovered: that of Dionysos or, according to Nietzsche's interpretation of Wagner, Dionysian music. Theology may inspire but it no longer mediates this break with representation. Poets having expelled the old gods, their images, their phraseology – in short, poetic diction – and, having instituted a more natural diction, the process of purification continues, not so happily, and the purified language proves to be as contaminated as ever. We see that the poetic diction once rejected had extraordinary virtues, including its non-natural character, its lucid artifice, the 'mirror-of-steel uninsistence' (Marianne Moore) by which it made us notice smallest things and ciphered greatest things, and gathered into a few terms, magical, memorable, barely meaningful, the powers of language.

Notes

1. In America Kenneth Burke is sensitive throughout his writings to the 'pure poetry' movement, and interesting polemical analyses can be found in R. P. Warren's 'Pure and Impure Poetry' (1942), reprinted in *Selected Essays* (New York, 1958); and Frederick Pottle's *The Idiom of Poetry* (1941), chap. 5. George Moore's *An Anthology of Pure Poetry* had been published in 1924; in his introduction Moore contrasts

didactic verse or thought with 'Greek' innocence of vision, claiming also that 'Shakespeare never soiled his songs with thought.' This antididactic strain in definitions of purity goes over into New Critical precepts, and is strongly influenced by Flaubert, Mallarmé, Gide, and the French Symbolists generally. See the extracts bearing on 'purification' in Ellmann and Feidelson's *The Modern Tradition* (New York, 1965). This perspective, however, leads back to Hegel's (later, Pater's) understanding of Hellenic 'purity' in art, and to Schiller's famous essay on *Naive and Reflective Art* (1795–96).

2. For American reflections on purity of style before the twentieth century, see *The Native Muse: Theories of American Literature*, vol. 1, ed. Richard Ruland (New York: E. P. Dutton), esp. pp. 32–33, 76–77, and 182–83.

3. I quote from the following sources: *Spring and All* (1923), *The Great American Novel* (1923), and 'Marianne Moore' (1925). The text used is that presented in *Imaginations*, ed. Webster Schott (New York, 1971).

4. The text of the poems as well as their numbering is taken from *The Poems of Emily Dickinson*, ed. Thomas H. Johnson (Cambridge, MA, 1955).

5. Dickinson likes to use 'counting house' terms: her lexicon, Noah Webster's American dictionary of the English language, includes the economic sense of 'engross' (s.v. 4 in the first, 1828 edition) as well as 'to copy in a large hand' (s.v. 5) and 'to take or assume in undue quantities or degrees; as, to engross power' (s.v. 6).

6. Sharon Cameron's *Lyric Time: Dickinson and the Limits of Genre* (Baltimore: Johns Hopkins University Press, 1979) has exact remarks on the stanzas as 'flashcards' suggesting 'the absence of any trace left from a previous moment/picture.' See her discussion of 'The Birds begun' and 'At half past three' on pp. 176–78. She calls 'begun' a 'strange preterite' (perhaps, I would add, a nominative absolute or pseudo-infinitive, though the 1828 Webster lists *begun* as an alternate preterite form) and points to the complicated grammar of the poem's last line.

7. See his 'Modern Poetry' (1929), published in *The Complete Poems of Hart Crane*, ed. Waldo Frank (New York: Liveright, 1933).

8. *Implere figuram* is the term in theology for the *kairos* moment, when history moves 'from shadowy Types to Truth' (Milton). The shadowy types are Old Testament figures or events, the Truth their repetition with fulfillment in the New Testament. This figural or typological perspective was extended to secular history in general: its happenings were similarly conceived as types or emblems for a superseding truth. The pattern of 'Forgotten, as fulfilled,' since it embraces 'Implement' as well as 'Element,' last and first, suggests a metatypological perspective, an overcoming of typology. Cf. Robert Weisbuch, *Emily Dickinson's Poetry* (Chicago: University of Chicago Press, 1975): 'the bird song is a foreshadowing type of the day, and yet we suspect that the introductory "forgotten" miracle is granted superiority over its fulfilment' (p. 122 and p. 193, n. 20). Roland Hagenbüchle's 'Dickinson Criticism,' *Anglia* 97 (1979): 452–74, may be consulted for others who have dealt with the issues of reference and indeterminacy.

Part II

Theory and History

Chapter 7

Pure Representation

Valéry once declared that truth in the raw state is more false than falsity. But having lingered with the poets in the foothills and between the fences of truth, we now face a peak that cannot be scaled except by a frontal assault.

This statement may be ventured as one of the few empirical truths concerning perception: the eye is the predominant (we do not say most essential) organ through which perception takes place. The eye, Plato writes, is of all the sense-organs the one that holds most sun.[1]

It is common experience that the faculty of sight is both the most oppressive and the most enlightening. Does the mind have any greater desire than to perceive with the directness and splendor of the eyes? But is the mind not sick with the multiplicity and irreducibility of phenomena entering by the eyes? 'O dark, dark, dark, amid the blaze of noon'!

Now symbols may be described as signs having the power to release the mind from the tyranny of the eye, as from all singular impressions. But the mind cannot ultimately distinguish symbol and sign according to kind: signs become symbols in its continuous context and insofar as the mind is not divided against itself. We say 'hair' is a sign, but who is interested in 'hair'? It is a discrete sign, it does not stimulate that *motus animi continuus* which gave Cicero his greatest human pleasure. Yet when Milton, in *Samson Agonistes*, writes 'the fatal harvest of his head,' the life of Samson is suddenly and in its entirety before the mind. Both sign and symbol, nevertheless, depend on something perceived through the senses, and especially the eyes.

Thus while the sign does not release the mind from visual perplexity – unless we are like a man suffering from extreme thirst who cries water, water and finds nothing but the image of water before his eyes – the symbol restores the mind to its paradise of motioned rest. To this end also the symbol often mobilizes other senses or relics of sense experience against the eye, until the mind's continuity is re-established.

How is one to describe the nature of this continuity assured by symbols to the mind? Critics rush in where poets fear to tread. One could say that it prefers chance to emptiness, event to chance, and emptiness to event; that it is a light which illumines without self-division or decrease, a power for which every-thing, beginning or result, seems fortuitous, but ultimately a game the reality of which rests beyond the player.

Yet the symbols which poetry has at its disposal are less immediate and unique than those of the other arts. A musical phrase may be heard without a distinct image forming in the mind, but a verse containing the word 'tree' cannot be heard without the formation, however fleetingly, of the image of a tree. The composer works directly with signs that have a highly arbitrary relation to the things they perhaps represent: sound answers to sound, and in many painters, color to color; but the poet, though he will treasure words, must respect the things they conventionally represent, and cannot use his signs as if they spoke directly or exclusively to ear and eye. Words do not answer to words.

If poetry cannot escape, if a good part of its power, even, stems from distinct representations, how may poetic symbols induce the unconditioned continuity of the mind? The poet will accept representation, but only for its own sake, desiring what may be called a *pure representation*. In pure representation, the poet represents the mind as knowing without a cause from perception, and so in and from itself; or he will represent the mind as no less real than the objects of its perceiving. For the mind that perceives, and accepts this fact, since it can never know the objects of perception entirely in themselves, would know itself in itself – free of the irreducible, objective, and inevitable cause of perception. However, since it can never know itself entirely in itself, it is seized by an infinite desire for the very externality perceived.

The mind, therefore, being most keenly aware through the dominant eye of that which is the cause of perception, pure representation will, at base, be the urge to construct that ideal system of symbols which relieves consciousness of the eyes' oppression but assures it of the eyes' luminosity. Is it necessary to say more? Valéry, working on *La Jeune Parque*, draws up a mock questionnaire, the seventh problem of which is

> What is to be thought of this custom: Piercing the eyes of a bird so that it may sing better. Explain and develop (3 pages).[2]

The four modern poets here studied (Wordsworth, Rilke, Hopkins, and Valéry) are united by their common striving for pure representation, which we have sometimes called the imageless vision; for poetry is at one with the other arts in seeking, though by varying means, visibility without image, audibility without sound, perception without percepts. In modern poetry, which relies much more on the immediate significance of sense perception, the theme of sight is often a conscious theme, and a work may be written to get rid of the tyranny, or realize the beauty of the bodily eye. We shall now examine each poet, his individual problem and solution; perhaps we can in this way gain an insight into the nature of the mind and of symbolic process, for it is difficult not to acknowledge that the perplexity of the eyes does not stand for a deeper, metaphysical perplexity. *Cur aliquid vidi?*

Notes

1. *Republic* Bk. VI, l. 508b.
2. *Lettres à quelques-uns* (Paris, La Nouvelle Revue française, 1952), 'à P. Louys,' 15 May 1916, p. 114: 'que faut-il penser de cette pratique: Crever les yeux à l'oiseau pour qu'il chante mieux. Expliquer et développer (3 pages).'

Chapter 8

The New Perseus

Ich habe kein Dach über mir, und es regnet mir in die Augen.
Rilke, *Malte Laurids Brigge*
(I do not have a roof over me, and it rains into my eyes.)

It is said that Perseus, when he went to slay the Medusa, was given by Athene a resplendent mirror to escape the monster's direct glance, which would have turned him into stone. Perseus, accordingly, looked in the mirror, cut off the Gorgon's head, and from her blood there sprang the winged horse Pegasus that with one stamp of its foot produced Mount Helicon's sweet fountain, dear to the Muses. The new Perseus is a different kind of hero. He disdains or has lost Athene's mirror, and goes against the monster with naked eye. Some say that, in consequence, he is petrified; others, that he succeeds but the fountain of Pegasus is a sweet-bitter brew.

As poets, Wordsworth, Hopkins, Rilke, and Valéry are at one in their quest for a pure representation. But as *modern* poets they are related by their effort to gain pure representation through the direct sensuous intuition of reality. Each has a greater or lesser trust in the unmediated vision; or it may simply be that Athene's mirror is irreparably broken. The eye and the senses are made to supply not merely the ornaments but the very plot of truth. The body itself becomes, in its contact with the physical world, the source and often the end of cognition. Not only the four poets here considered, but the majority of poets, beginning with the romantics, refuse any but human and sensory intermediaries to knowledge, seek the hellenic innocence of the senses, and create like Novalis a new communion hymn around an old question:

Wer hat des irdischen Leibes
Hohen Sinn erraten?
(Who has divined the high meaning of the earthly body?)

Their doubting of the mediated vision, moreover, suggests that though they are, like Novalis, often professed and active believers, these poets no longer understand a concept of divine creation operative in medieval Christian thought and reaching the zenith of its artistic expression in the period between Dante and Milton. An essential contribution of Judeo-Christian to Greek philosophy is a view of the world as directly created by God.[1] One of the finest passages in the *Confessions* tells how St. Augustine, seeking God by reflecting on the beauty of the earth, finds that all things on earth can give him only one answer: we are not He, yet He made us.

> I asked the earth, and it answered me, 'I am not He'; and whatsoever are in it confessed the same. I asked the sea and the deeps, and the living creeping things, and they answered, 'We are not thy God, seek above us.' . . . And I replied unto all the things which encompass the doors of my flesh; 'Ye have told me of my God, that ye are not He; tell me something of Him.' And they cried out with a loud voice, 'He made us.' (Chapter 10)

But the modern poet has suffered a distinct loss in the power to represent the world as a created thing. Milton is perhaps the last who, with nostalgic strength, can render the act of divine creation in its full imaginative splendor. Two ideas are basic to the medieval view of divine creation, and both are textually evident in the first chapter of Genesis: that of the world as a sequence of perfect creations, and that of man as the absolute creation. The first, of the world as an instant and complete creation, is given with glorious detail of sound and thought in the seventh book of *Paradise Lost*. When the sixth day comes, God speaks:

> The Earth obey'd, and straight
> Op'ning her fertile Womb teem'd at a Birth
> Innumerous living Creatures, perfet forms,
> Limb'd and full grown: out of the ground up rose
> As from his Lair the wild Beast where he wons
> In Forest wild, in Thicket, Brake, or Den;
> Among the Trees in Pairs they rose, they walked: (VII, 453 ff.)

The delight in pre-existent perfect forms, of nature or art, reached a last height in Milton, is sustained in the principles of the eighteenth century, but falls amid the general decay and indistinction of genres evident in the theory and practice of the romantic artists, a decay almost complete at the present time, when no philosophy – religious, historical or aesthetic – can restore a feeling for the *genre tranché*.

The second concept, of man as the absolute creation, that is, formed in the image of God, crown and master of created things, having nothing in common with these except the fact of createdness, and createdness out of dust, is equally emphasized in Milton, even more clearly than in the biblical accounts, and with prevenient pathos:

> Let us make now Man in our image, Man
> In our similitude, and let them rule
> Over the Fish and Fowl of Sea and Air,
> Beast of the Field, and over all the Earth,

> And every creeping thing that creeps the ground.
> This said, he form'd thee, *Adam*, thee O Man
> Dust of the ground, and in thy nostrils breath'd
> The breath of Life; and his own Image hee
> Created thee . . . (VII, 519 ff.)

Yet modern poets are haunted by the indifference of man and nature; the dust of the earth from which God formed the rest of creation by act of word, and the breath which he breathed into man by special act, are no longer separate but interpenetrating elements, and acts distinguished not in kind but in continuous time. Thus Wordsworth is strongly influenced by his feeling for continued revelation, and even the orthodox poet envies 'the horror and the havoc and the glory' which all creation with the seeming exception of man possesses; while Rilke almost goes so far as to reproach Christ for the resurrection of Lazarus, considering this a disturbance of natural process.[2] It is clear that a view of creation as immanent and continual has replaced the view of created things as instantaneously created, and of man as the absolute creation.[3]

The loss of the first concept, of instantaneous and perfect creation, brings to modern poetry its first major difficulty. The only thing that will spring up fully-formed to the unmediated vision is accidence or fortuitousness. Blake said that he could stare at the knot in a piece of wood until almost mad. We remember the 'smooth spoon' of Hopkins. Nerval never forgets a young English girl seen biting into a lemon; he must accommodate her in his myth-haunted consciousness. In Wordsworth the mystic moment is for the most part brought on by a commonplace event ('It was in truth an ordinary sight'). Some of the poets even construct theories on accidence. Rilke is the extreme case. He refuses to ignore any event, however slight; a dog, a bowl of roses, the stray sound of a violin – 'Das alles war Auftrag.' His concept of 'thing' is in response to such attempt, for the 'thing' is a fragmentary event, without determined contour, and simply that. The 'thing' resembles to a curious degree Hopkins's view of inscape and instress. With Hopkins the act of attention or caught attention receives value per se: 'All the world is full of inscape and chance left free to act falls into an order as well as a purpose: looking out of my window I caught it in the random clods and broken heaps of snow made by the cast of a broom.'[4] Valéry seems at first an exception. He is in direct reaction to the systematic accident-alism of Hugo and the mystical accidentalism of Nerval. Writing in 1920, Valéry realized that the symbolist movement provided only a short interlude of pure poetry. His successors 'have again opened on the accidents of being the eyes we had closed in order to make ourselves more akin to its substance.'[5] One need only compare the fine use of accident and accidence in Proust to the gross effects of chance in Balzac to perceive the advance in consciousness which has occurred, and which in modern psychology and increasingly in modern criticism is called (after Taine) the technique of significant detail. One could go on fairly endlessly, pointing out that the problem of accidence arises at the same time strongly in painting – the subordination of the detail to the whole is the main aesthetic preoccupation of Delacroix's *Journals*, and Baudelaire in an early 'Salon' compares Delacroix and Hugo to the detriment of the latter:

> Too materialist, too attentive to the surfaces of nature, M. Victor Hugo has become a painterly poet; Delacroix, always respectful of his ideal, is often without knowing it a poetic painter.[6]

But here we touch on the theories of local color and word-painting, which express the unmediated eye's attempt to grasp a physical reality by purely sensory means, theories which are variously denounced in the course of the century.[7] We should not forget to add that Valéry is only a seeming exception: he would use and reproduce by technical means the continual but rarely grasped parthenogenesis in consciousness of rhythm and word. Valéry is also responsible for a most perfect derationalization of sight: after him, the surrealists will free all the senses, and have their finest poet in Eluard whose main, inexhaustible theme is 'la vie immédiate.' Are not all these poets, in the words of Eliot, 'distracted from distraction by distraction'? Modern poetry would evolve a style dealing with 'immediate' rather than with 'general' nature.

The loss of the second concept, of man as absolute creation, brings a second major concern. The fear (sometimes the desire) arises that the physical world has a fatal influence on human life – 'Et la matière, hélas, devint fatalité.'[8] This concept of a material or environmental fatality has been popularized to such an extent by modern sociological theories that one does not always realize its relatively recent importance. Its authority lies, of course, in social, economic, and scientific developments. The concept presupposes a secret undifferentiation or even identity of organic and inorganic life, as is already set forth in Diderot's *Rêve d'Alembert* (1761) and Schelling's *Von der Weltseele* ('a hypothesis of the higher physics'). In Schelling's preface of 1806 one may find formulated in swift and imaginative manner themes that are obsessive and even tragic in poets like Novalis, Poe, Nerval, Baudelaire, and Hugo, themes that reach Rilke. These poets are all in one way or another haunted by the idea of reification.

But a third, perhaps most important, consequence, implicit in the loss of the Bible account of divine creation, is the modern poet's concern with the *inherent* arbitrariness of symbols. Although it was Adam who named every living creature, he did so at the behest and under the aegis of God (Genesis 2:19–20). Although words have a merely arbitrary or conventional relation to their referents, they are assured of a sacred origin. As words they are arbitrary, but as symbols divine; and the same holds for any other system of reference including that of the orders of creation, inasmuch as marked by the mark of God. As things they are what they are, but as symbols they are divine. The bread and wine on the tongue is, like the word, only bread and wine, and yet, as Claudel says, 'Chair de Dieu sur ma langue, consacre mon coeur et mon principe.'

However, those poets who have forsaken the literary and the spiritual authority of a sacred text not only feel the unavoidable inadequacy that dogs conventional ways of expression (a stimulus in all times for artistic creation), but feel this inadequacy as inherent in all the works of man, as his one constant dilemma, his pain from childhood on, his existential anguish. For nothing now declares God of itself, but all is the work of man, including the testaments; and all is profane as it is sacred, and cannot be more than his conceptions that remain conceptions. Symbols are only such by pretence, and the entirety of life is caught up in this pretence. Everything is *in potentia* equally sign and equally symbol.

In the romantic poets the leveling of symbols or the fusion of *genres* still has a distinct social and religious aim. Wordsworth's *Peter Bell* and *The White Doe of Rylstone* were written with the avowed attempt of showing the 'humblest departments of daily life' as suitable for both poetic and religious inspiration. The same motive works in *The Prelude*, which sacrifices the high argument of Milton for the personal history of a simple agrarian life. In France we have the somewhat later example of Lamartine's *Jocelyn*, itself in the line of Rousseau, and of course Victor Hugo acting as Christian Democrat in his famous preface to *Cromwell*. Germany has for its *cause célèbre*, besides Shakespeare, Goethe's *Wilhelm Meister*, which Novalis at first praises for its domestication of the marvelous, then condemns as a *Candide* against the poetic spirit. But Friedrich Schlegel already moves away from the consciousness of the social and religious cause when he describes the mingling of trivia and magnalia in *Wilhelm Meister* as an instance of romantic irony;[9] for romantic irony, as the expression of the artist's entire freedom vis-à-vis the materials of experience, already denotes a sense for the inherent inadequacy of all symbols as such, and leads to the now conventional stage tricks of Pirandello as well as to the present, almost universal, acceptance of the element of playfulness in art.

By the time of Hopkins, the dilemma is acute even in the orthodox religious artist. Though Hopkins may have been aware in 'The Windhover' of the significance of the falcon as a type of Christ, he suspends this knowledge, choosing indeed a falcon, but a local one. His poem testifies to the fact that the *res creatae* are no longer known as an object of contemplation leading the observer by degrees to God, but as one compelling him to God through the intuition of an inconceivable physical force felt present equally in every particular thing. Just as Van Gogh's conception of the starry night renders not so much this night with its indubitable peace as the despair of the artist in finding a visual form adequate to the mind's simultaneous perception of an immense calm and an equally immense power, so 'The Windhover' expresses by its asyndetic style and sprung rhythm not only the instress of the falcon, but also the artist's creative will to represent the divine as a physical force.

But not till Rilke and Valéry is the essential indifference of subject matter realized in full. No event seems now to have a greater intrinsic claim on the artist than any other. The subject of a poem, said Valéry, is as foreign to it and as important as his name is to a man. Rilke accepts and is able to poetize the most varied subjects, substantiating what phenomenology calls the original right of all data.[10] It is clear that there are no more 'poetic' objects. If Valéry's poetry centers on a minimum of symbols, the sea, the air, the sun, a tree, this is not an aesthete's prejudice but an arbitrary limitation which confers on them the power of abstract variables which recover individual meaning only if the *entire* system of signs wherein they participate is understood. The poetry of Mallarmé likewise forces the reader to the understanding of an entire system, which acts almost like a separate language, for what is denoted by the words is not, as Mallarmé has declared, the conventional thing itself, but the *effect* of a thing, and ideally, of its sign, that is, their [immediate] impact on the cleared consciousness.

What, therefore, started in romanticism as a religious and a social concern (is continued in realism as the humanitarian and positivist belief that 'whatever is worthy to exist is also worthy to be known')[11] reaches Hopkins as a problem in expression, and appears in Rilke and Valéry almost free from its religious, social, positivist, and expressionist foundations as a frank acceptance of the inherently arbitrary character of human symbols. *In the beginning was the fable.*[12]

There are two major paths taken by the poets in their struggle against the arbitrariness of symbols. The first is to accept the arbitrary basis of language and to make it both specific and total as in music. Poetry is to be purified of all effects not proper to it, that is to say, of all effects also found in other sign systems. One such effect is the utilitarian, another the emotional, a third could be the pictorial. What is left? First of all, absolute internal consistency, as in pure mathematics. That is why Valéry and Mallarmé cannot be understood except in their totality, but are then understood totally in every line. Second, effects which, though not as yet totally known, may be related to the imminent (rather than immanent) formations of consciousness.

This also has a bearing on another, often parallel path chosen by the poets to overcome arbitrariness, one which is an exploration of the inner motion and incipient meanings of human speech as such: the discovery of the *voice* of the spoken word. Only in this way can poetry rival the example of painting and the plastic arts to which it is so strongly attracted. Instead of giving conventional names to things, it would, like the painter, take them away and render instead the immediate 'figure' of the senses, which in this case especially is that of speech as pure voice. 'Wird euch langsam namenlos im Munde?'[13] The poetry of Rilke and Valéry are living instances of anominization; Hopkins also desires the 'inscape' of speech. But what both methods – the essentializing of the word's arbitrariness and the discovery of the spoken word's voice – have in common, is the attempt to find and to represent things *immediately* significant, *aesthetic* things, signs of the creative nature of perception.

The modern poet has committed himself to the task of understanding experience in its immediacy. He has neglected the armature of the priest – the precautionary wisdom of tradition – and often the inculcated respect for literary models. But therefore he only, and the more strongly, knows the need of mediation. The quest of the new Perseus becomes a quest for tokens of mediation, or 'immediation,' panentheistic symbols. The mirror must be restored. But the mirror remains Athene's gift, or that of God, in any case a supernatural gift. Does the modern poet's unarmed vision find its symbols of mediation?

Notes

1. See Étienne Gilson, *L'Esprit de la philosophie médiévale* (Paris, 1932), esp. chap. 4, 'Les Êtres et leur contingence.'
2. See Walther Rehm, 'Der Dichter und die Toten,' *Orpheus* (Düsseldorf, 1950), p. 563. This book has proved very informative on modern ideas of the poet as mediator, although its erudition at times obscures a great argument.
3. Charles Kingsley welcomed the *Origin of Species* with 'now they have got rid of an interfering God-a master-magician as I call it-they have to choose between the absolute empire of accident and a living, immanent, ever-working God.' I take this quotation from Charles E. Raven, the Gifford lecturer, who in his *Natural Religion and Christian Theology* (Cambridge, 1953) tries to discount St. Augustine's view of the natural world as a *massa perditionis*, insisting that original Christianity recognized the 'continuity of nature and supernature.' The finding of sufficient proof-texts to support this view is a major task for the modern theologian, and already quite apparent as early as Schelling and Coleridge.
4. See *Selections from the Notebooks of G. M. Hopkins*, ed. T. Weiss (New Directions, 1945).
5. *Variété I,* 113.
6. 'Salon de 1846,' article on Eugène Delacroix, in *Curiosités esthétiques*, ed. Jacques Crepet (Paris, 1923) pp. 106–7: 'Trop matériel, trop attentif aux superficies de la nature, M. Victor Hugo est devenu un peintre en poésie; Delacroix, toujours respectueux de son idéal, est souvent à son insu un poète en peinture.' Baudelaire will change his mind about Hugo in 'Réflexions sur mes Contemporains," *L'Art romantique.*
7. See especially the key article of Désiré Nisard, 'M. Hugo en 1856,' *Mélanges*, 2, 1868, 55 ff. The issue of the possibility of a material representation in literature was taken up with perspicuity by Irving Babbitt in his *New Laocoon*. Babbitt perceives that the originality of romantic and postromantic literature is in its word painting, its

use of 'local impressions,' but condemns this. The only academic critic to render it some justice before the present generation is Gustave Lanson in his *L'Art de la prose* (Paris, 1911), though this deals mainly with prose. 'Après Bernadin de Saint-Pierre, le mot, instrument de pensée ou de sentiment, est appliqué à la stricte notation de la perception des sens' (p. 207).

8. Hugo, 'Le Satyre.'
9. See his *Gespräch über die Poesie* (1800).
10. Edmund Husserl, *Ideas*, tr. W. R. Boyce Gibson (New York, 1952), paragraph 26. The original edition of the *Ideen* was published in 1913.
11. A dictum from Bacon's *Novum Organum*.
12. 'Au sujet d'Eurêka,' *Variété I*, 145.
13. *Sonnette an Orpheus*, Erster Teil, XIII. The immediate reference is to the taste of fruit.

Chapter 9

The Heroics of Realism

'I embrace ALL,' says Whitman, 'I weave all things into myself.'
Do you really! There can't be much left of *you* when you've done. When you've
cooked the awful pudding of One Identity.

D. H. Lawrence

The contemporary novelist displays an immense faith in the original right of all
data. Sense and nonsense are both admitted; little distinction is made between
public matters and private; no restricted or insignificant events remain. 'The
"proper stuff of fiction" does not exist,' wrote Virginia Woolf after seeing the
first fragments of *Ulysses*, 'everything is the proper stuff of fiction, every feeling,
every thought; every quality of brain and spirit is drawn upon; no perception
comes amiss.'

Such ranging or expansive sympathy is not new to literature. According to
Wordsworth, the only infallible sign of genius is 'a widening of the sphere of
human sensibility for the delight, honor and benefit of human nature'; and there
is no proof that Homer felt less widely than James Joyce. Yet whether or not the
modern writer has a broader range of feelings, he is somehow nearer or more
acutely receptive to them. 'He can no more cease to receive impressions,' to
quote Virginia Woolf again, 'than a fish in mid-ocean can cease to let water rush
through his gills.' This is, to say the least, a rather uncomfortable state of
existence.

For though no person is capable of responding infinitely to impressions, the
writer labors today under that a priori charge. He expects himself to be
constantly aware. Like Dostoevsky's Lebedyev, he becomes a blend of visionary
and voyeur: a know-all, a sense-all, a satanic kind of spying character, 'walking
up and down in the earth.' By the passkey of fiction he lets himself into every
door and most minds. His novels exfoliate in a leafy riot of impressions and
indiscretions. But they also prove that art dies where the focus of sensibility is,
on fixed principle, too wide.

The difficulty is usually stated in a different way. It arises as a question of how
form may be imposed on modern (limitless or chaotic) experience. But this is a
deceptive formulation with a touch of hysteria in it, as in Virginia Woolf's
further comment. 'Life is subjected [by the novelist] to a thousand disciplines

and exercises. It is curbed; it is killed. It is mixed with this, stiffened with that.' We recognize here the dogmatic factor in realism: its assumption that a direct contact with life — with things themselves — is always available. Forms are therefore a betrayal of life. A necessary evil, they stand arbitrarily between the novelist and life, to curb and kill.

Does life whelm the novelist in this manner? It is doubtful that we are as directly in touch with life as we would like to be. And the modern novelist does like to be: he suffers, more than ever, under an ideal obligation to the totality of experience. Yet though it is only ideal, it is no less an obligation, for the spirit of the time does not allow him to restrict his focus willfully. Everyone acknowledges, of course, that art cannot do without form and that forms restrict; but the sanction for those forms is no longer spontaneously social or religious: the sanction now rests almost completely with the individual artist. We hold him responsible whether he accepts the forms of his society or rejects them and makes his own. Whatever the forms, and whatever the subject, he is judged only in the light of that largest and most difficult abstraction — life itself.

Past novelists did not have to keep up with life. Change and novelty, before the industrial and technological revolutions, were rejected rather than accepted a priori. Despite this particular conservatism, art has always fostered larger perceptions; and the contemporary novel merely continues its general momentum toward a freer human sensibility. The coldest work of art still has its reversals and shocks: a falling of veils as in the Racinian *tu*, the illegitimate sympathy evoked by the Satan of *Paradise Lost*, the rare moments of almost physical illumination in the novels of Henry James. What we value in ancient as in modern art is precisely this power of sympathetic trespass: trespass against the society circumscribing the artist's range of feeling. The only difference, in this respect, between the two kinds of art is that this trespass previously coexisted with a narrow and now coexists with a broadening range of experience.

This difference, however, is more substantial than first appears. One might assume that literature before the present century had greater difficulties in transcending conscious or permitted limits. Are not social imperatives more persistent, and do they not prevent strange alliances of thought or feeling? Yet the truth is that the difficulty lies all on the side of modern literature. Not that the contemporary writer finds it harder to transgress; on the contrary, he finds it too easy. The reality of trespass is disappearing with the reality of convention; and the repressions on which great literature battens, from which it shapes the pressure of its scenes, is weakened. A generation's freedom to give its feelings away obviates that shuddering, magnanimous breakthrough of the conventional sensibility to excluded parts of life. When we know in advance that everything is permitted, what is there to reclaim? Just because their sensibility is (in principle, not always in fact) permissively open, modern writers are faced with having to renew the image of a redemptive transgression.

A trespass presupposes something to be breached, some strong convention between characters, or author and character, or author and audience. The novelist, before the present era, is allowed a potential omniscience but he will not use it beyond a certain point: he leaves many things unsaid or presents them obliquely. The ultimate reason for this may be aesthetic as well as social; it is difficult, in the traditional novel, to separate these motives. There is, moreover, a good deal of flexibility and ambivalence in the conventions: a breach of style, for example, a trespass of author against audience, may occur without breaching other conventions, as between characters – but this is a subject we do not have to consider at this point. What is generally true is that the author is restrained by social norms that affect directly his sensibility or the canons of his art; and this restraint, a limiting of focus and subject, makes every breach of appearances significant and allows a real emergence of dangerous sympathy.

Jane Austen's restraint is of the older kind. In *Persuasion*, two estranged lovers meet accidentally after many years, and we never doubt that their reconciliation will occur, any more than that Odysseus will reach home. They are kept, however, in tense separation and have to navigate social barriers and serious obstacles of self-esteem before they reach a new mutual accord. To collapse the space of separation too soon would be to collapse the novel, to sin at once against art, society, and some deeper sense of the necessity of a slow redemption, of having to buy back what had been estranged or wasted. Jane Austen's art is, in fact, so honest that we feel her to have ultimately written a fairy tale, something mellow and miraculous like *The Tempest*. So deeply does she make us perceive the emotional or social gulf between the lovers; so careful is she to respect a reality of time love might not have overcome.

The contemporary novel, however, precisely because its realism is a priori or formal, runs the danger of inducing too quickly a sense of intimacy with person and place. The initial or founding distance is gone. The heroine may lose her virtue or a character his mystery in a few pages. The novelist just can't help it: the promiscuity is less in the author than in the genre. Its impetus is demonic. Instead of proceeding toward intimacy, the writer must somehow manage to go from intimacy (Virginia Woolf's 'mid-ocean') to that natural estrangement which is Jane Austen's donnée. He must reveal the inauthenticity of every assumption of intimacy or find, as John Crowe Ransom once said, 'techniques of restraint' to replace the force of convention. To make lightning you must have charged poles and a distance to traverse; the conventions provided the distance, and the emotions did the rest. What provides that distance now?

Malamud's *The Assistant* can illustrate the problem. It falls patently into two parts, of which the first shows the distance between the main characters being destroyed, and the second a new distance being carefully realized. Like *Persuasion*, the novel's subject is a buying back, a redemption. Despite the gulf between Frank and Helen, one an Italian on the prowl and the other a Jew – a gulf made up of prejudice but also of genuine cultural difference – the two draw closer together. At the critical moment, however, Frank rapes Helen; and, in the catastrophe that follows, the assumption that a common humanity binds them together is removed. Frank is now at a much truer yet also more hopeless distance from Helen. It is only from this deeper estrangement that he can really win the 'Jewish' as well as 'human' Helen and redeem what he has lost.

Malamud also shows that the contemporary novelist is not naked of all social or inherited forms. He still has some access to traditions firmly held or to archaic cultures. He may also use the common rituals of his society; party, church-going, dinner, excursion, caucus, dating, interview. It is rather rare, moreover, that he chooses a perspective which so destroys the norm of distance that, as in Kafka, the relations between man and man become as precarious as those between believer and God after Protestantism had voided the intermediaries. Yet many of the rituals retained by the novelist – retained without anachronism – are no longer conventions of restraint. They are more in the nature of conventions of unrestraint, rapid transit communions. The modern picaresque is a flourishing genre because it recognizes this fact candidly: it is *the* genre of unrestraint. Sublime energies, said Thomas Mann, appear today only in the guise of the grotesque; but 'today' is a large category, one that stretches from *Don Quixote* to a Saul Bellow novel or to Mann's own finale, *Felix Krull*. The picaresque, however, breaches realism in so far as the hero is not altogether of the world in which he moves. He is a knight, a god of sorts; we cannot entirely draw him to our level.

Even when a writer stays entirely within realism, his novel must still estrange us, like the picaresque, from the intimacy of its mode. Malamud's Frank is no picaresque hero, yet he belongs to the archetype of the stranger, the person without a visible past, who is almost a fixture of the novel; and he is also, perhaps too obviously, a suffering servant figure. One can say that the writer's trespass is now against realism itself. If the novelist's mode commits him to the position that 'nothing real is alien to me,' his works break through to the fact that 'nothing real is familiar to you.' Realism being as great a tyranny as super-naturalism, a vital antithesis of mode and work appears, so that authors tend to beget otherness rather than intimacy, vision rather than common sense. How visionary Balzac's realism was is only clear today.

The re-achieved distance, in other words, whether aesthetic or mythical, is not established only to be annihilated again. It is a more positive, vital, visionary thing. To gain the world truly, one must first learn the measure of one's distance from it; and the dehumanization of art, noticed by Ortega y Gasset, is a general symptom of this necessary recreation of distance. Ortega's highest praise was to say, as of Proust, that he invented a new discrepancy between reality and ourselves. Dehumanization, however, is the wrong word. In the abeyance of self-justifying conventions, which limit the contact of persons and encourage a language intrinsically veiled, the artist makes room in the 'all too human' for a necessary angel (sometimes, a necessary devil):

> I am the necessary angel of earth
> Since, in my sight, you see the earth again,
> Cleared of its stiff and stubborn, man-locked set.
> Wallace Stevens

This humanistic attack on the anthropomorphic ('man-locked') intelligence fosters techniques of perception which are dissociative rather than associative in nature. They do not make the strange familiar but rather estrange the familiar. One such technique (there are a great many) is Faulkner and Robbe-Grillet's use of the 'estranged consciousness.' Even where it depicts an abnormal state of mind it does so by projecting reality as irreducibly, troublingly, *other*. Consciousness, for these writers, is little more than a rape, a wrong or premature intimacy. It needs, therefore, a moral as well as imaginative effort to reach the innocence of things or realize their independence vis-à-vis ourselves. Our narcissism is endless and essential, and only by various methods of dissociation that disrupt ordinary perception can we get beyond the self to a sense of the other.

In France, the surrealist movement, which had its effect on the novel, began a programmatic search for techniques of estrangement. 'La surréalité,' said André Breton, 'sera . . . fonction de notre volonté de dépaysement de tout.' The Parnassian coldness, the art for art's sake attitude, and Rimbaud's call for sensory experiments, were general forerunners. Much may even be attributed to the Romantics, especially the German branch, and that addition of strangeness to beauty in which Walter Pater saw the characteristic of their art. But to discuss the relation of the modern novel to poetry is not my purpose, though this relation is clearest in France. Let it suffice to say that the figure of the angel, used by both Rilke and Stevens, has a certain bearing. It tells us that the human, at a time like this, when sympathies are socialized and spread so wide as to become abstract, is often a fog of intimacy hiding the genuine difference; and that art must then make room for the other and even the divine. Art refuses to let us fall into one circumference.

I conclude with an example from the modern novel of how this genuine sense of difference, or otherness, is kept alive. It is related to what we have said about the mythic dimension of certain characters in the realistic novel. There is a highly complex kind of distancing that has recently come under attack. A new, self-generated convention, it is often considered the distinguishing mark of realistic fiction after Flaubert and Henry James. In objective or impersonal narration, as this convention is sometimes called, the author intrudes as little as possible, developing the story by means of reflectors (centers of consciousness) or some other dramatic method. Wayne Booth has made the first comprehensive and systematic critique of this mode in *The Rhetoric of Fiction*. He examines the impersonal novel with great patience and insight and discovers a flaw never before so carefully described.

This flaw he calls 'confusion of distance.' We know Jane Austen's attitude toward her characters, however nuanced it may be, but who can say precisely how an impersonal novelist stands in relation to his hero? How does Joyce consider Stephen Daedalus? Where does the truth lie in *The Turn of the Screw* – with the governess or the children? The author's attitude, of course, is complex. But should it not be sufficiently resolved, after due respect to mystery, so that contradictory answers (Joyce thinks Stephen is an ass; Joyce is deeply in sympathy with him) cannot be offered as they have been in a deluge of exegeses? Mr. Booth holds that this uncertainty about the author's true judgment is not due to any insufficiency of understanding in his critics, except as they are willing to tolerate an intolerably ambiguous author, but is an inevitable result of the impersonal mode of narration. Explicit judgments are not necessary, yet no author may fail to provide an implied standard without throwing his work to the winds of opinion.

Is there , however, a confusion of distance in the 'impersonal' modern novel? Perhaps the author does not stand in a relation of judgment to his characters? How then could he (or we) approve or disapprove? The reply that the author in creating, and we in reading, cannot but weigh the characters constantly, is not very convincing. Do we really judge Macbeth? Only by faint analogy can 'judging' be applied to what our minds do on confronting certain exceptional figures like Lear, Macbeth, Vautrin, or even Felix Krull. Tradition provides us, moreover, with a definite term for the person who is so much greater than we are, not morally perhaps but in mode of being – Nietzsche would have said he stands beyond good and evil – that our familiar, democratic judgment is suspended, if not disabled. We call that man or woman the *hero*.

Stephen Daedalus, I believe, is a hero in that sense: he embodies a special fate. The confusion of which Mr. Booth is aware arises when we see a character put almost beyond our judgment who is realistically portrayed as in no essential way superior to us. Camus's *étranger* is the extreme example of the hero who is only one of us, or even less, yet shakes off judgment by simply being what he is, as the trial at the end of the novel probably makes too explicit. By now such radically innocent characters are almost a convention. Between E. E. Cummings's *The Enormous Room* (enormously neglected) and John Cassavetes's film *The Shadows*, there lie two generations, a second world conflict, and a medium strongly challenging the novel, yet the characters in both have the same resilience, the same basic innocence, the same status beyond good and evil.

In fact, modern realistic fiction, with the exception of some eighteenth- and many nineteenth-century English novels (they provide *The Rhetoric of Fiction* with its truest ground), has kept its attachments to romance and myth, to characters that bear a daimon that cannot be morally or psychologically reduced. In Dostoevsky's *The Idiot*, Prince Myshkin exerts a disastrous influence. He destroys the two women he might have saved, and it would be impossible to say whether he is a saint, an idiot, an impotent, or all three. Yet if his character (a moral and psychological entity) is unclear, his mode of being (ontological) is transparent: he is human in all respects, and judgeable – except for his pity. That is his daimon, as anger is Achilles'. By that he is divine and disastrous, like Christ. The love others attribute to him is not love at all but a more-than-human pity, directed toward all suffers and therefore unable to make the exclusive love-judgments that Nastasya and Aglaya demand.

In what sense, however, is Daedalus a hero? Though he has no attribute as clear as that of Myshkin, Joyce's *Portrait* shows him moving toward the realization of his special fate. By the end of the book he has rejected all existential choices except that of being an artist. But this choice is not on a par with choosing love, the priesthood, patriotism. It means a fatal break with these. 'Silence, exile, cunning' is Stephen's motto henceforth. To be an artist has become a special fate involving the severance of familiar human ties. It may not have been so always; it could be argued that Stephen's act does not reflect more than an unfortunate historical situation, one that forces the artist into exile. Even so, at this point in history, whether it has passed today or not, the artist is often the form that the heroic takes. Like heroes of old Stephen moves from a matriarchal realm (family, church, Ireland) to the patriarchal aegis: 'Old father, old artificer, stand me now and ever in good stead.' New heroes may arise with the opposite trajectory.

Something of course remains dubious about Stephen. The hero is always a problem. Especially the realistic hero not separated from us by signs or status: we cannot escape double thoughts, and we try to bring him to our level by moralism and psychology. Nor can the hero himself escape them: he differs from his royal prototypes by being not only a problem to others but also to himself. His destiny may lift him beyond our final judgment, but he is not beyond self-judgment. In the *Brothers Karamazov*, Zossima, instead of adjudicating the case brought to him by Dmitri and his father, bows down before Dmitri. The novel begins in a withdrawing from, and leads into a miscarriage of, judgment. Yet Dmitri, like all Dostoevsky's characters, deeply and incessantly judges himself. Stephen, likewise, is quite self-critical. The hero is not abstracted from all judgment or in all respects. Joyce does, however, suggest a limit beyond which we should not go – unless we criticize his hero's daimon in the light of a religious concept. So a Christian might judge Achilles adversely as part of a world which still connects divinity and great wrath. Yet is not any religious criticism tantamount to setting up one daimon against another? Achilles gives way to Myshkin and a new fatality.

Impersonality in art can allow illicit sympathies or evade the problem of judgment. This is the threat of passivity, the opiate acceptance of monstrous fact secreted in novel or movie. It is the very thing that caused us to raise the question of the modern novelist who is (to quote Virginia Woolf once more) 'terribly exposed to life.' Yet confusion of distance – or, to speak less pejoratively, twofold vision – though often found together with impersonal or ironic fiction, is also a separate phenomenon, as the case of Myshkin shows. It is joined to impersonal narration not as an effect to its cause but as one method of self-generated distancing to another. They are both responses to a common problem, a serious contemporary exigency of realism.

When empathy becomes conventional, and the new or alien loses its aureole of sacred danger, it is increasingly difficult to admit transcendent personality or real difference. But art retains its power of making room for the strange, the different, and even the divine. It is the familiar world that must now be saved – from familiarity. Only in this light does impersonal narration find its reason. The author, staying within realism, keeps from too easy an intimacy with creation. The body of the world, the body of other persons, is a strange fact; their thoughts are a mystery; every relation includes shock and unveilings. The impersonal mode is clearly an effort at distance, one of many. It is an effort to hold back – by placing true imaginative obstacles before – the leveling and inquisitive mind. James obstacles himself; he refuses simply to know. Every mind tends to be viewed through another, and the desire to know positively (and can even the artist escape it?) is always presented as a vampirish act. A great novel does not breed familiarity; a bad novel is simply one that betrays the mystery, rapes the past, and lets us possess too quickly another person or mind.

Chapter 10

Literature High and Low:
The Case of the Mystery Story

The terms reversal (*peripeteia*) and recognition (*anagnorisis*) are well known. They name, according to Aristotle, the essential ingredients of complex plots in tragedy. Reversal he defines as a change which makes the action veer in a different direction to that expected, and he refers us to the messenger from Corinth who comes to cheer Oedipus and eventually produces the recognition leading to an opposite result. Recognition is often linked to this kind of reversal, and is defined as a change from ignorance to knowledge. 'Then once more I must bring what is dark to light,' Oedipus says in the prologue of the play – and does exactly that, however unforeseen to him the result. In most detective stories, clearly, there is both a reversal and a recognition, but they are not linked as powerfully as in tragedy. The reversal in detective stories is more like an unmasking; and the recognition that takes place when the mask falls is not prepared for by dramatic irony. It is a belated, almost last minute affair, subordinating the reader's intelligence to such hero–detectives as Ross Macdonald's Archer, who is no Apollo, but who does roam the California scene with cleansing or catalyzing effect.

I wish, however, to draw attention to a third term, left obscure in the *Poetics*. Aristotle calls it *tò pathos*, 'The Suffering,' or as Butcher translates it, the 'Scene of Suffering.' *Tò pathos*, he says – and it is all he says – 'is a destructive or painful action, such as death on the stage, bodily agony, wounds and the like.'[1]

Aristotle is probably referring to what happens at the conclusion of *Oedipus Rex*, though chiefly offstage: the suicide of Jocasta and self-blinding of Oedipus. Or to the exhibition of the mangled head of Pentheus by his deluded mother, in Euripides' *Bacchae*. He may also be thinking of the premise on which the tragic plot is built, the blood deed from which all consequences flow, and which, though premised rather than shown, is the real point of reference.[2] I wish to suggest that some such 'heart of darkness' scene, some such *pathos*, is the relentless center or focus of detective fiction, and that recognition and reversal are merely paths toward it – techniques which seek to evoke it as strongly and visually as possible.

I don't mean that we must have the scene of suffering – the actual murder, mutilation, or whatever – exhibited to us. In *The Chill*, and in Ross Macdonald's novels generally, violence is as offstage as in *Oedipus Rex*. (The real violence, in any case, is perpetrated on the psyche.) But to solve a crime in detective stories means to give it an exact location: to pinpoint not merely the murderer and his motives but also the very place, the room, the ingenious or brutal circumstance. We want not only proof but, like Othello, ocular proof. Crime induces a perverse kind of epiphany: it marks the spot, or curses it, or invests it with enough meaning to separate it from the ordinary space–time continuum. Thus, though a Robbe-Grillet may remove the scene of pathos, our eyes nervously inspect all those graphic details which continue to evoke the detective story's lust for evidence.

The example of Robbe-Grillet – I want to return to it later – suggests that sophisticated art is closer to being an antimystery rather than a mystery. It limits, even while expressing, this passion for ocular proof. Take the medieval carol, "Lully, lulley," and regard how carefully it frames the heart of darkness scene, how with a zooming motion at once tactful and satisfyingly ritual, it approaches a central mystery:

> Lully, lulley,
> The faucon hath born my mak away
>
> He bare him up, he bare him down,
> He bare him into an orchard brown.
>
> In that orchard there was an halle
> Which was hanged with purpill and pall.
>
> And in that hall there was a bed,
> It was hanged with gold so red.
>
> And in that bed there lith a knight,
> His wounds bleeding day and night.
>
> By that bed side kneleth a may,
> And she wepeth both night and day.
>
> And by that bed side there stondeth a stone,
> Corpus Christi wreten thereon.

Here we have a scene of pathos, 'death on the stage, bodily agony, wounds and the like,' but in the form of picture-and-inscription, a still-life we can contemplate without fear. It is a gentle falcon, even if it be a visionary one, that lifts us in this ballad from the ordinary world into that of romance. This is no bird of prey attracted to battlefield carnage. And though the heart of the romance is dark enough, it is also comforting rather than frightening because interpreted by the inscription. We do not have to overcome an arresting moment of pity or fear, we do not even have to ask, as in the Parsifal legends, 'What does this mean?' in order to redeem the strange sight. Its redeeming virtue is made clear to everyone borne away on this ritual trip.

The relation of the ballad to the modern mystery story is a complicated one; and my purpose here is not historical genealogy. The ballad revival had its influence not only on the gothic novel with its mystifications but also on the tension between brevity and elaboration in Melville's *Billy Budd*, the tales of Henry James, and the Gaucho stories of Borges. The modern elliptical ballad as well as the 'novel turned tale'[3] qualify the element of mystery in a definably new, even generic way.

Consider Wordsworth's 'The Thorn,' first published in a collection called *Lyrical Ballads* (1798). The movement of this ballad is so slow, the dramatic fact so attenuated, that we begin to sense the possibility of a plotless story. A line of descent could easily be established between pseudonarratives like 'The Thorn,' which converge obsessively on an ocular center of uncertain interest (has a crime been committed near the thorn, or is the crime an illusion to stimulate crude imaginations?) and lyrical movies like Antonioni's *Blow Up* or Resnais's *Marienbad*. The center they scan is an absence; the darkness they illumine has no heart. There is pathos here but no defined scene of pathos. Instead of a whodunit we get a whodonut, a story with a hole in it.[4]

Wordsworth's poem begins and ends with a thornbush seen by the poet

> 'on the ridge of Quantock Hill, on a stormy day, a thorn which I had often passed in calm and bright weather without noticing it. I said to myself, 'Cannot I by some invention do as much to make this Thorn permanently an impressive object as the storm has made it to my eyes at this moment?'

The narrator's eye, therefore, remains on the thorn, or the thorn (if you wish) in his eye: as always in Wordsworth the path from thing to meaning via an act of imaginative perception (an 'invention') is fully, almost painfully respected. Though consciousness moves toward what it fears to find, a scene of ballad sorrow and bloodiness, it never actually presents that beautiful and ominous 'still' which the Corpus Christi poem composes for us. The corpse has vanished and will not be found. The strange spot is not approached on the wings of a falcon, nor does it ever become a burning bush. Instead we approach it from within a peculiar consciousness, whose repetitive, quasi-ritual stepping from one object to another, from thorn to pond to hill of moss, as well as spurts of topographical precision – 'And to the left, three yards beyond,/You see a little muddy pond' – suggests we are behind the camera-eye of a mad movie maker, or . . . on the way to Robbe-Grillet.

But what exactly are we on the way to? Robbe-Grillet, after hints in Henry James, Gide, Faulkner, and Camus, has killed the scene of pathos. We all know that a corpse implies a story; yet Robbe-Grillet's contention that a story kills, that a story is a corpse, may be news for the novel. In his fiction the statement 'He has a past' is equivalent to 'He is doomed' or 'It is written.' So Oedipus, or a Robbe-Grillet hero, is safe as long as he has no past. So the detective in *The Erasers* commits the crime he is sent to solve: he enacts the prefigurative or formalistic force of traditional story-making which insists on its corpse or scene of suffering. If, moreover, we identify that scene of suffering with what Freud calls the primal scene – the 'mystery' of lovemaking which the child stumbles on – then we also understand why Robbe-Grillet is opposed to character or plot based on a psychoanalytic model. For him Freudianism is simply another form of mystery religion, one which insists on its myth of depth and hidden scene of passion. Robbe-Grillet formulates, therefore, what might be called the modern script-tease, of which Antonioni's *Blow Up* and *L'Avventura*, Bergman's *A Passion*, and Norman Mailer's *Maidstone*,[5] are disparate examples. What they share is the perplexing absence of *tò pathos*: one definitively visualized scene to which everything else might be referred.

I have brought you, safely I hope, from ancient to modern mystery stories by following the fortunes of the scene of pathos. But one comment should be added concerning this scene, and its structure. Comparing the scene of suffering with Freud's primal scene we gain a clue as to why it is able to motivate entire novels or plays.

It resembles, first of all, a highly condensed, supersemantic event like riddle, oracle, or mime. Now whether or not the power of such scenes is linked to our stumbling as innocents on sexual secrets – on seeing or overhearing that riddling mime[6] – it is clear that life is always in some way too fast for us, that it is a spectacle we can't interpret or a dumbshow difficult to word. The detective novel allows us to catch up a little by involving us in the interpretation of a mystery that seems at first to have no direct bearing on our life. We soon realize, of course, that 'mystery' means that something is happening too fast to be spotted. We are made to experience a consciousness (like Oedipa's in Thomas Pynchon's *Crying of Lot 49*) always behind and running; vulnerable therefore, perhaps imposed on. But we are also allowed to triumph (unlike Oedipa) over passivity when the detective effects a catharsis or purgation of consciousness, and sweeps away all the false leads planted in the course of the novel.

No wonder the detective's reconstitution of the scene of pathos has something phantasmagoric about it. So quick that it is always 'out of sight,' the primal scene's existence, real or imagined, can only be mediated by a fabulous structure in which coincidence and convergence play a determining role. Time and space condense in strange ways, like language itself, and produce absurdly packed puns of fate. What is a clue, for instance, but a symbolic or condensed corpse, a living trace or materialized shadow? It shrinks space into place (furniture, and so forth) exactly as a bullet potentially shrinks or sensitizes time. The underdetermined or quasi-invisible becomes, by a reversal, so overdetermined and sharply visible that it is once again hard on the eyes. Bullet, clue, and pun have a comparable phenomenological shape: they are as magical in their power to heighten or oppress imagination as Balzac's 'oriental' device of the fatal skin in *La Peau de Chagrin*.

Is it less oriental, magical, or punning when, in a Ross Macdonald story, the same gun is used for killings 15 years apart or the murders of father and then son take place in the same spot also 15 years apart (*The Underground Man*)? Or when, as in *The Chill*, a man's 'mother' turns out to be his wife? Or when, in Mrs. Radcliffe's *Romance of the Forest*, a marriageable girl happens to be brought to the very castle chamber where her true father was killed while she was still an infant? Recall also the speed with which things move in *Oedipus Rex*, how a messenger who on entry is simply a UPI runner from Corinth proves to be an essential link in Oedipus' past, part of the chain that preserved him from death and for a second death – the consciousness to befall him. There is nothing more fearfully condensed than the self-image Oedipus is left with 'A man who entered his father's bed, wet with his father's blood.'

I am haunted therefore by André Breton's image of 'le revolver aux cheveux blancs.' There has always been something like this greyhaired gun, some magic weapon in the service of superrealism. The movie camera that 'shoots' a scene is the latest version of this venerable gadget. Our reality-hunger, our desire to know the worst and the best, is hard to satisfy. In Sophocles' day it was oracular speech that prowled the streets and intensified the consciousness of men. 'This day will show your birth *and* will destroy you.' Try to imagine how Tiresias's prophecy can come to pass. A lifetime must depend on a moment, or on one traumatic recognition.

Tragedy as an art that makes us remember death is not unlike a memory vestige forcing us back to birth – to the knowledge that man is born of woman rather than self-born, that he is a dependent and mortal being. We become conscious of human time. The detective story, however, allows *place* to turn the tables on *time* by means of its decisive visual reanimations. The detective's successful pursuit of vestiges turns them into quasi-immortal spores; and while this resuscitation of the past partakes of the uncanny,[7] it also neatly confines the deadly deed or its consequences to a determinate, visualized, field.

This observation brings me to a central if puzzling feature of the popular mystery. Its plot idea tends to be stronger than anything the author can make of it. The *surnaturel* is *expliqué*, and the djinni returned to the bottle by a trick. For the mystery story has always been a genre in which appalling facts are made to fit into a rational or realistic pattern. The formula dominating it began to emerge with the first instance of the genre, Horace Walpole's *Castle of Otranto* (1764), which begins when a child who is the heir apparent of a noble house is killed by the enormous helmet of an ancestral statue which buries him alive. After this ghostly opening Walpole's novel moves, like its descendants, from sensation to simplification, from bloody riddle to quasi-solution, embracing as much 'machinery' as possible on the way.

The conservative cast of the mystery story is a puzzle. Born in the Enlightenment, it has not much changed. As mechanical and manipulative as ever, it explains the irrational, after exploiting it, by the latest rational system: Macdonald, for instance, likes to invent characters whose lives have Freudian or Oedipal explanations. In *The Underground Man*, the murderer turns out to be a murderess, a possessive mother with an over-protected son. The real underground man is the underground woman. With a sense of family nightmare as vivid as it is in Walpole, the novel advances inward, from the discovery of the corpse to the frozen psyche of the murderess, Mrs. Snow. All the characters are efficiently, even beautifully sketched, but they are somehow too understandable. They seem to owe as much to formula as the plot itself, which moves deviously yet inexorably toward a solution of the mystery.

A good writer, of course, will make us feel the gap between a mystery and its laying to rest. He will always write in a way that resists the expected ending: not simply to keep us guessing (for, as Edmund Wilson remarked, 'The secret is nothing at all') but to show us more about life – that is, about the way people die while living. What is uncovered is not death but death-in-life.[8]

Perhaps endings (resolutions) are always weaker than beginnings, and not only in the 'explained mystery' kind of detective story. What entropy is involved? Pynchon's *The Crying of Lot 49*, more imaginative than Mailer's *Barbary Shore*, and one of the few genuinely comic treatments in America of the detective story formula, suggests an answer. It is not simply a matter of beginnings and endings but of two sorts of repetition, one of which is magical or uncanny, the other deadly to spirit. Magical repetition releases us into the symbol: a meaning that sustains us while we try to thread secondary causes, trivialities, middles-and-muddles – the rich wastings of life in pre-energy-conserving America. As Pynchon's novel unfolds, we are literally wasted by its riches; those cries and sights; the treasure of trash; and to redeem it all only the notion of anamnesis, which reintroduces the idea of a 'first' cause, counterbalances the drag:

> *She was meant to remember . . .* She touched the edge of its voluptuous field, knowing it would be lovely beyond dreams simply to submit to it; that not gravity's pull, laws of ballistics, feral ravening, promised more delight. She tested it, shivering: I am meant to remember. Each clue that comes is *supposed* to have its own clarity, its fine chances for permanence. But then she wondered if the gemlike 'clues' were only some kind of compensation. To make up for her having lost the direct, epileptic Word, the cry that might abolish the night.

Oedipa's vision of being trapped in an 'excluded middle,' that is, having to desire always some first or last event that would resolve life in terms of something or nothing, meaning or meaninglessness, is reenforced, in the novel's last pages, by a haunting blend of metaphors:

> It was like walking among matrices of a great digital computer, the zeros and ones twinned above, hanging like balanced mobiles right and left, ahead, thick, maybe endless. Behind the hieroglyphic streets there would either be a transcendent meaning, or only the earth . . . either an accommodation reached, in some kind of dignity, with the Angel of Death, or only death and the daily, tedious preparations for it.

If Pynchon's novel ends strongly, it is because it doesn't end. 'It's time to start,' says Genghis Cohen, of the auction, and by a kind of 'honest forgery' (a sustained theme in the book) we find ourselves with Oedipa, absurdly, lyrically, at the threshold of yet another initiation.[9] This outwitting of 'the direct, epileptic Word' is like purifying the imagination of *tò pathos*; for the ritual 'crying' evoked but not rendered at the close of Pynchon's book is simply a version of that 'long-distance' call which perhaps began everything.

The detective story structure – strong beginnings and endings, and a deceptively rich, counterfeit, 'excludable' middle – resembles almost too much that of symbol or trope.[10] Yet the recent temptation of linguistic theorists to collapse narrative structure into this or that kind of metaphoricity becomes counter-productive if it remains blind to the writer's very struggle to outwit the epileptic Word. Take a less symbolic novel than Pynchon's, one in the European tradition of selfconscious realism. In Alfred Andersch's *Efraim's Book* the narrator generates an entire novel by writing *against* a final disclosure.[11] Efraim keeps interpolating new incidents although he knows the book will trump him in the end. A journalist shuttling between London, Berlin, and Rome, he is moved to write a book whose climax is the embarrassing secret he continually delays telling. Efraim is a post-Auschwitz Jew and uprooted intellectual who broods on the human condition, yet the secret obsessing him is simply that his wife is unfaithful. It is as if Andersch wants to reduce the dilemmas of moral existence in postwar Europe to a humiliating sexual disclosure.

We are not deceived by this deflation any more than by the inflated secret of detective stories. I prefer Andersch's novel, a work of political and artistic intelligence, to most mystery stories, but there is much in it that suggests it is in flight from the detective novel mood – from a 'mystery' too great to face. What if Efraim, after Auschwitz, had assumed the role of herodetective and inves-tigated that crime in order to fix its guilt with moral and visual precision? An impossible project: there is no language for it. Efraim thinks he is writing to delay facing a painful ending but he is really writing against the terror and intractability of historical events which the mind cannot resolve or integrate. He chooses a substitute secret, the infidelity of his wife, to keep himself writing, and moving into ordinary life. *Efraim's Book* has no formal ending other than the decision of the writer to accept himself: to accept to survive, in spite of Auschwitz and the defiling reality of posthumous existence.

Most popular mysteries are devoted to solving rather than examining a problem. Their reasonings put reason to sleep, abolish darkness by elucidation, and bury the corpse for good. Few detective novels want the reader to exert his intelligence fully, to find gaps in the plot or the reasoning, to worry about the moral question of fixing the blame. They are exorcisms, stories with happy endings that could be classified with comedy because they settle the unsettling. As to the killer, he is often a bogeyman chosen by the 'finger' of the writer after it has wavered suspensefully between this and that person for the right number of pages.

There exists, of course, a defense of the mystery story as art, whose principal document is Raymond Chandler's *The Simple Art of Murder*. In his moving last pages about the gritty life of the hero-detective, Chandler claims that mystery stories create a serious fictional world:

> It is not a fragrant world, but it is the world you live in, and certain writers with tough minds and a cool spirit of detachment can make very interesting and even amusing patterns out of it . . . In everything that can be called art there is a quality of redemption. It may be pure tragedy, if it is high tragedy, and it may be pity and irony, and it may be the raucous laughter of the strong man. But down these mean streets a man must go who is not himself mean, who is neither tarnished nor afraid . . . He is a common man or he would not go among common people. He has a sense of character, or he would not know his job. He will take no man's money dishonestly and no man's insolence without a due and dispassionate revenge . . . He talks as the man of his age talks – that is, with rude wit, a lively sense for the grotesque, a disgust for sham, and a contempt for pettiness. The story is this man's adventure in search of hidden truth.

Ross Macdonald has also defended the social and psychological importance of the detective story and described it as rooted 'in the popular and literary tradition of the American frontier.' Neither writer puts much emphasis on problem solving, on finding out who killed Roger Ackroyd. But as the claims grow for the honesty, morality, and the authentic American qualities of the detective novel, one cannot overlook the ritual persistence of the problem-solving formula.

Only in France has the eye of the private eye been throughly questioned. I have mentioned Robbe-Grillet; his collaboration with Resnais on films like *Marienbad* is also significant in this respect. What is missing from *Marienbad*, yet endlessly suggested, is *tò pathos*. Nothing moves us so much as when the image on the screen tries to escape at certain points a voice that would pin it down to one room, one bed, one time, one identity. Yet the screen image cannot be 'framed': by remaining a moving picture it defeats our wish to spot the flagrant act, or to have speech and spectacle coincide. The scene of pathos – call it 'Hiroshima,' 'Marienbad,' or 'Auschwitz' – eludes the mind it haunts.

A danger, of course, is the closeness of all this not only to mobile dreaming but also to erotic fantasy. The inbuilt voyeurism of the camera eye makes love and death interchangeable subjects. It cannot distinguish between these 'mysteries' because of the mind's hunger for reality, its restless need to spot, or give the lie to, one more secret. It seeks to arrest the eyes yet is never satisfied with the still or snapshot that reveals all.

After writers like Andersch and Robbe-Grillet, one turns with relief to Ross Macdonald and the naive reality-hunger of American detective fiction. In *The Underground Man* Macdonald keeps entirely within the problem-solving formula but broadens it by providing a great California fire as the background. This fire is an 'ecological crisis' linked more than fortuitously to the cigarillo dropped by Stanley Broadhurst, the murdered son. Stanley belongs to a 'generation whose elders had been poisoned, like the pelicans, with a kind of moral DDT that damaged the lives of their young.' By combining ecological and moral contamination Macdonald creates a double plot that spreads the crime over the California landscape.

California becomes a kind of 'open city' where everyone seems related to everyone else through, ironically, a breakdown in family relations that spawns adolescent gangs and other new groupings. The only personal detail we learn about the detective, Lew Archer, is that his wife has left him, which is what we might expect. Neither cynical nor eccentric, Archer resembles an ombudsman or public defender rather than a tough detective. He doesn't seem to have a private office, often being approached by his clients in public. One might say he doesn't have clients since anyone can engage his moral sympathy.

He is, then, as Chandler prescribed, a catalyst, not a Casanova, who sees more sharply than others do. It is curious how the detective, as a type, is at the same time an ingénue and a man of experience – his reasoning must take evil or criminal motives into account, but through his eyes we enjoy the colors of the familiar world. Like other realistic artists the good crime writer makes the familiar new, but he can do so only under the pressure of extreme situations. It is as if crime alone could make us see again, or imaginatively enough, to enter someone else's life.

Archer is not better than what he sees but rather a knowing part of it. His observations (acute, overdefined, 'Her eyes met me and blurred like cold windows') are those of an isolated, exposed man with a fragmented life. He finds just what he expects, people like himself, reluctantly free or on the run, and others equally lonely but still living within the shrinking embrace of an overprotective family. Yet just because Archer is so mobile and homeless he can bring estranged people together and evoke, as in *The Underground Man*, a consoling myth of community where there is none.

It is a myth only for the time being, perhaps only for the time of the book. Down these polluted freeways goes a man with undimmed vision, cutting through sentimental fog and fiery smog to speak face to face in motel or squalid rental or suburban ranch with Mr. and Mrs. and Young America! Superb in snapshot portraiture of California life, Macdonald gives us a sense of the wildlife flushed out by the smoke, the way people lean on one another when they fear crime and fire. They are neatly described by Archer, who moves among them as erratically as the fire itself.

This panoramic realism has its advantages. It is outward and visual rather than introspective, and so tends to simplify character and motive. There is a terrible urge – in Raymond Chandler even more than in Ross Macdonald – to make the most of gross visual impressions. Hence Moose Molloy in Chandler's *Farewell, My Lovely*, 'a big man but not more than six feet five inches tall and no wider than a beer truck' who 'looked about as inconspicuous as a tarantula on a slice of angel food.' The images flash all around us like guns, though we can't always tell to what end. Their overall aim is to make the world as deceptively conspicuous as Moose Molloy.

The detective (American style) tortures human nature until it reveals itself. People froth or lose their nerve or crumple up: the divine eye of the private eye fixes them until their bodies incriminate them. What can't be seen can't be judged; and even if what we get to see is a nasty array of protective maneuvers and defense mechanisms, the horror of the visible is clearly preferred to what is unknown or invisible.

There are, of course, differences of style among American mystery story writers. Macdonald's characters, for example, are more credible than Chandler's, because they are more ordinary, or less bizarre. Chandler is often on the verge of surrealism, of tragicomic slapstick: the first meeting between Marlowe and Carmen Sternwood in *The Big Sleep* goes immediately as far as a relation can go, short of complicity. The novels of Chandler and Macdonald have, nevertheless, the same basic flaw: the only person in them whose motives remain somewhat mysterious, or exempt from this relentless reduction to overt and vulnerable gestures, is the detective.

Yet Chandler's Marlowe is not really mysterious. Just as in his world punks are punks, old generals old generals, and the small guys remain small guys killed by small-time methods (liquor spiked with cyanide), so a detective is a detective:

'The first time we met I told you I was a detective. Get it through your lovely head. I work at it, lady. I don't play at it.'

When Marlowe is asked why he doesn't marry, he answers 'I don't like policemen's wives.' To marry Mr. Detective means becoming Mrs. Detective. Nothing here is immune from specialization: you can hire killers or peekers or produce sex or sell friendliness. Identities are roles changed from time to time yet as physically clear as warts or fingerprints. Your only hope is not being trapped by your *role* into an *identity*. Once you are marked, or the bite is on you, fun is over. It is, consequently, a clownish world: grotesque, manic, evasive, hilariously sad. Chandleresque is not far from Chaplinesque.

The one apparent superiority of the detective is that although he can be hired, he doesn't care for money (even if he respects its power). We really don't know whether the other characters care for it either, but they are placed in situations where they *must* have it — to make a getaway, for instance — or where it is the visible sign of grace, of their power to dominate and so to survive. What Marlowe says to a beautiful woman who offers him money is puzzlingly accurate: 'You don't owe me anything. I'm paid off.' Puzzling because it is unclear where his real satisfaction comes from. He seems under no compulsion to dominate others and rarely gets pleasure from taking gambles. What is there in it for him? The money is only expense money. We don't even learn who is paying off the inner Marlowe or Archer. Their motives are virtually the only things in these stories that are not visible.

We are forced to assume that the detective is in the service of no one — or of a higher power. Perhaps there is an idealism in these tough tales stronger than the idealisms they are out to destroy.

> I sat down on a pink chair and hoped I wouldn't leave a mark on it. I lit a Camel, blew smoke through my nose and looked at a piece of black shiny metal on a stand. It showed a full, smooth curve with a small fold in it and two protuberances on the curve. I stared at it. Marriott saw me staring at it. 'An interesting bit,' he said negligently. 'I picked it up the other day. Asta Dial's *Spirit of Dawn.*' 'I thought it was Klopstein's *Two Warts on a Fanny*,' I said.

This is merely a sideshow, but behind other and comparable scenes big questions are being raised: of reality, justice, mercy and loyalty. When Lew Archer says, 'I think it started before Nick was born, and that his part is fairly innocent,' he begins to sound theological, especially when he continues, 'I can't promise to get him off the hook entirely. But I hope to prove he's a victim, a patsy' (*The Goodbye Look*).

The moral issues, however, are no more genuinely explored than the murders. They too are corpses — or ghosts that haunt us in the face of intractable situations. So in *The Goodbye Look*, a man picks up an eight-year-old boy and makes a pass at him. Boy shoots man. But the man is the boy's estranged father and the seduction was only an act of sentiment and boozy affection. Grim mistakes of this kind belong to folklore or to high tragedy. The detective story, however, forces them into a strict moralistic pattern or, as in Ross Macdonald, into a psychoanalytic parable with complicated yet resolvable turns.

Since man does not live on tragedy alone, and since the crime story could be considered a folk genre, this may seem no condemnation. There is, however, an exploitative element in all this: our eyes ache to read more, to see more, to know that the one just man (the detective) will succeed – yet when all is finished, nothing is rereadable. Instead of a Jamesian reticence that, at best, chastens the detective urge – our urge to know or penetrate intimately another person's world – the crime novel incites it artificially by a continuous, self-cancelling series of overstatements, drawing us into one false hypothesis or flashy scene after another.

Thus the trouble with the detective novel is not that it is moral but that it is moralistic; not that it is popular but that it is stylized; not that it lacks realism but that it picks up the latest realism and exploits it. A voracious formalism dooms it to seem unreal, however 'real' the world it describes. In fact, as in a B movie, we value less the driving plot than moments of lyricism and grotesquerie that creep into it: moments that detach themselves from the machined narrative. Macdonald's California fire affects us less because of its damage to the ecology than because it brings characters into the open. It has no necessary relation to the plot, and assumes a life of its own. The fire mocks the ambitions of this kind of novel: it seems to defy manipulation.

Crime fiction today seems to be trying to change its skin and transform itself (on the Chandler pattern) into picaresque American morality tales. But its second skin is like the first. It cannot get over its love-hate for the mechanical and the manipulative. Even mysteries that do not have a Frankensteinian monster or superintelligent criminal radiate a pretechnological chill. The form trusts too much in reason; its very success opens to us the glimpse of a mechanized world, whether controlled by God or Dr. No or the Angel of the Odd.

When we read a popular crimi we do not think of it as great art but rather as 'interesting' art. And our interest, especially in the hard-boiled tale of American vintage, has to do more with its social, or sociological, than with its realistic implications. I don't believe for a moment that Chandler and Macdonald tell it like it is, but perhaps they reveal in an important way why they can't tell it like it is. The American 'realist in murder,' says Chandler, has purged the guilty vicarage, exiled the amateurs, thrown out Lord Peter Wimsey *cum* chickenwing-gnawing debutantes. We therefore go to the American tale expecting a naked realism. What do we find, however? A vision that remains as before, a mixture of sophisticated and puerile elements.

The American hero-detective is not what Chandler claims he is, 'a complete man.' He starts with death, it is true; he seems to stand beyond desire and regret. Yet the one thing the hardboiled detective fears, with a gamblerlike fascination, is being played for a *sucker*. In Hammett's *Maltese Falcon* the murder of Miles, who trusted Miss Wonderly, begins the action; Spade's rejection of Brigid O'Shaugnessy completes it. To gamble on Brigid is like gambling that love exists, or that there is, somewhere, a genuine Falcon. Spade draws back: 'I won't play the sap for you.'

No wonder this type of story is full of tough baby-talk. So Archer in *The Chill*:

'No more guns for you,' I said.
No more anything, Letitia.

Taking the gun from Letitia, at the end of *The Chill*, is like denying a baby its candy. It seems a 'castration' of the woman, which turns her into a child once more.

In Ross Macdonald's novels the chief victim is usually a child who needs protection from the father or society and gets it from Momma as overprotection – which is equally fatal. Enter the dick who tries to save the child and purge the Momma. Children are always shown as so imprisoned by the grown-up world that they can't deal with things as they are; and so the child remains a 'sucker.' There is often little difference between family and police in this respect. The psychiatrist is another overprotector. 'They brought me to Dr. Smitheram,' Nick says bitterly in *The Goodbye Look*, 'and . . . I've been with him ever since. I wish I'd gone to the police in the first place.' The detective alone is exempt from ties of blood or vested interest, and so can expose what must be exposed.

Both the arrested development of the detective story and its popularity seem to me related to its image of the way people live in 'civilized' society – a just image on the whole. For we all know something is badly wrong with the way society or the family protects people. The world of the detective novel is full of vulnerable characters on the one hand, and of overprotected ones on the other. Macdonald complicates the issue by emphasizing the wrong done to children, and especially to their psyches. Dolly in *The Chill*, Nick Chalmers in *The Goodbye Look*, and Susan Crandall in *The Underground Man* are as much victims of what Freud calls family romance (that is, family nightmare) as of society. We don't know what to protest, and sympathize with the adolescents in *The Underground Man* who kidnap a young boy to prevent him from being sacrificed to the grown-up world.

Yet 'protective custody' doesn't work. In *The Chill*, relations between Roy and Letitia Bradshaw are a classic and terrible instance of the man being forced to remain a man-boy as the price of making it. Roy, the social climber, marries a rich woman who can send him to Harvard and free him from class bondage. But the woman is old enough to be his mother and they live together officially as mother and son while she kills off younger women to whom her 'child' is attracted.

Protection, such novels seem to imply, is always bought; and much of the price one pays for it is hidden. Macdonald tends to give a psychological and Chandler a sociological interpretation of this. Chandler is strongly concerned with the need for a just system of protection and the inadequacy of modern institutions to provide it. He indulges, like so many other crime writers, in conventional woman hating, but suggests at the same time that women become bitches because they are overprotected. Helen Grayle, in *Farewell, My Lovely*, is the exemplary victim who (like the Sternwood sisters in *The Big Sleep*) is allowed to get some revenge on her 'protectors' before she is caught. Yet Chandler often lets his women criminals escape, knowing sadly or bitterly that they'll be trapped by the system in the end.

To avoid being a sucker and to expose a crisis in the protective institutions of society are psychological and social themes that are not peculiar to the American detective novel. They have prevailed since chivalric Romance invented the distressed damsel and her wandering knight. But the precise kinds of family breakup, together with new and menacing groups (similar to crime syndicates) which the detective is pitted against, give crime novels a modern American tone. That the detective is a *private* sleuth defines, moreover, his character as well as his profession, and makes him the heir to a popular American myth – he is the latest of the uncooptable heroes.

Yet detective stories remain schizophrenic. Their rhythm of surprising reversals – from casual to crucial or from laconic detail to essential clue – is a factor. The deepest reversals involve, of course, feelings about the blood tie. As in Greek tragedy *pathos* is strongest when there is death in the family. The thrill of a 'thriller' is surely akin to the fear that the murderer will prove to be not an outsider but someone there all the time, someone we know only too well – perhaps a blood relation.[12]

In Macdonald's fiction human relations tend to polarize: they are either quasi-incestuous (Roy and Letitia Bradshaw in *The Chill*) or markedly exogamous, exhibiting that inclination to strangers so characteristic of the hero-detective. It is as if our kinship system had suffered a crazy split. There seems to be no mean between the oppressive family ('I felt . . . as if everything in the room was still going on, using up space and air. I was struck by the thought that Chalmers, with family history breathing down his neck, may have felt smothered and cramped most of the time') and the freewheeling detective. Nothing lies between the family and the loner but a no man's land of dangerous communes: virile fraternities, like criminal mobs or the police, which are literally based on blood.

It is, then, an exceptional moment when we find Lew Archer lingering with

Stanley Broadhurst's widow and her young son, at the end of *The Underground Man*. For one moment the family exists and the detective is the father. The woman touches him lightly, intimately. It ends there, on that caress, which already has distance and regret in it. We must soon return, like the detective, to a world of false fathers and disabled mothers, to children as exposed as Oedipus or Billy Budd, and to a continuing search for manifest justice. 'O city, city!' (*Oedipus Rex*).

Notes

1. S. H. Butcher, ed. and trans., *Aristotle's Theory of Poetry and Fine Art*, 4th ed., XI.6 (1452b 9–13). There is a second brief mention at XIV.4 (1453b 17–22).
2. See Gerald Else, *Aristotle's Poetics* (Cambridge, MA, 1967), pp. 356–58.
3. See Jacques Barzun, 'The Novel Turns Tale,' *Mosaic* 4 (1971): 33–40.
4. The elliptical 'cuts' of Eliot's *The Wasteland* often produce a similar effect. Ellipsis joined to the technical principle of montage (in Eisenstein's conception) consolidate the international style we are describing.
5. *Maidstone* is a blatantly eclectic script-tease: it flirts with crime, sexploitation, politics, and film about film. Its plot consists of a wager by Norman T. Kingsley that the actors in the film will invent that scene of passion, he, the director, cannot or will not invent – that they will kill the King, that is, the director, that is, Norman.
6. For a straight psychoanalytic interpretation, see Marie Buonoparte, 'The Murder in the Rue Morgue,' *Psychoanalytic Quarterly* 4 (1935): 259–93; G. Pederson-Krag, 'Detective Stories and the Primal Scene,' *Psychoanalytic Quarterly* 18 (1949): 207–14; and, especially, Charles Rycroft, 'The Analysis of a Detective Story' (1957) reprinted in his *Imagination and Reality* (London, 1968). I emphasize in what follows the eye rather than the cry; but, as in Wordsworth's ballad, there is often something ejaculative or quasi-inarticulate (a 'tongue-tie,' to use Melville's phrase in *Billy Budd*) accompanying.
7. See Freud's 'The 'Uncanny'' (1919). His analysis of repetition, in relation to (ambivalent) reanimation may prove essential to any psychoesthetic theory of narrative. This may also be the point to introduce thematics, especially the thematics of the genius loci: animism, ghosts, ancestor consciousness, quasi-supernatural hauntings of particular places. Freud connects them either with memories of an intra-uterine (oceanic) state or with the later illusion of 'omnipotence of consciousness.' In Poe, one might speculate, the mystery story is intra-uterine gothic while the detective story is omnipotence-of-consciousness modern. See also note 8.
8. This almost inverts the sense of the gothic novel which Poe transformed into a modern tale of detection by dividing its mystery part from its rationalizing part. The mystery story, as he develops it, deals mainly with *vestiges* that intimate someone's *life-in-death*, and he exploits the horror of that thought. His detective stories tend to sublimate this theme of the 'living dead' by demystifying vestiges as clues: signs of

(and for) a persistent or mad or 'omnipotent' consciousness. Frederic Jameson's 'On Raymond Chandler,' *Southern Review* 6 (1970): 624–50, gives an interesting account of how the 'formal distraction' of the detective quest leads into genuine revelations of death-in-life.

9. Sterne's *Tristram Shandy* may be the original of this comic anamnesis which cannot begin (find the true starting point) and so cannot end.
10. See 'The Voice of the Shuttle' in this *Reader*.
11. Andersch is a distinguished German journalist and man of letters who has written several novels and was one of the original members of the famous postwar association of writers called 'Group '47.'
12. Charles Brockden Brown's *Wieland* (1797) remains the classic instance of a pattern which recalls Freud's understanding of family ambivalences.

Chapter 11

Romanticism and Anti-Self-Consciousness

The dejection afflicting John Stuart Mill in his twentieth year was alleviated by two important events. He read Wordsworth, and he discovered for himself a view of life resembling the 'anti-self-consciousness theory' of Carlyle. Mill describes this strangely named theory in his *Autobiography*:

> Ask yourself whether you are happy, and you cease to be so. The only chance is to treat, not happiness, but some end external to it as the purpose of life. Let your self-consciousness, your scrutiny, your self-interrogation exhaust themselves on that.[1]

It is not surprising that Wordsworth's poetry should also have served to protect Mill from the morbidity of his intellect. Like many Romantics, Wordsworth had passed through a depression clearly linked to the ravage of self-consciousness and the 'strong disease' of self-analysis.[2] Book 11 of the *Prelude*, Chapter 5 of Mill's *Autobiography*, Carlyle's *Sartor Resartus*, and other great confessional works of the Romantic period show how crucial these maladies are for the adolescent mind. Endemic, perhaps, to every stage of life, they especially affect the transition from adolescence to maturity; and it is interesting to observe how man's attention has shifted from the fact of death and its rites of passage, to these trials in what Keats called 'the Chamber of Maiden-Thought' and, more recently still, to the perils of childhood. We can say, taking a metaphor from Donne, that 'streights, and none but streights' are ways to whatever changes the mind must undergo, and that it is the Romantics who first explored the dangerous passageways of maturation.

Two trials or perils of the soul deserve special mention. We learn that every increase in consciousness is accompanied by an increase in self-consciousness, and that analysis can easily become a passion that 'murders to dissect.'[3] These difficulties of thought in its strength question the ideal of absolute lucidity. The issue is raised of whether there exist what might be called *remedia intellectus*: remedies for the corrosive power of analysis and the fixated self-consciousness.

There is one remedy of great importance which is almost coterminous with art itself in the Romantic period. This remedy differs from certain traditional proposals linked to the religious control of the intellect – the wild, living intellect of man, as Newman calls it in his *Apologia*.[4] A particularly Romantic remedy, it is nonlimiting with respect to the mind. It seeks to draw the antidote to self-consciousness from consciousness itself. A way is to be found not to escape from or limit knowledge, but to convert it into an energy finer than intellectual. It is some such thought that makes Wordsworth in the preface to *Lyrical Ballads* describe poetry as the 'breath and finer spirit of all knowledge,' able to carry sensation into the midst of the most abstract or remotest objects of science. A more absolute figure for this cure, which is, strictly speaking, less a cure than a paradoxical faith, is given by Kleist: 'Paradise is locked . . . yet to return to the state of innocence we must eat once more of the tree of knowledge.' It is not by accident Kleist is quoted by Adrian at a significant point in Mann's *Doktor Faustus*, which is *the* novel about self-consciousness and its relation to art.

This idea of a return, via knowledge, to naïveté – to a second naïveté – is a commonplace among the German Romantics. Yet its presence is perhaps more exciting, because suitably oblique, among the English and French Romantics. A. O. Lovejoy, of course, in his famous essay on the 'Discrimination of Romanticisms' (1924), questions the possibility of unifying the various national movements. He rightly points out that the German Romantics insist on an art that rises from the plenitude of consciousness to absorb progressively the most sophisticated as well as the most naïve experience. But his claim that English Romanticism is marked by a more primitivistic 'return to nature' is weakened by his use of second-rate poetry and isolated passages. One can show that the practice of the greater English Romantics is involved with a problematical self-consciousness similar to that of the Germans and that, in the main, no primitivism or 'sacrifice of intellect' is found. I do not mean to deny the obvious, that there are primitivistic passages in Chateaubriand and even Words-worth, but the primary tendency should be distinguished from errors and epiphenomena. The desire of the Romantics is perhaps for what Blake calls 'organized innocence,' but never for a mere return to the state of nature. The German Romantics, however, for a reason mentioned later and because of a contemporaneous philosophical tradition centering on the relations between consciousness and consciousness of self (Fichte, Schelling, Hegel), gained in some respects a clearer though not more fruitful understanding of the problem. I cannot consider in detail the case of French Romanticism. But Shelley's visionary despair, Keats's understanding of the poetical character, and Blake's doctrine of the contraries reveal that self-consciousness cannot be overcome; and the very desire to overcome it, which poetry and imagination encourage, is part of a vital, dialectical movement of soul-making.

The link between consciousness and self-consciousness, or knowledge and guilt, is already expressed in the story of the expulsion from Eden. Having tasted knowledge, man realizes his nakedness, his sheer separateness of self. I have quoted Kleist's reflection; and Hegel, in his interpretation of the Fall, argues that the way back to Eden is via contraries: the naïvely sensuous mind must pass through separation and selfhood to become spiritually perfect. It is the destiny of consciousness or, as the English Romantics would have said, of imagination, to separate from nature so that it can finally transcend not only nature but also its own lesser forms. Hegel in his *Logic* puts it as follows:

> The first reflection of awakened consciousness in men told them they were naked . . . The hour that man leaves the path of mere natural being marks the difference between him, a self-conscious agent, and the natural world. The spiritual is distinguished from the natural . . . in that it does not continue a mere stream of tendency, but sunders itself to self-realization. But this position of severed life has in its turn to be overcome, and the spirit must, by its own act, achieve concord once more . . . The principle of restoration is found in thought, and thought only: the hand that inflicts the wound is also the hand that heals it.[5]

The last sentence states unequivocally where the remedy lies. Hegel, however, does not honor the fact that the meaning he derives from the Fall was originally in the form of myth. And the attempt to think mythically is itself part of a crucial defence against the self-conscious intellect. Bergson in *The Two Sources of Morality and Religion* sees both myth and religion as product of an intellectual instinct created by nature itself to oppose the analytic intellect, to preserve human spontaneities despite the hesitant and complicated mind.[6] Whether myth-making is still possible, whether the mind can find an unselfconscious medium for itself or maintain something of the interacting unity of self and life, is a central concern of the Romantic poets.

Romantic art as myth-making has been discussed convincingly in recent years, and Friedrich Schlegel's call in 'Rede über die Mythologie' (1800) for a modern mythology is well known. The question of the renewal of myth is, nevertheless, a rather special response to the larger perplexities of reflective thought. 'The poet,' says Wallace Stevens in 'Adagia,' 'represents the mind in the act of defending us against itself.' Starting with the Romantics this act is clearly focussed, and poetry begins to be valued in contradistinction to directly analytic or purely conceptual modes of thought. The intelligence is seen as a perverse though necessary specialization of the whole soul of man, and art as a means to resist the intelligence intelligently.

It must be admitted, at the same time, that the Romantic themselves do not give (in their conceptual moments) an adequate definition of the function of art. Their criterion of pleasure or expressive emotion leads to some kind of art for art's sake formula, or to the sentimentalism which John Stuart Mill still shared and which marks the shift in sensibility from Neoclassic to Romantic. That Mill wept over the memoirs of Marmontel and felt his selfhood lightened by this evidence of his ability to feel, or that Lamartine saw the life of the poet as 'tears and love,' suggests that the *larmoyant* vein of the later eighteenth century persisted for some time but also helped, when tears or even joy were translated into theory, to falsify the Romantic achievement and make Irving Babbitt's criticism possible.

The art of the Romantics, on the other hand, is often in advance of even their best thoughts. Neither a mere increase in sensibility nor a mere widening of self-knowledge constitutes its purpose. The Romantic poets do not exalt consciousness per se. They have recognized it as a kind of death-in-life, as the product of a division in the self. A mind that acknowledges the existence or past existence of immediate life knows that its present strength is based on a separation from that life. A creative mind desires not mere increase of knowledge, but 'knowledge not purchased by the loss of power' (*The Prelude*, Book 5). Life, says Ruskin, is the only wealth; yet childhood, or certain irrevocable moments, confront the poet sharply and give him the sense of having purchased with death the life of the mind. Constructing what Yeats calls an anti-self, or recovering deeply buried experience, the poet seeks a return to 'Unity of Being.' Consciousness is only a middle term, the strait through which everything must pass; and the artist plots to have everything pass through whole, without sacrifice to abstraction.

One of the themes which best expresses this perilous nature of consciousness, and has haunted literature since the Romantic period, is that of the Solitary, or Wandering Jew. He may appear as Cain, Ahasuerus, Ancient Mariner, and even Faust. He also resembles the later (and more static) figures of Tithonus, Gerontion, and *poète maudit*. These solitaries are separated from life in the midst of life, yet cannot die. They are doomed to live a middle or purgatorial existence which is neither life nor death, and as their knowledge increases so does their solitude.[7] It is, ultimately, consciousness that alienates them from life and imposes the burden of a self which religion or death or a return to the state of nature might dissolve. Yet their heroism, or else their doom, is not to obtain this release. Rebels against God, like Cain, and men of God, like Vigny's Moses, are equally denied 'le sommeil de la terre' and are shown to suffer the same despair, namely, 'the self . . . whose worm dieth not, and whose fire is not quenched' (Kierkegaard). And in Coleridge's Mariner, as in Conrad's Marlow, the figure of the wanderer approaches that of the poet. Both are storytellers who resubmit themselves to temporality and are compelled to repeat their experiences in the purgatorial form of words. Yeats, deeply affected by the theme of the Wandering Jew, records a marvelous comment of Mme. Blavatsky's: 'I write, write, write, as the Wandering Jew walks walks, walks.'

The Solitary may also be said to create his own, peculiarly Romantic genre of poetry. In 'Tintern Abbey,' or 'X' Revisited, the poet looks back at a transcended stage and comes to grip with the fact of self-alienation. The retrospective movement may be visionary, as often in Hölderlin; or antiquarian, as in Scott; or deeply oblique, as in lyrical ballad and dramatic monologue. In every case, however, there is some confrontation of person with shadow or self with self. The intense lyricism of the Romantics may well be related to this confrontation. For the Romantic 'I' emerges nostalgically when certainty and simplicity of self are lost. In lyric poem it is clearly not the first-person form that moves us (the poem need not be in the first person) but rather the I toward which that I reaches. The very confusion in modern literary theory concerning the fictive I, whether it represents the writer as person or only as persona, may reflect a dialectic inherent in poetry between the relatively self-conscious self and that self within the self which resembles Blake's 'emanation' and Shelley's 'epipsychidion.'

It is true, of course, that this dialectic is found in every age and not restricted to the Romantic. The notion of man (as of history) seems to presuppose that of self-consciousness, and art is not the only major reaction to it. Mircea Eliade, following Nietzsche, has recently linked art to religion by interpreting the latter as originating in a periodic and ritually controlled abolition of the burden of self, or rather of this burden in the form of a nascent historical sense. It is not true, according to Eliade, that primitive man has no sense of history; on the contrary, his sense of it is too acute, he cannot tolerate the weight of responsibility accruing through memory and individuation, and only gradually does religious myth, and especially the Judaeo-Christian revelation, teach him to become a more conscious historical being. The question, therefore, is why the Romantic reaction to the problem of self-consciousness should be in the form of an aggrandizement of art, and why the entire issue should now achieve an urgency and explicitness previously lacking.

The answer requires a distinction between religion and art. This distinction can take a purely historical form. There clearly comes a time when art frees itself from its subordination to religion or religiously inspired myth and continues or even replaces them. This time seems to coincide with what is generally called the Romantic period: the latter, at least, is a good *terminus a quo*. Though every age may find its own means to convert self-consciousness into the larger energy of imagination, in the Romantic period it is primarily art on which this crucial function devolves. Thus, for Blake, all religion is a derivation of the Poetic Genius; and Matthew Arnold is already matter-of-fact rather than prophetic about a new age in which the religious passion is preserved chiefly by poetry. If Romantic poetry appears to the orthodox as misplaced religious feeling ('spilt religion'), to the Romantics themselves it redeems religion.[8]

Yet as soon as poetry is separated from imposed religious or communal ends it becomes as problematic as the individual himself. The question of how art is possible, though post-Romantic in its explicitness, has its origin here, for the artist is caught up in a serious paradox. His art is linked to the autonomous and individual; yet that same art, in the absence of an authoritative myth, must bear the entire weight of having to transcend or ritually limit these tendencies. No wonder the problem of the subjective, the isolated, the individual, grows particularly acute. Subjectivity – even solipsism – becomes the subject of poems which qua poetry seek to transmute it.

This paradox seems to inhere in all the seminal works of the Romantic period. 'Thus my days are passed/In contradiction,' Wordsworth writes sadly at the beginning of *The Prelude*. He cannot decide whether he is fit to be a poet on an epic scale. The great longing is there; the great (objective) theme eludes him. Wordsworth cannot find his theme because he already has it: himself. Yet he knows self-consciousness to be at once necessary and opposed to poetry. It will take him the whole of *The Prelude* to be satisfied *in actu* that he is a poet. His poem, beginning in the vortex of self-consciousness, is carried to epic length in the desire to prove that his former imaginative powers are not dead.

I have already confessed to understanding Coleridge's *Ancient Mariner* as a poem that depicts the soul after its birth to the sense of separate (and segregated) being. In one of the really magical poems in the language, which, generically, converts self-consciousness into imagination, Coleridge describes the travail of a soul passing from self-consciousness to imagination. The slaying of an innocent creature, the horror of stasis, the weight of conscience or of the vertical eye (the sun), the appearance of the theme of deathlessness, and the terrible repetitive process of penitence whereby the wanderer becomes aware through the spirits above and the creatures below of his focal solitude between both – these features point with archetypal force to the burden of selfhood, the straits of solitude, and the compensating plenary imagination that grows inwardly. The poem opens by evoking that rite de passage we call a wedding and which leads to full human communion, but the Mariner's story interposes itself as a reminder of human separateness and of the intellectual love (in Spinoza's sense) made possible by it.

To explore the transition from self-consciousness to imagination and to achieve that transition while exploring it (and so to prove it still possible) is the Romantic purpose I find most crucial. The precariousness of that transition naturally evokes the idea of a journey; and in some later poets, like Rimbaud and Hart Crane, the motif of the journey has actually become a sustained metaphor for the experience of the artist during creation. This journey, of course, does not lead to what is generally called a truth: some final station for the mind. It remains as problematic a crossing as that from death to second life or from exile to redemption. These religious concepts, moreover, are often blended in and remind us that Romantic art has a function analogous to that of religion. The traditional scheme of Eden, Fall, and Redemption merges with the new triad of Nature, Self-Consciousness, and Imagination – the last term in both involving a kind of return to the first.

Yet everything depends on whether it is the right and fruitful return. For the journey beyond self-consciousness is shadowed by cyclicity, by paralysis before the endlessness of introspection, and by the lure of false ultimates. Blake's 'Mental

Traveller,' Browning's 'Childe Roland to The Dark Tower Came,' and Emily Dickinson's 'Our journey had advanced' show these dangers in some of their forms. Nature in its childhood or sensuous radiance (Blake's 'Beulah') exerts an especially deceptive lure. The desire to gain truth, finality, or revelation generates a thousand such enchantments. Mind has its blissful islands as well as its mountains, its deeps, and treacherous crossroads. Depicting these trials by horror and by enchantment, Romanticism is genuinely a rebirth of Romance.

In the years following World War I it became customary to see Classicism and Romanticism as two radically different philosophies of life and to place modernism on the side of the antiromantic. André Malraux defined the classical element in modern art as a 'lucid horror of seduction.' Today it is clear that Romantic art shared that lucidity. Romanticism at its most profound reveals the depth of the enchantments in which we live. We dream, we wake on the cold hillside, and our sole self pursues the dream once more. In the beginning was the dream, and the task of disenchantment never ends.

The nature poetry of the Romantics is a case in point. Far from being an indulgence in dewy moments, it is the exploration of enchanted ground. The Romantic poets, like the Impressionist painters, refuse to 'simplify the ghost' of nature. They begin to look steadfastly at all sensuous experience, penetrating its veils and facing its seductions. Shelley's 'Mont Blanc' is not an enthusiastic nature poem but a spirit-drama in which the poet's mind seeks to release itself from an overwhelming impression and to reaffirm its autonomy vis-à-vis nature. Keats also goes far in respecting illusions without being deluded. His starting-point is the dream of nature fostered by Romance; he agrees to this as consciously as we lie down to sleep. But he intends such dreaming 'beyond self' to unfold its own progressions and to wake into truth. To this end he passes from a gentler to a severer dream-mode: from the romance of *Endymion* to the more austere *Hyperion*. Yet he is forced to give up the *Hyperion* because Saturn, Apollo, and others behave like quest heroes instead of gods. Having stepped beyond romance into a sublimer mode, Keats finds the quest for self-identity elated rather than effaced. It has merely raised itself to a divine level. He cannot reconcile Miltonio sublimity with the utterly human pathos that keeps breaking through. The 'egotistical sublime' remains.

It was Wordsworth, of course, whose poetry Keats had tried to escape by adhering to a less self-centered kind of sublimity. 'Let us have the old Poets, and Robin Hood.' Wordsworth subdued poetry to the theme of nature's role in the growth of the individual mind. The dream of nature, in Wordsworth, does not lead to formal Romance but is an early, developmental step converting the solipsistic into the sympathetic imagination. It entices the brooding soul out of itself, toward nature first, then toward humanity. Wordsworth knew the weight of self-consciousness:

It seemed the very garments that I wore
Preyed on my strength, and stopped the quiet stream
Of self-forgetfulness.

Prelude (1850), 5.294 ff.

The wound of self is healed, however, by 'unconscious intercourse' with a nature 'old as creation.' Nature makes the 'quiet stream' flow on. Wordsworth evokes a type of consciousness more integrated than ordinary consciousness, though deeply dependent on its early – and continuing – life in rural surroundings.[9]

The Romantic emphasis on unconsciousness and organic form is significant in this light. *Unconsciousness* remains an ambiguous term in the Romantic and Victorian periods, referring to a state distinctly other than consciousness or simply to unself-consciousness. The characteristic of right performance, says Carlyle in *Characteristics* (1831), is an unconsciousness – 'the healthy know not of their health, but only the sick.' The term clearly approaches here its alternate meaning of unselfconsciousness, and it is to such statements that Mill must be indebted when he mentions the 'anti-self-consciousness theory' of Carlyle. In America, Thoreau perpetuates the ambiguity. He also prescribes unconsciousness for his sophisticated age and uses the word as an equivalent of vision: 'the absence of the speaker from his speech.' It seems to me that the personal and expressive theory of poetry, ascribed to the Romantics, and the impersonal theory of poetry, claimed in reaction by the moderns, answer to the same problem and are quietly linked by the ambiguity in *unconsciousness*. Both theories value art as thought recreated into feeling or self-consciousness into a more communal power of vision. Yet can the modern poet, whom Schiller called 'sentimental' (reflective) and whom we would describe as alienated, achieve the immediacy of all great verse, whatever its personal or historical dilemma?

This is as crucial a matter today as when Wordsworth and Coleridge wrote *Lyrical Ballads* and Hölderlin pondered the fate of poetry in 'Der Rhein.' Is visionary poetry a thing of the past, or can it coexist with the modern temper? Is it an archaic revelation, or a universal mode springing from every real contact with nature? 'To interest or benefit us,' says a Victorian writer, 'poetry must be reflective, sentimental, subjective; it must accord with the conscious, analytical spirit of present men.'[10] The difficulties surrounding a modern poetry of vision vary with each national literature. In England the loss of 'poesy' is attributed by most Romantics to a historical though not irreversible fact – to the preceding century's infidelity to the line of Chaucer, Spenser, Shakespeare, and Milton. 'Let us have the old Poets, and Robin Hood,' as Keats said. Yet for the German and the French there was no easy return to a tradition deriving its strength from both learned and popular sources. 'How much further along we would be,' Herder remarks, 'if we had used popular beliefs and myths like the British, if our poetry had built upon them as whole-heartedly as Chaucer, Spenser and Shakespeare did.'[11] In the absence of this English kind of literary mediation, the gap between medieval romance and the modern spirit seemed too great. Goethe's *Faust* tried to bridge it, but also, in his *Wilhelm Meister*, anticipated a new type of literature which subsumed the philosophical character of the age and merged myth and irony into a 'progressive' mode. The future belonged to the analytic spirit, to irony, to prose. The death of poetry had certainly occurred to the Romantics in idea, and Hegel's prediction of it was simply the overt expression of their own despair. Against this despair the greater Romantic poets staked their art and often their sanity.

Notes

1. *Autobiography* (1873), chap. 5. Mill says that he had not heard, at the time, Carlyle's theory. The first meeting between the writers took place in 1831; Mill's depression lasted, approximately, from autumn 1826 to autumn 1828. Mill called self-consciousness 'that demon of the men of genius of our time from Wordsworth to Byron, from Goethe to Chateaubriand.' See Wayne Shumaker, *English Auto-biography* (Berkeley and Los Angeles, 1954), chap. 4.

2. Excessive thought as a disease is an open as well as submerged metaphor among the Romantics. There are many hints in Novalis; Schelling pronounces naked reflec-tion (analysis) to be a spiritual sickness of man (*Schellings Sämtliche Werke*, ed. K. F. Schelling [Stuttgart, 1856–61], 2: 13–14); the metaphor is explicit in Carlyle's *Characteristics* (1831) and commonplace by the time that E. S. Dallas in *The Gay Science* (1866) attributes the 'modern disease' to 'excessive civilization and over-strained consciousness.' The *mal du siècle* is not unrelated to the malady we are describing. Goethe's *Die Leiden des Jungen Werthers* (1774) may be seen as its terminus a quo, and Kierkegaard's *Sickness unto Death* (1849) as its noonday point of clarity.

3. Wordsworth, 'The Tables Turned' (1798). For the first peril, see Kierkegaard's *Sickness unto Death*, and Blake: 'The Negation is the Spectre, the Reasoning Power in Man;/This is a false Body, an Incrustation over my Immortal/Spirit, a Selfhood which must be put off & annihilated alway' (*Milton*, Bk. 2). This last quotation, like Wordsworth's 'A reasoning, self-sufficient thing,/An intellectual All-in-All' ('A Poet's Epitaph'), shows the closeness of the two perils. For the second, see also Coleridge: 'All the products of the mere reflective faculty [viz. the 'understanding' contradistinguished from what Coleridge, knowing something of Kant, calls the 'reason'] partook of DEATH' (*Biographia Literaria*, chap. 9): Benjamin Constant's definition of one of the moral maladies of the age as 'the fatigue, the lack of strength, the perpetual analysis that saps the spontaneity of every feeling' (draft preface to *Adolphe*); and Hegel's preface to *The Phenomenology of Mind* (1807). Hegel observes that ordinary analysis leads to a hardening of data, and he attributes this to a

persistence of the ego, whereas his dialectic reveals the true fluency of concepts. Carlyle most apodictically said: 'Had Adam remained in Paradise, there had been no Anatomy and no Metaphysics' (*Characteristics*, 1831).

4. *Apologia Pro Vita Sua* (1864), chap. 5. In the same chapter Newman calls reason 'that universal solvent.' Concerning Victorian remedies for 'this disease/My Self' (Marianne Moore), see also A. Dwight Culler, *The Imperial Intellect* (New Haven, 1955), pp. 234–37.

5. *The Logic of Hegel*, trans. from the *Encyclopedia of the Sciences* by W. Wallace, 2nd ed. (Oxford, 1904), pp. 54–57. The first sentences given here come from passages in the original later than the remainder of the quotation.

6. *Les Deux Sources de la Morale et de la Religion* (1933), chap. 2. Both religion and 'la fonction fabulatrice' are 'une reaction défensive de la nature contre le pouvoir dissolvant de l'intelligence.' (Cf. Newman, cited in note 4.) As Romanticism shades in modernism, a third peril of over-consciousness comes strongly to the fore – that it leads to a Hamlet-like incapacity for action. Bergson, like Kierkegaard, tries to counter this aspect especially.

7. 'I lost the love of heaven above,/I spurned the lust of earth below' (John Clare, 'A Vision'). By this double exile and their final madness, two poets as different as Clare and Hölderlin are joined. See Coleridge's intense realization of man's 'between-ness,' which increases rather than chastens the apocalyptic passion: 'O Nature! I would rather not have been – let that which is to come so soon, come now – for what is all the intermediate space, but sense of utter worthlessness? . . . Man is truly and solely an immortal series of conscious mortalities and inherent Disappoint-ments' (*Inquiring Spirit*, ed. K. Coburn [London, 1951], p. 142). But to ask death instead of life of nature is still to ask for finality, for a quietus: it is the bitter obverse, also met at the beginning Goethe's *Faust*, of the quest for absolute truth.

8. I have omitted here the important role played by the French Revolution. The aggrandizement of art is due in no small measure to the fact that poets like Wordsworth and Blake cannot give up one hope raised by the Revolution – that a terrestrial paradise is possible – yet are eventually forced to give up a second hope – that it can be attained through direct political action. The shift from faith in the reformation of man through the prior reformation of society to that in the prior reformation of man through vision and art has often been noted. The failure of the French Revolution anchors the Romantic movement or is the consolidating rather than primary cause. It closes, perhaps until the advent of Communism, the possibility that politics rather than art should be invested with a passion previously subsumed by religion.

9. Mill, Hazlitt, and Arnold came to approximately the same estimate of Words-worth's poetry. Comparing it to Byron's, they found that the latter had too much fever of self in it to be remedial; they did not want their image cast back at them magnified. Carlyle prefers to compare Goethe and Byron ('Close your Byron, open your Goethe'), yet his point is the same: Goethe retains a strong simplicity in a tormented and divided age, while Byron seems to him a 'spasmodically bellowing self-worshipper.'

10. R. M. Milnes, *Palm Leaves* (London, 1844).

11. *Von Ähnlichkeit der mittlern englischen und deutschen Dichtkunst* (1777). Cf. Louis Cazamian on French Romanticism: 'Le romantisme n'a donc pas été pour la France, comme pour l'Angleterre, un retour facile et naturel à une tradition nationale, selon la pente du tempérament le plus profond.' *Essais en Deux Langues* (Paris, 1938), p. 170.

Chapter 12

Text and Spirit*

> The face-to-face with the text has replaced the face-to-face with God.
> Edmond Jabès, *Le parcours*

Even a casual observer of the worldly scene or of news that besieges ears and eyes and becomes increasingly a confusing talk show with endlessly extemporized sense and nonsense, even you and I, who are that casual observer, cannot fail to notice how often the supernatural turns up as a topic. Let me excerpt a moment close to Christmas 1997. 'In Books, It's Boom Time for Spirits,' runs a headline of 'The Arts' section of *The New York Times* (November 11, 1997). The very next week, this same section, devoted to Robert Gobert's installation piece in the Los Angeles Museum of Contemporary Art, features a Madonna standing on a drainage grate with a cruciform pipe through her belly, which elicits the curious headline 'Religion That's in the Details' (not only entrails) and adds 'A Madonna and Drain Pipe Radiate an Earthy Spirituality.' The number of best-sellers on near-death or out-of-body experiences is well known; spirit raptors proliferate; and the recovered memory syndrome has insinuated not only devastating suspicions about family values but also made stars of obscure people who claim to have lived previous lives as saints, warrior-heroes, and Amazonian queens.

Serious scholars, too, turn from their literary preoccupations to write, as Harold Bloom has done, on *The American Religion* and, with the approach of the millennium, on omens, angels, avatars, and such. Bloom's survey of Christian and heterodox movements since 1800 envisions the year 2000 as the triumph of an unacknowledged, specifically American religion, in which the 'soul stands apart, and something deeper than the soul, the real Me or self or spark, thus is made free to be utterly alone with . . . a free God or God of Freedom' who loves every American with a personal love. Bloom would like to stand aloof, but finds he too is part of this scene – as American as Emerson or Whitman. 'Religious criticism,' he says, 'even if it seeks to banish all nostalgia for belief, still falls into the experience of the spiritual, even as literary criticism cannot avoid the danger of falling into the text.'[1] Although there is nothing new in the antics of hucksters and televangelists, or meeting the Lord in the air (in a spaceship, no less, according to Louis Farrakhan), or weeping statues, or miracles on Broadway

(Tony Kushner, *Angels in America*), or the amazing ease with which both preachers and skinheads claim to have heard the call of God, it is time to reflect on this bullishness in the spiritual market.

Did the mere approach of the year 2000 act as a magnet? My initial thought is that there is enough craziness in traditional religion itself, I mean imaginative, poetic craziness, so that this sort of human circus is unnecessary. At the same time, I agree with William Blake that imagination is religion's birth mother, always trying to free its offspring, the poets, from strictures of doctrine. But then one remembers a different aspect of the spiritual impulse, that it is never entirely free or disinterested. It often breaks through as the compulsive side of those whose disgust with the human condition – with themselves or others or politics – becomes intolerable and who tend to advocate purgative schemes of reform.

To write adequately about spiritual experience – or what is called such – would need the tolerance and comprehensiveness of a William James.[2] Indeed, the task of distinguishing between spirituality and spiritism seems endless. The question of where spirituality is today is also complicated by the increasing predominance of visual texts, particularly movies. How 'spiritual' is a film like *Seven* (1995), written by Andrew Walker? It is one of many staging the city as an evil place that requires purification through a punisher or avenger. Based on the Christian typology of the Seven Deadly Sins, it tracks a murderer's grisly serial killings in pursuit of a spiritual quest. The killer himself imposes the scheme of the Seven Deadly Sins on randomly chosen victims, and the surprise is that, while outwitting the police, he allows himself to be killed at the end as a sacrifice to his own scheme – because he embodies one of those sins. There is no spiritism here of the supernatural kind; but there is a borderline sense of the uncanny, as in so many detective stories, where a fiendish force seems to outmanoeuvre human reason. The rational wins only because the murderer (or author) wants it to, in order to save the concept of motivation. *Seven* cannot be dismissed as the gothic exploitation of religious mania; it is a ghastly hyperbole demonstrating how sinister that mania becomes when the spiritual life runs amuck, when its claim to mark and fight evil is seized by a despairing intensity that leads to flamboyant acts of proclamation.

In general, the detective-story format of looking for clues that do not yield easily to looking, and mock in their cunning character the noisy, clumsy pursuit of the police, points to the need for a different kind of *attention*. In such films, there is a glut – gluttony – of sight that cuts across all attempts to render these moral fables spiritual. Perhaps the spiritual can only be caught at the margin, glimpsed, not focussed on; it evades being incorporated, or fixed as a purely visual event. In *Seven*, there is a short moment in a police station where, quite implausibly, strains of classical music are heard – an allusion, perhaps, to a more striking scene in another film, *The Shawshank Redemption* (1994), in which music of that kind transports the prisoners in the yard to a world they have not known and may never know again. Brushed by the wings of that music they stand still, in their inner space, attentive; then the miraculous notes evaporate into the grim round of their daily existence.

My aim is to cover only one aspect of spiritual experience, that which involves 'listening' to texts. This aspect of spirituality is linked to my previous examples through the quality of attention that texts, canonical or non-cano-nical, foster. In what follows I begin with literature, and the reason is personal, coming both from my training and the fact that Jews are still a text-centered community.

Many have claimed that something read, even as fragmented as a single sentence come upon by chance, has made a radical difference and set them on a new course with spiritual implications. This happened most famously to Augustine; the *tolle lege* ('take up and read') episode from his *Confessions* recalls the magical practice of the *sortes Virgilianae* or *sortes* based on the Bible in which you opened Virgil or the Bible and decided on a course of action by taking the first verse that met your eye as an oracle. The practice survived into Methodism and was known to George Eliot, whose Dinah Morris in *Adam Bede* seeks divine guidance 'by opening the Bible at hazard.'[3] Saul Lieberman, a distinguished scholar of the Talmud, speculated that this sort of divination was also behind the curious notion of *bat kol*, 'daughter [or echo] of the voice [of God],' heard in an era when He was no longer audible, or, as the Bible puts it, when open vision had ceased – the era of postprophetic teachers who between the second century B.C.E. and the fifth C.E. were the founding fathers of orthodox Judaism.[4]

The perplexed soul would go out of the house of study into the street, and words accidentally heard (often Scripture verses) were to be a deliverance, indicating the path to be followed. (To 'follow a *bat kol*,' an expression based on Isaiah 30:21, is mentioned several times in both the Jerusalem and the Babylonian Talmud.) Some of these sounds must have penetrated the scholar's house; but perhaps his devoted attention, his *kavanah*, kept them out. The celestial *bat kol* could also appear in dreams or daydreams. This audism has something desperate about it; it is clear, from such incidents, that 'the spirit blows where it lists,' or that, to cite Bob Dylan, the answer is blowing in the wind.

In order to respect secular experience, to see in it a potential hiding place of the spirit – not unlike the way art after Marcel Duchamp values trashy occasions – we eavesdrop everywhere. Chance disrupts or challenges, as so often in novelistic plots, a potential ethics. The surrealists say that such encounters reveal a *hasard objectif*. Today we don't necessarily consult Virgil or the Scriptures and turn these into a lottery; but the world, the very world from which we seek refuge, still opens to divulge accidental epiphanies. Modern Age spiritism of this kind may have begun with Baudelaire's *Fusées* (Fireworks): they describe a type of trance that parallels a depth experience also yielded by hashish but extends it like a magical varnish over anything and everything, including 'la première phrase venue, si vos yeux tombent sur un livre' (the first-come phrase, if you happen to look into a book).[5] Poetry itself, Baudelaire suggests, is the product of an intelligence lit up by an intoxication of this kind.

Often today, our learned psychedelic adventurers, instead of consulting the *bouche d'ombre* of a sacred volume, mix yoga-like meditational practices with conventional forms of ecstatic prayer and chanting. The act of emerging from a period of concentration, of isolated study or brooding, into the promiscuous clamor of the street or the sad variety of books one admires and cannot make one's own, seems to hide a sensuous need, the wish for a *coup de foudre*, a choice as absolute as Emily Dickinson's

> The soul selects her own society
> Then – shuts the Door –
> To her divine Majority –
> Present no more – [6]

Grace, akin to love, amazes, because it occurs involuntarily among the impossible diversity of human beings with whom one wishes to be intimate. Indeed, as we have also seen with the Branch Davidians or the Jonestown suicides, the need to love or to cleave to a strong, ordering voice, whether that of gurus or the text they claim to embody, is essential to this kind of communal spirituality. Many are deceived when the promise of life, of rebirth, produces its own *rigor mortis*: in Dickinson's words, a closing of the valves of attention 'Like Stone.'[7]

Myself, I have never graduated beyond Fortune Cookies; and even those lost their charm when I opened one and received the all-too-probable message: 'What you have eaten isn't chicken.' But I admit that as a student of literature, and as one who reads a lot, in the canon as well as miscellaneously, there are times when a passage has taken my breath away: when I have been tempted to call the impact of such a text spiritual, and supposed that others would call it such. The first case I will take up is perhaps too good, in that the subject matter is already in the religious realm.

I read Cardinal Newman's *Gerontius* again, a play structured as a viaticum, or ultimate rite of passage. It describes the individual soul passing from the instant of death to the judgment seat. It was not so much Newman's daring conception that held me, as he shows the dying man moving like a somnambulist along that fatal path, accompanied by the voices of the funeral mass and the intercession of orders of angels. What held me was an early moment in this process, when Gerontius expresses his terror: terror of dying, *timor mortis*, but also of God's judgment closing in. Newman places heroism at life's end, as it is overwhelmed by pangs related to the physical agony of death, pangs that contain an intuition of damnation:

> I can no more; for now it comes again
> That sense of ruin, which is worse than pain,
> That masterful negation and collapse
> Of all that makes me man . . .

In this prayerful monologue Gerontius does not address himself to God, Christ, Mary, or other intercessors – until seized once more by a spasm of fear. The comfort of address, of being called or being able to call upon, is removed, as he begins a free fall, dying alone, without steadying hand or voice:

> as though I bent
> Over the dizzy brink
> Of some sheer infinite descent;
> Or worse, as though
> Down, down for ever I was falling through
> The solid framework of created things . . .[8]

Like Gerontius, at that moment, we realize how ordinary life bears us up; so that if the term 'spiritual' can enter appropriately here, it also refers to the gratitude one owes created or material things for their support. The earth generally does not give way; and we trust our body, for a time. There are intimations, however, that this confidence cannot last: at the end of our life, or at the end of days, or indeed at any time in the course of individual existence, we are deserted, a trapdoor opens, the pit yawns. It is then that spirits enter or reenter and the immediate frontier becomes death.

In considering the colorful aspects of a free-floating spirituality as well as one closely linked to religion, I will try to avoid cornering myself into a decisive definition of the phenomenon itself. Like Nathaniel Hawthorne in 'The Celestial Railroad,' I am anxious not to become a Mr. Smooth-it-away. I suggest, then, that we often seize on one event, whether disturbing or exhilarating or both, that cuts across a relatively careless, wasteful, ignorant life. We focus on what was revealed – on what turned us around, not necessarily from bad to good but toward a sense of purpose and identity. The quality of attention so aroused is not necessarily the outcome of a religious exercise: it can involve the act of attention as, in Malebranche's phrase, 'the natural prayer of the soul.' Or there is Keats's wonderful analogy: 'I go among the Fields and catch a glimpse of a stoat or a fieldmouse peeping out of the withered grass – the creature hath a purpose and its eyes are bright with it.'[9]

Readers, poetically inclined, yet also distracted by passages that seem to stand out, must find a way to go where these lead. Such readerly absorption is, I think, becoming rarer, not just because books have multiplied and the World Wide

Web is there to be browsed, but also because film has become a major art form; and film is panoramic, requiring a more diffused as well as exigent attention, one that hypnotizes through a variable zooming and focussing. The tyranny of the eye, the simple pleasure of filmic omnipotence, combines distraction with a faux-semblant of concentration.

Of course, some intensity of the visual has always existed; the use of religious icons or the meditative 'exercises' of Ignatius tell us how important images, inner or outer, have been. Or, as in D. H. Lawrence's 'Bavarian Gentians,' written a few months before his death, the coming darkness renders the visible more visible, counterpart of a kindly light purely and intensely nature's own. The poet calls the dark blue flowers black lamps from Dis, the god of the Underworld. Their burning darkness contrasts with Demeter's pale lamps and acts as the poet's spirit guide or *psychopompos* to the region of the dead.[10]

Yet unless the discipline of reading has first come about, without being routinized by print culture, it is doubtful we can even approach an analysis of spiritual value, at least in our civilization. In many conversion experiences, as William James has shown, terror and turmoil are allayed (or incited and allayed) when a voice is heard uttering Scripture words.[11] Poetry's dense phrases have a parallel effect: they often induce a contemplative mood, asking to be carried longer in the womb of the mind, and do not bring a premature and disenchanting clarity to birth.

Is spirituality, then, linked to the sense of the individual as such being found, or found out? That those affected feel directly called or addressed is probably more important than recognizing whose voice it is or the exact content of the call. A sudden, mysterious utterance outflanks the resistance to being identified or known too well. Is not the oldest – and youngest – game that of hide-and-seek? Shock, surprise, self-consciousness, unanticipated arousals of guilt or joy, even a negative correlative of these, 'Blank misgivings of a Creature/Moving about in worlds not realized'[12] – such radical moments, not always verbal, although demanding a verbal response or a temporal, sustained act of consciousness, may not constitute the spiritual as such or bind it to the ordinary life we lead. Yet they furnish a disruption from which we date a conscious birth.

The individual is always singled out, is always one of three stopped by an Ancient Mariner, transported by a musical phrase, 'looked at' by a work of art, as when the archaic torso of Apollo admonishes Rilke: 'You must change your life.'[13] There is a heightened sense of place or virtual embodiment. The spiritual in those moments approaches ecstasy yet does not leave the body except to enter, at the same time, a specific visionary space. So Jacob at Beth-el: 'How full of awe this place!' (Genesis 28:17). Compare the flashbacks of trauma: 'I think I would have no trouble even now locating the spot on the median strip of Commonwealth Avenue [in Boston] where they [the repressed experiences of

many years ago] emerged out of that darkness . . .'[14] Krzystof Kieslowski's film
The Double Life of Veronica (1991) intimates how strong and sensuous the pull is
toward union with a second self that is always somewhere else, and whose
absent presence is felt as a loss, even a disembodiment. This ghostly, complementary other is as endlessly mourned as its reintegration is desired.
Aesthetics classifies such ecstasies as sublime; religion, as full of awe. They
exalt, terrify, and humble at the same time.

Individuation of this sort seems to be essential even when the newly minted
person flees from it into the arms of a brotherhood, sisterhood, or God. It is
notoriously difficult, as we all know, to distinguish the sense of election from
mania. Then how do we get from such instances of spiritual experience to a
communal bond without betraying or falsifying them? To hear voices is a form
of madness; random textual surprises are borderline cases that involve the reader
and can be amplified as inner quotations, cryptomania, or internalized commands. Yet once we have redeemed that madness by turning to methodical
exegesis, are we still in the precarious domain of being singled out, or do we
simply confirm by falling back on doctrine what was revealed? Have astonishment and awe turned into dogmatic faith?

We should not underestimate the importance, negative or positive, of
hermeneutics in religion: an activity that flexes the meaning of a canonical
text. The methodical character of hermeneutics tries to minimize eccentric
responses by establishing a true, authoritative, original meaning. Yet everyone
who has ventured into the field of interpretation, even when it represents itself
as a discipline or a science, knows the polyphony if not cacophony of exegesis
and how endlessly interesting it is to try to meet the challenge of texts. Although
we take for granted that the voice of God is no longer heard in the way the boy
Samuel heard it, or which would make the interpreter reply 'Here I am,' a part
of us returns to certain texts as to vestiges in which strength of spirit condenses
itself and could achieve what Robert Frost memorably called 'counter-love,
original response.'[15]

I have given my essay the title 'Text and Spirit' because it has always puzzled me
how dependent spirituality is, not only on books – necessary for cultural
transmission, once there is dispersion, or as the oral tradition becomes too
complex – but on textual issues. The rivalry of religion with religion could not
continue without systems of interpretation that activate in specific ways the faith
community's Scripture, which may be a book shared by several religions.

It must already be clear, in any case, that there is a link between text and spirit
when textual incidents, in the form of fragments, are like a voice falling into us,
taking hold of us. Although elaborated and restored to their first or another
context, such audita remain snatches from a ghostly conversation or a more
absolute book. I have represented this receptivity to spiritualized sound as a

psychic and existential fact. Moreover, I have stressed its contingency, as religion itself often does when it depicts a divine intervention: a prophet is unexpectedly called, a commanding voice is heard, a rebus or inscription appears.

But I have also said that the orthodox hermeneutics we have inherited, while respecting life-changing responses to source texts with canonical status, seeks to limit these.[16] Although some passages are more astonishing than others, and through as yet unknown mediations even ordinary biblical pericopes can have a startling effect, both religious and literary theories of exegesis take much pride in the doctrine of context – a predetermined context, shielding the reader from subjectivity and speculative excess. Similarly, in evangelical or charismatic movements, where startling conversions – even convulsions – are expected, what takes place is, as it were, programmed in and becomes a sacred or, at worst, sacrilegious mimicry.

The force of the fragment, then, surprises, because it comes from outside, even when that outside is within us. It does not matter how we analyze the psychic fact; what is important is that a metonymic textual condensation, this appearance of word as vision, *leads back* to a source text, or is the germ, as in creative writing, of a *leading forward*, a transformative moment that creates its own narrative support.

In talking of spirit, we have an obligation to go first to where the word *ruach* appears in the Hebrew Bible. After 'In the beginning God created the heaven and the earth,' Genesis discloses that 'the earth was unformed and void, and darkness was upon the face of the deep.' The *ruach elohim*, which 'hovered over the face of the waters,' is close to that darkness on the face of the deep. But this might suggest that chaos, the *tohuvabohu* of unformed earth and water, may have preexisted; in which case the creation would not be *ex nihilo*, out of nothing, but only a form-giving event. The Bible's opening phrasing defeats that thought; and the 'spirit of God,' with the formless darkness mere backdrop, manifests itself as a commanding voice instantly originating light. Yet even here, in this place of power, as John Hollander has remarked, 'Light is called, not torn forth.'[17]

In the second chapter of Genesis, there is a subtle parallel to the spirit hovering over the face of the waters: 'there went up a mist from the earth, and watered the whole face of the ground' (2:6). This is a transitional sentence that could be joined either to the previous verse describing the barren, soon-to-be-fertile, earth or to the next, which retells the creation of humankind: 'Then the Lord God formed man of the dust of the ground, and breathed into his nostrils the breath of life; and man became a living soul.' The words for breath and soul are not *ruach* but respectively *neshamah* and *nefesh*. As a picture of the creative act, there is something gentler here and more intimate: a proximity of divine to human that is not felt in the first creation-of-man account (Genesis 1:26–29) despite the theme of *zelem elohim*, of being created in God's image.

In fact, where we might expect the *ruach* to reappear, as in Genesis 3:8, we find instead a voice, 'the voice of the Lord God walking in the garden.' The earlier depiction showed the spirit of God as a hovering force in the formless darkness; in the later picture, however, the mist rising from the ground and watering the face of the earth is an image taken directly from nature, and the creation that follows is distinctly anthropomorphic, in that its subject is literally the shaping of a man, while the very art of description is friendly and naturalistic. Genesis 3:8, moreover, augments the idea of a relation between *ruach elohim* and voice, the voice that generates light. Without, to be sure, a definite body, that *ruach* voice now addresses and interpellates the lapsed human being, an act that can be said to call it to consciousness or conscience.

If my analysis is correct, *ruach* is not anthropomorphic (it is, if anything, close to theriomorphic); yet as a speaking and intelligible voice it moves toward a pathos at once human and sublime. *Ruach* never forfeits its quality as a numinous, awe-inspiring source. This is borne out when we enter the later, more historical era of Judges, where the voice of God, while still manifest, often escapes those who search for it. The episodes that focus on the relation among Samuel, Saul and God are particularly disturbing: indeed, here the verb *lidrosh*, the root of *midrash*, meaning to seek out the voice, first appears.[18]

The episodes are disturbing because while God's relation to Samuel remains familiar, allowing responsive words or obedience, the pressure on Saul is terrifying. Saul is an *am ha'aretz* (a simple, earth-bound fellow) going to the seer for a mundane, bumpkin-like purpose, 'Can you give me guidance where my asses are?' and being confronted by a fearful demand, a question that is not a question at all but an astonishing, exalting imposition: 'And on whom is all the desire of Israel? Is it not on thee, and on all thy father's house?' (1 Samuel 9:20). Samuel then predicts Saul's journey home, which culminates in his joining a band of prophets: 'And the spirit of the Lord will come mightily upon thee, and thou shalt prophesy and be turned into another man' (1 Samuel 10:1–7), where 'come mightily upon' translates *zalachat*, 'seize' thee or 'fall upon' thee (cf. 1 Samuel 11:6 and 16:13). A power of transformation is evoked, akin to that of the *ruach* in the first lines of Genesis.

Clearly, the open vision and voice are passing from Israel. The presence of God returns in the prophets, but with more violence, ambivalence, chanciness, and – in Abraham Heschel's formulation – pathos: so the *devar adonai* is like a burning fire consuming Jeremiah's heart and bones (Jeremiah 20:9). God's *ruach* reverts to something of its aboriginal manifestation: We are made to feel its incumbent mystery and transformative violence more than its intimacy.

It is well known that the sealing of the canon of Hebrew Scripture is linked to the recession, if not disappearance, of prophetic voice and vision. With the destruction of the First Temple, then decisively with the destruction of the

Second and Bar Kochba's defeat, inquiry of God must go through *midrash*. The Sages may still be looking for asses, but these include the Messiah's donkey. Those rabbis are not shy; they assert on the basis of Deuteronomy 30:11–15 that the Law is not in heaven but among them in the earthly tribunal; indeed, they abjure the authority of the *bat kol* and seek to shut down the prophetic impulse, even as Saul banished the witches whom he was nevertheless forced to consult. This means, in effect, that spirit has become textualized; inquiry of the Lord, in the post-prophetic and post-priestly era, is mediated by the recitation, reading, and contemplative study of Talmud Torah.

This multilayered commentary continues to call itself an oral tradition, however, and claims descent from Sinai; the image of direct transmission, through the voice of God or 'daughter' of that voice, is never entirely given up. To read in the Talmud, or to extend its inquiry, becomes a religious experience itself.[19] Priest and prophet are replaced by the figure of the rabbi of exemplary learning who walks with the Law (*halakhah*, the path), even as the righteous of old had walked and conversed with God.

The rabbinic revolution, as it has been called, seals the canon and draws the consequences of that closure. In the Sages' own hyperbole, God is made to say of an errant Israel, 'Would that they abandon me but keep my Torah!'[20] This expresses, of course, a fear that *God* has forsaken the community; in captivity and dispersion, only the Torah remains. But whatever dryness of spirit ensues, whatever constriction and narrowness of purpose, the act of reading strengthens and takes on a quality of prayerful recitation – of a crying to God in words of the canonized text as well as a listening for His response.

One might think that how *Midrash* usually atomizes Scripture would diminish the latter's eloquence. Such divisions certainly sin against plot or story, the very features that entice us to look at the Bible as literature. What matters in *Midrash* is the verse, or part of the verse, even a single word or letter. Meaning is achieved by the montage of biblical patches. Gershom Scholem once called this 'mosaic style' of the great halakhists 'poetic prose in which linguistic scraps of sacred texts are whirled around kaleidoscope like.'[21]

What I have tried to do is sketch a minimalist theory of spirituality influenced mainly by the Jewish commentary tradition. Some will be disappointed by this modest approach. Spirituality is a word with great resonance, yet I have not extracted large, exalted structures of sensibility or discourse. Were I to do so, I would have to respect an entire midrashic sequence or collection and show how words dim the eyes as well as refresh them, insofar as visuality and idolatry may be linked. I would also have to deal with the issue of anthropo/gyno/morphism, or divine pathos: a fertile, if always disputed, well spring of religious energy. I would have to stay longer with the way *ruach* breaks into voice, becomes voice-feeling; and, close to the heart of the throat, threatens to turn the human response into a stammer. I would also have to recognize that, in Judaism, with a

Messiah who tarries, 'hope' must be a central theme, wherever and however it manifests itself. The very word 'spirituality,' moreover, still seems somewhat foreign to traditional Jewish thinking and observance: it got preempted by Pauline Christianity. Only to Levinas might it be applied: his theology evokes a vigilance, even an insomnia, that keeps human finitude, traumatized by the infinite, from enclosing itself in 'the hegemonic and atheistic self' for which life reduces to equanimity.

There is one further generalization I want to venture. It returns to something almost as equivocal as dreams, namely the gift of speech and what Dante and also the German-Jewish religious thinker Franz Rosenzweig call its 'grammar': voiced thinking that becomes writing and seeks a coincidence of spirit and letter. That coincidence is rare and demands a price – an engagement that takes time, perhaps a lifetime. For there is no guarantee that poetic words, ancient or modern, will make sense, or the same sense, to different readers throughout history. In fact, the more earnest our attention to language, the more the conventional links dissipate, and a nakedness appears in the words as words, one that both arouses and threatens the process of intellection.

We often feel, then, that biblical words say too much to be received: their anagogical force, while breaking what Rosenzweig calls the shell of the mystery, can make us feel as poor as Edward Taylor, the Puritan poet:

> In my befogg'd dark Phancy, Clouded minde,
> Thy Bits of Glory, packt in Shreds of Praise
> My Messenger [his poetry] doth lose, losing his Wayes.[22]

We cannot presume to win spiritual coherence lightly, when the spirit itself is so often figured as a preternatural, disruptive intervention. The not-foundering of communication under that pressure is unusual, for speech could turn into nothing more than a contiguous mass of alien sounds. Perhaps, then, shards, *klipot*, Edward Taylor's 'Bits of Glory Shreds . . . of Praise,' must suffice.

Let me end by recounting what happened to Martin Buber. His path to the great Buber-Rosenzweig translation of the Bible was very complex, but one episode stands out.[23] Well-acquainted in early youth with the Hebrew original and then with several translations, including Luther's, he noticed shortly after his Bar Mitzvah that he read the Bible with literary enjoyment – a fact that upset him so much (!) that for years he did not touch any translation but tried to return to the *Urtext*, the original Hebrew. By then, however, the words had lost their familiar aspect and seemed harsh, alien, confrontational: 'sie sprangen mir ins Gesicht' (they dared me to my face).

Thirteen years later – one thinks, therefore, of a second Bar Mitzvah – he attended the funeral of the founder of modern Zionism, Theodor Herzl, and came home feeling oppressed. Reaching for one book after another, everything seemed voiceless and meaningless (*stumm*). Then, as if by chance, and without expecting much, Buber opened the Bible – and happened upon the story of how King Jehoiakim had Jeremiah's scroll read and consigned piece by piece to a brazier's fire (Jeremiah 36:21 ff.); this went to Buber's heart, and he began to face the Hebrew once more, conquering each word anew, as if it had never been translated. 'I read [the Hebrew] aloud, and by reading it this way I got free of the whole Scripture, which now was purely *miqra'* [vocal reading].' A few years later, while again rereading a biblical chapter out loud, the feeling came over him that it was being spoken for the first time and had not yet been written down, and did not have to be written down. 'The book lay before me, but the book melted into voice.'[24]

Buber has not left us a reflection on why the 'found' passage from Jeremiah affected him so powerfully, and he does not refer explicitly to the *bat kol*. But his stated wish to 'get free of' Scripture by first converting it into an aural experience is remarkably candid. The Hebrew root *qara'* in *miqra'* may have helped as a first step toward a retranslation of the Bible that challenges Luther's strongly vernacular version. *Qara'*, as in *qryat sh'ma*, denotes the action of calling, of a crying out or reciting, as well as naming: The content of this prayer is, after all, a naming of God. *Qara'* as 'reading' never loses its residual meaning of 'calling out.' Moreover, in the episode from Jeremiah, the verb *qara* (when spelled with ayin rather than aleph) is a near homonym of 'tearing' – a sacrilegious act on the part of the King and which recalls two distantly related events. First, the destroyed scroll is rewritten by Jeremiah's scribe Baruch, a doubling that could recall that of Sinai's tablets as well as raise the issue of the relation of written to oral Torah. Both Buber and Rosenzweig try to express the link between text and spirit in a radical way, one that goes through the restitution of its oral or aural resonance, but otherwise they do not seek to transform the Bible by any type of spiritualizing interpretation. '*Schrift ist Gift* [Script is poison],' Buber quotes Rosenzweig, from a letter shortly before their work of translation began, 'holy *Schrift* included. Only when it is translated back into orality can I stomach it.'[25]

The episode from Jeremiah, moreover, leads intertextually to 2 Kings 22, in which Hilkiah the High Priest discovers a Book of the Law (*sefer hatorah*) in the temple and Shaphan the scribe reads it to King Josiah; but there the King tears his clothes,[26] not the scroll, and has it read aloud to the assembled people. Near its inception 2 Kings had recounted the story of Elijah and Elisha: how Elijah ascends in a whirlwind and perhaps leaves to his disciple a 'double portion of . . . *ruach*.' Here, too, we go once more from prophecy as open vision to the discovery of a scroll that must provide vision by inquiry, by a midrashic process linked to recitation and research. The fiery chariot and horses carrying Elijah away, become, when Elisha is lamented (2 Kings 13:14–15), no more than a figurative allusion, an exclamation ('My father, my father, the chariots of Israel and the horsemen thereof!') expressing a fear that the *ruach* will depart from Israel with Elisha's passing. Despite the sporadic persistence of prophecy, the spirit will now have to reside mainly within the temple of a text.

I leave the last word to Levinas, who suggests that talmudic and midrashic literature shows that 'prophecy may be the essence of the human, the traumatism that wakes it to its freedom.' Thought itself is an elaboration of such a moment.

> It probably begins through traumatisms to which one does not even know how to give a verbal form: a separation, a violent scene, a sudden consciousness of the monotony of time. It is from the reading of books – not necessarily books of philosophy – that these initial shocks become questions and problems, giving one to think.[27]

The prophetic consciousness, reading, and the ethical converge, wherever self-identity, challenged by otherness, instructed and roused by it, becomes 'la spiritualité de l'esprit.'

Notes

* The Tanner Lecture for 1999 at the University of Utah.

1. Harold Bloom, *The American Religion: The Emergence of the Post-Christian Nation* (New York: Simon and Shuster, 1992), 15, 256–57.

2. *The Varieties of Religious Experience: A Study in Human Nature* (New York: Longmans, Green, 1902).

3. George Eliot, *Adam Bede* (London: Oxford University Press, 1996), 33.

4. Saul Lieberman, *Hellenism in Jewish Palestine: Studies in the Literary Transmission, Beliefs and Manners of Palestine in the 1 Century B.C.E.–IV Century C.E.* (New York: Jewish Theological Seminary of America, 1950), Appendix I, 'Bath Kol,' 194–99.

5. Baudelaire, 'L'homme dieu' in *Paradis Artificiels, Oeuvres Complètes*, ed. Y. G. le Dantec (Paris: Gallimard, 1964), 376.

6. Emily Dickinson, 'The soul selects her own society.' Poem 409 in *The Poems of Emily Dickinson, Variorum Edition*, ed. R.W. Franklin (Cambridge and London: The Belknap Press of Harvard University Press, 1998). First published in 1890.

7. Ibid.

8. John Henry Newman, *The Dream of Gerontius* (London: Burns, Lambert, and Oates, 1866), 115–16, 118–20. 'As though I bent' corrected in the 1904 edition to 'as though I went.'

9. The Keats quotation comes from a letter of March 19, 1819 to George and Georgiana Keats. See *The Letters of John Keats 1814–1821*, ed. Hyder E. Rollins (Cambridge, MA: Harvard University Press, 1958), 2:80.

10. D. H. Lawrence: 'Bavarian Genetians' in *Selected Poems*, ed. Jan Todd (Oxford: Oxford University Press, 1993), 97–98. Originally printed in Lawrence's *Last Poems* of 1932.

11. James, *Varieties of Religious Experience*, Lecture IX, 'Conversion.'

12. William Wordsworth, 'Ode: Intimations of Immortality' in *Selected Poems*, ed. John O. Hayden (New York: Penguin, 1994), 144.

13. Rainer Maria Rilke, 'Archaic Bust of Apollo' from *Der Neuen Gedichte Anderer Teil* (*New Poems: Second Part*), first published in 1908.

14. Brooke Hopkins, 'A Question of Child Abuse,' *Raritan Review*, Winter 1993, 35.

15. Robert Frost, 'The Most of It' in *A Witness Tree* (New York: Henry Holt, 1942).

16. The opposite is true of the Kabbalah, which often 'relativizes' the letters in Scripture, claiming the Torah was originally, as one mystic claimed, 'a heap of unarranged letters' combining in different forms according to the state of the world. See Gershom Scholem, *On the Kabbalah and its Symbolism*, tr. Ralph Mannheim (New York: Schocken, 1977), 74–83.

17. John Hollander, *The Work of Poetry* (New York: Columbia University Press, 1997), 27.

18. See 1 Samuel 9:9, perhaps interpolated; but Saul's name in the Hebrew suggests 'asking,' most clearly after Saul's death in 1 Samuel 28:6: 'When Saul inquired of the Lord [*vajish'al Shaul beadonai*], the Lord answered him not, neither by dreams, nor by Urim, nor by prophets,' which leads into the episode of the ghost-seer of Endor.

19. A good account of this development is found in Moshe Halbertal, *People of the Book: Canon, Meaning, and Authority* (Cambridge, MA: Harvard University Press, 1997).

20. *Lamentations Rabbah: An Analytical Translation*, Jacob Neusner (Atlanta: Scholars Press, 1989), 14, in Petihta Two (II.i.5.B).

21. See Scholem, *Walter Benjamin: The Story of a Friendship*, tr. Harry Zohn (Philadelphia: Jewish Publication Society, 1981), 107.

22. 'Meditation Twenty-Eight' in *The Poetical Works of Edward Taylor*, ed. Thomas H. Johnson (Princeton, NJ: Princeton University Press, 1971), 139.

23. I am indebted for this example to Herbert Marks. See his 'Writing as Calling,' *New Literary History* 29 (1998), 15–37. The Buber episode is available in Martin Buber and Franz Rosenzweig's *Scripture and Translation*, tr. Lawrence Rosenwald and Everett Fox (Bloomington: Indiana University Press, 1994), 205–19.

24. Buber and Rosenzweig, *Scripture and Translation*, 208.

25. Buber and Rosenzweig, *Scripture and Translation*, 211.

26. Elisha tears his clothes at the passing of Elijah (2:12), as does the King of Israel after having read Naaman's letter (5:7) which might portend a disaster. To this day the *q'ria* is a ritual tearing of clothing following the death of a close relative or a public calamity.

27. Emmanuel Levinas, *Éthique et Infini: Dialogues avec Philippe Nemo* (Paris: Fayard, 1982), 15. See also his *Beyond the Verse: Talmudic Readings and Lectures* (London: Athlone, 1994) and *Nouvelles Lectures Talmudiques* (Paris: Éditions de Minuit, 1996), passim.

Chapter 13

Midrash as Law and Literature

My motives in studying Midrash are not pure. I am a raider of the lost ark looking for treasure. It is not for the sake of heaven I study but to bring back voices and types of interpretation of which that ark is as full as Noah's was of beasts. In an era of restitutions, such a restocking of identity through a historical and compensatory search is common enough. But in the case of Midrash — by which I always mean a method of exegesis as well as the collections formed by it — another motive enters. I cannot forget how these writings were slandered, and how public ignorance abetted such slander in the Nazi era. Jews were demonized at a time when Talmud and Midrash were available yet remained a closed book even to the educated. And for centuries before that, theological anti-Semitism had misrepresented the spirit of Jewish law: non-Jews were taught to see only a crass and stubborn literalism, a mean-spirited, materialistic frame of mind, rather than what David Weiss Halivni has called the predilection of Midrash for justified law, which heaps interpretation upon interpretation.[1] That era of prejudice and ignorance should be approaching its end.

Yet to make sure of its demise will take a concerted effort. Those who live within the walled garden are often so absorbed by its pleasures and duties that they do not open it to others. And those like myself who sneak through the wall like a thief in the night cannot emerge with more than fragments wrongly detached from a living environment. I am not discouraged, however, because the need is so great — the need of those in my generation who 'have the Bible and their great poets, but no longer understand how to use their imaginations in reading them.' These are Northrop Frye's words forty years ago, describing how William Blake felt two hundred years ago.

You can imagine my mixed feelings when I read in Ralph Waldo Emerson's journal the following entry:

> If Minerva offered me a gift and an option, I would say give me continuity. I am tired of scraps. I do not wish to be a literary or intellectual chiffonnier. Away with this Jew's rag-bag of ends and tufts of brocade, velvet, and cloth-of-gold; let me spin some yards or miles of helpful twine, a clew to lead to one kingly truth, a chord to bind wholesome and belonging facts.[2]

On the level of tradition I, too, want continuity, and on the level of intellectual, especially literary analysis, that desired continuity translates into a search for the formal unity of the Hebrew Bible and correlatively of midrashic method. Yet the first lesson Midrash itself teaches the apprentice is to be wary of over-unifying its words or of unifying them in a totalizing way. It is comforting to anticipate with Emerson 'a clew to lead to one kingly truth,' and it is intellectually imperative to keep that possibility in mind. The Hebrew Bible, however, is not a classical work of art, nor is Midrash a Patrologia in which a supersessionist revelation draws everything into that regal unity of 'wholesome and belonging facts.' Emotionally and intellectually I am with Emerson, but empirically and spiritually I am closer to the point at which Midrash and Kafka intersect.

Let me return to Emerson's image of the Jew's rag-bag. It does not have to be an insult or an indication of abject poverty. Many contemporary scholars accept a documentary hypothesis which views the Hebrew Bible as a glorious patchwork, and that the seams show through, as in modern collages, can be an artistic, though not a theological, virtue. Since with Midrash and Talmud there is – perhaps all the more – a marked effort to preserve every significant tradition and law, however elliptical or unclear, many sayings or exegeses are agglutinated: having been stored in a collective memory – the Oral Tradition – and waiting to get into the written text at the appropriate moment, if no such moment comes along, they sneak in nevertheless. The founding rabbis, in short, can be considered as law-rhapsodes, and the halakha as a severe poetry.[3]

The literary study of Midrash makes us aware that what is meant by the literary has not been clearly defined. Does it neatly preclude this memorial and encyclopedic dimension of rabbinic literature? One reason for the modern interest in both Bible and Midrash is their apparent carelessness about literary effects associated with the concept of genre and formal unity. What we call 'rhetoric' and 'poetics' – arts indebted to Greek and Roman thought – did not separate out as technical branches of knowledge during the formative period of talmudic Judaism. It would be exciting to know what the paidea of the sages involved, and while we know something about the rabbinic academies, we do not know enough. But it seems that, despite the impact of Hellenistic learning in the area of dream interpretation or hermeneutics,[4] poetics played no role. Even today, the elements of Midrash are taught mainly through immersion. The best an essay can do is to smear a little honey on this or that text.

My essay may not be different in this regard. But I do want to raise the issue of what happens to that cornerstone of poetics, the concept of unity, when Midrash enters the picture. Consider J. B. Soloveitchik's 'The Lonely Man of Faith.'[5] The essay rejects source criticism (the documentary hypothesis) as an attaint to the unity and integrity of the divine text. This rejection does not entail, however, a denial of contradiction in Scripture. What ensues – what

Soloveitchik liberates himself into – is a strong midrash on the two stories of Adam's creation. Their incongruity is not a textual accident (as the Higher Criticism proposes) but points to a real contradiction in the nature of man. Soloveitchik develops the two accounts into a picture of Adam the first and Adam the second.

These two categories allow him to pursue a sensitive contrast that builds into an entire moral and social philosophy. It sets against the intellectual and scientific dignity of man the crisis-feeling of being overpowered by God or the world, a feeling which radically deepens the quest for redemption. The first Adam is lonely because he is committed to an ideal of mastery that results in dominion over the cosmos yet separates him from it; the second Adam is doomed to explore that loneliness as a loss which can only be illuminated by the dimension of faith and the covenantal idea. The muteness and indifference of an alienated cosmos now sharpen Adam's consciousness of separation; for each 'I' is ontologically lonely – that is, incomplete – and so the 'natural work community' of Adam the first cannot solace this ordained lack of connection. Hence a turn from cosmos to covenant. 'Our sages said that before Abraham appeared *majestas dei* was reflected only by the distant heavens and it was a mute nature which "spoke" of the glory of God. It was Abraham who "crowned" Him the God of the earth, i.e., the God of men.'[6]

By a surprising return to the text Soloveitchik then suggests that Elohist and Yahwist (distinguished by the documentary hypothesis) do express very different *source experiences*. The craving of covenantal man for a personal and intimate relation with God cannot be realized through the cosmic 'E-lohim encounter,' so that the locus of transcendental experience must shift to where 'the finite "I" meets the infinite He "face to face." '[7] This more communal relation between man and God is symbolized by the Tetragrammaton in the Biblical account of Adam the second.

I do not apologize for spending time – little enough – on part of Soloveitchik's essay. It participates in an intelligent revolt against modernity; it acknowledges yet does not accede to the claim made on us by modern categories. Here is someone acquainted with the language of contemporary philosophy, who knows that Jewish thought has often flourished within a foreign environment, and who will not accept the fact that philosophy speaks only Greek. His brilliant rejection-conversion of Higher Criticism seems to come right out of the lineaments of midrashic style. It is true that he does not call his procedure 'midrashic,' yet there is no question that it is so. It explores an incongruity, it puts into play proof-texts and associated authorities in a potentially endless dialogue, one that brings the Bible closer to us even as it brings us closer to it. The essay's fusion, moreover, of homiletic dependence on Scripture with an analysis of contemporary spiritual problems culminates in an appropriation of 1 Kings 19 that makes Elisha into a typical representative of the natural work community, an Adam the first transformed by his sudden encounter with Elijah into an Adam the second. Covenantal mankind replaces majestic mankind.

There is, however, one disconcertingly superficial aspect to this modern orthodox scholar. What he says about the literary is both minimal and wrong. The Higher Criticism, he alleges, based itself on 'literary categories invented by modern man.' Now contemporary critical theories do use stylistic criteria to distinguish sources, but no literary scholar would stop there. It is precisely the issue of the unity or coherence of art that has exercised poetics since Aristotle. Using the example of Greek tragedy, Aristotle defined a unity that was non-episodic, that did not depend, like epic, exclusively on the presence of a hero but was the outcome of an 'action' involving all elements. It seems impossible to apply Aristotle's scheme to the Bible, which remains episodic and, though it is said to have been given to Moses, is not unified around Moses as hero, or 'one greater man.' The unity of Scripture supported explicitly and unreservedly by Soloveitchik obviously suggests different criteria and forms of analysis. To discover them is also a task of contemporary literary theory.

Recent literary thinkers have challenged the simple location of unity in art.[8] They rejoice, like Midrash, in the 'interpretive bounty' of a text;[9] they accept the mediacy of linguistic and interpretive structures. A full-scale rethinking of the dichotomy of creation and commentary is in process, which has already modified our picture of what constitutes unity. So Claude Lévi-Strauss engages, like Soloveitchik, disparate creation myths, from Greek literature and South American folklore, because interest has shifted from elegant ideas of artistic coherence to the making and sustaining of traditions. A consensus is building that cultures stabilize contradictions in their belief-system by the interpretive extension of foundational texts. On this view, commentary is not, or not only, a by-product of these texts but is itself a functional revelation. The structure of first (Scripture) and second (Midrash/Interpretation) is modified into a hendiadys or syzygy. Dan Sperber, the French anthropologist, has said succinctly: 'Exegesis is not an interpretation but rather an extension of the symbol and must itself be interpreted.'[10]

This understanding of the relation between text and commentary is important for Judaism, where commentary becomes the authorized form of creative thought.[11] We have no statement more radical in this respect than that both Oral and Written Law were given on Sinai, for this legitimates talmudic commentary as strictly coterminous with Scripture. Therefore the daring intimacy of Midrash with Bible. Remember Moses in Akiba's school room, marveling at what he hears, and just a little bemused. Instead of a magisterial theology expressed in Aristotelian treatises, our main inheritance is the composite, heteroglossic supplement of Midrash: a supplement that converts exegesis into law finding (halakha) or a literature of justification (aggada).

Of course, literary commentaries and midrashic ones have their differences. But these are not easy to define except by pseudo criteria. The very advance of contemporary theory toward Midrash makes Jewish scholars more zealous to avoid contamination. There is fear that the motive for Midrash will be mistakenly reduced from *Everything is in the text, and what the text signifies is its relevance to the actions or thoughts of the interpretive community,* to: *Everything is text, and the text is a structure of imaginary relations, a tissue without issue.* I acknowledge the danger, but why be frightened by those who insist on being superficial?

The literary establishment has its anxieties, too. Is it not foolhardy to extend from sacred to secular texts the principle that an apparent incoherence signals an overarching integrity? Yet every good literary interpretation takes precisely that risk. It comes upon an obvious or less obvious difficulty: a crux, a deviation from the norm, a contradiction. On that evidence it either impugns the authority of the work, or it values the anomaly and so augments the authority of the work.

The secular critic, of course, has a choice between negative and redemptive approaches, while the religious interpreter does not. The darshan cannot stay in the negative. His inventiveness is spent on ways to redeem the text's negative features (incoherence, ellipses, the disparity of historical fact and religious expectation, gaps between tenor and text). His basic choice may be character-ized as follows. Does the harmony evoked in order to repair the text point to a higher unity? Or is the truth plainer, a *rectification*, even polemically directed against a *mystification*, one that comes from our need to think of the sacred in sublime rather than down-to-earth terms?

In brief, though the words of the Torah can be made to fly up, more often Midrash infers from ellipses or condensations a very human story and introduces dialogues that draw God deeper into the affairs of mankind. Let me bring an example from Midrash *Tanhuma*, which has parallels in Genesis Rabbah and the Babylonian Talmud (Berakhot 60a).

Genesis 30:21–22 reads: 'Afterwards she [Leah] bore him [Jacob] a daughter and named her Dinah. And God remembered Rachel and listened to her and opened her womb.' Here there are four possible ellipses: 'Afterwards' could raise the question, Precisely after what? 'Dinah' is not followed by an explanation of the name, as is the norm in Genesis (the name Joseph is explained in verses 23–24 of the same chapter).[12] The transition from Leah to Rachel is abrupt. And, Leah as well as Rachel could be referred to by 'God . . . listened to her.'

Here is how *Tanhuma* interprets the verses:

> After Leah had given birth to six sons, she saw by way of prophecy that there would be twelve tribes in the future emerging out of Jacob. She had already given birth to six sons and was pregnant with her seventh. The two maid servants [Bilhah and

Zilpah] had given birth to two sons each, hence a total of ten. Leah arose and called out to the Holy One, blessed be He: 'Master of the World, twelve tribes in the future will arise out of Jacob; I already have six sons and am pregnant with my seventh and the maid servants have two each. If my next child is a male, my sister Rachel will be even less than the maid servants!' Immediately, the Holy One, blessed be He, listened to her prayer and transformed the fetus within her into a female, thus it says: 'Afterwards, she bore him a daughter and named her Dinah . . .' Why did she name her Dinah? Because Leah the righteous stood before the Holy One, blessed be He, seeking a judgment (*din*) and the Holy One, blessed be He, said to her, 'You are *rahmanit* [kind person, merciful person] and so I will be merciful to her, hence: 'Now, God remembered Rachel.'[13]

The interpolated story, typical of a patriarchal society, makes the ellipses fertile, and suggests that Leah, after giving birth to six sons and carrying a seventh, remembers the plight of her sister and calls on God to grant Rachel the next male child. God converts the fetus in Leah's womb to a female, while mercifully (a pun intervenes here linking the word for mercy with that for womb) granting Joseph to Rachel as her first male offspring. Whereas the Bible story mentions nothing about Leah's frame of mind and, indeed, has God abruptly 'remember' Rachel after Leah has given birth, the midrashic writer ascribes that 'remembering' first to Leah and then uses it as a charming psychological touch to explain the meaning of the name Dinah. In brief: he assumes that Leah has an open line to God and can influence Him. He also shows God making a decision not autocratically, or in a great consult with his angels, but after a plea from a mortal. Leah's *rahmones* seems to activate his own.

Is there a literature from that time which is so down-to-earth? It may be strange to call Midrash literature since it remains a mode of commentary explicitly linked to the very words of Scripture. Yet we recognize the creative and parafictive result of its interpretive elaborations. Moreover, at a certain level Midrash is *not* satisfied with the text as it stands, and while it refuses to produce a new or transformed writing it looks for more of the original in the original, for more story, more words within the words.[14] Moreover, this potentiality in the sacred text is rarely treated as a mysterious void. Leah, as she stands before God, exerts a theurgic force, however weak,[15] and such force, such pressure, is also what the darshan exerts on and through the Bible. The rabbinic interpreter is characterized by *participation exégètique*.

That Midrash is not satisfied with the text — in the sense that it wishes for something more, not something different — means that its labor of the negative can be very daring. Gaps or obscurities, everything that could be characterized as indeterminate, are emphasized before being resolved by one interpretive or interpolative *davar* after another. And though what is potential is usually understood in accord with the dictum that the language of the Bible addresses the normal person's capacity for understanding, in the tricky area of theurgic interpretation text moves close to theory in one respect: it must be 'falsifiable' (in the Popperian sense of that word).

Let me clarify this scandalous idea. The midrashic skill, for instance, that divides up words or verses, together with an ingenious repunctuation (revoweling) of phrases, is a combinatory art that questions the canonized letters before us. While these letters have a received meaning on the *grammatical* level of word and sentence, they are taken to be, at the same time, *anagrammatic*, in the sense of constituting the elements of a divine name coterminous with the Torah and guaranteeing every mark in it. This perspective is made explicit by the Kabbalah. 'The whole Torah is the Name of the Holy One,' we read in the *Zohar* (Yithro 87a); the letters of the Torah, the Ramban comments, were written continuously, without break of words, which makes it possible to separate them into Divine Names when read by that 'path' (Nachmanides, *Commentary on the Torah,* Introduction to the Book of Genesis). Scholem remarks that these names of God constitute a language without a grammar.[16]

The established link between signifier and signified can therefore be heuristically modified by viewing the signifier anagrammatically as a combination of letters that yield, by permutation if necessary, another signifier. So 'Israel,' Yod, S, R, 'L is reinscribed as 'Y-SAR-EL' to reveal the mystical number 10 (Y = 10) which points to, in the series of Sephirot or separate intelligences, the tenth and last emanation (Prince of the Presence, or SAR EL).[17] The extreme of this combinatory art is found in Abulafia and the prophetic Kabbalah, but normative Midrash never loses sight of that potential.[18]

Isaac Heinemann, it is well known, sees Midrash as 'creative philology.' The difference, even known to Milton, between *kri* (the voiced text) and *ktiv* (the written, consonantal text) permits pun and paranomasia, such as substituting 'builders' (*bonecha*) where the received text has 'sons' (*banecha*), and far more startling shifts. Such revoweling contains an entire allegory, extracted by readers alert to the inner flow, the lava as it were, of the Sinaitic text. Even consonants can be changed, or transposed, at the level of *kri*. So in Jacob's struggle with the angel, *wayyasar*, he 'fought' (and prevailed), is repunctuated to turn the letter 'sin' into a 'shin' to yield the meaning 'he sang' (and prevailed) – suggesting a significant fusion of the roles of patriarch and angel (alluding to the angel's request to leave before break of dawn, which aggadic midrash interprets as having to leave in order to sing before God's throne at dawn, each dawn reminding us of the birthday of creation).

There is usually, of course, a homiletic or moralistic aspect to this play with words. Indeed, the segmentation of the Bible for the sake of commentary may have produced fragments memorable enough to circulate as proverbs or to pass more fully into the common language as well as the common understanding.[19] The creation, by an art of division and combination, of quotable fragments ('citemes,' as Arnold Goldberg calls them)[20] allows their recitation in the most varied circumstances: released from their immediate context, the interpreter or preacher can find new frame narratives for them in any Bible episode or invent conversations between Israel and God. This has the effect of renewing Scripture words in startling ways. They come at us now from another context as if it were their original site or as if a later text (their source) had lodged in an earlier one, emanating from it as Midrash itself does at a still later point.

Consider how, in the *Mekhilta* de' R. Ishmael, the verse from Song of Songs, 'O my dove that art in the clefts of the rock, let me hear thy voice,' is applied to Israel caught between Pharaoh and the Deep Red Sea. 'What were the Israelites at that moment like? Like a dove fleeing from a hawk, and about to enter a cleft in the rock where there is a hissing serpent. If she enters, there is the serpent! If she stays out, there is the hawk! In such a plight were the Israelites at that moment, the sea forming a bar and the enemy pursuing. Immediately they set their mind upon prayer. Of them it is stated in the sacred writings [Kabbalah]: O my dove that art in the clefts of the rock,' and so on.[21]

Through this re-citing (resiting) of citations we seem to hear something speaking from the 'cleft' of the Torah's words. In this uncanny sense also 'there is no earlier or later.' Contextual unities of time, place, narrative, or grammatical meaning are overruled by a dynamic that points to an intertextual coherence. When the midrashic author associates a passage from the Writings (*ketuvim* or *kabbalah*) with a passage from the Pentateuch, this synoptic method works because the special authority of the Pentateuch actually promotes a sense that the earlier contains the later – a sense that extends itself (for this reader at least) to Midrash, as if *mikrah* (the canon) were always already Midrash or as if, were we to lose *mikrah*, it could be largely reconstructed through the 'distributive justice' of interpreters whose proof-texting skills have opened the canon to a text-faithful imagination.

I return to the relation between the Bible as, on the one hand, a language of sacred names and, on the other, a language of common words adapted to human capacities. The interpreter's emphasis on names is based, formally, on etymological traditions that explain place names like Penuel or personal names like Israel and Joseph. The name is converted into a paraphrase and comes with a story. It functions like a hook for memory, whether or not that was the formal intention. What is important from a hermeneutic perspective is that the name-paraphrase-story pattern can suggest a transformation from story and paraphrase back to name, from signified back to a material yet numinous signifier. In that way the common words, under hermeneutic pressure, may disclose an un-common language, the presence of sacred name or alphabet. And when that occurs, exegesis moves closer to prayer and becomes *participation exégètique*.

Midrash, in brief, can motivate and potentiate words as if they were names. By 'motivate' I mean that an opaque piece of language, like the proper name

'Dinah' in the passage from *Tanhuma*, is explained by an etymological byword or narrative, and by 'potentiate' I mean that this motivation sensitizes the reader to a numinous element in all Scripture words, as if they originated in theophoric voicings. What is evoked is a reversibility that recovers the divine names within Scripture's accommodated language.

Consider once more the passage from *Tanhuma*. It comments on the Bible via a mishnaic rule about a certain kind of prayer. The Mishnah (which became Judaism's major legal codification) discourages the wish for a male child – so strong in patrilinear societies – once conception has occurred. A prayer expressing that wish is considered *tefilat shav*: pointless or worthless. Yet both in the Talmud and in *Tanhuma* the mishnaic stricture is not accepted without qualification. The Gemora (major commentary on and clarification of the Mishnah) asks, 'Is there no room for mercy [*rahmana*]?' that is, Surely God's decision is modifiable? The question seems humorous to the contemporary mind, and a pun linking 'mercy' and 'womb' may be active. Yet the theological coherence of the mishnaic ruling has been challenged, and the Talmud meets the challenge.[22]

Rabbi Yosef, for instance, supports the worth of the disputed prayer, arguing that it was after (*v'ahar*) Leah's appeal to God, not immediately after her son Zevulun's birth, that God 'remembered' Rachel. This argument for the worth of the prayer is rejected, however, on the ground that '*en maskirin ma'aseh nisim*, the precedent of miracles is not accepted for the making of halakha. But the Talmud does proceed to discuss in detail what prayers *are* permitted and when: in the first three days one may wish that conception take place, from the third to the fortieth day that the child be a male, and so forth. (Rabbi Yosi goes even further in the *Tanhuma*, insisting that such prayers are not worthless until the moment the woman is actually on the birthing stool.) After rejecting, that is, an imputed miracle as the basis of law, the rabbis revise an apodictic Mishnah in the light of their own human and empirical knowledge. A timetable is suggested as in the recent abortion debate.[23]

Seen in context, then, *Tanhuma*'s midrash still develops in the shadow of a legal restraint that reaches deeply into personal, albeit socially conditioned, attitudes. Whether that conception of law appeals or appals is not at issue here. Nor whether it leads to a mingling of sublime and trivial.[24] The field of halakha is obviously very broad, and the field of so-called aggadic or nonauthoritative Midrash equally so. Like secular types of imaginative prose, aggadic Midrash is overdetermined. Its relation to Mishnah, folklore, and the Bible itself exceeds a unity imposed by talmudic law finding. We can rarely claim that a passage from aggada has been introduced for only one reason.

What I want to emphasize, however, is the wordplay that animates midrashic discussion. Such wordplay enters not as a disposable device but as a crucial aspect of the traditionary materials. The continuity of the *Tanhuma* midrash with its talmudic and halakhic counterpart revolves less on a dissident opinion than on the retelling of a heart-warming story and the reinforcement of linguistic devices that allow the story in. What is said about Leah is grounded verbally in the Bible: close reading, similar to that of modern language-obsessed exegetes, discovers a textual opacity and correlates it with a hidden – though not esoteric – meaning. What the darshan does with the language of Scripture (with '*ahar/aheret, Dinah* and *rahmah*) provides a glimpse into a level of action that is more personal and comforting, more 'anthropopathic' than what transpires at the explicit narrative level. The midrashic habit of segmentation, moreover, works here so brilliantly that it seems to be a technique inspired directly by the text rather than ingeniously imposed on it. We are encouraged to read *wajishma 'eleyha* ('and He listened to her') as if the verse had Leah and not Rachel as the object of the verb, a reading motivated by hearing in '*eleyha* the name 'Leah.' The process that enriches meaning (the signifier-signified axis) also enriches the word as a phonemic rather than semantic entity (the signifier-signifier axis), for since there is no obvious agrammaticality the verbal thickness is rather an anagrammatic discovery of the interpreter. Sensitized by this kind of reading, every word in Scripture could become a name or a crux open to elaboration.

Thus *Tanhuma*'s commentary centers on an adverb ('*ahar*); a noun (*rahmah*) not in the Bible episode but introduced through talmudic discussion; also perhaps the root *zakhor*, male, with its link to *jizkhor* (He remembered, i.e., 'maled' Rachel); the name 'Dinah' construed as a verb ('she strove') and the name 'Leah' heard in an inflected pronoun ('*eleyha*). No one can read such interplay of Bible, Talmud, and Midrash without slowing up at every word and marveling how this augmenting of Leah's name contributes to God's name, which the Bible writes out, as it were, in every particle of its language.

There is, then, a double movement, which maintains at one and the same time the familiar, grammatical sense of the Bible words *and* suggests that any or all of them are open to an anagrammatic, divinatory reading.[25] The secular reader also knows about this doubleness, for it is different only in degree and not in kind from his own interpretive ventures. Ferdinand de Saussure's experiment with 'hypograms' and such coinages as Walter Benjamin's 'Agesilaus Santander' – perhaps inspired by Jewish name mysticism via Gershom Scholem – are dramatic instances that point in the same direction. Midrash invalidates the distinction between the muses as Daughters of Memory – here textual memory – and Daughters of Inspiration.

Can I gather what I have said into a single hypothesis? The attempt to put imagination in the service of memory reverses an emphasis in Hellenistic culture, if we recall the opening invocation of the *Iliad* and characterize fiction as putting memory in the service of imagination. More technically stated: the art of memory that Midrash may reflect depends on textual instances (topoi or citemes) rather than images (*imagines*) or places (*loci*). This is no more than a guess on my part; yet the mnemotechnics operative here do not seem to rely on 'visual impressions of almost incredible intensity.'[26] The visuality directs itself to, and perhaps breaks itself on, scriptural words and letters, even their shape. I describe a tendency, of course, not something invariable. What is important here is that imagination, whether it sponsors or represses images, is disciplined by and yoked to the sacred *in the form of a text*, at least during the Talmudic era. So the sharpness and imaginative acuity shown by Midrash, its fertility and wit, remain commentary; they find their way back to the words of the Bible, and, however many meanings are discovered, these never replace Scripture. While some interpreters play with fire, they continue to recognize the Torah as God's Promethean gift to man. Moreover, though passages may be defamiliarized (which can actually aid memorization) by being taken out of their immediate context and paired intertextually through the devices of *gematria* or pun and paranomasia, the 'infinity' of interpretation suggested does not – in rabbinic Midrash – favor mystical over everyday kinds of meaning. (The balance shifts with Kabbalah, but that is another story.) Like a good psychoanalyst, the redactor allows his attention to float or distribute equally: the impression, in fact, is that stories and similes from daily life predominate. As in Soloveitchik's reading of the two accounts of creation, Midrash speaks with Bible or God in intelligible, even intimate terms and, so, produces either a halakha or an aggadic flourish that puts the strangest experience within reach.

From a simple starting point, the literary study of Midrash, we have arrived at a complex result. Let me summarize and conclude. Literary study that has Midrash as its subject faces a number of difficulties. The first of these is that contemporary thought is moving away from the literary – from essentialist definitions that are said to be ideologically motivated and favor a fixed, eurocentric canon. The very existence, at the same time, of a writing like Midrash, that cannot be said to have a literary purpose yet is intensely textual and intertextual, helps to expand the contested notion of the literary. What interests literary scholars in Midrash is, therefore, that it cannot be constituted as literature, that it challenges narrow aesthetic or genre-conscious theories.[27]

Another way of stating the originality of Midrash is to point out its exceptional position as a form of commentary, with strong residues of oral transmission that elude a concept of the literary based on manuscript and especially print culture. Midrash, even in the age of manuscript culture, is allowed a freedom characteristic of oral tradition, which does not congeal the transmitted communication but leaves room for diversity of performance. In Midrash, as in oral forms, 'the integrity of the past [is] subordinate to the integrity of the present.'[28] With one crucial exception: the integrity of the letter of Scripture must be preserved. The text commented on is accorded sacred status and, though itself reflecting earlier forms of oral transmission, is not allowed further change. Thus Midrash, which tends toward a retelling of the Bible that might eventually have replaced it, becomes instead a spiritual means to preserve a letter-perfect Hebrew Scripture.

A further difficulty springs from pious fears about secular misuse. Yet the scholarly study of Midrash was among the first fruits of the nineteenth-century 'Wissenschaft des Judentums.' Zunz's book on the rabbinic homilies remains a classic.[29] What is strange and exciting is that in our time a form of close reading has developed which displays some features of Midrash. So far, however, the similarities between rabbinic Midrash and this new Midrash, inquisitive, open, highly text-dependent, have elicited more antagonism than sympathy.[30] There is already an attempt to disqualify the secular mode by imputing to it mystification or privatism: ingenious academics and punsters should not be compared, we are told, with rabbis whose utterances are historically situated and make a truth claim.[31]

These turf-protecting charges assume that the historical situation of those who are evolving the new Midrash is not worth examining. Yet why do para-midrashic readers come on the scene? And why, long before Derrida, is there a revival of interest in Patristic typological commentary as a complex literary form and, beyond that, in a critique of any method of reading that insists on 'unity' as the literary work's highest value despite ambiguity, polysemy, and complexity of reference?

If we are troubled today by unifying modes of commentary, it is because, in the past, they have been triumphalist. Midrash, however, is subtle in this regard. It encourages the intellect to find room in the strictest laws or else to support by proof-texts the most imaginative turn on Scripture. It is as if the original text had become unreadable except through an extreme fragmentation that paradoxically confirms its unity. The fragmentation deconstellates phrases and words, producing what Maurice Blanchot has called an '*écriture du désastre*' yet installing all the more firmly the law of citation. 'If citation,' Blanchot writes, 'in its fragmenting force, destroys in advance the text from which it is not only torn but which it exalts to the point of being nothing but this having-been-torn-away, then the fragment without text or context is radically uncitable.'[32]

It is crucial to separate the concept of unity from that of triumphalism by a hermeneutics of the faithful fragment, and the disaster of the *hurban* may have contributed to just this separation in Jewish commentary. The multivocal or aspectival qualities of Midrash do not seem to be the result only of historical distance – of our ignorance of the mode, its forms or genres. Goldberg can talk of the 'aporia' of midrashic texts and their special linguistic and literary characteristics.[33] How to interpret that 'aporia' without oversimplifying it by referential history or a purely contemporary appropriation, is the critical task.

Yet we need not give up all speculation about the mimetic character of midrashic style, as long as it is heuristic rather than dogmatic. The impact of the *hurban* has to be considered, but also the shift in *contemporary* intellectual life from identity-philosophies to theories of difference based on an appreciation of the intertextual character of writing, and the light this throws on psyche and structure of belief. If quality of belief matters in midrashic texts as well as belief itself, if interpreters test themselves and their listeners over and again, this would recall a modern revolt against the automatism of creeds. 'No forcing of image, plan or thought,' writes A. R. Ammons, admiring how nature undoes art. At the same time he senses, as we do in Midrash, a darker side to this apparent freedom:

> . . . all possibilities
> of escape open: no route shut, except in
> the sudden loss of all routes . . .[34]

It is true that there is also a deeply unmodern aspect to Midrash. For the self-consciousness we characterize as 'modern' often seeks to estrange itself through the deceptive 'anti-self-consciousness' of fiction. Every trace of secondariness is then displaced or denied. 'To forget the text which has engendered the text. We write starting from that forgetfulness.'[35] There is no such forgetting in either the old or the new Midrash, which are citational to an extreme degree. They reject amnesia and cryptomnesia. Even when, as in Jabès, the absolute authority of Scripture is lost, words of the other are recalled, or simulacra that continue to haunt us.

Once the religious thinker understands that the literary study of Midrash does not turn everything into aggada or fable, and then into a web of language-inspired forms (that linguistic aspect is fascinating, of course, and poses an obvious challenge),[36] then it is possible for Midrash to be studied comparatively, as an exceptional form of commentary. It is exceptional because of its close yet supple relation to a canonical text, because of the way exegesis turns into exegesis plus, or 'literature' – in short, because of matricial qualities that allow us to see a creative yet text-permeated mind at work. The dichotomy between (primary) text and (secondary) interpretation is alleviated: exegesis augments instead of displacing the received symbols and words. There is fictional momentum, but it does not become freestanding even in the *mashal*, the midrashic parable, a form that goes farther in devious naiveté than the Homeric simile. Just as the *mashal* can be accused of stylistic insubordination, so Midrash is an insubordinate type of exegesis,[37] a wonderfully inventive yoking of one text to another by a virtuosity that saves the whole: in Soloveitchik's words, the 'unity and integrity' of Scripture.

As for the future, and the field that may eventually be created by the awareness that Midrash and literary study take of each other, I can say only one thing with confidence. A knowledge of Midrash will prove more interesting for the literary critic than a knowledge of literary criticism for the scholar of Jewish texts. Ask not what deconstruction may do for Midrash; ask what Midrash may do for deconstruction.

Notes

1. David Weiss Halivni, *Midrash, Mishnah, and Gemara: The Jewish Predilection for Justified Law* (Cambridge, MA: Harvard University Press, 1986).
2. See Bliss Perry, ed., *The Heart of Emerson's Journals* (New York: Dover, 1958), 267.
3. I allude, of course, to Giambattista Vico's famous description, in *The New Science* (1725–44) of the Roman Law, chanted by the decemvirs and still memorized by the schoolboy Cicero.
4. See Saul Lieberman, *Hellenism in Jewish Palestine* (New York, 1950).
5. J. B. Soloveitchik, 'The Lonely Man of Faith,' *Tradition* 7 (1965): 5–67.
6. Ibid.
7. Ibid.
8. Northrop Frye indicates the problem while trying to obviate it. He writes: 'Unity, a primary principle of works of art since Plato's time, also indicates the finiteness of the human mind, the *care* that works toward transforming the "imperfect" or continuous into the "perfect," the form achieved once and for all. The Bible, however unified, also displays a carelessness about unity, not because it fails to achieve it, but because it has passed through it to another perspective on the other side of it' (Northrop Frye, *The Great Code: The Bible as Literature* [New York: Harcourt Brace, 1982], 207).
9. Harold Fisch, 'The Hermeneutic Quest in *Robinson Crusoe*,' in *Midrash and Literature*, ed. G. H. Hartman and S. Budick (New Haven, CT: Yale University Press, 1986), 230.
10. See Dan Sperber, *Rethinking Symbolism*, trans. Alice L. Morton (New York, 1975). In *The Voice of Jacob* (Bloomington: Indiana University Press, 1990), Leslie Brisman demonstrates how sensitive biblical interpretation can be, when it accepts the documentary hypothesis (its modification of the Bible's inspirational or authorial unity) yet brings the documents (here J and E/P) into dialogue. To do this requires (1) a definition of the literary as 'the primacy of intertextual, as opposed to sociological or political, motives for invention' (p. xiii), and (2) a midrashic sense of how late voices have a standing, how a kind of firstness can be drawn from secondariness.
11. The best discussion of the innovative and revelatory role of commentary in Judaism is that of Gershom Scholem. See his 'Offenbarung und Tradition als religiöse Kategorien im Judentum' (Revelation and tradition as religious categories in Judaism), *Judaica*, vol. 4 (Frankfurt: Suhrkamp, 1984). The English translation appears as *The Messianic Idea in Judaism* (New York: Schocken, 1971).
12. It is also rare, moreover, that a female child is given a formal naming phrase.

13. I am grateful to Barry Holtz for drawing my attention to this passage in an interesting talk held at a Midrash colloquium at Yale.

14. God Himself, in Menahot 29b, the famous story about Moses already cited above, is shown ornamenting the letters of Scripture (making crowns or wreaths for them). Scholem in 'Revelation and Tradition' interprets Moses's query to God, 'Who is restraining you?' to mean, 'Why are you not satisfied with the letters as you have constituted them, so that you add to them crowns, that is, the hooks which are found on certain letters in the Torah scrolls?'

15. If 'theurgic' is objected to, a different word should be found; I am not interested here in the differentiation of theurgy and magic or whether 'theurgy' comes in only with a Neoplatonic influence.

16. Scholem, 'Revelation and Tradition.' Scholem's further remark, that Revelation is essentially that of the name or names of God (linked to the signatures or *rishumim* found in created things), suggests how intrinsic the mystical mode of commentary is that reached exoteric status with the Kabbalah.

17. The fullest account of such practice in the Kabbalah may be found in Moshe Idel's *Kabbalah: New Perspectives* (New Haven, CT: Yale University Press, 1988). For *gematria* in Midrash, see, e.g., Rabbi H. Freedman and Maurice Simon, eds., *Midrash Rabbah: Numbers* (London: Socino, 1939), 2:734–39, especially on the *yod*. For information on Abulafia and on the Kabbalah I am indebted to conversations with Moshe Idel as well as to Gershom Scholem's chapter in his *Major Trends in Jewish Mysticism*, 3d. revised ed. (New York: Schocken, 1939). Scholem first pointed out the crucial importance to the Kabbalah of mitzvot and halakha as more than 'allegories,' indeed, as often resembling mystery rites of cosmic importance. Idel, in his revision and extension of Scholem, distinguishes between ecstatic Kabbalah (ascendental and unitive) and theurgical Kabbalah (descendental, working more through the mitzvot to harness divine powers).

18. The hermeneutic devices of Midrash, as they border on permutation, are described by Saul Lieberman in his chapter 'Rabbinic Interpretation of Scripture,' in *Hellenism in Jewish Palestine* (n. 4 above).

19. I owe this observation to Moshe Greenberg. Compare Kenneth Burke on proverbs, *The Philosophy of Literary Form*, 3d ed. (Berkeley: University of California Press, 1973), pp. 2. 294 ff.: 'Could the most complex and sophisticated works of art legitimately be considered somewhat as "proverbs writ large"?'

20. Arnold Goldberg, 'Der verschriftete Sprechakt als rabbinische Literatur,' in *Schrift und Gedächtnis*, ed. A. Assman, J. Assman, and Chr. Hardmeir (Munich: Wilhelm Fink, 1983).

21. Jacob Z. Lauterbach, ed., *Mekilta de-Rabbi Ishmael* (Philadelphia, 1942), 1:211. My attention was drawn to this passage by Daniel Boyarin's suggestive essay on intertextuality, allegory, and the meaning of Midrash by way of 'handles' provided by the Song of Songs. See his 'Re-citing Scripture,' *Orim: A Jewish Journal at Yale*, vol. 3, no. 2 (1988); cf. his *Intertextuality and the Reading of Midrash* (Bloomington: University of Indiana Press, 1990), chap. 7. Does this Midrash recall a speculation that the Song of Songs was revealed to Israel at the Red Sea?

22. See the Babylonian Talmud, Tractate X, Mishnah 3, and Tractate Berachot 60a.

23. Yet what is science here, and what theology, is hard to say: for Thomas Aquinas, too, a male child becomes a soul by the fortieth day. (For a girl it takes longer!)

24. The tendency to interpret down as well as up, and perhaps the redactors' unwillingness to let go of any interpretation that illustrates human behavior, can lead Midrash aggada to include silly or dubiously humorous exegeses. For example, see the following, in the Buber edition of the *Tanhuma*: '(Genesis 30:23) *Then she said: God has taken away my shame*. What is the meaning of *Has taken away?* Simply that before a wife gives birth there is shame found within her house. How? When she breaks a vessel in her house, whom does she have to blame? When she gives birth, she blames her child. She therefore said: *God has taken away my shame*' (Salomon Buber, ed., *Midrash Tanhuma* [Vilnius: Wittwe & Gebrüder Romm, 1885]).

25. Another way of putting this is that in Midrash (but not, perhaps, in the extreme permutations of prophetic Kabbalah) the idea of a divine (pure, absolute) language did not lead to a rejection of the accommodated or current language. A strictly analogous problem in contemporary thought is the relation of scientific language (in its as yet unrealized perfection) and ordinary discourse. The perfect language or metalanguage of science, writes Henri Lefebvre, 'would be a "pure" construction, closer to an elaboration in logic pushed to its final term than the natural and spontaneous "expression" of feelings, emotions, passions, images. It could turn out . . . that this perfectly rational language is characterized by the displacement or elimination of stops, blanks, cuts, pauses, which abound in our spoken or written language. The latter segments and punctuates our "expressiveness" in language; it introduces articulations but also haltings, uncertainties, choices that are doubtless arbitrary (between words, turns of phrases, ways to compose a discourse) . . . A mathematical demonstration is obviously not spaced and articulated like a discourse. Its continuity follows through without gaps.' See his *Le langage et la societé* (Paris: Gallimard, 1966), chap. 1.

26. See Frances A. Yates on 'The Classical Art of Memory,' in her *The Art of Memory* (Harmondsworth: Penguin, 1966), 19. David Stern suggests, however, that some elements in the important type of parable called the king-*mashal* 'represent the literary equivalent in Rabbinic Judaism to the pictorial art of early Christianity.' See his *Parables in Midrash: Narrative and Exegesis in Rabbinic Literature* (Cambridge, MA: Harvard University Press, 1991), pp. 94–97.

27. This does not mean, of course, that important types of discourse like the *peticha* (proem) should not be isolated and defined; 'literary' indicates a development of form-criticism liberated from source-criticism, though not from a speculation about the genesis of structures that could provide insights into their historicity.

28. Walter Ong, *Orality and Literature: The Technologizing of the Word* (London: Routledge, 1982), 48.

29. Leopold Zunz, *Gottesdienstliche Vorträge der Juden* (Frankfurt am Main: J. Kauffmann, 1892).

30. Exceptions are Susan Handelman's *The Slayers of Moses: The Emergence of Robbinic Interpretation in Modern Literary Theory* (Albany, NY, 1982); and Boyarin's *Intertextuality and the Reading of Midrash*.

31. Howard Eilberg-Schwartz, in an important article, 'Who's Kidding Whom? A Serious Reading of Rabbinic Word Plays,' *Journal of the American Academy of Religion*, vol. 55 (1988), reads rabbinic paranomasia from the perspective of 'linguistic assumptions (that) would have made a dichotomy between activities called philology and word-plays inconceivable. Any linguistic transformation that we might designate as a pun or word-play would constitute, from the rabbis' linguistic understanding, a reasonable interpretation of a word.' It is 'reasonable' because they believed in the pre-existence of Hebrew and Torah and the inter-dependence of both. This belief produced what he usefully calls a 'molecular' analysis of biblical Hebrew in terms of consonantal recombination and re-voweling: 'There is a seemingly unproblematic level that tells a story. But the words that comprise this narrative are linked in various ways to one another and thus force the reader onto the level of commentary.' I can follow Eilberg-Schwartz so far. But the rabbinical assumptions he offers as *superintending* the interpretive process do not *determine* it. His anxiety about the notion of play leads him into a restrictive intentionalism that deprives the interpreter of a freedom within those assumptions (not just against them), a freedom without which the entire rabbinic enterprise of interpretation would lose much of its interest and integrity – for if the divine words were totally presignificant, they could not be used to argue with or even 'defeat' God in the drama that plays itself out between God and man but also between conflicting interests in the community (e.g., the Schools of Hillel and Shammai), each of which claims authority.

32. Maurice Blanchot, *The Writing of the Disaster*, trans. Anne Smock (Lincoln: University of Nebraska Press, 1986).

33. Goldberg (n. 23 above), 139. In his careful 'Introduction: Law as Literature,' to *Semeia*, vol. 27 (1983), William Scott Green points out that halakha too should be studied as a cultural construction, as texts that are 'sources' rather than simply data. He emphasizes the 'literary strategy of juxtaposing opposites without resolution' in halakhic law finding, which makes it difficult to treat it as mimetic, as an unmediated form of actual rabbinic practice. 'Indeed, the structure and form of rabbinic writings suggest that our first reading of these documents must see them not as records of collective behavior or institutional legislation, but as works of intellect and imagination.'

34. A. R. Ammons, *Corson's Inlet: A Book of Poems* (Ithaca, NY: Cornell University Press, 1965).

35. 'Oublier le texte qui a enfanté le text. Nous écrivons à partir de cet oubli.' E. Jabès, *Le livre du dialogue* (Paris, 1963).

36. If the anagrammatical reading of Scripture points to a 'revelation' of the divine names or to a mystical alphabet, a *logos* that created the world and still has creative (or destructive) force, then there is a strange convergence with a radical kind of deconstruction that sees literature as 'revealing' nothing more and nothing less than the remarkableness of the alphabet we already have, and by whose combinations everything that we do or think is articulated.

37. David Stern's *Parables in Midrash: Narrative and Exegesis in Rabbinic Literature* (Cambridge, MA: Harvard University Press, 1991), in a section called 'Theorizing

Midrash' (63–67), shows finely how 'in midrash, exegesis may be the mashal's occasion, but its exegetical occasion does not exhaust the mashal's meaning, which goes far beyond both exegesis and narrative alone, lying instead in their intersection.'

Chapter 14

The Voice of the Shuttle

Aristotle, in the *Poetics* (16.4), records a striking phrase from a play by Sophocles, since lost, on the theme of Tereus and Philomela. Tereus, having raped Philomela, cut out her tongue to prevent discovery. But she weaves a tell-tale account of her violation into a tapestry (or robe) which Sophocles calls 'the voice of the shuttle.' If metaphors as well as plots or myths could be archetypal, I would nominate Sophocles' voice of the shuttle for that distinction.

What gives these words power to speak to us even without the play? No doubt the story of Tereus and Philomela has a universally affecting element: the double violation, the alliance of craft (cunning) and craft (art), and what the metaphor specifically refers to: that truth will out, that human consciousness will triumph. The phrase would not be effective without the story, yet its focus is so sharp that a few words seem to yield not simply the structure of one story but of all stories in so far as they are telltales. Aristotle, in fact, mentions Sophocles' kenning during his discussion of how recognition scenes are brought about; and it is interesting that other examples cited by him share the characteristic of seeming to exist prior to the plays that embody them, as if they were riddles or gnomic words imposed by tradition and challenging an adequate setting. Take, for example, 'So I too must die at the altar like my sister' (Orestes); or 'I came to find my son, and I lose my own life' (Tydeus); Or, again, 'Here we are doomed to die; for here we were cast forth' (Phineidae, *Poetics* 16.6). These phrases, overheard, bring about a recognition. Like the voice of the shuttle they have little meaning without a story that sets them. Yet once a story is found, their suggestiveness is not absorbed but potentiated. And this, perhaps, is what *archetype* means: a part greater than the whole of which it is a part, a text that demands a context yet is not reducible to it.

Can a rhetorical analysis of this phrase clarify its power? 'Voice' stands for the pictorial legend of the tapestry by a metonymic substitution of effect for cause. We say similarly, if less dramatically, that a book 'speaks' to us. 'Shuttle' stands for the weaver's instrument by the synecdochal substitution of part for whole, but it also contains a metonymy which names the productive cause instead of the product. Thus we have, in the first term (voice), a substitution of effect for cause, and in the second (shuttle), of cause for effect. By this double metonymy the distance between cause and effect in an ordinary chain of events is significantly increased, and the termini of this chain are over-specified at the expense of intermediate points (Fig. 14.1). What this etiologic distancing means is not clear from the expression taken out of context. You and I, who know the story, appreciate the cause winning through, and Philomela's 'voice' being restored; but by itself the phrase simply disturbs our sense of causality and guides us, if it guides us at all, to a hint of supernatural rather than human agency. (The inanimate speaks out, cf. blood crying from the earth in Genesis 4.)

Figure 14.1

A rhetorical analysis, therefore, brings us quickly to a limit. But we learn certain things from it. The power of the phrase lies in its elision of middle terms and overspecification of end terms. This could bear on two features every theory of poetic language seeks to explain: 'aesthetic distance' which usually favors the cool, reflective, nonrepresentational virtues; and 'iconicity' which usually abets the concrete, motor, representational ones. These features, however, are no more dissociable than are periphrasis and pointedness in Sophocles' figure. We find ourselves in the presence of an antinomy which is restated rather than solved by calling art a concrete universal. The tension of this figure from Sophocles is like the tension of poetics.

I make this large claim in a purely heuristic spirit. There is something cross-eyed about the figure and something cross-eyed about every explanatory poetics. 'It must be visible or invisible,' says Wallace Stevens in *Notes toward a Supreme Fiction*, 'Invisible or visible or both / . . . An abstraction blooded, as a man by thought.' Now while Nature, according to an old saying, loves mixtures ('la nature aime les entrecroisements'), science does not. I must therefore steer an ambiguous course between nature and science and sketch for you a playful poetics: one that asserts nothing directly about logic, ontology, or linguistic science yet brings together the smallest literary patterns with the largest, the analysis of single metaphors or verses with the comprehensive kind of anatomy practised by Aristotle in the *Poetics*. So far all we have learned is that figures of speech may be characterized by overspecified ends and indeterminate middles, that this structure may explain the shifting relations of concrete and abstract in poetics, and that (I add this now) the very elision or subsuming of middle terms allows, if it does not actually compel, interpretation. I mean that the strength of the end terms depends on our seeing the elided members of the chain (e.g., the full relation of Tereus and Philomela); the more clearly we see them, the stronger the metaphor which collapses that chain, makes a mental bang, and speeds the mind by freeing it from overelaboration and the toil of consecutiveness. A great verbal figure gives us the second wind of inspiration; it makes us sure, after all, of overtaking the tortoise.

I begin with a line from Milton: 'Sonorous metal blowing martial sounds' (*Paradise Lost*, 1.540). A balanced line, with adjective–noun phrases flanking the pivotal verb. The syntactical sequence (1 2 1 2) is counterpointed, however, by a chiastic pattern of alliteration (1 2 2 1, s m m s). Milton, too, it seems, 'aime les entrecroisements.' Yet it is hard to make something significant of such formal patterns, which are not unusual in Milton. Suppose, however, you take the line as complete or self-balanced: an inspired throw of the verbal dice. We may then look at it as generated from a redundant concept, 'sonorous sounds,' which we recover by collapsing the ends. The verse, from this perspective, is the separating out of 'sonorous sounds'; a refusal, by inserting a verbal space between adjective and noun, to let them converge too soon. 'Sonorous' is divided from 'sounds' and assigned to 'metal'; while 'metal,' as it were, gives up 'martial' which is assigned to 'sounds' by syntactical transfer. Here metaphor is as much a function of syntax as syntax of metaphor. While the chiastic alliteration, moreover, helps to overcome the redundance of 'sonorous sounds,' the syntactical parallelism lightens the secondary redundance of 'martial metal.' These two features, previously mentioned, distribute and differentiate the sonic mass like God dividing elemental matter in order to get the sixfold creation.

Figure 14.2

sonorous		sounds
raven		darkness
mon		o(n)cle
sa		tyros
i	(eve)	ll
brim	(in a flash)	full
what	(torn ship)	soever
a		sloe
rolling		air
Humpty		Dumpty

Compare now Sophocles' metaphor and Milton's line. In Milton the middle terms need not be recovered by interpretation: his line effects its own middle by separating the ends (Fig. 14.2). What is created in both is a breach or space – an opening with the sense of freedom implicit in that word – but while in Sophocles this space functions as etiologic distancing, as a suspension of normal causality, in Milton it allows the emergence of words out of sheer sound and is linked to a distancing intrinsic to language, one which differentiates sounds as meaning by a 'diacritical' (Saussure) or 'binary opposition' (Jakobson) method.

The idea of space now introduced is not the same as aesthetic distance, nor the tendency of the Miltonic or Sophoclean figure to collapse into a strong redundancy or tighter than normal idea of causation the same as iconicity. I doubt we can reach these very general concepts except by approximation. But we already glimpse what makes the 'tension' of single figures or the literary work as a whole. Take a second, and more ambitious, Miltonic figure. In *Comus* music is heard 'smoothing the Raven doune/Of darkness till it smiled.' Here 'smoothing' and 'smiled' converge slightly, but the real interest lies in the central metaphor, the raven down of darkness. The most likely model of how it originated is to posit a seed-phrase, 'the raven of darkness,' a simple imaginative concept justified by Virgil's 'bird of night' (cf. *Aeneid*, 8.369), and with a tang of redundancy which can be brought out by translating it as 'the dark bird of darkness.' Some such overlap exists in any metaphor, in so far as it is analogical; and Milton diminishes the redundance by the syntactical insertion of a second figure which distances 'raven' from 'darkness.' This figure, the 'down of darkness,' has nothing conceptually redundant in it. A surprising trope, it is linked to one terminus – 'darkness' – by alliteration and to the other – 'raven' – by imagistic extension.[1] Thus the linear, syntactical insertion of this second metaphor works exactly like the 'metal . . . martial' segment which was also linked by consonants. In Milton, syntax differentiates metaphor just as metaphor differentiates something more massive which it continues to express.

The 'transformational' poetics here emerging can be clarified by polarization: going, on the one hand, to the microstructures of literature, entities studied by linguists, and on the other hand to the macrostructures studied by all of us. In a phrase like 'le monocle de mon oncle' the redundancy of sounds is obvious, yet there is no semantic redundancy. Indeed, the wit of the phrase is that a slight difference in sound (between 'monocle' and 'mon oncle') releases such vast, if dubious, difference of meaning. It's like a man slipping on a banana peel – cause and effect are totally disproportionate. Technically defined the difference in sound is a slight distortion of quantity but primarily a matter of what linguists call 'boundary' or 'juncture' – here typographically indicated by 'monocle' dividing into two words, 'mon oncle.'[2] What metonymy is to the 'voice of the shuttle' or syntax to Milton, juncture is to this witty title from Wallace Stevens (Fig. 14.2).

Juncture is simply a space, a breathing space: phonetically it has zero value, like a caesura. But precisely because it is such a mini-phenomenon, it dramatizes the differential or, as Saussure calls it, diacritical relation of sound to meaning. In any crucial arrangement of words, a small change goes a long way, as we learn through slightly mistranslated words in diplomatic messages. Split the atom of sound (and speech is fission) and you detonate an astonishing charge of meaning. With juncture we may have reached an analogue on the level of speech to aesthetic distance in art, especially as it remains linked to that explosive, if harnessed, *enargeia* (picture power) which we sometimes name iconicity.

The importance of zero values like juncture becomes more obvious when we turn to the smallest literary unit, the pun. Artemidorus records in his *Oneirocritica* that when Alexander of Macedon was besieging Tyre he dreamt he saw a satyr dancing on his shield. By dividing the word into sa-tyros, 'Tyre is thine,' this became a favorable omen for the siege. Freud, who cites the story and is fascinated by the immense role words play in dreams, gives many examples of what he calls 'condensation.' The image of the satyr, for example, is a visual condensation of a compound phrase (sa-tyre), but when the form of condensation remains verbal, we get punning or portmanteau phrases like Joyce's 'mamafesta.' Joyce extraverts the fact that language itself has its dream work which dreams seem only to imitate. This dream work shows itself, before Joyce, in naming rather than nouning, and especially in the resonant appeal of mythic names:

> Abhorred *Styx* the flood of deadly hate,
> Sad *Acheron* of sorrow, black and deep;
> *Cocytus*, nam'd of lamentation loud
> Heard on the rueful stream; fierce *Phlegeton*
> Whose waves of torrent fire in flame with rage
>   *Paradise Lost*, 2.577 ff.

Each of these lines is, at it were, a decontraction of the name.

This leads to the thought that nouns may be demythologized names. We are told that under the Hebrew word *TeHOM* in Genesis 1 (translated 'the deep') the divine Babylonian monster *TIAMAT* may be couchant, reduced by the Bible from monster to mere noun. How are the mighty fallen, into syntax! What is true of nouns may be true of language in general. For Emerson language is fossilized metaphors; Saussure thought that grammatical systems might have originated in anagrammatic distributions of a sacred name; and Shelley asserted 'language itself is poetry . . . Every original language near to its source is itself the chaos of a cyclic poem.'

Whatever the truth of these speculations, they share a common feeling. Reading a poem is like walking on silence – on volcanic silence. We feel the historical ground; the buried life of words. Like fallen gods, like visions of the night, words are erectile. A poet can 'speak silence' as simply as Chatterton did by opening up words through a mock-archaic spelling: 'When joicie peres, and berries of blacke die,/ Doe daunce yn ayre, and call the eyne arounde . . .' That 'joicie' is Joycean. Joyce's more Freudian understanding of words simply brings literature abreast of language: he dramatizes the language jam in which we are stuck, the intrinsic duplicity, racial mix, and historically accreted character of living speech. 'Mamafesta' not only mocks patriarchal imperatives but plays on the structural impurity of language, which mingles, like any doctrine or myth, opposing strains. There is the mother tongue (mama) and the learned, generally latinate layer (manifesto). English is especially prone to this happy impurity, not having suffered, like French or Italian, a decisive neoclassical sublimation of the vernacular. The division of language into sounding words or periphrases (e.g., 'the deep backward and abysm of time,' a Shakespearean blend of colloquial and learned) and its contraction into those resonant vocables from which, like dream interpreters of old, Milton draws new meanings, are part of one and the same rhythm. It compounds 'the imagination's Latin with/The lingua franca et jocundissima' (Wallace Stevens).

It is a far cry, of course, from mystical semantics to modern semiotics. Both, however, respect the function of silence, those zero values of juncture, elision, and decontraction which play so vast yet intangible a role in poetry. It is not mystical to call poetic language the voices of silence. Let us watch Milton creating meaning out of zero values in a famous pun: 'O Eve in evil hour . . .' (*Paradise Lost*, 9.1067).

The pun again involves a name, though the latter does not release a new meaning by juncture. Instead, as is characteristic of Milton, it distributes itself in linear fashion by transfer or contamination. To go from 'Eve' to 'evil' is metaphor on the level of sound. But is the direction of the transfer from 'Eve' to 'evil,' or from 'evil' to 'Eve'? Milton, it could be argued, does not need the word 'Eve' except to spell out a pun that is not particularly good. He adds reader insult to language injury. But the double 'Eve-evil' gives us the sense of a third term or matrix, a common root from which both might have sprung. Thus juncture may be involved after all: whatever the matrix malorum is, it contains at this fateful hour both 'Eve' and 'evil.'

This hypothetical matrix is like the redundant concept, 'sonorous sounds,' which generated a verse-line already studied. The present half-line is also curiously, beautifully redundant. The more we listen to it, the more it becomes one modulated crying diphthong – a breaking or ablauted Oh. The end terms O and *hour* stand in the same intensified relation as the chiastic middle terms 'Eve' and 'evil.' It is fanciful, yet true to the sound-shape of the line, to say that 'evil' is 'Eve' raised a phonetic rather than a grammatical degree, an impression reinforced by the fact that both 'evil' and 'hour' are quantities hovering between one syllable and two so that 'evil' can be heard as a decontraction of 'ill' (Fig. 14.2). The semantic energy and affective pitch of the line is again determined by properties that approach zero value (O . . . hour; Eve . . . evil).

From juncture, usually represented by a slash, it is only a step to the grammatical figure of tmesis, best represented by a dash. Tmesis, from the Greek 'to divide' (cf. *atom*, 'the undividable'), can be as simple as in Gerard Manley Hopkins's 'Brim, in a flash, full.' Two words conventionally joined, are disjoined to accommodate an intruded middle (Fig. 14.2). The effect is that of interjection, of bursting in, but it gives extra value to the enclitic 'full,' which otherwise would have been slurred. The end terms are stressed ('in-stressed,' Hopkins would say) by their being distanced, crowded away from each other. This is not unlike what happens through metonymy in the voice of the shuttle.

The continuity of juncture and tmesis is best shown by a graded series of examples. The enjambment in

> I have
> Immortal longings in me

is a hovering kind of juncture and depicts Shakespeare's Cleopatra on the point of crossing a fearful divide. She crosses it wishfully, by a mere breathing or aspiration. Donne's running speech, his self-persuasive eloquence, tries to leap a similar divide, but the strain is more evident:

> thinke that I
> Am, by being dead, Immortal . . .

At once nervous and peremptory, this 'I Am Immortal' asserts itself in quick sequence against the line-end severance of subject and copula and a tmetic severance within the copula. Severance may seem too strong a word for pauses ('I/Am') or suspensions ('Am . . . Immortal') natural to spoken speech. Tmesis here is not a violent or artificial device but a more difficult enjambment, a heightened form of juncture which continues to individuate the basic words as they incline toward finality, carried by the proleptic verve of speech. Severance is the right term, however, when we look beyond speech to poetry. The qualified haste, the precarious finality of Donne's poetry is also that of religious hope. How to 'cross-over' – or the dangers of passage – is the central theme:

> In what torn ship soever I embark
> That ship shall be my emblem of thy ark.

'Whatsoever' opens and swallows 'torn ship' as the poet severs the grammatical bond to interject his fear. But 'embark' also opens to let a saving rhyme, 'emb(lem) . . . ark,' emerge as the poet converts fear into hope by further prolepsis.

A more complicated form of tmesis distends the syntactical bond almost beyond repair. The normative adjectival space in 'a lush-kept plush-capped sloe' is strained to the utmost; in fact, by the internal rhyming of the twofold compound adjective Hopkins reverses ends and middles, since rhyme is characteristic of line endings. Wishing to restore, in *The Wreck of the Deutschland*, our sense of the scriptural 'In the beginning was the Word,' which he opposes to the understated habit of English speech, Hopkins creates these hysteron-proteron formations (the Word, i.e., Christ as the Word, which is always confessed last, should be uttered first by us). We can see another result of this upbeat style in a line which describes the Windhover riding 'The rolling underneath him steady air' (Fig. 14.2). The introversion of all these modifiers between the adjective ('rolling') and the noun ('air') parallels the trick of inversion in classical imitators or neoclassical rhymers. The middle of the line is so strong, compared to the conventional ends, that it almost jumps out like the word 'Buckle' in the same poem, which, escaping its grammatical tie like a chemical its bond, becomes plosive:

> Brute beauty and valour and act, oh air, pride, plume, here
> Buckle!

'Buckle' (the first word of the second line) is as true a rhyme word as 'here' (the last word of the first line) because it at once condenses and detonates the sound pattern of the preceding words with their complex chiastic alliteration. The last becomes the first once more.[3]

It is strange that the ultimate form of a zero value like tmesis should be a surplus value like rhyme. But tmesis, you will remember, splits a conventionally bonded phrase by means of an assertive middle term, creating stronger poles as well as intruding a strong middle. Now in rhymed poetry the poles regress to a line-end position, becoming *bouts rimés*, while the rest of the verse is inserted between these rhymed ends. We see by this that Milton's rejection of rhyme is related to Hopkins's freeing rhyme from its fixed terminal position and making the last first (in sound-shape, not merely line-place). The end terms of Milton's figures tend, in fact, to be redundant like perfect rhymes; and he uses syntactical tmesis to distance them, to insert phrases that remain bonded to the poles. A Miltonic middle, which separates, for example, 'sonorous' and 'sounds' or 'raven' and 'darkness,' is a brilliant modification of redundancy, the distribution of an overly-rich mental or aural concept.

Thus rhyme is not an isolated phenomenon. Every birth of meaning has, like rhyme, a binary form, since meaning emerges through the opposition of similar-sounding entities. Consider 'Humpty-Dumpty': it suggests, like 'Eve . . . evil,' a unitary word embracing the divided elements – yet nothing can put Humpty-Dumpty together again. Humpty-Dumpty is the portmanteau word that failed, but its fortunate failure reveals the binary form. The hyphen joining Humpty and Dumpty is at once disjunctive and conjunctive; we may interpret it as the generalized tmetic sign which points to the middle between all *bouts rimés*. When a pun or portmanteau word sorts itself out, and similar sounds are put in line-end positions, we get rhyme. Rhyme is but another example of a figure with overspecified ends and an indeterminate middle. Is all poetical or figurative speech of this structure? Is it all a modified punning?

You can define a pun as two meanings competing for the same phonemic space or as one sound bringing forth semantic twins, but, however you look at it, it's a crowded situation. There is too much sound for the sense or too much sense for the sound. This aspect we have named the redundancy principle, and it makes poetry radically oblique in terms of sign function. Poetry either says too much – approaches the inexpressible – or too little – approaches the inexpressive. 'The voice of the shuttle' could be an inflation of the proper term, an inane periphrasis for tapestry (cf. 'fruit of the loom'). It could also be a miraculous condensation so packed with meaning that it skirts the oracular. Poetry will always live under a cloud of suspicion which it discharges by such lightnings.

We don't know, to be honest, what a perfect verbal system is like. But we do know language develops by what Coleridge calls desynonimization and the structuralists call binary opposition. A breathing space, a division within redundancy, appears and makes room for us, for our word. So Tiamat, its mythological fatness, is degraded from name to noun, and from monster to vague mystery. But the artist, like God, broods on the deep noun and makes it pregnant. A new meaning comes forth, a new word, a new world.

You probably feel as impatient with me, and all this talk about zero values, as Bishop Berkeley did with Newton's infinitesimals. He called these entities, calculable only by Newton's theory of fluxions, the 'ghosts of departed quantities.' I now turn from minims to maxims, and to more tangible values.

No critic can refrain from having his say on the *Oedipus*. I am tempted to build on it not only a theory of life, like Freud, but a theory about what makes literature vital to life. Freud never brought his theory of 'dream-work' together with his theory about Oedipus. Yet it is clear that what he calls 'condensation' is crucial to a tragedy which compresses life to coincidence and the smallest possible freedom. For, talking now about plot, mythos, and such maxistructures, we can say that Oedipus, killing his father and marrying his mother, simply elides individual identity and is allowed no being properly his own. The oracle takes away, from the outset, any chance for self-development. Oedipus is redundant: he is his father, and as his father he is nothing, for he returns to the womb that bore him. His lifeline does not exist.

Except for the illusion that it exists, which the play relentlessly negates. This illusion is important, it is all Oedipus has to develop in. Achilles' career is also limited by a prophecy: short life and glory, or long life and none. But it is not 'condensed' like a Greek epigram in which the marriage bed is also the deathbed. Oedipus converges on his fate like an epigram on its point or a tragedy on its recognition scene. The etiologic distancing collapses, the illusion bursts, the supernatural leaves the natural no space. The placenta of illusions has been eaten by the stichomythia.

Human life, like a poetical figure, is an indeterminate middle between overspecified poles always threatening to collapse it. The poles may be birth and death, father and mother, mother and wife, love and judgment, heaven and earth, first things and last things. Art narrates that middle region and charts it like a purgatory, for only if it exists can life exist; only if the imagination presses against the poles are error and life and illusion – all those things which Shelley called 'generous superstitions' – possible. The excluded middle is a tragedy also for the imagination.

In human history there are periods of condensation (or concentration, as Matthew Arnold called them) where the religious spirit seems to push man up tight against the poles of existence. Middles become suspect; mediations almost impossible. Things move by polarizing or reversing (peripeteia) or collapsing. 'The best lack all conviction, and the worst/Are full of passionate intensity,' as Yeats said, seeing the center breaking up. The Reformation was an era of this kind, and it produced, in its purity, a most awesome concentration of human consciousness on a few existentials. The space filled by boughten mercies and mediations is collapsed into a direct, unmediated confrontation of the individual and his God. What does art do in this situation? Does it – can it – save the 'ghost of departed mediations'? Is there any authentic way of inserting a middle strong enough to satisfy a now extremist imagination?

Emily Dickinson often begins with death, or a moment near it. Her poems are as laconic as tombstones that speak from the wayside. In the following poem she has come to a way-station called Eternity. The poem 'condenses' at that point:

> Our journey had advanced –
> Our feet were almost come
> To that odd Fork in Being's Road –
> Eternity – by Term –
>
> Our pace took sudden awe –
> Our feet – reluctant – lead –
> Before – were Cities – but Between –
> The Forest of the Dead –
>
> Retreat – was out of Hope –
> Behind – a Sealed Route –
> Eternity's White Flag – Before –
> And God – at every Gate –

These are strangely detached, inconclusive verses for all their exactitude. We are told that the soul must pass through death ('the forest of the dead') to the city of God. Yet though you cannot reach Eternity except through death, the poet opened by saying that she was near Eternity to start with, while in the last stanza Eternity precedes the soul with a safe-conduct. In this little quest-romance Eternity is always *before* you.

The difficulty may lie in the very idea of Eternity, which cannot be represented by space or time categories. This does not explain, however, why Emily Dickinson is haunted by a conception impossible to depict. The conception, obviously, is a motivating one in terms of the poem. The poet sees to see. Her mode is infinitive. Each stanza infers that one step which is not taken – into epiphany, or visibility. Nothing is at once more and less visible than white: 'Eternity's white flag before.' There is, to quote Wallace Stevens once more, a 'seeing and unseeing in the eye.' The God at every gate multiplies an opening through which we do not pass.

It is a poem, therefore, which three times brings us to a limit and three times displaces that limit. Our feet had 'almost' come (st. 1); 'The forest of the dead' intervenes (st. 2); the gate god appears, as concrete as eternity's color (a 'colorless all-color') is vague (st. 3). The limit is also, of course, a limen or threshold; yet the imagination that moves to cross it and see God does no more than see limits. Will God open or block the gate? And is not his very appearance, finally, as gate god, the block? Eternity becomes seeable only at that risk: the poet has advanced, if she has advanced at all, from Terminus to Janus. Her destiny – or is it her choice – seems to be to stay profane: *profanus*, on the threshold of vision.

The space Sophocles wrested from the gods was the very space of human life. That space is illusory, or doomed to collapse as the play focuses on the moment of truth which proves the oracle. In Emily Dickinson, predestination corresponds to the oracle. No wonder 'Our pace took sudden awe.' That next step, into death, is also, according to the faith of her fathers, a step into destination – into judgment and eternity. Protestantism has shrunk the breathing space between death, judgment, and apocalypse, so that the last things are one thing, and purgatory is no more. Like an oracle, in fact, judgment is already there at birth; death only justifies it or renders it visible. What is life, then, except death's threshold? Since the 'ocular proof' comes with death, the life of the mind is centered on that moment, which is any moment. A person should live as if it were the moment preceding judgment. One is always, to quote the absolute opening of another poem, 'The man – to die – tomorrow.' We anticipate for whom the bell tolls; the time is always zero minus one.

Yet Emily Dickinson's tone is unhurried, as if there were time to puzzle 'that odd fork in Being's road.' Placing 'Eternity' near 'term' even shows, in the following line, a bookish wit. The mind remains slightly apart or off-center, like the rhymes; off-center also to the body. The impersonal constructions – 'our journey,' 'our pace,' 'our feet' – elide the agony of self-consciousness and suggest a speaker positioned above the vehicular body. There is a distance between her and her feet compounded at once of awe and detachment. Her attitude is almost spectatorial.

Can we define that attitude exactly? It is clear that Emily Dickinson's art creates a space. It allows the threshold to exist; it extends the liminal moment.

The poet's minutes are our days and hours. If rhymes are there, it is not because they condense, but because verse should be orderly, even in extreme situations. They decondense rather; especially the last and best of them: 'god . . . gate.' Here off-rhyme moves from line-ending into the midst of the verse. Some will hear in 'god . . . gate' the echo of a closing door: she fears she may not be admitted. But it is better to leave it, like the rhyme itself, slightly ajar.

That her feet are 'toward eternity' does not alter, radically, the poet's state of mind. She is carried off, perhaps, but she does not give herself. As the journey takes her along, her poem remains a bourgeois ledger, an extension of Christian watchfulness. To remain what she is, steadfastly, unterrified, amounts to an election of self: she will not change utterly. Thus personality is not pushed beyond the human sphere as in Greek tragedy. Behind Philomela – the weaver – looms, like an oracular or archetypal shadow, the figure of fate. Fate too spins. On her shuttle she divides and spins the thread of human existence. But also, possibly, a sound: is not Sophocles' 'the voice of the shuttle' a symbol for oracular utterance? Fate alone could tell all, and Philomela, when her voice is restored through art, participates for a moment in divinity. She triumphs over a terrible doom, yet the recognition she brings about continues a tragic chain of events. Emily Dickinson does not 'tell all'; there is no staring recognition in her poetry. Her fate is to stay profane, outside the gates, though in sight of 'the promised end.'

Interpretation is like a football game. You spot a hole and you go through. But first you may have to induce that opening. The Rabbis used the technical word *patach* ('he opened') for interpretation. Gershom Scholem has shown that the extravagance of the Kabbalah is linked to its opening Scripture to the suffering and concreteness of secular history. Deucalion's interpretation of the 'bones of his mother' as the 'stones of the earth' is similarly an imaginative wager that saved a race.

We have art, said Nietzsche, so as not to die of the truth. A vital hermeneutics, it limits the sacred or makes room for life in life. The truth mediated by art is deadly because it is too present, too specific. The truth-seeker is like the child who sees exactly 'a hundred and three' sheep in a landscape; the artist like one who knows that what was seen is 'about a hundred over there *and* three here': '103' is shown to be a hendyadis, or a poetic diction, which overspecifies the ends (cf. 'finny tribe,' 'the voice of the shuttle') yet saves the sense of a middling.

Naming, like counting, is a strong mode of specification. It disambiguates the relation of sign to signified, making the proper term one end and the thing that is meant the other. Two terms complete the act; signification itself is elided, or treated as transparent (Fig. 14.3). Naming of this kind does not draw attention to itself. Literary speech does, however; and not by an occult quality (a secret third term), but rather by structures like periphrasis which under- and overspecify at the same time. Poetical figures habitually take away the proper term: 'The sun must bear no name.' Yet when Stevens adds 'gold flourisher' he suggests how creative this decreation is, how his 'abstraction' compounds under- and over-specification.[4]

Figure 14.3

The final hermeneutics art practices on itself. 'It is written' or 'everything has been said' is the somber oracle that denies the individual talent. In stories there is a period of error or quest, that wonder-wandering which makes them stories and evades an eternally fixed world. In this 'wonder and woe' youth becomes '*mündig*' – is given its proper voice. Old names are cleansed; new tongues flicker. Creative error makes the blue darter hawk (it is blue and it darts) into a 'blue dollar hawk,' 'the outmost sentinel of the wild, immortal camp.' Tribal imperative remain, however: individuality is wrested from the overwhelming presumption that we have a duty in common. Stories begin, therefore, with something that means too much: a corpse (as in *Hamlet* or the latest thriller), an oracle, an archetype, an overdeterminable symbol. Art does not add itself to the world of meanings: it makes room in meaning itself.

It is an axiom of contemporary poetics that a word is not simply a meaning: 'A poem should not mean/But be.' Confusion sets in, however, as soon as we attempt to define how words are released from their bondage to meaning. The alternative to meaning must be within the aura of meaning, even part of its structure: so Kant's 'purposiveness without purpose' remains within the aura of teleology. Meaning is everywhere; the problem is that of fullness rather than emptiness, of redundancy and insignificant signification. Things come to us preinterpreted: Stevens asks the sun to shine in a heaven 'that has expelled us and our images.' Superfetation of meanings in our world is like the proliferation of gods and spirits in the ancient world. 'And still the world pursues' – no wonder Mallarmé wished to evoke an 'objet tu' by means of an 'ombre exprès.' There is always something that violates us, deprives our voice, and compels art toward an aesthetics of silence. 'Les yeux seuls sont encore capable de pousser un cri,' René Char writes about his experiences in the Second World War. And Nelly Sachs, alluding to the suffering of her people:

> Wailing Wall Night
> Carved in you are the psalms of silence.

Bibliographical Note (1969)

On 'condensation,' see Freud, *The Interpretation of Dreams* (Vienna, 1900). The satyros story is mentioned on p. 99 of the 1911 edition. On the glamor of grammar, see C. Brooke-Rose, *A Grammar of Metaphor* (New York, 1959); Morton W. Bloomfield, 'The Syncategoremic in Poetry: From Semantics to Syntactics,' in *To Honor Roman Jakobson* (The Hague, Janua Linguarum Series Major 31, 1967), 1: 309–17; and T. Todorov, 'La grammaire du récit,' *Langages* 12 (1968): 94–102. A. J. Greimas's remarks on the 'syntactical distance' between defined and solving word in crossword puzzles may have implication for poetics through the intermediate notion of periphrasis (*To Honor Roman Jakobson*, 1: 799–815). W. K. Wimsatt, Jr., notes Milton's syntactical 'dislocations' in 'One Relation of Rhyme to Reason,' *The Verbal Icon* (Lexington, KY, 1954).

Owen Barfield in *Poetic Diction* (London, 1928), pp. 66 ff. and 116 ff., has genial remarks on the making of meaning through abridgment or etymological development. He utilizes Emerson's essay on 'Language' and Shelley's 'Defense of Poetry.' De Saussure's notes on words within words and anagrammatic grammar are analyzed by J. Starobinski, *Mercure de France* (Février 1964); and in *To Honor Roman Jakobson*, 3: 1906–18. Kenneth Burke's 'On Musicality in Verse,' *The Philosophy of Literary Form* (Baton Rouge, 1941), studies concealed alliteration in Coleridge and approaches De Saussure. His 'A Theory of Terminology,' in *Interpretation: The Poetry of Meaning*, ed. R. Hopper and D. L. Miller (New York 1967) pp. 88 ff., summarizes much of his concern with tautology and graded series. For 'Joyce as Philologist,' see Richard M. Kain, *Mosaic* 2 (1969): 74–85, and the relevant works of David Hayman and J. S. Atherton. I have previously tried a structuralist analysis in *Hopkins: A Collection of Critical Essays* (Englewood Cliffs, NJ, 1966), pp. 8–9.

In Lewis Carroll's *Through the Looking Glass* Humpty-Dumpty defines a *portmanteau* phrase as 'two meanings packed up into one word.' See also Carroll's preface to the 1896 edition of that book. His story 'Novelty and Romancement' is based on the misapprehension of 'boundary.' The ontological role of error in figurative speech is the subject of Walker Percy's 'Metaphor as Mistake,' *Sewanee Review* 67 (1958): 79–99. I take from him the example of the 'Blue Darter Hawk.' Sigurd Burkhardt's *Shakespearean Meanings* (Princeton, 1968), esp. chap. 2, discusses the 'bondage of meaning' and how poetry breaks the 'semantic identity' of words. Cf. Elizabeth Sewell, *The Structure of Poetry* (London, 1951), esp. p. 16. The modern 'Aesthetics of Silence' is discussed by Susan Sontag in *Styles of Radical Will* (1969). Also, for the basically oblique relations between literary sign and signification, see Maurice Merleau-Ponty, 'Le langage indirect et les voix du silence,' in *Signes* (Paris, 1961). On the possibility of a 'science de la littérature' based on a linguistic model, see Roland

Barthes, *Critique et vérité* (Paris, 1966), pp. 56–63. The Russian Formalists' distinction between the significant (phonemic) and nonsignificant (phonetic) relation of sound to meaning is summarized by V. Erlich, *Russian Formalism*, 2nd ed. (New York, 1965), pp. 218 ff.

Of the many areas omitted in this essay, the most important perhaps is that of the sociology of language, or rather 'literacy.' The work of Kenneth Burke, Roland Barthes, Michel Foucault, George Steiner, and others complements in this field philologists like Karl Vossler, Leo Spitzer, and Erich Auerbach. The notion of an 'écart stylistique' is essential to them. Some studies of particular interest: A. Van Gennep, 'Essai d'une théorie des langues spéciales,' *Religion, moeurs et légendes* (Paris, 1909); J. Huizinga, *The Waning of the Middle Ages* (London, 1924); Ernest Jones, 'A Linguistic Factor in English Characterology,' *Essays in Applied Psycho-Analysis* (London, 1923); Wilhelm von Humboldt, *Schriften zur Sprachphilosophie* (Wissenschaftliche Buchgesellschaft, Darmstadt, 1963).

Notes

1. The possibility that 'doune' puns on the adverb ('At every fall [of music] smoothing down the Raven of darkness') increases, if anything, its tmetic force.
2. I am not attempting an exact linguistic analysis: *juncture* is used only as the best available term, and I am aware that 'oc' and 'onc' contain a different phoneme. However, the impression occurs that as 'mon' separates from 'ocle' the latter compensates by expanding into 'oncle.' Elizabeth Sewell calls such impressions the 'sound-look' of words.
3. Compare the relation of 'west' and 'Waste' in: 'Her fond yellow hornlight wound to the west, her wild hollow hoarlight hung to the height / Waste' 'Spelt from Sibyl's Leaves'.
4. This holds true even when abstraction is attacked. The *New Republic*, wishing to restore the proper term, spells it like it is: A + B + M = Lunacy. The scientific form loses its cool; it is made to collapse into the colloquial, like technical into ordinary language philosophy. An abstract ABC adds up to a Luna – C. One side of the mock equation, by overspecifying the 'proper' term, reveals a deceptive underspecification in the other.

Part III

Positions

Chapter 15

Practical Criticism

A Short History of Practical Criticism

What at present preoccupies scholars and students in the literary humanities is clear: the lack of interaction between their profession and the mainstream of society. Though this is a recurrent problem, I. A. Richards had thought to find a secure place for literary studies by denying the existence of a 'phantom aesthetic state' and basing the critic's work on two pillars. 'The two pillars upon which a theory of criticism must rest are an account of value and an account of communication' (*Principles of Literary Criticism*, 1924). Having established these principles, an eminently 'practical criticism' became possible; the book *Practical Criticism* appeared in 1929; and the term, in its modesty and common sense, helped to assure the success of literary techniques of close reading.

Although in William Empson's *Seven Types of Ambiguity* (1930) this effort at close and discriminating reading already showed a quasi-theological strain, and signalled trouble ahead for those who wished to 'bound the infinite' of interpretive studies, certain developments of the 1930s led to an institutionalization of the 'practical' approach to literature, which came to be known as the New Criticism. First, the political and economic unrest of that time made it important to protect the study of art from imperious demands of an ideological nature, emanating from politics but also from positive philosophy and science; then, a move toward mass education, speeding up significantly after World War II, meant that teachers could not rely as much on the patience or privileged background of their students. Teachers had to educate as well as initiate; and new textbooks were developed to give students, more quickly than proved possible, a modest mastery of the cultural goods.

The expansion of literary studies within an academic framework meant that English took its place beside history and the 'moral sciences' (a translation of the term *Geisteswissenschaften*) as a school to train the judgment. *Practical Criticism* was subtitled 'A Study of Literary Judgment,' and literary judgment was deemed to be the best or most liberal preparation for other kinds of judgment in the practical world. This attitude was especially prevalent at Cambridge University, where F. R. Leavis's emphasis on the greatness of the native tradition, of vernacular literature, sought to replace the mystique still surrounding the Classics. A counter-mystique soon arose, with Leavis at its center: resisting the growing culture industry, the mindless media, the trend to uniformity. A new and militant clerisy tried to prevent the dulling of judgment and further corruption of society by modern techniques of management and rationalization.

In America a stronger process of democratization (among other factors) prevented a new mystique from being formed, although a few courses at Amherst, Columbia, Harvard, and Yale influenced deeply the minds of teachers who came into their own in the late 1950s and early 1960s. Sir Thomas Browne admired the Heathen who, deprived of Revelation, 'sucked divinity' from nature; and so the American student was taught to extract meanings from literary texts independently of any higher or abstruse theory concerning language, art, and society. The student was, in fact, admonished to respect the mystery of those texts – even if that word was not used, but rather their 'autonomy,' 'mode of existence,' or 'limits' – really the student's own limits. Literature was not politics, not religion, not philosophy, not science, not rhetoric, etc. These were real but extrinsic factors; instead an intrinsic approach to the mode of existence of the literary work of art had to be found (see René Wellek and Austin Warren, *Theory of Literature*, 1949). Yet no theorist of the time was able to define the differentiating 'nothing.'

That 'nothing' has plagued us ever since. It acted as an unacknowledged theological restraint. The end of literary studies was not knowledge but rather a state of secular grace. That 'nothing' also enforced the scientific notion that if literature was to be studied seriously it would have to be delimited as a department or field specialization, on the one hand; and a rigorous prohibition on the other (though couched as a principle of decorum), impeded the speculative contamination of art with anything else and led to an emptying out of the literary-critical enterprise. In the 1970s we find a growing awareness that 'practical criticism' may have failed, both vis-à-vis society at large and, more peculiarly, within the academy.

We no longer see what is 'practical' about practical criticism, except that as a reading technique it could help to stem a renewed tide of illiteracy. But as such it is already in competition with other, patently scientific techniques. A new 'philosophy of composition,' for example, has already subsumed Richards's 'theory of criticism' and its two pillars of evaluation and communication. Leavis had relied on English as a native yet cultured language with its own long-nurtured and organic virtues: by a natural contagion the practised reader of the great vernacular works would learn how to write and think a living English. But in America today English is increasingly subject to community standards, if not community control. And where it is most vital it escapes most standards, because new vernaculars are emerging, creole fashion. Practical criticism is relatively powerless in the face of these developments: it is a desperate search for reading and writing techniques that continue the study of grammar by other means. A gap opens up between advanced studies, which now seem quite impractical, and everyday classroom teaching, which is more elementary and disputatious than ever.

In this situation our self-doubt comes to the fore, even a tendency to self-blame. This alienation, this lack of effective interaction with society is, we think, our own fault: we have not done enough. Instead of deepening the idea of interpretation we turn against it. At best a new science, whether structuralism or semiology, is called upon to curb the adventurism or subjectivism of the reader; and it joins forces with those who denounce multiplying interpretations, seeing them as an economic need of the publishing professor rather than as an authentic literary and intellectual task. At worst, and spurred by retroactive idealization, the New Criticism is called upon as modest, practical, good enough, and set against the cerebration now going on, its philosophic pretensions, its conceptual armory and galloping jargon. Is not the new theoretical criticism destroying what might be saved of the practical side of our discipline?

To accept this line of thought is to inflict an additional wound on ourselves. We would be asking 'the wild, living intellect' (Cardinal Newman) not merely to check itself but also to accept other social forces that continue unchecked. We would take it for granted that the other professions – law, business, science, social science – have so imperative or intimate a relation to the commonweal that they should continue to grow, or at least not hold themselves back. But if we have anything to blame it is not the life of the mind, or the striving of those in literary studies who are trying out new perspectives or saving the older ones – who are trying to understand philosophy (European or American) or thinking about exegetical traditions prior to science and as persistent as religion itself. If we must blame ourselves it should be for holding too narrow a conception of what is practical.

For we have not been able to persuade ourselves – and therefore whom can we persuade in society at large? – that what we are professing is as essential to society's well-being as law or business or the performing arts. Our best and most deserving publicist was the late Northrop Frye. His system is less a system than an influencing machine: an evangelical battery in an escalating mental war. But, in general, all our touted skill in rhetoric consumes itself in the polemic of critic with critic and school with school. That can be fun, and may sharpen some issues; yet now is also the time to examine the failure of practical criticism in terms of our narrowed conception of what is practical in the humanities and beyond them. Practical criticism never grew up.

Chapter 16

The Sacred Jungle

In the conclusion to his comprehensive work *The Symbolism of Evil,* Paul Ricoeur calls us 'the children of criticism,' who 'seek to go beyond criticism by means of a criticism that is no longer reductive but restorative.' The intellectual scheme revealed by those words goes back to the German Romantics. It presupposes that as moderns we aim at a second naiveté in and through critical reflection. It also presupposes that the concepts of immediacy and of the sacred ('the immediacy of the symbol') are identical and that it is the aim of restorative criticism to disclose that identity. Criticism, as a form of romantic irony, rediscovers hermeneutics, for its very negativity leads to discovery. True irony, Friedrich Schlegel writes in his notebooks, is not merely a striving for something without end ('Unendlichkeit'); it is the attempt to possess it by a micrological thoroughness in both poetical and philosophical matters. This education toward living in the Universal ('Bildung zum Unendlichen') Schlegel also characterized as 'applied mysticism.'

Ricoeur is a late if effective proponent of insights into the way that the negative converts itself and allows our penchant for interminable analysis to understand and even appreciate its apparent opposite: religious or enthusiastic forms of closure. 'I can still today communicate with the sacred,' affirms Ricoeur, 'by making explicit the prior understanding that gives life to the interpretation. Thus hermeneutics, an acquisition of "modernity," is one of the modes by which that "modernity" transcends itself, insofar as it included forgetfulness of the sacred.' Alluding to Heidegger by way of Bultmann, Jung, and others, Ricoeur continues: 'I believe that Being can still speak to me – no longer, of course, under the precritical form of immediate belief, but as the second immediacy aimed at by hermeneutics.'

Words like these remain in touch with Romantic philosophies of history which predicted that we would emerge from the dark passage of an age of doubt and criticism into a new, more organic or total belief.[1] A similar 'principle of hope,' though shadowed about by the image of gyres or the cyclical and eternal wheel of time, continues to shape Yeats's *A Vision.* A beautiful machine converting old myth into fresh credence, Yeats's prose poem is a construction looking toward the same change as these speculative histories, which he turns into a unanimous philosophy of symbols. But there exist, in our time, and stretching back at least a hundred years, countless if less vigorous testaments for the rebirth of the supernatural through intellectual and even technological means. When we read in 1935 that the true potentiality of film lies 'in its unique faculty to express by natural means and with incomparable persuasiveness all that is fairylike, marvelous, supernatural' (Franz Werfel), we find ourselves back in the Romantic period, in the days of *Lyrical Ballads* (1798), when Wordsworth's new realism aimed to 'excite a feeling analogous to the supernatural,' while Coleridge would take supernatural events and procure for them a provisional belief.

To connect the issue of achieving a second immediacy ('to reestablish response in depth through conceptual mediation')[2] with that of the reanimation of symbols from art or religion, clarifies the importance of the Romantic movement as well as its subsumption by Hegel. 'The principle of restoration,' he wrote, 'is found in thought, and thought only: the hand that inflicts the wound is also the hand that heals it.' That hand haunts modern artists and intellectuals alike. Though merely a figure of speech, it points to the literal hand that writes the figure being reanimated.

That I move so quickly, using quotations, should not obscure the great divide that opened between Continental and Anglo-American thought in the nineteenth century. The distrust in England and America of Hegelian or 'conceptual' mediation was never entirely allayed by French intermediaries, of whom Ricoeur is only one of the latest. Nor could a poet succeed, even when as strong and influential as Yeats. At the confluence of French and British traditions, Yeats's system, articulated most fully in *A Vision*, tried to revive the ancient, moribund symbols for a hyperconscious readership. Only by ancient symbols, he said, can a 'highly subjective art escape from the barrenness of a too conscious arrangement into the abundance and depth of nature.'

Yeats proved to be too mannered-magical; or it became obvious that his beautiful machine was driven by a Gothic motor. The situation in England and America between the two World Wars was, in any case, so complex that I can only guess at causes that lay behind an evident result. Anglo-American critics did not see *through* French culture to German lines of thought with which the Symbolist precursors of Yeats and Eliot were still in touch. They continued to follow an anti-self-consciousness tradition of their own, which placed the 'dissociation of sensibility,' or the unfortunate and purely hypothetical separation of thinking and feeling, or saying and being, somewhere in the seventeenth century. It seemed to be post-Donne or post-Shakespeare or – in one polemical version – the work of Milton, his inhibiting and antivernacular effect on the living language.

The revaluation of Romanticism is a special feature of post-New Critical or revisionist criticism in America. The term 'revisionist,' in fact, is perhaps most appropriately applied to the rethinking of literary history now going on, which questions a periodization that has given 'modernity' a polemical and prestigious life separated from Romantic origins. But the revision that is occurring is not a matter of redressing the balance, or adjusting claims, or seeing continuities rather than discontinuities: it thrusts us back into an awareness of the problematic persistence of enthusiastic, poetic, and even archaic forms in contemporary life.

I cannot summarize what so many scholar-critics have worked at faithfully over the past fifty years. Nor can I put together the jigsaw-puzzle relationship of European and Anglo-American thought in the area of literary under-standing. But it is possible to describe as a foreshortened historical sequence the forgetting of Romantic, and especially German Romantic, thinking. To recover from the 'forgetfulness of the sacred' we have first to remember that other attempt to deal with an apparently archaic or daemonic subject matter in a 'modern' way. It is not, of course, the German element that is crucial, and it would need, in any case, a more specialized study to show why German Romanticism was seminal. We would also need a consideration of the role of French thinkers, both artists and critics, in mediating radical German thought; and other European figures, like Croce and Ortega, might be considered. Even in England the turn away from German Romantic thought was not absolute; an expansive and focal mind like Walter Pater's, able to refine so much strange knowledge, from pagan times to Hegel, throws a prose bridge over those severed traditions and allows a resonance of their accommodation to persist in subsequent thinkers. Not only Yeats but also Stevens echoes Pater's mode of philosophical criticism: unschematic, re-fracted, mobile, though more persistently profiled than Emerson's.[3] I hope that the ensuing historical sketch can suggest the intricate relation of critical and creative, and sometimes critical and religious, elements in post-Enlight-enment society.

> What is lacking in England, and has always been lacking, that half-actor and rhetorician knew well enough, the absurd muddle-head Carlyle, who sought to conceal under passionate grimaces what he knew about himself: namely, what was *lacking* in Carlyle – real *power* of intellect, real *depth* of intellectual perception, in short, philosophy.
>
> Nietzsche, *Beyond Good and Evil*

In England, the most sophisticated anti-Romanticism came from Matthew Arnold. He claimed that while the English Romantics were writers with great energy and creative force, they did not 'know' enough, and so missed the chance of becoming universal figures, like Goethe. They could not transcend their national and parochial base.[4] T. S. Eliot, in an introduction to his first collection of essays, *The Sacred Wood* (1920), quotes Arnold on the Romantics and adds: 'This judgment . . . has not, so far as I know, ever been successfully controverted.' In *The Use of Poetry and the Use of Criticism* a dozen years later, he expands Arnold's list.

> We should be right too, I think, if we added that Carlyle, Ruskin, Tennyson, Browning, with plenty of energy, plenty of creative force, had not enough wisdom. Their culture was not always well-rounded; their knowledge of the human soul was often partial and often shallow.

Who, then, will escape whipping? If there is one criterion that distinguishes the present movement in criticism from that prevailing, more or less, since Eliot, it is a better understanding and higher evaluation of the Romantic and nineteenth-century writers.

In Arnold's estimate of the Romantics, there is more irony than truth. For revisionist studies have shown that these same Romantics were clairvoyant rather than blind precursors of later movements that tended to disown them while simplifying the radical character of their art. The irony deepens when we recall that philosophical criticism in the German style was *almost* introduced to England via Coleridge's *Biographia Literaria*. But Coleridge broke off the attempt with the excuse that he wished to reserve such 'Constructive Philosophy' for his never-written *Logosophia*. Chapter 13 of the *Biographia* is interrupted by what might be called a *letter* from Porlock (Locke? Poor Luck?); that is, from a very prudent, practical-minded friend advising Coleridge not to proceed further in his kind of hypostatic discourse. Philosophical criticism, therefore, which had attained a first flowering in the work of Schiller, Fichte, Schelling, and the Schlegels, was to develop chiefly within a German matrix. It became increasingly alien to the English mind.[5] While the two countries remained, for a while, eager to learn from each other in matters of art, in matters of criticism a serious split – a real 'two cultures' situation – soon emerged.

It manifests itself as early as Carlyle's *Sartor Resartus*, composed in 1830–31, only fifteen years after Coleridge's *Biographia*. Here, indeed, English is a 'Babylonish dialect' made of Germanisms, Swiftian gusto, and a baroque simulacrum of the earthy, archaizing diction of northern England. The book's crazy, mockingbird style is meant to be a nauseous cure or asafoetida for British empiricism. 'Teufelsdröckh,' the name of its hero-author, means devil-dirt, or possibly devil-print. 'Diogenes,' his first name, means divinely born.

Matthew Arnold, recognizing the un-English character of the style, issued the warning: 'Flee Carlylese as you would the devil.' The rough, Germanizing wit of *Sartor* shows not only that, as in medieval times, wit and mystery go together, but it inserts an English work into a tradition which remains almost exclusively Teutonic, and leads from Luther through Jean Paul Richter to Nietzsche and Thomas Mann (compare the latter's *Dr. Faustus*). Nietzsche, though always keeping his distance from Carlyle, may have owed to him part of his awareness that no previous age was as prepared 'for a Carnival in the grand style, for laughter and a high-spirited revelry, for transcendental flights of sublime nonsense' (*Beyond Good and Evil*). In 'The Function of Criticism' of 1923, Eliot quotes from the editorial columns of an unspecified newspaper which not only associates 'humorous' with 'nonconformist' qualities, but also attributes this combination to 'the unreclaimed Teutonic element' in the English character.

Carlyle's remarkable style, I am suggesting, is an aspect of his covert transfusion of Northern religious enthusiasm (directly described by Walter Scott when dealing with the Covenanters in *Old Mortality*) into German nature-enthusiasm and its transcendental symbolics. Carlyle maintains, of course, a defensively humorous distance from Teufelsdröckh's exotica by pretending to be his editor. But the problem of distance is a complex one: it involves defining the genre of a book that is at once commentary and fiction.

The 'Clothes Philosophy' of *Sartor* stresses mediation: it distances humanity from nakedness, nature, even from the textual source (Teufelsdröckh's German manuscript, supposedly discovered by the 'editor'), which is presented in *Sartor* only in an excerpted or retailored ('resartus') form. 'We never get Teufelsdröckh unmediated,' says G. B. Tennyson. But no writer who goes through the detour of a text gets himself unmediated.

Carlyle's disgust, moreover, at this potentially infinite regress of mediation – even though it provides a saving distance from absolute inwardness or solipsism – is quite obvious. His solution is to foreground the mediatory process, to make the writer's distance from any source so palpable that the retailored text is endowed with a factitious presence of its own. The very feel of *Sartor* depends on the 'fragments, the titles, the passages taken from here and there, the works unfinished or stopped in midpassage . . . double and single quotation marks for passages cited, and editorial interpolation in the midst of quotations' (G. B. Tennyson). It is as if something groundless were being foregrounded – which, taken out of metaphysics or German *Naturphilosophie,* and articulated as a theory of language, could evoke Heidegger and Derrida.

The formal effect, in any case, is a fading of the distinction between original and commentary. Quotation is king, yet everything is quotation. In *Sartor* criticism has found its carnival colors. Carlylese, instead of being a metalanguage, merges with the idiom of its source: its originality is its impurity, the contamination of gloss and original. But since the source is invented, Carlylese is actually a self-educing prose, maintained by the fiction not of a source alone, but of a source that needs an editor-translator-interpreter. Here is feigning indeed, though in the service of criticism.

Yet equally – this is the Puritan joker – in the service of religion. For Carlyle's attitude toward Teufelsdröckhian metaphysics is exploitative as well as empathic. German metaphysics, he wrote, is 'a disease expelling a disease.' He thought of it as literally a medical *crisis* and providentially appointed cure in the long illness of unbelief or excessive self-consciousness. It would eventually consume itself. He too may have the disease, since it is contagious, part of the 'Spirit of the Age'; but the fever of his style has its creative as well as suffering aspect.

Sartor, then, is the Age of Criticism producing – out of itself as it were – a fiction. The Negative is converted into Being, to echo Hegel; and this holds for the verbal style and genre of the book as clearly as for its famous journey from 'The Everlasting No' to 'The Everlasting Yea.' We are dealing not with a historical curiosity but with a creative historiographical act – a revision of the English language which succeeded more in America (if we think of Melville's prose) than in England. Carlylese is a richer, rougher English, one that pretends to be contaminated by German; yet the German source is simply a device that motivates a different critical idiom. An enthusiastic type of criticism replaces an English type which was, and continues to be despite Carlyle, a critique of enthusiasm.

The issue of enthusiasm is not separable from that of religion, and could draw us into a complex analysis of the relation of literary style to religion and politics. The relation of enthusiasm to political fanaticism is a fearful reality that hovers over English history and the establishment of *via media* institutions from the reign of Elizabeth on. Literary criticism like everything else became a *via media* institution. Though a fear of enthusiasm gradually receded into the *angustiae* of the Gothic novel, it was given a temporary renewal by the French Revolution with its regicide, its Reign of Terror, and its atheistic religion of reason.

It seems hardly credible, therefore, that the future author of *The French Revolution* (1837), who began *Sartor* in the year of the July revolution (1830), and failed to place his book with a publisher, perhaps because of the Reform Bill agitation, should so neglect the French scene. But the Northern (Anglo-*Saxon*) and Calvinist axis was the essential one for him in respect of the difficult relation of literature, religion, and enthusiasm. Eighteenth-century Paris had been a mere *hortus siccus*, the 'most parched spot in Europe,' and even French revolutionary turmoil served only to reveal the poetry in history. It heaved up huge symbols of repressed religiosity that pointed to the real creative ferment of mankind – religious rather than secular, religion struggling with the secular, and criticism with belief.

That *Sartor* uses one culture to criticize or complete another is not the important thing, however daringly performed. Its recovery of the relation of criticism to enthusiasm – to the religious question – and its understanding of what is common to criticism and fiction are more crucial. In these matters Carlyle is a genuine precursor of the philosophical critics of today.

Criticism differs from fiction by making the experience of reading explicit: by intruding and maintaining the persona of editor, reviewer, reader, foreign reporter, and so forth. Our struggle to identify – or not to – with an imaginative experience that is usually in the form of a story, is what is worked through. Both paradigmatically and personally the critic shows how a reader's instincts, sympathies, defences are now solicited and now compelled. The psychological drama of reading centers on that aroused merging: a possible loss of boundaries, a fear of absorption, the stimulation of a sympathetic faculty that may take over and produce self-alienation.

This is felt to be too threatening even now whenever a critic fudges the line between commentary and fiction – this *merging*, which most criticism methodically *prevents*, but which Carlyle *represents*. After Carlyle, the 'explicit reader' enters certain American authors (Poe and Melville, for example) in the fictional guise of a narrator who has barely escaped a visionary merger, or else as too palpable an authorial presence. In a counter-tradition, that of Flaubert and James, the author disappears, or evokes what has been called an 'implicit author.' But the emphasis remains on the sympathetic imagination, or on an enthusiast always about to merge, out of idealism, with the destructive element.

Should we discount the psychic danger of merging – the anxiety it evokes even in such formal activities as reading – an obverse difficulty may appear. This is the tendency to distance oneself too much, to make of distance a defence by claiming that origins are fake or contaminated or (at best) motivating fictions. It can lead to something that parallels Gnosticism's separation of the pure origin or pure good from a world created by the usurping demiurge; so 'Teufelsdröckh' and his 'editor' find themselves in unexpected theological company. The issue such an analysis raises is, again, the relation of fiction, criticism, and theology.

How much is implied by Emerson's famous statement in 'Self-Reliance' (1841) that in reading others our rejected thoughts return with a certain alienated majesty? Could it imply identity with the pure origin, and a falling away from it when we lack self-reliance? 'By our own spirits are we deified,' Wordsworth wrote of poets in their strength: it is an extreme form of Gnosticism from its optimistic, even manic side.

'But thereof come in the end despondency and madness,' Wordsworth adds. There is a dark obverse to the quest for autonomy and originality. What Emerson says of our reading can also be said of our dreams. We eventually recognize them as our rejected thoughts returning with a fearful or majestic luster. The question is whether we *can* acknowledge them as ours. To do so is to take responsibility for them; to take on, for good or bad, a certain sublimity. In his optimistic moments Emerson sees no problem in this. Yet the distortions of the dream-work itself, and the many anti-self-consciousness theories that spring up in the nineteenth century, indicate there is a problem. So Carlyle talks in *Characteristics* of the 'ideal unconscious,' a strange notion when we think of how Freud viewed the unconscious at the end of the century.

Notes

1. This positive nihilism had already reached a high point in Novalis's 'Genuine anarchy is the generative element of religion' ('Wahrhafte Anarchie is das Zeugungselement der Religion'), which comes from his essay 'Christianity or Europe' (1799), written with the experience of the French Revolution in mind. Heine, looking back on those romantic, all-embracing nihilists, remarked nastily that Friedrich Schlegel was so inclusive in his perspective because his vantage point was really a church tower.

2. See Terence Des Pres, 'Prophecies of Grace and Doom: The Function of Criticism at the Present Time,' *Partisan Review* 42 (1975): 277. Cf. my 'Romanticism and Anti-Self-Consciousness' in this *Reader*. A powerful defence of Hegelian conceptual mediation ('denkende Vermittlung') comes when Hans-Georg Gadamer criticizes historicist or objectivist reconstruction as a mode of self-forgetfulness in his *Truth and Method*.

3. Pater's *The Renaissance* (1873), his remarkable Bildungsroman *Marius the Epicurean* (1885), and even *Plato and Platonism* (1893) transcend apology, tract, and familiar essay. They provide, after Coleridge, the first English (rather than German) instances of 'philosophical literature.' It is no accident that the inaugural quotation in *Plato and Platonism* is from the *Cratylus* dialogue that discusses 'in what proportion names, fleeting names, contribute to our knowledge of things.' Like Shelley, Pater understands the coexistence of sceptical and visionary thought in Plato. The complex arc that joins Shelley (especially his *Defence of Poetry*, composed in 1821 but not published till 1840) to Emerson and Pater and curves back to Heideggerian philosophy as well as to French 'Travels in Cratylia' is suggested by a comment on Socratic irony in Chapter 7 of *Plato and Platonism*. Noting how often 'it may chance to be' is used in Plato, Pater comments: 'The Philosopher of Being, or, of the verb "To be," is after all afraid of saying "It is".'

4. See 'The Function of Criticism at the Present Time' in *Essays in Criticism* (1865): 'It has long seemed to me that the burst of creative activity in our literature, through the first quarter of this century, had about it, in fact, something premature . . . the English poetry of the first quarter of this century, with plenty of energy, plenty of creative force, did not know enough. This makes Byron so empty of matter, Shelley so incoherent, Wordsworth even, profound as he is, yet so wanting in completeness and variety.'

5. 'I have read some of Hegel and Fichte, as well as Hartley . . . and forgotten it. Of Schelling I am extremely ignorant at first hand, and he is one of the numerous authors whom, the longer you leave unread, the less desire you have to read' (Eliot, *The Use of Poetry and the Use of Criticism*).

Chapter 17

Radical Art and Radical Analysis

'The Religions of all Nations,' Blake declared, 'are derived from each Nation's different reception of the Poetic Genius, which is everywhere called the Spirit of Prophecy.' The struggle for an American reception of the Poetic Genius, from Emerson, Whitman, and Emily Dickinson to William Carlos Williams, continues this line of thought; and insofar as it has to choose, it prefers itself primal and reprobate rather than Christian and Humanist.

We have not seen the last American Puritan. D. H. Lawrence's *Studies in Classic American Literature* (1922) expresses that truth as violently as Williams or Pound – or, for that matter, Van Wyck Brooks. The Puritan tradition, reinforced by the founders of America, continues its embrace. Kenneth Burke struggles out of it, like a fly in ointment or religious unction; whereas Northrop Frye, raising Blake's identification of poetry with divinity to a legitimating axiom for literary studies, accommodates more easily both Scripture and its extension into a secular canon, or what we call literature.

The fact that religion or society condemns the poetic genius in its midst cannot change, according to Frye, this identity of literature and divinity. Culture-politics of the repressive kind exists, but is an evil child, vision gone bad, as Blake's epics demonstrate. What is crucial is the relation of art as a whole to society as a whole. The critic sees, of course, the present weakening of religion (at least in the West) as a structure of belief, yet hopes that the identity of imaginative religion with art will modify the impotence of both in modern life. Frye completes Arnold by returning to Blake, who said that the imagination is eternal; and he corrects Eliot by arguing that what is important in religion can be communicated, especially today, only through art.

> The arts, which address the imagination, have, ever since the Romantic movement, acquired increasingly the role of the agents through which religion is understood and appreciated. The arts have taken on a prophetic function in society, never more of one than when the artist pretends to depreciate such a role, as, for instance, T. S. Eliot did. (*The Modern Century*)

Should we set Kenneth Burke against Northrop Frye? With his catastrophic view of the history of religious and purifying ideals, Burke cannot legitimate art as an after-religion. Humorous (in the old sense) rather than unifying, he turns to the drama and particularly Shakespearean drama to find some paradigm of true community. Where, if not in Shakespeare, do we find represented both the vicious cycle of order and guilt, the 'Iron Law of History/That welds Order and Sacrifice,' and a hoped release from it? The relation of literature to politics, including modern political religions, from Puritan theocracies to the totalitarianisms of Left or Right, is Burke's burden even when he seems to be literary in the most technical sense. Let us imagine, then, what Burke might have said on behalf of Shakespeare in explaining to a politicized age a 'trifling' song from *The Tempest*:

> *Ariel's Song*
> Come unto these yellow sands,
>   And then take hands:
> Curtsied when you have, and kissed
>   The wild waves whist:
> Foot it featly here and there,
> And sweet sprites bear
>   The burthen . . . Hark!
>   Hark!
> *Burthen* [*dispersedly*]. Bow-wow!
> *Ariel.* The watch-dogs bark:
> *Burthen.* Bow-wow!
> *Ariel.* Hark, hark, I hear
>   The strain of strutting chanticleer
>   Cry –
> *Burthen.* Cock a-doodle-do!

The song is airy, like Ariel; and it passes from revel to dirge (to the second, even more famous song, 'Full fathom five thy father lies . . . Those are pearls that were his eyes . . .') by the gentlest sea-and see-change. We are made to intuit the mood of Ferdinand, who thinks his father shipwrecked in the tempest and seems to hear the waves soothing his loss and their own fury. And we are made to forget the bad vibes of Caliban, his equation (in the previous scene) of speaking and cursing – for it is always language itself ('My language! heavens!' is Ferdinand's cry on hearing Miranda speak) that is recovered and rediscovered in this play. A delicate balance is created between so many things: woe and wonder, dreaming and waking, curse and blessing.

Yet even out of context that first song has a charm of its own. It suggests, capped by a curious refrain, the light-hearted integration of animal spirits, a unity that preserves in sublimated form the hierarchic order being 'silenced' by a ritual dance which is pure moonshine, which takes place before dawn. 'Bow' in 'Bow-wow' is the command of the barker, the one who calls the tune, invisible *magister ludi*; but it is also what Ariel takes it to be, a barking sound: peremptory, disruptive, mocking. It is the voice of clown-master or King of Fools; it is, more generally, the lunatic fringe of rhyme or rhythm, sheer performative energy of language, onomatopoeia, mimicry. It cannot be resolved into orderly meaning but signals a discordant ending, a discontinuity between the real and the elfish as dawn breaks. Cock-crow, next, with its edge of obscene incitement ('cock adoodle-do') reinforces barking, as the sun rises on a barnyard world and a pecking order that imposes once more the 'burthen' of labor and language. The revel is about to end.

Where, then, is Shakespeare's paradigm of community? What we seem to have is the opposite, a momentary charm, a pure interlude, fraying into impure noise and silly puns. The lyric, like the magic circle of Romance itself, cannot really hold up time. Break or bark of day returns, and the adult nursery form is undone. This is true, no doubt; poetry does not, cannot, bridge the painful distance between master and slave, freedom and servitude. But it does bridge, in Shakespeare, the distance between literate and illiterate on the basis of a shared imaginative belief or desire: Ariel's song is mythmaking in a learned *and* folkloric way, it is motivated by courtly *and* popular tradition. There is, moreover, something extravagant in the whole scheme of this Romance of a Comedy, which the burthen asks us to share: wishing to appeal to the entire audience (like Prospero's epilogue), it turns an antithetical pun into a piece of nonsense verse as if meaning in language were less important than a performative and contagious energy. Even 'ding-dong, bell,' the closing refrain of the second song, is not as congruent as it seems. It alludes, of course, to the death-knell being rung. But one can imagine Ariel, or the invisible conductor, gesturing at that point for a bell-sound from the musicians. The play-acting, that is, spreads out from the visible scene to the 'wings': to the extended stage of life, where all are actors, the audience too; and to the offstage master of these charms, to Prospero or Shakespeare himself. There is a vanishing point where the master-slave relation is dissolved, or where we all participate equally in the human condition.

Great art is radical: our understanding of this fact in relation to religion has been advanced by Frye and Burke. But art's contribution to the political sphere remains difficult to formulate. What kind of 'act' is art, independent of its subject matter, which can range from the most conservative beliefs to libertine thought, from Ariel's 'airy tongue' to satirical rage? Historical evidence is inconclusive. Sometimes a writer hits home, like Brecht; more often not. Intent and reception, program and influence, seem to have separate destinies. Thirties-minded critics (I steal Kenneth Burke's phrase), like Edmund Wilson and Burke himself in America, Adorno and Benjamin in Germany, Malraux in France (indeed, almost every leading intellectual was involved) struggled constantly with the issue of art and politics.

On one level there is no mystery: by not conforming, art slanders an established order, good or bad. Its very existence is often a resistance, it gives the lie to every attempt to impose a truth by state-sponsored power. Shelley's Beatrice in *The Cenci* is an absolute symbol for this resistance. But on another level there is a mystery. However opposed art may be to religion, hierarchy, or the very idea of the sacred, it exhibits the kind of energy, concentration, and compulsive structure we associate with its despotic opponents. Fueled, psychoanalysis would say, by the Unconscious, it is the product of an exceptional alliance between conscious and unconscious or driving thoughts.

Even apparently conformist art can burst, with grotesque power, through the eggshell of its beliefs. But this precarious alliance of conscious and unconscious thoughts shows up in other areas too: in religion and politics especially. What we appreciate as exemplary in art we admire and fear as 'charismatic' in public life. If it is hard enough to tell charlatan from genius in art, it often seems impossible to distinguish between creative and destructive portions of the spirit in a significant politician or religious leader.

Art cannot escape that shadiness, that ambiguity; but once published it also cannot cease exposing itself. No formula may pre-empt what the effect of its openness will be. The reader-critic is deeply involved in not allowing art to be shunted aside or co-opted by the newest ideology. Take the formula, as old as Herder, that the greatness of English literature (he was thinking particularly of Shakespeare) was its ability to build on folk traditions, to avoid the sterilizing discontinuity between learned and unlearned art that had afflicted French Classicism. But the phenomenon of the *Anstreicher* (house painter), as Brecht called Hitler, of the artisan and man-of-the-people who would form a powerful coalition of all classes and transform work into a joyful, satisfying activity akin to art – that ideology is not wholly distinct from the animus in my previous account of Ariel's song from *The Tempest*.

A scrutiny of the religious motives underlying such words as order, unity, and community is essential, therefore; and it was practised by the Frankfurt School, which understood the appeal of totalitarianism in terms of an upsurge of messianic or religious politics, and connected demagogic movements with a rhetoric that relied on what Burke called 'a bastardization of fundamentally religious patterns of thought.' Burke used this phrase in his essay on Hitler's *Mein Kampf* – an analysis contemporary with the work of Walter Benjamin and writers conveniently grouped as the Frankfurt School. But religion is itself a mixed matter, a complex phenomenon not easily reduced to ideals of purity, totality, or askesis. For Nietzsche, these ideals were indeed religious but also in the service of an ultimate will to power. Totalitarianism, moreover, according to Adorno and Horkheimer, is a consequence of the Enlightenment, which *believed* in Reason and dominated the disorder of history by means of a concept of uniformity and the purging of all non-rational – in effect, non-bureaucratic, non-conformable – ideas. It proved to be a counter-religion, a religion of absolute secular progress.

I have discussed elsewhere (see 'Purification and Danger in American Poetry' [in this *Reader*, pp. 128–41)] the relation of ideals of purity to concepts in literary theory. For the moment I want to focus on the difficulty of reducing art to political statements and the related problem of discerning its sociopolitical influence. I have hinted that these difficulties come from the fact that it is too radical. But how is this radical character of art to be conceived?

Burke, in the analysis of *Mein Kampf* already mentioned, suggests a connection between rhetoric as a strategy of persuasion and rhetoric as the art of endowing voice with absolute magnitude. Those impatient with the 'contrary voices' of parliament, or similar 'houses of confusion,' Burke remarked, find it tempting to 'wish for the momentary peace of one voice, amplified by social organizations, with all the others not merely quieted, but given the quietus.' It is surely this 'sinister unifying' of all voices that cannot extend to art, except through overt repression or *dirigisme*. Ariel, in his song, incorporates by a delightful and dispersed mimicry the voices that break in; and even if it is argued that it is he, after all, who directs and plays his own song, those impure echoes and puns remain, testifying to an energy of sound, a discordant concord of voices, that cannot be further reduced. Such voices, when internalized or subdued as 'inner' voices, show a potentially compulsive, eruptive character. With psychoanalysis, moreover, we have moved closer to understanding the role of images of voice in the total psychic life of the person, so that the concept of inner voice itself becomes a bridge helping us to connect the driven genius of artist, religious leader, and politician.

Revolutions could be considered as festivals in which these voices break out and cannot be contained. They become pentecostal, but in a political way. The voices inflame, and fire is but their objective correlative. Paradoxically, therefore, the engagement of the Romantic artists with the French revolution – as of Milton with the Puritan revolution – can hinder our grasp of art's relation to the sociopolitical sphere if the political event is given priority or made the exclusive focus. For the radical character of art is then overshadowed by a fixed point of reference that excludes too much else in thought. What is meant by the radical character of art, in isolation or in conjunction with other types of radical activity, can only be demonstrated by a close analysis of the rhetorical and symbolic dimension. (Carlyle attempted something of this nature in his books on Cromwell and the French Revolution.) This analysis is not possible without literary experience: we must learn not only to read between the lines but also to hear the words, the words in the words and the images of voice they evoke. The institution of writing itself, at the level of complexity literature reveals, is presupposed, and the link between writing and ideation can no longer be ignored.

The productive force of close analysis has already enabled certain Romantic and post-Romantic writers to enter our consciousness in new and startling form:

Rousseau, Blake, Wordsworth, Shelley, Hölderlin, Michelet, and Nietzsche have benefited. Others, Ballanche, Carlyle, Emerson, Thoreau, Melville, Hugo, are being revalued. After a painful separation that limited, supposedly for its own good, the understanding of literature – 'literature' became only that, and was resolutely dissociated from thought-systems of a religious, political, or conceptual kind – we are returning to a larger and darker view of art as mental charm, war, and purgation.

Chapter 18

The Critical Essay between Theory and Tradition

Contemporary literary analysis exposes, once more, the ambiguity of language; and it does so not to impugn words and induce new schemes for a 'real character,' a more stable and truthful language-structure, but to heighten our awareness of a complex resource already in place. 'Where the old Rhetoric,' I. A. Richards writes in his *Philosophy of Rhetoric*, 'treated ambiguity as a fault in the language, and hoped to confine or eliminate it, the new Rhetoric sees it as an inevitable consequence of the powers of language . . .' Ambiguity, at least in art, confirms these 'powers,' and suggests that modes of reading which assert the possibility of literal or unmediated expression are terrible simplifications.

These simplifications, however, enter a vicious cycle reactive to freer modes of reading. While it is liberating to celebrate ambiguity as indeterminacy, the very ease of doing so exacerbates the fever of fundamentalism that chronically ravages the body politic. The polemics of the situation do not work for the critical spirit unless we can make a case on behalf of the negative energy of intellect all around us. 'The mind of man,' Christopher Smart wrote, 'cannot bear a tedious accumulation of nothings without effect.' So we may ask ourselves: Is Derrida's 'atheology' perhaps the equivalent of a negative theology? Are we in the presence of a 'negative classicism,' as André Malraux defined the unconventional strength of modernist painting? Should we accept a philosophy of history like that of the Saint-Simonians, who took comfort in the fact that after each sceptical age there would arise an organic and myth-filled age? Do we credit Michel Foucault's insight, developed above all in his *History of Sexuality*, that all our liberated talk about repression and censorship is merely a way of extending and intensifying the directorial powers of church and state that now penetrate via our own 'critical' claims into the innermost recesses of a private sphere they were intended to guard? Can even art escape being propaganda?[1]

I take it for granted that we remain in an Age of Criticism, but one traversed by a return to religious faith, to clear commitments and often to fundamentalist kinds of faith. Now it is hard to get one's historical bearings on the frequency of these cycles: T. S. Eliot announced in 1929 his return to religion and conservative politics; the same year Walter Lippmann published *A Preface to Morals*, analyzing the dissolution of the ancestral order and suggesting that neither modernism nor fundamentalism could lead to that 'religion of the spirit' appropriate to a 'Great Society.' We know too well, also, that fascism displayed apocalyptic traits and a fervor of adhesion that have typically characterized the more fanatic religions. So that the evidences of a return from the 1960s on to either cultic or conventional religion need not surprise.

Whatever reasons for contemporary reactions to 'Whirl is King' (Aristophanes), the problems that affect literary and cultural criticism remain the same as in other eras. I will single out the problem of doing interpretations at a time when texts seem overly porous – so ambiguous or variable in the history of attributed meanings that the cry is heard, why should we study literature? A time too when, obversely, the import of texts is decided by authority, with the aid of the idea that there is one meaning, often defined as 'literal.'

We can turn once more to Richards for a modern focus on this dilemma. He asks criticism to foster an 'intellectual tradition' that 'tells us . . . how *literally* to read a passage.'[2] If he had said: how not to read literally, the emphasis would have fallen on the interpretive complexity of art. Yet a modern prejudice, linked to the change of hermeneutics into criticism, makes him put his statement the other way. He is, of course, a realist rather than a fundamentalist, one who admires that stubborn and commendable streak in us which links literature to life, not only to more literature. Like Wallace Stevens, he too keeps 'coming back and coming back/To the real: to the hotel instead of the hymns / That fall upon it out of the wind.' Yet by the end of the paragraph what is deplored is not a loss of reality but a loss in interpretive flexibility. This is where theory comes in, as a supplement to the recovery of a skill. Our age, Richards suggests, is 'losing its skill in interpretation' and 'begins the reflective inquiry which may lead to a theory by which the skill may be regained – this time as a less vulnerable and more deeply grounded because more consciously recognized, endowment.'

Richards also posits a time near the beginning of modern English where we actually 'read aright.' He connects the adroitness of later sixteenth- and much seventeenth-century writing to social and religious causes that coincide with the flourishing of English: the wide circulation of sermons as well as plays, letters as well as poetry, controversy as well as fiction and translations.[3] By the end of this period, certainly, the very prose Richards himself writes, as well as the genre of essayistic criticism, has been created.

But we have little evidence of how the literature of that period was interpreted (*Rezeptionsgeschichte* not having been invented); what evidence there is belongs to the history of taste and does not take the form of sustained analysis. Certain prefaces and some self-commentating sermons or works, like those of Donne, seem to constitute an exception, but is that enough to make up for the lack of a global view of seventeenth-century culture or a better grasp of the way art reflects on itself and its text-milieu? These questions point to what has in fact developed since Richards: (1) reader-reception theory; (2) a new historicism that wishes to ascertain the 'episteme' (Foucault) of a culture by appreciating all its signifying *and* repressive practices, not only canonized works; and (3) a more general awareness of how cultures augment their fictions through interpretation and obversely their interpretive discourse through fiction (Frank Kermode's subtitle to *The Genesis of Secrecy*, 'The Interpretation of Narrative,' could as easily read 'The Narrative of Interpretation.') Together the three tendencies expand the definition of what literature is, redeem the isolation of belles-lettres, and shift attention to unfreedoms of speech challenged by forceful though oblique or marginalized cultural practices. A further movement, puzzling and influential deconstruction, is a critique of all canonical as well as historiographical schemes that put a bit of weight behind interesting allegories, turning them once more into comprehensive symbols or paradigms.

I am trying to inch forward from Richards to the contemporary scene by also constructing such a historical overview, but one that avoids progressive claims and impatient judgments. The loss of interpretive skill that Richards responds to, whatever its ultimate cause, is still with us. It obliges us to expand our view of the history of criticism, and to see that we cannot start it around 1700. What we call criticism is only the tip of the iceberg compared to the vast commentary tradition stretching back to Midrash and Patristic exegesis, and beyond that to Alexandria and Philo. The age of criticism is a distinctive though very late development. Yet one can hold to Richards's distinction between skill and theory, as between nature (i.e., vulnerable endowment) and its conscious reinforcement (i.e., a more thoroughly grounded, immunized endowment). Together with the utopian premise that attaches to Richards's notion of educability, there emerges a pragmatic caution that projects the skill to be grounded not as something given or gained once and for all but as a second nature, a habit of the flexible and reflective intelligence. Even though Richards uses one period as a touchstone for his conception of interpretive mobility, his attitude toward that skill is anti-foundationalist. The literal for him always stands in relation to other modes of reading, and the critical spirit itself is clearly more than an auxiliary and subordinated gift.

It is here that I sense a real difference between our present work, which remains close to that of Richards and others in Eliot's generation or the American New Criticism. As promoters of modernism, the New Critics brought contemporary literature into the university and linked it to what they called 'the tradition.' It was a pedagogically progressive yet culturally con- servative movement. The New Critics were also surprisingly conservative in their attitude toward the critical spirit. Like Eliot, they stressed its capital importance in the work of creation but remained wary of its freelance and sometimes autonomous character. They overlooked, as it were, Oscar Wilde's deflation of the artist. 'I am always amused,' he wrote, 'by the silly vanity of those writers and artists of our day who seem to imagine that the primary function of the critic is to chatter about their second-rate work.' In the Eliot tradition the critical spirit was considered dangerous, corrosive, too self-conscious, when left to its own recognizance. It was safer leaking from art as irony, paradox, or ambiguity. Uneasy about the creative potential in criticism, Eliot remarked in 1956: 'These last thirty years have been, I think, a brilliant period in literary criticism in both Britain and America. It may even come to seem, in retrospect, too brilliant.' What might he have said of the next thirty or fifty years?

The emphasis has shifted from integrating high modernist art into the canon, to the work of reading that helped to establish the canon and can therefore also modify it. Our picture of the literary universe is no longer that of great, autonomous, quasi-Scriptural books clustered at the center, attracting into their orbit satellite and epigonal works of Interpretation. That picture can never be entirely effaced; it has, let us say, a Ptolemaic value. But our concept of what is creative projects today a more eccentric, or decentered map. It is not only that social movements gathering momentum in the 1960s have overturned hierarchy, patriarchy, academy, monogamy, in the realm of letters. That is the surface, I think, of a tidal change that began when structuralism, joining anthropological and linguistic findings, reformed Western concepts of creativity by rationalizing episodic compilations, from folklore to South American myths. Using binary opposition as a structural principle, Lévi-Strauss explained how meaning was made and remade: how cultures dealt with contradictions in their belief-systems. So primary creation and secondary interpretation lost their rigid boundaries; though to expand the canon does not mean the proportional representation of every ethnic group but an acknowledgment (that must stand the test of time) of the devoted work of commentators and critics. The significant new work of art is gathered in, if at all, by them: we no longer maintain the image of the perfect work or objectified mind over there, and the consumer or interpreter desirous of communion with that brilliant object over here.

In these matters Richards was in advance of Eliot, or more democratic and experimental. *Practical Criticism* (1929) showed that art was not all that available even to acculturated students; that education had to undo both mental simplification and cultural prejudice; and that especially in a competitive modern era, where consumables replace the more difficult experience of art, the culture had to find a way of 'endowing' criticism. It may seem like a small thing, but despite recent complaints about bringing criticism into the university and so over-institutionalizing it (as if each year the universities were aborting Edmund Wilsons and Kenneth Burkes), to write and read critical texts with the same care that we give to literature – to bring, as it were, even the literature of criticism into the canon – is an achievement we are still working on.

Most of us, I have found, do not think criticism very productive, or read it with much pleasure. It has too many undeveloped allusions and ricochets. Within the casual flow of critical words there is a charged and overdetermined quality. Like pastoral, criticism seems always to glance at greater matters, and Richards's prose is a case in point. It evades fixed terminologies and never seems indebted to a central discipline. Yet it is steeped in the vocabulary of the social sciences. This absence of one fixed doctrine is crucial; it explains both the suggestiveness of criticism and the fact that there is this sort of writing able to avoid dogmatic resting points and explicitly systematized argument.

It is quite possible, then, even necessary, to subject critical prose to explication. The first who did so in a sustained manner, who took it to have a texture, was John Crowe Ransom in *The New Criticism*, the title lending its name to the movement he discussed. Other New-Critical practitioners applied close reading exclusively to fiction, and insisted with Eliot that 'you cannot fuse creation with criticism as you can fuse criticism with creation.' Our recent, more acute awareness of intertextuality, which has lessened the a priori ranking of fiction over commentary and enabled us to see the mediated and redacted nature of all texts even when a named author originates them, is making us more medieval and midrashic in studying criticism as a creative yet text-dependent activity.

Take Richards's opening once more: 'Intellectual tradition tells us . . . how *literally* to read a passage.' It sets up a shifting series of ideas. Is Richards raising the issue of what might restrain interpretation (the chapter is entitled 'The Bridle of Pegasus'), or rather what might liberate it? Is he calling for the rediscovery of hermeneutics as a discipline, but within a non-religious, that is, primarily intellectual frame? That is the direction Heidegger will go, with the difficult aim to depragmatize meaning and to explore (if not explain) why we cannot speak 'being' at the present time, like Scripture or a few great poets. Is not 'intellectual tradition,' however, an oxymoron, since traditions are notoriously resistant to rationalization? Does 'intellectual,' then, intend 'secular' – in which case the critic would be seeking an alternative tradition to the one that sustained the religious if unstable society of seventeenth-century England? The subject-phrase that opens the paragraph is impersonal, evoking like Eliot does an authoritative guide.

We are on a train that must switch from one rail to another, yet our journey takes us along both. It is essential (1) to explore the antagonism between theory and tradition, which Richards accommodates by the notion of 'intellectual tradition.' It is also essential (2) to explore the question of critical style, that is, how to read *criticism* aright, which leads us to acknowledge a conflict between the essayistic mode and descriptive poetics.

Yet we can relate (2) to (1). The growth of a science of literature that looks down on the familiar essay replays the antagonism of theory to tradition. Essayistic criticism is held to be merely impressionistic or epigonic (parasitic) by scientific critics. It is accused of using the resources of figuration in a lax or self-contaminating way. From it, consequently, no rules can be derived for reading aright the auxiliary prose that exists to help us read literature aright.

> Figurative language [a typical statement runs] is a stereotype of 'essayistic' criticism. It is a symptom of its epigonic character: 'essayistic' criticism imitates the semantics of its object language because it is unable to develop its own descriptive language; therefore, it cannot rise above the level of paraphrase or parody.' (Lubomir Dolezel)

Practically speaking, the contradiction between descriptive modes and essayistic ones is less formidable than it appears. For however inventive of categories and technical words the science of literature may be, it relies – like literature itself – on the critical essay to integrate and familiarize its terms. Is it not, in fact, a sin against literary science to forget that the social and pedagogical prose we use in most discussions originates in the essayistic criticism of the latter half of the seventeenth century and the beginning of the eighteenth? That prose was inspired by the proto-democratic ideal of the 'honnête homme' or gentleman, and it has remained almost totally stable as an ethos and a style from the time of *Tatler* and *Spectator* to that of the *New York Review of Books*. Indeed, the return to technical poetics is often a protest, one of several, against the demi-intimacies of this style that pretends to a conversational equality of author and reader and subdues class distinctions as well as the signs and trappings of expertise. Even Hans-Georg Gadamer is tempted to put his key concept of a 'fusion of horizons' (*Horizontverschmelzung*) under its aegis. That fusion of horizons, he claims, is 'the full realization of conversation, in which something is expressed that is not only mine or my author's but common.'

In addition to a science of literature, or integral to it, we need a sociology. Important as the conversational imperative was in forming communicative prose, it drifted into a bad gentility promoting chit-chat or causerie even in professional circles. While not bad in itself, since one can only praise what James Boswell described as 'gaiety of conversation and civility of manners,' the habit was unfortunate in the way it censored both enthusiasm and the scientific spirit. Its decorum tyrannized over large tracts of French and English letters.[4] Richards's insistence on theory is clearly a provocation to the genteel and amateur tradition: it calls for research, protocols, professionalism, empirically tested principles. The title of his first book, *Principles of Literary Criticism* (1924), gains resonance against the background of the parodic Jane Austen opening of R. H. Tawney's *The Acquisitive Society* (1920): 'It is a commonplace that the characteristic virtue of Englishmen is their power of sustained practical activity, and their characteristic vice a reluctance to test the quality of that activity by reference to principles. They are incurious as to theory . . .' Richards lifted a Cloud of Unknowing from the humanities at the risk of admitting scientific and artisanal ideals. *Chariots of Fire* (1981), the Hugh Hudson film about life at

Cambridge in the 1920s, renders the situation against which the emphasis on theory protested.

There surely is an 'ordeal of civility' (J. Cuddihy) which the founders of the 'sciences humaines' — Marx, Freud, Lévi-Strauss — and their followers had to undergo. The genteel tradition of learning was also, moreover, a gentile tradition. To jump forward a little, when Harold Bloom used Buber's 'I and Thou' as a framework for the mythmaking in Shelley's poetry or Gershom Scholem's understanding of Kabbalah to argue for his theory of misreading, the jittery dovecotes of English studies did not coo with pleasure. An eloquent article denouncing Bloom and one of his colleagues, entitled 'The Herme-neutical Mafia: After Strange Gods at Yale,' not only alludes to one of Eliot's most Christian books but makes it clear that something not quite gentlemanly was going on in the Old School. Essayistic criticism, in short, is not always part of the tradition but fights an internal battle by fashioning an iconoclastic style. When we read Coleridge on 'the modern Anglo-Gallican style,' which he despised because it was without 'the hooks and eyes of intellectual meaning, never oppressing the mind by any after-recollection,' do we not suspect that it was to redress such attenuation that Jacques Derrida — *enfin* — appeared?

A neglected aspect of the ordeal of civility concerns women. Though the conversational ideal is attached to the 'gentleman,' in France it is also perpe-tuated by the salons. The civilizing power of women over men was, in any case, a chivalrous cliché that came into the Renaissance via legends and books of courtesy. The cliché intimated also the other side of woman: her seductive potential that could lead men to break out of the bonds of conventional behavior. For Virginia Woolf the issue posed itself in terms of the domestication of women; and in that domestication, in the tying down of the wildness, in confining her to the role of consort, mother, housekeeper, the conversational ideal played its part. It was not gossip (often subversive) but social chit-chat that kept the emotions in check, albeit at the cost of trivializing overt relationships.

Woolf's short stories, *Monday or Tuesday* (published in 1921, augmented and republished after her death) show that kind of conversation eating into woman's soul. She even seems to cooperate with it: the Mrs. Dalloway figures in Woolf's fiction are as reticent about their true feelings as the men. So 'Together and Apart' depicts the impasse of small talk as it unseals yet soon freezes a momentary affection. Words are frigid, they fail to betray (in the sense both of express and give away) persons who must hunt and haunt each other by these wary, destabilizing tokens. Alongside this Jamesian theme another prevails at the level of near-caricature: tags of poetry and gilded phrases rise up in the female soul — even identifying themselves as that soul — to create a prose poem that counter-points an asthenic causerie. This rape by reverie, by golden speech ('Thinking thus, the branch of some tree in front of her became soaked and steeped in her admiration for the people of the house; dripped gold; or stood sentinel'), is as disconcerting as the more prosaic impositions of society. Each stream of thought, color it gold or gray, is composed of clichés and keeps language within an airless realm of signifiers. Sasha Lasham, we read,

> was glad she was with Bertram, who could be trusted, even out of doors, to talk without stopping . . . he chattered on about his tour in Devonshire, about inns and landladies, about Eddie and Freddie, about cows and night travelling, about creams and stars, about continental railways and Bradshaw, catching cod, catching cold, influenza, rheumatism and Keats . . .

For woman's soul, 'by nature unmated, a widow bird,' this distancing of the outdoors by pseudo-intimate talk at once preserves virginity and disastrously confirms its violation. 'At that moment, in some back street or public house, the usual terrible sexless, inarticulate voice rang out; a shriek, a cry. And the widow bird startled, flew away . . .' ('A Summing Up').[5]

At this point I wish to propose a historical generalization. If the history of commentary spans more than two millennia, then the period René Wellek describes as 'Modern Criticism' is dominated by closure and premature synthesis. From about 1660 to 1950 (I choose dates that should be modified by a knowledge of national traditions) a neoclassical decorum triumphed, despite traumatic breaks and perhaps because of them. Even when art was adventurous, criticism remained reactionary. It requires, of course, more than the pop sociology I can offer to indicate how many factors conspired to produce that loss or limitation of interpretive skill which was Richards's point of departure.

The closure characterizing that period involves an ethos of language refinement that goes back in England to Charles II and the 'Augustan' age, and is still notable in Richards's mentor, C. K. Ogden, who published Bentham's attack on legal fictions and wrote a tract against 'word-magic' entitled *Debabelization* (the occasion was the Basic English project, which Richards too supported). Sacred hermeneutics are marginalized; there is a general weakening of multivocal diction and a consensus in favor of plain or common speech and whatever genres and formal unities could be derived from Aristotle. The 'limitary tone of English thought,' as Emerson called it, is formed.

There is nothing original in identifying such a period of closure. Nor in suggesting that a fear of enthusiasm, which leaves its stamp on Swift's greatness, is the scarlet thread that runs through an age in which a *via media* decorum spread to all matters in hopes of damping the fires of controversy and preventing a recurrence of bloody schisms. Mikhail Bakhtin, taking Continental rather than English literature as his text, sees a similar period characterized by the attempt to repress vernacular energies and popular – especially mocking and so potentially revolutionary – speech. My sense is that this period continues much longer in criticism than in art, and with fewer exceptions.

So decisive, in any case, is the disintoxication of prose and the suspicion of visionary poetry beyond Spenser, Shakespeare, and Milton, that Somerset Maugham can assert of the King James Bible that it has been harmful to English prose. 'The Bible is an oriental book. Its alien imagery has nothing to do with us. Those hyperboles, those luscious metaphors, are foreign to our genius.' The latter consisted, according to Maugham, in plain speech. 'Blunt Englishmen twisted their tongues to speak like Hebrew prophets.' He concludes: 'To write good prose is an affair of good manners . . . good prose should resemble the conversation of a well-bred men.' Though written in the late 1930s, these lines might have been redacted in Will's Coffee House where the Tatler held forth in the first decade of the eighteenth century.

I am under no illusion that in pursuing the question of style, and pitting theory against gentility, I have resolved the larger issue of the relation of theory to tradition. My purpose was to suggest that in this area too we do not know we are talking in prose – how complex and historical a medium it is.

Notes

1. For some reflections on the rise of propaganda, see my 'From Common to Uncommon Reader: Theory and Critical Style,' in *Révue Internationale de Philosophie: Philosophical Aspects of Literary Criticism,* 41, pp. 398–413.

2. The paragraph from I. A. Richards's *Coleridge on Imagination* continues as follows: 'It guides us in our metaphorical, allegorical, symbolical modes of interpretation. The hierarchy of these modes is elaborate and variable; and to read aright we need to shift with an at present indescribable adroitness and celerity from one mode to another. Our sixteenth- and seventeenth-century literature, supported by practice in listening to sermons and by conventions in speech and letter-writing which made "direct" statement rare to a point which seems to us unnatural, gave an extraordinary training in this skill. But it was skill merely; it was not followed up by theory . . .'

3. Richards quotes Coleridge's praise of 'Shakespeare's time, when the English Court was still foster-mother of the State and the Muses; and when, in consequence, the courtiers and men of rank and fashion affected a display of wit, point and sententious observation, that would be deemed intolerable at present – but which a hundred years of controversy, involving every great political, and every dear domestic interest had trained all but the lowest classes to participate. Add to this the very style of the sermons of the time, and the eagerness of the Protestants to distinguish themselves by long and frequent preaching, and it will be found that, from the reign of Henry VIII to the abdication of James II, no country ever received such a national education as England.' See *Coleridge on Imagination.*

4. See *After Strange Texts: The Role of Theory in the Study of Literature,* eds. G. S. Jay and D. L. Miller, for a fuller account. Stanley Cavell prefaces his *Themes out of School* (subtitled 'Effects and Causes') with a defense of the causerie that modifies 'causes' by the idea of the casual (topical) conversation and even the ungenteel shmooz. He reinstitutes a tension between origin and occasion, between the formal or scientific discourse on origins (causes) and the idling power of the occasional essay. Richard Rorty, in a similar revolt against the truth claims of his profession, also prefers the idea of philosophy as a conversation. The rediscovery that there is a question of style in philosophy brings about a conversational anti-style (with a Jamesian formality in Cavell), and shows that philosophy and literary studies, as professions, are running parallel yet out of sync with each other.

5. 'Sexless' is puzzling. It describes more, surely, than the cry's indeterminate gender. Does the indeterminacy suggest a dehumanizing erosion of gender difference? Or does 'sexless' imply (despite Woolf's dislike of D. H. Lawrence) a Lawrentian critique? Lawrence's till recently unpublished *Mr. Noon,* written in the 1920s, uses authorial intrusions to mock the 'Gentle reader, gentille lecteuse' tradition and its desexualized 'dummy' values. Indeed, Lawrence prefers to address the woman reader as more capable of removing false sublimations. 'The sterner sex either sucks away at its dummy with such perfect innocent complacency, or else howls with such perfectly pitiful abandon after the lost dummy, that I won't really address the darling any more.' Woolf's 'usual terrible sexless . . . cry' may evoke the world of the prostitute, curiously if powerfully intruding on virginal and majestic Sasha. One is made to feel that both worlds are sexless, but that, if anything, the dutiful chatter which Sasha tolerates and even abets is more sadly empty.

Chapter 19

Literary Commentary as Literature

'I am always amused,' Wilde says characteristically, 'by the silly vanity of those writers and artists of our day who seem to imagine that the primary function of the critic is to chatter about their second-rate work.' The problem is what to do about first-rate work, or that which is great enough to reduce all critical comment to chatter.

The English tradition in criticism is sublimated chatter; but it is also animated by a fierce ability to draw reputation into question. Even Shakespeare had once to be made safe; and Milton is restored, after Leavis, to his bad eminence. This power to alter reputations is formidable, and it shows that criticism has an unacknowledged penchant for reversal in it, which is near-daemonic and brings it close to the primacy of art. This penchant, of course, can be dismissed as the sin of envy: as a drive for primacy like Satan's or Iago's. Yet, as Lukács remarked, there *is* something ironic about the critic's subordination of himself to the work reviewed. At best he keeps testing that work, that apparent greatness, and by force of doubt or enthusiasm puts it more patently before us. He plays the role now of accuser and now of God. A judicious rather than judicial criticism will, needless to say, not try for a single verdict: like Dr. Johnson, it exposes virtues and weaknesses, strong points and failings together. But it can also frighten by opening a breach – or the possibility of transvaluation – in almost every received value. Even irony, therefore, seems unable to digest Wilde's insouciance. 'The fact of a man being a poisoner is nothing against his prose.'

Wilde means, of course, a poisoner in life, like Thomas Wainewright.[1] But can we help thinking, at the same time, of the poison or immorality that may lodge in art, and that made Plato compare a certain kind of rhetor to a dangerous cook? A breach is opened by Wilde between morality and art parallel to that between morality and religion in certain pronouncements of Christ or, for that matter, Blake and Kierkegaard. This parallel may put too great a strain on art, as Eliot feared; and it may also put too great a strain on the critic, who knows that poisons can be remedies.[2] Still, at least since Wilde (with anticipations in Poe and Baudelaire), the theory of art has been striving to understand the daemonic artist, even the artist-criminal. Not as an empirical or social phenomenon so much as a theory-enabling fiction that could reveal the problematic depths of *persona* and *intention*.[3] Wilde tears apart face and mask, while modern persona theory tries to repair the breach. Yet the issue of an intention too faceless to be envisaged still defeats us; and for that reason Derrida suggests that we should substitute the word *sfeinctor* for *author*.

Nor is it an accident, then, that Derrida interests himself in Genet and the 'precious bane' of his style. Derrida's *Glas*, a work in which commentary becomes literature, by interweaving philosophical discourse, figurative elaboration, and literary criticism, begins one column with Genet's evocation of a 'Rembrandt déchiré.' But the theme of the torn picture (namely, manuscript) does not express an iconoclasm nourished by the simple opposition of art-appearance and reality (*Dorian Gray*), or art and religion, or art and a claimant absolute. It expresses, rather, the insufferable coexistence, even crossover, of holiness and profaneness in art. This crossover tears the distinction apart; and we imaginatively take our revenge by tearing at it, or prudently and hygienically – by means of a *genre tranché* critical theory – denying the crossover, and separating the demonry of art from the civility of criticism, or discursive from literary discourse, or persona from person, and so forth. Yet everyone has known the feeling that in Henry James or Sartre, let alone Borges, criticism is not independent of the fictional drive. The more insidious question is whether any critic has value who is only a critic: who does not put us in the presence of 'critical fictions'[4] or make us aware of them in the writings of others.

What I am saying – pedantically enough, and reducing a significant matter to its formal effect – is that literary commentary may cross the line and become as demanding as literature: it is an unpredictable or unstable genre that cannot be subordinated, a priori, to its referential or commentating function. Commentary certainly remains one of the defining features, for it is hardly useful to describe as 'criticism' an essay that does not review in some way an existing book or other work. But the perspectival power of criticism, its strength of recontextualization, must be such that the critical essay should not be considered a supplement to something else. Though the irony described by Lukács may formally subdue the essay to a given work of art, a reversal must be possible whereby this 'secondary' piece of writing turns out to be 'primary.'

We have viewed the critical essay too reductively, just as, in the history of literature itself, we often find types of fiction defined by arbitrary rules from which they break loose. Let us remember, too, that instrumental music, before a certain time, was strictly subordinated to text or programmatic function. Later the instruments become speculative. The same holds true of criticism: its speculative instruments are now exercising their own textual powers rather than performing, explaining, or reifying existing texts. What is happening is neither an inflation of criticism at the expense of creative writing nor a promiscuous intermingling of both. It is, rather, a creative testing and illumination of *limits*: the limits of what Hegel called 'absolute knowledge' and John Dewey the 'quest for certainty.'

I have argued previously that the more pressure we put on a text, in order to interpret or decode it, the more indeterminacy appears. As in science, the instruments of research begin to be part of the object viewed. All knowledge, then, remains knowledge of a text, or rather of a textuality so complex and interwoven that it seems abysmal. There is an 'echappé de vue ins Unendliche,' as Friedrich Schlegel quaintly says. Or, as Derrida puts it, the act of reading to which we are 'abandoned' by the critic forbids a single theme or resolution to emerge. 'Laissez flotter le filet, le jeu infiniment retors des noeuds.' We see that English and French waves have an inspiration in common: whatever the difference – and it is considerable – Derrida's radical attention to the skein of language is still part of the 'repudiation of the metaphysics' also aimed at by Ogden and Richards in *The Meaning of Meaning* (1923). But now the starting point in France is the pataphysical heritage[5] as well as a linguistic critique of metaphysics, or Hegel's 'absolute knowledge.'

There is no absolute knowledge but rather a textual infinite, an interminable web of texts or interpretations; and the fact that we discern periods or sentences or genres or individual outlines or unities of various kinds, is somewhat like computing time. We can insist that time has a beginning and an end; or, more modestly, that Romanticism, for example, began circa 1770 and ended circa 1830; but this is a silly if provoking mimicry of providential or historical types of determinism. Such linearity is precisely what stimulates Derrida and others to cross the line: to accept, that is, the need for lineation and delineation, but in the form of a textuality as disconcerting as a new geometry might be.

Against Derrida's *Glas*, a clear example of literary commentary as literature, it can be urged that bad cases make bad law. Exceptional this work certainly is, but can it represent criticism in any save an extreme contemporary form? It is not for me to decide that question. What seems extreme today may not be so a decade or a century hence. Books have their own fate; and I am sufficiently convinced that *Glas*, like *Finnegans Wake*, introduces our consciousness to a dimension it will not forget, and perhaps not forgive. It is not only hard to say whether *Glas* is 'criticism' or 'philosophy' or 'literature,' it is hard to affirm it is a book. *Glas* raises the spectre of texts so tangled, contaminated, displaced, deceptive that the idea of a single or original author fades, like virginity itself, into the charged Joycean phrase: 'Jungfraud's messonge book.'

Two cautionary remarks. The first is that, in criticism, we deal not with language as such, nor with the philosophy of language, but with how books or habits of reading *penetrate* our lives. Arnold's 'The Function of Criticism at the Present Time,' still a classic essay for our discipline in terms of its quality of self-reflection, takes its power from the courage of adjudicating between English and French literature – *literature* in the broadest sense, as the character displayed by our laws, our magazines, our political writings, as well as poetry and criticism.

My second caution (still thinking of Arnold) is that a hundred years or even two hundred years is not long in the eyes of God or recorded history, if endless in the eyes of each generation. One can exaggerate the newness of the present moment in criticism. There has certainly been some speed-up in the rhythm of events even if we discount such extreme statements as Péguy's, on the eve of the Great War: 'The world has changed less since Jesus Christ than in the last thirty years.' Arnold himself was struck by the speed-up, and his very focus on the function of criticism acknowledges it. He sees the critic aiding the creative mind to find its proper 'atmosphere,' which lies 'amidst the order of ideas' and beyond the provincialism of its era. And he welcomed the 'epoch of expansion' that was opening in England. Yet he also feared the example of France, where the Revolution had produced a commitment to 'the force, truth and universality of the ideas it took for its laws.' For these ideas were not really free, but imprisoned by particular ideologies, by the French 'mania for giving [them] an immediate political and practical application.' My caution is that things have not changed all that much since Arnold's essay of 1864; that despite the increased tempo and complexity of modern life, what was true in his contrast of France and England may still be so.

In fact, even Lukács's notion of the essayist as a precursor type may have a direct relation to Arnold. Lukács substantializes the idea of a critic and puzzles over the paradox of a social type whose essence is transience. For Arnold too the critic is a precursor, but Arnold does not claim an interest in the critic as such. His view is determined by concrete historical considerations, in particular by the stirring up of ideas in the era of the French Revolution. That stirring up is part of a great stream of tendency and must be for the good, but criticism itself is not that good. Arnold therefore makes a sharper distinction than the young Lukács between precursor-critic and creative genius, insisting that criticism merely prepares the ground for the latter by stimulating a living current of ideas. It was because that current had not been sufficiently present in England when the Romantics wrote that they failed to match the glory of the writers of the Renaissance; and Arnold ends 'The Function of Criticism' by foreseeing a new epoch of creativity that the movement of modern criticism will usher in. 'There is the promised land, toward which criticism can only beckon. That promised land will not be ours to enter, and we shall die in the wilderness: but to have desired to enter it, to have saluted it from afar, is already perhaps the best distinction among contemporaries.' To which one can only reply: Ah, Wilderness. It is precisely that precursor or purely functional notion of criticism, or any great divide between criticism and creation, which is now in dispute.

Notes

1. See 'Pen, Pencil and Poison,' in *Intentions*.
2. Cf. Jacques Derrida's 'La pharmacie de Platon,' in *La dissémination*.
3. There is a convergence, at this point, of the problem of intention in a secular context with the same problem in a sacred context. The depth interpretations of sacred hermeneutics, whether rabbinical or patristic or kabbalistic, are based on divine revelations that are close to being faceless, i.e., 'dark with excessive bright.'
4. *Critical Fictions* is the title of Joseph Halpern's book on Sartre's criticism (1976).
5. For a fine account of this heritage, see Roger Shattuck, *The Banquet Years*.

Chapter 20

Words and Wounds

Hypothesis

Let me suppose that words are always armed and capable of wounding: either because, expecting so much of them, looking to them as potentially definitive or clarifying, we are hurt by their equivocal nature; or because the ear, as a *psychic* organ, is at least as vulnerable as the eye. What is unclear about the first hypothesis is why we should expect so much of words. This overestimation, which may turn of course into its opposite, into contempt of talk, can suggest that words themselves caused the hurt we still feel, as we look to them for restitution or comfort. (Where there is a word cure, there must be a word-wound.) I prefer, initially, the other way of stating our hypothesis, that within the economy of the psyche the ear is peculiarly vulnerable or passes through phases of vulnerability. The 'cell of Hearing, dark and blind,' Wordsworth writes in *On the Power of Sound*, is an 'Intricate labyrinth, more dread for thought/To enter than oracular cave.'

Every literary interpreter and some psychoanalysts enter that cave when they follow the allusive character of words, their intentional or unintentional resonance. 'Strict passage,' Wordsworth continues, describing the auditory labyrinth, 'through which sighs are brought,/And whispers for the heart, their slave . . .' Othello's speech fills Desdemona's ear: '[She'd] with a greedy ear/Devour up my discourse.' There exists a lust of the ears as strong and auspicious as the lust of the eyes about which so much has been written since Saint Augustine. The two are, doubtless, interactive: the Story of the Eye (as in George Bataille's pornosophic novella of that title) always turns out to be, also, the Story of the Ear. But whereas 'the ineluctable modality of the visible' (Joyce) has been explored, especially by analysts interested in primal scene imagery, the ineluctable ear, its ghostly, cavernous, echoic depth, has rarely been sounded with precision.

Wordsworth's phrase 'strict passage' points to the constricted or narrowing, and therefore overdetermined, character of the sounds that make it through, but also to a moral dilemma. The ear must deal with sounds that not only cannot be refused entry, but penetrate and evoke something too powerful for any defence:

Wordsworth suggests it is akin to sexual lust or the intoxication of a blood sport, 'shrieks that revel in abuse/Of shivering flesh.' The *percéphonic* power of poetry, song or music to undo this wounding, 'warbled air,/Whose piercing sweetness can unloose/The chains of frenzy, or entice a smile/Into the ambush of despair,' suggests a sweet piercing that counters or sublimates a bitter one.[1]

'Chains of frenzy' tells us how close we are to the theme of madness; 'the ambush of despair,' how close to depression. Moreover, to 'entice a smile / Into the ambush of despair' is ambiguous, and 'unloose/The chains of frenzy' has a double-negative effect that could undermine rather than reinforce the idea of a liberating cure. These phrases, like the ear itself, are constricted; and even should we attribute that feature to the condensed diction of the Pindaric ode Wordsworth is imitating, this merely rehearses the entire problem and does not bring us a step forward. For while imitation can be therapeutic it can also be compulsive, or expressive of a word-wound that still binds the hearer. At this point, obviously, clinical material on the relation of word and wound should be adduced; not being a clinician I shall fall back on literary examples.

Names and Wounds

> No wound, which warlike hand of enemy
> Inflicts with dint of sword, so sore doth light
> As doth the poysnous sting, which infamy
> Infixeth in the name of noble wight.

So Spenser, in the sixth book of *The Faerie Queene*, alluding to the wound inflicted by the Blatant Beast, enemy to courtesy and an allegory of slander. Psychology and anthropology agree on the importance of the motif of the *wounded name*. To achieve a good name, or to maintain it, has been a motivating force in both heroic and bourgeois society. Fiction corresponds to life at least in one respect, that slander and rumor – hearsay more than sightsay – determine the drama of errors that besets reputation. A peculiar and powerful theory of what it means to redress a wounded name is developed by Jean-Paul Sartre. He speculates that his contemporary Jean Genet, a convict turned writer, fashioned his identity out of a 'dizzying word' addressed to him when he was a young boy.

The word was a vocative, an insult, a common malediction like 'You thief!' flung at him by a foster parent. It is said to have made Genet aware of his radically disinherited state. Genet was an illegitimate child; his mother too was a thief, or of the insulted and despised. That phrase, therefore, became a call, a vocation, which helped not only to establish a negative identity for Genet but redeemed that of his mother through him. A chance remark becomes, in

Kierkegaard's words, 'the infernal machine which sets fire to the tinder which is in every soul' (*Journals* of 1837). Genet grows up a thief, a homosexual, a powerful writer with his own Magnificat and gospel: John ('Jean') becomes Saint John. The connections are complex, and it takes Sartre a voluminous and immensely dialectical book to account for what happened.[2]

I am interested more in the elements that go into the theory than in the exact truth-value of the theory itself. What in Sartre's view wakes the child to the problem of identity is not a sight, an ocular fixation as in the famous case of Augustine's friend Alypius, but an *aural experience*.[3] Moreover, the verbal structure of what Genet hears is a vocative, and ritually it approaches an act of nomination or even annunciation. Identity is bestowed on Genet by a ghostly scene of naming, a curse converted by him into an act of grace.

Genet, then, is word-wounded by the insult or curse, but he makes it into an identity badge by a psychic reflex, and then by a lifelong fixation. And the tinder, the inflammable material rendering him vulnerable, is the very absence of an authentic name – an absence that provokes endless fillers or substitutes.

'You thief!' while only one such filler, happens to suggest that Genet must *steal* a name if he is to own one. For 'Genet' is a name that points to the absence of a 'proper' name: it is the mother's surname, and suggests moreover a figurative origin because it is a 'flower of speech.' Genet, that is, takes *genêt* ('broom flower,' Leopardi's *ginestra*) and turns it via his ritualistic and flower-name-laden novels into a literal figure; into something truly his own.

'Flowers of speech' is a designation for the figures or metaphors that characterize literary discourse and distinguish it from apparently straighter or more scientific kinds of writing. Genet links figurative language, or flowers of speech, with the 'language of flowers,' or the principle of euphemistic and courtly diction. He depicts what are criminal events in the eyes of bourgeois society by a sublime and flowery style. No one is deceived, of course: the reader sees through to the sordid wound and understands this inverse Magnificat.

Yet Genet steals back his name less to magnify himself than the absent mother, or rather mother tongue. His name, elaborated, founds an artificial diction that is his only source of healing and salvation.[4] This stealing back of a name is not as naive or exceptional as it seems, for those who have a name may also seek a more authentic and defining one. The *other* name is usually kept secret precisely because it is sacred to the individual, or numinous (*nomen numen*): as if the concentrated soul of the person lodged in it. A perilous or taboo relation may arise between the given (baptismal) name and the truly 'proper' name, and then a psychic search unfolds for this hidden word under all words, this spectral name.[5] It is a quest that often leads to the adoption of pseudonyms and nicknames, and even to anonymity. So Malcolm Little erases his family name by an X like the mark of the illiterate slave yet which he endows with a redemptive meaning:

The Muslim's 'X' symbolized the true African family name that he never could know. For me, my 'X' replaced the white slave-master name of 'Little' which some blue-eyed devil named Little had imposed upon my paternal forebears. The receipt of my 'X' meant that forever after in the nation of Islam, I would be known as Malcolm X. Mr. Muhammad taught that we would keep this 'X' until God Himself returned and gave us a Holy Name from His own mouth.[6]

Twelve years later Malcolm gives himself that name, or a likeness of it, from his own mouth, when he calls himself, having gone on a pilgrimage to Mecca, El-Hajj Malik El-Shabazz.

Names against Wounds

I would to God thou and I knew where a commodity of good names were to be bought.

(*I Henry IV* I.ii.80–83)

'Call me Ishmael.' We don't know the original name of Melville's storyteller. Perhaps there is no original name; or it is extirpated, like Pierre's family name by the end of the novel *Pierre*. Only the act of self-naming is apparent. Yet the adopted name is not empty, of course: if not as grand as Malcolm's, it still points East, to the Orient or the Oriental tale, to a lost origin, or a compelled sympathy with exile and alien.

Ishmael, the ending of which rhymes (at least approximately) with the first syllable of Melville's name, may evoke the homophonic word *male*. The trouble with this kind of rhyming, this illness of the ear, as W. H. Auden once defined poetry itself, is its infectiousness. What if 'Melville,' when heard with 'Ishmael,' elicits further echoes? Male(v)ill, Male Will? Or should the ear pick the assonance of *el* as the deceptive key, in its Hebrew meaning of 'God' and its Arabic force as definitive article: the 'the'?

Though names, then, may be medicinal, they are never simples. Yet the class of proper nouns, or names, comes closest to having the magical force of certain herbs called *simples*. Why should that be?

An observation of Saussure's on the semiotic structure of names may be relevant. Whereas ordinary nouns, *table* and *chair*, not only point to a referent in the world of things but rely on a concept of table and chair in order to signify, names seem to be pure signifiers that have only a referent (the indicated person or place) but no concept or signified. We cannot conceptualize names unless we make them into trade names (like Kodak) or type names (like calling a woman a Griselda).[7]

Naming does have a spectral dimension if we seek to perpetuate someone by calling a child after him or her. (It makes the child a *revenant*, Freud said.) A gap opens, nevertheless, between name and meaning; and this is clearest in etymological speculation, extending from Isidore of Seville or the *Legenda Aurea* (*Golden Legends of the Saints*) with their beautiful and fantastic elaboration of the meaning of saints' names, to Derrida's punning transformation of *Hegel* (the philosopher's name) into *aigle* (the bird's name).

This would suggest that words become magical the closer they move to the status of pure signifiers or name equivalents. Approaching the character of an 'acoustical image' (Saussure), names accrue the mystery or magic of an *Open Sesame*. We can make believe that there exists a naming formula, anagram, or password to pierce the opacity of our ignorance and open the treasure house of meaning.

Perhaps the second-order discourse we call 'metalanguage' – terms of art, explanatory or classifying schemes, and words about words – aspires to the same magic, that of pure signification. Here Linnaeus, who established the Latin nomenclature for plants and animals in his *Systema Naturae* (1735; 10th ed., adding animals to plants, 1758), was crucial. The virtue of flowers (birds, etc.) was joined to the virtue of Latin to produce a (re)naming of all creatures in a manner at once scientific and fantastic. The Latin appellation, in its very strangeness and strictness, merely succeeded in putting the vernacular name of the creatures in relief, and so induced a more complex verbal consciousness, a doubling of signifying systems: the Latinate order (itself binominal in Linnaeus) as well as the common language designation. But the wound inflicted on language, through this propagation of names, analogous to the wound inflicted by Linnaeus's discovery of sexual characteristics in plants (on which his nomenclature was partially based, and which gave a shock to the 'language of flowers') – this wound proved fortunate in some respects. The new, more complex name could be used as a stronger potion for the perturbed spirit.

Take Christopher Smart's liturgy, which, aware of Linnaeus, impresses the various names of the creatures as if to heal language itself after its fall from simplicity:

> Let Shallum rejoice with Mullein Tapsus barbatus good for the breast.
> For the liturgy will obtain in all languages.
> Let Johnson, house of Johnson rejoice with Omphalocarpa
>   a kind of bur. God be gracious to Samuel Johnson.
> Let Adna rejoice with Gum Opopanax from the wounded root
>   of a species of panace Heracleum a tall plant growing to be
>   two or three yards high with many large wings of a yellowish
>   green – good for old coughs and asthmas.[8]

I don't think we can know the 'smart' that 'Christopher' bore, except to say on the evidence of the text before us that it had to do with his sense of 'existimation,' a word that seems to conflate *exist, estimate,* and *esteem.* 'For my existimation is good even among the slanderers and my memory shall arise for a sweet savor unto the Lord.' The wound dressed or redressed is associated with naming, and this would not exclude, of course, the 'smart' of love or the 'smart' use of words to achieve or re-establish reputation.

So naming and the problem of identity cannot be dissociated. So literature and the problem of identity cannot be dissociated. Literature is at once onomatopoeic (name-making) and onomatoclastic (name-breaking). The true name of a writer is not given by his signature, but is spelled out by his entire work. The bad or empty name or nickname may be countered by the melodious and bardic magic of art:

> There is nothing in a name. The name Menschikoff, for instance, has nothing in it to my ears more human than a whisker, and it may belong to a rat. As the names of the Poles and Russians are to us, so are ours to them. It is as if they had been named by the child's rigmarole, *lery wiery ichery van, tittle-toltam* . . . At present our only true names are nicknames . . . We have a wild savage in us, and a savage name is perchance somewhere recorded as ours . . . I seem to hear pronounced . . . [the] original wild name in some jaw-breaking or else melodious tongue. (Thoreau, *Walking*, 1862)

Look with thine ears (*King Lear*)

The motif of the wounded name, that at first seemed rather special, leads into the crucial problem of self-identity and its relation to art and writing. But let us also consider the issue from the reader's point of view.

It may prove hard to say anything definitive about the capacity of words to wound. Or about the obverse effect, their medicinal, defensive qualities. The whole theory of defences, originated by Freud, is involved in metaphor, and becomes ever more elaborate. Moreover, we have to recognize that hearing – a receptive and, as overhearing, involuntary act – is already within the sphere of hurt. We are in bondage to our ears as to our eyes. We are all like Shakespeare's Emilia in *Othello* (V.ii) when it comes to the aggressing power of words. Emilia to Iago: 'Thou hast not half that power to do me harm/As I have to be hurt.' That statement is itself a covert threat and suggests how much depends on hearing what is said in what is being said.

Yet this is where the study of literature enters. Reading is, or can be, an active kind of hearing. We really do 'look with ears' when we read a book of some complexity. A book has the capacity to put us on the defensive, or make us envious, or inflict some other narcissistic injury. When literary critics remark of literature, 'There's magic in the web,' they characterize not only what distinguishes the literary from the merely verbal, but what distinguishes critical from passive kinds of reading. Critical reading, then, which almost always leads to writing, allows us to estimate words as words, to use rather than abuse their affective powers, to determine as well as be determined by them. These things are obvious, and I feel preachy repeating them; but too often we conceive of reading as a scrutiny of content or form rather than more generally of the status of words in the psyche and the environing culture.

What active reading discloses is a structure of *words within words*, a structure so deeply mediated, ghostly, and echoic that we find it hard to locate the *res* in the *verba*. The *res*, or subject matter, seems to be already words. Even images, as Freud noticed in his analysis of dreams, turn out to have the form of a *rebus*, or words (parts of words) that appear in the disguise of things. These reified verbal entities must then be translated back into the original sounds, like a charade. But words themselves, of course, may reify, by being taken too literally or absolutely. Psychoanalysis, with its emphasis on the overdetermined or ambivalent symbol, and semiotics, with its disclosure of the radical obliquity of signification, undertake to correct that abuse.

Writing and reading of the active sort are certainly homeopathic vis-à-vis the 'wound' left by literalism *and* the 'wound' that literalism seeks to cure: equivocation. The search for the absolute word, or minimally for the *mot juste*, is like that for the good name. There is bound to be a non-correspondence of demand and response: an inadequacy or lack of mutuality that relates to our drive to make words into things. However precise words may seem, there is always understatement or overstatement, and each verbal action involves itself in redressing that imbalance.

'Nothing' as the *Mot Juste*

Take Cordelia's famous 'Nothing,' which sets going one of the bloodiest of Shakespeare's plays. It is only ponderable when we think about the status of words. Cordelia exercises, of course, her power of non-receiver, of not responding to a 'Speak' that would enjoin the very words to be spoken. But within this paralegal situation her 'Nothing' raises a more basic issue. Lear wants to exchange power for love; initially words of power for words of love. Cordelia's reply contains not only a judgment that the quality of love cannot be constrained but that there may be something disjunctive in language itself that makes such an exchange – or reversal, if Lear, who wants to 'crawl unburdened toward death,' desires a licensed regression to childhood – as unlikely as reconciling love and power in the real world. Lear's fiat, his quasi-divine command, remains naked of response, therefore; and since the original fiat in Genesis was answered not only by obedience ('Let there be . . . And there was') but also by recognition and blessing ('And God saw it was good' 'And God blessed . . .'), Cordelia's 'nothing' has, in its very flatness, the ring of a curse.

Lear gives all, Cordelia nothing. The disproportion is too great. In Lear's view, order itself is threatened, and his great rage is just. But order, here, is the order of words, the mutual bonding they establish. Lear is asking no more than his daughter's blessing; which is, moreover, his one guarantee in a situation where he is about to divest himself. And instead of word-issue Cordelia utters something that sounds as sterile to him ('Nothing will come of nothing') as a malediction. It is painful to recall how much of the ensuing drama is curse, rant, slander, and impotent fiat:

> Hear, Nature, hear: dear goddess, hear:
> Suspend thy purpose if thou didst intend
> To make this creature fruitful.
> Into her womb convey sterility,
> Dry up in her the organs of increase,
> And from her derogate body never spring
> A babe to honor her
>
> (I.iv.265 ff.)

> You nimble lightnings, dart you blinding flames
> Into her scornful eyes! Infect her beauty,
> You fensucked fogs drawn by the pow'rful sun
> To fall and blister
>
> (II.iv.160 ff.)

> Blow, winds, and crack your cheeks! rage! blow!
>
> (III.ii.1)

Cordelia's 'Nothing' proves to be sadly prophetic. It exhibits the power of words in seeming to deny them.[9] As such it may be representative of all word-wounds, given or suffered, as they approach the status of *curse* or the incapacity to *bless*. Our speculations are becoming a shade more definitive.

Curse and Blessing

'I will not let thee go, except thou bless me.' And he said unto him, 'What is thy name?'

Genesis 1:32

> [He] in the porches of mine ears did pour
> The leperous distilment
>
> *Hamlet* I.v.63–64

Curse and Blessing are among the oldest types of formalized speech. Like oaths and commandments, to which they are akin, they seek to bind the action of those to whom they are addressed, yet unlike oaths or commandments they are resorted to when legal instruments are not appropriate or have failed. Legal codes may contain curses as a reinforcement or obversely seek to limit a curse – but it is clear that curse and blessing have a psychological aspect, as well as a legal or ritual role.

Supposing the psyche demands to be cursed or blessed – that it cannot be satisfied, that it cannot even exist as a nameable and conscious entity – as ego or self – except when defined by direct speech of that kind, then we have a situation where the absence of a blessing wounds, where the presence of a curse also wounds, but at least defines.

Perhaps direct speech itself is the problem here, the desire for a fiat, an absolute speech act. The evil eye, for instance, as in Coleridge's *Ancient Mariner* – the 'glittering' eye, or 'stony eyes/That in the moon did glitter' – is surely a curious form of that direct speech which is so condensed that *sema* is *soma*. (Do all word-images have a similar structure?) It 'shoots' with as unerring an effect as the crossbow with which Mariner killed albatross. Time is punctured in this poem of intolerable moments of stasis, which also features as its main speaker a constricted persona. Curse is primary, blessing secondary; the one must be drawn out of the other, like story and story time out of a negative and arresting fiat. The very desire for a fiat is at the heart of this compulsive narrative, with its fit-like motion.

I have inferred a verbal cause, or placed the wound in the word. But it turns out that by *wounding* I mean principally the expectation that a self can be defined or constituted by words, if they are direct enough, and the traumatic con-sequences of that expectation.[10] To quote from *Othello* once more, 'the bruised heart was pierced through the ear.' Moreover, because the demand to be cursed or blessed stems from the same source, and life is as ambivalent in this regard as words are equivocal, the psyche may have to live in perpetual tension with its desire to be worded. It may turn against as well as toward words. The equivocations put into the mouth of Shakespeare's clowns or fools are, thus, a babble that breaks language down because it cannot draw a 'just' or 'definitive' statement out of the crying need to curse or bless or to do both at once.

> Do you hear how Fury sounds her blessings forth?
> Aeschylus, *Eumenides*[11]

Lear opens with something like a curse, a decreating as well as a deflating word. Ordinary language, influenced perhaps by literary stereotypes, teaches us to think of 'a father's curse' and 'a mother's blessing.' It is as if the action of *Lear* strove toward 'a mother's blessing' but could only attain 'a father's curse.'

Shakespeare, in fact, is so puissant because he is explicit, because everything becomes utterable as direct speech. There is an Aeschylean and cathartic quality in him absent from most other poets. The defining wound is always before us, in every brazen word. And the dramatic action is as direct as the words. When Edgar, disguised as Tom o'Bedlam, meets Gloucester, his blind and beggared father, he utters a foolish cry that manages to word a terrible wound. 'Bless thy sweet eyes, they bleed' (*King Lear* IV.i.54).

This outrageous pun, one of several about eyes, suggests on the basis of a link between 'blessing' and 'bleed' (the etymological meaning of blessing is to mark with blood in order to hallow) that *since* the eyes bleed, *therefore* are they blessed. Shakespeare moves repeatedly toward imagining the worst in the form of a divestment, a making naked, a making vulnerable, of which one symbol is this castration of the eyes. But when Shakespeare calls on that darkness, in his play's general *fiat nox*, the curse the action labors under can still generate a bearable blessing.

Blessing and curse, euphemism and slander, praise and blame undermine statement. However neutral or objective words seem to be, there is always a tilt of this kind, produced by the very effort to speak. There are those who must curse in order to speak, and those who must bless in order to speak: some interlard their words with obscenities, some kill them with kindness expressions. These are the extreme cases that suggest how close we are to muteness: to not speaking at all unless we untangle these contrary modes. Their tension is, for the purpose of literature at least, more basic than any other; and it needs no witch doctor or psychiatrist to tell us that despite our will to bring forth unambiguous issue, words that point one way rather than the other, we remain in an atmosphere as equivocal as that of the witches' chorus in *Macbeth*: 'Fair is foul and foul is fair/Hover in the fog and filthy air.'

Let me also refer to Aeschylus's *Eumenides*: how, by a retrospective myth, it founds a city-state on a transfiguration of the cursing principle. The judicial process instituted by Athena is merely a breathing space or asylum in the play, like the navel stone or her idol. The real issue is the breathless rush of the Furies, unremitting, unrelenting.

> We are the everlasting children of the Night,
> Deep in the hall of Earth they call us Curses.

The final chorus, therefore, has to convert the Curses into an energy that is equal and contrary. It must honor the Furies in terms they understand, which affirms them in their onrush, their dark and eternal function:

> You great good Furies, bless the land with kindly hearts,
> you awesome Spirits, come – exult in the blazing torch, exultant in our fires, journey on.
> Cry, cry in triumph, carry on the dancing on and on!

Flowers of Speech

How thoroughly the human condition is a verbal condition! The medicinal function of literature is to word a wound words have made. But if we have learned something about the limit of poet as medicine man, we have also learned something about the limit of all verbal expression. Objectivity in language is always a form of 'You great good Furies': a neutralizing or musicalizing of badmouthing. The very production of speech may depend on a disentangling of blessing and curse, on the outwitting of that eternal complex.

Everything we say has to bind the Furies in the fetters of benevolence. Flowers of speech, as Baudelaire made explicit (laying the ground for Genet), are also flowers of evil. These equivocal flowers or figures characterize the literary use of language.

I give two examples of how a great writer outwits the intolerable tension of curse and blessing, and founds a language of his own that enables, and sometimes disables, ours.[12]

In *Finnegans Wake* James Joyce's (or Jeems Joker's, as he signed himself) hero is HCE. This acronym, though given various interpretations, may be a truncated reversal of E-C-H-O, reinforcing HCE's name of 'Earwicker.' The ear does become ineluctable in this book, which is the extended ballad of *Perce-Oreille*. Joyce methodically exposes the vulnerable ear by showing the unvirginal or contaminated state of language. In his 'mamafesta' no phrase remains simple. Sexual innuendo subverts or thickens every sentence, as it often does in Shakespeare. Words *are* jokes: they betray their compound or compoundable nature; they are not from eternity but rather created and adulterated, of equivocal generation, beautiful in corruption. 'In the name of Annah the Allmaziful, the Everliving, the Bringer of Plurabilities, haloed be her eve, her singtime sung, her rill be run, unhemmed as it is uneven!'

Yet here the wounded name is joyfully plural. Language has suffered a fortunate fall ('O fortunous casualitas'). Blasphemy is reconciled with good humor, and lust sings in echoes that perpetually hollow and hallow this prose, as in the following 'joycing' of the language of flowers:

> Bulbul, bulbulone! I will shally. Thou shalt willy. You wouldnt should as youd rememser. I hypnot. 'Tis golden sickle's hour. Holy moon priestess, we'd love our grappes of mistellose! Moths the matter? Pschtt! Tabarins comes. To fell our fairest. O gui, O gui! Salam, salms, salaum! Carolus! . . . I soared from the peach and Missmolly showed her pear too, onto three and away. Whet the bee as to deflowret greendy grassies yellowhorse. Kematitis, cele our erdours! Did you aye, did you eye, did you everysee suchaway, suchawhy, eeriewhigg airywhugger?

An ancient belief held that there was in nature a 'general balm' (John Donne, 'A Nocturnal upon St. Lucie's Day') with the virtue of sealing all wounds. A related group of superstitions considered excretions like sweat or blood or even excrement as therapeutic. Joyce releases into language a 'Thinking of the Body' that would be unthinkable but for a 'language of flowers.' Literature sweats balm, and heals the wound words help to produce.

My second example, then, is an episode from *King Lear*. In Act IV, scene vi, Lear enters 'fantastically dressed with wild flowers.' The scene is marked by ear-piercing puns as well as moments of terrible pathos. At one point Lear's rambling language, itself tricked with wild figures, culminates in the dialogue:

> *Lear* . . . Give the word.
> *Edgar*. Sweet marjoram.
> *Lear*. Pass.

What is being reenacted by Lear in his traumatized and defenceless condition is a type-scene of defence: getting past sentinel or guard. Also being re-enacted is the first scene of the tragedy, his command to Cordelia, the 'Speak' that led to 'Nothing.' But Edgar plays along, and the password he gives is taken from a language of flowers close to the mother tongue. 'Sweet marjoram.' Literature, as figurative language, extends that password.

The Language Exchange

> The stutter is the plot
> Charles Olson, on Melville's *Billy Budd*

Edgar's word *recognizes* the game Lear plays; its meaning resides in this act of recognition rather than its semantic appropriateness. It is not quite a nonsense word, but almost any word would have done. That it is drawn from the language of flowers converts the royal, now all-too-human, challenge into a childlike game, like riddle or charade. Infancy is close: the king still leads, but as 'His Majesty, the child.'

That 'marjoram' is a near-palindrome, related to vernacular feelings or beliefs, aids this sense of a redemptive word that has retained a link with childhood. To keep talking, in this situation, is not only to allow Lear to keep up appearances but to maintain a trust in words themselves. *La séance continue.*

Such speech acts remind us how much responsibility is on the respondent, on the interpreter. Dialogue itself is at stake, and the medium becomes the meaning at this crucial point. Literary speech, quite obviously, is not eloquent for the sake of eloquence; if eloquence plays a part it is because mutism, the failure to speak or to trust in speech, is never far from the deceptive flow of words. Every strong instance of verbal condensation is as much a stutterance as an utterance and skirts aphasia, like a riddle does.

A word, then, on riddles. Do they provoke a response or silence? Riddles divide into a silent and pointed part (the presumed answer), a periphrastic and overtly expressed part. They have been called a simple form (A. Jolles), but they are rarely found except as components of developed and complex literary structures. Lear's 'Give the word' is like the demand of the sphinx, and yet very unlike, since the implied riddle is so general (life as the mystery, Lear's fate as the mystery) that any word of recognition, of response, might do. We realize that even in less pathetic circumstances this contradiction between word as meaning and word as act of speech prevails. For do we not address many situations with words that are essentially passwords: signs of obeisance or identity or mutual recognition? When Lear tests Cordelia and her sisters, the word he demands, the giving of it, seems all too easy. A verbal satisfaction is necessary, as in a rite of passage; and the link between survival and readiness of speech is publicly affirmed.

Wit, the presence of mind in words, is the opposite of a failure to speak. Yet wit, pointed or periphrastic, is often felt as a wounding of language, of 'natural' language. Wit is called for in moments when words might fail as meanings: when the code is unknown, or when it is in such danger of devaluation that it must be rescued by surcharge. Love produces such dangerous moments. It beggars words, as Cordelia knows, yet it continues to demand them. The language of love can become, therefore, a cliché, as in the periphrastic language of flowers; or it can fall pointedly silent.

Goethe's commentary on his own *West–East Divan* (imitations of Oriental poetry) includes a section entitled 'Exchange of flowers-and-signs' ('Blumen- und -Zeichenwechsel'). The flowery diction associated with Oriental style is shown to be a necessity rather than a luxury. It brings things and words into a single system of signs, and so facilitates the exchange of feelings. This type of diction, which also characterizes the lover's discourse in the West, is established in the following way. The lover sends a gift to the beloved (a flower or other object deemed to be precious) who must pronounce its name and figure out which among the rhymes of the word designating the received object completes the message and solves the riddle. 'Amarante: Ich sah und brannte' ('Amaranth: I saw and burnt'). 'Jasmin: Nimm mich hin' ('Jasmin: Take me with you'). 'Seide: Ich leide' ('Silk: I suffer').

It is not possible – though Goethe refuses to say so openly – to guarantee this private code, for the code is always in the process of being established. It depends on a twofold gift: that of flower or precious object, and of responsive word ('Give the word'). Thus the skill or will of the interpreter is essential: his skill in playing, his will to find or else to impose a meaning. Goethe calls this literary game a 'passionate divination.' It brings ear and wit into play and may occasionally create a short novel by the establishing of a 'correspondence' – Goethe means, probably, of word and thing, of word and rhyming word, as well as of the feelings of the lovers in a letter-like exchange.

There are analogies here to the interpretive situation generally. Emily Dickinson could call her poems 'my letter to the world'; so the literary text or artifact is a gift for which the interpreter must find words, both to recognize the gift, and then to allow it to create a reciprocating dialogue, one that might overcome the embarrassment inspired by art's riddling strength.

Goethe does not develop these analogies; nor does he explore an important contradiction. Each exchange of things-and-words involves a private language that at its limit is intuited; and each exchange involves the contrary, a public and highly stylized word-system. He simply apposes these two aspects: in the next section of his commentary on the *Divan*, entitled 'Codes' ('Chiffer,' literally 'Ciphers'), he reports how in Germany around 1770 the Bible was so crammed into educated youth that many were able to use it wittily to 'consume Holy Writ in conversation.' It was possible, therefore, to 'make a date with a book' ('ein Buch verabreden'), that is, by a ciphered system of allusions to make it the textual intermediary to a secret rather than open exchange of thoughts. This conversion of a public system of signs into a sort of *trobar clus* also enters Goethe's section on the exchange of flowers and words, for Goethe suggests there that the 'passionate divination' he has described could return to the speechlessness in which it began: the silence not of embarrassment, concealment, or evasion, but of perfect divinatory understanding.

> Lovers go on a pleasure trip of several miles and spend a happy day together; returning home they amuse themselves with charades. Not only will each guess immediately what is intended as soon as it is spoken, but finally even the word that the other has in mind, and intends to cast into the form of a verbal puzzle, will be anticipated and pronounced by immediate divination.

How much Goethe takes for granted! That love needs secrecy and a code, or a special system for exchanging tokens and thoughts, is not explicitly related by him to any psychic or social condition (to the danger of persecution, for example, or the sense of self-esteem). He describes what is, not the reason for it, since this Eastern phenomenon is understandable in the West, and has its own parallels there. Goethe is valuing established genres as archetypes or primal phenomena. He does not wish to repristinate or orientalize what is current in the West, because his understanding can intuit the same pattern there without an explanatory or analytic scheme. He sees the genre in the idea of it.

Yet this intuitive procedure (Goethe sometimes called it *Anschauung*) papers over the problematic breach between private and public language, as between intuition and expression. It is necessary to reflect that the happiness associated with being intuitive, with the intimacy of understanding or being understood, may be the obverse of not being understood, or of having been understood and betrayed. Betrayal, breach of promise, breach of trust, misunderstanding, misinterpretation, persecution – these are equal realities. The more intimacy, the more potential misery. Goethe's 'correspondence' – the exchange and the system of meaning built on it – cannot be guaranteed, intellectually or socially. It is always a dangerous liaison.

One should not talk of understanding, therefore, as if it were a matter of rules or techniques that become intuitive and quasi-silent. There is, of course, internalization; but the life-situation of the interpreter has to deal with riddles as well as puzzles: what is sought is often the readiness to take and give words in trust, rather than the answer to a problem. 'Language,' Iris Murdoch writes, summarizing Sartre, 'is that aspect of me which, in laying me open to interpretation, gives me away.' Troth rather than truth: the ability to exchange thoughts in the form of words; to recognize words of the other; or to trust in the words to be exchanged. One breaks words with the other as one breaks bread. What is guaranteed by recognition, in the political sphere too, is the language exchange itself.

The art of divination Goethe describes can indeed be cultivated by parlor games whose purpose is to diminish shyness or strangeness. But this parleying aspires to recognition and not to absolute knowledge; and indeed, there is much to be said against being known by others. The other's words, which may be riddling – inherently so, if words are not subject to pure anticipated cognition – these words are allowed to create value by means of our own reception, by our formal willingness to interpret them. Each transaction consists of exchanging words for words as well as sounding out the words in words.

Partial knowledge is the *normal* condition, then, of living in the context of words. Words themselves help us tolerate that state: recognition must precede as well as follow cognition. To put the entire emphasis on the cognitive function (*connaissance*) will damage the recognitive function (*réconnaissance*) and the language exchange as a whole. Values continue to be created that may seem purely ritual, or not entirely perspicuous. Even when art represents a movement from ignorance to knowledge, it is not for the sake of clearing up a simple misunderstanding or emending the human mind in an absolute manner. Tragedy, for instance, hinges on a mistake that questions the very possibility of language exchange: in the case of Oedipus, a human understanding mistakes the language of the gods. Oedipus is faced with an oracular statement that forces interpretation to go blind, to stumble along by means of tense, stichomythic exchanges, 'epitaphic comments, conflictingly spoken or thought' (cf. Melville, *The Confidence Man*, chap. 2). The oracular allows no development, no capacious response.

Or tragedy flows from a scene of non-recognition, deliberate rather than the result of ignorance or mischance. In Faulkner's *Absalom, Absalom!*, Sutpen (unlike King David, who laments aloud over his estranged son, calling him by name) refuses to recognize a son of mixed blood, to accord him the honor of the family name. That non-recognition may expose its victim to the elements, to a position outside the law. The very possibility of having one's words regarded may then be lost.

Simple misunderstandings are not the proper topic for comedy, either, and barely for jokes. Jokes based on mistaking the sense of words produce a forced laughter; to be effective they must be deliberate and dangerous *jests*, and so they skirt tragedy again. Therefore, in *Love's Labour's Lost*, Berowne is sentenced by his lady Rosaline to a year's jesting in a hospital ('To move wild laughter in the throat of death'), so that his indiscriminate mockery, his 'wounding flouts,' may heal instead of hurt, or proving impotent will be self-cured. In a jest the laughter is ultimately on words: at the expense of language that can't and must be trusted.

Trusting and words: there is a scene of passionate divination in Tolstoi's *Anna Karenina* (part 4, chap. 13). Levin is together with Kitty, who had rejected him at the time she was in love with Vronsky. Their conversation turns on the vanity of arguments and what causes them to end so suddenly. Levin explains his theory to Kitty who

> completely grasped and found the right expression for his badly expressed thought. Levin smiled joyfully: he was so struck by the change from the confused wordy dispute with his brother and Pestov to this laconic, clear and almost wordless communication of a very complex ideal.

Kitty then goes to a table covered by a green cloth in preparation for a game of cards and begins drawing on it in chalk. Levin wants to propose to her a second time, and is afraid to do so in so many words; yet he must find the words. A private game follows in which he chalks on the same cloth the initials of the words he wishes to utter; she divines them and answers with initials of her own. He takes the lead, but Kitty overtakes him; and though the initials are a kind of stutter, because of Kitty's intuitiveness the potentially hurtful words are twice-born, and the language exchange is restored:

> He sat down and wrote out a long sentence [in the code]. She understood it all, and without asking if she was right, took the chalk and wrote the answer at once. For a long time he could not make out what she meant, and he often looked up in her eyes. He was dazed with happiness. He could not find the words she meant at all; but in her beautiful eyes, radiant with joy, he saw all that he wanted to know. And he wrote down three letters. But before he had finished writing she read it under his hand, finished the sentence herself, and wrote the answer: 'Yes.'[14]

Notes

1. Wordsworth's lines are themselves already allusive: they echo the ending of Milton's *L'Allegro*, the 'Cheerful Man,' which is paired with the poem of *Il Penseroso*, the 'Melancholy Man.' On 'le nom tout à la fois floral et souterrain de Perséphone [percé-phone]" (Michel Leiris), see Jacques Derrida's 'Tympaniser – la philosophie,' the overture to his *Marges de la philosophie*.

2. See J.-P. Sartre, *Saint Genet: Actor and Martyr*, trans. B. Frechtman. See also Hartman, *Saving the Text* (Baltimore: Johns Hopkins University Press, 1981), chap. 4. The obverse theme, that of a "speaking wound," becomes therefore the literary conceit par excellence: it at once offers and negates the possibility of muteness. See Julia's address to Eusebio in Calderón's *Devoción de la Cruz*, or Northumberland's speech to Morton in the second part of *Henry IV* (I.iii).

3. Alypius succumbs to a spectacle in the Circus: 'As soon as he saw that blood, he drank down savageness with it; he did not turn away but fixed his eye and drank in frenzy unawares, delighted with the guilty combat, intoxicated with the bloody sport,' *Confessions*, book 6, chap. 8. It is significant, however, that his eyes open when he hears the crowd shout. Augustine's own conversion was initiated by a voice, or the aural event 'tolle, lege.' See also Hans Robert Jauss, *Aesthetische Erfahrung und literarische Hermeneutik*, pp. 136–60, which defines Alypius' experience as a perverted form of *compassio* (sympathetic identification) and connects it with the role of catharsis in aesthetic experience.

4. A remarkable (true or not) account of the rejection and countercreation of a mother tongue is found in Louis Wolfson, *Le schizo et les langues*. Kenneth Burke's criticism abounds in speculations on the psycholiterary role of proper names: see, e.g., the remarks on 'Thomas' Eliot, and on a character in one of his own stories, in *Attitudes toward History* 1: 109–11 and 2: 108–10.

5. I develop the idea of a spectral name more fully in *Saving the Text*, ch. 4: 'Psychoanalysis: The French Connection.' See also below, 'Lacan, Derrida, and the Specular Name.' In applying the idea to Genet I owe a debt to Derrida's *Glas*. Concerning the relation of spectral to 'absent' name, cf. Lacan: 'The neurotic has been subjected to imaginary castration from the beginning; it is castration that sustains the strong ego, so strong, one might say, that its proper name is an inconvenience for it, since the neurotic is really Nameless.' *Ecrits: A Selection*, trans. Alan Sheridan (New York: Norton, 1977), p. 323.

6. From *The Autobiography of Malcom X* (as told to Alex Haley), chap. 12.

7. The point can be made in different ways, with different implications. Bertrand Russell says, 'Only such proper names as are derived from concepts by means of *the* can be said to have meaning, and such words as *John* merely indicate without meaning.' Leo Spitzer remarks in an essay on Villon that (I translate) 'there is a poetry inherent to proper nouns . . . one can enjoy a name as *matière sonante*, as the material basis for reverie.' Cf. Roland Barthes, 'Proust et les noms,' in *To Honor Roman Jakobson*.

8. I excerpt from W. H. Bond's edition of *Jubilate Agno*. To go into the aetiology of Smart's disturbance would mean to go beyond the boundary of what is empirical –

as Freud did, toward the end of *Totem and Taboo*, a book as deeply concerned as Smart's poem with the 'primal deed' or 'primal wound' from which culture may have sprung, and which may still echo in feelings of guilt and ambivalence.

9. Cf. Theodor Reik on psychoanalysis, which 'reveals the power of the word and the power of withholding the word, of keeping silent.' 'Die psychologische Bedeutung des Schweigens' (1926) in *Wie Man Psychologe Wird*. Reik's essay is a short yet remarkably comprehensive analysis of the emotional interdependence of 'Sprechen' (speaking) and 'Schweigen' (keeping silent), and raises the possibility that silence is always, to some degree, deathlike.

10. What is more effective with regard to self-definition, curse, or blessing? *The Ancient Mariner* shows a man still laboring under a curse, yet promulgating a message of blessing, a good spell. Set against the 'merry din' of a marriage feast, the poem seems to affirm, almost as a blessing, our *manque à être*: the peculiarly human sense of incompleteness, of ontic lack and separation from 'bird and beast,' together with the desire for completion, or rejoining the community of creatures. Perhaps, as Freud surmised, too much of human development takes place outside the womb, so we feel intrinsically premature, untimely separated from sustaining nature.

11. All renderings of Aeschylus are from the Robert Fagles translation of *The Oresteia* (Harmondsworth: Penguin, 1977).

12. The cycle of words-and-wounds continues, because great writers so often reduce us to muteness, or else require us to echo them deviously. The creative way in which this 'curse' of the precursor's greatness weighs on later poets is the subject of Harold Bloom's work on the 'anxiety of influence.' I should also pay tribute here to Kenneth Burke's concern throughout *The Philosophy of Literary Form* with the connection of art to homeopathic 'medicine.' The quotations from Joyce's *Finnegans Wake* that follow in the next paragraphs are taken from the definitive eighth edition (New York: Viking, 1958), pp. 44, 175, 104, 360.

13. Iris Murdoch, *Sartre: Romantic Rationalist* (New Haven: Yale University Press, 1959).

14. In quoting Tolstoi I use the Louise and Aylmer Maude translation.

Chapter 21

Reading, Trauma, Pedagogy

1.

What is the relevance of trauma theory for reading, or practical criticism? This much is known: in literature, as in life, the simplest event can resonate mysteriously, be invested with aura, and tend toward the symbolic. The symbolic, in this sense, is not a denial of literal or referential but its uncanny intensification. The reason for this convertibility of literal and symbolic is the 'traumatizing' already mentioned, which constantly shatters basic trust yet always, in a symbolic mode, picks up the pieces.[1] The theory, moreover, does contribute very specifically to an analysis of human time, clarifying its repetitious structure as a mode of negative narratability that alternates with highly charged moments, such as Wordsworth's 'spots of time.' These may return as flashbacks, but are also, at least in Wordsworth's description (and later in Proust's), revivifying beacons from a period of greater intensity, which had seemed lost.

In short, we gain a clearer view of the relation of literature to mental functioning in several key areas, including reference, subjectivity, and narration. I would have said 'disturbed mental functioning' but that would give rise to a misunderstanding. For the disturbance in question is not an unfortunate departure from normalcy, though it may involve anguish and ask for relief; it is, rather, a very human though compulsive doubt, an obstinate questioning that cannot be methodized or reduced to an affirmative structure like the Cartesian cogito. Instead, spurred by a residual idealism, it grapples, again and again, with issues of reality, bodily integrity, and identity. It is a doubt (sometimes a brooding ecstasy) which afflicts reference (is this the real or at least a sign of the real?), subjectivity (saying 'I' and the possibility of meaning it), and memory or story (being in control of the 'plot' of one's life rather than part of some other, unknown but fatal, narrative).[2]

I have mentioned these factors because they play a specific role in the study of imaginative literature. What reality-reference do poems or novels have; who is the 'I' that tells the story or claims authorial privilege; and why should we believe so fantastic a tale or mode of telling, one that, even when it respects criteria of realism, is marked by coincidences and a just-under-the-surface fabulous structure – which is precisely what appeals?

Not that trauma theory, at least when it works within the orbit of literary studies, has definitive answers. But instead of seeking premature knowledge, it stays longer in the negative and allows disturbances of language and mind the quality of time we give to literature. The questioning of reference, or more positively our ability to constitute referentiality of a literary kind (with a symbolic or polysemic dimension), indicates the nearness of dream or trauma; negative narratibility defines a temporal structure that tends to collapse, to implode into a charged traumatic core, so that the fable is reduced to a repetition-compulsion not authentically 'in time';[3] and the subjection of the subject, when it is not given an exclusively political or erotic explanation, evokes what Lacan defines as the 'fading' of the I before the Other. This fading always indicates a disturbance vis-à-vis the symbolic order.[4]

2.

In one basic area the yield for literary theory is already substantial. The epistemological bias – which not only favors a progressive view of knowledge and the effects of knowledge, but sees the complex structure of our coming-to-know mainly as the clearing away of subjectivity – this bias is shown to have distorted the reader/text relationship. We habitually view literary interpretation as a binary process, one that takes place between object-like texts and subject-like readers. We try to call this process a dialogue, or claim, using a conventional prosopopeia, that texts 'speak' to us. But the animating metaphor in this is all too obvious. It betrays the fact that while we feel that books are alive, we cannot find a good model, a way to picture that. The more we try to animate books, the more they reveal their resemblance to the dead – who are made to address us in epitaphs or whom we address in thought or dream. Every time we read we are in danger of waking the dead, whose return can be ghoulish as well as comforting. It is, in any case, always the reader who is alive and the book that is dead, and must be resurrected by the reader. The reader's forceful exegesis, however, does not remain at the conversational level but becomes a text which must itself be revived at a later point. The exegetical conversation is unable to maintain itself as oral tradition. It finds a different, a literary mode of transmission.

Ambitious thinkers, of course, not only want their work to stay alive but wish to supervise the future meaning of their teachings. This is the most obvious reason for Plato's devaluation of the medium of writing, which takes authority away from the author and places it in unknown hands – at best in those of a particular tradition or school. At worst, of course, in the hands of the State: this is what Nietzsche saw happening, and he fought as vigorously as he could against that. Nietzsche's critique of the university and its claim of academic freedom depicts a perversion of the ear through the lecture system: 'One speaking mouth, with many ears, and half as many writing hands – there you have, to all appearances, the external academic apparatus; there you have the University culture machine [*Bildungsmaschine*] in action.' Behind this machine at a 'careful, calculated distance' stands the State: Derrida points out that this picture of an educational State Apparatus, 'which dictates to you the very thing that passes through your ear and travels the length of the cord all the way down to your stenography' tends to conflate umbilical and ear. Uncannily 'an umbilical cord . . . create[s] this cold monster that is a dead father or the State.'[5]

Leaning on Nietzsche and Derrida, but also on insights culled from such different writers as Bataille, Bourdieu, Lacan, and Levinas, the new ethical theory tries to break down the reproductive tyranny of the educational system, its creation of a pseudo-ear that fosters the mere illusion of democracy and objectivity.[6] It acknowledges the problem of transferring to books, to writing as an institution, the pedagogical vitality of the teaching relation and orally transmitted knowledge. Texts are not simply the objects of a cognitive process; their 'moment' includes teaching as well as teachings.[7] Teaching is here understood in a broad sense as a performative activity, as interpretation that wishes to change the person, and so a world. The reader, similarly, is not simply a subject who reads, but a teacher or a student; something of both, perhaps. If we superimpose the interactive relation of teacher and student on that of reader and text, literary study loses some of the chill which cognitive or constative theories have cast on it, and reading is restored as ethical (or metaepistemological). Ethical, because the readings are addressed, and not only formally (through an explicit or implicit dedication, or an analogy of literature and letters) but to the other as a responsive, vulnerable, even unpredictable being. Through a criticism that 'reads the wound' and does not deny it (Paul Celan's phrase is *wundgelesenes*), the original text, itself vulnerable, addresses us, reveals itself as a participant in a collective life, or life-in-death, one sign of which is tradition or intertextuality.[8]

3.

I have some questions about this revival of a notion of paidea, which today includes, and often focuses on, women's experience. But it does invite us to rethink our relation to literature without superseding it in the fervor of our commitment to social justice. One reservation I have is that what is called the ethical may turn out to be, once again, a displaced evangelical intensity. The 'memento trauma' aspect is not all that far from a 'memento mori.' Is this conception of criticism as a secondary testifying a religious phenomenon, though one that has renounced the totality claim of religion? Does it seek a hermeneutics of modern, fragmented being? Susan Handelman writes explicitly that 'hermeneutics and homiletics cannot be separated and . . . are brought together under the category of the pedagogical.'[9]

A question therefore remains about how this ethical perspective can differentiate itself from advocacy teaching: from the strong personalism that has invaded the classroom and the profession as a whole, and which, as in politics, succeeds not so much by astringent evidence or humane conversation as by scandal, publicity, and sheer force of display in a 'society of the spectacle.' I certainly don't mean that Cathy Caruth, or Susan Handelman, or Barbara Johnson, or Jill Robbins, or Avital Ronell, or Cynthia Chase – or, in the previous generation, Shoshanna Felman, Jacqueline Rose, and Julia Kristeva – take that path. In fact, they are exemplary in not setting up a counterideal to 'mastery,' or a mocking feminist reversal of that hierarchical and complacent mode of teaching. But it will be necessary to spell out how their 'recuperation of the Pedagogical Moment' can avoid politicization or cultic personalism.

A step toward that comes when we remind ourselves that, so far, the discourses explored by this reintroduction of the pedagogical moment are psychoanalysis (or medicalized speech generally) and midrash, as well as literary criticism. Feminism enters as a critique of both psychoanalytic and literary discourse. It exposes in analyst, critic, and artist a distortion of gender issues. We confront potentially traumatic questions bearing on sexual identity and the tyranny of psychosocial constructs.[10] Getting personal, feminism breaches the barrier between autobiographical reflection and institutional concerns.

My remarks are limited here to 'the pedagogical moment,' and what can be learned from it to alter the reader/text relationship. Reception theory, for example, whether or not it is prompted (as in Norman Holland, David Bleich, Jane Tompkins) by psychoanalysis, is intensely pedagogic. It offers a way of slowing reading by allowing the student's opinions, prejudices, and positions to emerge, and subduing the teacher's own rage for order. The potential impact of midrash on literary criticism is a more complex case. Midrash originally flourished in a legal-religious, and so authoritarian, context. Yet it is the very freedom of this form of commentary which appeals, the creative response to a Writing that remains, all the same, sacred and unalterable. There is, very often, a challenging of the symbolic order and, simultaneously, its recuperation. I suspect that the response of midrash can be so daring because of the relation between orality and aurality. The pseudo-ear is challenged; we find ourselves in a commentary that restores an elided and intricate type of hearing. Rabbinic interpreters often discover or reconstruct a virtual text, words within words that yield new meaning through oto-matic ('eary') punning.

Where, in fact, does the received text lodge: in the text or in ourselves? It is hardly satisfactory to resolve the issue by saying the text is in the text but its meaning is in us. We soon get lost again in epistemological niceties. It is better to admit that a traumatic or enthusiastic element may enter secular exegesis, as it does midrash or the religious relation to Scripture. We sense it in such comments as Levinas's 'Teaching is not reducible to maieutics [the Socratic method]; it comes from the exterior and brings me more than I can contain,'[11] and Norman O. Brown's 'The book sets the reader on fire.'[12] Emerson's humanistic dictum, that in reading others we recognize our own 'alienated majesty,' also provides this insight.

Rabbinic midrash is a remarkable blend of ecstatic and maieutic practices. After Sinai, and all the more after the hurban (the destruction of the Second Temple, leading to the Jewish diaspora), the community has received the law, that is, accepted it once and for all, so that this law is not, or is no longer, heteronomous. The obligation to interpret and transmit it rests now on the teachers of the community, even though the otherness of God remains. Methods of study evolve which are, at once, commentary (constative) and prayer (performative). They encourage communal inquiry and intense intellectual exploration but do not exclude the possibility of inspired or mystical readings. The text is now more in the text than ever, rather than in God, yet it is 'revealed' through both legal and freer kinds of midrash, through Scripture's active 'reception' – even consumption – by rabbinic interpreters.[13]

Something like this reception theory, at once introspective and enthusiastic, also motivates the secular practice of literary criticism, without being acknowledged. What is assumed by the theory is that reception goes hand in hand with teaching and transmission, that the materials being studied are contagious, and that there will be a transference between teacher and student. (A wonderful example of textual contagiousness – typical of the way literature works, with or without a teacher – comes when Lacan, commenting on the dream recorded by Freud, characterizes the child's address to the father, 'Don't you see I am burning?' as a 'firebrand.') We have an obligation, of course, to analyze that transferential process, and to recognize the 'subject position' as, also, a limiting fact. But the hope is that literary studies, in contemplating spurned ancestral modes, and thinking back through trauma theory to religious experience, might become more imaginative rather than more pious.

4.

My own interest in the relevance of psychoanalysis to literary studies has not centered on trauma. The poets were there before, as Freud once declared, so I prefer to talk of 'psychoaesthetics' and 'representation-compulsion.'[14] But I share with trauma studies a concern for the absences or intermittences in speech (or of conscious knowledge in speech); for the obliquity or residual muteness of 'flowers of speech' and other euphemic modes; for the uncanny role of accidents; for the 'ghosting' of the subject; for the connection of voice with identity (the 'appeal' in cryptonymy, punning and specular names); for interpretation as a feast not a fast; and for literature as a testimonial act that transmits knowledge in a form that is not scientific and does not coincide with either a totally realistic (as if that were possible) or analytic form of representation.[15]

How does traumatic knowledge become transmissible – how can it extend into personal and cultural memory? Though Wordsworth evokes the role of 'mute, insensate things' in the growth of the mind, rather than a psychogenesis of speech, he records early 'spots of time' which become the support of 'far other' experience. In *Wordsworth's Poetry* I associated trauma with such eidetic and referential flashbacks. A 'spot syndrome' that fortified the youngster for the mystery of individuation marked even the mature poet's mind, haunting it with particular objects or places ('And there's a tree, of many one').[16] These places, mythic and realistic, never lose their aura entirely; indeed, Wordsworth's 'Where shall I seek the origin?' inspires him to evoke quasi-sacred sites of 'first encounter,' binding contacts between his imagination and earth, as if earth had omphaloi, specific localities that could restore poetic strength and lead to a future as strong as the past. The forming and deforming power of such fixations could be creative symptoms of trauma linked to reality-hunger, or a compulsive desire for 'the real.'[17] They are to nature what scenes of pathos are to tragedy, according to Aristotle.

Considerations like this foster a nonreductive psychology. At the same time, it is possible to move from Wordsworth to the present. There is something very contemporary about trauma studies, reflecting our sense that violence is coming ever nearer, like a storm – a storm that may already have moved into the core of our being. The reality of violence, not simply as external fate, but intrinsic to the psychological development of the human species, and contaminating its institutions (the Law system not excluded) is 'the fateful question' posed by Freud in the closing pages of *Civilization and Its Discontents*. Today we must add to Freud's insight an enlargement of the fact of violence through technical resources that relay powerfully both fiction and news. Audiovisual media pressure a mind that is no longer allowed to 'sleep' but must continually react. Wallace Stevens already defined imagination as a violence from within responding to a violence from without. Soon there will be no versions of pastoral; Wordsworth's may have been the last viable one, at the threshold of modern industrialization and urbanization. The interest in trauma, moreover, goes together with an interest in testimony as a genre that indeed presses back with the courage and patience of memory.

Notes

1. The symbolic, in Lacan, is not a cure of the real but is itself a kind of trauma. For the child's developmentally necessary transition from the phase of the imaginaire (essentially narcissistic, or a two-body, nurturer-child relationship) to the three-body phase of the symbolic (correlative with the onset of the oedipal complex) is always traumatizing. The symbolic order must cure itself; and it does so by missing the real or accepting it as missing. D. W. Winnicott, however, has a much simpler view of the relation between traumatic and symbolic. If the mother–child dyad, as he conceives it, develops transitional objects that are 'a symbol of the union of the baby and the mother (or part of the mother)' – that is, objects located at that point in mental time and space where separation or contiguity replaces union or continuity – then trauma occurs when such symbol-making is disabled. See Winnicott, *Playing and Reality* (New York, 1971), esp. 'The Location of Cultural Experience,' pp. 95–103.

2. Oliver Sacks, in *The Man Who Mistook his Wife for a Hat* (New York, 1990), mentions Wittgenstein's *On Certainty*, and remarks it might have been titled *On Doubt*, being marked by doubting no less than affirming: '[Wittgenstein] wonders whether there might be situations or conditions which take away the certainty of the body, which do give one grounds to doubt one's body, perhaps indeed to lose one's entire body in total doubt' (p. 43).

3. It is interesting that in neoclassical aesthetic theory what Aristotle called the scene of pathos (a potentially traumatizing scene showing extreme suffering) was not allowed to be represented on stage. It could be introduced only through narration (as in the famous récits of Racinian tragedy). An important type of psychoanalytic literary criticism, moreover, consists in discovering and thematizing a childhood fantasm, which may have a phylogenetic as well as ontogenetic element. A perhaps unintended effect of this kind of analysis is that it suggests the relative inauthenticity or very limited autonomy of the individual's psychic development. The earliest, now classic, example is Marie Bonaparte, 'L'Identification d'une fille à sa mère morte,' in which a hallucinatory swan appears; the insight is deployed literarily on a large scale by Charles Mauron in *Des métaphores obsédantes au mythe personnel* (Paris, 1963).

4. Compare '[T]he distance between self and other is always disturbed, or being disturbed . . . there is always some difficulty of self-presentation in us . . . therefore, we are obliged to fall back on a form of "representation." ' Geoffrey H. Hartman, The *Fate of Reading* (Chicago, 1975), p. 74.

5. Jacques Derrida, 'Otobiographies,' in The *Ear of the Other: Otobiography, Transference, Translation*, ed. Claude Levesque and Christie McDonald, tr. Peggy Kamuf (Lincoln, NE, 1988; original French ed., 1982). The Nietzsche extract I reproduce comes from educational writings in his *Nachlass*, in English as *On the Future of our Educational Institutions*, tr. J. M. Kennedy (New York, 1964).

6. Fred Botting, in an issue of the *Oxford Literary Review* with the title 'Experiencing the Impossible,' evokes the importance of Bataille's heterology and quotes Denis

Hollier's *Against Architecture*: '[T]here has never perhaps been any other theory than theories of the other, as Jacques Derrida has suggested, since all theory is deployed along the pioneer frontiers of assimilation, intervening at points where homogeneity perceives that it is threatened.' Botting suggests how, through Bataille and Derrida, theory becomes the sustaining enemy to theory, a 'factor in the process of disturbance . . . the shattering of the pedagogical narrative which popularized and institutionalized French writings in Britain by means of an apparently unified thread connecting structuralism, psychoanalysis, Marxism and poststructuralism.' *Oxford Literary Review*, 15 (1993), 206. On the negative aspect of literary pedagogy, see also John Guillory, *Cultural Capital: The Problem of Literary Canon Formation* (Chicago, 1993) and Kwame Anthony Appiah, *In My Father's House: Africa in the Philosophy of Culture* (New York, 1992), p. 55.

7. Compare Susan Handelman, 'The "Torah" of Criticism and the Criticism of Torah: Recuperating the Pedagogical Moment,' *Journal of Religion*, 74 (1994), 356–71. Handelman astutely contrasts Levinas and de Man, casting the latter as epistemological villain – but she neglects de Man's interest in 'blind' knowledge, his critique of the arrogance of insight, and his struggle to describe the aporia of performative and constative. Compare with Handelman Barbara Johnson's critique of de Man's impersonality in 'Deconstruction, Feminism, and Pedagogy,' in her *A World of Difference* (Baltimore, 1987), pp. 42–46.

8. The text is vulnerable because of its very historicity, not only because it was produced by a mortal person. See Thomas Greene, *The Vulnerable Text: Essays on Renaissance Literature* (New York, 1986). For a reconception of literary history close to the spirit of this paragraph, see Sanford Budick, 'The Experience of Literary History: Vulgar versus Not-Vulgar,' *New Literary History*, 25 (1994), 749–77. Budick restricts his understanding to one kind of tradition (that of the West, and in particular its effective founding through a Roman or Vergilian *translatio studii*). His chiastic frame of mind, moreover, connects the 'life-in-death' of reinscribed words (that is, intertextuality) with the experience of a death-in-life, 'unrecuperable loss' that makes literary history, as the record or recovery of previous life, something potential rather than fully realizable. 'The representation of this experience entails the claim that an unrecuperable loss within thought is a condition of one kind of experience of literary history (and one kind of tradition)' (767).

9. Handelman, 'The "Torah" of Criticism,' 364. My discussion does not resolve, of course, the issue of metalanguage (or a language of description separate from the object language) in literary criticism. While the situation in literary studies is not the same as in medicine, Kathryn Hunter's chapter on 'Narrative Incommensurability,' in *Doctors' Stories*, (Princeton, 1991), pp. 123–47, is very suggestive.

10. See, for example, Elaine Showalter's continuing work on (male) hysteria and such sensitive explorations of tone in poetry as Susan J. Wolfson's 'Lyrical Ballads and the Language of (Men) Feeling: Wordsworth Writing Women's Voices,' in *Men Writing the Feminine: Literature, Theory and the Question of Genders*, ed. Thaïs E. Morgan (Albany, 1994), pp. 29–57. Susan Eilenberg, *Strange Power of Speech: Wordsworth, Coleridge and Literary Possession* (New York, 1992), shows these voices as a passion, something strange within the poet, and usurping. This strangeness or

otherness can be but is not inevitably linked to gender issues. The issue of the identity of voice (or how voices reinforce or undermine identity) connects also with legal ownership questions and perhaps the copyright issue.

11. From *Totality and Infinity*, quoted in Handelman, 'The "Torah" of Criticism,' 362. Levinas retains, however, an ideal of mastery, defined as 'the coincidence of the teaching and the teacher.' This is, precisely, the ideal of an embodiment that exceeds epistemological inquiry and founds exemplarity.

12. Norman O. Brown, *Apocalypse – And/Or – Metamorphosis* (Berkeley, 1991).

13. The burning bush of Scripture is never consumed, however. It is illuminating to recall in this respect both Bataille's theory that conspicuous consumption, or the disposal of excess resources, is an (anticapitalistic) religious phenomenon, and Derrida's theory of dissemination as a writing that cannot return to the father (original author).

14. See, for example, 'I. A. Richards and the Dream of Communication,' in my *The Fate of Reading*, pp. 20–40, and 'Christopher Smart's "Magnificat": Toward a Theory of Representation,' pp. 74–98 reprinted in this *Reader*.

15. What an irreducibly literary knowledge means is clarified by Gabriele Schwab, 'Das ungedachte Wissen der Literatur,' *Deutsche Vierteljahrsschrift für Literaturwissenschaft und Geistesgeschichte,* 68 (1994), 167–89.

16. I stress the depiction of childhood trauma, but when Wordsworth describes political betrayal he must be said to suffer an adult trauma. When Britain declares war on France in 1793, or when it accepts the Convention of Cintra in 1808, an imagery enters that, while not entirely different from what is found in the 'spots of time,' is distinctive. I quote from the opening paragraph of the poet's pamphlet *Concerning the Convention of Cintra*: 'Yet was the event [of the Convention] by none received as an open and measurable affliction: it has indeed features bold and intelligible to every one; but there was an under-expression which was strange, dark, and mysterious – and . . . we were astonished like men who are overwhelmed without forewarning – fearful like men who feel themselves to be helpless, and indignant and angry like men who are betrayed.'

17. We glimpse there a Wordsworth/Coleridge difference. For Coleridge, as I have tried to show, the obscure object of desire is symbolic, and it is the symbolic order that must be repaired.

Part IV

Culture

Defining Culture

Let me state my argument. 'Culture' at present, the ring and function of the word, its emotional and conceptual resonance even when it is abusively applied, keeps hope in *embodiment* alive. Consciousness, as ghostly as ever, cannot renounce that hope in a living and fulfilling milieu. 'We live in a place that is not our own,' Wallace Stevens writes; such honesty, however, is a torment. He continues, therefore: 'And hard it is in spite of blazoned days.'[1]

I need not emphasize that the strongest imaginative needs are also those most likely to be trivialized, even deliberately 'wasted.' Whenever a novel, biography, news story or new historical essay begins in the manner of 'It was a cold and foggy evening . . .'[2] this is a repetition of a venerable technique, called 'composition of place,' that continues to stir us deeply and tritely. It is also a fact that with the advent of television a new kind of communal memory is created, promoting false embodiments, charged images that are the equivalent of fixed ideas. Artists must work with these as well as against them. Yet historically each super-realism proves to be a phantom. Ideologies of culture, which are as dangerous and effective as the art they inspire, also exploit our reality hunger by proposing 'a cure of the ground' (Stevens, 'The Rock').[3]

That phrase, 'a cure of the ground,' remembers culture as cultivation. But in Stevens it is also a euphemism for death. Nothing, he implies, can relieve us of imagination except imagination itself, even as that faculty conceives, ironically, its own demise and so approaches both the 'plain sense of things' and an absence of the imagining self close to death. I take that to be the meaning of 'a cure of ourselves, that is equal to a cure/Of the ground, a cure beyond forgetfulness.' The rock – from which Stevens's poem derives its title – exists, but not as a foundation; it is, necessarily, the motive for metaphor. A restless imagination localizes itself by a pseudo-specification that is not unlike love's fantasia. This rock, or 'the grey particular of man's life,' is transformed, humanized; its barrenness becomes, through poetry, 'a thousand things.' The spirit seeks, that is, the local, not the literal: indeed, to advocate that cure of the ground as a literal 'blood and soil' doctrine would curse the ground.

Yet we should not ignore the political backdrop of this distinction between local and literal. The cosmopolitan ideal of 'civilization' – the Enlightenment picture of the world citizen – has proved to be too vague, has not engaged our full imaginative and symbolic powers. 'If we are dreaming of a "national culture" today,' Van Wyck Brooks writes in 1918, 'it is because our inherited culture has so utterly failed to meet the exigencies of our life, to seize and fertilize its roots.' And, he adds sarcastically, 'that is why we are so terribly at ease in the Zion of world culture.'[4] Indeed, intellectual history teaches us that 'culture' achieves its pathos as a counter-concept to 'civilization,' especially in Germany. Consider Max Weber's famous definition: 'Culture is something finite, excerpted by human thought from a senseless and boundless world history, and invested with sense and meaning.'[5]

In such definitions the feeling of non-presence I have described seeps back and infects the very ideas intended to exorcise it. We continue to sense an incipient nihilism. This nihilism can turn against culture as well as nature, renounce all hope in secular incarnation, and become near-apocalyptic.[6] Theology and metaphysics have always engaged with a desire that is distinct from mere need in that it cannot be assuaged. The relation between idealism and skepticism, as in Plato, or of spiritualism and the anxiety of being perpetually excluded from true knowledge, as perhaps in Descartes, also points to a phantomization that lies just beneath the proud architectonics of philosophy, religion, and art and leads to the Pandemonium of political theologies.[7] Moreover, sociology has recently suggested that the dominant class creates and sustains itself by a principle of aesthetic distinction that limits both use and exchange value, a principle I interpret as a way of pursuing embodiment through a continually reinforced self-inclusion.[8] By a systematic, continuous, and institutionalized closure, we remain insiders. No wonder Bourdieu writes: 'There is no way out of the game of culture.'

So, after documenting the modern explosion of 'culture' as word and idea, I want to ask: are not images of embodiment that haunt us, and feelings of abstractness or non-embodiment that tell us we are not real enough, or that we inhabit the wrong body, the post-religious source of ideologies whose explanatory and remedial strictures increase rather than lessen abstraction and too often incite a cannibalistic violence greater than that of Hegel's animals?

It is here, also, with this kind of question, that one encounters Marx's strength as an imaginative and consequent thinker. He would claim that my emphasis on non-embodiment and the phantomization of reality describes the 'ghostly objectivity' of reified life under Capitalism, 'Monsieur Le Capital and Madame La Terre ghost-walking,' but divorces it from its foundation in the socioeconomic by depicting the ghost feeling as independent and permanent, 'as the timeless model of human relations in general.'[9] Like Hegel, I have stood matters on their head and not understood that my suspicion of postreligious ideologies is itself deeply ideological. Marx's vivid sense of alienated labour and damaged life brings a specific formula for reform and so for hope; unfortunately, all attempts to embody that reform by revolutionary change, to remove the false mystique of reified gods or human goods, have so far not exorcised the ghost feeling but continue to water it with blood.

Culture speech is an aspect of our culture: everything now tends to be seen in culture terms. 'Culture' has become our most prevalent 'complex word,' to use Empson's striking phrase.[10] There is no mystery about its linguistic development, starting with Cicero's metaphor 'cultura animi': culture of the soul, rather than of earth or deities associated with agriculture. (The transferred meaning, as Hannah Arendt points out, fortifies the intuition that the soul needs a human habitation, a dwelling place that does not simply subject nature to man.)[11] The well-known ambiguity of the genitive allows the construction 'the culture of' to go in two semantic directions. One is the dynamic or functional meaning, as when we construe Rémy de Gourmont's 'culture of ideas' to mean 'cultivating the ideas,' developing, understanding them better; the dynamic meaning is also aptly caught by John Stuart Mill, when he praises the 'culture of the feelings' transmitted by Wordsworth's poetry. The other direction of the genitive focuses on the formal product, the 'culture' produced by this activity. When a police department claims that it is 'the culture of the agency' to undertake certain procedures, the second kind of meaning has taken over, though the first persists.[12]

A world in which a Paris street still bears the name 'La culture de Sainte Cathérine' and that advertises a book *Beyond Beef: The Rise and Fall of the Cattle Culture* remains unified in the sense that we catch the connection between cult and agriculture;[13] at the same time the gap between provincial and global; between the church as a toponymic institution (however universal its hopes) and mass technology, can jar us into a sense of nostalgia about local attachments. The same is true when writers try to suggest a link between place and spirit, as if 'culture' were continuous with soil and climate: 'the peculiar flavor,' we read, 'of that old New England culture, so dry, so crisp, so dogmatic, so irritating.'[14] Even if such expressions as 'mass culture,' 'popular culture,' 'working-class culture,' and 'inmate culture' (Erving Goffman) make a certain sense – because they point to a sizable group, a quantitative spread, and because they are often applied in a provocative or questioning way (is *this* what or where culture is today?) – surely the quantitative factor is not defining, except as an undertone of anxiety, in such offshoots as camera culture, gun culture, service culture, museum culture, deaf culture, football culture, bruising culture (boxing, and all who follow the sport), the 'insistently oral culture of Washington' (i.e., gossip and slander), the culture of dependency, the culture of pain, the culture of amnesia, etc.[15] Why has this word taken over, like a linguistic weed? I will add some examples of its proliferation.

An average day. In the *New York Times*, after the Jefferson High School killings, there is mention of a 'culture of hidden weaponry.' *My London Review of Books*, just out, describes a new theory speculating that the origin of culture was in a 'sex strike,' during which the females, in order to defeat the 'alpha male,' a macho type capable of inseminating many of them one after the other, devised a way of hiding their ovulation. This so-called strike gave the averagely sexed male a chance and increased female control of the entire matter. Here culture does not mean lifestyle but the control of nature.

But what does 'Adjusting to Japan's Car Culture' mean, a headline on the first page of the next day's business section? Does it refer to the role cars play in the life of the Japanese, with a suggestion that cars run them (an inversion of culture managing nature)? The article actually describes the 'corporate culture' of Japanese industry and the difficulty American executives have fitting in. (Headlines are the one place in a newspaper where condensation permits striking and even malicious ambiguities. Perhaps we should talk of a 'headline culture.') 'Culture,' in the cases just cited, generally takes on the meaning of a habitual way of doing things that claims to express a basic national or group trait, as if it were 'the nonhereditary memory of the community.'[16] But principally the word serves as a means to age a modern practice instantly, to give a product – obviously of our making – traditional status.

This is problematic, of course. The anthropological meaning of 'culture' as a traditional way of life[17] is now extended to cover what is merely a lifestyle, whose legitimacy does not derive from tradition but precisely from what challenges tradition: modern technology. It is ironic that a word that Nietzsche had defined as 'a unity of artistic style manifest in all the vital activities [*Lebensäusserungen*] of a people'[18] and that for the greater part of its semantic career in English denotes 'the harmonious development of the whole person' (Raymond Williams), a development compensating for scientific and industrial specialization, now presents that specialization itself as the basis of a way of life.[19]

While one is tempted to see this antithetical extension of meaning as parody rather than paradox, it could not have prevailed without something attractive in the very notion of cultural history. What is suggested, beginning with Vico, is a view of history (he says 'civil society' and 'the world of nations') as human creation, a history, therefore, that we can understand, reinvent, and even control. The diversity of historical event, as well as the creative energy of a historical writing that changes nature from indifferent background to cultural milieu, raises the hope that Stevens will be proved wrong in his rearguard action on behalf of the universe: 'It is the human that is the alien,/The human that has no cousin in the moon.' Yet has our knowledge of history and nature as it leads to power over them worked to our benefit? This is the great post-Enlightenment issue, which confronts us daily.[20]

For this entrepreneurial vision of human development could be an illusion fostered by advanced capitalism; it is not, moreover, entirely absent from Marxism.[21] Whereas 'culture' used to point to the way we organized our leisure time (the culture page of the newspaper, which sees no difference between culture and entertainment, reflects and abets that meaning), a not-so-subtle reversal has recently taken place. It makes 'changing the culture' shorthand for an alteration in habits of work rather than of leisure, an alteration, for example, that might benefit the national economy or industrial policy.[22] Thus it includes the recognition that we now have greater powers to shape the environment but also that habits of the workplace carry over into our free or leisure time. As a result, the concept of leisure as the realm of freedom (freedom from governmental or social interference as well as from toil) weakens, even though our power to alter nature or society has significantly increased. Culture, I read, 'is imagined as a plastic medium which politically powerful social elites may rework and remould at will'; indeed, when such 'reworking' is shorn of its exclusively economic goal, such as improvement of productivity in the workplace, then 'culture' moves very close to the sense it has in contemporary culture studies.

'Culture is thought of as directly bound up with work and its organization; with the relations of power and gender in the workplace and the home; with the pleasures and the pressures of consumption; with the complex relations of class and kith and kin through which a sense of self is formed; and with the fantasies and desires through which social relations are carried and actively shaped . . . It is not a detached domain for playing games of social distinction and 'good' taste. It is a network of representations – texts, images, talk, codes of behaviour, and the narrative structures organizing these – which shapes every aspect of social life.'[23]

> That same day, entering Phelps Gateway at Yale, I see a metal coat hanger with the inscription: 'This is not a medical instrument.' I think: to understand a symbol like this requires some knowledge of a specific cultural context. Damn it, culture again, in the cultural studies aspect of a 'network of representations' that shapes social life. What has to be recalled is, first, the abortion debates of fin-de-siècle America. Then, to savor the exhibit fully, Magritte's well-known picture of a pipe with the motto: 'This is not a pipe.' For something like the metal hanger is, alas, too often used as a medical instrument. The hanger is not a clever symbol drawing attention to the difference between art and reality but an object highlighting an underground practice that society denies or refuses to take responsibility for. The negative ('This is not . . .') serves to affirm the existence of the practice.
>
> Here 'cultural context' points not only to a specific social situation but also to a scandalous mode of representation that made toilets into works of art and generally disrespected boundaries, especially those between private and public, popular and sophisticated, marginal and established. (Picasso's *Venus de Gaz*, a burner framed as a fetish, mocks our own art fetishism.) But this mode – related to Murray Krieger's 'fall of the elite object'[24] – cannot entirely control the meaning of the symbols it creates: their transgressive character transcends any assigned, stable significance, so that the cheap wire hook that stands for the endangering and demeaning of women forced

into back-alley abortions may also evoke a violence intrinsic to all acts of abortion, whatever the instrument. The pro-choice symbol becomes ominous when it links up with an unlimited claim to control nature, with the idea that culture reinvents nature and could desanctify or instrumentalize life.

Now science enters, as Bacon's improvement of nature, implicit even in such common phrases as 'cell culture,'[25] but also as it tends to challenge, by alternatives, long-established social patterns. A prochoice fantasy, a feminist tract as visionary as Erasmus Darwin's *Love of the Plants*, is entitled *Simians, Cyborgs, and Women: The Reinvention of Nature*.[26] It describes a potential liberation of the body more radical than N. O. Brown's *Life against Death* or *Love's Body* by treating physical intercourse as an evolutionary stage, with the present state of affairs as stodgy as the nuclear family. For literary readers Donna Haraway writes a form of science fiction based, like Ferenczi's *Thalassa*, on biological (now sociobiological) data. But where Ferenczi was interested in the genealogy of sexual feelings and drives, in how our evolutionary past has influenced present comminglings, Haraway is resolutely future-oriented and therefore ends with the conviction: 'Science is culture.' Not a culture, mind you, as in C. P. Snow's *The Two Cultures,* which deplored that the specialization endemic to modern society had divorced scientists and humanists.[27]

Of course, not all uses of 'culture' converge. But whatever the word touches receives at present a sort of credibility. One hears of a smokers' culture, of [Australia's] beach culture: do such things really exist? The point is that the term bestows, like rights language run amok, a certain dignity, one that is based not so much on numbers as on a sense that a *meaningful nucleus of life, a form of social existence, has emerged or is emerging.* And we pay attention to it, I suggest, because social fragmentation means two things that together amount to a disabling paradox: the general culture seems too distant or alien, while the hope for some unity of being – which I call embodiment – can migrate to groupings often held together by parochial, sectarian, self-serving, and even antisocial interests.[28]

These interests range from the folklore of indigenous or immigrant cultures, or the practices of a religious cult that has broken with a mainstream denomination, to the lifestyle of gay people or the agenda of political, commercial, and even criminal organizations (a tv report on the Bank of Credit and Commerce International talked as easily of 'BCCI's criminal culture' as of a 'Washington culture'). So abusive is the extension of the word, so strong and vulgar its pathos, that I begin to understand an Africanist claim about the West. It is alleged that an ingrained Cartesianism has *ghosted* the colonizers, abstracted them from life, so that 'culture' becomes a dream for what is missing, a phantom or proxy comforting the 'white-man-who-has-problems-believing-in-his-own-existence.'[29]

Yet, to repeat, not all uses of 'culture' converge. In fact, the proliferation of the word in the sense I have singled out is only part of the picture, albeit a part that seems to have taken over. The *other* major sense of the word, as in 'high culture' or 'a cultured person' or Arnold's *Culture and Anarchy*, has almost an antithetical resonance. Often an elegiac aura surrounds it. 'To say, "Here we no longer use citation" means the end of our culture, in the West, as we have known it, more or less, since the PreSocratic thinkers.'[30] This threatened 'culture' is, so to say, less culture-bound; a distinct cosmopolitan perspective enters. *Bildung* (liberal education leading to self-development) rather than *Erziehung* (systematic or specialized training) is emphasized, while an aesthetic element or prestigious 'je ne sais quoi' is tolerated. So a French philosopher, writing for a general audience, fudges elegantly when he says that his book presupposes 'une certaine culture, un certain acquis philosophique.' You acquire this culture actively, as a modification of some natural traits; at the same time, you make it seem natural, as if breeding and background had predisposed you to receive it. Sainte-Beuve claims that it pervades, because of the classical tradition, French literary life, which 'consists in a certain principle of reason and culture [*un certain principe de raison et culture*] that has over time penetrated, and modified, the very character of this gallic nation.'[31] The word still suggests an integrated way of life, although what is integrated is understood to be artificial, even consciously highbrow ('kulcha').[32]

Culture in this older sense goes together with affluence or social climbing, for it is freedom from ordinary conditions of a material, parochial, or ideologically exigent kind that invests the word with promise.[33] The relation between being cultured and being free is one of the great commonplaces of humanistic (or 'liberal') education. (Kant, in an especially subtle move, claims that the real end of culture is freedom rather than happiness and that it promotes the former by instilling an affection for thoughtfulness.)[34] Yet despite culture's 'free play of ideas,' a respect for embodiment continues to prevail, and nation or religion or ethnic identity is often viewed as a necessary form of local attachment. Toward the end of his life Coleridge wrote in his notebook that 'the self is in and by itself a Phantom'; nonetheless, it was 'capable of receiving true entity by *reflection* from the *Nation*.' Both the self and mankind were, as graspable, psychological notions, too abstract. The nation, however, was 'something real to the imagination of the citizen' and became distinct 'in relation to the personalities of other nations.'[35] The *other* idea of culture, then, while stressing the play of ideas and its effectiveness in modifying or even (as Matthew Arnold hoped) gradually doing away with the class structure, was not free of a tension between culture and nation, or culture and society (which gives Raymond Williams's crucial study of the word its title).[36]

The creation of a cultural sphere within society or nation-state, a sort of free zone for the market of ideas, can be traced back to the *honnête homme* concept, promoted by the salons of Parisian society in the eighteenth century. The salons themselves were a development of courtesy ideals that emanated, as the word suggests, from the court. In the seventeenth century, culture moves closer to urbanity, the culture of cities. The new decorum joins courtiers and significant personalities from the bourgeoisie to create an ideal public of court and town ('la cour et la ville').[37] Within that charmed circle of sociability, and within it alone, people of different ranks and professions mingled and talked freely, affirming values characterized as *honnête*, that is, *unaffected*, in the twofold sense of unpretentious and independent of vested interests. A premium was placed on an intelligence that could see matters from a broad perspective and did not specialize itself in turn: that remained conversational and not excessively ostentatious.

That this ideal degenerated into a new 'culture of wit' was inevitable; and Rousseau's attack its far-from-simple 'honesty' as merely another form of hypocrisy revealed the problem. Still, in this ideal of the *honnête homme*, which Erich Auerbach already associates with Montaigne as the self-reflective essayist who is more interested in being a writer than a gentleman – an ideal infiltrating the citified and robuster café society of *The Tatler, The Spectator,* and the beginnings of English literary journalism – we catch a glimpse of Matthew Arnold's understanding of how culture promotes a wholeness of being that might overcome the divisiveness and parochialism of the class structure. Also adumbrated is Karl Mannheim's definition of intellectuals as an interclass stratum. Although from a socially stratified and class-conscious point of view intellectuals appear to be deracinated airheads (*Luftmenschen*), they alone may be in a position to demystify the conversion of special interests into universals.

To define these two major senses of culture – the one denoting *a* culture, that is, a specific form of embodiment or solidarity;[38] the other (*culture* without any article) pointing to a general ideal, held despite class, profession, or broader allegiance (religion, race, collectivity, nation) and positing a shared human heritage, a second or accrued nature[39] – is to differentiate contrasting and perhaps contradictory concepts.

My purpose in examining the resonances of 'culture' is critical as well as historical. There are, no doubt, other sexy words around – 'community,' 'identity' – that exude a similar promise.[40] But the historical semantics of 'culture' clarify what we are experiencing in literary studies at this time. The conversion of literary into cultural studies arises, certainly, from an urgent and growing concern with social justice and what may be called *species thinking* (now that we know so much of our history, what does it tell us about the human species?). Yet it also arises from an imaginative need that operates at all levels of life, private as well as public. Our hope that culture can provide an embodiment to satisfy a ghostly hunger, as devouring as a vampire, persists despite an impasse. The intimacy of the small or homogeneous group, of an extended family that promises to transmit and foster a tradition, runs up against other such formations and requires, in order to prevent a perpetual war between communities, a larger and transpolitical perspective, a universal culture. This other 'culture' has the mission to make what seems intransitive transitive again. The very effort, however, leads to a further contradiction, perhaps because it takes place primarily in another relatively small group, an international elite, including universities that are never the communiversity we hope for. As we debate the issues, a highly specialized discourse is produced, a *Fach* that sins by its technical diction and aggressive bearing against the very qualities that 'culture' as a historical and progressive movement is meant to achieve: qualities of accessibility and participatory momentum.[41]

Today there are those who see the 'general culture' as hegemonic. If we acknowledge, however, the antinomy between 'a culture' and 'culture,' then the right conclusion would be that it is 'a culture' that tends towards hegemony, while 'culture,' understood as the development of a public sphere, a 'republic of letters' in which ideas can be freely exchanged, is what is fragile.[42] In this area, things are very complex. On the one hand, the general culture can deceptively claim to be on the side of breadth and generosity, while it is actually imperious or imperialistic. On the other hand, 'a culture' can be deeply conformist and seek to limit individual rights, which it may even denounce as a *culte du moi*, as excessive individualism. So Maurice Barrès plays on the organicist and agricultural analogy to express his belief in the necessity of a culture grounded in French soil: 'J'ai besoin qu'on garde à mon arbre la culture qui lui permet de me porter si haut, moi faible petite feuille' (I need culture to conserve my tree and to allow it to carry me, a feeble, small leaf, upward).[43]

With Burckhardt and Nietzsche the historical image of Greece begins to change, and 'culture' is now seen as a precarious, even heroic, achievement against great odds, a sort of tragic *agon* always threatened by decadence. It does not solve anything, therefore, to denounce 'culture' as 'high culture,' that is, as elitist and obsolete. Herbert Marcuse called this move a 'repressive desublimation,' and he insisted on the importance of 'aesthetic incompatibility.' Although the main target of his attack was mass culture, his words on the 'flattening out of the antagonism between culture and social reality through the obliteration of the oppositional, alien, and transcendent elements in the higher culture' remain cogent.[44]

Perhaps Václav Havel is a better guide here than either Marcuse or T. S. Eliot. Coming from the republic of letters to politics, he insists that 'civility,' or what he renames 'the culture of everything,' must penetrate the political sphere as well. The notion of a high or autonomous sphere of culture is neither conceptually protected nor attacked by him: his argument is that manners must become *moeurs*, a second nature or tradition, if everyday life in post-Marxist society is not to be ravaged once more by regressive nationalisms or an all-usurping economic imperative.[45]

The question that remains, however, is whether Havel's ideal can accrue enough imaginative force to displace the appeal of political religions and their uncompromising, spiritualistic demand for total devotion, sacrifice, embodiment. Civility, as Havel uses it, comes close to what Hannah Arendt called 'classic virtues of civic behavior' that distinguish 'a responsible member of society, interested in all public affairs' from a bourgeois, 'concerned only with his private existence' and who becomes too easily a 'functionary' of the state.[46] Nationalism, in Arendt's view, is not genuine patriotism at all but eliminates open public discussion in favor of a propagandized mass ideology. My provisional conclusion about Havel's civic ideal is pessimistic. Once the nation-state or a faith community has appropriated what might be called the superego ideal of culture by promising embodiment and exacting collective obedience, civility is often viewed as a minor virtue to be sacrificed on the altar of a higher destiny.

Notes

1. 'Notes toward a Supreme Fiction.' Another side of the organic feeling of harmony, 'of an indissoluble bond, of being one with the external world as a whole' (*Civilization and Its Discontents*, trans. and ed. James Strachey (New York: Norton) 12), linked by Freud to the experience of the child in the maternal body, is developed by Julia Kristeva and others who seek to understand the role of a pre-Oedipal stage in human development. The oceanic feeling may explain a basic anxiety in the grown child, insofar as it continues to sense a lack of ego boundaries and at once delights in and fears to be engulfed by the 'ocean.'

2. 'One evening in 1919, a short, shy fellow named Irving Caesar [to become Irving Berlin], who was just short of his 25th birthday, sat close to the stage of one of the cavernous theaters on Times Square and took in a performance of the song "Swanee" ' (*New York Times Book Review*, 3 May 1992, 22). ' "It was a fine autumn evening in 1922. I was a notary's clerk in Marommes" ' (J.-P. Sartre, on narratable 'reality,' in his novel *Nausea* [1939]). Even putting the date after the title of a novel reveals a certain nervousness of the same kind, a minimal gesture of emplacement.

3. Embodiment should be, strictly speaking, a 'cure of the body,' as the erotic imagination always demands, or as the poetic imagination strives for, giving voice a body or not being satisfied with imperfect words. This aspect, neglected here, points to Ovid and the Ovidian tradition in the West. Cf. Lynn Enterline, *Pursuing Daphne: Body and Voice in Ovid and Renaissance Ovidian Poetry* (Stanford: Stanford University Press, 1997). The complex task of sexualizing and gendering embodiment is taken up by Sandor Ferenczi in *Thalassa: A Theory of Genitality*, trans. H. A. Bunker (Albany, NY: Psychoanalytic Quarterly, 1938), and Erich Neumann in *Apuleius: Amor and Psyche, the Labors of the Feminine* (New York: Pantheon, 1965).

4. *Letters and Leadership* (New York: B. W. Huebsch, 1918).

5. 'Kultur ist ein vom Standpunkt des Menschen aus mit Sinn und Bedeutung bedachter endlicher Ausschnitt aus der sinnlosen Unendlichkeit des Weltgeschehens' (*Gesammelte Werke zur Wissenschaftslehre*, quoted in Aleida Assmann and Jan Assmann, 'Kultur und Konflikt: Aspekte einer Theorie des unkommunikativen Handelns,' in *Kultur und Konflikt*, ed. Jan Assmann and Dietrich Harth [Frankfurt-am-Main: Suhrkamp, 1990], 35). My translation. For a short history of the culture/civilization distinction, see appendix 1 in my *The Fateful Question of Culture* (New York: Columbia University Press 1997), 205–240.

6. Harold Bloom, after a life of studies centering on Shelley, Blake, Yeats, and Stevens, has recently revised his earlier critique (inspired by them) of 'Natural Religion.' He has identified the primordial feeling of ghostliness, as it becomes a conviction and a religion, with the ancient gnostic heresy that the Nature we know is the work of another power than God, that the Creation is already a Fall, and that we have a spiritual existence apart from any such embodiment, apart from the secular world. See *The American Religion: The Emergence of the Post-Christian Nation* (New York: Simon and Schuster, 1992).

7. Stanley Cavell has linked philosophy to literature (especially through his readings of Shakespearean tragedy) by disclosing in both an alive and pervasive *skepticism* as the provocative workings of a ghost feeling surely similar to the one I have described. Descartes's philosophical and Shakespeare's tragical method at once acknowledge and avoid a dispossession: the unavailability of our own private world (a skepticism from the fact that we cannot know ourselves intimately enough) and of public reality (a skepticism from the fact that the minds of others, or of whoever orders the world, also may be closed to us). Yet writers like these continue to *dare to know*. I sin against Cavell's patient elaborations with this instant summary and send the reader to, above all, *The Claim of Reason: Wittgenstein, Skepticism, Morality, and Tragedy* (New York: Oxford University Press, 1979).

8. Pierre Bourdieu, *La distinction: Critique sociale du jugement* (Paris: Editions de Minuit, 1979).

9. See Georg Lukács, *History and Class Consciousness: Studies in Marxist Dialectics*, trans. Rodney Livingstone (Cambridge, MA: MIT Press, 1971), 95. Lukács supports Marx's attempt to disenchant the 'mysticism of commodification.' Derrida traces Marx's pervasive recourse to spectral metaphors in the *Specters of Marx*. Lucien Goldmann suggests that Heidegger's concept of *Dasein* responds to Lukács's *Verdinglichung* (reification), itself developed from Marx's basic intuition about the historical rather than permanent status of a world of things, of objects standing against the subjectivity of the worker with a spuriously independent life.

10. Cf. Raymond Williams, *Keywords: A Vocabulary of Culture and Society* (New York: Oxford University Press, 1976), 76: '*Culture* is one of the two or three most complicated words in the English language.'

11. See the suggestive survey of the word in Hannah Arendt, 'The Crisis in Culture,' *Between Past and Future* (New York: Viking, 1961), 211 ff.

12. An early analysis of the historical semantics of the word, with some remarks on its grammatical development, is Joseph Niedermann, *Kultur: Werden und Wandlungen des Begriffs und seiner Ersatz-begriffe von Cicero bis Herder* (Florence: Libreria Editrice,

1941). It provides an indispensable survey but does not touch sources beyond Herder. For later uses of the word, see A. L. Kroeber and Clyde Kluckhohn, *Culture: A Critical Review of Concepts and Definitions* (New York: Vintage, 1963). A further, but contemporary, linguistic factor favoring the spread of the word promotes all subcultures to cultures by dropping the prefix *sub*, as if it were infra dig, or a carryover from 'subversive.' On the culture/civilization antithesis as it coincides with national self-imagining in Germany and France, see Norbert Elias, *The Civilizing Process* (Cambridge: Blackwell, 1994), 3–41, and Hartman, *Fateful Question*, Appendix 1.

13. Cf. Jack Goody's *The Culture of Flowers* (New York: Cambridge University Press, 1993), which examines, according to the advertisement, 'the secular and religious uses of flowers across a wide range of cultures, from ancient Egypt to modern China.'

14. Van Wyck Brooks, *America's Coming-of-Age* (New York: B. W. Huebsch, 1915).

15. Cf. Assmann and Assmann, 'Kultur und Konflikt': 'Als Suffix kann [Kultur] nahezu jede Konstellation eingehen' (35).

16. Y. M. Lotman and B. A. Uspensky, 'On the Semiotic Mechanism of Culture' (1971), *New Literary History* 9 (winter 1978): 211–32.

17. 'By "culture", then, I mean first of all what the anthropologists mean: the way of life of a particular people living together in one place. That culture is made visible in their arts, in their social system, in their habits and customs, in their religion' (T. S. Eliot, *Notes towards the Definition of Culture* [London: Faber and Faber, 1948], 122). We see here how infectious the anthropological meaning is: we have slipped from 'tradition' (as in his well-known essay 'Tradition and the Individual Talent') to 'traditional way of life" to 'culture.' Eliot does not specifically argue that culture, in this sense, is the only way of conferring identity; that stage, with its 'determination to respect art only within the ground rules of culture" and stemming 'from a prior definition of culture that ties it to the social or anthropological group, rather than individual taste or judgment' is attacked by a recent critic as 'cultural idolatry.' See David Bromwich, *Politics by Other Means: Higher Education and Group Thinking* (New Haven: Yale University Press, 1992), 12 ff.

18. See the first of his 'Untimely Observations' of 1873.

19. While in the modern era complaints about the 'machinery' of living increase (see n. 36 below), there is evidence that specialization can also simplify the multi-cultural demands of traditional societies. As Ganash N. Devi has pointed out, 'The English term "culture" is not sufficiently large to cover the semantic scope' of India's cultural situation, where people live 'within a bilingual and even multilingual cultural idiom' and have to switch their culture codes according to the needs of their social situations ('The Multicultural Context of Indian Literature in English,' in *Crisis and Creativity in the New Literatures in English*, ed. Geoffrey Davis and Hena Maes-Jelinek [Amsterdam: Rodopi, 1990]). Multi-culturalism, which represents subcultures as cultures, tries to restore a complexity that was removed by modern political and scientific streamlining. For how these complexities turn into perplexities when a modern national culture tries to control a traditional multicultural situation, see Clifford Geertz, 'Thick Descrip-

tion: Towards an Interpretive Theory of Culture,' *The Interpretation of Culture* (New York: Basic Books, 1973), 3–30.

20. Both Michel Foucault and Michel de Certeau are of importance here. See, especially, Certeau's remarks on 'l'articulation nature-culture' in *L'écriture de l'histoire* (Paris: Gallimard, 1975), 82 ff. Certeau emphasizes how history, as a discipline, actively moves 'natural' elements into the 'cultural' domain, making them more available, for instance, for a literary transformation into symbols: 'Of waste materials, of papers, of vegetables, even glaciers and "eternal snows," the historian makes *something else*: he makes history out of them . . . He participates in the work which changes nature into environment and modifies in this way man's nature.' Ernst Cassirer, in his *Logic of the Humanities* [Kulturwissenschaften], trans. C. S. Howe (New Haven: Yale University Press, 1961), credits Vico (followed by Herder) with a 'logic' that 'dared to break through the circle of objective knowledge, the circle of mathematics and natural science, and dared instead to constitute itself as the logic of the humanities – as the logic of language, poetry, and history' (54).

21. If we adduce Althusser's concept of 'Ideological State Apparatuses,' or the way the dominant class reproduces through superstructural organizations such as schools and churches, opinions favorable to its control of the modes of production, then such proliferating talk about 'corporate culture,' the 'culture of the agency,' etc., could be seen as spreading a deceptive idea of human creativity yet favoring the actual 'State Apparatus': business, police, and so forth. (Marxism has its own, competitive understanding of how human creativity, as a means to mastery over nature, is to be developed.) In *L'état culturel: Essai sur une religion moderne* (Paris: Fallois, 1991), Marc Fumaroli describes a similar technique of control. He documents the 'elephantine' growth and spread of the word 'culture' in contemporary France and charges that it has become the name of a state religion, permitting 'the flattering illusion that administrative and political activity applied to the arts is in itself of artistic and genial quality.' The 'creative' *dirigisme* of the state in cultural matters reduces culture to client status: it is the extension, the Frankfurt School might say, of administrative reason and celebrates a state apparatus rather than the liberal arts. 'Abstract and sterile, the Culture of cultural politics is the insinuating mask of power, and the mirror in which it wishes to take pleasure [*jouir*] in itself' (my translation). See Chapter 3, 'La Culture: Mot-valise, mot-écran.'

22. During the pope's visit to the United States in October 1995, I heard in the media that his speeches aimed at 'changing the culture,' which now meant the moral culture, worldwide. And consider the following, from Meaghan Morris's *Ecstasy and Economics: American Essays for John Forbes* (Sidney: Empress, 1992): 'During the 1980s, the word "culture" began to be used in a rather peculiar sense. In 1990, a week after the worst company crashes in Australian history had ended a decade of financial mismanagement and "de-regulated" corporate crime, a groveling tv current affairs show host asked Rupert Murdoch (back home to shut down a couple of newspapers) what "we" could do to save "our" economy. The mighty multinationalist replied, "Oh you know – change the culture." . . . What Murdoch "meant" was a cliché: a 1980s media commonplace that Australia's biggest problem

is the lazy, hedonist, uncompetitive, beach-bound, lotus-eating ethos of the ordinary people' (124). Morris's entire essay 'On the Beach' should be of great interest to cultural studies.

23. From the introduction to John Frow and Meaghan Morris, eds., *Australian Culture Studies* (St. Leonards, New South Wales: Allen and Unwin, 1993). Cf. Morris's *Ecstasy and Economics*, 124 ff. A *New Yorker* portrait of Colin Powell, which contrasts him with Jesse Jackson, shows both leaders using the 'culture' word in a similar way. Powell, Jackson says, is 'flowing with the culture . . . He's created a comfort zone among the guardians of the culture.' Powell is reported to say 'As a culture, the Airforce . . .' Jackson, though oppositional, 'counter-cultural' to 'the dominant culture,' must still express himself in culture terms. See Henry Louis Gates Jr., 'Powell and the Black Elite,' *New Yorker* 71 (September 25, 1995): 64–80.

24. Murray Krieger, *Arts on the Level: The Fall of the Elite Object* (Knoxville: University of Tennessee Press, 1981).

25. A December 1992 article in the *New York Times* on the popularity of vampire movies is headlined 'Blood Culture' (Frank Rich, "The New Blood Culture," *New York Times*, 6 December 1992, sec 9, 1). This brings together the scientific connotation with the ordinary sense of art-as-culture but also, wittily and ominously, with the claim that, because of AIDS, an entire subculture is being created of people united by their concern with that disease.

26. Donna J. Haraway (London: Free Association Books, 1991).

27. Further signs of the times: I receive a reader's catalog from the University of Chicago Press. It lists the following titles or subtitles: *Cultural Misunderstandings*; *Cultural Aesthetics*; *Culture and Anomie*; *Reenvisioning Past Musical Cultures*; *Women's Culture, Occultism, Witch-craft, and Cultural Fashions*; *Symbolic Action and Cultural Studies*; *The Culture of Politics and the Politics of Culture in American Life*; *The Cultural Politics of Race and Nation*; *Science as Practice and Culture*; *Women, Achievement, and College Culture*; *Culture Wars*. Or consider this, from a 16 July 1994 *New York Times* op-ed piece on a city kid by Barbara Nevins Taylor: 'He didn't bother with his homework and fell behind. The culture of the housing projects and the hormones of adolescence collided with the culture of the school' (21).

28. A theory recently put forward is that we have become a *Kulturgesellschaft*, the German word demonstrating the symptom that it seeks to describe. It defines 'a society in which cultural activity functions increasingly as a socializing agency comparable to and even often against the grain of nation, family profession, state' (quoted in Huyssen, *Twilight Memories: Marking Time in a Culture of Amnesia* (New York: Routledge, 1995), 31 ff).

29. Wole Soyinka, *Myth, Literature and the African World* (Cambridge: Cambridge University Press, 1976), 138–39. Yet 'culture' appeals just as strongly to Africanists; it stands for an original cohesion, an organic community, that the colonizers are said to have destroyed. A fuller discussion would begin with Frantz Fanon's 'On National Culture' in *Les damnés de la terre* (Paris: François Maspero, 1961; published in English as *The Wretched of the Earth*, trans. Constance Farrington [London: MacGibbon and Kee, 1965]), which delineates in compelling detail the situation of the 'colonized intellectual' who participates in the project of decolonization. Here I

wish only to note the abundance of body or embodiment metaphors in Fanon's essay. Commenting, for instance, on the style of the conflicted intellectual who is freeing himself from the colonial culture but has not integrated with ('faire corps, c'est à dire, à changer de corps, avec' [to become one with, that is, to become one body with]) European civilization, Fanon writes: 'Style nerveux animé de rythmes, de part en part habité par une vie éruptive . . . Ce style, qui a en son temps étonné les occidentaux, n'est point comme on a bien voulu le dire un caractère racial mais traduit avant tout un corps à corps, révèle la nécessité dans laquelle s'est trouvé cet homme de se faire mal, de saigner réellement de sang rouge, de se libérer d'une partie de son être qui déjà renfermait des germes de pourriture. Combat doulour-eux, rapide où immanquablement le muscle devait se substituer au concept' [The animated, nervous style of rhythms, inhabited everywhere by an eruptive life . . . This style, which has in its time astonished Westerners, is not, as one would like to say, a racial characteristic, but conveys above all something physical, reveals the necessity in which this man found himself to do himself harm, to really bleed, to release his being from a part which already contained the germs of rot. Painful, reactive combat, in which muscle inevitably replaces idea].

30. George Steiner, in Pierre Boutang and George Steiner, *Dialogues: Sur le mythe d'Antigone/sur le sacrifice d'Abraham* (Paris: Lattès, 1994), 154. My translation.

31. 'De la tradition en littérature, et dans quel sens il la faut entendre,' *Causeries du Lundi*, vol. 15 (Paris: Garnier Frères, 1857–62). My translation.

32. In 'The Crisis of Culture,' Hannah Arendt adopts Herbert Marcuse's famous attack on the 'affirmative culture' of a bourgeoisie that reduced Schiller's 'aesthetic education' to climbing out of the lower regions into 'the higher, non-real regions, where beauty and the spirit supposedly were at home.' See Arendt, *Between Past and Present* (New York: Viking, 1961), esp. 201–5. See also Herbert Marcuse, 'The Affirmative Character of Culture' (1938), in *Negations: Essays in Critical Theory* (Boston: Beacon, 1968).

33. There is a third meaning of 'culture' that lies uneasily between the two I have mentioned. Perry Anderson, in a well-known critique of 'National Culture' in 1968, draws up a devastating inventory of what culture amounts to in England at that date. He exempts the hard sciences and the arts from this inventory, which – as he admits in a later statement – belies the 'national' in his title or confuses culture with what happens in the academy or gets absorbed through that conduit. Yet Anderson did make the point that the British university had become an inertial system in which innovation came largely from Central European refugees and that even these innovations had been only selectively successful, the criterion of success being whether they could be accommodated to an inertial 'Englishness.' The inventory meaning of 'culture' thus cannot avoid a critical edge: Anderson, like Marcuse, uses non-national cultural achievements to challenge the national status quo, to rouse the national consciousness to equal achievements. Moreover, Anderson's emphasis on *academic* culture as an inertial system promoting 'national' values parallels the more scientific and elaborated analyses by Pierre Bourdieu, which show how the French educational establishment reduces culture to style rather than substance, to a 'relation to culture' that perpetuates the *honnête homme*

ideal of the seventeenth century and reproduces a pattern of social distinction paradoxically based on the attempt of the upper class (the 'dominant culture') to make its imposed values seem natural or invisible ('une certaine culture'). See Perry Anderson, 'Components of the National Culture,' *New Left Review*, no. 50 (July–August 1968): 3–58; and Pierre Bourdieu, 'Literate Tradition and Social Conservation' (written with Jean-Claude Passeron), in *Reproduction in Education, Society and Culture* (London: Sage, 1990: original French ed.: Pierre Bourdieu and Jean-Claude Passeron, *La reproduction: Eléments pour une théorie du système d'enseignement* [Paris: Minuit, 1970]).

34. For the ramifications of this, see Cassirer, *Logic of the Humanities*, Chapter 5, 'The "Tragedy of Culture," ' and cf. Arendt, 'Crisis in Culture,' where she brings Cicero and Kant together: 'The humanist, because he is not a specialist, exerts a faculty of judgment and taste which is beyond the coercion which each specialty imposes upon us' (225).

35. David P. Calleo, *Coleridge and the Idea of the Modern State* (New Haven: Yale University Press, 1966), Chapter 5, 'The Psychological Basis of the State.'

36. *Culture and Society: 1780–1950* (London: Chatto and Windus, 1958). Leonard Woolf, continuing his autobiography under the title *Principia Politica: A Study of Communal Psychology* (London: Hogarth, 1953), suggests that politics, by which he means 'constructing the framework or manipulating the machinery of government or society,' became more inevitable and preoccupying during his lifetime. 'There is something strange in the fact that so much of [my life] has been occupied, not with living, but with the machinery of living. But the strangeness does not end there; it is not limited to my particular experience, for it is part of a general strangeness, a new and fantastic pattern, which has appeared in human life during the last 50 or 100 years. This pattern has been determined by the encroachment of the machinery of life upon living and the art of living' (9–10). The values implied by 'culture' seem to offer an antidote to this fact. But Woolf himself, interested in the relation of communal psychology to sociopolitical action, rehabilitates the word 'civilization': 'What determines whether a society is civilized is its material standard of life, its intellectual and spiritual standards of life, and its contributions to art, science, learning, philosophy, or religion' (53). He refuses to value 'culture' (as the fine arts) and its products higher than the other civilized standards.

37. My account is primarily indebted to Erich Auerbach, 'La cour et la ville,' now in *Scenes from the Drama of European Literature* (Minneapolis: University of Minnesota Press, 1984), 133–82. See also Elias, *The Civilizing Process*, 32: 'The *homme civilisé* was nothing other than a somewhat extended version of that human type which represented the true ideal of court society, the *honnête homme*.' Hannah Arendt concurs in interesting and sardonic remarks on the origin of 'good society': *Between Past and Future*, 199–200. Rémy de Gourmont is characterized as an *encyclopédiste honnête homme* in the introduction to essays translated from his *La culture des idées*: see *Decadence and Other Essays on the Culture of Ideas* (New York: Harcourt, Brace, 1921).

38. 'Solidarity' is the word Raymond Williams uses as a near-equivalent of what I call 'embodiment': I introduce it deliberately here. See, e.g., *Culture and Society*, 332: 'The feeling of solidarity is, although necessary, a primitive feeling.'

39. While I cannot accept Arendt's sharp dichotomizing – assigning culture to objects and the world and separating it from entertainment that relates to people and consumable life – she makes a charge that still needs answering: 'Culture is being threatened when all worldly objects and things, produced by the present and the past, are treated as mere functions for the life process of society, as though they are there only to fulfill some need' (*Between Past and Present*, 208). Her intuition that cultural objects have a 'thingness' and can only be evaluated by their permanence (to which she says life is indifferent), while it saves culture from the philistine or from consumer society generally, points once more to the desire for embodiment, one that is associated with durability rather than reification. What the 'function' of this desire may be or that of art objects 'which every civilization leaves behind as the quintessence and lasting testimony of the spirit which animated it' (201) is not clarified by her.

40. For 'identity' as a 'plastic word,' see Lutz Niethammer, 'Konjunkturen und Konkurrenzen kollektiver Identität. Ideologie, Infrastruktur und Gedächtnis in der Zeitgeschichte,' *PROKLA: Zeitschrift für kritische Sozialwissenschaft* 96 (1994): 377–99.

41. Not only the study of culture but culture itself as a separate and quasi-autonomous sphere is subject to this paradox pointedly expressed by Guy Debord in *La société du spectacle* (Paris: Buchet/Chastel, 1967): 'La culture est le lieu de la recherche de l'unité perdue. Dans cette recherche de l'unité, la culture comme sphère séparée est obligée de se nier elle-même' (149). See also Hartman, *Fateful Question*, Chapter 1.

42. A good historical treatment of the concept of a 'republic of letters' is found in Michael Warner, *The Letters of the Republic: Publication and the Public Sphere in Eighteenth-Century America* (Cambridge: Harvard University Press, 1990). For contemporary thought, the strongest development of the idea is Hannah Arendt's notion of 'world' as a public sphere in which political action can be freely debated and a communal sense (Kant's *Gemeinsinn*) is made manifest, 'a faculty of judgment which, in its reflection, takes account . . . of the mode of representation of all others' (*Critique of Judgment*, trans. Werner S. Pluhar [Indianapolis: Hackett, 1987], 294; translation modified). See Kant, *Critique of Judgment*, paragraph 40. I comment on Arendt's 'republic of letters' in 'Art and Consensus in the Era of Progressive Politics,' *Yale Review* 80 (1992): 50–61. Habermas's magisterial treatise on *Öffentlichkeit* is well known.

43. Cited by Alain Finkielkraut, *La défaite de la pensée* (Paris: Gallimard, 1987), 61. My translation.

44. Herbert Marcuse, *One-Dimensional Man: Studies in the Ideology of Advanced Industrial Society* (Boston: Beacon, 1964), Chapter 3. Cf. Frederic Jameson's *Postmodernism; or, The Cultural Logic of Late Capitalism* (Durham, NC: Duke University Press, 1991), which expresses Marcuse's complaint in terms of a new and disorienting cultural space that requires our mapping. After noting what he calls the 'dissolution of an autonomous sphere of culture' in the form of an 'explosion,' that is, a 'prodigious expansion of culture throughout the social realm, to the point at which everything in our social life – from economic value and state power to practices and the very structure of the psyche itself – can be said to have become "cultural," ' he admits

that no leftist theory of cultural politics has been able to do without 'a certain minimal aesthetic distance, of the possibility of the positioning of the cultural act outside the massive Being of capital.' But he then goes beyond these theories (and beyond Adorno) in asserting that 'distance in general (including "critical distance") has very precisely been abolished in the new space of postmodernism' and that the task of theory is to find out the historical reality of that new global space. Jameson seems to position himself at once as a scientist observing an objective phenomenon and an explorer charting unknown seas of thought – for purposes of *disalienation*, or 'the practical reconquest of a sense of place' (47–51).

45. 'The Culture of Everything,' *New York Review of Books* 34, no. 10 (28 May 1992): 30.

46. Arendt's distinction is already put into play in 'Organized Guilt and Universal Responsibility,' a discussion of 'real political conditions which underlie the charge of collective guilt of the German people,' published in 1945. See Hannah Arendt, *Essays in Understanding, 1930–1945*, ed. Jerome Kohn (New York: Harcourt Brace, 1994), especially 128–32.

Chapter 23

The Question of Our Speech

The true Man is the source, he being the Poetic Genius
William Blake

It is important to bring poetry, or literature generally, into the fold of cultural discourse. Not only does poetry often express the same themes, but it can also challenge the quality of that kind of talk. At one level, of course, poetry has no bearing on cultural critique. It cannot confirm or disconfirm specific remedies concerning social and political reorganization that may be drawn from theories about our imperfect transition from feudal and rural conditions to an industrial society. It may take sides, of course, through passionate impersonation; what it does most convincingly, however, with its famous 'concreteness' or illustrative energy, is to provide counterexamples to disembodied thought and unearned abstraction.

I bring literature (and the literary sense of language) directly into the debate for other reasons as well. Comparing Schiller's *Letters on Aesthetic Education* with Raymond Williams's *Culture and Society*, a difference of style appears that should be meaningful. But has there been progress, or is that too crude a notion for changes between 1795 and 1958? One admires 'The Development of a Common Culture,' William's conclusion to *Culture and Society*, for its careful stopping at keywords, its verbal massage, its pragmatic probing that understands how stiff our mental habits are, and a historical semantics that broadens cultural memory. Yet at the end of *Culture and Society* do we not feel – despite our assent to these good words and our relief that dogmatism and prophecy have been displaced – that the underlying situation may not have changed? Is not Williams's question, for example, of whether there can be a 'compatibility of increasing specialization with a genuinely common culture' as urgent and insoluble as ever, despite his addendum that the question is 'only soluble in a context of material community and by the full democratic process'?[1]

The adjective-noun compounds in the above sentence are as distinctive and obscurely affecting as 'poetic diction' was in the eighteenth century or sublime-sounding hypostases were in Schiller. A High Church vocabulary has been exchanged for a Low or Broad Church one, altar has become table, but otherwise there remains a muffled drumbeat, an insistence, in these last subdued yet eloquent pages of William's book, on something close to a jargon of commonality. This may be preferable to the 'jargon of authenticity' Adorno charges Heidegger with, but it nonetheless raises a rhetorical issue beyond that. What will persuade us that it is all right to live within our means, to quicken our response to low-profile words rather than wishing to be moved by thaumaturgic ones? *Mundus vult decipi*: because there is a biological play instinct; because the imagination, which partakes of it, does not really want a puritanical common-wealth; because, as Blake said, 'One Law for the Lion and the Ox is Oppression,' what should we do with our surplus imagination, its *uncommon* culture, which is playful, extravagant, dangerous, often both sublime and a bit crazy?

This problem does not lessen my appreciation of the plain or middle style, but it makes a place for another more high-flown or high-tech, which has its own historical and continuing achievement and is part of 'the common need.' There is, however, what Williams has named a 'Long Revolution,' whereby industry and democracy, helped by this emphasis on culture, successfully shift away from a 'dominative mood,' marked by 'the theory and practice of man's mastering and controlling his natural environment.' 'We are still rephrasing this,' Williams adds, using an odd metaphor, 'as we learn the folly of exploiting any part of this environment in isolation . . . learning, slowly, to attend to our environment as a whole, and to draw our values from that whole.' This is an unexceptionable thought, because the feeling that a totality has been lost, that the individual has shrunk into specialization or sectarian folly – become, to quote Blake, a 'Human Abstract' – does indeed determine both Schiller's restorative concept of culture and that of the English critics to whom Williams's book is devoted. Exceptional, however, is that odd metaphor of 'rephrasing,' which tells us that Williams considers words as part of the harmed environment. So this is where literature comes back, finds its value: the ability to 'rephrase,' to think experience and words in tandem, to experience words as well as to word experience. His penultimate sentences say too much but say it slowly.

> The evident problems of our civilization are too close and too serious for anyone to suppose that an emphasis is a solution . . . Yet we are coming increasingly to realize that our vocabulary, the language we use to inquire into and negotiate our actions, is no secondary factor, but a practical and radical element in itself.[2]

Despite their more forceful theorizing and historicizing and their skepticism about progress, Adorno and Horkheimer would be in general agreement.

A further reason to keep literature in mind is that while cultural theory has a clear focus, it is often tendentious, as sure as the doctrine of original sin of the nature of humanity's fall. Literature, however, captures such elegiac themes as the loss of the organic community, or the loss of totality, or the mutilation and reification of human relations in modern (capitalistic, industrial, modern, post-modern) society in a way that is not predetermined by a casuistic ideology or causal system. Art is neither didactic nor pedagogical, except by fits and starts. Whatever its purposes may be – and they do not exclude the expression of strong beliefs – it does not strive for a univocal solution, catechism, or definitive means–end relation. And though Williams thinks of culture instrumentally, as a very special means of social education and progress, the difference between the tradition he carries forward and overt authoritarian *dirigisme* is found in his sense of culture as a 'tending of natural growth' that reforms society and the state by means of a 'Long Revolution.' Culture never loses for him either the agri-cultural or process-oriented – *cultura/culturans* – meaning.[3] This chapter, then, will not be devoted to the Henry Jamesian question of how, if at all, immigrant speech or emergent vernaculars might be integrated into an existing culture; James had always feared that America had no culture at all, in the Arnoldian sense, and his essay of 1905, responding to the influx of East European Jews after the Russian pogroms of the 1880s, only restates that fear acutely.[4] My concern is to advance a point of view that would see literature itself as cultural discourse, in that way getting beyond lip service or a purely abstract esteem for art. This aim involves showing precisely the relation between literary instance and cultural crisis.

Art, like cultural theory, wishes to liberate the 'Human Abstract.' In Blake, art fights the system: it discloses how ideologies manacle the mind and distort everything creative: modes of thinking, imagining, writing. The question of our speech arises because poems like 'The Tyger' are spoken from *within* the system, from within a totalizing and forceful ideology that has corrupted the very idea of creation. Blake's depiction of a self-induced and paralyzing astonishment before the sublime of that mind-boggling creature is at once seductive and demys-tifying:

> Tyger, Tyger, burning bright
> In the forests of the night,
> What immortal hand or eye
> Dare frame thy fearful symmetry?

The questioner, as this apparently orthodox praise of creation proceeds, becomes increasingly dizzy:

> What the hammer? what the chain
> In what furnace was thy brain . . .
> What the anvil? What dread grasp . . .

The seeming inadequacy of terms derived from human and especially manual labor (hands, feet, and tools) is used satirically to project the tiger as a sublime and mystical thing, *as if there were no analogy possible between divine creation and human labor*. The end of such rapturous exclamation is the worship of established power or a submissive silence like Job's, after God has spoken from the whirlwind and reprimanded him ('Where wast thou when the world was created . . . ?'). Yet Blake, because he wishes to save rather than deflate visionary perception, rejects a merely ironic or satirical stance. His fantasy is polemical *and* defamiliarizing, 'unlike,' as Wallace Stevens might say:

> It must be that in time
> The real will from its crude compoundings come,
> Seeming, at first, a beast disgorged, unlike,
> Warmed by a desperate milk.[5]

The project of overcoming the Human Abstract, and placing our kind (the human species) once more into its larger 'organic' community, embraces 'Animal Forms of Wisdom' like the Tyger; and it is with them that Blake's hero, the Man, converses at the end of *Four Zoas*. In Blake's wondrous and sprawling epic about the four 'creatures' the biblical Book of Revelation had developed out of the prophecies of Ezekiel, the poet expresses astonishment at things created but undoes (how many times!) the rapt paralysis that befalls his 'dizzy questioner.' These 'compoundings,' Blake's cosmic fabliaux, are as sophisticated as the return to the ballad in Coleridge and Wordsworth.

Coleridge's 'Rime of the Ancient Mariner,' for example, which literary taxonomists classify as a supernatural ballad, is basically a story about *phantomization*, about the way the human in us is emptied out. The poem's plot first separates the protagonist from society and then restores him to it via a larger, communitarian consciousness of 'man and bird and beast.' Tradition tells us that when the soul leaves the body, or genius its natural element, a sound of lamentation is heard. So poetry, in this pivotal period of romanticism, is the sound of a disembodied spirit trying to come back, to redeem imagination from abstraction.[6]

The case of Christopher Smart, however, the greatest if also most idiosyncratic poet to offer a visionary representation of the restored human link with the *res creatae* (animal, vegetable, or mineral) and who wrote around 1760 the strange and long-neglected lines published only in 1939 as *Jubilate Agno*, shows that a strict literary-historical periodization is deceptive. Yet Wordsworth's nature poetry is particularly intriguing as a new rhetoric of community, or as an attempt to repair – in a style very different from that of Smart – the breach between nature and culture.[7]

Romanticism, Walter Pater observed, added strangeness to (classical) beauty. This strangeness comes at first through a predilection for the Gothic, a style that the romantics refined. They used the spectral as a device, a technique to disclose psychic states that required interpretation rather than dismissal. They heeded the internal weather of ominous feelings and imagistic flashes that induced prognostic and even prophetic intimations about the disturbed relation between nature and mankind. The spectral was often a shadow cast over ecology, over nature as man's home. In terms of conventional classicist representation the question became: Will nature outlast the physical or mental ravages of War, Industry, and City? Would the genius loci of woods, rivers, sky, and field depart forever into utopian memory? Wordsworth fought a tremendous rearguard action against the bad signs. Why should Paradise, the Elysian Groves, the Fortunate Fields, he asks in a famous passage, be 'A history only of departed things,/Or a mere fiction of what never was?'[8] *Lyrical Ballads*, Wordsworth and Coleridge's early and most famous collection, was, among other things, a project to keep the genius from parting by accommodating supernatural intimations, especially the aura of particular places. To compare Wordsworth's 'Hart-Leap Well' with both Coleridge's 'Ancient Mariner' and Bürger's 'The Wild Huntsman' is to understand the continuing appeal of Gothic incident and the way different poetics merge it with place, landscape, nature, cosmos. In Wordsworth the notion of a threatened (sometimes threatening) spirit of place assumes a central role: from juvenilia, in which it is a gothicized cliché, to his autobiographical *Prelude*, where its more subtle presence is linked to the themes of personal identity, poetic election, and growth. But in all the poets I have mentioned (and Milton would have to be added) the venerable topos of a sympathetic Nature – a Nature with feelings – is fading.

Wordsworth still tries to keep it alive, even if he rejects anthropomorphic personification and resorts to scrupulously negative formulations. He writes of the hunted creature in 'Hart-Leap Well,' 'This beast not unobserv'd by Nature fell,/His death was mourn'd by sympathy divine.' An animistic superstition that had supported many poetieal conceptions in the past becomes as threatened as the Rainbow is according to Keats; its vanishing is an 'Enlightenment' that foreshadows a further and final flight of Milton's 'parting genius.' Yet paradoxically this is the time when an *imagination* increasingly tagged as 'sympathetic' makes its appearance and refuses to accept nature's total disenchantment.

Only now does the imagination tolerate the real world as the premier source for its representations. The great and conscious proposers of this change are Wordsworth and George Eliot. A new complexity enters, however, since the traditional myths and visionary forms lose their hold just when, in terms of fears about nature, they are most needed. Do they really disappear from both the world and poetry?

Surely the crisis poem after Wordsworth still tries to 'simplify the ghost' of nature, to meet it in some startling, adventurous form. Failing that, poets represent its loss as the basis of a new quest romance: even as the supernatural ballad dies out, both poetry and the novella find new ways of throwing the lights and shadows of the uncanny over the realism now filling the pages of fiction. A concern prevails that if the common aspects of life in nature are not cultivated by imaginative rather than instrumental reason, nature will cease to be an object of vital interest and eventually render us homeless. 'The sun strengthens us no more, neither does the moon,' is D. H. Lawrence's lament. By cultivating nature through the feelings – it is this quality in Wordsworth that relieved John Stuart Mill's intellectual crisis – we are bonded to 'the world, which is the very world/Of all of us:'[9] Lacking this 'culture of the feelings,' however, our imaginative energies face increasing alienation, to the point of becoming spectral, even apocalyptic, as when Wordsworth encounters imagination after crossing the Alps, and the disembodied power is compared to a sudden mountain mist, an 'unfathered vapour.'[10]

What is impressive here, and in romanticism generally, is not the discovery of a new truth (it isn't new) but a greater honesty and force in representing it. This also holds for traditional forms like the ballad. Revived less as a naive than as a native genre, the ballad now expresses the experience of phantomization as a modern and intelligible fact. In many ballads and folktales a ghost too vengeful or desirous enters. Cold by nature, this ghost needs human warmth and seeks to combine with, to rape if necessary – so I understand Goethe's 'Erl-King' – a human companion. In Goethe's 'Bride of Corinth,' a female ghost, denied fulfilment in life because of religious repression, demands that life back and becomes a vampire.

Though it is faddish to discourse on vampires, let me stay with a more general Halloween, a sort of low-grade, permanent spookiness. The most formal reaction to the sense that nature and imagination are falling away from each other, that the link of nature has weakened, is a fetishistic and extreme cathexis named by Ruskin the 'pathetic fallacy.' It leads far beyond Tennyson's 'cruel, crawling foam.' If beauty, at least classical beauty, is marked by balance and correspondence, a perfect matching of subjective and objective, of shape and spirit, then the 'pathetic,' that is, sympathetic, fallacy breaks the mold or shows a crack in this ideal. Visionary or hyperbolic forms, of course, had always sinned against that ideal: Milton's *Lycidas* and Donne's *Anatomy* are sustained pathetic fallacies. But when the sympathetic imagination acts up yet is deprived of traditional visionary symbols, then a new tension emerges between hyperbolic pathos and realistic narrative, most noticeably in the shorter fictional forms.

Consider the way Virginia Woolf, for example, pans in her short story 'Solid Objects' from 'one small black spot' in the distance, which turns out to be a boat on the water, to her main character, John, who gives up a political career after finding a lump of green glass, a discovery that leads to his endless fascination with the beauty and solidity of found objects. This panning is a complex defence against empathizing too much, against moving into the secrets of matter or mind in order to compensate for the consumerism and insubstantiality of ordinary social life.[11] It happens that one of the starting points of Wordsworth's earliest mature poem, 'The Ruined Cottage,' is a speck of glass:

> I crossed this dreary moor
> In the clear moonlight, when I reached the hut
> I looked within but all was still & dark
> Only within the ruin, I beheld
> At a small distance on the dusky ground
> A broken pane which glitter'd to the moon
> And seemed akin to life.[12]

Wordsworth circumvents the pathetic fallacy, though not pathos, by scrupulous phrasing. He draws from this fragment the entire story of 'The Ruined Cottage,' a tale of broken sympathies leading to the mutual abandonment of man and nature and so to the destruction of the very notion of *milieu*. The artistic problem raised by this ghostly moment is not only how to resist extreme pathos or spectral symbolism in order to prevent narrative space collapsing but also how to express, here as elsewhere, the relation of 'mute, insensate things' (including, crazily, that speck of glittering glass) to the sympathetic imagination.

'The Ruined Cottage' is the site of the tale of Margaret, abandoned by a husband who cannot bear to see his family starve and so sells himself into the army during the Napoleonic Wars, leaving her to waste away silently in hope of his return. The story is conjured up from that site by a wandering Pedlar and told to the Poet (Wordsworth himself) who has met him there. The speech situation, then, becomes quite complex: at the center is a silent ruin, a symbol of inarticulate suffering that resists, even as it redemptively elicits, the fluency of moral reflection:

> And never for each other shall we feel
> As we may feel[,] till we have sympathy
> With nature in her forms inanimate[,]
> With objects such as have no power to hold
> Articulate language. In all forms of things
> There is a mind.[13]

On one level, Wordsworth succeeds: the story of Margaret becomes a vivid reminder of how human sympathies develop. Nature, he implies, serves as a transitional object; eventually her 'gentle agency' turns us from love of the rural to love of humanity, even to the passion of Margaret. However, at the level of language itself, there is much less clarity. What remains untheorized in Wordsworth's argument is argument itself: the 'power to hold/Articulate language.' How does language enter the developmental process? How do we pass from 'mute dialogues' with the mother (1850 *Prelude* 2.269), and then with nature, to articulate language, especially poetic expression? Wordsworth assumes (and Coleridge will challenge the assumption) that rural speech embodies a special quality, a counter-urbanity that reflects nature's influence on human development.

As a philosopher – a role Coleridge imposed – Wordsworth remains confused.[14] Yet his moral position is quite clear: poetry articulates a silent sympathy and prevents language from becoming a 'counter-spirit.' So the Pedlar's decorum of disclosure, his respect for the near-muteness of things, for their opaque and quietistic mode of being, limits the audistic pleasure we take in hearing about suffering and catastrophe. The result is a displacement from tale (vicarious adventure, vicariously experienced suffering) to teller, from narrative action to narrator: the slowness of the story, its retardations, are antitheatrical devices serving to reduce voyeurism and to make us thoughtful about the character of poet or storyteller, their attraction to the heart of darkness.

At any point, so Wordsworth would like us to believe, his story could lapse, become silent, merge back into a reticence of nature from which the Pedlar's watchful ear and eye have drawn it. This turning toward nature has struck some critics as a turning away from human suffering, but it is, after all, the poet who uncovers the story, who rescues it from nature's 'oblivious tendencies.' The creation, moreover, of a narrative space is also the virtual creation of a community: storyteller and listener – Pedlar and Poet, and then the poet and those who receive his poetry – form a special bond. They bring an understanding of how 'mute, insensate things' affect imagination and convey 'the still, sad music of humanity.' A common destiny of nature and mankind is affirmed. Within this frame the Pedlar, as the poet's mentor, transmits an ethos, a consistent, integrated, exemplary way of conducting one's life.

The thought of such a legacy – passing from Pedlar to Poet – is important to Wordsworth. The Pedlar is similar to the Peasant in 'Hart-Leap Well,' or to the poet himself in 'Michael.' Wordsworth enters the prologue to that poem in his own person: he negotiates a threatened breach between rural and modern by becoming, as it were, Michael's heir. He reacts to the changes in rural England, which are seen as deceptively slow and immensely sad. Another great work of time is being ruined: English nature itself.

Wordsworth always means by nature an entire complex of feelings and perceptions: precisely what we would now call a culture. But the changes in that culture, as the enclosure movement gains momentum and industrialization transforms country into city, do not signal something new that has its own integrity. Instead they prompt the fear that nature as a whole will fade from the human imagination, that an immemorial compact between mind and world, nature and imagination, is in danger of being dissolved. This compact, deeper than any religion, involves what for the Enlightenment is a superstition: the idea that nature has feelings, even 'passions,' as Wordsworth will say, using a favorite word ('The sounding cataract/Haunted me like a passion').[15]

Readers who demystify his focus on nature and charge that it hides an antisocial streak, a deeply troubling solipsism, mistake the task he has set himself, or the immensity of the shift in sensibility that is occurring as Wordsworth constructs a new vision of community. It may be true that he is as solipsistic as any of us. But his subject, the growth of a poet's mind, cannot be reduced to the psychological and compensatory trick of someone who has trouble growing up, who cannot turn his imagination to social life and politics. If Wordsworth has survived such criticism, from Matthew Arnold, who accused him of averting his eyes from 'half of human fate' (in 'Stanzas in Memory of the Author of "Oberman" ' [1849]), to certain New Historicists, it is because he is the only writer to carry forward a *pastoral culture* as a fully modern poet. Humble as it may seem, this feat, if successful, would amount to a *translatio studii*: the significant transmission of a culture into a new era.[16] The modernizing impetus of other English romantic poets is not a *translatio*: they are either forthrightly urbane (like Byron and, to an extent, Shelley), or creatively nostalgic (evoking, like Keats, 'Flora and Old Pan' while seeking to go beyond the fairy way of writing), or deliberately local and provincial (like John Clare). Wordsworth alone rescues for a modern sensibility what can – or in his view, must – be saved.

No doubt his effort too is retrospective; it is, in Schiller's sense, sentimental rather than naive. In *A Guide through the District of the Lakes*, mainly written in 1810, Wordsworth claims to have given a faithful description of 'a perfect Republic of Shepherds and Agriculturalists,' indeed an 'almost visionary moun- tain republic' as it existed for centuries, 'until within the last sixty years.' What I have called a pastoral culture is a construct, but that does not mean it has no basis in fact.[17] Wordsworth's well-known letter to Charles James Fox, sent with the second edition of *Lyrical Ballads* and inviting the politician to pay special attention to 'Michael' and 'The Brothers,' expresses forcefully his admiration for the independent farmers called 'statesmen,' as well as for the 'sacred property' of the poor. It is 'sacred' because property, especially landed property, is essential to 'the feelings of inheritance, home, and personal and family independence.'[18] At this point Wordsworth does not identify with a specific social class; he represents a more general ethos and claims for the poet an independent privilege, a 'Power like one of Nature's' (1850 *Prelude* 13.307–311).[19]

Such portents as Goldsmith's *The Deserted Village*, published in 1770 (the year of Wordsworth's birth), which describes the depopulation of the English countryside as the enclosure movement creates more itinerants and industry draws workers into the cities, and daily evidence around Wordsworth that 'even in the most sequestered places, by manufactures, traffic, religion, law, inter- change of inhabitants, etc., distinctions are done away which would otherwise have been strong and obvious'[20] do not seem to affect Wordsworth's faith in a trustworthy rural imagination. *It is my view that the failure to give this imagination a modern form, the failure to translate into a modern idiom a sensibility nurtured by country life, creates – less in England, because of Wordsworth, than in continental Europe – an unprogressive, overidealized, image of what is lost, and thus a deeply anti-urban sentiment.* After 1815, when the worst aspects of capitalistic farming and the industrial revolution begin to be felt, Wordsworth's influence increases but can also be used for reactionary purposes. It is on the continent, however, that pastoralism eventually distorts cultural thinking and leads to serious political consequences.[21] I would like to give an impression of the virulence of this utopian and unintegrated ideal and how it has affected the issue of the 'inexpressive' or 'silent' in poetic language.

There is – let me begin by admitting this – something absurd in seeing the Pedlar or Michael or other protagonists of Wordsworth's 'Pastoral' as culture bearers. A faint absurdity like that hovers over *Lyrical Ballads* as a whole. Applying the concept of tradition in its strong form of a *translatio studii* (the transmission of learning from one nation or culture to another) is a way of characterizing at once Wordsworth's originality and his incongruity. His *translatio* is not based on a complete pass-through of an older culture or on a Renaissance-type of modernization, of making illustrious a dialect or vein of folklore by an expertise derived from the classics (a pattern sometimes described as new wine in old bottles). Nor – and this is a more serious matter – does Wordsworth infuse the city, the urban landscape, with any kind of splendor, however intermittent.[22] A vision of the culture of cities is not within his reach. Instead, Wordsworth's culture bearing tries to cut across the nature/culture divide by conveying the still unmediated, accessible, and integral – yet barely so – presence of a half-perceived and half-created mode of life, one that is rapidly disappearing as a 'culture' with more authenticity than most.

It was Lionel Trilling who introduced the idea of authenticity in order to characterize the inexpressiveness of Michael. His touchstone, like Arnold's, is the verse that describes how the shepherd would sit an entire day by the sheepfold 'and never lifted up a single stone':

> Michael says nothing; he *expresses* nothing. It is not the case with him as it is with Hamlet that he has 'that within which passeth show.' There is no within and without: he and his grief are one. We may not, then, speak of sincerity. But our sense of Michael's being, of – so to speak – his being-in-grief, comes to us as a surprise, as if it were exceptional in its actuality, and valuable. And we are impelled to use some word which denotes the nature of this being and which accounts for the high value we put on it. The word we employ for this purpose is 'authenticity.'[23]

Sincerity involves the test of speech: it is because speech can be hypocritical or ambiguous and because it is always for show – even when not explicitly audience-directed and rhetorical – that the issue of the character behind the speech arises, and even a question of whether speech, distinct from the unfathomable person, can ever be sincere. A suspicion may also be voiced that speech is always impersonation, that someone else (the 'ghost' I have previously introduced) is speaking us or in us. Plato's attempt to distinguish oral from written by attributing a sincerity he names truth to the oral mode cannot be sustained. The idea of authenticity moves the issue away from speech toward other evidences, such as character, though these evidences too are not truly silent or self-evidential but continue to depend on report. There is a regress of evidence until we reach a religious or mystical stratum: authenticity suggests a mode of being so self-coincident, so integral, that it signals the absence of internal division, or of the intellectual consciousness we associate with such division. Authenticity means living only in the eye of God or Nature.[24]

In overflow passages to 'Michael' Wordsworth struggles with the issue of both the shepherd's language and nature's language. The language of nature was, of course, a topos of long standing: nature is said to 'speak' to us by signatures or symbols. God has given us this second 'Book' (of Nature), which expands the truth of Scripture to all eyes. The religious background of the authenticity concept surfaces here. That something of Bible or liturgy may affect the diction of 'Michael' only strengthens its own authenticity. Yet when Wordsworth, in an alternate beginning to the poem, tries to convey this language of nature, he fails, because intention demands articulacy and what he shows remains sub-articulate:

> There is a shapeless crowd of unhewn stones
> That lie together, some in heaps, and some
> In lines, that seem to keep themselves alive
> In the last dotage of a dying form.
> At least so seems it to a man who stands
> In such a lonely place.

This fragment may have been discarded because the image of a mysterious intention arising directly from nature (an appearance of mystery resolved later in the poem), or the image of an obscure feeling *in* the stones, is just too close to a crazy empathy, to an extreme form of the 'pathetic fallacy.'[25] Other fragments refer to the shepherd's attempts to express himself, to the peculiar integrity of his language. Yet Wordsworth has to admit a residual silence or even idiotism:

> No doubt if you in terms direct had ask'd
> Whether he lov'd the mountains, true it is
> That with blunt repetition of your words
> He might have stared at you, and said that they
> Were fearful to behold, but had you then
> Discours'd with him in some particular sort
> Of his own business, and the goings on
> Of earth and sky, then truly had you seen
> That in his thoughts there were obscurities,
> Wonders and admirations, things that wrought
> Not less than a religion in his heart.[26]

The near-muteness of Leech-gatherer and Idiot Boy comes to mind. Can we really talk of a *culture*, or what should sustain it, when its language is so sparse ('simple and unelaborated') and has to be purified of 'all lasting and rational causes of dislike and disgust'? I am now quoting, of course, from the 1800 preface to *Lyrical Ballads*, which introduces the topic of a more natural language for poetry, one that is taken from 'low and rustic life.' Coleridge will quarrel with his friend's formulation of the matter in Chapter 17 of the *Biographia Literaria*.

There is no need to interrogate that quarrel, Coleridge's response is strong and correct, yet not entirely to the point. Wordsworth's attempt to justify the diction of poetry in mimetic terms – by claiming, in the preface, that he wishes to introduce 'the real language of men' – may indeed be inept, for he is advocating a quality not based primarily on speech. It is clearly not language as such but rather an ethos or a culture the poet wishes to save. That culture, while it is peculiarly English, has not yet *emerged* into poetry; speech, therefore, can become a 'counter-spirit' to it. Hence Wordsworth is compelled to use mimetic terms in such an equivocating manner. If he were asked bluntly what characterizes that culture, which is relatively mute and very near subsistence level, the answer would have to fall back on the 'authenticity' of passions and affections[27] that focus on 'nature': on landed property, rural homestead, or patrimony as the minimum gage for freedom of spirit and family independence.[28]

At this point what I have called a pastoral culture, which *fades into memory before it has emerged into maturity, like the twilight presence of Lucy*, seems to unmask itself as a cultural politics defending property rights. Such emphasis on property is not new in English political thought. Yet Wordsworth's concept of property qualification is quite different from the standard use of it to justify restricted voting rights or citizenship, though he opposed the Reform Bill of 1832 'as giving a grace to an industrial, propertyless society.'[29] It is true that property, in both Wordsworth's and the standard philosophy, is thought to foster a reality relation and individual dignity. A man without property becomes too easily a man without properties (qualities, *Eigenschaften*): deracinated, lacking local attachments, abstract in his thinking – a space cadet, we would now say. But Wordsworth's focus on the rural scene and on the modest or the poor is not ipso facto a defence of larger holdings. Property has no value for him except as a need of the soul, close to the need for roots. It is not fungible in the ordinary sense; it must remain *in nature*, merging with it, tied to an imaginative community of beings, to a living, interactive nature culture. To achieve a spiritual home requires associative links to a specific place and a sensitivity to 'gradations' that cannot occur without a material homestead. As a poet Wordsworth does not presuppose this fact on the basis of received ideas: he creates or recreates it as the 'cultured Vale' we find in his nature poetry.[30]

The sense that we exist in *this* world, that we are not ghosts and strangers on earth, doomed to wander about in exile, is called by both Rousseau and Wordsworth the 'sentiment of being,' and Trilling, in associating it with authenticity, names it an 'unassailable intuition.' It is assailed, of course, all the time. Yet such 'moments of being' are attested by imaginative residues in our speech. 'To be' itself, Trilling adds, is used by Wordsworth as if he were conscious that it enters the name of God ('I am that I am'). Such simple words, carrying a reservoir of silence, though not less capable of betrayal than complex words, raise the issue of whether we can ever fuse being and meaning through language. Heidegger looks in that direction; he is always 'on the way to language' (*Unterwegs zur Sprache*). Yet we know how vulnerable he was to a political doctrine that stressed the organic community and the possibility that it could be recovered by a decisive historical act. Is Heidegger's language, so close to poetic paranomasia, an advance over Wordsworth's as cultural discourse?

In the conclusion to the *Letter on Humanism*, written for a French admirer soon after the Second World War, Heidegger links future thought to an ending (the end of metaphysics) and a beginning (a 'more originary' thinking). But he seems careful about prospecting the future. Cultural prophesy – including his own brand of decisionist rhetoric that for a time credited the Nazi *Aufbruch* as exposing the neediness and inauthenticity of his era – had hastened rather than prevented catastrophe, and his emphasis now reverts to the relation of thought and language. Still, the style of the concluding paragraph remains promissory:

> Das künftige Denken ist nicht mehr Philosophie, weil es ursprünglicher denkt als die Metaphysik, welcher Name das gleiche sagt. Das künftige Denken kann aber auch nicht mehr, wie Hegel verlangte, den Namen der 'Liebe zur Weisheit' ablegen und die Weisheit selbst in der Gestalt des absoluten Wissens geworden sein. Das Denken ist auf dem Abstieg in die Armut seines vorläufigen Wesens. Das Denken sammelt die Sprache in das einfache Sagen. Die Sprache ist so die Sprache des Seins, wie die Wolken die Wolken des Himmels sind. Das Denken legt mit seinem Sagen unscheinbare Furchen in die Sprache. Sie sind noch unscheinbarer als die Furchen, die der Landmann langsamen Schrittes durch das Feld zieht.[31]

> (Future thought is no longer philosophy, because it thinks more originally than metaphysics, whose name means the same. Yet future thought also cannot any longer, as Hegel demanded, lay aside its name of 'Love for Wisdom' and become wisdom itself in the form of absolute knowledge. Thought is descending into the poverty of its temporary mode of being. Thought gathers language into simple speech. Language is the language of being as clouds are the clouds of heaven. Thought places with its speech unapparent furrows in language. They are even more unapparent than the furrows made in the field by the slowly striding peasant.)

The apparent simplicity and pastoralism of this prose are not accidental. The war is over, including a very real culture war between Germany and France that

I have not had the time to describe. It focussed on the *Kultur/Civilisation* antithesis.[32] That this war is still going on despite Heidegger's much-subdued style (there is pathos in this paragraph, but not *pathos* in the oratorical sense, that is, the heroic-pathetic vein of some Heidegger writings in the Nazi period), is suggested by the fact that he continues to shun words derived from the Latin or Romance stratum. But at least he does not indulge in the violent punning whereby he used to furrow words, claiming to recover a more original meaning. The tone has changed, for the time being, and the only etymological move is a very old one, which derives the idea of linear writing from the pattern of the furrow.[33] When we think, however, of Vico's magnificent interpretation of Roman law – that 'severe poem,' as he called it – or E. R. Curtius's defence of *romanitas* in the magisterial *European Literature and the Latin Middle Ages* – written during the Nazi period and demonstrating the immense Latin heritage that Goethe transmitted to modern German literature – one can only wonder at Heidegger's provincialism.

Heidegger's rejection of Latinity is, nevertheless, a philosophically complex act. It preceded the political change in Germany and was based on his judgment that the language of philosophy was not the language of thought and that both had become inauthentic. The abstraction that has invaded modern life is denounced as an occultation of Being. The history of our thinking about Being, enmeshed in categories supplied by language, requires therefore an aggressive mode of analysis (*Destruktion*) that must alter the diction of philosophy and thought as a whole. Heidegger rejects, in short, not the classical heritage as such but its faulty mediation of more radical Greek intuitions. He returns to the possibility of a direct German-Greek axis of linkage. In a strange parallel to Wordsworth, there is the hope in a new *translatio*, an original and originative thinking that will restore language to simplicity and human life to its unalienated place in nature, so that 'humanism,' with its secularist, antisacred pretensions, becomes superfluous. Heidegger's 'Thought gathers language into simple speech,' together with the final image of the philosopher-peasant cultivating a speech with unapparent furrows, has a relation to Wordsworth's own cure of language.

Unfortunately, as I have suggested, the very absence on the continent of a Wordsworth or a Wordsworth reception removed what might have moderated a cultural and political antimodernism vulnerable to vicious dichotomies. Political thought, especially in Germany, pitted the archaic *numen* of *Kultur* against the superficial classicism and cosmopolitanism of *civilisation* and exaggerated the organic relation of man to nature (also, mysteriously, to nation) in country life, in order to set that pastoral culture against urban deracination.[34] It is not possible to read Heidegger's final evocation of the peasant without thinking of the polemic in fascist thought against *bodenloses Denken* or 'groundless thought.' This overdetermined phrase is applied by Heidegger to 'metaphysics' as the wrong kind of unworldiness but also, more generally, to deracinated and deracinating speculation. The paragraph is an example of what Lyotard has called Heidegger's *impensé paysan*.

'Groundless thought,' interpreted as the mentality of the person without property or who does not feel he has a hereditary national stake, motivates from the late nineteenth century on the intersecting discourses of anti-intellectualism and anti-Semitism. It would be easy to cite a masterpiece of *ressentiment* like Maurice Barrès's *Les Déracinés* (The Uprooted) to illustrate the exploitation of a regionalistic and rural nostalgia. Or to examine how Nazi ideology played on the suffering of the peasantry and attracted that group by promises of equality with other professions or estates (*Stände*) in the new *Volksgemeinschaft*. Or to show how Edouard Drumont, the arch anti-Semite, linked finance capitalism and a corrupting city life to deracinated immigrant Jews, accused of dispossessing native citizens and turning the good old country (*le vieux pays* or *la France d'alors*) into *la France juive*. Even when Jews are praised, it is for their ability to deal with abstractions, a talent that is said to derive from their having been excluded throughout Christian history from work on the land and other 'productive' professions and therefore having to turn to the handling of 'abstract money' and the institutions associated with it.[35]

Nor is it difficult to cite less prejudiced texts haunted by the Human Abstract. Count Keyserling declares roundly in 1926: ' "Abstract Man" was the invention of the eighteenth century.'[36] F. R. Leavis quotes 'Rilke on Vacuity,' protesting American commodification:

> Now there come crowding over from America empty, indifferent things, pseudo-things, dummy-life . . . A house, in the American sense, an American apple or wine, has nothing in common with the house, the fruit, the grape into which the hope and pensiveness of our forefathers would enter . . . The animated, experienced things that share our lives are coming to an end . . . We are perhaps the last to have still known such things.

Rilke wishes to preserve 'their human and Laral worth.'[37] The ancient authorities guiding our morals were blended, according to Walter Lippmann, 'with the ancient landmarks, with fields and vineyards and patriarchal trees, with ancient houses and chests full of heirlooms, with churchyards near at hand and their ancestral graves.' But modern man is an 'emigrant who lives in a revolutionary society,' who can find no fixed point outside his conscience and does not 'really believe there is such a point, because he has moved about too fast to fix any point long enough in his mind.'[38] Commenting on the modern intellectual, Trilling adds: 'It is a characteristic of the intellectual life of our culture that it fosters a form of assent which does not involve actual credence.'[39]

The painter R. B. Kitaj, born in Ohio and now living in London, makes an identity out of all this. He calls himself a Diasporist.

> I've come to make myself a tradition in that Diaspora . . . as a real American rootless Jew, riddled with assimilationist secularism and Anglophiliac-Europist art mania, besieged by modernisms and their sceptical overflow, fearful at the prospect and state of Wandering, un-at-homeness, yet unable to give myself to Ohio or God or Israel or London or California.[40]

But in most cases, when fear of modern life, of an exponential growth of this identitarian nonidentity, combines with the charged themes of emigrant, Jew, and intellectual, an explosive situation is created.

No one needs to be reminded how much greater the panic about refugees is today than even between the world wars. The chief propagandist of Le Pen's National Front, an 'unassuming, baby-faced technocrat,' according to a report in the *Wall Street Journal*, can suddenly change and bark out a doctrine of racial venom, asserting

> a world-wide 'cosmopolitan' conspiracy that seeks to abolish national identity and infect the world with the AIDS virus. He says that racial integration has corrupted the U.S. He mocks those in French politics with Jewish-sounding names – pronouncing the names in an exaggerated way.[41]

Yet the most inflammatory element in this rhetoric that seeks to halt the reign of *bodenloses Denken* or universalist abstraction is the memory of a rural culture. Maurice Bardèche even sees its loss *legislated* by the Nuremberg Tribunal, which recognized a 'humanity' above and beyond the national state. The nation, the patria, the patrimonial culture (whether of country or town) is devalued, Bardèche claims, in favor of a general *Personne Humaine*. He gives the gist of what the new law imposes in the following extraordinary peroration:

> You will be a *citizen of the world*, you too will be packaged and dehydrated, you will cease to hear the rustling of the trees and the voice of the clock-towers, but instead you will learn to listen to the voice of the universal conscience: shake the earth from your shoes, peasant, that earth is worth nothing any more, it is dirt, it is embarrassing, it prevents the making of pretty packages. Modern Times have come. Listen to the voice of Modern Times. The Polish handyman who changes employ a dozen times each year is as much a man as you are; the Jewish Old Clothes dealer who has just come from Korotcha or Jitomir is as much a man as you are; they have the same rights as you in the country [*sur la terre*] or the town; respect the negro, o peasant. They have the same rights as you and you will make place for them at your table and they will enter into council with you and teach you what the universal conscience is saying, which you do not hear as well as you should. And their sons will be *messieurs* and will be appointed judges over your sons, they will govern your town and buy your field, for the universal conscience gives them expressly all these rights. As for you, peasant, if you consult your friends and if you regret the time you only saw boys from the canton at village festivals, know that you are murmuring against the universal conscience and that the law does not protect you from the same.[42]

In a similar spirit, but focussing on what he calls postwar aesthetic taboos, Hans Jürgen Syberberg, creator of *Hitler: A Film from Germany*, sees Nazi 'Blut und Boden' propaganda as a distortive populist incarnation of a premodern rural culture (*ländliche Kultur*) that had been aristocratic (Blut = blood = lineage; Boden = landed property). He suggests that, because of the postwar taboos, we have repressed rather than come to terms with a still valuable aesthetics. 'Heidegger,' he asserts, 'to the day of his death, was in all his judgments on poets from Hölderlin to Rilke, and in all his philosophic discoursing, a man of this culture that drew its nourishment from the soil.'[43]

> The countryside, the silent universe of ill-hap . . .
>   *I, Pierre Rivière . . . A Case of Parricide in the Nineteenth Century*

> Let Tola bless with the Toad, which is the good creature of God, tho' his virtue is in the secret, and his mention is not made.
>   Christopher Smart

There are three correlative issues that any analysis of the language of cultural criticism must take up. One is its authenticity, meaning by that the quality Trilling ascribes to Michael, Wordsworth's near-silent peasant and 'statesman.' Cultural rhetoric is noisy and explicit; its very aim is often to give voice to the voiceless, representation to those who are anonymous and marginalized. Wordsworth talks of 'mute, insensate things' whose influence on thought and emotion he wishes to evoke, but people like Michael, or those still more humble or oppressed, are mute and *sensate*, and the visionary poetry of the romantic period focusses on the animal creation, which is equally subjected, and not always, as Scripture has it, 'in hope' (Roman 8:19–23). From this point of view Wordsworth's 'Hart-Leap Well' and *The White Doe of Rylstone* are as central to his oeuvre as 'Michael,' 'The Pedlar,' or *The Prelude*. What is *quietly* conveyed in Wordsworth's poetry, too quietly for some, is the misery of the rural poor in the countryside or those displaced into the cities; part of this misery is that, being treated no better than animals, and sometimes worse, they are also deprived of the very pleasures Wordsworth depicts: a freely exercised and excursive imagination, a sense for both animal and meanest flower, sympathy for 'Nature.'

There were differences between the condition of English peasants and those in the rest of Europe. Every country had its own specific problems, especially as capitalistic farming developed.[44] The scholars assembled by Foucault to understand Pierre Rivière's butchery of his mother and two siblings at Aunay-sur-Odon in 1835 move from that crime and Pierre's bleak though articulate testimony to a frightening picture of rural life, in some ways worsened when peasants became full citizens after the Revolution. The kind of bloody particulars printed up in contemporary French broadsheets are very unlike the incidents described and reflected on in Wordsworth's ballads, though by calling them 'lyrical' he signaled that their content would differ from the usual sensational contents of the popular ballad. Reporting ominous symptoms of Rivière's 'silent universe of ill-hap,' the authors of a note in Foucault's volume headed 'Blood and Cry' put a question that barely arises when reading Wordsworth: the 'acts [of murderers like Pierre] were discourses; but what were they saying and why did they speak this terrifying language of crime?'[45]

It proved difficult, clearly, for these authors to find the right voice – the right rhetorical emphasis – for their own discourse. They are concerned, beyond saving from oblivion the historical facts and a significant text, with creating testimony of their own. They do not want to leave the scene 'without an echo' by simply adding particulars to particulars or writing a becalmed social history. They too, one senses from their style throughout, want a 'terrifying language.'

It remains to be determined, as I have said, how different the situation of the rural poor was in the France in the 1830s from that in the Lake District during the Napoleonic Wars. But surely there was great suffering in both places; as to silence, both good and bad, there might have been more in England, given that the exemplary incident recovered by Foucault was aggravated by endless quarrels in the Rivière family over contractual property rights.[46] Wordsworth's poetry, if culturally significant, cannot be spared a juxtaposition with Pierre's 'blood and cry,' yet to compare them does not displace his (or my) understanding of how to preserve a reticence that, close to nature's own in the poet's depiction, might prevent language from becoming a 'counter-spirit.'

A second question affecting cultural discourse is the difficulty of forging progressive words that would not simply reverse the signs ('devil' and 'angel' in Blake's *The Marriage of Heaven and Hell*; 'culture' as cosmopolitan and 'culture' as racist in National Socialist Germany). To work the system against itself is to risk that sooner or later one's own revision will appear as merely a variant of the system. Blake attempted to make a virtue of this difficulty; he refused to abandon corrupted or trivialized visionary categories, instead compounding them into a new 'system' by creating a super-sublimity and often a wicked inversion of traditional dichotomies. Raymond Williams's prose, I have suggested, remains in the verbal orbit of idealism, despite his improved understanding of the 'material community.' Another interesting case is Walter Benjamin's avoidance of such terms as 'creative' and 'genius' in 'The Work of Art in the Era of Mechanical Reproduction,' because they were bourgeois clichés appropriated by Nazi rhetoric. Yet Benjamin has not escaped a fierce critical debate on whether his language betrays a materialistic or a mystical orientation.

The deception of hoping to be objective about one's culture through criticizing it is raised by Adorno: 'By such exclusivity [*Vornehmheit*] the cultural critic assumes a privileged position and establishes his legitimacy, even while contributing to that culture as its salaried and honored gadfly.'[47] In his *Aesthetic Theory*, Adorno holds that art can stand in opposition to modern society only by identification with that against which it rebels. He falls back on a homeopathic view of art's effect, mentioning its 'admixture of poison' and recalling the ancient topos of the spear of Achilles, which alone can heal the wound it inflicts.[48]

Recently Derrida, also fascinated by the 'gift' (*pharmakon*) of speech, has explored the 'polysemic mobility' and 'all [the] sources for reversal' in an early Benjamin text and has even suggested that there was a complicity – 'specularity' is the better word – between the best and worst cultural discourses in the Nazi era, as they engage with German nationalism.[49] Let me also cite Leo Spitzer's comment regarding a fellow scholar of Romance literature, Karl Vossler. In 1936 Vossler, receiving an honorary degree in Madrid, gave a speech in which he declared that his study of Spanish culture was founded on an aversion to materialistic and positivistic theses. But a London paper reporting the event pointed out that antimaterialism and antipositivism were Nazi slogans. 'So ambiguous,' remarks Spitzer, 'had humanistic studies become in Germany.'[50]

This question of 'our' language is further bedeviled by the fact that every social and political philosophy of modern times makes the same virtuous claim: it seeks the reconstruction or recovery of community, culture, nation-state. Yet at the same time the question of what *rhetorical* devices become necessary to cohere people of some diversity, to encourage them to agree or even sacrifice to that common purpose, tends to be suppressed in liberal-democratic thought. Isn't it clear enough from elections we have gone through that either the words of candidates for office are discounted, and some other criterion such as 'character' or 'charisma' tends to prevail, or the most manipulative slogans are greeted with applause and roars of approval? We uphold the fiction of the thoughtful voter while always doubting the honesty of the candidate seeking that vote. In this strange rhetorical situation, all the frankness, as Wyndham Lewis observed, is on one side,

> and that is not on the side of the West, of democracy. All the traditional obliquity and subterranean methods of the Orient are, in this duel, exhibited by the westerner and the democratic regime. It is *we* who are the Machiavels, compared to the sovietist or the fascist, who makes no disguise of his forcible intentions, whose *power* is not wrapped up in parliamentary humbug, who is not eternally engaged in pretences of benefaction.[51]

The last problem is the expanding and overdetermined nature of the word 'culture' itself. We have seen it become a talisman against the abstract life, against a feeling of increasing and encroaching unreality, all the more so when an available doctrine links that condition causally to a social or political condition. The rhetoric of culture is then associated with a corrective politics and may become revanchist. An intrinsic utopianism often surfaces: the memory of a *temps perdu*, of a pastoral moment in personal or collective history. However delusive, this belief in a vanished and more unified mode of life that once graced a homeland, a place that is our own, a prior ecological innocence, conspires with ideologies that seek a cure of the ground and wish to sacralize a community in its land. The archaic and allegorical forces of the genius loci may then be appealed to, as blood (race) and soil (nation, patrimony) become identifying slogans.

The cultural situation in the United States is not quite as dangerous. There is a constitution that spells out an ideal: it would safeguard, for each of us, life, liberty, and the pursuit of happiness. Still, happiness – a substitute, in the preamble, for the more traditional 'property' – was always the most questionable of the triad. We pursue something that would bind gently and invisibly, tie us to, into, a community, without tying anyone down. Property, humanely defined as home, subsistence, family ties, fortified by guarantees of freedom of association and expression, as well as equality before the law, is indeed essential to life. The problem arises when cultural ideas become a property substitute, compensating those who have too little yet need to embody and define themselves.[52]

For the plight of the poor is not a transcendental but a real homelessness. Foucault's recovery of Pierre Rivière's testimony proves doubly relevant: it explodes rural idealism and demonstrates what may happen when those in nature, yet little more than chattel, revolt against 'enduring the unlivable, day in day out.'

> The enclosed horizon of the hedgerows was from time immemorial a profusion of lives devoid of all future, deprived of all prospects . . . For the mute horror of the daily round, for the predicament of dumb beast and dupe, [Pierre] has substituted a more flagrant horror, protest by hecatomb. And he thereby assumes the right to break the silence and speak at last. To speak the heart of the matter like one returned from the dead.[53]

Deprived of a vital milieu even while alive, it is no wonder that so many of the poor felt trapped in an unreal reality. Because they have never fully lived in the world, they may become, like the undead, vengeful spirits.

Notes

1. Raymond Williams, *Culture and Society*, 1780–1950 (London: Chatto and Windus, 1958), 333. The complaint against specialization can be found as early as Socrates, of course. But in a political rather than philosophical context an early locus is Rousseau's 'Discours sur les sciences et les arts' (1750): 'Nous avons des Physiciens,

des Géometres, des Chymistes, des Astronomes, des Poètes, des Musiciens, des Peintres; nous n'avons plus des citoyens; ou s'il nous en reste encore, dispersés dans nos campagnes abandonnées, ils s'y périssent indigens et méprisés.' [We have physicians, mathematicians, chemists, astronomers, poets, musicians, painters; we no longer have citizens; or if there remain any among us, they are dispersed amidst our abandoned countryside, where they perish poverty-stricken and despised]. I should add that in the 1960s and 1970s Williams got to know continental Marxist thinkers more thoroughly and that he goes much further in specifying what he calls 'material community' by refusing to consider cultural history (intellectual life and the arts) as merely secondary or superstructural. See the introduction to his *Marxism and Literature* (New York: Oxford University Press, 1977).

2. Williams, *Culture and Society*, 336–38.
3. For a forthright critique of an instrumental view of culture, see Hannah Arendt, 'The Crisis in Culture,' in *Between Past and Future: Eight Exercises in Political Thought* (New York: Penguin, 1977), 197–226.
4. 'The Question of Our Speech,' in *The Question of Our Speech; The Lesson of Balzac: Two Lectures* (Boston: Houghton, Mifflin, 1905), 3–52.
5. Wallace Stephens, 'Notes Toward a Supreme Fiction,' *It must give Pleasure*, VII.
6. The expression is from Yeats, describing the effect of Chaucer on him. The role of Chaucer during the romantic period, his significance compared to that of Spenser and Milton, deserves fuller treatment. In the quest, moreover, for an imagined (and lost) community, which underwrites the many stirrings of nationalism at this time, the genius loci figure appeals for its archaism rather than its neoclassical elegance. It is gothicized, as in Walter Scott's *Waverley*.
7. 'No poet is more emphatically the poet of community. A great part of his verse . . . is dedicated to the affections of home and neighborhood and country, and to that soul of joy and love which links together all Nature's children, and "steals from earth to man, from man to earth" ' (A. C. Bradley, 'Wordsworth,' in *Oxford Lectures on Poetry* [London: Macmillan, 1909], 143–44).
8. 'Prospectus to *The Excursion* (1814).
9. 1850 *Prelude* 11.142–3.
10. 1850 *Prelude* 6.595.
11. Cf. Douglas Mao's analysis of the episode in *Modernism and the Question of the Object* (Ann Arbor: umi, 1994), 17–20.
12. *The Ruined Cottage and The Pedlar* (The Cornell Wordsworth), ed. James Butler (Ithaca: Cornell University Press, 1979), 87.
13. From the Alfoxden manuscript, quoted in *The Ruined Cottage*, 15.
14. There is no sustained consideration in Wordsworth on the origin of language, as in Rousseau's essay or Herder's. The latter was written for the Berlin Academy's contest of 1770: 'Are men, left to their natural faculties, in a position to invent language . . . ?' Interesting remarks in John P. Klancher's *The Making of English Reading Audiences, 1790–1832* (Madison: University of Wisconsin Press, 1994) bring a sociological perspective to the problematics of language and cultural transmission in Wordsworth. Klancher explores what the poet meant by tasking himself with 'creating' the public taste by which he would be appreciated. But

Klancher's conclusions, very different from mine, are that Wordsworth found his nineteenth-century audience only by displacing 'the real cultural and historical conflicts of the early nineteenth century with an essentialized "Romanticism" [Klancher essentially repeats here Jerome McGann's charge that there was, and still is, a "Romantic ideology"] and Wordsworth, among others, successfully established the terms for that subliming of the historical in the ideal' (150). Klancher does add that Wordsworth 'did not do so without great pain.' Klancher's remarks on the romantic mystification of ideal (virtual) reader and audience (5) can be compared with Gary Harrison's more specific analysis of middle-class appropriations of Wordsworth's poetry in his 'Postscript' to *Wordsworth's Vagrant Muse: Poetry, Poverty, and Power* (Detroit: Wayne State University Press, 1994), 173–93. There is, obviously, a methodological problem as well as a moral issue here: not only, do we hold an author accountable for misuses or partial uses of his text? but also, do these (ideologized) uses really represent the accumulative force of his poetry on readers and the way it opens a problematic that others then attempt to control or close?

15. From 'Tintern Abbey' (1798). A quasi-human sensitivity, according to this ancient idea, animates the entire cosmos. The mechanical fancy might put a genie in the waterfall, but this trivializes the belief. By Wordsworth's time such neoclassical machinery has clogged the arteries of an imagination that must work harder than ever to keep the idea of a sympathetic nature alive. Nor can the poet revert to an older, explicitly visionary mode of figuration, because that is just as injurious to nature's integrity.

16. A literary-sensitive description of the *translatio studii* idea is found in Frank Kermode, *The Classic: Literary Images of Permanence and Change* (New York: Viking, 1975). The relation of a predominantly rural culture to the form of literary transmission, in particular to an 'artisanal form of communication' like that between Pedlar and Poet, is described by Walter Benjamin in 'The Storyteller'; see *Illuminations: Essays and Reflections*, ed. Hannah Arendt, trans. Harry Zohn (New York: Schocken, 1968), 91. Yet Wordsworth's *translatio* is best understood as a fidelity to the 'immemorial compact' previously mentioned: it resembles the feudal *homage* applied to the relation between man and nature. The poet becomes, so to say, nature's 'man.' On the feudal *homage*, see Marc Bloch, *La société féudale* (1939; rev. ed., Paris: Albin Michel, 1942), 223–37. Needless to say, this analogy is only approximate: the dedicated poet feels liberated by his discovery of a bond with nature, which had been made 'for him' and to which he rededicates himself.

17. The complexity of this construct, related to the linked fortunes of pastoral and georgic as literary genres, is delineated by John Murdoch, 'The Landscape of Labor: Transformations of the Georgic,' in *Romantic Revolutions: Criticism and Theory*, ed. Kenneth R. Johnston, Gilbert Caitin, Karen Hanson, and Herbert Marks (Bloomington: Indiana University Press, 1990). Murdoch spins a fascinating *political* tale by combining social history and the history of pictorial representation, arguing that 'the absorption of the Georgic into the collective cultural consciousness, into a region almost *beyond* consciousness' – which assimilated, in effect, the georgic to the pastoral – was a deliberate concealment of the ethos of 'hard, unremitting labor' as

well as cultural propaganda for the progressive state that had given up the golden age and 'primal otium.' The 'landscape of Labor,' he concludes, 'is being transformed into the landscape of Nature' (190, 184, 192). Yet Murdoch does not consider Wordsworth and does not discuss the imaginative truth of such 'constructs,' only their presumed *real-politik* origins. Michael H. Friedman's *The Making of a Tory Humanist: William Wordsworth and the Idea of Community* (New York: Columbia University Press, 1979), especially Chapter 5, is a more judicious consideration of the changes and forces against which Wordsworth conducts what Friedman considers a rearguard politics that weakens him as a poet. The classic and relatively neglected work of Kenneth MacLean, *Agrarian Age: A Background for Wordsworth* (New Haven: Yale University Press, 1950), delineates very carefully the poet's relation to a declining peasantry and the agricultural changes in England. Words-worth, according to MacLean, does not simply maintain a 'ruralism classical in spirit' but remains 'faithful throughout to the ideal of an agrarian society of small proprietors,' while deploring the suffering caused to domestic cottage industry by the disappearance of home spinning (see in general Chapter 3). One should compare with Murdoch's ideology critique the following assertions of MacLean as an alternate point of view: 'Poetry is not men's trades and tackle and gear. Poetry is the science of feeling. The georgic element in Wordsworth's peasant poetry was only incidental. His first duty as a poet was to interpret the emotional character of peasant life' (96). The real change, as Raymond Williams has shown, has to do with the notion of pastoral itself as a literary genre affecting perception and ideology. In *The Country and the City* (New York: Oxford University Press, 1973), especially chaps. 2 and 3, he shows what must be demystified and what can be salvaged of this perspective. For a balanced survey of rural myths and value, see Christiana Payne, *Toil and Plenty: Images of the Agricultural Landscape in England, 1780–1890* (New Haven: Yale University Press, 1993), Chapter 2; and Harrison, 'The Discourse on Poverty and the Agrarian Idyll in Late Eighteenth-Century England,' in *Words-worth's Vagrant Muse*, 27–55.

18. See *Wordsworth's Literary Criticism*, ed. W. J. B. Owen (Boston: Routledge and Kegan Paul, 1974), 99–102. For this 'ruralism classical in spirit,' as MacLean calls it, Walter Scott is also important. There are important affinities between Wordsworth and Scott in this linking of rural and national character. See especially Katie Trumpener's 'National Character, Nationalist Plots: National Tale and Historical Novel in the Age of Waverley, 1806–1830,' *ELH* 60 (1993): 685–731, and her *Bardic Nationalism: The Romantic Novel and the British Empire* (Princeton: Princeton University Press, 1997).

19. He understands, moreover, that the competition is not primarily with a sublime and resilient classicism, as was the case in Germany and later in France. For him, the georgic and pastoral style of Virgil, itself a recreation marked by urbanity, points to a vision partially realized by the mixed rural and urban culture of British life, now endangered.

20. Letter to John Wilson, 7 June 1802.

21. There is nothing in continental Europe to compare with Raymond Williams's *The Country and the City* for a careful, engaged, and at the same time politically conscious

description of country life and its fatal alteration. Cf. also John Barrell's more narrowly construed but powerfully focused books, such as *The Idea of Landscape and the Sense of Place, 1730–1840: An Approach to the Poetry of John Clare* (Cambridge: Cambridge University Press, 1972). Yet there is, between the wars, Marc Bloch's great study of rural France in feudal times (useful to Barrell); see *Feudal Society* (Chicago: University of Chicago Press, 1963). There is also Foucault's remarkable edition of Pierre Rivière's memoir that recalls the suffering and annulled humanity of French peasants, both before and after the Revolution. (Their abject status and universal poverty, however, were not primarily the result of industrialization.) Recently, moreover, the attempt to understand the rise of fascism has focused on the fact that the movement gained its strongest hold in places where industrialization threatened the greatest loss of the past or where preindustrial traditions resisted modernization. Consult, e.g., H. Stuart Hughes, *The Sea Change: The Migration of Social Thought, 1930–1965* (New York: Harper and Row, 1975), 130–32. I should also remark that Germany and France industrialized (and became *functioning* nation-states) later than England. On this matter, see especially Gregory Jusdanys, *Belated Modernity and Aesthetic Culture: Inventing National Literature* (Minneapolis: University of Minnesota Press, 1991); and Eugen Weber, *Peasants into Frenchmen: The Modernization of Rural France, 1870–1914* (Stanford: Stanford University Press, 1976).

22. There are exceptional moments, such as the Westminster Bridge sonnet. See Geoffrey Hartman, *The Unremarkable Wordsworth* (Minneapolis: University of Minnesota Press, 1987), 211.

23. Lionel Trilling, *Sincerity and Authenticity* (Cambridge: Harvard University Press, 1972), 93.

24. Cf. the conclusion of Wordsworth's 'The Old Cumberland Beggar': 'As in the eye of Nature he has lived,/So in the eye of Nature let him die!' The fundamentalism of the late Tolstoy in such tracts as 'What Is Art?' is another (I think unfortunate) response to the nature/culture divide on the Continent that over-idealizes the ethos of the peasant.

25. The passage, nevertheless, is not all that removed from the affect of the famous dejection scene that opens Keats's *Hyperion*. In Wordsworth, however, there is no classical machinery.

26. The two passages are found in E. de Selincourt, *The Poetical Works of William Wordsworth* (Clarendon: Oxford University Press, 1940–49), 2:482. On 'rural idiocy' and romantic localism generally, see the fine pages in David Simpson, *The Academic Postmodern and the Rule of Literature: A Report on Half-Knowledge* (Chicago: University of Chicago Press, 1995), Chapter 6, especially 139–41, on William Cobbett.

27. The word 'passion' often connotes in Wordsworth a strong affection trying to express itself in words.

28. Susan Eilenberg, in *Strange Power of Speech: Wordsworth, Coleridge and Literary Possession* (Oxford: Oxford University Press, 1992), successfully combines economic issues of property, sociopsychological ones of identity or propriety, and literary ones of speech, diction, and genre. She links, for example, Wordsworthian matter-of-

factness and propriety as an element of style to 'the epitaphic coincidence of property and identity at the spot (*topos*) at which the earth is not only *where* it is but also *what* it is' (29).

29. MacLean, *Agrarian Age*, 102.

30. J. G. A. Pocock has emphasized the survival of republicanism and its rhetoric of civic virtue in the eighteenth century. A major conflict arose between it and the ideology of commerce; as Robert Griffin has pointed out, what was at stake was not 'a division of property between the haves and the have-nots' but a 'dispute between two types of property.' He quotes from Pocock's 'The Mobility of Property' (*Virtue, Commerce and History* [Cambridge: Cambridge University Press, 1985]): 'We are contrasting a conception of property which stresses possession and civic virtue with one that stresses exchange and the civilization of the passions' (115). See Robert J. Griffin, *Wordsworth's Pope: A Study in Literary Historiography* (Cambridge: Cambridge University Press, 1996), 12. It seems clear that Wordsworth attempted to merge civic virtue and rural virtue and that the 'cultured Vale' was more civilizing for him than the city as the encroaching hub of commerce.

31. Heidegger, *Brief über den Humanismus* (Frankfurt-am-Main: Klostermann, 1946), 47. My translation.

32. See also Hartman, *The Fateful Question of Culture* (New York: Columbia University Press, 1997), appendix 1, 205–24.

33. I have previously discussed this Heidegger passage in *Minor Prophecies: The Literary Essay in the Culture Wars* (Cambridge: Harvard University Press, 1991), 9–10.

34. 'Wordsworth' stands here as a metonymy for a complex development, somewhat less divisive and bloody in England than elsewhere. The issue of the peasantry in modernity remains vital and difficult today, especially in South Africa, if we listen to the Ugandan political theorist Mahmood Mandani, as quoted by Breyten Breytenbach: 'If we are to arrive at a political agenda that can energize and draw together various social forces in the highly fragmented social reality that is contemporary Africa, we need to devise an agenda that will appeal to both civil society and peasant communities, that will incorporate both the electoral choice that civil society movements seek and the quest for community rights that has been the consistent objective of peasant-based movements' (*New York Review of Books*, 26 May 1994, 4).

35. See, e.g., the Marxist comment by David Rousset – his *L'univers concentrationnaire* (Paris: Pavois, 1946), a description of the structure of Nazi concentration camps in which he was himself a political prisoner, is a classic – who understands the fate of the Jews through the prism of their forced role as 'magicians of abstract money': 'With a truly remarkable sureness of reaction, the vast majority of this people [the Jews], formed and maintained in its originality [?] by its traditional historical practice of merchant and usurer, awkward in acting directly on things but skilful in recognizing their abstract relations, will engage in the complex maze of worldwide commerce, will find its vocation in speculations on modern law,' etc. (preface to F. J. Armorin, *Des juifs quittent l'Europe* [Paris: La Jeune Parque, 1948], 9, 10–11; my translation). For an ambitious speculation of how the Jew becomes, for Nazism, the personification of the principle of abstraction behind the evil of capitalism and rapid industrialization, see Moishe Postone, 'Nationalsozialismus und Antisemitismus:

Ein theoretischer Versuch,' in *Zivilisationsbruch: Denken nach Auschwitz*, ed. Dan Diner (Frankfurt-am-Main: Fischer, 1988), 242–54.

36. Hermann Keyserling, in his preface to his *Menschen als Sinnbilder* (Darmstadt: Reichl, 1926), 9. Cf. Wyndham Lewis's far more interesting remarks throughout *The Art of Being Ruled* (London: Chatto and Windus, 1926), e.g., 'Our minds are still haunted by that Abstract Man, that enlightened abstraction of a common humanity, which had its greatest advertisement in the eighteenth century. That No Man in a No Man's Land, that phantom of democratic "enlightenment," is what has to be disposed for good' (375).

37. R. M. Rilke to Rudolf Bodlander, 23 March 1922, quoted by J. B. Leishman in his introduction to *New Poems*, ed. J. B. Leishman (New York: New Directions, 1964), 18.

38. Walter Lippmann, *A Preface to Morals* (New York: Macmillan, 1929), 59.

39. *Sincerity and Authenticity*, 171.

40. R. B. Kitaj, *First Diasporist Manifesto* (London: Thames and Hudson, 1989), 115.

41. *Wall Street Journal Europe*, 23 March 1992, 1.

42. Maurice Bardèche, *Nuremberg: ou, La terre promise* (Paris: Les Septs Couleurs, 1948), 246–47; my translation. The intellectual roots of this attack go back to the critique of the *Declaration of the Rights of Man* by conservative or counterrevolutionary political thinkers, who claim that the 'l'homme en soi' assumed by the *Declaration* is purely abstract, a metaphysical entity. See Hartman, *Fateful Question*, Chapter 6, 'A Culture of Inclusion', 165–203 and cf. Wyndham Lewis, *The Art of Being Ruled* (1926), ed. R. W. Dasenbrock (Santa Rosa: Black Sparrow, 1989). In France, the rural culture to which Bardèche appeals was indeed slow in being displaced by an urban mentality, but it was hardly the peaceable realm he evokes. For a description of peasant life in France, its resistance to administrative measures of the central state, and its gradual change and assimilation to such nationalization, see Weber, *Peasants into Frenchmen*.

43. H. J. Syberberg, *Vom Unglück und Glück der Kunst in Deutschland nach dem letzten Kriege* (Munich: Matthes and Seitz, 1990).

44. See, e.g., Max Weber's review of West European communities, and especially Germany, in 'The Relations of the Rural Community to Other Branches of Social Science,' as translated in *Congress of Arts and Science, Universal Exposition, St. Louis* (Boston: Houghton-Mifflin, 1906), 8:725–46.

45. *I, Pierre Rivière . . . A Case of Parricide in the Nineteenth Century*, ed. Michel Foucault, trans. Frank Jellinek (Lincoln: University of Nebraska Press, 1982; original French edition, 1973), 183. Wordsworth's early 'Salisbury Plain,' however, written but not published in 1793, moves in the same direction.

46. The condition of the French peasant around the time of the French Revolution, in terms of landholding, almost complete freedom from serfdom, yet oppressively heavy taxes and punitive legal discrimination, is described by Alexis de Toqueville in *The Old Regime and the French Revolution* (1856), pt. 2, chaps. 1 and 12. See also Georges Lefebvre, *The Coming of the French Revolution*, trans. R. R. Palmer (1939; reprint, New York: Vintage, n.d.), pt. 4, 'The Peasant Revolution.'

47. 'Kulturkritik und Gesellschaft' (1949), collected in *Prismen* (Berlin: Suhrkamp, 1955). My translation. *Vornehmheit* could also be translated as 'distinction,' in Bourdieu's sense of the word.

48. *Ästhetische Theorie* (Frankfurt-am-Main: Suhrkamp, 1970), 201–2. His main examples are Baudelaire and Poe, but an earlier example of this purposeful contamination could be Blake.

49. Jacques Derrida, 'Force of Law: "The Mystical Foundation of Authority," ' *Cardozo Law Review* 11 (July/August 1990): 919–1047.

50. Leo Spitzer, 'Das Eigene und das Fremde: Über Philologie und Nationalismus,' *Die Wandlung* 1 (1945–46): 576–95.

51. Lewis, *Art of Being Ruled*, 74–75.

52. A problem of the Republican Party in the 1992 presidential elections, most starkly exhibited at the party's August convention in Houston, was defining these so-called non-economic values designated as 'family values' and as 'cultural.' Most notoriously, figures like Pat Buchanan proclaimed a 'cultural' and even 'religious' war to affirm those values. The economic issue was almost entirely sidestepped. Interestingly enough, through the proclamational rhetoric that marks conventions, the term 'value' began to move toward open and flamboyant statement, toward credo-like assertion, shedding the sense of something quietly and unassumingly active.

53. Jean-Pierre Peter and Jeanne Favret, 'The Animal, the Madman, and Death,' in *I, Pierre Rivière*, 176–77 (trans. slightly modified). The irony in this case is that the misery of Rivière's family does not come primarily from poverty but from quarrels about property between wife and husband and the dignity available to them through contract legalisms. '[Pierre's father] identified himself with the being of the Contract, alienated himself in it, and lost himself in it' (180).

Chapter 24

Pastoral Vestiges

We justify the contemplative in terms of the active life. Yet it is possible to argue for the contemplative life even if knowledge is uncoupled from startling practical results, and interpreting the world has little bearing on changing it. One would have to stress a negative virtue: that thought is often pleasurable in itself and does not add to the world's harms even when it discovers more of them. Not a lofty argument, to be sure, but not unconstructive either, since ordinary life might benefit, and a Thoreau can make his beanfield a blessing (a 'bene'). *Walden*'s nature-consciousness becomes the token of a human independence and freedom too often spoiled – as is nature – by more coercive and prophetic types of speculation.

In Thoreau we touch of course the persistence of the pastoral convention in literature. The prophet, especially the American visionary in the Puritan tradition, becomes a shepherd again. Yet can pastoral survive, once we identify its contemplative attitude with the bystander – with the marginal poet, for example? Pastoral presupposes a natural or necessitated life of leisure, song crafted from the position of either apprenticeship or exile. The greater world is there, its pressure is felt, a more potent voice beckons. But pastoral glances at that world through the art of minimalized reference, through a piping that takes pleasure in evoking what a more heroic existence rejects. In 'Soonest Mended' John Ashbery welcomes an unheroic generation, convalescing from the burden of the past, and released into the ordinary:

> To reduce all this to a small variant,
> To step free at last, minuscule on the gigantic plateau –
> This was our ambition: to be small and clear and free.

Today the figure of the bystander is deeply problematic. It has been damaged by the European Holocaust, whose memory revives with every devastating book or testimony. Given the passivity of so many who knew or could have known, is it possible now to 'stand and wait?' Recall Milton's *Lycidas*, where the poet turns to Nature as if its agency could have intervened. I mention Milton because of the enormous difference between the tragedies, and so to recall Adorno's haunting question: Can there be poetry after Auschwitz?

The damage seems to spread from pastoral to poetry, and so to art in general.

To single out the Holocaust does not mean that all other suffering, all other injustice, is depreciated. On the contrary, now the issue of intervention poses itself all the time. 'We cannot not know,' Terrence des Pres has written. A major cultural figure like Havel did not become a bystander at a later time.

The attempt to examine an injustice as extreme and unforgivable as genocide needs a certain coldness, a barrier to rage; and it is possible that pastoral could provide it, if only as an alienation-effect. But the thought that penetrates every defence is that the bystanders remained inert, or even exploited the expulsions and the killings. The civilized world rather than Nature (as in *Lycidas*) was in complicity or stood by. Milton was able to save the pastoral axiom of a sympathetic cosmos by giving it an ornamental farewell – mourning, as it were, over the conceit as well as over his dead poet-friend, exhibiting a style that had been discredited but not entirely disenchanted. Can one, after a tragedy of such different scope, recover the courage for art?

The pastoral mask has fallen, I said at the beginning. If the fate of art is linked to the fate of pastoral – a large claim, not to be substantiated here, and in which pastoral stands over against total demystification – then it is important to seek vestiges of pastoral. All the more so if pastoral restrains, even while it acknowledges, the 'dread voice' of prophetism. Should pastoral fail as a style, as a significant element in perception, what will prevent poetic fury from becoming apocalyptic and turning – as at times in Milton – against the imaginative pluralism of art itself?

Chapter 25

Realism and 'America'

The present debate over the New Journalism, a genre that blurs the boundary between reportage, and fictive interpolation passed off as reportage, helps to focus our increasing sense that realism too is artifice. John Hersey, commenting on Norman Mailer and others, has called himself a 'worried grandpa' of this trend, and he insists that his pioneering book *Hiroshima* (1946) is journalism uncontaminated by fiction. Yet Mailer is not unaware of the problem. He adds a final section to *The Armies of the Night* that moves from a short chapter entitled 'A Novel Metaphor' to a last chapter entitled 'The Metaphor Delivered.' He does not want to write a novel yet feels driven to it by the supermedia effect that haloes every publicized event.

> The mass media, [he writes], which surrounded the March on the Pentagon created a forest of inaccuracy which would blind the efforts of an historian; our novel has provided us with the possibility, no, even the instruments, to view our facts and conceivably study in that field of light which a labor of lens-grinding has produced.

'Dark with excessive bright thy skirts appear,' Milton writes of God enthroned. The correlative, secular darkness that besets the modern reporter is a powerfully expectant emptiness, created by sheer technique: a dazzling 'field of light' which awaits or creates the star-hero that should fill the scene, yet also produces a doom of confusion through overexposure, and blinding, trivial details that disintegrate every starry focus.

So absurd and magnetic is this confusion that a John Hinckley and a Jody Foster, who have no connection, gravitate into the same field of light. Things falling apart induce a crazy causality, as in detective novels. The detective novel, in fact, is one of those fictions emerging to grasp the pseudo-event or eschatological center that cannot hold. As in Nathanael West, as in Pynchon, as in Mailer, the metaphor for this center – America – is never 'delivered' but remains an Andromeda writhing in the male novelist's imagination.

Have you ever looked into Michel Butor's *Mobile*, subtitled 'Étude pour une représentation des États-Unis' (Sketch for a representative Picture of the U.S.) and dedicated to the memory of Jackson Pollock? In this sort of writing there is no 'milieu': there is a repetitive plurality of place names or personal names disclosed by the black spotlight of print as it moves from stage to stage in an orgy of telecommunications. You can break images but you can't break this square eye that penetrates like a blind focus the privacy of every place and sets up an insatiable claim for up-to-date relevance. 'Only connect' then becomes the inhuman injunction of media mentality: if Derrida is prevented from being offered a chair at Nanterre, and Althusser kills his wife, and MacCabe is denied upgrading at Cambridge, the international desk of a famous weekly sniffs out the truffle of a conspiracy and suddenly professes an interest in the hitherto supposedly cloistered academic life. A stringer appears at Yale to tie it all up.

No wonder representation becomes unreal, and must change or purge itself constantly in a kind of permanent revolution. Our reality hunger seeks bigger and better modes of fast-breaking news – until art regains its authenticity through sheer force of askesis. Two directions, then, of representational practice can be identified: the wasting of older forms of realism, since they turn out to be, in retrospect, strongly encoded forms of fantasy; and the salvaging or purification of some of the same forms, as if they were restorative archetypes.

Let me – very briefly – illustrate these two tendencies. In the same year as Butor's *Mobile*, Philip K. Dick publishes *The Man in the High Castle*, usually classified as science fiction. It is by no means the author's best work, and it may not be science fiction: it has no space or time machines. But it is about an alternate version of reality, being set in a postwar world where Germany and Japan as victors have divided the globe between them.

To read *The Man in the High Castle* is a curious experience. By any standard it is bad as art and uninteresting as history. Yet the themes of art and history are all-pervasive. Art and history are made to lose their monumental, fixed, authentic character: they dilapidate into a horribly stylized prose (post-Hemingway, telegraphic, pseudo-elliptical imitation Japanese) that fascinates only conceptually. Two quotations will suffice. Their context is the possibility of an 'American' type of art in a world where Americans have lost the war and are thought incapable of creating anything of value. The only objects appreciated by the occupying Japanese are prewar antiques: old firearms, Mickey Mouse watches, and so forth.

> Getting up, he hurried into his study, returned at once with two cigarette lighters which he set down on the coffee table. 'Look at these. Look the same, don't they? Well, listen. One has historicity in it.' He grinned at her. 'Pick them up. Go ahead. One's worth, oh, maybe forty or fifty thousand dollars on the collector's market.' The girl gingerly picked up the two lighters and examined them. 'Don't you feel it?' he kidded her. 'The historicity?' She said, 'What is "historicity"?'
>
> 'When a thing has history in it. Listen. One of those two Zippo lighters was in Franklin D. Roosevelt's pocket when he was assassinated. And one wasn't. One has historicity, a hell of a lot of it. As much as any object ever had. And one has nothing. Can you feel it?' He nudged her. 'You can't. You can't tell which is which. There's no "mystical plasmic presence," no "aura" around it.'

'The hands of the artificer,' Paul said, 'had wu, and allowed that wu to flow into this piece. Possibly he himself knows only that this piece satisfies. It is complete, Robert. By contemplating it, we gain more wu ourselves. We experience the tranquillity associated not with art but with holy things. I recall a shrine in Hiroshima wherein a shinbone of some medieval saint could be examined. However, this is an artefact and that was a relic. This is alive in the now, whereas that merely remained. By this meditation, conducted by myself at great length since you were last here, I have come to identify the value which this has in opposition to historicity . . . To have no historicity, and also no artistic, esthetic worth, and yet to partake of some ethereal value – that is a marvel. Just precisely because this is a miserable, small, worthless-looking blob; that, Robert, contributes to its possessing wu. For it is a fact that wu is customarily found in least imposing places, as in the Christian aphorism, "stones rejected by the builder." One experiences awareness of wu in such trash as an old stick, or a rusty beer can by the side of the road. However, in those cases, the wu is within the viewer. It is religious experience. Here, an artificer has put wu in the object, rather than merely witnesses the wu inherent in it . . . In other words, an entire new world is pointed to, by this. The name for it is neither art, for it has no form, nor religion. What is it? I have pondered this pin unceasingly, yet cannot fathom it. We evidently lack the word for an object like this. So you are right, Robert. It is authentically a new thing on the face of the world.'

Walter Benjamin's concept of a type of presence he too calls 'aura' and which is lost in the Era of Mechanical Reproduction raises a similar issue. But the context, in Dick, is peculiarly American. Is there an American vulgate? Or are we simply in the degenerate presence of the vulgar? Henry James posed exactly the same question almost a century before and created a compensatory elegance. Dick feels himself to be as vulgar as Henry James; he doubts America as a milieu in which art might flourish. The reader is led to an analogy between Dick's novel and the handicrafts or fakes so important to its theme. The style it offers is crafted from a mixture of precious and trashy materials (from *I Ching*, or *Book of Changes*, and from detective fiction, from the good and the bad in Poe, from Nathanael West, etc.) by a shady artisan in abject surroundings. Dick's novel, at the same time, wants to make a strong and especially American statement. It depicts a period in which art, however contemporary, is doomed to be valued only as always already a collectible, as the relic of a material culture. These modern antiques are basically what they always were, that is, commodities, but now their fetishistic character is clarified. The second excerpt is even more revealing than the first in its iconoclasm: 'wu' is exactly like art or grace – without works. It has passed into an arbitrary body and emanates a dubious charm. It functions like the oracle game that dominates this novel's pseudo-Japanese, quasi-American culture with its elliptical sayings: fortune-cookie formulas derived from the *Book of Changes* via Hammett, Chandler, and the tough tale.

How are we to understand Dick's vulgar but effective attack on our best idols, those of (1) historicity, and (2) realistic representation? There is certainly, as in all science fiction, a release from gravity, celebrated in another context by Norman O. Brown. Yet the mind released from the 'aura' of things uniquely attached to place and time feels a threat of disembodiment. Becoming too light, it projects a total loss of presence – the terror of losing face, here interpreted by Tagomi, the main Japanese character, as losing place. This terror foresees a displacement without remedy, without any cure of the ground. We approach the point – a kind of vanishing point – where representation has lost all face value.

Realism in art – especially the doctrinaire realism of the great novel from Balzac through Proust and Mann – may already be fetishistic, or an aesthetic movement of Restoration. Flaubert's importance, certainly, is that he extroverted the link between realism and its vanishing point – between a fascination with local color and lived reality as the ground of all face value, and the speciousness of every such value. The book, therefore, is but a solid vertigo, expressive of an epileptic rather than epic kind of world.

> I would like to write a book about nothing, a book without external links, which would be held together by the internal force of its style . . . just as the earth without being suspended moves in the air, a book which would have almost no subject-matter, or at least whose subject would be almost invisible, if that is possible.

Sartre links this to the 'internal hemorrhage of being' in Flaubert; and Fredric Jameson to the derealizing effect of a *société du spectacle*. 'Abolishing the real world, grasping the world as little more than a text or sign-system – this is notoriously the very logic of our consumer society, the society of the image or the media event.'

I turn from the wasting to the salvaging of representational form. The obverse of science fiction – its strange jazz-like vortex into which every image of woe and wonder descends – is the askesis of ballet. What is more solid than a Degas painting of those fugacities? Is the surprising later growth of ballet in the midst of media superfetation merely the product of a bourgeois nostalgia, the re-creation of a lost innocence at highbrow level? Is Ballanchine's Candyland another Disneyland, or what Doctorow, in *The Book of Daniel*, names 'Autopia'?

Ballet was never merely pastoral. It is, as it was, a strict competitive genre. Despite its spectacular stage dazzle, the courtliness of this form simplifies complex and sloppy bodies, even the body of desire itself, until light – Mailer's 'field of light' – mingles with pathos to produce a rigorous and self-purgative art. The abstractness of ballet, like that of silhouettes, combines gravity and levity in an orchestrated world that, though full of puppets, dolls, and courtiers, seems animated by the purest kind of mimicry when compared to that other stage world of relentlessly roving and chattering cameras. Ballet is nonfigurative art sustained by the trot of a simple story line.

This counterpoise of ballet's musical automatism to the compulsive and climactic newsworld is not the sole reason, of course, for its appeal. But it is just possible that ballet has become the ascetic and semiotic art we are seeking: one that restores to abstract signification its representational base. For in ballet legs as well as arms become pointers, they write as well as represent the score being performed. This signing or writing by rearticulated limbs suggests a perpetual enjambment, a poem composed for some multiple-membered god of the East. That pen and penis may have a relation through the finer rigidity of ballet, that this physical writing mutes composed bodies without too strong an aura of mutilation but rather of compensation, is a barely conscious factor, though a factor nevertheless.

Chapter 26

The Reinvention of Hate

Rimbaud said that love must be reinvented. But in the century just past hate was reinvented.

It will not be a surprise that even hate has a second nature or constructed aspect. Yet it remains a scandal how far some regimes have gone to culture, as well as acculturate, hate. I refer to the deliberate growth and development, as in test-tube culturing, of an instinct whose origins remain obscure, though it seems closely linked to aggressive self-preservation. I refer also to a culture of hate that is the organized result of such a process.

Usually hate is something we hide; we feel ashamed of it. But this shame may also exacerbate a hate officially sanctioned by party or state. Hate then turns against shame; xenophobia becomes pitiless; the humiliated self scapegoats a group – gets rid of own sense of shame by heaping it on someone else, who is treated as evil by nature, at once responsible and abjectly other. Not all personal shame can be removed, of course – there is too much around – but a specific taboo, such as anti-Semitism, when lifted can become a cultural imperative.

In that case, however, what was once dammed threatens to overflow and flood everything. Because repression and the guilt or shame that accompany it are common psychical facts in civilized society, the hate released is massive. But it feels like a renewal of virility, like breaking through a social lie. Clear identification of the enemy promises true conflict, the establishment of irreducible principles as politics turns fundamentalist. Politically acceptable hate, no longer just instinctive, becomes a rationalized passion supported by ideology. In Nazi Germany it was used as a weapon, even against civilians, both by the military and by a coordinated bureaucracy. Triumphant Nazi documents record a chilling disregard, a ferocious contempt, for the humanity of the victims. Thus civilization succeeds not in diminishing hate but in making it dirigible.

Hatred, linked to anger, is not always ignoble. It inspired the oldest epic in the canon, Homer's *Iliad*, and has a complex tie to revenge as an instrument of justice. Achilles's fury makes him appear larger than life and comes close to being a prophetic attribute. Whether or not poetic furor shares in this attribute, everyone, I will assume, feels a thrill in reading or seeing – at a safe distance – expressive candor breaking through restraint.

Jonah's flight from the mission of prophecy, and the readiness of the Athenians to impose fines on playwrights who offended them, indicate the problematic nature of forceful speech, whatever its motivation or affect. Extreme humor, too – bawdy, or Mikhail Bakhtin's carnivalesque – puts itself as well as its subject at risk. Consider how William Blake plays with strange fire, though he is usually admired (shielded by his canonical status) rather than questioned in this regard.

Blake's 'Proverbs of Hell,' such sayings as 'Prisons are built with stones of Law, Brothels with bricks of Religion,' show him to be a 'Tyger of wrath' rather than a 'horse of instruction.' Indignation as well as a particular rage – against hypocrisy – plays its part in his fierce social critique. (He would have cursed William Bennett for prescribing self-censorship based on 'constructive hypocrisy.') Yet is Blake himself free of a *libido destruendi*, the aggression Freud described in *Civilization and Its Discontents*? His savage clairvoyance, cutting through euphemism and piety, could be motivated by a resentment of the instinctual sacrifices that civilized behavior demands. A libidinal anger certainly animates not only many of his proverbs ('He who desires but acts not, breeds pestilence'; 'Sooner murder an infant in its cradle than nurse unacted desires') but also his over-long allegories of fiery, apocalyptic purgation. They are fuelled by the sevenfold mayhem of *Revelations*: poetic and prophetic fury merge in repeated descriptions of the 'human harvest' at the end of days. The poet intersperses pastoral songs of liberation, singing 'Odors of life,' as he calls them, with orgiastic portrayals of how the new human wine is extracted:

> In the Wine Presses the Human grapes sing not nor dance,
> They howl & writhe in shoals of torment, in fierce flames consuming,
> In chains of iron & dungeons circled with ceaseless fires,
> In pits & Dens & shades of death, in shapes of torment & woe;
> The Plates, the Screws & Racks & cords & fires & floods,
> The cruel joy of Luvah's daughters, lacerating with knives
> And whips their Victims . . .
>
> (*The Four Zoas, Night the Ninth*)

The secret we would like to learn is what makes this fury creative rather than sadistic.

Blake, it must be stressed, attacks the system – priest, king, government, the ideology of natural religion – rather than a scapegoated group. And he claims that his poetic pyromania is really a depiction of 'mental fires.' Yet at what point, or under what circumstances, does figurative speech explode into literal belief and harmful performance?

Allow me a passage *à la limite* by way of an incongruous comparison – for Blake's cutting speech and a military commander's savagery seem at first worlds apart. In an official report it was disclosed that the Bosnian Serb commander General Mladic, had summoned U.N. peacekeepers and ordered a pig's throat slashed in front of them to show how he would evacuate the Muslims from the safe haven his forces had taken, if his conditions were not met. Is this symbolic speech, or a form of terrorism? We know that the threat in this figure was fulfilled. A rictus followed rhetoric's open mouth.

Having found a sanctioned target, uncivil hatred relishes naked expression. It was hard for contemporaries to take literally the venomous rage of a Louis-Ferdinand Céline or the shameless, vituperative journalism that sprang up in Germany and Occupied Europe under the influence of National Socialism. It is hard to believe even now that the language found in, say, the newspaper *Je Suis Partout* was meant, as well as meaningful, and that it intimidated and infected a mass of people. Leon Poliakov, in his *Bréviaire de la haine* (Harvest of Hate), recalls how a Wehrmacht guard reacted in 1940 when a prisoner (Poliakov himself) said he was a Jew: 'But why do you tell me this? In your place I would rather die of shame than admit it.' Such a reaction could not have come about without a relentless propaganda that segregated the Jews as unclean, shameless and irremediably evil in a Manichaean world strictly and comprehensively divided into sacred and profane.

Jews became not only legal outcasts but objects of sacred horror. As Robert Kanters (quoted by Poliakov) has pointed out, 'From the simplest to the most important act, from entering a café to marrying, [a German] can do nothing without first taking care to recognize the barrier that separates the two worlds.'[1] Blacks in the United States and South Africa have been subjected to a similar apartheid, but in Germany the war against the Jews was all the more vicious because, almost indistinguishable in physical and cultural characteristics from other Germans, they had to be marked to prevent them from 'passing.' Yet nothing could mark the assimilated Jews adequately. Julius Streicher's caricatures were sadly, laughably crude and relied mainly on claiming to expose the Jews' two-facedness – their cunningly disguised Orientalism under the assimilated surface. The attempt to separate Jew from German escalated from defamation to isolation, then to Jews' being expelled from the professions and stigmatized by a special passport stamp, a tribal name (Israel, Sarah), and the yellow star. Eventually all were deported, imprisoned in ghettos and concentration camps, subjected to slave labor, torture, random murder, and, finally, systematic extermination.

I shall return to this fatal usurpation of all life by a political religion. My initial and more innocuous question is: Can we learn anything from literature about a social order based on hate and hate speech?

There is a telling moment in Milton's *Paradise Lost*, when Satan first sees Eden, the earthly paradise. The fallen angel addresses the sun in a powerful and peculiar monologue, culminating in a curse that contains a reluctant blessing:

> to thee I call,
> But with no friendly voice, and add thy name
> O sun, to tell thee how I hate thy beams
>
> (4.35–37)

Satan's naming, though not unlike Adamic naming, is also a parody of it and transforms acknowledgement into hate. Satan spits out the name. Outcast and spoiler, he recalls his former sunlike state and is afflicted beyond despair by a sort of protest against beauty and innocence, a protest close to jealousy. Involuntarily, therefore, he hails the creation.

Hate, as this depiction suggests, need not lack a connection to love. An equivocation of words or ambivalence of feeling may enter – but this is an undesired or unconscious complication that incites even more ferocity in the attempt to purge the emotion of anything except itself. Let me instance a dramatic gesture in Shakespeare's *Troilus and Cressida* (it should be compared to the Serb general's strategy and chilling warning). Achilles conceives a sinister desire to look at Hector before their fight. He summons the Trojan and gloats over him to locate exactly where he will inflict the fatal wound:

> Tell me, you heav'ns, in which part of his body
> Shall I destroy him? Whether there, or there, or there,
> That I may give the local wound a name;
> And make distinct the very breach whereout
> Hector's great spirit flew.

In this symbolic aggression (a boast that seeks to weaken the enemy hero, to break his spirit) the virtual wound is on the way to becoming a real wound, whether through magic, psychological warfare, or imitation of the divine fiat. The directness, moreover, of Achilles' speech, its vicious, spear-like pointedness, mimics something that is intrinsic to hate as a passion. It has found its object; its aim is now unambiguous; the conversion seems complete of a powerful emotion that could have gone in the direction of love (here, homoerotic love) but is expressed as hate and contempt. I am not sure hate can be isolated, as in a chemical table of elements, from other destructive emotions, yet if we allow the similarity of anger and hate, we spot the obverse of its passionate simplification in Jakob Boehme's 'Love is wrath quenched.'

In any attempt to grasp the passion of hate, two aspects, then, must be recognized. First there is the simplification effected by hate and hate speech. They combine to find a very specific target. Naming is used as a fatal weapon to stigmatize the person or group. Naming and shaming merge. Then there is the link of hate with repressed jealousy, with the resentment of a creative power or glory (even an election) from which the hater feels excluded. But like a demiurge, the hater creates a counter-domain, in reality or fantasy. This domain is a hell rather than a chaos. The hater, that is, strives to solidify it as a counterworld with clear if bloody confines. It is not nothing, and not limbo; it is the hater's heterocosm, a sacred space that has definitively broken with pieties and substitutes rigid rituals. The one thing this alternate reality cannot be is indirect – teeming with ambiguous situations, uncertainties, unintegrated elements , like the world in which we ordinarily live. Given this intolerance of the human condition, Theodor Adorno's hyperbole shocks but also makes sense. 'Genocide,' he wrote, 'is absolute integration.'

It is uncomfortable to recognize the frustrated creativity in hate, the idealism gone bad. But at least this insight saves us from another simplification, itself not devoid of resentment. Inspired by Marxism, it attempts to explain the hierarchical hell of the Nazi camps as an inverse, demystified image of capitalistic society, a stripping naked of its exploitative nature. This perspective is found, for instance, in David Rousset's remarkable *The Other Kingdom* (L'univers concentrationnaire), written immediately at the end of the war. Yet Rousset was right in calling the camps a universe and in describing how precise their rituals were. The amazing pseudo-legality by which so many areas functioned in the Third Reich achieved its deadliest triumph in the camps. Hierarchy and regulation, however arbitrary, were all in all. Nothing, supposedly, was left to chance; every action was in principle dictated or bureaucratically automated. Yet even in the death camps accidents, or a sudden intervention, could save a life, or, rather, defer a death. Hate is reversible, in spite of the mental and emotional walls it deliberately constructs so that no ambivalence or 'uncharted' desire can penetrate.

There is some truth, then, in popular fictional representations of the criminal world as a social order with its own rules – much more 'clean-cut,' on the whole, much less ambiguous, than rules in our own grey ambivalence-ridden life. Within that new order, of course, something always breaks down and betrays it, because the dirt of love enters the machinery of hate, or something unanticipated and sentimental, perhaps a striving to get from the artificial to the real light, or a memory of the 'outside,' infiltrates disruptively. The criminal's totalizing fantasy, the illusion of creating a personal world, secure, heroic, invulnerable, is as improbable as the movies that exploit it, and needs ever stronger fantasies to shore it up.

Varlam Chalamov, a survivor of Kolyma, protests literary depictions of the underworld by Victor Hugo and Fyodor Dostoyevsky, who had never known, as he had in Stalin's Gulag, the career criminal. He says they romanticize him and make him attractive by suggesting the survival of a core of charity within his coldness and ruthlessness. Although such charitable 'weakness' may exist, the underworld's attraction is quite different, according to Chalamov. He confirms that organized crime is a cosmos, even in prison: a highly structured order, and with a blood tie that is achieved not necessarily by having blood on one's hands but rather by a family-like submission to a veteran in-group.

The young, according to Chalamov, are particularly vulnerable to the world of crime. Its fascination goes beyond cloak and dagger and secret rites. More crucial is their recognition of a powerful group that has thrown off the scruples and cares that preoccupy their families at home; and they escape, in particular, the torment and queasiness of adolescence. By a real and bloody game, whose psychological tension is far more addictive and defining than disciplinary brotherhoods in the legitimate world – the police, the military, the Society of Jesus – they are forced, and wish to be forced, into premature manhood. Chalamov's picture of the young initiate is, I think, reliable testimony, and I wish to quote a small part of it:

> Penetrating with beating heart the underworld, the youngster associates with people who terrify his parents. He observes their pretended independence, their false liberty. He mistakes their bragging and bravado for cash. He considers them as men who have challenged the existing social order . . . He does not think of the pain of the other, of the shed human blood which represents what his hero has stolen and which is present without accountability . . . He dreams about the final touch, his definitive affiliation with the order: the prison, which he has been taught not to fear.[2]

Hatred as a principle of order divides humanity coldly into friend or enemy, family member or alien, and builds this division, this split, into an easily recognized, all-encompassing mode of existence, one that has no room for equivocation or straying sympathies. We rediscover at this point the disconcerting fact that cultures often see themselves founded on a schizophrenic simplification: on a crime, like a war or a massacre, that is at best ambiguous or unintelligible, at worst morally unredeemable, yet must become an unchallenged foundation. We also pass here from a special development within nation or collective, from how a counterculture of hate takes hold, to a theory on the formation of cultures generally.

In spite of recent efforts to envisage a multicultural nation with a wide tolerance for difference and dissent, political history shows rather that the greater the disunity or fear of civil war, the louder the call for a clear rededication to oneness through symbols of order that stigmatize opposition and even criticism as fatally subversive. The brave experiment of parliamentary democracy aims, of course, at overcoming this anxiety about pluralism. But our fearful imagination is not assuaged. It always senses behind what is firmly established the threat of a return of the repressed, of anarchic terror of some kind; and the ensuing tension requires – at least symbolically – an object of 'sacred horror' to relieve it, to delimit the fear by giving it shape. Every unsolved murder also incites that fear, which may be related, in addition, to the sporadic outbreak of witch-hunts and scapegoating. To illustrate the role of sacred horror, I turn briefly to a poet's reaction to the civil war in seventeenth-century Britain.

Andrew Marvell, reflecting on Oliver Cromwell's career after the regicide, adduces a strange episode from the founding of Rome:

> So when they did design
> The Capitol's first line
> A bleeding head where they begun
> Did fright the architects to run;
> And yet in that the state
> Foresaw its happy fate.[3]

The king's beheading, Marvell suggests, provides that bleeding head for his own era. It is a happy omen in spite of the 'fright' it elicits, and legitimates the new order. The decisive event is here shielded by a symbol, an augury whose sacred horror consecrates Cromwell's continued forceful actions. It sends a message that wounds of this kind are fortunate and necessary, that the integrity of the body politic is paradoxically secured by them. Yet Marvell's irony or equivocal poise, though its edge is keen, refuses to take sides, to speak for the future, to 'cut' through the issue.

Terror – the terror of war, murder, bloodshed, and violence, but interpreted as a sacrificial necessity – is basic to national myths of birth or rebirth. Perhaps the emblem of Greater Serbia should be a pig's bleeding head. In much the same way the New Germany made the Jew into a desecrating horror to be removed from the *Volksgemeinschaft* by expulsion or, if necessary, bloody purification. Decisive foundational events often center on such a redemptive purge. Especially in terms of nation-building: the new or renewed culture wants to be absolutely clear – clearer than nature itself – about who is pure and who a contaminant. It pretends there is nothing in common between itself and the racial enemy.

Yet, as the proverb states, 'Nature loves mixtures.' Race purity, as a foundation of the new Reich, was doomed to fail, though not before exacting its sacrifice. There were many 'Aryan' look-alikes; ironically, it was the assimilated Jews who at that time disproportionately supported Germany's high culture. A ridiculous bureaucracy developed, therefore, as well as blade-runners called the S.S., devoted entirely to the detection and liquidation of the Jew.

A fascinating moment in the film *Shoah* comes when Claude Lanzmann interviews Franz Grassler, second in command of the 'Jewish District' (that is, ghetto) of Warsaw. Why were the Jews walled in? To control typhus and other epidemics, Grassler answers. But, Lanzmann retorts, quoting Adam Czerniakow, the Jewish head of the ghetto, hadn't the Germans always identified the Jews with typhus? 'Yes, it is possible.' A figure had become literal fact and metaphor murder. The Jews were disease itself; the entire state bureaucracy was based on racial hygiene. Such rage for order, incited by an ineradicable ambiguity, is merely an exaggeration of what Chalamov discerns as lust for 'definitive affiliation' with 'the order.' Intellectuals, I must add, are as tempted by extreme political solutions as anyone else; perhaps even more, insofar as they suffer from hermeneutic perplexity and the endlessness of judgment.

Let me conclude by recalling an example I have written about before, which illustrates how a deliberate culture of hate is created. The plot of a typical Nazi-sponsored work, published in 1938, *Rabauken! Peter Mönkemann haut sich durch* (Rowdyism! Peter Mönkeman fights his way through), takes the form of a Bildungsroman. Peter, a young veteran of World War I and the Freikorps, copes with the disorder of the Weimar Republic and discovers that at all levels it is dominated and corrupted by Jews. To fight his way through and expose them demands that the true German modify his feelings and cultivate a murderous hate. But will this not produce a paralyzing self-disgust and spread over the human image in general? The novel suggests that only a diseased or noxious member is targeted, as in surgery. Yet there is no 'safe hate.' Given the explosive nature of anger and hate, to release those emotions is a tricky process. *Rabauken*, with its vulgarized Nietzschean message, is far from being stupid or irrational; it solves the difficulty by presenting the German character as innately sensitive and so requiring the suspension of that sensitivity where Jews are concerned. Nazi propaganda cultivated the image of a new stern breed of German who is asked to kill without mercy to 'create [by genocide] a better and eternal Germany for our descendants.'

Consider Mönkemann's outburst, when Dr. Singer, an influential Jew, mocks the notion that a small number of Jews (less than 1 percent of the population) could harm Germany:

> If someone notices the first sign of lice in his lodgings, and does not immediately fumigate – radically so, with poison gas and other substances – his pad will later be full of them and he won't be able to save himself from the vermin. Then the lice become masters in his own house. And this fumigation, [Mönkemann] adds, feeling the pressure and the hate, we have forgotten about. Unfortunately, it just didn't occur to us idiots.

The protagonist feels besieged or under pressure (in *Bedrängnis*) because he cannot entirely repress (*verdrängen*) an oversensitive conscience. This prevents the truth about Jews from getting through and has made the Germans forget their native virility. The lice-imagery and other bestial tropes, moreover, which dehumanize the Jews, are like an expression of peasant anger that remains ineffective as long as it is purely personal, without popular support and organizational backup. The anger must become policy: cold, calculated anti-Semitism.

At the same time, instinctive rage and outrage free the hero from repression and exalt him beyond enervating restraints. At one point he takes over the stage of a nightclub to denounce the Jewish danger to a startled audience:

A young warrior [Recke] stands there – who can divine the agony of his soul and the greatness of the hate goading his blood – a young churl, built like the son of a god, with flashing eyes of fire, ready to pounce like a panther, and as if he were already measuring the distance between himself and his deadly enemy.

So this is the New Man – in embryo, of course, since he symbolizes a frustration and powerlessness that only organization (the party) will redeem.

However unpleasant it is, we have no choice but to study the structure of these demagogic ideas. Mönkemann's outburst touches on deep feelings: losing one's home, losing control, pollution, radical disgust. We are but a step away from the propaganda films of 1940 and 1941, which develop his analogy by depicting the Jews as a repulsive swarm of plague-bearing rats. Metaphor becomes murder when the dehumanization takes effect and poison gas is no longer a figure.

Why was this pornography of hate tolerated? How could such crude propaganda be effective? We do not know how many Germans actually believed what they were fed. Freedom of expression disappeared very quickly after 1933: passive collaboration, opportunism, and fear make it hard to judge the true state of conviction on this matter. Yet we can infer from anti-Semitic strata in France and Belgium what was effective as a rationale, and it had to do with the idea of a defence of culture. Where we detect a nearly fatal attack on culture, intellect, and civilized values, these strata, in their xenophobia and anti-Semitism – which was their only unifying bond, for many in France were anti-German – saw themselves as saviors of a degenerate society. French anti-Semites represented the exposure and expulsion of foreign elements as a Defence of the West, even though the Nazi ideal often presented itself as anti-French and anti-Western. (From the left, too, the cry arose that civilization had to be defended – against fascism.)

The rationale of anti-Semitism, then, was quite clear. It appealed to a widely shared anxiety about national decadence and even genetic degeneration. Novels like *Rabauken* insinuated what Nazi slogans disseminated stridently: the culture of the *Kulturvolk*, its potential as a *Herrenvolk*, is endangered, especially from within. The nation must be alerted to this danger, because in its very humanity the German character is reluctant to recognize the evil. Only if the Germans are instructed by ideology and the new racial science to look closely enough, only if they overcome liberal sentiments – about human equality, pity, and successful Jewish assimilation – will they penetrate beyond the mask, perceive irredeemable difference, and end equivocation. The Nazi *Kulturkampf*, in short, claimed to be a defence of culture, not its nemesis. Deliberate, organized hatred became a sanctioned principle of order, and we know with what result.

Notes

1. Léon Poliakov, *Harvest of Hate* (Syracuse, NY: Syracuse University Press, 1954).
2. Varlam Chalamov (or Shalamov), *Kolyma Tales*, trans. John Glad (New York: Norton, 1980).
3. Marvell, 'An Horatian Ode upon Cromwell's Return from Ireland.'

FILM

Chapter 27

Jeanne Moreau's Lumière

The movies are our epics; and the formulaic or quotational nature of artistic transmission can be studied there to effect This is because of the voracious demands of the medium, which must be fed, if necessary, by recycled plots and images, its wide dissemination (one can hardly not undergo the influence of particular movies), and the closed character of the international community created in the process of filming.

Jeanne Moreau's *Lumière* is yet another story about the actor's life. Its special twist is that Jeanne Moreau herself has written and directed it – but such a twist or trope is not my concern. I am interested in the fact that a film as derivative or quotational as *Lumière* – so full of what might be called movie diction – can be a powerful statement.

To examine the resemblance between Moreau and Bergman is not sufficient, though it may be one beginning for appreciation. *Lumière* is a film that catches the imposed or self-willed discontinuities in the actor's life: the 'cuts' (Moreau, who plays the actress Sarah Dedieu, collects knives) that are of the essence in cinematic composition. In a typical Bergman film, and most brutally perhaps in *Face to Face*, habitual life is suddenly invaded by a radical uncertainty. This sudden arrest of the natural rhythm is not motivated any more than a heart attack might be, and Bergman uses psychoanalytic inserts for their imagistic rather than explanatory power. Existence is cut, formally, by something known only through its effects: even clock-time cannot be trusted; persons must talk themselves, as a mother does with her child, into trusting the next step; the simplest words have to be recovered; no relation holds. We classify what happens in *Face to Face* as a 'psychotic episode,' but it resembles very closely what actors provoke in themselves as they switch back and forth between a daily self and the framed self-image which they assume in front of the camera.

Correlative with the tyranny of 'Cut!' is the imperative 'Lights!' and Moreau's film has chosen to develop the resonances of that figure. Her film is luminous. More subdued and tender than Bergman's usual mode (his camera can caress, but when his characters caress it tends to draw blood), it is indebted to Truffaut's conception of the romantic thriller. Yet Moreau's touch, however womanly, does not disguise the hard glare of the action. We learn how the person in the actor responds to an exposure demanded by those 'lights,' an exposure outrageously justified by an ethos of total submission to auteur or director or the wish to transcend all shame.

It is a world, then, where identity is created out of nakedness. Careers may begin with pornography and rise into loftier blues. And they knew that they were naked: that trauma, or desire, is repeated in various ways by the actors' willingness to live within a circle of fire created by the searchlights of camera and set.

Lumière depicts this intensification of the human condition. After an awkward expository scene introducing us to Sarah Dedieu and three other women, we are switched to Paris and the 'fatal week,' whose focus is to time what spotlight is to character. The awarding of the 'Prix Diamant' to Sarah is to climax that week, and it reunites her with three women friends: two of them young actresses at different stages of their careers, and Laura, an older Italian friend of fifteen years' standing. Scenes from Sarah's life of scattered intimacies are shown as they converge on the award ceremony, which also brings together the men in her orbit. The awarding of the prize is made to coincide with Sarah's attempt to commit herself to marriage, or a steady relationship; but in the aftermath, which includes the death of one of the men she relies on, Sarah returns to her cinematic role of 'femme fatale' – that is, to the next 'shooting.' Despite the film's stereotyped plot and its reliance on Jeanne Moreau as the only developed character, it sets up a moving contrast between the dehumanizing demands of the cinematic medium and the residual womanliness brought by Sarah to each relation (with women even more than with men).

I come now to a crucial moment of formal quotation in the film. The play on names (consider Heinrich Grun, Saint-Loup, Sarah Dedieu) prepares us for it, as does the affecting scene where Grun, a German novelist who wants to live with Sarah, hands her a torn page with scribbled lines of faulty French, which Sarah proceeds to read to him. His love letter speaks for him through her voice: his muteness allows or demands (auteur-like) her complicity. It is the test or trial for a 'shooting' that may not take place. Writing, in short, precedes the complicity of the individual in its utterance, approximately as a given or proper name defines the person who bears it.

The crucial moment I refer to arrives as the action verges on a death. By certain devices Jeanne Moreau makes us feel that death is imminent – there is too much insomnia around, and the act of love seems to have lost its dream-like power to entice or extend sleep. The need for rest becomes absolute, although we are unable to say who must die in order to achieve rest for us. We anticipate a suicide, a Liebestod of some kind, motivated by a despairing or frustrated imagination.

Just before death chooses Grégoire (a fatherly friend of Sarah's, associated with a detached attitude toward death because of his clinical study of tumors), an apparently unmotivated scene occurs. We accept it because it fits in with the atmosphere of an actor's life. Someone plays a recorded voice reciting in French: 'La Trobe leant against the tree, paralyzed. Her power had left her. Beads of perspiration broke on her forehead. Illusion had failed. "This is death," she murmured, "death." '

The intrusion of this voice is ghostly, gratuitous, premonitory. We sense, if only casually, an 'It is Written.' The action that is going on, and about to reach a climax, has gone on before, is going on elsewhere too: we are dealing with a universal drama. The recorder's uncanny expansion of the frame of reference could be compared to that of the chorus in Greek tragedy. What there is stylized and apodictic – a voice powerless to intervene yet often movingly banal – is here a technical input, and recognized at first only as something cut out of another frame (and cut off). In short, a quotation.

Yet it is an allusion as well as a quotation; and to recognize that precipitates discovery. The voice is reciting a passage from Virginia Woolf's *Between the Acts*, a novel she had almost completed at the time of her suicide. One of the young directors in Moreau's film is called Saint-Loup. Moreau is herself directing this film: so she is 'Sainte Loup' – that is, 'Virginia Woolf.' As in *Between the Acts* there is a question whether the director has the power or inspiration to bring the play to its end. The 'Hour of the Wolf' has come, that indeterminate moment which Sarah actually talks about and which Bergman has used effectively in a film of that title. The action falters, it needs a death, and perhaps it falters because of that realization.

Hearing of Grégoire's death on waking up after a night of love – at last she has slept well – Sarah complains of the light for the first time: of the 'Lumière' of the sun entering her bedroom. She understands how her life between the acts is infected by acting, which is a light to prevent the real light from coming in. We rarely see Sarah in sunlight: she is a screened figure, moving about in the movie world's artificial day and night. Now the sunlight punishes her or makes her as guilty as Racine's *Phèdre*. It reveals the devouring character of a theatrical and usurping light that is far more exposing, that leaves an actor no hope of cherishing a secret, whether 'Grégoire' or a child in the womb. An actress is by definition without child – a sterile Sarah.

Finally, of course, the quotation from Virginia Woolf stands for 'Virginia Woolf.' It is a charged symbol for the career or life of the woman writer aspiring to room, child, a creation: this film of her own. *Lumière* takes leave of Jeanne Moreau, alias Sarah Dedieu, as she submits to the next act, to the hysteria of makeup, lights, directors; as she handles the gun that symbolizes the crime passionelle which, in this film, we never get to see – perhaps because it is really a crime against herself already committed, perhaps because it is the trivial implicate of all those shooting lights.

Indeed, the metaphor of 'shooting,' which transfers a property from gun to camera, suggests that art starts beyond that crime or invests it in the formalistic power of the medium. Moreau's spectacle about spectacles contains, therefore, an unavailing scruple. To be seen is to be sinned against: the drive toward visibility or exposure is almost a religious passion, a suffering that must be undergone. Why? To break the images, to see 'Nothing that is not there and the nothing that is' (Wallace Stevens), or to transcend the self-images called roles and again achieve a kind of invisibility. Perhaps invulnerability, for to be seen is also to die – of shame; but only so that shame may die. In the Moreau of this film there is a tender coldness, as if she had become clairvoyant. The subdued darkness of this Snow Woman is especially remarkable in her voice, which moves deliberately fast and glitters like a gun you see, then don't see.

The end of all this shooting is that a new self is born, free as a 'star.' Yet the star must be a woman again, and the reverse metamorphosis is not completed in *Lumière*, though aspired to. A star and yet a woman too – Moreau has tried to create a work of art in which the character of actress is 'half-hidden from the eye,' and nurturance, shelter, motherhood, are not excluded. The pathos of the film resides in that hope which her friend Laura (pregnant, monogamous, family-centered) represents.

The generalizing power of quotation and allusion mediates raw visual desire: the image-centered, even pornographic wish that films struggle with. In terms of an extension of Aristotle's poetics to film dramaturgy, this wish coincides with what is there called the 'scene of pathos' or 'the suffering,' and it may parallel Freud's 'primal scene.' The poetic – that is, artistic – cinema works against the grain of its own power to represent graphically – as flesh-writing – scenes of this kind. Films are, like surgery, so crude yet sophisticated an intervention that their potential to expose the psyche to phantasms of every kind calls for a Rousseauistic scruple; and it is interesting that Jeanne Moreau has drawn this out of a reflection on the woman writer and woman actor.

Her film, in its deliberate cosmopolitanism, wanted to make contact with Virginia Woolf, but what it represents is a New Eloise, a woman who realizes like Rousseau's Julie 'the nothingness of human affairs.' She differs from her, of course, in agreeing to marry the cinema, as nuns marry the Church. Jeanne Moreau, in her film, embodies a fatality closer to the spirit of Rousseau's novel than to Laclos's *Liaisons Dangereuses*, or fictions inspiring her other roles.

Chapter 28

Spielberg's Schindler's List

As a film that conveys to the public at large the horror of the extermination, *Schindler's List* is entirely successful. The mass scenes are heart-rending: the liquidation of the ghetto, the enticement and deportation of the children from the camp, the mothers rushing the convoy, and later, the exhumation and burning of the bodies (a scene from hell). The scale is deliberately varied: from the brilliant opening, matching the smoke of the extinguished candle and the smoke of the locomotive, to Schindler's hilltop observation of the exterminating action, to the close-ups in the apartment buildings (the chaos of terror made physically painful to the viewer's eyes by handheld, unsteady cameras, as if the eyes had to be punished for what they could not feel). Then back to the hilltop and the extraordinary glimpse of the little girl in the red coat wandering alongside and apart from the murders and roundups, as if on an ordinary kind of walk. Then the desperate effort of the boy to find a hiding place, and ending in a sewer. The sheer assault on the lifeworld of the Krakow Jews as well as on their persons could not be rendered more effectively than when the contents of the suitcases are emptied, first at the deportation center, where the spoliation is clear, then during the ghetto's liquidation, when even spoliation ceases to matter, and the contents and then the suitcases are contemptuously thrown over the banisters.

We have learned that technique is never just technique: it retains a responsibility toward the represented subject. This link of responsibility distinguishes Spielberg here. The difference between close-ups and long shots is utilized again and again: uncomfortably but tellingly we sometimes see the action as if through the telescopic sights of Goeth's (the Nazi commander) murderous rifle. The imperative to make everything visible is not modified by such distancing; rather, the viewers' eyes are more fully implicated. We are made aware of our silent and detached glance as spectators removed in time and place. Neither the creator of this film nor its viewers can assert, like the chorus in the *Oresteia*: 'What happened next I saw not, neither speak it.'

Yet, as I realized later, the premium placed on visuality by such a film made me deeply uneasy. To see things that sharply, and from a privileged position, is to see them with the eyes of those who had the power of life and death. There is no convincing attempt to capture a glimpse of the daily suffering in camp or ghetto: the kind of personal and characterizing detail which videotestimony projects record through the 'lens' of the survivors' recollections.

Nor is there an attempt to explore the behavior of the main protagonists. Spielberg has been commended for not making Schindler transparent or seeking to illuminate the mystery of his compassion. While we do not need or want an 'explanation,' both Schindler and Goeth remain stylized figures that fail to transcend the handsome silhouettes of the average Hollywood film. The madness of Goeth is made believable simply by the madness of the war and particularly this war against the Jews; and there is no conversion or turn in Schindler that is expressly highlighted. Seeing the brutal liquidation from the hilltop may have played its part; but it is only when 'his' Jews are fated to be sent to Auschwitz that he shifts decisively from making money to spending his money to buy them back. The scene in the cellar between Goeth and Helen Hirsch, and in Goeth's house between Schindler and the drunken camp commander on the subject of power, are psychologically credible, but their frame remains a crude and deadly game of power.

Goeth's offhanded, as if casual murderousness, moreover, especially when he toys with sparing the young boy who has sinned against cleanliness (the neurosis is barely hinted at), can be perversely humanizing. Against our will, we are made to identify with the hope that something in this man is redeemable, and that the boy will be saved.[1] The pathology against the Jews, moreover, is always expressed in actions rather than words, as if no argument or introspection were needed. Only in defence of Schindler, imprisoned for kissing a Jewess, does Goeth trot out some garbage about the spell cast by those women, which betrays his own acted-out fascination with Helen Hirsch. The film's pace remains that of an action movie which tolerates no diversion except to increase suspense: it 'clicks' from shot to shot, from scene to scene, with the occasional mechanical failure symbolizing a chance for human feelings to reenter the sequence.

Spielberg is always precise, with a special ability to translate history into scene and synecdoche. Yet his tendency toward stylization is both distancing and disconcerting. The wish to encompass, through the episode of 'Schindler's List,' the enormity of what happened in Krakow and Plaschow, leads to moments approaching Holocaust kitsch. The SS officer playing the piano during the liquidation of the ghetto, and the 'Is it Bach? No, Mozart' comment of the soldiers who hear him, is an unnecessary touch; I feel the same about the scene with the 'Schindler women' in the showers at Auschwitz, which is melodramatic and leaves the audience confused (like the terrified prisoners, in that crucial moment of uncertainty, when the lights go out) about the issue of disinfecting showers and gas showers. The episode, however, in which Goeth vaunts that he and his troops are making history, because the Jews who settled in Krakow six centuries ago will have ceased to exist by day's end, is important, and recalls Himmler's Poznan speech.

Poster effects, that make this very much a Hollywood film, will show through even more with the passage of time. While a certain flatness in the characters may be inevitable in a panorama of this kind, and strengthens the mass scenes and 'actions' that convey so ferociously Nazi callousness and terror, the focus on Goeth on the one hand and Schindler on the other is too clean, like the killings themselves, which are quick and neat, though always shocking in their cold-blooded nature. Two of the three endings of the film are also Hollywood: the farewell scene in the factory is stagey, and Schindler's breakdown (concerning his not having saved enough Jews: had he only sold his car, his gold Nazi pin, etc.) detracts rather than adds; the survivors walking en masse toward the sunset with 'Jerusalem the Golden' sung by an angelic offstage chorus (in Israeli showings of the film, I understand the song was changed to 'Eli, Eli'), while giving a certain comfort after all those scenes of mass victimization, is again Hollywood or fake Eisenstein. This sentimentality is redeemed only by the final sequence; it takes us out of docudrama, and presents the survivors, the Schindler remnant, together with the actors who played them, as they place a ritual pebble on Schindler's tombstone in the Jerusalem graveyard.

Claude Lanzmann takes a radical position in a comment on *Schindler's List*, writing that the Holocaust, 'is above all unique in that it erects a ring of fire around itself . . . Fiction is a transgression. I deeply believe that there are some things that cannot and should not be represented.'[2] I too believe in the possibility of reticence: that there are things that should not be represented. Yet because our modern technical expertise is such that simulacra can be provided for almost any experience, however extreme, it is more today a question of should not rather than cannot. What should not be represented remains a moral decision; a choice that does not have to be aggravated by a quasi-theological dogma with the force of the Second Commandment.

It is true that the more violence I see on the screen, through real-time reporting or fictional re-creation (all history sooner or later returns as film, to use a phrase Anton Kaes has popularized), the more I rediscover the wisdom of a classical poetics that limited direct representations of violence or suffering, especially on the stage, and developed instead a powerful language of witness or indirect disclosure. The idiom of violence should not be routinized and become, as so often in the movies, an expectation, even a default setting. Though genius may breach any decorum and overcome our abhorrence, as Shakespeare does when he shows Gloucester's blinding on stage, it is clear that repeated depictions of *to pathos*, as Aristotle names those bloody scenes, will desensitize rather than shock, especially when art enters the era of mechanical reproduction. The Rodney King tape, shown over and over again, turns into an icon, a barely expressive metonymy.

In short, Spielberg's version of *Schindler's List* can be faulted on two counts.

One is that it is not realistic enough. It still compromises with Hollywood's stylishness in the way it structures everything by large salvational or murderous acts. The stylishness, in fact, leads often to stereotype and visual cliché. But the second is that the very cruelty and sensationalism of the event, reconstructed through a spectacular medium, exerts a magnetic spell that alone seems able to convey the magnitude of the evil. Viewers of this powerful film are surely troubled by the question that Adorno has renewed concerning the pleasure we take in tragedy; or they may wonder how its spell, so close to voyeurism, could have been modified. The 'ineluctable modality of the visual,' with its evacuation of inwardness, fixates imagination more than the formulas of oral tradition. Artists have always, in one way or another, rebelled against the tyranny of the eye.[3] A self-conscious commentary intruded into such a movie is no solution: it would merely have weakened its grip as docudrama, or postmodernized the film. Spielberg has created a fact on the screen, and the moral challenge passes to the viewers. Can we, either during the movie, or as those images recall themselves in the mind, become like the Percival of legend, who must decide what to ask or not to ask of an extraordinary sight? There is no guarantee, of course, that the questions we ask – not only about how the Holocaust could have happened, but what is to be done now that it has happened – will be redemptive.

In the debate about this film the major issue becomes: What are the characteristics of an authentic depiction of the Shoah? 'Authentic' is a heartfelt yet slippery word. I have to rephrase the question: How should we value a graphic, cinematic realism of Spielberg's kind, seemingly unconscious of itself (that it remains a fiction of the real) and which elides (except for the last scene) the passage of time and the relation of memory to reality?

To answer this question I seek the help of two other well-known films about the Holocaust. Claude Lanzmann in *Shoah* rejects all archival images or simulacra (except the model sculpture of the gas chambers and crematoria): he keeps the film in the present, the time of composition reuniting survivors and the original (now deceptively peaceful) scene of their suffering. He animates that scene by an action of the survivors' own memory, and even – as in the case of Bomba, the Auschwitz barber – by using props to assist a painful return of the past. In this radical and principled work, the presence of the past is evoked primarily through human speech, through testimony; and so the film is anything but archival, or a historical simulacrum.

Lanzmann too is very much, in his presence as director and questioner, a part of this present. His questioning can become, not just with the perpetrators but also with the victims, a pressured interrogation. Occasionally this creates a problem. For he does not appear to be all that interested in the survivors' afterlife – the way their daily reality is still affected by a traumatic past. Instead, with relentless directorial insistence, he recovers and communicates every detail of how the 'Final Solution' was implemented, every aspect of the death machinery's working, of the technological Mammon that demands its sacrifice. That is the 'reality' he brings home in all its technical and bureaucratic efficiency. Stunning, disconcerting, obsessive, and either hypnotic or tedious, *Shoah* is a film that does not entirely spare Lanzmann himself, who is shown to be – in the service of his cause – ironic, manipulative, and anything but likeable. To his credit, however, he does not seek to explain the obscene facts by a Marxist or any other thesis. 'There is no Why here,' he quotes (in a later comment on the film) a concentration camp guard's welcome, recorded by Primo Levi.

In Haim Gouri's trilogy that opens with *The Eighty-First Blow*, precisely what Lanzmann rejects is the very base of the representation. Reality is depicted exclusively through archival images. But individual memory does enter, via the voice-over of survivors who comment on the events – a tangle of voices with its own richness and variation, and in no simple way subordinated to the photomontage. These images and voices have to speak for themselves: though sequenced, there is no other effort to bring them into compositional time, which Lanzmann never departs from. Yet the director's didactic if invisible hand remains palpable. In *Flames in the Ashes*, for example, the part of Gouri's trilogy that deals with resistance, the issue of why Jews did not put up more fight is 'answered' by footage of defeated Russian soldiers, columns of them stretching to the horizon in an endless line, utterly dejected, guarded by very few Germans, and scrambling abjectly, like animals, for cigarette butts or food.

Neither Gouri's nor Lanzmann's films are primarily about memory in its relation to reality. Although Lanzmann composes his film as an oral history, his interviews are used to reconstruct exhaustively and exclusively one aspect of the Shoah only – the most terrible one, its end-phase, the 'Final Solution,' together with the technology and temperament that made it possible. Gouri's focus is more varied, less obsessive, but he must compose the visual track mainly in the 'idiom' of the perpetrators, since most of the photos at his disposal (especially in *Flames in the Ashes*) were made by the Nazis themselves for propaganda documentation.[4]

The very format of voice-over adopted in Gouri's trilogy is reminiscent of newsreels shown in the old movie theatres. Goebbels's propaganda machine exploited the format blatantly in such films as *Der Ewige Jude*. But in Gouri the excited and triumphant monologue of the announcer has given way to a spirited montage of voices. His documentary gains its integrity from the fact that it invents or reconstructs nothing. It struggles, rather, with a mass of received materials: utterances, images, musical score.[5] They are all 'clichés.' Gouri is symphonic, a conductor rather than a director; and though his emphasis remains on reportage, the structural gap between visual footage and voice-over makes the film both less unified in its realism and more interesting from a formal point of view. A picture, here, is not worth a thousand words but requires these words (the voices of the survivors, in their timbre as well as their message) to humanize it, to rescue it from voyeuristic hypnosis.

Yet Gouri never develops his technique in order to portray memory as either its own place, evolving its own stories or symbols, or in a competitive situation. The relation of cinematic image to voice-over (voix-off, the French say) is not problematized as in the *Hiroshima, Mon Amour* of Alain Resnais and Marguerite Duras. Different lifeworlds – that of the Japanese man and the French woman, that of the aftermath of the atomic bomb and the aftermath of the Nazi occupation – are juxtaposed in that film; while soundtrack and image are sometimes at odds. Today, as we recede from the original event, and identity – personal or collective – is increasingly based on publicized memories, there is bound to be an even greater tension between different 'cultures.' These are now defined by what is rescued from oblivion or singled out for remembrance by modes of representation, reception, and transmission.

However different their films, both Lanzmann and Gouri avoid an invasive technological gaze. We have become painfully aware of that gaze since Vietnam, Biafra, Somalia, Bosnia, Rwanda.[6] For it is no longer unimaginable that some of the terrible scenes reconstructed by Spielberg might have been filmed in real time – as if that present were our present – and piped almost simultaneously into our homes.[7] Those who watch *Schindler's List*, therefore, face the dilemma I have already mentioned. How do we respond to such sights? In our very impotence, do we protest and turn away, or find some other defence? Have we no choice but to demand that these representations be labelled unpresentable? How can we morally accommodate the fact that 'what others suffer, we behold'?[8]

Schindler's List has not only achieved popular acclaim but is being prepared for widespread use in the schools. This suggests that all my reservations and questions have missed a very basic point: as the Greeks (though not the Hebrews) maintained, a clear picture of what is feared can moderate that fear. It may be fundamentally affirming to 'sing in the face of the object' (Wallace Stevens) as Spielberg incredibly seeks to do.

Yet even Spielberg cannot pass beyond the limits of realism. Although there is a bona fide attempt to follow the facts and to be accurate about the Jewish milieu depicted (how much his errors or compromises detract from the overall picture will remain in dispute), so much in the movie is structured like a fiction, so much is like other action films, even if this one is based on documented history, that the blurring of history with fiction never leaves us free from an interior voice that murmurs: 'It is (only) a film.' This happens not simply when the film is most vulnerable – when it is not about the Holocaust at all but stages a homoerotic psychodrama, scenes of tense mutual jockeying between Goeth and Schindler – but also when episodes like the liquidation of the ghetto force us into a defensive mode by the sheer representational power displayed. Visual realism can induce an 'unreality effect.' Hans Jonas is reported to have said that 'At Auschwitz more was real than is possible.'

Though Spielberg's gaze seems to me problematic, we should explore the questions it raises. And while I prefer Gouri's and Lanzmann's alternate modes of representation, almost the obverse of each other and more respectful than Spielberg of the action of memory and the issue of presentability, there is no need to insist dogmatically on a single type of realistic depiction. I want to describe briefly other exemplary modes, especially those that respect the action of memory.

In the case of Aharon Appelfeld (whose novels have not yet been filmed) memory is an absent presence. We are made to feel the scorching flame that animates his characters but we never see it consciously displayed as a haunting or unbearable force. We know something has displaced their life or basic trust or vital faith, yet memory's 'fire,' as Appelfeld calls it, is subject to a perpetual curfew.

His novels stand out, in fact, for not singing in the face of the object; he does not describe the Shoah directly, only before and after. The survivor is often his theme, but not the specificity of Holocaust memory. He refuses the slightest hint of melodrama, focussing instead on the daily life of human beings who have difficulty living in this world after what they have gone through, yet cannot escape into political or religious mysticism. They want to do something with a life, their life, that was spared, but continue to feel guilty and out of focus.

Like Helga in *The Healer*, there is always a sick person who seems to take on herself the symptoms of an obscure illness; but that illness is intermittent, cut across by an extraordinary earthiness and a horizon where that earthiness is not opposed to faith. Yet there has been a fatal separation between faith and feeling, orthodoxy and assimilation. Jewish emancipation has not fulfilled Jewish needs. If we ask, given his characters' lack of orientation, where are they going, it is tempting to answer with Novalis: 'Immer nach Hause,' 'Always home.' That underlying nostalgia is close to a death-drive.

A sense of spiritual waste emanates from Appelfeld's stories, exacerbated by the shiftless biological energy his characters display, and by strong, though discontinuous moments of physical pleasure in nature, in just being alive. There is no purposeful dying but also no rebirth. Yet it is rebirth that is at the horizon of all this aimless wandering. The irony in many Appelfeld novels, from *Age of Wonders* and *Badenheim* on, is that a post-traumatic condition, which requires no extreme effects of art to represent it, begins to resemble the human condition as a whole. So the insouciance or innocence of his assimilated Jewish characters (a trait that makes them sleepwalkers in an increasingly hostile environment) is not unlike that of camp inmates who have passed through the worst. Both groups display a hypnotic alertness, where everything is registered by the senses yet meaning and affect seem rarely to get through. A movie in their mind (which we cannot see) makes the survivors wander about restlessly, up and down, back and forth, ever wakeful though wishing to sleep it off. In the case of the assimilated, pre-Holocaust Jews, the restlessness seems to come from a haunting lack of memory: they are described as 'ego floating on the surface of consciousness.' For both groups, then, getting away from the past, its fullness or emptiness, is not enough: they crave a distraction – even an ecstasy – as deep as nature itself, or an anti-self-consciousness principle as subsuming as art.

Often, therefore, Appelfeld evokes a magical but recuperative sleep, midway between amnesia and gestation. Of the youngsters who finally reached Israel, he writes: 'After years of wandering and suffering, the Land of Israel seemed like a broad, soothing domain, drawing us into deep sleep. Indeed, this was our desire: to sleep, to sleep for years, to forget ourselves and be reborn.'[9] An extended psychic absence is the necessary prelude for healing, for a rebirth that has a distinctly aesthetic dimension, in that empathy returns to what was previously merely observed.

'We must transmit memory,' Appelfeld has written, 'from the category of history to that of art.' A question arises concerning that program: do his novels veil historical memory too much or do they save the specificity of art in an age of brutal realism? The problematic reaches beyond Holocaust-centered representations. A film like Resnais's *Last Year at Marienbad* is distinguished by its deliberate, stylized entanglement with the absence rather than presence of memory – with memory-envy. In its chill and elegant way, it parallels Appelfeld's distancing: a decisive event is presupposed, a virtual lieu de mémoire that cannot be brought to life, that refuses to become a living encounter.[10] Yet that there was, once, a place and a time of real encounter continues to exert its seduction. The French classicism of the film is, by way of both the sterile setting and the actors' deportment, a protest against another kind of seduction, that of contemporary realism. At the same time, it succeeds in starkly shifting the focus to a man and a woman who must perform their minuet with little to help them except a memory that is more unreal than real: memory here remains the mistress of illusions.

In a similar yet also startlingly different way, the German filmmaker Alexander Kluge refuses to allow the 'forces of the present' – our programmatic realism – 'to do away with the past and to put limits on the future.' His movies come to terms with the past and its continuing pressure by incorporating images of ruined or deserted Nazi architecture. These negative lieux de mémoire, once glorified by Nazi films, serve as a reminder of the 'eternity of yesterday.' Symptoms of a fatal collective dream that has not really passed away, they play on in the *Kinotier*, the 'cinema animal' (Kluge's phrase) we have become.[11]

What is to be done with that cinema animal: how can it be nurtured, but also trained? Memory and technology have become correlative themes. If, by a new fatality, everything returns as film, then not only is the present endangered as a site of experience, but also the past. The Soviet joke that 'the past is even less predictable than the future' takes on a broader significance, one that encompasses us too. The authenticity of past and present is imperilled not only by Enlightenment philosophies of progress, which elide everything for the sake of the future, nor just by the selfishness of each Now Generation, but also by a subversive knowledge that information technology can infiltrate and mediate everything, so that our search for authentic or unmediated experience becomes at once more crucial and desperate.[12]

That context strengthens the importance of a new genre of representation, the videotestimony, which is cinematic and counter-cinematic at the same time. Formally, videotestimonies make a double claim: they convey 'I was there,' but also 'I am here' – here to tell you about it, to take that responsibility despite trauma and pain, despite the divide between present and past. The 'I am here' is the present aware of the past but not seeking its grounding there – for it finds not a ground but a destabilizing abyss, a murderous ditch like the one victims were forced to dig for their own corpses. Thus the position of the Holocaust survivor expresses a much more difficult juxtaposition of temporalities than past and present. In the survivors, aware of new generations, aware of their own decimated community, truth and transmissibility enter into conflict. Some such tension has always existed: Gershom Scholem senses it in the veiled procedures of the mystic, and Walter Benjamin in the peculiar world of Kafka's imagination. But this time we know from photos, from film, from documents, very precisely what happened, and what makes the story so difficult to tell. The chilling facts, however, are not the only thing the witnesses seek to give, or what we want from them. Rather, their 'I am here' balances the 'I was there' and recalls the humanity of the victim who has to survive survival. There was life in death then, there is death in life now: how is that chiasmus to be honestly recorded?

It is here that technology both helps and hinders, and we see a new genre emerging. The video-visual medium has its own hypnotism, but it becomes clear, when one views the testimonies, that its effect is, in this instance, more semiotic than hypnotic, that the medium both identifies and differentiates persons who have been through a wasting and dis-identifying experience. Every time we retrieve an oral history in this form, even when, tragically, it tells of Treblinka or Auschwitz, technology helps to undo a technology-induced sameness. For the more fluent we become in transmitting what we call our experience, the more similar and forgettable the experience becomes. What had previously to pass through the resistant channels of tradition is now mediated by a superconductive technical process that seems to promise absence of friction and equal time (equal light) for everyone. Hence a subversive feeling about the interchangeability and replication of experiences – a replication implicit in the technological means of their transmission.[13]

Testimonies are, as a genre, not limited to recording witnesses of the Holocaust: 'testimonial video' is a more general contemporary phenomenon that links memory and technology in order to rouse our conscience and prevent oblivion. But the relation between memory and technology is especially problematic when the experience to be transmitted is traumatic. As I have indicated, the more technically adept we are in communicating what we call our experience, the more forgettable the latter becomes: more interchangeable and easily simulated. Yet Holocaust testimony, in particular, uses video to counter a video-inspired amnesia. A homeopathic form of representation is being developed.

While not exempt from error and unconscious fabulation (especially forty and more years after the events), these audiovisual documents allow occasional spontaneous access to the resurgence of memory as well as to significant details of daily life and death, which conventional history used to pass by. Memory is allowed its own space, its own flow, when the interview is conducted in a social and non-confrontational way, when the attempt to bring memories of the past into the present does not seek to elide a newer present – the milieu in which the recordings took place. Since the period in which they will be viewed is not the period in which they were recorded, just as the period of recording is not the time of the original experience – a pattern challenged by 'real-time' video, or 'The Assault of the Present on the Rest of Time' – a temporal complexity is created very close to the dimensionality of thought itself, and which undermines the attempt to simulate closure, or any kind of eternity-structure.[14]

Let me give an example of that temporal complexity, inseparable from the rhythm of memory when expressed in words. In one of the Yale videotestimonies a woman tries to describe her state of confusion during a Nazi 'action.' She wraps her baby in a coat, so that it appears to be a bundle, and tries to smuggle it by a German guard who is directing the Jews to left or right. She says she holds the bundle on her left side, thinking she will rescue it that way; but that memory is already a confusion, showing the strain she was under in making choices. As she passes the guard, the baby, who is choking, makes a sound; the guard summons her back, and asks for 'the bundle.'

At that point in her story she utters a 'Now,' and creates a distinct pause. It is as if by that 'Now' she were not only steeling herself to speak about what happened next, but seeking to recapture, within the narrative, the time for thought denied her in the rushed and crucial moments of what she had lived through. She goes on to describe her traumatic separation from the baby: she wasn't all there, she claims, or she was numb, or perhaps, she implies, she is imagining she had a baby – perhaps she has always been alone. Even Jack, her husband, she says later on – slipping to another nowtime as the camera pans to him (and for a moment we think she is saying that even with Jack she has remained alone) – even Jack didn't know her story, which she revealed to him only recently, though he too is a survivor. When, just before this moment, she admits she gave the officer the baby, she does not say 'the baby' but 'the bundle' (a natural metaphor, sad and distancing, yet still affectionate, perhaps a Yiddishism, the 'Paeckel'): 'He stretched out his arms I should hand him over the bundle and I hand him over the bundle and this was the last time I had the bundle.'[15]

I remember in a shadowy yet haunting way a moment in one of Resnais's films (I believe it was *Muriel*, set in the period of the Algerian war and revelations of torture by certain elements of the French army), when a home movie is inserted, and the muteness of the medium seems to heighten our sense of the mutilation (physical, psychological, or both) inflicted on the woman who is its subject. Emptied of sound, those scenes screamed all the more. I also remember them in black and white, and contrasting with the color film; but I may be wrong about that. The crude tape was like a play within a play, and I thought of the mime in Hamlet, that serves to catch the conscience of the king. Here as there the irruption of an archaic medium takes us out of the temptation to smooth over or aestheticize what happened. Breaking the frame suggests that a crude form of realism may be closer to the truth than its sophisticated version. Silenced memories live on silently.[16]

That Spielberg shoots in black and white has an archaic effect and could have been a temporal distancing, but it seems post-color, so rich a tonality is achieved. Spielberg made the right choice; yet the film needed also an internal contrast to relieve what I have called its invasive technological gaze and to respect unglossy aspects, the graininess and haltings of memory. So Gouri, at the end of *Flames in the Ashes*, presents an epic array of photos, creased rather than glossy, and in a static flow of images quite unlike the film's erratic though fluent montage up to that point. But Spielberg seems always in a hurry, or in love with mimesis, with the motion and hugeness of a medium that has retained its magic, and which he stages, whatever the subject, for the sake of the child in us – for the children whose murder, though not directly shown, is his most terrible and poignant theme.

It is the child in the adult that remains Spielberg's theme even here: the abused and disabused child. Cinema addresses that sin against the child – not only, as in *Schindler's List*, by terrifying us with pictures of a mass infanticide, but also, in general, by reviving a link between the adult memory and the childlike imagination.[17] For our increased ability to recover the past through historical research or psychotherapy is abetted by technology's proficiency with simulacra. Yet Spielberg's art is not primarily retrospective, because the child and the adult differ as 'cinema animals.'

The child (in us) still learns through wonder; for young people the past can never catch up with the future, with freedom, with possibility. Who can forget, in Spielberg's *Close Encounters of the Third Kind*, the boy's face when his toys spontaneously light up, start up, come alive? That mixture of innocence and wonder, an expectant gaze that says 'I always knew you were real, you were alive' is unforgettable. Whatever our age, when we enter the cave and become 'cinema animals,' we also re-enter a realm of possibility. Our feelings are freed – even for the sinister subject, for a film like *Schindler's List*, which reconnects them with a knowledge we had desensitized or relegated to footnotes. But the adult, as distinct from the child, is a 'cinema animal' also in a more disturbing way.

Now the ability to reproduce simulacra, or to think we see memories – in fact, to call them up and project them onto the wall of the cave – can make us their prisoner. They are no longer toys, companions, comforters, masks endearing rather than frightening, whose silent smiles or grins disclose, ever so intimately, a mysterious realm. In a society of the spectacle, strong images are what property or the soil is often said to be: a need of the soul. If the incidence of recovered memory seems to have increased dramatically in recent years, it may be that images of violence relayed hourly by the media, as well as widespread publicity on the Holocaust that leads to metaphorical appropriations (Sylvia Plath is a famous case), have popularized the idea of a determining trauma. It is understandable that many might feel a pressure to find within themselves, and for public show, an experience equally decisive and bonding, a sublime or terrible identity mark. The wound of absent memory may be greater than the wound of the memory allegedly recovered, and which, however painful, recalls a lost intensity, a childlike aura.

In a powerful and precise essay, 'La mémoire trouée' or 'The Memory Full of Holes,' the French writer Henri Raczymow speaks of a double vacancy that affects his identity as a Jew.[18] There is the loss of traditional Judaism, which Bialik captures in his poem 'On the Threshold of the House of Prayer.'[19] The Haskalah or Jewish Enlightenment had already created, before the war, a diaspora within the diaspora: many Jews could participate only intellectually and nostalgically in a communal life which, viewed from a threshold never crossed, seemed warm and appealing. This loss is made more rather than less acute by the realization that the mourned reality was a sentimental construct, and could not now be expressed except in fiction, or 'by sewing scraps together.' But the second loss for Raczymow's generation (the children and grandchildren of the survivors) is what Nadine Fresco has called 'the diaspora of ashes': the physical and cultural destruction of Jewish communities, especially in Eastern Europe.

Raczymow, whose family came from Poland, does not seek to impose his sense of an absent or ashen memory on anyone else. But the way he situates himself as a writer helps us to think about the fact that Spielberg too must be situated. There is no universal or omniscient point of view, however objectifying the camera-eye may seem to be. So the brilliance of *Schindler's List* reflects a specifically American kind of optimism. This optimism does not make a statement about human nature (presenting Schindler as a hero need not cancel out Goeth, or atrocities never before depicted so vividly) but rather a statement about film as a technology of transmission which differs from writing as Raczymow conceives it.[20] For Spielberg the screen must be filled up; he brings to life what we know of the documented history – in that sense he does not 'recover' memory at all but enables its full transmission as imagery. Raczymow, in contrast, both as a Jew and a writer, lives the paradox of having to express a double void, and becomes, in the words of Maurice Blanchot, 'the guardian of an absent meaning':

> My books do not attempt to fill in empty memory. They are not simply part of the struggle against forgetfulness. Rather, I try to present memory as empty. I try to restore a non-memory, which by definition cannot be filled in or recovered. In everyone there is an unfillable symbolic void, but for the Ashkenazi Jew born in the diaspora after the war, the symbolic void is coupled with a real one. There is a void in our memory formed by a Poland unknown to us and entirely vanished, and a void in our remembrance of the Holocaust which we did not live through. We cannot even say that we were almost deported.[21]

Notes

1. This insidious optimism is reinforced by the structuring theme of the film. J. Hoberman points out in a symposium on *Schindler's List* in the *Village Voice* (March 29, 1994) that Spielberg chose a story in which the meaning of the camps' deadly selection ritual is reversed: 'The selection is "life," the Nazi turns out to be a good guy . . .'
2. *Manchester Guardian*, March 3, 1994, 15, translated from *Le Monde*.
3. For this and the next paragraph cf. Chapter 10, 'Holocaust Testimony, Art, and Trauma,' in Hartman, *The Longest Shadow* (Bloomington, IN: Indiana University Press, 1996).
4. An exception is footage of the Eichmann trial in Jerusalem, which deeply influenced him (see his *The Man in the Glass Booth*), as well as many of his compatriots.
5. In Alain Resnais's *Night and Fog*, one of the early (1955) if not the earliest attempt to work with archival footage (much of it familiar now, through that film), what one feels most is the dilemma: what can be done, morally, visually, with such atrocious images? In Resnais's 'essay,' then, scenes appear sometimes too composed, and the recited monologue that serves for voice-over too poetic, even if deliberately so.
6. '[T]his is what the white ones cannot understand when they come with their TV cameras and their aid. They expect to see us weeping. Instead they see us staring at them, without begging, and with a bulging placidity in our eyes.' 'I opened my eyes

for the last time. I saw the cameras on us all. To them, we were the dead. As I passed through the agony of the light, I saw them as the dead, marooned in a world without pity and love.' From the *New York Times* op-ed column of January 29, 1993, by Nigerian novelist Ben Okri.

7. According to journalist Richard Schickel, Spielberg said that he 'wanted to do more CNN reporting with a camera I could hold in my hand'; he also reportedly told his cast 'we're not making a film, we're making a document,' *Time* (December 13, 1993): 75.

8. See Terrence des Pres, *Praises and Dispraises*. An unsparing use of archival footage can also, of course, raise that question, as in Resnais's *Night and Fog*. But this seminal movie intended to shock viewers out of their ignorance or indifference. Its assault on the viewer is only modified by an 'essayistic' effect, achieved by Resnais's formal virtuosity of composition and Jean Cayrol's voice-over.

9. 'The Awakening,' in Hartman, ed., *Holocaust Remembrance: The Shapes of Memory* (Oxford: Blackwell, 1993), 149. Also Appelfeld, *Beyond Despair*, introduction and Lecture One. In the case of survivor immigrants to Israel, the 'sleep' was induced by a suppression from without as well as a repression from within: Zionist ideology had, on the whole, contempt for Old World Jews and insisted on refashioning them.

10. Appelfeld's American contemporary, Philip Roth, refuses to fast in the French way – which remains quite sumptuous – and does not give up anything of his own art and comic gift, because the Holocaust is not his theme. He manages to endow Anne Frank with an alternate life as Amy Bellette, the focus of Nathan Zuckermann's fantasies in *The Ghost Writer*, just as he transposes Kafka into a Czech refugee who outlived his work and becomes an unknown Hebrew school teacher in New Jersey. See the fine article of Hana Wirth-Nesher, 'From Newark to Prague: Roth's Place in the American Jewish Literary Tradition,' in *What is Jewish Literature?*, ed. H. Wirth-Nesher (Philadelphia: Jewish Publication Society, 1994).

11. See the presentation of Kluge's thought in 'The Assault of the Present on the Rest of Time,' *New German Critique*, 49 (1990): 11–23.

12. Gertrude Koch observes, in the *Village Voice* symposium (March 29, 1994), how even the 'realism' of *Schindler's List* is mediated by film history: 'he recycled every little slip of film that was made before to produce this film.' She thinks Spielberg tricks us into believing – through a 'rhetoric' presenting powerfully what we seem to know or have actually seen before in other Holocaust movies – that it happened exactly like this. But this is a problem with every realistic film, although it can be argued that the stakes here are higher. I prefer to treat this problem as one concerning Spielberg's elision of the perspective of personal memory.

13. Critical thought, therefore, looks for residues of technology in every product, in case the truth has been modified to achieve transmissibility. The era of simulacra is necessarily an era of suspicion. Walter Benjamin is the literary source for these reflections, extended by Guy Desbord and Jean Baudrillard.

14. On testimonial video generally, see Avital Ronell, 'Video/Television/Rodney King: Twelve Steps beyond The Pleasure Principal,' in *Differences: A Journal of Feminist Cultural Studies*, 4 (1992): 1–15.

15. Bessie K., Holocaust Testimony (HVT-205), Fortunoff Video Archive for Holocaust Testimonies, Yale University. See also Lawrence L. Langer, *Holocaust Testimonies: The Ruins of Memory* (New Haven: Yale University Press, 1991), 49.

16. Since writing this, I was able to see *Muriel* again. The home movie projected in the film is indeed silent, but it does not show Muriel's torture directly. Bernard (the French soldier who has returned from Algeria) narrates the abuse as a voice-over that accompanies images of the daily life of the soldiers, as they fight or train, mingle with civilians, mug for the camera. A powerful and typical Resnais counterpoint is created between two incompatible memories: a series of harmless images, picture postcards in motion, and a hauntingly absent – fantasized or covered up – reality. It is interesting to recall that this film, subtitled 'Le Temps d'un Retour,' and with a screenplay by Jean Cayrol, was released ten years after *Night and Fog*.

17. Historians like John Boswell in *The Kindness of Strangers* have begun to document the prevalence of infanticide. They make us aware how deeply the love of children is accompanied by a fear and resentment of them. Deborah Dwork, in *Children with a Star*, records the pain of children caught up in the Holocaust, but also the love that saved them, and she establishes the importance of the oral history of child survivors. Judith S. Kestenberg's 'International Study of Organized Persecution of Children' has created an important archive. Finally, I might mention Jean-François Lyotard's *Lectures d'enfance*, which are basically meditations on the 'infans': the relation in the human being of mute to representable, a relation that can never satisfy a haunting 'debt' contracted at birth.

18. Originally presented as 'Exil, mémoire, transmission,' and translated (slightly modified here) from 'La mémoire trouée,' *Pardès*, 3 (1986): 177–82, as 'Memory Shot Through with Holes,' in *Yale French Studies*, 85 (1994): 98–105.

19. The word 'Beit Hamidrash' in Bialik's title means 'House of Study' as well as 'House of Prayer' and points to an integration that is among the things now lost.

20. The concept of writing, in Raczymow, is certainly influenced not only by the post-war 'New Novel' (which he mentions) but by a longer genealogy that includes Mallarmé and Proust. The cultural revolt in French literature against realism – and often within it – was more programmatic and consequent than in England and America. Moreover, several important authors, some Jewish, some not – they include Blanchot, Jabès, and Derrida – link the integrity of writing to its 'Hebraic' questioning of (realistic) image-making.

21. Raczymow, *Yale French Studies* 85 (1994): 104.

The Interpreter's Freud

Freud alone proves Emerson's observation that a significant institution is the shadow of a great thinker. We cannot understand Freud without understanding the peculiar quality of his greatness: that quality which made him, which still makes him, a scandal, a shadow we negotiate with. He has imposed on us with the force of a religion. 'One must have a very strong and keen and persistent criticism,' Wittgenstein remarked about Freud, 'to see through the mythology that is offered or imposed on one. There is an inducement to say, "Yes, of course, it must be like that!" A powerful mythology.'

Freud, however, wished to found a science of mind and not a mythology. His first major book on *The Interpretation of Dreams* planted the banner of rational and methodical inquiry in the very swamp of unreason, where few had ventured and, of those, very few had come back, their sanity intact. Yet these rationalist aspirations of psychoanalysis by no means disprove its redemptive and communitarian nature. Though psychoanalysis is not a religion, it still exhibits many features of past religions, including reasoning about unreason, about the irrational forces we live with and cannot entirely control.

Where is language in this field of forces? Especially the language of the interpreter as it takes for its subject other language constructs presenting themselves as textual, like literary artifacts, or as a mysterious code belonging also to another medium, like hysterical symptoms or dream images. It is not necessary to overemphasize what we have learned about language since Freud and again since Lacan. The discourse of the analyst remains within the affective sphere of the discourse it interprets; it is as much a supplement as a clarification; and instead of an ascetic and methodological purism, which isolates the interpreter's language from the so-called object-language, creating in effect two monologues, we have to risk a dialogue in which our own often unconscious assumptions are challenged. 'The analysand's discourse,' André Green has written, 'is a stream of words that . . . the analyst cannot shut up in a box. The analyst runs after the analysand's words.'

In psychoanalysis especially, because it involves transference and counter-transference, because it puts the interpreter, not only the text or person interpreted, at risk, this exchange of words does not always lead to an urbane dialogue. The word dialogue, in fact, is deceptive, for there may be, in this situation, more imposition and resistance, more 'crisscross' or crazy connections than when Dostoevsky or, for that matter, Hitchcock, gets strangers together on a train. The Romance of the Railroad penetrates the interpreter's discourse, which hurtles toward its uncertain destination along a branching track of words with exotic expectations, mysterious switches, and – hopefully – good brakes.

To understand Freud's power as an interpreter (whether or not we agree with his findings or their claim to be scientific) it is necessary to read him with an attention solicited by his own immense culture, in which a sensitivity to language stimulated by literature played its part. I begin, therefore, by taking a sample from *The Interpretation of Dreams* to give it a close, literary reading. It is equally important, however, to gauge the transferability of Freud's interpretative method. The second half of my essay, then, will take up a nonanalytic text, a poem of Wordsworth's, and do two things: see it in a Freudian context, but also see Freud in its context.

It is a striking truth that literary analysis, like Freud's dream analysis, does no more and no less than disclose a life in images or words that has its own momentum. Ambiguities, overdetermined meanings, and strange linkages are more obvious than the coherent design they seem to flee from. 'My thoughts crowd each other to death,' Coleridge wrote. He finds himself in the grip of what he named 'the streamy nature of association'; in his Notebooks, especially, not only the dreams he puts down but also his speculative etymologies and related word chains accelerate into a futile 'science of the grotesque' (a phrase I take from Kenneth Burke's fine essay on Freud, in *The Philosophy of Literary Form*). But many writers acknowledge explicitly an experience similar to that of 'racing thoughts.' 'I often felt the onset of madness,' Flaubert confesses. 'There was a whirl of ideas and images in my poor mind, and my consciousness, my ego, seemed to be foundering like a ship in a storm . . . I played with fantasy and madness, as Mithridates did with his poisons.' Or Keats, in a lighthearted vein:

> I must be quaint and free of Tropes and figures – I must play my draughts as I please . . . Have you not seen a Gull, an orc, a Sea Mew, or any thing to bring this Line to a proper length, and also fill up this clear part; that like the Gull I may dip – I hope, not out of sight – and also, like a Gull I hope to be lucky in a good sized fish – This crossing a letter is not without its associations – for chequer work leads us naturally to a Milkmaid, a Milkmaid to Hogarth Hogarth to Shakespeare Shakespeare to Hazlitt – Hazlitt to Shakespeare and thus by merely pulling an apron string we set a pretty peal of Chimes at work.

'A pretty peal of Chimes . . .' Keats's insouciance puts us at an equal distance from the purely formal character of rhyme, as it suggests a flirtatious harmony, and the tongue-tying phenomenon of clang associations. When Freud encouraged 'free' association in himself and his patients, he simply took the burden of self-judgment away, so that this inner speech, to which Flaubert and Keats allude, might be fully disclosed. *The Interpretation of Dreams* remains a disconcerting work because of this: Freud's interpretive method is not as separate as one might expect from the dream which is its object. Both dream and dream analysis are streamy, associative structures. The only difference between reported dream and analytic commentary is that the dream is more elliptical in the way it passes from sentence to sentence or image to image. Freud's interpretation fills up these ellipses or 'absences' in the dream; as Keats too is aware of having to fill in spaces by moving figures across a chequer board without being checked.

Quite often too, like Keats, Freud introduces explanatory material that branches off with a digressive life of its own – especially when that material is a name. An example will be helpful here. In trying to understand a dream about three women, one of them making dumplings (Knödel), Freud recalls the ending of the first novel he had ever read, in which the hero goes mad and keeps calling out the names of the three women who had brought him the greatest happiness – and sorrow. One was called Pélagie; and by a path at least as eccentric as that of Keats, the three women become the three Fates; Pélagie becomes a bridge to the word 'plagiarize,' which then also throws light on Knödel as a name (the name of a person) rather than a common noun. Suddenly everything alliterates or 'chimes.' Here is a portion of Freud's analysis from the section on 'Infantile Material as a Source of Dreams' in Chapter 5.

> In connection with the three women I thought of the Fates who spin the destiny of man, and I knew that one of the three women – the inn-hostess in the dream – was the mother who gives life, and furthermore (as in my own case) gives the living creature its first nourishment. Love and hunger, I reflected, meet at a woman's breast . . . So they really were Fates that I found in the kitchen when I went into it – as I had so often done in my childhood when I was hungry, while my mother, standing by the fire, had admonished me that I must wait till dinner was ready. – And now for the dumplings – the Knödel! One at least of my teachers at the University – and precisely the one to whom I owe my historical knowledge . . . would infallibly be reminded by Knödel of a person against whom he had been obliged to take legal action for plagiarizing his writing. The idea of plagiarizing . . . clearly led me to the second part of the dream, in which I was treated as though I were the thief who had for some time carried on his business of stealing overcoats in the lecture-rooms. I had written down the word 'plagiarizing' without thinking about it, because it just occurred to me; but now I noticed that it could form a bridge [Brücke] between different pieces of the dream's manifest content. A chain of associations (Pélagie – plagiarizing – plagiostomes or sharks . . . – a fish's swimming-bladder) connected the old novel with the case of Knödel and with the overcoats, which clearly referred to implements used in sexual technique.

This is not the end: a further train of thoughts immediately takes off from the 'honored name of Brücke,' leading ('as though the need to set up forced connections regarded nothing as sacred') to the memory of Fleischl (Fleisch: meat), a second respected teacher, linked to Freud's experiments with cocaine in what he calls the Latin Kitchen (the dispensary or pharmacy).

In literary studies we often ask what the genre of a work may be. It is a question raised when the reader confronts a new or puzzling form; and it certainly arises when we read *The Interpretation of Dreams*. It is hard to call the book a work of science, and leave it at that. Often the fugual connections and especially the word chains are not furnished by the manifest content of the dream: and though they may belong to the dream thoughts they do so only by virtue of an analysis which is interpolative and like an elaborate joke. One is reminded of Freud's own aphorism: 'The realm of jokes knows no limits.' What, then, is the genre of this book?

My quotation from the Knödel dream suggests that Freud finds a strange and original way to write a Confession. I mean an autobiography that lays bare whatever it may be – certainly sexual wishes, guilt feelings, and social envy, as well as the infantile emotions that spur the quest for scientific fame. *The Double Helix* is nothing compared to Freud in disclosing the libido of science. 'Freud's frankness,' Kenneth Burke wrote, 'is no less remarkable by reason of the fact that he had perfected a method for being frank . . . what for him could fall within the benign category of observation could for [others] fall only within its malign counterpart, spying.'

It is the reversal of malign into benign and vice versa, which risked, as Burke saw, a 'drastic self-ostracizing act – the charting of the relations between ecclesia and cloaca.' Freud's Confession, entitled *The Interpretation of Dreams*, even transcends Augustine's and Rousseau's, because in addition to a very moving if oblique narrative of self-justification, it launches an extraordinary mode of reading, one that is both wilder and more daring in its very rage for order than either rabbinic exegesis or the figural and typological method of the Church Fathers. Freud's way of interpreting dreams becomes a powerful hermeneutics, rivalling that of the great Western religions. Though his dreambook is an unlikely candidate for a Scripture – being, I have suggested, more like a Confession – it fashions a secular key out of phenomena that this same civilization had repressed by calling them sacred, then irrational, then trivial. Freud not only redeems this excluded mass from insignificance, he also introduces strange new texts for our considerations: texts neither literary nor Scriptural but whose discovery throws doubt on the transcription of all previous inner experience. Freud reveals much more than a code for the decipherment of dreams: he invents a new textuality by transcribing dreams in his own way. It is not just the dream which is important, but also the dream text. After Freud we all have Freudian dreams; that is, we report them that way – except for those chosen few who are Jungians.

Psychoanalysis, then, creates new texts as well as transforming our understanding of those already received. Yet because the religious systems of the past also disseminated methods of interpretation that were radically revisionary, it is important to emphasize two features that distinguish psychoanalytic interpretation from these influential modes.

The first difference concerns the transactive relation of text and commentary. The dream text is not an object with Scriptural fixity. Scripture itself, of course, or the many books (biblia) we now call the Bible, had to be edited and fixed by a succession of interpretive communities. But Freud allows us to see the commentary entering the text, incorporating itself with the dream: what he called his self-analysis, working on dreams he had, so invests and supplements an original version that it becomes less of an object and more of a series of linguistic relays that could lead anywhere – depending on the system of rails and who is doing the switching. The dream is like a sentence that cannot find closure. Freud keeps coming up with fragments of something already recounted, as well as adding meaning to meaning. This extreme indeterminacy, even if it was there in what we now call Scripture, is no longer available to us, despite suggestive residues of freedom in the early rabbis whose midrashim exposed every inconsistency or gap in the sacred text, or who elicited new interpretations by changing speculatively the received voweling, the *nekudoth*.

A second feature that distinguishes psychoanalytic interpretation is its kakangelic rather than evangelic nature. I admit to coining this discordant word. The New Testament claims to bring good news, and reinterprets the Old Testament – that is, the Hebrew Bible – in the light of its faith. If the Gospels emphasize mankind's guilt, they also counter it by the possibility of salvation. But Freud brings bad (kaka) news about the psyche, and offers no cure except through the very activity – analysis – which reveals this news. 'A single Screw of Flesh / Is all that pins the Soul' Emily Dickinson wrote; and her homely metaphor keeps the hope open that on the other side of the 'Vail' or 'Gauze' of the body, her soul could enter into its freedom and see God or the loved one in full presence. Yet in Freud the 'Screw of Flesh' or "la chose genitale" (Charcot) cannot be totally sublimated, not even through the noncarnal conversation which psychoanalysis institutes. For it is precisely through this conversation that the patient becomes more aware of the 'mailed [maled] Nerve' (Dickinson) as something – pin, penis, pen – without which there is no soul, no signification, good or bad.

The dream analysis I have previously cited reflects this kakangelic vision, this 'inverse Freudian piety toward the sinister' (to quote Philip Rieff). Knödl, Fleischl, and Brücke do not appear as proper names in the dream, yet Freud's interpolative commentary dwells on the dream's misuse of such names. He calls it 'a kind of childish naughtiness' and an act of retribution for witticisms made about his own name. He also mentions a mock-heroic verse written by Herder about Goethe. 'Der du von Göttern abstammst, von Gothen oder vom Kote' ('Thou who art the descendant of Gods, of Goths or dung'), and he answers it in the name of Goethe by quoting from the latter's *Iphigenia*: 'So you too, divine figures, have turned to dust!' That Freud takes it on himself to answer Herder's quibble with a line of such pathos (it alludes to the death of many heroes during the siege of Troy) indicates something more than a regressive sensitivity about one's name. The dialogue of those two verses makes a little drama whose subject is the ambivalence that surrounds great men who have become ego ideals; and the ease with which their names can be profaned, dragged in the dust, causes Freud to balance Herder's childish punning with a compensatory impersonation. In *Totem and Taboo* the avoidance of the name of the dead in primitive societies, though more elaborately explained, still hinges on the same kind of envy or ambivalence. Freud has realized, in short, the profaning power of dreams; yet not of dreams only, but of language as it allows that chiming to mock and madden anything sacred. He has to decide whether Goethe or Kot, ecclesia or cloaca, evangelism or kakangelism is to be the dominant trend of his commentary. It happens that two members of that strange trinity comprising Knödl, Fleischl, and Brücke are sacred to Freud; yet the dream degrades them from proper to ordinary nouns. As ordinary nouns, however, they can become quiet conduits for the dream work; though the plot thickens when we ask what the dream work is seeking to reveal.

For the teaching of two of these men nourished Freud's scientific ambitions: they were among his male Fates. We do not learn particulars of what they taught him, since the dream is after something more universal. If we suppose that the dream conspires with Freud's wish that dream analysis be recognized as a science, then a hieratic form of discourse must appear, analogous to the hieroglyphs the dream itself presents. Yet the dream's mode of expression remains distinctly vernacular rather than hieratic – that is, without terms from the Latin Kitchen. While the language of the dream, then, forged in the real kitchen of women and dumplings, reaches for a mysterious vernacular, or mother tongue, the chain of associations characterizing the language of the interpreter fails to transform the dream text into the 'purer' discourse or sacred instrument of the scientist: his white overcoat or sublime condom.

Freud is brought back to his childlike if ambivalent veneration for Brücke, Fleischl, etc. He also experiences a related anxiety, that he may be a plagiarist like Knödl and so must clear his name. The dream discloses what infantile jealousies still prop the scientific project; but part of that project – not analyzed by Freud – is the ideal of a flawless discourse, a Latin of the intellect, a dream-redeeming sacred commentary. Not the dream is holy but the power of the interpretation as it methodizes and universalizes itself.

'Behold, the dreamer cometh.' That is said mockingly of Joseph in the Pentateuch; yet Joseph gains fame not as a dreamer but as a dream interpreter.

We glimpse in Freud the dreamer rising to fame not through vainglorious dreams but through the art or science of dream interpretation, which he called 'the royal road.'

The name 'Sigmund Freud' is indeed a misnomer. For in wrestling with the angel of the unconscious, with the evasive dream thoughts, Freud strips away so many layers of idealization, so many euphemistic formulas, that only wounded names are left. But through his unconsciousness-raising we learn what we are up against: profanation, defamation, self-slander, equivocation, distortion, ambivalence, displacement, repression, censorship. Freud neither curses nor blesses that hard-won knowledge; and so his greatness, finally, may be his moral style, that he neither palliates nor inculpates human nature.

From Freud I turn to Wordsworth, respecting his own statement that 'The poets were there before me.' My text is from the Lucy poems, a group of short lyrics on the death of a young girl, which is a motif that goes back to the Greek Anthology and evokes three highly charged themes: incompleteness, mourning, and memory.

> A slumber did my spirit seal;
> I had no human fears:
> She seemed a thing that could not feel
> The touch of earthly years.
>
> No motion has she now, no force;
> She neither hears nor sees;
> Rolled round in earth's diurnal course,
> With rocks, and stones, and trees.

'A slumber did my spirit seal.' After that line one would expect a dream vision. The formula is, I fell asleep, and behold! Yet there is no vision, or not in the expected sense. The boundary between slumber and vision is elided. That the poet had no human fears, that he experienced a curious anaesthesia vis-à-vis the girl's mortality or his own, may be what he names a slumber. As out of Adam's first sleep an Eve arose, so out of this sealed but not unconscious spirit a womanly image arises with the same idolatrous charm. Wordsworth's image seems to come from within; it is a delusive daydream, yet still a revision of that original vision.

There is, however, no sense of an eruption from the unconscious: brevity and condensation do not lead, as they do in dreams, to remarkable puns, striking figures, or deviant forms of speech. Nor is it necessary to be psychoanalytic to recognize that the trance is linked to an over-idealization of the loved person. The second stanza, which reports that she has died, should, in that case, express disillusionment. Yet remarkably this does not occur: the poet does not exclaim or cry out. Both transitions, the passage from slumber to dream, and the breaking of the dream, are described without surprise or shock.

Is there nothing that betrays how deeply disturbing the fantasy may have been? Perhaps, if the emotion was strong, it is natural enough that the words should seek to understate and to seal the impression. There is, however, an uncanny displacement on the structural level that is consonant with what Freud calls the omnipotence of thoughts and a general overestimation of psychical acts attributed by him to primitive cultures and, in contemporary civilization, to art.

This displacement is, rhetorically speaking, also a transference: in the initial stanza, the poet is sealed in slumber; in the second that slumber has passed over, as if intensified, to the girl. She falls asleep forever; and her death is specifically portrayed as a quasi-immortality not unlike what his imagination has prematurely projected onto her. 'Rolled round in earth's diurnal course,' she indeed cannot 'feel/The touch of earthly years.' This subtle transfer, this metaphor as extended structure rather than punctual figure of speech, is anticipated by at least one local condensation. 'Human' in 'I had no human fears' is a transferred epithet. The line should read: 'I had no such fears as would have come to me had I considered her a human – that is, mortal – being.' We do not know which way the transfer goes: from the girl to the poet or vice versa. And yet we do know: surely the illusion took rise in the poet and is an error of the imagination. Yet Wordsworth leaves that illusion its moment of truth as if it were natural, and not in any way out of the ordinary. He does not take pains to demystify it. Nature has its own supernatural gleam, however evanescent it is.

The supernatural illusion preserves the girl from a certain kind of touch, 'of earthly years' in the first stanza, but in the second she is totally distanced. Coleridge surmised that the lyric was an imaginary epitaph for Wordsworth's sister, and F. W. Bateson seized on this to claim that 'A slumber' (and the Lucy poems as a whole) arose from incestuous emotions and expressed a death wish by the brother against the sister. The poem removes an object of love by moving it beyond touch. In all but one important respect it confirms Freud's analysis about the way neurotics evade reality. Freud shows how the whole world is eventually embargoed, put beyond touch or contact by a widening fear of contagion. The only difference is that in Wordsworth the whole world enters in the second stanza as an image with resonances that are more positive than sinister.

Wordsworth's poem, moreover, practically offers itself for inclusion in a section of the dreambook that contains Freud's most famous literary interpretation. In 'Dreams of the Death of Persons of whom the Dreamer is fond' (Chapter 5) he discusses the story of Oedipus. We readily respond to the death of Oedipus, says Freud, 'because it might have been ours – because the oracle laid the same curse upon us before our birth as upon him.' That curse is understood to be an unconsciously fulfilled wish, a pattern we also suspect is present in 'A slumber.' But the question for literary criticism, even as it engages with psychoanalysis, is why such a wish, at once idealizing and deadly, and as if fulfilled in the second stanza, does not disturb the poet's language more. Even if the death did not occur except in idea, one might expect the spirit to awake, and to wonder what kind of deception it had practised on itself. Yet though the poem can be said to approach muteness – if we interpret the blank between the stanzas as another elision, a lesion in fact – Wordsworth keeps speech going without a trace of guilty knowledge. The eyes of the spirit may be open, but the diction remains unperturbed.

I want to suggest that Wordsworth's curious yet powerful complacency is related to euphemism: not of the artificial kind, the substitution of a good word for a bad one, or the strewing of flowers on a corpse, but an earthy euphemism, as it were, a balm deriving from common speech, from its unconscious obliquity and inbuilt commitment to avoid silence. To call it euphemism may be inadequate but the quality I point to resists overconsciousness and demystification.

It is generally the task of the critic to uncover euphemism in any sphere: literary, psychological, political. When Freud tells a patient the meaning of one of her flowery dreams, 'she quite lost her liking for it.' A kakangelic unmasking may be necessary, although not many would go as far as Kenneth Burke, who praised Freud's method as 'an interpretive sculpting in excrement' and put praise in action by suggesting we read Keats's 'Beauty is Truth, Truth Beauty' as 'Body is Turd, Turd Body.' What makes Wordsworth's poetry so difficult to psychoanalyze is its underlying and resistant euphemism, coterminous with ordinary language, and distinguished from the courtly and affected diction of the time.

Consider the word 'slumber' as such a euphemism. Then consider the entire second stanza as a paraphrase for 'she is dead.' The negative aspect of these phrases can be heightened. The 'slumber' may remind us of bewitchment or fascination, even of hypnosis. It could be a hypnoid state in which one hears voices without knowing it, or performs actions on the basis of these voices. In another Lucy poem, 'Strange fits of passion,' such automatism is strongly suggested, and a voice does intrude at the end in the form of an incomplete sentence that expresses, in context, a premonition, but in itself is more ambiguous: 'If Lucy should be dead!'

That we may be in the domain of voices is made more probable by the word 'passion' in 'Strange fits of passion': it meant an outcry under the impact of strong emotions. Yet to pursue this analysis would mean to go from the issue of euphemism to how language is a synthesis not only of sounds but of speech acts, and especially – if we look to infancy – of threats, promises, admonitions, yeses and nos that come to the child as ideas of reference in vocal form, even if (or because) not every word is understood. Such an analysis would also oblige us to explore the text of poetry as an undoing of that synthesis, or a partial recovery of the elements behind the deceptive neutrality of language. Ordinary speech, from this perspective, is a form of sleep-walking, the replication of internalized phrases or commands without conscious affect; poetic speech is an exposure of that condition, a return to a sense of language as virtually alive – in any case with enough feeling to delay our passage from words to things. Poetic speech re-enters an original zone of stress and inhibition and becomes precarious.

That precariousness is both acknowledged and limited by Wordsworth's euphemism. The second stanza of 'A slumber,' unlike the end of 'Strange fits,' does not cry out: as a periphrasis for 'she is dead' it amplifies and even embellishes that reluctant phrase. It is hard to think of the lyric as a stark epitaph skirting aphasia. And though the traumatic or mortifying event may occasion the euphemism, it cannot be its cause. We must find a 'feeding source' (to use one of the poet's own metaphors) elsewhere; and we can find it only in the other threat to speech: the near-ecstasy depicted in the previous stanza. A common source of inarticulate or mute behavior, such ecstasy, whatever its nature, carries over into the second stanza's euphemia.

Epitaphs, of course, are conventionally associated with consoling and pleasant words. Here, however, not all the words are consoling. They approach a negative that could foreclose the poem: 'No . . . No . . . Neither . . . Nor . . .' Others even show Wordsworth's language penetrated by an inappropriate subliminal punning. So 'diurnal' (line 7) divides into 'die' and 'urn,' and 'course' may recall the older pronunciation of 'corpse.' Yet these condensations are troublesome rather than expressive; the power of the second stanza resides predominantly in the euphemistic displacement of the word grave by an image of gravitation ('Rolled round in earth's diurnal course'). And though there is no agreement on the tone of this stanza, it is clear that a subvocal word is uttered without being written out. It is a word that rhymes with 'fears' and 'years' and 'hears,' but which is closed off by the very last syllable of the poem: 'trees.' Read 'tears,' and the animating, cosmic metaphor comes alive, the poet's lament echoes through nature as in pastoral elegy. 'Tears,' however, must give way to what is written, to a dull yet definitive sound, the anagram 'trees.'

Pastoral elegy, in which rocks, woods, and streams are called upon to mourn the death of a person, or to echo the complaint of a lover, seems too extravagant a genre for this chastely fashioned inscription. Yet the muted presence of the form reminds us what it means to be a nature poet. From childhood on, as the autobiographical *Prelude* tells us, Wordsworth was aware of 'unknown modes of being' and of strange sympathies emanating from nature. He was haunted by an animistic universe that stimulated, shared, and called upon his imagination. The Lucy poems evoked a nature spirit in human form, perhaps modelled after his sister, and is a forerunner of Cathy Linton in *Wuthering Heights*. It makes no sense to suppose a death wish unless we link it to the ecstatic feelings in this poetry. Yet where do these feelings come from? Wordsworth does not actually say he projected his starry emotions upon the girl. It is, rather, our habit of giving priority to the psychological state of the writer, our inability to consider his euphoria as a contagious identification with the girl, that makes us assume it is a dream and a delusion. For to think otherwise would return us to the world of pastoral elegy or even to a magical universe, with currents of sympathy running along esoteric channels – the very world described as primitive in *Totem and Taboo.*

Reading Freud through Wordsworth now brings us closer to a critique of Freud. The discovery of the role played in mental illness by large-scale wishful thinking, by omnipotence of thought, is a proven achievement. Yet Freud's description of the thought process of primitives and their licensed contemporary relic, the artist, is for once not reflective or dialectical enough. Freud wants so badly to place psychotherapy on a firm, scientific foundation that he exempts himself from an overestimation of psychical acts. At the same time he has made it hard for us to value interpretations not based on the priority of a psychological factor. Animism is accepted as a functional belief only in fiction – in Jensen's *Gradiva* or Wordsworth's poems or *Wuthering Heights* – but is considered dysfunctional in terms of mental health unless demystified by psychoanalysis. Perhaps the decisive matter here is not a compulsion to demystify (to be kakangelic) but a failure to draw a certain type of experience into that special dialogue established by psychoanalysis. For the problem with art as with nonclassical anthropological data is that interpretation cannot find enough associations for them. Psychoanalysis distrusts, with good reason, the appearance of autonomy in such artifacts even while recognizing their force, which is then labeled 'primitive.'

Yet Freud could acknowledge, in passing, that his persistent, even obsessive, mode of interpretation might share the delusional character of superstitions it sought to analyze and dispel. He himself may have suffered from a fear of contagion that placed, as Jacques Lacan and others have claimed, too many protective barriers between his hermeneutics and religious hermeneutics. Those barriers are coming down, or do not seem as impenetrable as they once were. Indeed, in the first part of my talk, I suggested some analogies that made religion and psychoanalysis enemy brothers. But I can be somewhat more specific, in conclusion, about what Freud saw yet tried to close out.

He was always distrustful and demystifying towards eudemonic feelings, the kind that Wordsworth expressed in 'A slumber.' He considered them a 'thalassal regression' (to use Ferenczi's phrase), an attempt to regain an inertial state, the nirvana of pre-oedipal or undifferentiated being. Wordsworth's attitude was very different. In all his most interesting work he describes a developmental impasse centering on eudemonic sensations experienced in early childhood and associated with nature. Whether beautiful or frightening, they sustain and nourish him as intimations of immortality; and though Wordsworth can be called the first ego psychologist, the first careful observer of the growth of a mind, he shows the strength and usurpation of those ecstatic memories as they threaten the maturing poet who must respect their drive. If there is a death wish in the Lucy poems, it is insinuated by nature itself and asks lover or growing child not to give up earlier yearnings – to die rather than become an ordinary mortal.

This developmental impasse is quite clear in the present poem. Divided into two parts, separated formally by a blank and existentially by a death, the epitaph does not record a disenchantment. The mythic girl dies, but that word seems to wrong her. Her star-like quality is maintained despite her death, for the poet's sense of her immutability deepens by reversal into an image of 'participation mystique' with planet earth. There is loss, but there is also a calculus of gain and loss which those two stanzas weigh like two sides of a balance. Their balancing point is the impasse I have mentioned: such a death could seem better than dying into the light of common day. Yet to think only that is to make immutability of such value that human life is eclipsed by it. Ideas of pre-existence or afterlife arise. My analysis has tried to capture a complex state of affairs that may resemble religious experiences or pathological states but which Wordsworth sees as an imaginative constant, ordinary and incurable. For those who need more closure in interpretation, who wish to know exactly what the poet felt, I can only suggest a phrase from his famous 'Ode; Intimations of Immortality from Recollections of Early Childhood.' The meanest flower, he writes, can give him 'thoughts that do often lie too deep for tears.' The girl has become such a thought.

Even here we meet a euphemism once more. Naming something 'a thought too deep for tears': is that not a remarkable periphrasis for the inability to grieve? This inability seems to be a strength rather than a weakness, if we take the figure literally. 'Too deep for tears' suggests a place – a mental place – beyond fits of passion or feelings, as if Wordsworth desired that grave immunity. Yet to call the words euphemistic is to acknowledge at the same time that they are so affecting that mourning is not absent but continued in a different mode. The work of writing seems to have replaced the work of mourning. Is there a link, then, between writing and grieving, such that writing can be shown to assist those Herculean psychic labors Freud described for us, whose aim is to detach us from the lost object and reattach us to the world?

My main concern has been to understand yet delimit Freud's kakangelic mode of interpretation. Wordsworth enabled me to do this by showing that euphemism can be an ordinary rather than artificial aspect of language, especially when the work of mourning is taking place, which is pretty much all the time. I have argued that this euphemism cannot be demystified because it is not simply a figure of speech covering up naked truth. Looking closely at a poem by

Wordsworth reveals a far more complicated situation. The strongest euphemisms in Wordsworth are also the most naturalized; they seem to belong to language rather than being imposed on it. They are not in the service of evading reality or putting the best face on things. They have an energy, a force of their own, one that counters a double threat to speech: expectedly, that which comes from loss; but unexpectedly, that which comes from ecstasy, even if it is a remembered ecstasy, and so touched by loss. I have sometimes talked of euphemia rather than euphemism, both because we are dealing with a feature basic to language, and not simply to one poet's use of language; and also because the aphasia it circumscribes remains perceptible. Wordsworth's euphemia, in short, is nourished by sources in language or the psyche we have not adequately understood. They bring us back to an awareness of how much sustaining power language has, even if our individual will to speak and write is assaulted daily by the most trivial as well as traumatic events.

This sustaining power of language is not easily placed, however, on the side of goodness or love (eros) rather than death. Writing has an impersonal, even impersonating quality which brings the poet close to the dead 'whose names are in our lips,' to quote Keats. *Personare* meant, originally, to 'speak through' another, usually by way of an ancestral mask, which made the speaker a medium or an actor in a drama in which the dead renewed their contact with the living.

It is not surprising, therefore, that there should be a hint of the involuntary or mechanical in stanza 2 of 'A slumber': a hint of the indifference to which the girl's difference is reduced, and which, however tragic it may be, obeys a law that supports the stability a survivor's speech requires. 'O blessed machine of language,' Coleridge once exclaimed; this very phrase is symptomatic of the euphemia without which speech would soon cease to be, or turn into its feared opposite, an eruptive cursing or sputtering as in Tourette's syndrome. Coleridge has to bless the machine as a machine; yet his blessing is doubly euphemistic, for he knew too well what the machine could do in its unblessed aspect, as an uncontrollable stream of associations which coursed through him by day and especially by night.

It is here we link up once more with Freud, who created a new hermeneutics by charting compulsive and forced connections which 'regarded nothing as sacred.' Someone said of a typical lecture by Emerson that 'it had no connection, save in God.' Freud's kakangelic method removes all vestiges of that final clause. The recovered dream thoughts have no connections save in the negative fact that their capacity for profanation is without limit. All other connections are the result of a secondary process extending from the dream work's disguises and displacements to more conscious revisions. At times, therefore, the manifest dream content may appear saner than an interpretation that reverses the dream's relatively euphemistic bearing or disintegrates its discursive structure. Instead of completing dream texts, or by extension literary texts (or, like Jung, encouraging their synthesis), Freud makes them less complete, less fulfilling. The more interpretation, it seems, the less closure.

But did Freud himself regard nothing as sacred? I have already suggested that if the dream is unholy, and is shown to be so by the interpretation, the power of that interpretation as it methodizes and universalizes itself is something very near to holy. One wonders how else Freud could have continued his work without falling mute, without being overcome by the bad news he brought. The dream peculiar to Freud, as interpreter and scientist, a dream that survives all self-analysis, is of a purified language that remains uncontaminated by its materials, that neither fulfills nor represses an all-too-human truth. I hope Freud's shade will understand this parting remark as a blessing on the only scientist I have ever been able to read.

Note

* The 1984 Freud Lecture at Yale, an annual event sponsored by the Kanzer Seminar for Psychoanalysis in the Humanities, the Western New England Psychoanalytic Society, and the Whitney Humanities Center.

quoi du reste aujourd'hui, pour nous, ici, maintenant, d'un Hegel?

Pour nous, ici, maintenant : voilà ce qu'on n'aura pu désormais penser sans lui.

Pour nous, ici, maintenant : ces mots sont des citations, déjà, toujours, nous l'aurons appris de lui.

Qui, lui?

Son nom est si étrange. De l'aigle il tient la puissance impériale ou historique. Ceux qui le prononcent encore à la française, il y en a, ne sont ridicules que jusqu'à un certain point : la restitution, sémantiquement infaillible, pour qui l'a un peu lu, un peu seulement, de la froideur magistrale et du sérieux imperturbable, l'aigle pris dans la glace et le gel.

Soit ainsi figé le philosophe emblémi.

Qui, lui? L'aigle de plomb ou d'or, blanc ou noir, n'a pas signé le texte du savoir absolu. Encore moins l'aigle rouge. D'ailleurs on ne sait pas encore si *Sa* est un texte, a donné lieu à un texte, s'il a été écrit ou s'il a écrit, fait écrire, laissé écrire.

On ne sait pas encore s'il s'est laissé enseigner, signer, ensigner. Peut-être y a-t-il une incompatibilité, plus qu'une contradiction dialectique, entre l'enseignement et la signature, un magister et un signataire. Se laisser penser et se laisser signer, peut-être ces deux opérations ne peuvent-elles en aucun cas se recouper.

Sa signature, comme la pensée du reste, enveloppera ce corpus mais n'y sera sans doute pas comprise.

Ceci est — une légende.

Non pas une fable : une légende. Non pas un roman, un roman familial puisque s'y agit la famille de Hegel, mais une légende.

Elle ne prétend pas donner à lire le tout du corpus, textes et desseins de Hegel, seulement deux figures. Plus justement deux figures en train de s'effacer : deux passages.

Sa sera désormais le sigle du savoir absolu. Et l'IC, notons-le déjà puisque les deux portées se représentent l'une l'autre, de l'Immaculée Conception. Tachygraphie proprement singulière : elle ne va pas d'abord à disloquer, comme on pourrait croire, un code c'est-à-dire ce sur quoi l'on table trop. Mais peut-être, beaucoup plus tard et lentement cette fois, à en exhiber les bords

reste à penser : ça ne s'accentue pas ici maintenant mais se sera déjà mis à l'épreuve de l'autre côté. Le sens doit répondre, plus ou moins, aux calculs de ce qu'en termes de gravure on appelle contre-épreuve

column a

« *ce qui est resté d'un Rembrandt déchiré en petits carrés bien réguliers, et foutu aux chiottes* » se divise en deux.

Comme le reste.

Deux colonnes inégales, disent-ils, dont chaque — enveloppe ou gaine, incalculablement renverse, retourne, remplace, remarque, recoupe l'autre.

L'incalculable de *ce qui est resté* se calcule, élabore tous les coups, les tord ou les échafaude en silence, vous vous épuiseriez plus vite à les compter. Chaque petit carré se délimite, chaque colonne s'enlève avec une impassible suffisance et pourtant l'élément de la contagion, la circulation infinie de l'équivalence générale rapporte chaque phrase, chaque mot, chaque moignon d'écriture (par exemple « *je m'éc...* ») à chaque autre, dans chaque colonne et d'une colonne à l'autre de *ce qui est resté* infiniment calculable.

A peu près.

Il y a du reste, toujours, qui se recoupent, deux fonctions.

L'une assure, garde, assimile, intériorise, idéalise, relève la chute dans le monument. La chute s'y maintient, embaume et momifie, monu-mémorise, s'y nomme — tombe. Donc, mais comme chute, s'y érige.

column b

Figure 1 Jacques Derrida, *Glas* (Paris: Editions Galilée, 1975), p. 7. The columns were not labeled in the original, this has been added to aid reference.

Chapter 30

Lacan, Derrida, and the Specular Name

In a glass darkly. Jacques Lacan discovers a 'stade du miroir' (mirror phase) in the early development of what is to be the child's ego. By the complaisance of the mirror, the child sees itself for the first time as a coordinated being and, triumphantly, jubilantly, assumes that image. But what is found by means of this play ('je-jeu') with the mirror is really a double rather than a differentiated other. The myth of Narcissus is given clinical verisimilitude. The other (Rimbaud: 'Je est un autre') is necessary for self-definition, but in the mirror is simply an illusory unification. The 'corps morcelé,' moreover, the fragmented or uncoordinated body image prior to the mirror phase, is only suspended. It remains active in the domain Lacan names the verbal or symbolic in contrast to the nonverbal or imaginary.

Beyond these observations lies a difficult psychopathology that we need not oversimplify except to say that the concept of a 'corps morcelé' (cf. Derrida's *Glas*, 'un Rembrandt déchiré,' in figure 1) is connected with Lacan's understanding of the castration complex, or how the phallus or the body part that 'represents' the sexual foundation of otherness is enmeshed in an extraordinary developmental series of differential yet substitutive (compensatory) mechanisms. Acceptance of the (absent) phallus, or of the (absent) father, or, basically, of the mediacy of words, allows a genuine recognition of difference.

Since the mirror phase, although using gestaltist and biological evidence, is not securely based on experimental data (especially when compared to the painstaking work of Piaget) it might be better to call it the Marienbad complex. Not only is Marienbad where the hypothesis was first made public, but also Resnais's film *Last Year at Marienbad* expresses Lacan's mirror domain as a fact of the imagination: the image or heroine in that film's mobile mirror seems to quest for a specular yet totally elusive identity, for some unique reduction to one place, one time, one bed, one fixative spectral event.

The mirror phase, then, deals with images, with thing rather than word representation. (In *Last Year at Marienbad*, the sound track is dissociated from the life of the images, running nonparallel with it, as an arbitrary or contrapuntal yet related experience. It is like the somewhat mysterious juxtaposition, in Lacan, of symbolic and imaginary spheres.) The notion of a 'corps morcelé' does, however, connect with the differential system of a psycholinguistics. The question therefore arises: is there anything comparable to the mirror stage on the level of language?

Lacan's emphasis on the birth of language out of a 'symbolic' rather than 'imaginary' sphere seems to moot this line of inquiry. He suggests that the specular image, as the base of other imagery that serves an integrative or unifying function, is an illusory modification of a deeper or prior system, inherently differential. Thus, the question of what corresponds to the mirror phase on the level of language (to its unifying if illusory effect) may seem unanswerable in terms of Lacanian psychiatry.

Yet there is the well-known magical or religious ambition to possess the word. Does not the concept of Word or Logos in religion, or in such artists as Hölderlin, provide a clue? And is not the Lacanian psychopompos, who recovers an interior signifier, of that tradition? We are looking for a correlative in language to the specular image. The logos understood as that in whose 'image' whatever is is signifying seems to motivate a logocentric phase of development – the very thing Derrida seeks to expose.

Or consider the importance of the proper name in Shakespeare. 'Had I it written, I would tear the word,' Romeo says to Juliet, referring to his family name. The wounding of a name is too much like the wounding of the body not to be significant. We don't know why Genet tore 'Rembrandt' (see the illustration in this book of the first page of *Glas*), but the effacing or defacing of the proper name suggests that there may be such a thing as a specular name or 'imago du nom propre' in the fantasy development of the individual, a name more genuinely one's own than signature or proper name. Signatures can always be faked. Is there something that cannot be faked? 'The signature is a wound, and there is no other origin to the work of art' (*Glas*, 207b). Is it possible to discern a specular word, logos phase, or imago of the proper name in the development of the individual?

Derrida's reflections on Hegel, in *Glas*, open with a play on the idea of 'naming' or 'nomination,' a theme fully elaborated in his juxtaposed column on Genet. He implies, without calling it so, an imago of the proper name on the basis of what we know of the haunting, fixative, unifying effect of 'being named.' Just as the specular image produces a jubilant awareness, tested and affirmed by the child's mirror mimicry, so the specular name can produce a hallelujah and magnifying language that mimics a sublimity associated with the divine logos. This is so even if the identifying name, the 'nom unique' or ' nom propre,' is accusatory. Indeed the scene of nomination (my own phrase) is bound to be accusative as well as nominative, or includes within it a reflexive, intense response to the act of vocative designation. 'You are a thief,' that commonplace accusation, that merest insult addressed to Genet as a child, strikes inward as a divine apostrophe and perhaps founds the perverse high ritualism of his style.

In such a scene of nomination, then, the mirror speaks. We suspect, of course, that our primary narcissism had already spoken to it, like the queen in Snow White. But whatever question has been put remains obscure: only the mirror's response is clear, indeed so clear that it obliges us to assume its answer as an identity, to construct or reconstruct some feature in us clarified by this defining response. At the same time, the specular name or identity phrase – our true rather than merely proper name – is reaffirmed in time by a textual mimicry, joyful, parodistic, or derisory, of the original magnification. The repetition of the specular name gives rise to texts that seem to be anagrammatic or to conceal an unknown-unknowable key, a 'pure' signifier. These texts are called literature.

Can we assert that the specular name 'exists'? Derrida knows that such words as 'exist' and 'is' point to a static order of things, and he tries to avoid the trap of this inbuilt language-metaphysic. He suggests, instead, that if there is a Hegelian Sa ('savoir absolu') it may be incompatible with the Sa ('signifiant') we call a signature: the proper name (Hegel) affixed to a text as its authenticating seal.

A similar counterpointing of proper and specular name is suggested in Genet's case. The 'antherection' of his name in a given passage (that is, the flowery style that alludes to his flower name, 'genêt') makes a tomb of it: as in Saussure's anagrams, the text generated by the name is bound to enlace and so to bury it. Like a child who will not believe his parents are his real parents but engages imaginatively in a 'family romance,' so the proper name, or signature, is always being 'torn up' in favor of a specular name, whether or not it can be found:

> The grand stakes of discourse (I mean discourse) that is literary: the patient, tricky, quasi animalistic or vegetative transformation, unwearying, monumental, derisive also, but turning derision rather against itself – the transformation of the proper name, rebus, into things, into the name of things. (*Glas*, 11b)

More radically still: writing is coterminous with that canceling movement, 'la nécessité du passage par la détermination biffée, la nécessité de ce tour d'écriture.' Every return, then, as in Genet, to a scene of nomination, must be unmasked as a figure. It introduces a factitious present or fictitious point of origin that may not be taken literally ('livré à la police') unless we are in search of an 'ordinateur secret' leading back to baptism or birth.

> A text only exists, resists, consists, represses, lets itself be read or written if it is elaborated [travaillé] by the unreadability [illisibilité] of a proper name. I have not said – not yet – that such a proper name exists and that it becomes unreadable when it falls [or is entombed, a play on 'tombe'] into the signature. The proper name does not

ring forth [résonne], lost at once, save at the instant of its débris, when it breaks – embroils – checks itself on touching the signature [seing]. (*Glas*, 4lb)

Glas ends, therefore, with the words 'le débris de' [Derrida] – that is, it touches, without actually stating, a signature ('seing'). The proper name seems to have been 'disseminated': 'Glas' has told (tolled) its demise. This concept of dissemination moves to the fore in Derrida's writings after the *Grammatology*. It is essential for his critique of Lacan or Sartre or any hermeneutics that relapses into a thematics (even a polythematics) by its insistence on an explanatory 'key.' In his grimly funny way, Derrida compares this procedure of 'slipping the universal passkey into all lacunae of signification' to a police action. 'It would mean arresting once again, in the name of the law, of veracity, of the symbolic order, the free movement [marche] of an unknown person' (*Glas*, 36b).

The signature, which denotes propriety through the proper name, is the 'cas limite' of this arrest. Only courts of justice should insist on it, with their cumbersome machinery of registration, verification, ceremonial gravity, etc. Dissemination is, strangely enough, a pastoral though totally uninnocent protest against such restrictive or paralegal types of hermeneutic. It is the obverse, in fact, of classification. 'What makes us write is also what scatters the semes, disperses signacoupure and signacouture' (*Glas*, 192b).

The passage from cl (for class, clé, clue) to gl (for glas or glu) analogizes these contraries: classification and dissemination. 'At the very moment,' Derrida continues,

> we try to seize, in a particular text, the workings of an idiom, linked to a chain of proper nouns and actual denotative configurations, 'glas' also names classification, that is, their inscription in networks of generalities infinitely articulated, or in the genealogies of a structure whose cross-weaving, coupling, switching, detouring, branching can never be derived merely from a semantic or a formal rule. There is no absolute idiom or signature . . . The bell tolls always for the idiom or the signature. For the absolute precursor [aïeul absolu: perhaps 'primal father']. (*Glas*, 169b)

Thus, we enter a chain of secondary elaborations stretching to infinity. There is no way of tracing them to an origin, to a logos that may have been 'In the Beginning.' When, in a quasi-heraldic moment – talking arms of character, Lacan might say – Nerval's 'Desdichado' recites, in the opening sonnet from *Chimères*, 'Je suis le ténébreux, le veuf, l'inconsolé,' we know that the family name 'Labrunie' has been cast out in favor of a specular identity that is the widowed logos itself: the babel of 'à la tour abolie.' The appropriate herme-neutic, therefore, is like the interminable work of mourning, an endless affectional detachment from the identity theme as such, whether that is linked to the (absent) logos or to a maternal and sexual presence distanced by the logos into the idea of an Immaculate Conception.

Perhaps the most persistent – obsessive – theme in *Glas* is the Immaculate Conception. It surges into the opening page before its time. No sooner has the author said, in the margin, 'Sa will henceforth be the mark ['sigle'] of absolute knowledge,' than he adds, 'And IC, let us note it already, because the two portals [i.e., columns on the page] represent each other mutually, the mark of the Immaculate Conception.' The notion of 'sigle' (of words represented by their first letter) enters a series including 'signature' and 'seing' (seal or mark at the end of a text, representing the signatory, with a possible interlingual pun on seing/sein/Sein: seal/breast/Being). This tripling could be explained by the special function assigned each term, but Derrida is more concerned with how language moves by marginal differentiation through a signifying series that can never quite circumscribe, or comprise, a body (corpus).

The term Sa, therefore, which he institutes as an abbreviation for Hegel's 'absolute knowledge' ('savoir absolu') but which is homophonic with Saussure's abbreviation for signifier ('signifiant'), although it is composed of first and last (of initial letters that denote an end state) is neither a first or last term, for it enters an indefinite sequence that includes other words already mentioned, as well as signe, ensigner, enseigner. (Sa is also a feminine possessive pronoun, and as SA stands for 'Société Anonyme,' in English 'Inc.' for Incorporated.) Writing *Glas* in two columns, or beginning with two Hegel passages, reinforces our awareness that the 'scene of writing' never takes place in one place: its locus (corpus) is always also 'ein anderer Schauplatz,' as Freud put it: displaced from right to left, to a supplementary comment or even into a physical symptom, which Lacan rightly analogizes to a 'truth' already written down elsewhere and therefore in part missing from present discourse. There is, in short, no absolute or transcendental Sa (signifier) any more than an absolute or certain Sa (knowledge of what is signified). We cannot say 'This is my body,' without being enmeshed in a complex symbolic or semiotic system.

From the start of *Glas*, then, we are presented with two illusory moments of ecstatic identification some eighteen hundred years apart (1) absolute knowledge, Hegel's vision of an end to dialectic and alienation in the thought process of the philosopher who has internalized history, and (2) the phantasm of the Immaculate Conception. Why the latter? What bearing has it, as developed in the column on Genet, on the Hegelian 'legend' unfolded opposite? And why emphasize, of all literary writers, Genet? Among Anglo-American readers the juxtaposition will cause a resistance that even the brilliance of the result may not remove.

Every literary narrative contains another narrative: however continuous or full the one seems to be, the other is discontinuous and lacunary. Jean-Luc Nancy has called this 'other' narrative the 'discours de la syncope.' Given that our minds tend to overestimate, even when wary or ashamed of it, fictional writing, the reader is usually forced into the position of having to recover the 'discours de la syncope,' that is, the precariousness of all transitions, or the undecidability of fiction's truth. Every story is like Isabel's in Melville's *Pierre*, and every authoritative title or naming should be treated on the analogy of *Pierre, or The Ambiguities*.

This deepening sense of an endless or ungrounded or noncontinuous discourse is not purely cautionary or subversive. There is something we can take away with us: a perception similar to that offered by myths and positive interpretation. Our vision of the psyche's vulnerability broadens and intensifies; it extends into the bowels of language, from images to names and to the pathos that insistently attends the giving or calling out of a name. However different the Gothic gloom of Melville's *Pierre* and Faulkner's *Absalom, Absalom!* both novels turn on the seductive centrality of a scene of recognition – of naming and acknowledgment. The concepts of vocation, initiation, and identity run parallel yet subordinate to that central hinge that Aristotle in the *Poetics* already discerned as essential to Greek tragedy.

The desire for a 'here and now,' fixed image or defining word, mystic portrait or identity-imposing story, is not dissociable, according to psychiatry, from family romance: the recognition scene is always a displaced or sublimated family scene. It is no different with the Christian scandal of the 'Presence of the Word' (*logos spermatikos*) in the Immaculate Conception, or more precisely, in the Annunciation. Let me, therefore, recenter these reflections on the most famous scene of nomination in our culture: the Annunciation.

There are, of course, other scenes that show the Word of God coming to earth with vocational force. But this episode is particularly relevant to Genet because it 'magnifies' a woman; indeed, Mary's hymn, called the Magnificat after its Latin version, and recorded in Luke, has become part of Christian liturgy. Not only is the Presence of the Word in this scene of nomination also the Word of the Presence ('Hail, O favored one, the Lord is with you,' Luke 1:28), but the transcendental signifier, as we might truly call it, issues in a Magnificat because it takes away a curse: of infertility, and more generally, in reference to woman, of impure, because infertile, menstruation. Mary's condition, moreover, could have shamed her (Matt. 1:18–20; Luke 1:24), but through the intervention of the angelic word a potential denunciation becomes an annunciation.

In Genet, profanely, the same structure holds. Denunciation is converted into Annunciation; the curse (perhaps that of being born of woman, or male seed considered as impure, as a menstrual flow, unless made fertile in the woman) is taken away; and the Magnificat of a convict's style results. How 'you are a thief' should become functionally equivalent to the sanctifying 'you are with child' is the psychic puzzle that Sartre and Derrida try to resolve.

★   ★   ★

'You are a thief' can only stand for 'You are with child' if, at some level, Genet is trying to steal the womb itself – whereas he can at most, if we trust Ferenczi's bioanalysis in *Thalassa*, steal into the womb and give something to that death in order to live. Genet is not successful in modifying even imaginatively the logocentric enclosure: he simply erects a subversive, symmetrical counterpart, the image of male fulness of grace, 'L'Annonce fait à Jean-Marie.' Sound-reasoning on his flowery or anthographic style must include the thought that flowers such as the lilies of the field or those associated with the Annunciation are pure in the sense that Hegel caught when he posits a nonagonistic 'religion of flowers': they can grow and multiply as if by grace, without the curse of labor (cf. Gen. 3:16 ff.). The commandment, by place the first in the Bible, 'Be fruitful and multiply,' is death to hear, as Adam remarks in Milton's *Paradise Lost* (X.731), for it means, after the Fall, a multiplying of deaths or, for Genet, genitality with no grace except as it 'blesses' a woman. His family of thieves and murderers is erected in vain opposition to the survival of the 'onto-theologic' model in secular society.

Genet's mirror image of the Holy Family, then, expresses a reversal rather than a transvaluation of values. Given the conservative character of the institution of language, it is doubtful that there could be transvaluation. We can reverse or use the trope of catachresis, we can deploy all the subversive flowers in the anthology of speech, or we can reverse in another sense, by deconstruction, and expose the fallacy that every great artist's mind passes on itself – the result remains a secret recognition scene. As Genet himself has written: 'The world is turned inside out like a glove. It happens that I am the glove and I understand at last that on the day of judgment God will call me with my own voice: "Jean, Jean" ' (*Glas*, 220b). Or Lacan:

> The Word always subjectively includes its own reply . . . The function of Language is not to inform but to evoke. What I seek in the Word is the response of the other . . . In order to find him, I call him by a name which he must assume or refuse in order to reply to me.

'The allocution of the subject entails an allocutor . . . even if he is speaking "off" or "to the wings." He addresses himself to ce (grand) Autre whose theoretical basis I have consolidated.'

Even the most deliberate counter-annunciation yet conceived, Mallarmé's mirror scene in the *Herodiade*, can only use the language of flowers against itself. 'Vous mentez, o fleur nue de mes lèvres.' Herodiade's specular cries know they have no issue. Devoted to sterility, Herodiade is Mary's opposite in the drama of the logos that eventuates so curiously in Genet's (or Derrida's) image of the mother as 'bourreau berceur.' The logos as the 'relève' (Aufhebung/fulfillment) of metaphor reifies metaphor and suppresses language fertility. Christ and Herod become co-conspirators in this Genet-ic massacre.

Figure 2 Jost Ammann, *Aus dem Geschlechterbuch der Familie Tucker* (1589)

Figure 3 Johann Hiltensperger, Logocentric Labyrinth (18th century)

Figure 4 William Blake, Name painting from *Milton* (1808)

Figure 5 William Blake, Title page to *Milton* with signature (engraved 1808). "Milton," separated by the figure, and read from right to left, spells "Lim[b] not".

His adventure is having been named.

Sartre, *Saint Genet*

[T]he difficulty begins with the name.

Ralph Waldo Ellison, 'Hidden Name and Complex Fate'

The subject too, if he can appear to be the slave of language, is all the more so of a discourse in the universal movement, in which his place is already inscribed at birth, if only by virtue of his proper name.

Lacan, 'The Agency of the Letter'

The idea that literature is the elaboration of a specular name is not meant to encourage a new substantialism of the word. Since the specular name is always already a fiction – hidden or forgotten or cancelled, or motivated unconsciously by a life that dies into allegory – it can determine autobiographical quests only in the manner of Plato's theory of anamnesis. The quest, as it becomes lifelong and remains indeterminate, recuperates esoteric traditions: stories about the magic of names, anagrammatic intuitions, scenes of nomination or annunciation, and, in short, to steal the title of Karl Abraham's early essay, 'the determining force of names.'

Gershom Scholem published a strange name fantasy of Walter Benjamin's, written at Ibiza, Spain, in 1933. It involves Paul Klee's picture *Angelus Novus* (a personal icon for Benjamin, who owned it) and the ancient tradition of the natal genius or personal angel whose name is hidden but who represents one's true identity and secret self. Benjamin's allegory, close in some respects to a Kafka parable and in other respects to a Baudelaire prose poem, was deeply linked to his situation at that time: his troubled relation to women, his Jewish ancestry, and his sense of being born under Saturn (he had written *The Origin of German Tragic Drama* and was steeped in Baudelaire). Scholem's beautiful and thorough interpretation has brought this out in a definitive way, and I cannot add to what he has said.

My interest lies elsewhere; in Benjamin's fantasy as a particularly revealing example of how autobiography is determined by the idea of a hidden – spectral or specular – name. I will quote only the opening paragraphs, which constitute about half of this interesting document, but they suffice to show how Benjamin verges on a complex scene of nomination: an angelus-annunciation that turns not only on the magical force of an occult name but also on what might happen when that name is or must be betrayed.

Agesilaus Santander

When I was born the thought came to my parents that I might perhaps become a writer. Would it not be good, then, if not everybody noticed immediately that I was a Jew. That is why they gave me in addition to the name by which I was called ['Rufnamen'] two further, exceptional ones, from which it couldn't be perceived either that a Jew bore them or that they belonged to him as first names ['Vornamen']. Forty years ago no parents could have proved more far-seeing. What they considered a remote possibility has come true. Except that the precautions by which they meant to counter fate were set aside by the one most concerned. That is to say, instead of making it public together with his writings, he treated it as the Jews the additional name of their children which remains secret. Indeed, they only communicate it to them when they reach manhood. Since, however, this manhood can occur more than once in a lifetime, and the secret name may remain the same and untransfigured only for the pious, so to whoever is not pious the change of name might be revealed all at once, with the onset of a new manhood. Thus with me. But it remains the name, nevertheless, which binds together the vital forces in strictest union, and which must be guarded against the unauthorized ['Unberufenen'].

Yet this name is not at all an enrichment of the one it names. On the contrary, much falls away from his image when that name becomes audible. His image loses above all the gift of appearing to be human. In the room I occupied in Berlin, before he stepped – armed and encased – out of my name into the light, he fixed his picture on the wall: New Angel. The Kabbala relates that in every instant ['Nu'] God creates a numberless number of new angels, all of whom are only destined, before they dissolve into nothing, to sing for a single moment the praise of God before His throne. Such an angel the New one pretended to be before he would name himself. (My translation)

What emerges with startling clarity is the aura of being named or imaged. Benjamin also said: 'Things made of glass have no "aura" ' ('Die Dinge aus Glas haben keine "Aura" '). So the world he projects in his Romance of Being Named resists translucence or glassification: the very word 'Agesilaus' strikes one as the opposite of the word 'Glas' – it contains g-l-a-s, in fact, and becomes, as it were, its antonym. Recalling Benjamin's interest in anagrams, Scholem suggests that the title of his fantasy should be deciphered as 'Der Angelus Satanas' (The Angel Satan), and he links it to the New Angel of Klee's picture that continued to haunt Benjamin. (See, especially, the ninth of Benjamin's 'Theses on the Philosophy of History,' written not long before his death.) But one should add that the insistence of this picture in the writer's life is itself 'demonic': it reveals a specular fixation on Benjamin's part, and seems to be transposed from German Romantic fiction or the Gothic novella. However we unriddle it, 'Agesilaus Santander' remains an abracadabra phrase that aims at reviving the aura of names, or of a naming with ritual and fixative power.

I doubt, then, that this title is decipherable in a single way. The difference in sound shape, for example, between Agesilaus and Angelus (Novus) could foreground the syllable 'laus,' to remind us of the Latin word for praise; if so, a relation might suggest itself between 'Age'/'Ange' plus 'laus' and the Kabbalistic angel whose essence is to praise God a single moment, an 'Augen'-blick.

Other decipherings may be possible, but I will try only one more. Benjamin thinks of himself as a refugee: he has abandoned the orthodoxy of his fathers; he is in Spain, from which the Jews were expelled and one former home of the Kabbalists whose mystical reflections on names was known to him through

Scholem; the Nazis have come to power; and he ponders angels whose essence is not permanence but transience, whose newness is their nowness, or their flight from Nu to Nichts, as they praise and wait to be dissolved. Considering, then, that this scholar was doomed to wander and flee, and that his major work had been on seventeenth-century German literature, might he not have remembered the poet of that era who took the pseudonym 'Angelus Silesius' for his *Der Cherubinischer Wandersmann* (The Cherub Wanderer), a collection of epigrammatic mystical verses? 'Agesilaus,' though a real and not a made-up name, seems to scramble 'Angelus Silesius' into a single word, and Santander could suggest the mixed Santa/Satanic quality of Benjamin the pilgrim or some desired relation to Southern (Spanish and Kabbalistic) rather than Northern spirit of place through the name of this town.

What we are given, then, is the aura of a name: 'Agesilaus Santander' is the quintessence of an anagram rather than a univocally decipherable writing. The scrambling is permanent and the meanings we recover are fugitive constructions, like the 'new angels' in contrast to the old. The name may even accuse the maker of the name: it is satanic also in that. For it stands as the product of an artificial mysticism that evokes an 'aura artificiel' in the manner of Baudelaire's 'paradis artificiel.' It betrays a fallen aura, mere aroma of aura, the whiff of a Turkish cigarette and Eastern mysteries. Like 'Xanadu' and 'Kubla Khan' the name is an authentic fake, a given or proper name consumed by the imagination, the scar of a signature that belongs to no one. 'Its traits had no human likeness.' Benjamin's fantasy could be part of a book on hashish he meant to write. He continued to look, patiently and yet in flight, to the origin of all names in the garden God had planted eastward of Eden. Psychoanalysis: the Eden connection.

Part V

Memory

Chapter 31

Public Memory and its Discontents

I want to raise the issue of how to focus public memory on traumatic experiences like war, the Holocaust, or massive violations of human rights. You might think this is not an issue at all; that we are, in fact, too absorbed in such painful matters. I have often heard objections claiming that the study of the Holocaust, in particular, is displacing among Jews a learning-tradition two thousand years old. There may be some truth to that charge; it is easy to become fascinated with cruelty and violence, with the mystery of such extreme inhumanity. But we cannot turn away from the world in which this happened; and the question of what impedes our focus is complicated by the very efficiency of modern media, their realism and representational scope.

The substantial effects of film and telecommunications are having their impact. An 'information sickness,' caused by the speed and quantity of what impinges on us, and abetted by machines we have invented that generate endless arrays, threatens to overwhelm personal memory. The individual, we complain, cannot 'process' all this information, this incoming flak: public and personal are not being moved closer together but further apart. Can public memory still be called memory, when it is increasingly alienated from personal and active recall?

Among the symptoms of this malady of our age are philosophic discussions about the existence or nonexistence of a 'post-humanist subject,' a conference on 'The Uses of Oblivion,' and the fear, openly expressed, that 'our past will have no future in our future' (David Rieff). Even as our senses are routinely besieged, the imagination, traditionally defined as a power that restores a kind of presence to absent things, has its work taken away, and is in danger of imitating media sensationalism. It becomes, as Wallace Stevens said, a violence from within pressing against the violence from outside. In the midst of unprecedented realism in fiction and the public media, there is reason to worry about a desensitizing trend, one that keeps raising the threshold at which we begin to respond.

How do we keep our sensitivity alive, when such vivid and painful events become our daily fare? How do we prevent denial or indifference from taking over? We have known for a long time that there is great suffering in the world, suffering impossible to justify. Such knowledge must have been with us at least since the Book of Job was written. But we also know from the time of Job's so-called friends to that of Holocaust deniers, that suffering is explained or rationalized against all odds.

Today we have entered a new period. Until recently, perhaps until news from Bosnia reached the screen, we clutched at the hope that had the indifferent masses in Germany or America known what was going on in the concentration camps, known with the same graphic detail communicated today by TV, surely the atrocities could not have continued. There would have been an outcry of the popular conscience and so much protest that the Holocaust would have had to stop.[1]

Yet right now we are learning a new truth about human indifference. As the media make us bystanders of every act of violence and violation, we realize that this indifference or lack of focus was not so incomprehensible after all. For we glimpse a terrible inertia in ourselves and can even find reasons for it. We register the fact that no event is reported without a spin, without an explanatory or talky context that buffers the raw images; and we realize that pictures on TV remain pictures, that a sort of antibody builds up in our response system and prevents total mental disturbance. Even while deploring and condemning the events, we experience what the poet John Keats called 'the feel of not to feel it,' as we continue with everyday life.

It is not my intent to add to our already considerable sense of guilt or powerlessness. My point is that the media place a demand on us which it is impossible to satisfy. Paradoxically enough, their extended eyes and ears, so important to informed action, also distance the reality of what is perceived. Terrible things, by continuing to be shown, begin to appear matter-of-fact, a natural rather than manmade catastrophe. Zygmunt Bauman has labelled this the 'production of moral indifference.'[2]

For our sensibility, however compassionate, is not superhuman: it is finite and easily exhausted. Sooner or later coldness sets in, admitted or not. We remain deeply engaged, however, because official morality does not cultivate that coldness. This is an important difference between our situation and that of Germans under the Nazi regime, so that viewer reaction splits schizophrenically into responding passionately to images of global misery and an exhausted self-distancing. Those images, for all their immediacy, become too often electronic phantoms.[3]

A desensitization of this kind (Robert Lifton calls it 'psychic numbing') was already noted by Wordsworth near the beginning of the Industrial Revolution. He complained in 1800 of a 'degrading thirst after outrageous stimulation' blunting 'the discriminating powers of the mind' and reducing it to 'a state of almost savage torpor.' People were losing their ability to be moved by ordinary sights and events, by 'common life,' because of 'the great national events which are daily taking place, and the increasing accumulation of men in cities, where the uniformity of their occupations produces a craving for extraordinary incident which the rapid communication of intelligence hourly gratifies.'[4] Wordsworth created, in response, a minimalist poetry, a 'lyrical' ballad which reduced the narrative or romance interest to near zero, and urged the reader to 'find a tale in everything.'

Since Wordsworth's time psychic numbing has made considerable progress. The contemporary problem is not Bovaryism or Quixotism – seeing the real world (defensively) with an imagination steeped in romance – but looking at whatever is on the screen as if it were unreal, just an interesting construct or simulation. Actuality is distanced by a larger than life violence and retreats behind all those special effects. While Adorno discerns an 'obscene merger of aesthetics and reality,' it is not surprising that art historian Robert Rosenblum should defend what he calls Warhol's 'deadpan' by claiming that it reflects a 'state of moral and emotional anaesthesia which, like it or not, probably tells us more truth about the realities of the modern world than do the rhetorical passions of Guernica.'[5]

But if the present has now less of a hold, if abstractness and psychic numbing have indeed infected us, how can we remain sensitive to the past, to its reality? Spielberg's *Schindler's List* won its acclaim in part by getting through to us, by lifting that anxiety – though not without deploying spectacular means.

Consider a related problem intensified by the media: whether we can trust appearances. Because our technical power of simulation has increased, but forgetfulness has not decreased – the speed with which events fall into 'the dark backward and abysm of time' has, if anything, accelerated – the greatest danger to public memory is official history. Even the dead, as Walter Benjamin declared, are not safe from the victors, who consider public memory part of the spoils and do not hesitate to rewrite history . . . or re-image it. Milan Kundera in the opening episode of *The Book of Laughter and Forgetting* recalls how a discredited Communist leader was airbrushed out of a famous historical photo – so readily is history falsified and public memory deceived.

You may have seen a movie that is set in Argentina under the military dictatorship. It could also have been set in Eastern Europe during the time of Soviet domination. Puenzo's film, *The Official Story*, tells a tragic and typical narrative of public deceit and personal discovery. It is the story of a mother who learns that her adopted child was stolen from a 'disappeared' Argentinian woman. At first the mother does not suspect the truth, but a small doubt punctures the basic trust she has in the system: that doubt grows and grows, the search for the truth grows and grows, until – as also in *Oedipus the King* – a hidden past is revealed. But, tragically, her resolute pursuit of the truth breaks up the family and endangers the child.

What I have described comes close to being a universal kind of plot, as old as the historical record itself. What is the difference, then, between past and present? The contemporary difference can be summed up in Emerson's famous dictum: 'We suspect our instruments.' The very means that expose untruth, the verbal or photographic or filmic evidence itself, is tainted by suspicion. All evidence is met by a demystifying discourse or charges of manipulation. The intelligent scrutiny to which we habitually submit appearances becomes a crisis of trust, a lack of confidence in what we are told or shown, a fear that the world of appearances and the world of propaganda have merged through the power of the media. To undo this spell and gain true knowledge would then be more tricky than in gnosticism, which distrusted nature and tried to gain a knowledge of the true god behind the god of nature.

What I have argued is that there is a link between epistemology and morality, between how we get to know what we know (through various, including electronic, media) and the moral life we aspire to lead. My account has been pessimistic: it implies that the gap between knowledge and ethical action has not grown less wide for us. The pressures to be politically correct, to say and do the right thing, have increased, but neither our thinking nor our actions have adjusted to the challenge so clearly stated by Terrence des Pres, who said that, after the Holocaust, 'a new shape of knowing invades the mind,' one that opens our eyes – beyond the Holocaust – to the global extent of political misery.[6] In a democracy, moreover, and once we are in the electronic age, while there is more realism, there is also the liability that goes with that: a gnawing distrust of public policy and official memory. The free speech that is one of the foundations of truth in the democratic 'marketplace of ideas' leads to a continual probing, testing, and even muckraking that has an unexpected effect on the integrity of the public life it was intended to assure.

Indeed, the more that official history is disputed by scholarship or media-journalism, the more an insidious and queasy feeling of unreality grows in us. What are we to do, for example, with all the speculations about Kennedy's assassination that parade as investigative journalism or docudrama? It is as if the political realm, and possibly all of public life, were inauthentic – a mask, a Machiavellian web of continuous deception.[7] This negative insight also undermines the gravity and uniqueness of lived events, and encourages a deep scepticism about the world – or a relentless, compensatory belief in something fundamental and unfalsifiable, a something which often takes the form of nationalistic or religious fanaticism.

My aim in raising this issue of the relation of morality to knowledge in a democratic and electronic age is, frankly, moralistic. I seek to draw some conclusions, not only to describe as clearly as possible a contemporary dilemma. Terrence des Pres, again, states that dilemma with the precision of a proverb: 'Thanks to the technological expansion of consciousness, we cannot not know the extent of political torment; and in truth it may be said that what others suffer, we behold.'[8] The triumph of technology has created two classes which can coexist in the same person: those who suffer, and those who observe that suffering. This fact cannot be touted as moral progress, but there is one gain from it. Given our new eyes for the pain of others, and given that 'we cannot not know,' all monopolistic claims about suffering do not make sense.

'What others suffer, we behold' is like a second fall from innocence, a second bite of the fatal apple. It removes all excuse by taking away our ignorance, without at the same time granting us the power to do something decisive. Often, therefore, we fall back on a religious feeling, as President Reagan did at Bitburg, though in his case it served the bottom line of NATO policy. At Bitburg, Mr. Reagan's reconciling memorial perspective equated fallen German soldiers, including Waffen SS, and the civilians they killed, many of them Jewish victims. This 'dead' perspective short-circuits reflection on a torment des Pres called political, because of its manmade rather than inevitable nature.

Even when the politics are not so obvious, sceptical contemporary thought sees them everywhere: in religion, in memory, in art. But that insight too has no activist or redemptive value. It simply confirms des Pres's hellish vision of universal political torment. When we ask, haunted like Tolstoi by such suffering, 'What is to be done?' no course of action proposes itself as entirely credible. Rather, the ethical impasse breeds, I have suggested, desperate and manichean solutions, post-Tolstoi fundamentalisms, whether religious or political.[9]

A related reaction is cultural revolution and its instrument, the politicized memory. In flight from human and hermeneutic complexities, this kind of politics saturates everything with ideological content and claims redemptive power for a purified vision of the past. I have previously mentioned the role of official history, promoted by the apparatus of state. It manipulates memory like news.

Now it is true that a war is always going on to modify memory, and we all wage it in ourselves first: who does not remember moments of altering (or rationalizing or shading) experiences painful to self-esteem? When waged in public, however, such warfare leads to an institutionalized and bogus recollection, a churlish denial of the history of others (covering up, for instance, at Theresienstadt and Auschwitz, the Jewish identity of most of the victims), or an artificially inseminated perspective. A single authorized narrative then simplifies not just history but the only active communal memory we have, made of such traditional materials as legends, poetry, dances, songs, festivals, and recitations, the sum of which helps to define a 'culture,' when combined with various interpretive traditions.

Art as a performative medium – art not reduced to official meaning or information – has a chance to transmit this inheritance most fully. When art remains accessible it provides a counterforce to manufactured and monolithic memory. Despite its imaginative license, art is often more effective in 'embodying' historically specific ideas than the history-writing on which it may draw. Scientific historical research, however essential it is for its negative virtues of rectifying error and denouncing falsification, has no positive resource to lessen grief, endow calamity with meaning, foster a vision of the world, or legitimate new groups.[10] But art remains in touch with or revives traditional materials that satisfy our need for community without repressing individualist performance.

We start indeed with a cultural inheritance, yet that cannot be fixed as immutably as doctrine is in theology. Memorial narratives asserting the identity of nation or group are usually modern constructs, a form of anti-memory limiting the subversive or heterogeneous facts. Invented to nationalize consensus by suggesting a uniform and heroic past ('O say, can you see . . .'), they convert 'great memories' into political theology. Cults and myths do not go away in modernity; on the contrary, revolution, national rebirth and the drive for political legitimation make blatant ideological use of paradigms from the past. So Marx objected in *The Eighteenth Brumaire* to the French Revolution's historical masquerade: its archaic revival of symbols from the Republican phase of the Roman Empire.[11] This tendency, taken to its extreme, views the culture of a community not as its 'nonhereditary memory' but as a pristine essence to be repristinated, a foundation with biological or mystical force that determines history.

What is viable, then, in the notion of collective memory tends to be artistic rather than nationalistic; and unless we keep in mind this link between art and memory – recognized when the Greeks made Mnemosyne the mother of the Muses – national or ethnic politics will reduce culture to a tyrannous and frozen difference, a heroic narrative demanding consent.

A sense of the nation as vital to cultural memory arose in Romanticism. Throughout Europe, artists and scholars tried to free literature from the yoke of 'foreign' classics by retrieving (and counterfeiting if necessary!) a native tradition. This literary nationalism was often a reconstruction, motivated by visionary nostalgia. 'A people who lose their nationality create a legend to take its place,' Edwin Muir wrote about Walter Scott's attempt to carry on a tradition that had lost its continuity. The ideal culture, according to Romantic historicism, was produced by the spirit embodied in a people, a spirit of the folk (Volksgeist) which expressed the true, distinctive voice of each nation among the nations.

Collectors and antiquarians hunted for old stories, songs, and ballads: relics of a past disappearing too quickly, and to which popular or archaic strength was imputed. A lively interest arose for anything regional rather than cosmopolitan: the buzz words were 'local attachment,' 'local romance,' even 'local superstition.' Hence Wordsworth's 'Hart-Leap Well,' a self-consciously recreated ballad, typical of a return to stories represented as an emanation of particular places – places impressed on the collective memory and still part of the imaginative life of ordinary people.[12]

These legends about place stretch back to the Bible and seem to reflect traces of a popular memory. Being topocentric (subordinating time to place) they also lessen our anxiety that the ancient rapport between singer and audience, or artist and community, may have broken down.

> We have no institutions, [Alasdair MacIntyre declares] through which shared stories can be told dramatically or otherwise to the entire political community, assembled together as an audience, no dramatists or other story tellers able to address such an audience . . . Our audiences are privatized and dispersed, watching television in homes or motel rooms . . .

This panicky view shows how deep the nostalgia for a collective memory runs. Since it is indeed difficult to humanize modern urban spaces, to invest them with a historically charged sense of place, the picture arises of a story-less modern imagination moving from non-place to non-place, and even enjoying the anonymity of highways, airports, large hotels and shopping malls. It looks as if each sacred memory-place ('lieu de mémoire') is emptied out to become what Marc Augé defines as a nowhere-place ('non-lieu').[13] Yet the old myths die hard: Michael Kammen in *Mystic Chords of Memory* notices 'the remarkable way in which local events can be conceptualized to conform to paradigms of religious tradition or to the totally secular needs of a modern state struggling for existence.'

Before I discuss three recent literary ventures that respond to the challenge of reattaching imagination to the collective memory, or creating a communal story under modern conditions – conditions described in the introductory part of this chapter – let me add a few words to define contemporary public memory in its difference from the traditional collective memory.

Maurice Halbwachs, killed at Buchenwald, viewed the collective memory as a 'living deposit' preserved outside academic or written history. 'In general,' he writes in his posthumous book, 'history begins only at the point where tradition ends, at a moment where social memory is extinguished or decomposes . . . [T]he need to write the history of a period, a society, even of an individual does not arise until they are already too far removed in the past' for us to find many living witnesses.[14]

Although these lines were probably composed in the 1930s, they already seem dated, for today we feel a need to record everything, even as the event is occurring; and the media not only make this possible but encourage it. A nervous effervescence marks modern experience and the rise of public memory in distinction from collective memory. The loss or subsumption of the past in the present, a present with very little presence beyond the spotlight moment of its occurrence – which wearies itself out of the mind by its violence or is almost immediately displaced by another such moment, sound-bite, or instantly-fading image – this self-consuming present, both real and specious, vivid and always already a trace, is curiously like the collective memory in that it has, to quote the historian Yosef Yerushalmi, 'not the historicity of the past but its eternal contemporaneity.' (Yerushalmi offers the example that in Jewish liturgy the destruction of the First and Second Temples is conflated, as if it were the same destruction; and the Holocaust is often assimilated as the third 'hurban'.) Of course, public memory is also utterly different: it strikes us as a bad simulacrum, one that, unlike the older type of communal or collective memory, has no stability or durée, only a jittery, mobile, perpetually changing yet permanently inscribed status.[15] Hence my opening question on what could focus public memory on the traumatic events it is busy recording.

Halbwachs's observation that we are motivated to write things down only when they are in danger of fading entirely can be made relevant to his own project: today the collective memory is in this danger. Doubly so: It is weakened because public memory, with its frantic and uncertain agency, is taking its place; and because a politicized collective memory, claiming a biological or mystical permanence, tries to usurp the living tie between generations.[16]

With this remark we return to literature. One reason literature remains important is that it counteracts the impersonality and instability of public memory, on the one hand, and, on the other, the determinism and funda-mentalism of a collective memory based on identity politics.[17] Literature creates an institution of its own, more personal and focussed than public memory yet less monologic than the memorializing fables common to ethnic or nationalist affirmation. At the same time, because today the tie between generations, the 'living deposit' or 'passé vécu,' as Halbwachs calls it, is jeopardized, creative activity is often carried on under the negative sign of an absent memory (Ellen Fine) or 'mémoire trouée' (Henri Raczymow).[18] A missed encounter is evoked, through a strenuous, even cerebral exercise of the imagination, as if the link between memory and imagination had been lost.

I turn first to Toni Morrison's *Beloved*. Its epigraphs suggest not only a comparison between the political suffering of blacks and Jews but also that the pathos and the covenant have passed to the former. One epigraph is a dedication: 'Sixty million and more.' The second alludes through a New Testament quote to the concept of the Chosen People: 'I will call them my people, which were not my people; and her beloved, which was not beloved' (Romans 9:25).

It is no exaggeration to call *Beloved* that people's 'zakhor' ('Remember!').

Where in black history is there something comparable to a genealogy of 'begats,' or the millennia of myths, chronicles, scriptures, and scriptural interpretations that characterize the collective memory of the Jews? (Concerning the begats, Julius Lester reminds us, on the dedication page of *To Be a Slave*, that 'The ancestry of any black American can be traced to a bill of sale and no further. In many instances even that cannot be done;' and John Edgar Wideman prefaces *Damballah* with 'A Begat Chart' and a 'Family Tree.') African American memory remains to be recovered. But more important still, where is the conviction of being loved that makes memory possible? What kind of story could have been passed on, or who stayed alive long enough to remember a suffering that destroyed those who might have been tradents, a suffering that allowed no development of person, family or ethnic group? 'Anyone Baby Suggs knew, let alone loved, who hadn't run off or been hanged, got rented out, loaned out, bought up, brought back, stored up, mortgaged, won, stolen or seized.'

Between Baby Suggs, or Grandma Baby as she is also called, and Beloved, the little girl killed by her mother, there is no growth or normal history or significant genealogy. The child whose life was aborted at less than two years, and who preternaturally re-enters the mother's house as a young woman (now able to talk and carry on conversations of the most affectionate kind), is a ghost from folklore who expresses hauntingly the unlived life, a love that never could come to fulfilment except in this fantasy-form. Morrison's startling use of the revenant, the spirit-figure that returns in many a romantic ballad (a genre that itself needed 'revival'), challenges us to a suspension of disbelief. Not so much, I would suggest, disbelief affecting the preternatural return of Beloved – for that partly pagan, partly Christian myth has 'a foundation in humanity,' as Wordsworth would have said – but disbelief concerning the atrocities suffered by African Americans, that ghost which we have not entirely faced.

African American history discloses, then, in a novel like Morrison's, a special difficulty concerning its 'absent memory.' The subject of that history, the black community, is so scattered by suffering, so 'disremembered and unaccounted for,' that the story to be passed on 'is not a story to pass on,' and Morrison can only represent it by a ghostly 'devil-child,' a fantasy-memory of the love or election this people has not known. In search of that reversal of fate, *Beloved* becomes a Song of Songs, the Shulammite's scripture.

My second example of absent memory is very different. The postmodern work of art, to which I now turn, cultivates that absence and does not seek to recover the very possibility of memory itself – of 'rememory' as Morrison names it. Raymond Federman, for example, tries to do without resonant names and local romance in *To Whom It May Concern*, though he too, like Morrison, subverts an unfeeling realism. He uses gimmicks (as he admits) to fight 'the imposture of realism, that ugly beast that stands at bay ready to leap in the moment you begin scribbling your fiction.' He renounces realism even in a novel that recalls the great roundup and deportation of Jews from Paris in July 1942, and its impact on two children who escaped. His self-defeating venture takes courage from experiments, starting with Sterne and Diderot, which portray life as an infinite detour rather than a punctual drama or epiphany: something less than heroic, composed of accidents, small gestures, and simple, even insignificant words. Thus the 'non-lieu 'gains a sort of authenticity. 'The grim story of Sarah and her cousin should be told without any mention of time and place. It should happen on a timeless vacant stage without scenery. No names of places. No decor. Nothing. It simply happened, sometime and somewhere.'

Federman is indebted to the New Novel that evolved in postwar France, and such films as *Last Year at Marienbad*. They depict memory as a mode of seduction – as a narrative of past encounter suggesting that the human condition is so empty or forgetful, so deprived of sacred space ('lieu de mémoire') and therefore so needy, that it cannot be redeemed except by the construction and imposition of an imaginary history. This deliberate recourse to a perhaps fictional past returns us, of course, to the province of the collective memory, except that *Marienbad* seeks to erode the latter's historical and nationalist pretensions (the Versailles-like decor in the film is meant to be only that, a decor) in favor of the private, imaginative needs of one man and one woman. Federman, like Resnais or Robbe-Grillet, refuses to give his characters more memory than they have. The wound of an absence remains. In this he speaks for an entire postwar generation that lost parents or relatives, while they themselves missed the brunt of the war. 'They suffered from not suffering enough,' he writes of his escaped children.

My last example is a genre that in documentaries such as *Eyes on the Prize* or Lanzmann's *Shoah* or the witness-accounts in Yale's Video Archive for Holocaust Testimonies is also oriented toward an 'absent memory.' Personal testimony has long been a significant part of both religious and secular literature, and is usually considered a type of autobiography. Videotaped oral testimony, however, is partly a creation of modern technology and so has a chance of influencing that environment. As history it seeks to convey information, but as oral witness it is an act of remembrance. And as this spoken and more spontaneous mode, which can be recorded without being written down, it contributes to a group biography through highly individual yet convergent stories. The collective memory thus becomes a collected memory (James Young), at once a private and a public legacy, and through video itself counters video's dispersive flow.

Each testimony is potentially an act of rescue, as the Israeli poet, Haim Gouri, observed when covering the Eichmann trial: a rescue 'from the danger of [survivors] being perceived as all alike, all shrouded in the same immense anonymity.' Moreover, by recording an experience collectively endured, by allowing anyone in the community a voice – that is, not focussing on an elite – a vernacular and many-voiced dimension is caught.[19] Memory collected this way is too plural and diverse to be politicized or sacralized. But I can characterize the genre of these testimonies best, and the Archive of Conscience they are building, by saying that they accept the presence of memory, however painful, rather than its absence.[20]

The amnesia that invades characters in postmodernist fiction (think of the difference between Beckett and Proust), creating a limbo in which the tape of memory starts and crashes, again and again – this amnesia may reflect a public memory that has become primarily space instead of place, anonymous and occupied by impersonal networks of information. As memory, then, it is purely virtual if not absent. In oral testimonies, however, a burdened recollection asserts itself and fashions a complex relation to the rupture between the positivism of historical experience and the symbolic stores of collective memory. Not only do memory's informative and performative (or ritual) functions try to unite again, but time present, in these testimonies, becomes more than a site of loss or nostalgic recuperation: more than the place which reveals that our capacity to experience has diminished, or that the past must be forgotten to be survived.[21]

Even if memory, as Rimbaud said of love, has always to be reinvented, this does not alter the truth that some kinds of memory are better than others. Though Plato suggested that writing would be harmful to recollection, it proved essential for transmitting thought, both in manuscript and print. Writing a thing down meant passing it on, for a communal or generational recipient. But who is the addressee of the new electronic writing, with its capacity for near-instantaneous reception and transmission? Every TV program is implicitly addressed 'To Whom It May Concern,' which begs the question of who must be concerned.

Videotaped oral history is an important compromise because it comes on the cusp between generations, addresses those still growing up, and at a time when the collective memory is fading into the quasi-timeless, panoramic simultaneity of public memory. From Abel Gance and Walter Benjamin to Jean Baudrillard, this impact of technology on memory-institutions such as art and history has been a subject of intense reflection. I have emphasized the difficulty, moral as well as cognitive, of responding to the images before our eyes in a critical or affective manner when the audio-visual mode becomes ineluctable and bypasses or floods time-bound channels of personal memory.[22]

I have also suggested that there is such a thing as memory-envy. It shows itself in writers who seek to recover an image of their community's past – a past deliberately destroyed by others or which was not allowed to form itself into a heritage. Memory-envy also touches a generation that feels belated: the 'generation after' which did not participate directly in a great event that determined their parents' and perhaps grandparents' lives. Memory is lacking in both cases as a basis for the integrity of person or group. At the level of the collective, moreover, memory-envy can take the form of foundation narratives, myths of origin that fortify group identity. Some of these decisive but also imposed identity-fictions must be labelled false memories.

Increasingly, politicized and simplified aspects of the collective memory take over from an actual artistic heritage. We still have the arts, and literature in particular, to recall that each of us is a being made of many beings, and that the heritage of the past is pluralistic and diverse. But as the collective memory weakens, political religions (Eric Voegelin's name for totalitarian regimes) falsify the complexity of the past and cultivate an official story that seeks to reawaken ancient hatreds. This falsified memory, with its foundation myths, or funda-mentalist notions of national destiny and ethnic purity, is the enemy. We cannot allow it to masquerade as history, as is happening with the Pamyat movement in Russia, the attempt to rehabilitate Tissot in Slovakia, and nationalistic nostalgia, whether in Bosnia or the Middle East. The outbreak of unreal memory can be fought, but only if younger bystanders, whether artists or scholars, bring testimony of their own, ballads of their own, before our eyes. And only if, like the Carribean poet Derek Walcott, they accept the scarred rather than sacred, the fragmented rather than holistic nature of what he names 'epic memory,' which has to be recomposed – performed – again and again. For oral tradition, however monumental its aspiration, remains an art of assemblage. To reconstruct 'this shipwreck of fragments, these echoes, these shards of a huge tribal vocabulary, these partially remembered customs' needs a special love. 'Nothing can be sole or whole/That has not been rent,' Yeats's Crazy Jane tells the Bishop. 'Break a vase,' says Walcott, 'and the love that reassembles the fragments is stronger than the love that took its symmetry for granted when it was whole.'[23]

Notes

1. The shock factor seemed greater during the Vietnam War, the Biafra famine, and even occasionally before that. In 1941, filmed Japanese atrocities in China, or, in the 1960s, pictures of southern brutality against blacks during the Civil Rights move-ment, caught the attention of the American public.
2. See Bauman, *Modernity and the Holocaust* (Ithaca: Cornell University Press, 1989). The context of his discussion is Nazi bureaucracy and Hannah Arendt's thesis on the banality of evil. Concerning immediate media coverage of the Bosnian conflict, Slavenka Drakulic asks in the *New Republic* (June 21, 1993): 12: 'here they are,

generations who have learned at school about concentration camps and factories of death; generations whose parents swear it could never happen again, at least not in Europe, precisely because of the living memory of the recent past. What, then, has all the documentation changed? And what is being changed now by what seems to be the conscious, precise bookkeeping of death?'

3. No wonder many in the younger generation, who are the most susceptible, are drawn to the unreality of fiction, to horror movies and other artificial plots, ever more crude, gothic, and violent: one can pretend that these, at least, are mere fantasy.

4. Preface to *Lyrical Ballads*. Compare Goethe's notation circa August 8, 1797, in *Reise in die Schweiz*: 'Sehr merkwürdig ist mir aufgefallen, wie es eigentlich mit dem Publikum einer grossen Stadt beschaffen ist; es lebt in einem bestaendigen Tummel von Erwerben und Verzehren.' (It seems to me very peculiar and worthy of notice, the quality of public life in a great city; it is marked by a constant tumult of acquiring and consuming.) (Cf. Wordsworth's famous line, 'Getting and spending, we lay waste our powers') He goes on to mention, in particular, theater and the inclination of the reading public toward novels and newspapers as the major distractions. These early symptoms of a consumer culture show that, from the outset, sensations are among the commodities being produced and consumed.

5. 'Warhol as Art History,' in *New Art*, ed. A. Papadakis, et al. (New York: Rizzoli, 1991). Henri Lefebvre's theory of 'everydayness' diagnoses a 'generalized passivity' that accompanies the increasing uniformity of everyday life (itself a functionalist result of the industrial and electronic revolutions) and is often veiled by the surface of modernity. 'News stories and the turbulent affectations of art, fashion and event veil without ever eradicating the everyday blahs. Images, the cinema and television divert the everyday by at times offering up to it its own spectacle, or sometimes the spectacle of the distinctly noneveryday, violence, death, catastrophe, the lives of kings and stars – those who we are led to believe defy everydayness.' For Lefebvre, see 'The Everyday and Everydayness,' *Yale French Studies* 73 (1987): 7–11. Or cf. Gianni Vattimo on what he characterizes as a 'growing psychological dullness': 'Technical reproduction seems to work in exactly the opposite sense to shock. In the age of reproduction [the reference is to Walter Benjamin's essay of 1936 on that subject], both the great art of the past and new media products reproducible from their inception, such as cinema, tend to become common objects and consequently less and less well defined against the background of intensified communication.' Gianni Vattimo, *The Transparent Society*, trans. David Webb (Baltimore: Johns Hopkins University Press, 1992), 47–48.

6. Des Pres, *Praises and Dispraises: Poetry and Politics, the 20th Century* (New York: Penguin, 1989), Prolog.

7. The result of this can also be comic: think of the energy some expend on seeking to prove that Shakespeare was really Francis Bacon or the Earl of Essex, or consider that even children's literature is beginning to exploit this revisionism, as in *The True Story of the Three Little Pigs*, by Alexander T. Wolf.

8. *Praises and Dispraises*, Prolog (my emphasis). That which 'we cannot not know' is 'the real,' according to Henry James.

9. Such as blaming the 'white devil' or the Jew for the world's suffering, or the notion of an evil empire. One of the few treatises to take up the possibility of ethics in a technological age, Hans Jonas's *Das Prinzip Verantwortung* (Frankfurt a/M: Insel, 1979) argues that our sense of technological power has led to utopian expectations: that it is all too easy to conceive of action on the pattern of technical progress, and that we need, therefore, a new 'modesty' as the basis of moral activism: 'In view of the quasi-eschatological potential of our technical processes, ignorance about ultimate consequences becomes itself a ground for responsible hesitation – a second-best quality, should wisdom be lacking.' In America, at the same time, televangelism spawns its own sublime simplicity: the sinful past can be overcome by turning to a savior figure. The sense of universal suffering conveyed (painfully) by the media is here relieved (painlessly) by the media.

10. Indeed, Jean-François Lyotard defines our 'postmodern' condition as 'incredulity toward metanarratives' produced by progress in the sciences. There is often a rupture, then, between the increasingly scientific history of the historians and the culture of the community, that is, collective practices structured by group memory. In Judaism this separation from communal ways of remembering becomes painfully clear after the Holocaust. The command 'zakhor,' 'remember!' that resounds throughout the Bible and Jewish tradition, used to refer to observances that stressed, in Yosef Yerushalmi's words, 'not the historicity of the past, but its eternal contemporaneity.' Today the same 'remember!' documents in volume upon volume a genocide that has weakened Jewish continuity. A form of memorizing rather than remembrance, and information rather than performance oriented, it is very different from the liturgical memory, the collectively recited lamentations, petitions and hymns, or the scripture study, by which Jews as a community healed or at least integrated the catastrophes in their past. Amos Funkenstein reintroduces the notion of 'historical consciousness' to show that the split between historical and liturgical memory is not, today or in earlier times, as absolute as Yerushalmi represents it: see 'Collective Memory and Historical Consciousness,' *History and Memory* 1 (1989): 5–27.

11. Two more contemporary examples. (1) East Germany's foundational cult, centered on the prewar Communist leader Thaelmann. There is evidence that Thaelmann was brought to Buchenwald and executed there toward the end of the war. To magnify Buchenwald as the symbol of German resistance to fascism, the East German government identified the cell where he was killed, made it a cavernous shrine, and used it to initiate young devotees of the youth movement. The Thaelmann cult excluded all perspectives on the Nazi era except that of heroic Communist revolt, and became a sterile and self-exculpatory 'god-term' for East Germany, one that allowed its inhabitants to transfer guilt for fascism and war crimes exclusively to the citizens of the other (West) Germany. (2) The rebirth of Israel, as Saul Friedlander and Alan Mintz (among others) have shown, activated a 'paradigm retrieval' which had long ago linked catastrophe and redemption. 'The national historian,' Funkenstein writes, 'who in the nineteenth century enjoyed the status of a priest of culture, and whose work, even professional, was still read by a wide stratum of the educated public . . . even created some of [the symbols], some almost

from nothing, such as the legend of Hermann, the victorious Cheruskian hero of early Roman-Germanic encounter.' 'Collective Memory,' 21.

12. The stories often crystallize or cluster around proper names, especially place-names (Hart-Leap Well; Beth-El; Wessex; Balbec; Paris, Texas; Ole Kentucky; Chelm; Homewood). Some of these are fictional places; but such is the power of art that names outlive in our imagination referents they may never have had.

13. Pierre Nora, *Les lieux de mémoire: La République. La Nation.* (1984–), and Marc Augé, *Non-Lieux: Introduction à une anthropologie de la surmodernité* (Paris: Seuil, 1992). The conception of 'non-lieu' plays with the legal term by which courts refuse to receive a complaint or else nullify its basis in law. Cf. Claude Lanzmann, 'Le lieu et la parole,' in *Les Cahiers du Cinéma*, 37 (1985). He describes there how he develops a technique to overcome the 'non-lieu de la mémoire.' For MacIntyre, see *After Virtue: A Study in Moral Theory* (Notre Dame: Notre Dame University Press, 1984).

14. *La mémoire collective*, 2nd ed. (Paris: Presses Universitaries de France, 1968), 68–69. Halbwachs's 'collective memory' is a broader concept than 'communal memory': no memory, according to Halbwachs (in the wake of Durkheim and Marc Bloch), is purely individual but always depends, to be a memory, on an 'affective community' (which need not be religious or ritual). Edward Shils in *Tradition* (Chicago: Chicago University Press, 1981) makes the case that there is a sense of the past which is inculcated early and which is important as a general 'sensibility to past things' as well as for its specific contents.

15. 'Commentators on American culture note that a sense of historicity is shifting away from singular stories that are forever true – away from story-lines that are hero-oriented and confrontational. There are fewer authentic moments of "catastrophe time".' See Don Handelman on 'media events,' in *Models and Mirrors: Toward an Anthropology of Public Events* (Cambridge: Cambridge University Press, 1990), 266ff.

16. Jacques Le Goff, in describing the work of Pierre Nora on memory-places, and a new history 'which seeks to create a scientific history on the basis of collective memory,' does not entirely confront this difference between public and collective memory in his rather optimistic assessment. '[T]he whole evolution of the contemporary world, under the impact of an immediate history for the most part fabricated on the spot by the media, is headed toward the production of an increased number of collective memories, and history is written, much more than in earlier days, under the influence of these collective memories.' *History and Memory*, trans. Steven Rendall and E. Claman (New York: Columbia University Press, 1993), 95.

17. Cf. the description of what J. Assmann names 'das kulturelle Gedächtnis,' which seeks a stability beyond the saeculum of oral history and the span of Halbwachs's collective memory. 'Kollektives Gedächtnis und kulturelle Identität,' in *Kultur und Gedächtnis*, ed. Jan Assmann and Tonio Hölscher (Frankfurt a/M: Suhrkamp, 1988). Funkenstein, 'Collective Memory,' sees the difference between a purely liturgical memory and a more dynamic, heuristic collective memory emerging in the historical consciousness. The latter, according to him, appears in the hidushim

(new insights) of rabbinic (halakhic) law-finding, as well as in literature – but he does not provide us with a conceptualized understanding of the difference between 'the liturgical incantations of a dynasty of tribal leaders' and 'the poetry of Homer or the Book of Judges.'

18. See Ellen S. Fine on post-Holocaust Jewish writers (especially the children of survivors) in 'The Absent Memory,' *Writing and the Holocaust*, ed. Berel Lang (New York: Holmes & Meier, 1988). Also Nadine Fresco, 'Remembering the Unknown,' *International Review of Psycho-Analysis*, 11 (1984): 417–27. For Henri Raczymow, see 'Spielberg's *Schindler's List*,' in this Reader.

19. Videotape adds to that dimension by allowing the recording of 'stylistic' and 'prosodic' features, such as gestures, visually accented pauses, etc. As in photography generally, more detail previously thought of as incidental or accidental is included.

20. Claude Lanzmann, in 'Le lieu et la parole,' *Cahiers du Cinéma* (1985), goes so far as to say that his film seeks an 'incarnation.' 'Le souvenir me fait horreur: le souvenir est faible. Le film est l'abolition de toute distance entre le passé et le présent' (374) (Recollection disgusts me: it is so weak. The film aims at the abolition of all distance between the past and the present).

21. I must leave aside, here, the more general issue of the revival, through history or art, of memory-places. For the sensibility, for example, that joins Wordsworth to Milton in understanding memory-place, see *Paradise Lost*, IX, 320–29. In terms of academic transmission the lieu de mémoire becomes a 'topos'; but the boundary between discourse, on the one hand, and poetry and even living performance, on the other, is quite porous, as was shown by E. R. Curtius's magisterial book *European Literature*, trans. William Trask (Princeton: NJ: Princeton University Press, 1953) on the way the classical tradition reaches modern European literature, and by the famous research of Parry and Lord on the formulaic compositional methods of Yugoslav bards. For Halbwachs's interesting treatment of 'Religious Space,' see *La mémoire collective*, 145–46 and 160–65. Monuments too are 'lieux de mémoire,' involving, like stories, real or legendary places.

22. For Hegel it would have needed the entire history of the world, together with an intellectual odyssey of millennia, before mind is mind, free of its subservience to sense perception, and able to retrieve all its memory-stages in the activity of thought. Meanwhile (i.e., in everyday rather than visionary temporality) interesting makeshift solutions are found. I have mentioned Alexander Kluge; Claude Chabrol's *L'oeil de Vichy* (1993) raises the spectator's consciousness of visual dependence by creating a film purely out of archival propaganda images, countered only by a dry historical commentary placing them in context. And Wilfried Schoeller has written: 'Every museum, every monument, every memorial site recalling the Nazi era should reserve a moment of discretion, should leave something open and perhaps even claim the status of ruin or artifact, so that the imagination can still be active toward something in it.'

23. Walcott, Nobel lecture, 'The Antilles: Fragments of Epic Memory,' in the *New Republic*, December 28, 1992: 27. However, in emphasizing the performative dimension we need to distinguish between an opportunistic recomposing of the

collective memory, motivated by identity politics, and the creative-heuristic use of its traditions in art. Such notions as Schiller's 'aesthetic education' may provide a beginning for theorizing that difference. The formalist's de-instrumentalizing emphasis on what is distinctively literary also responds to the need for a critical perspective.

Chapter 32

Tele-Suffering and Testimony

Why was the sight
To such a tender ball as the eye confined?
John Milton, *Samson Agonistes*

Television is a mechanism bringing us images from far away while making itself as invisible as possible. To be effective, it cannot relinquish this magical realism, this counterfeit transparency. Arguably, TV shares that characteristic with print or other media: To cite a common definition of imagination, they render what is absent, present. Yet TV's difference from a verbal or literary medium is quite clear. Novels, or histories in book form, respect the absence of those absent things more: Their distance is factored in, not only by deliberate devices that expose a (relatively) invisible author's rhetorical manipulations but also by the difference between the mental activities of viewing and reading. TV, to generalize, conveys the illusion not of making absent things present but present things more present (than they are or can be). Even when devoted to information rather than fiction, TV emits a hyperbolic form of visuality.

Of course, like literature, TV can become self-conscious and blow the cover of its magic by showing within its pictures a camera taking pictures or a monitor reflecting them. But it does so, usually, only to increase its authority as an objective mediation, or rather to make us think of it as a medium rather than a mediation. Showing the camera is showing what you shoot with: It is no longer a concealed instrument.

Those opposed to the modern world's iconomania can shun the cameras but would find it futile to smash them. Cameras are not icons but productive of them, and the network by which they send images is redundant rather than place-bound, so that any damage would be merely symbolic. In fact, although a religious rhetoric denouncing the lust of the eyes is still heard, many faiths have succumbed to the medium and adopted it for profitable evangelical propaganda.

I do not want to give the impression that TV is purely a mechanism. It is, indeed, the most powerful means we presently have for the production of images (if we consider the downloading of images on the Internet simply a further extension of TV's potency). Yet behind the mechanism there are its directors or agents, removed by the magic – the automatism – of photography.

The interaction of TV's image production and those who coordinate or manipulate it is a lively and self-complicating topic. Not without reason has journalism (now dominated by TV's influence on the general public) been called the Fourth Estate. Sociologists and others have begun a full-scale critique of the managers who set the conditions of reporting and viewing for the medium: They suspect a 'structural corruption' that makes it ineffective to try to modify by discursive means (such as this essay) what goes on.

There exist, no doubt, genial filmmakers who attempt to criticize the image through the image; and I will soon describe the Yale Video Archive's further attempt to do just that. But it is hard not to agree with French sociologist Pierre Bourdieu that anyone who goes on television will suffer a loss of autonomy and that the self-analysis occasionally nurtured by TV journalists only feeds their 'narcissistic complaisance.'

Now and then a murderous incident like the 1999 Columbine School massacre by two Colorado teenagers incites a flurry of speculation about the influence of the imagery video brings into the home. The television set or a computer with video games has become, as it were, a new hearth. But is it a controlled, domesticated fire we have brought into the castle of our privacy?

As parents, my generation tried to limit the viewing of TV primarily to prevent neglect of homework or a sidelining of intellectual and socializing influences. Increasingly, though, the problem does not involve only the proper allotment of leisure time. What is viewed comes into question, and the very modality of watching. For not only are violent films available on a 24–hour basis, but newscasting itself, on the same continuous basis, transmits daily pictures of violence, suffering, and destruction. One of the simplest axioms of psychoanalysis holds that hyper-arousal leads to trauma or inappropriate psychic defences: It seems clear enough that, while human responses are not uniform, and our psyches are quite resilient, this intensification has its impact. We live in an artificially enhanced visual culture, but it is premature to claim that we have visual culture.

The issue of TV's responsibility for social violence is a complicated one. The medium does not present a seamless web of images. Its hypnotism is far from unalloyed. The medium is more talky, in fact, than most cinematic composition: It adds layers of words to juxtaposed visual excerpts. In addition to the words and snatches of music that come with the relayed images, we have the anchorperson's or moderator's commentary. News, talk shows, music montages (MTV), and documentaries, therefore, may be the ultimate TV, rather than retailed Hollywood-type films. Moreover, while films usually hide the fact that they are episodic and present themselves as wholly new and startling (although playing on continuities bestowed by famous actors or character types), TV not only likes to serialize programs but allows arbitrary breaks for advertising that disturb our concentration without quite dehypnotizing it.

We take our eyes away from a book in order to think, or else to rest them, letting what has been read go deeper. In contrast, TV offers (also because of the ease of channel surfing) not real breaks or reflective pauses but one audiovisual representation after the other. Its 'flow,' in short, at once isolates certain sequences and distracts us from them. The reality effect of its imagery, therefore, is heightened and diminished at the same time. This is one reason why it is hard to generalize about the contagious effect of TV violence: It all depends on whether your inner reception is tuned to what tries to invade you and won't let go or, alternatively, to the interruptions – visual and verbal – that dissipate it.

One clear danger, however, should not be overlooked. Increasingly, as on-the-spot news reporting and other live broadcasts, especially the wilder kind of talk show ('My sister has two lovers') gain TV share, the reality effect of what is viewed verges on an unreality effect. The reason may be stated as follows. When reading fiction or seeing it in cinematic form, we adopt what S. T. Coleridge called a 'suspension of disbelief.' We know those multiple gory deaths in action movies are faked and that a considerable supply of ketchup is used. But what can keep addicted viewers, especially young ones, from a more fatal 'suspension,' which consists in looking at everything live as if it were a reality that could be manipulated? The unreality effect that turns what we actually see into electric phantoms is a new and insidious psychic defence.

Good fiction quietly posts many signs that imply 'No Way Through to Action.' It constructs reflective detours that convert reading into a many-levelled interpretive act and remind us we are dealing with simulacra. The problem with TV, however, is that, only a click away, and an intimate part of home, it becomes a treacherous servomechanism conspiring with a residual, delusory omnipotence of thoughts. While for most of us TV simply hard-copies the eye, making the 'tender ball' less vulnerable, for some it may produce a mental atmosphere that makes it appear as if the very place we live in also came from that box. 'Televised reality,' Norman Manea has written, 'becomes a self-devouring "proto-reality" without which the real world is not confirmed and therefore does not exist.'[1] The world is then no more and no less incredible than what confronts us in the news or ever-more horrific movies.

It is not that there must be a direct link between violent scenes depicted on TV or film and the brutal acts of teenagers; we surely know how confusing, precarious, and potentially catastrophic the passage from adolescence to maturity is, independent of a supposedly malignant TV effect. But there probably is a derealization of ordinary life that causes some youngsters to act out – like a game or drama whose roles they assume – their pain, disillusion, or mania. Animated gadgets rather than people inhabit a world of that kind, and it is easy to fall into the Manichean mind-set of 'them and us' or 'the good and the bad guys,' fostered also by increasingly formulaic and ferocious movies. Youthful idealization of certain role models often goes together with an underestimation or even scapegoating of a despised group.

Concerning this derealization, it is astonishing to reflect that only forty years ago, one of the most significant books about the cinema, Siegfried Kracauer's *Theory of Film*, bore the subtitle *The Redemption of Physical Reality*. It argued with great cogency that

> Film renders visible what we did not, or perhaps even could not, see before its advent. [Film] effectively assists us in discovering the material world with its psycho-physical correspondences. We literally redeem this world from its dormant state, its state of virtual nonexistence.[2]

Kracauer dealt with film as the fulfilment of the realistic effect of black-and-white photography. The cinema, he claimed, was animated by 'a desire to picture transient material life, life at its most ephemeral,' whether 'street crowds, involuntary gestures' or 'the ripple of the leaves stirred by the wind.'[3]

Compared to this view of the medium, what we see in movie houses today should be called *photoys*. They are ghostings of reality, not its redemption. What, for example, is being rendered – made visible – by *The Matrix*? There are, no doubt, some strong 'psycho-physical' sensations produced by this film's mastery of special effects: the way, for example, it carries the tendency of a body-piercing generation to an extreme by undermining the integrity of personal flesh. So, in addition to the doubling and out-of-body experiences intrinsic to its story line, near the beginning of the film there is a brilliant visual pun when the movie's reluctant hero is 'bugged' by a disgustingly alive mechanical insect inserted via the navel into his innards. This inverted parturition recalls Nietzsche's insight that all preconceptions arise in the entrails. It is as if we had to return there to see the world without prejudice.

Yet ordinary sense data enter this film only in the form of incongruous scenes: of a here-and-now that can no longer be securely confined to a single location. As Christian painters often surrounded earthly events with heavenly figures, doubling the locus of the action, so every significant adventure of the hero, however external or apparently objective, has its echo in an invasive internal change dramatized as physical agony or the labor pains of rebirth. Moreover, a devious topology leads to defamiliarized interiors that remain absurdly familiar. The contraption to which people are strapped before they undergo their psycho-physical journey is a conflated image of a dentist's chair, an electric chair, and how astronauts are buckled up before the launch. Similarly, although we traverse seedy if potentially mysterious passageways to get to the Oracle, when we meet her she is in an ordinary kitchen baking cookies. And, despite the importance to the film of mobile communication, at a crucial final moment the hero steps into the interior of an old-fashioned phone booth, a retro effect that recalls (affectionately enough, but hardly realistic) Superman's transfiguration. In a sense we never get outside – outside of the movie studio producing all these effects.

What kind of reality, then, are we shown? Interestingly enough, we are not as far from Kracauer's 'redemption' as might first appear. It is precisely a redemption of physical reality that is being aimed at – radically, comically, ingeniously, despairingly – by movies like these. The motif of redemption, in fact, governs *The Matrix's* plot: to find 'the One' who has the guts to free us from a world of appearances that limits or controls human perception and presumably keeps us from experiencing the *real* real world.

Yet in truth the movie offers only an engineered reality – an assemblage of phantasms, of illusionistic contraptions that seek to get under our skin yet rarely do so. In fact, in order to remain in the human, it relies on a few sentimental or fairy-tale episodes, such as a life-giving kiss. When Kracauer, then, writes that the cinema is uniquely equipped to 'redeem this world from its dormant state, its state of virtual non-existence,' he lays bare the ghostliness of existence revealed by cinematic photography's own counter-gnostic, technological quest romance. I continue to prefer poetry's economy of means, as in these (admittedly imploding) stanzas of Emily Dickinson:

> I heard, as if I had no Ear
> Until a Vital Word
> Came all the way from Life to me
> And then I knew I heard –
>
> I saw, as if my Eyes were on
> Another, till a Thing
> And now I know 'twas Light, because
> It fitted them, came in.
>
> I dwelt, as if Myself were out,
> My Body, but within
> Until a Might detected me
> And set my kernel in.[4]

It may have been my own reality hunger, as well as the duty of memory, that made me take part in a project to film Holocaust survivors. Founded in 1979 by a New Haven grassroots organization, the project was adopted by Yale, which created in 1981 the earliest Video Archive for Holocaust Testimonies. Working with the archive, I became more aware of the power and limits of film and video.

Our aim to record on video the stories of survivors and other witnesses proved more complex than we had assumed. The idea was to put people with direct knowledge of those grim events before the camera and let them speak with the least possible intervention. A series of authentic autobiographical accounts would emerge and contribute to the collective memory of a time passing away together with the eyewitness generation. That time would soon be available only through history books.

The project was instinctively right in seeking to extend the oral tradition by means of video testimony and in allowing the voices of witnesses to be heard directly in an embodied, audiovisual form. But we only gradually understood the communal implications of the enterprise and its potential impact on memory and the communicative environment.

Let me illustrate what we learned by discussing a number of practical issues that arose. How does a venture like this balance the seductive magic of photorealism – expressive of the wish to make the survivors and their experience more evidential – with an anxiety about intrusion and voyeurism? Should we not hold such an archive to be a sacred deposit and shield it, for a time at least, from the merely curious or prying? We turned to a law school professor who wrote an opinion quoting Justice Brandeis's 'Sunlight is the best disinfectant.' We obtained informed consent from each of the interviewed and made sure they understood that their testimony would be a public act of witness open to all who came to consult it in the university library. Moreover, visitors to the Yale Archive were asked to read a statement that laid out the reasons for the testimony project.

When I look back at the first two years of filming, I realize what made the issue of privacy more sensitive. The survivors who came to be interviewed were totally supportive; but others – a few historians as well as some survivors not yet interviewed – felt uncomfortable watching the tapes. What disturbed them was partly the emotional, intimate texture of these oral histories, but chiefly their video-visual aspect.

Indeed, among the almost two hundred testimonies initially recorded, I now see inspired but also, at times, irritating camera work. Wishing to project the act as well as narrative of witness, we often sought what one of the project's founders, adopting a legal term, called 'demeanor evidence.' The result was excessive camera movement. The supposedly 'imperturbable' camera (Kracauer's word) zoomed in and out, creating Bergmanesque close-ups. Eventually we advised that the camera should give up this expressive potential and remain fixed, except for enough motion to satisfy more naturally the viewers' eye.

Another decision also involved the visual sense. Should witnesses be recorded in a studio or at home? Our choice was at first forced on us rather than thought out, yet proved to be fortunate. There was so little funding that space provided free on the unoccupied floor of a building became a makeshift studio and more feasible than transporting equipment and interviewers from one home to the other. The makeshift studio was sparsely furnished: chairs as necessary, a backdrop curtain, and sometimes a plant. What we sacrificed was the kind of colorful, personal setting we would have found in the survivors's home, and which helps when videography has a film in mind; what we gained (this realization came later, and we stuck with our ascetic decision) was not only simplicity or starkness but a psychological advantage. The interviewees, in a sparse setting, entered their memories with less distraction, or, to put it differently, they could not divert their attention to this or that familiar object. There were also fewer disruptions – such as a child crying, a dog barking, a telephone ringing – to disconnect the flow of thought.

Another decision was for the camera to focus exclusively on the witness and not show the interviewers. In retrospect, I think we might have included at least an initial verification shot of the interviewers; but we were determined to keep the survivor at the center, visually as well as verbally. Despite TV's disdain for 'talking heads,' that is exactly what we aimed for. The survivor as talking head and embodied voice – a more sophisticated technique would merely distract viewers. We were not filmmakers, even potentially, but facilitators and preservers of archival documents in audiovisual form. In short, our technique, or lack of it, was homeopathic: It used television to cure television, to turn the medium against itself, limiting even while exploiting its visualizing power.

I suppose we did sacrifice by this effacement of the interviewers – heard and not seen, and trained to ask only enough questions to make the witnesses comfortable, to keep them remembering, and sometimes to clarify a statement – a certain amount of transparency. For interviewers have a special importance in this kind of oral history. They are positioned quite differently from investigative journalists. Yes, they do seek to elicit information, often of historical value. Yet basically their purpose is to release memories of what happened 'in the deep backward and abysm of time': not yesterday or a short time ago, but as far back as forty years when the project started in 1979, and sixty by today.

This act of recall cannot be accomplished without respecting the Holocaust's continuing impact on the life of the witnesses. Afterthoughts and associations often arise in the very moment of giving testimony; the past is not confined to the past. The best interviews result from a testimonial alliance between interviewer and interviewee; a trust relation forms, in which the search for facts does not displace everything else. Such an alliance, however, is a framing event that lies beyond the scope of the camera. It cannot be made transparent (in the sense of visually readable) but needs the sort of meditation author and psychiatrist Dori Laub and others who know the Yale project have given it. When I talk of the project's communal frame, a return of trust, a wounded trust, is involved. The interviewers – indeed, all persons associated with the project – form a provisional community and become representative of a larger community, one that does not turn away from but recognizes the historical catastrophe and the personal trauma undergone.

Memory, we have learned from Maurice Halbwachs, and again from Pierre Nora, always has a milieu. How do you photograph a memory, then, how do you give it visibility, when that milieu has been destroyed by Holocaust violence as well as the passage of time? But experiences do remain imprinted on the mind, set off by the very absence of what inhabited the original space. Our foreknowledge of mortality may even enhance what has vanished. The quiescent or subdued memory image endows photos with a physical aura. The effect is that of a still-life (even when the camera is in motion): A ghostly presence emerges, an unquiet spectral demand for reintegration that lends credence to Kracauer's film theory.

Holocaust videography, of course, to achieve a return of memory through photographed testimonial speech, can place the victims back in what is left of their milieu of suffering, as Claude Lanzmann often does in his film *Shoah*. It pictures, for example, a field or grove of trees, now quite innocent, and which defeats the camera-eye as in Michelangelo Antonioni's *Blow-Up*. Lanzmann even arranges a remarkable mise-en-scène by placing a barber, whose duty in the camps was removing the prisoners' hair, into an ordinary barber shop. However effective this device may be, we sense its artifice. It is best to resuscitate memories by simply raising the internal pressure with the assistance of non-aggressive interviewers.

Ideally, these interviewers become more than questioners: They comprise, to use Halbwachs's expression, a new 'affective community' that substitutes, however inadequately, for the original and tragically decimated milieu. But here an unresolved contradiction casts its shadow over the video testimony project in the dot-com era. Will the work of memory retrieval and its communitarian aspect withstand the 'imperturbable' camera, its cold, objectifying focus, and now, in addition, the impersonal market forces of electronic recall and dissemination?

I have suggested that survivor videography does build in some resistance by counteracting the glossy or ghostly unreality of seemingly realistic yet increasingly surrealistic TV programs. In part this is because the testimonial words do not fade out, replaced by a cinematic simulacrum of the events being described. Although the testimonies range over time and space, the camera's mobility, as well as its visual field, remains restricted to a person speaking in a particular place, at a particular time. While presenting testimonies in audiovisual format may add an expressive dimension, even that is not an essential feature – for the speaker's bearing and gestures could also distract from the story being told. What is essential is the mental space such minimal visuality ('I see a voice!') allows. Witnesses can 'see' better into, or listen more effectively to, themselves; and viewers too respond to that intimacy.

All our efforts at Yale were directed, then, to capturing the personal story; and to maximize the witnesses' autonomy during the taping process, we did not limit the time of the interview or impose any conditions whatsoever. Yet our decision in this regard was based less on sophisticated thinking about TV than on the fact that victims of the Shoah had been brutally deprived of precisely their personal autonomy. The camera, also, because it focussed on the face and gestures of the witnesses, was anything but cold: In fact, it 're-embodied' those who had been denied their free body image in the camps.

I am less sure, however, about the success we will have in taming post-production procedures. As distance learning becomes standard and machine-readable cataloguing takes over, archives of conscience like ours may not be able to resist being turned into megabytes of information, electronic warehouses of knowledge that marginalize the other values I have mentioned. This greed for more and more information, for positivities, which has already accumulated an extraordinary and melancholy record on the Holocaust, has not yielded appreciable ethical lessons. The heaping up of factual detail may even be an excuse to evade the issue of what can be learned. Yet it is not enough to say 'nothing' can be learned; that no lesson can stand up to the enormity of what happened. If only because such a position neglects the testimonial act as such, and the gulf that appears, in the aftermath of Auschwitz, between the possibility of testimony – which extends to visual and verbal representation generally – and Sarah Kofman's axiom: 'Speak one must, without having the power.'[5]

Having described the communal frame of memory retrieval and the potential impact of survivor videography on the medium, I am tempted to make a final and very broad generalization. It shifts the focus from the survivors to those who look at their testimony and ultimately to the quality of our gaze. 'What others suffer, we behold,' Terrence des Pres (a brilliant, literary-trained cultural observer) wrote of the modern condition – with reference, in particular, to the increased technical power of optical transmission.[6] We become, through the media, impotent involuntary spectators; it was so with the events in Bosnia, and then in Kosovo. It is no longer possible not to know. But the effects of this traumatic knowledge, this tele-suffering – Luc Boltanski, a French sociologist, has named it 'souffrance à distance' – are beginning to be felt.

One difficult effect is that of secondary traumatization, through a guilt, perhaps a shame, implanted by becoming aware of evil or simply of such suffering. We know more about identification with the aggressor than identification with the victim; a bond sometimes grows between persecuted and persecutor, between the kidnapping victim, for instance, and the abductor. Sympathetic identification with the victim, however, is taken for granted, so that strong side-effects have drawn less attention. In the humanities, where the subject of trauma has only begun to be recognized, we spend more energy criticizing psychoanalysis than dealing with what is fruitful in trauma theory.

That we learn through our own suffering is a cliché that targets abstract or book knowledge: the real issue is whether we can learn from the suffering of others without overidentifying. To overidentify with the victim may have consequences as grave as to identify with the aggressor. Indeed, I suspect there may be some convertibility in the form of a movement toward coldness or cruelty when it becomes too hard to take in something that so intensely wants to be forgotten or mastered. We fear not just the image of suffering itself but also the sense of powerlessness that accompanies it – the obsessive thoughts and a drift toward desensitization. Without empathy no art, especially no fiction; yet the management of empathy is not easily taught.

The Holocaust testimony project, an active if belated response, relays terrible stories, yet in a bearable way, most of the time. It, too, creates a bond, as I have already said. In the telling, the psychologist Judith Herman has remarked, the trauma story becomes a testimony; and in the hearing of it the listener, who as interviewer enables the telling, is a partner in an act of remembering forward that obliges us to receive rather than repress inhuman events.

So the worst returns to haunt later generations. But it also gives them a chance to work it through. That is still a crude way of putting it, however. We know from Primo Levi's *The Drowned and the Saved* that the 'ocean of pain' for the survivors rose instead of ebbed from year to year and that many among them were afflicted with a shame that could not be cleansed.[7] In fact, as these stories circulate, in the form of video testimonies, and generally as written memories or fictionalized accounts – as they gradually, and not always in a conscious manner, reach the public, we see the beginning of a rather astonishing phenomenon.

I have called it memory envy. An extreme case may be that of Binjamin Wilkomirski, whose *Fragments* was hailed as the most authentic depiction so far of a child survivor of the Holocaust.[8] Yet the chances are that Wilkomirski was brought up in Switzerland and never saw the inside of a concentration camp.[9] His identification, nevertheless, with survivor experiences is quite convincing. The author internalizes what he has heard and read, and it emerges as his own experience. Here the creative and the pathogenic are hard to tell apart. Some deep envy is at work, particularly in those who have no strong memories themselves – 'strong' also in the sense that the memories bestow social recognition. The pressure to own a distinctive identity, however painful, plays into this: better to recover false memories than none, or only weak ones.

An equally interesting though very different case is Harold Pinter's play *Ashes to Ashes* (1996). It depicts a woman, Rebecca, who is being interrogated by her husband about the sadistic practices of a former lover. Rebecca seems to have tolerated or been hypnotized by them. Perhaps she is still under their spell. The

Holocaust is never mentioned, but her mind, like Sylvia Plath's, lives in its penumbra – in a memory, perhaps a fantasy, dominated by male violence, the loss of babies and of the innocence they evoke. Her husband is unable to bring her back; his very questioning becomes another kind of violence. As in the setting for survivor testimony, the stage is bare of props and the only action is a (tormented) interview. It comes as a shock to hear Rebecca repeat, at the end and climax of the play, the words of a woman who had her baby taken away (I quote verbatim here but leave out the 'Echo,' which, in the play, repeats the last words of each phrase):

> They took us to the trains
> They were taking the babies away
> I took my baby and wrapped it in my shawl
> And I made it into a bundle
> And I held it under my left arm
> And I went through with my baby
> But the baby cried out
> And the man called me back
> And he said what do you have there
> He stretched out his hand for the bundle
> And I gave him the bundle
> And that's the last time I held the bundle
> And we arrived at this place
> And I met a woman I knew
> And she said what happened to your baby
> Where is your baby
> And I said what baby
> I don't have a baby
> I don't know of any baby[10]

The words were a shock because they reproduce with omissions and slight changes those of a survivor in a Yale testimony.[11] I read them first in a *New Yorker* review of Pinter's play after it was staged in America two years later. We glimpse here how diffusion occurs: how Holocaust memory influences affectively a wider public. For it is improbable that Pinter could have seen the Yale testimony in question. It is far more likely that he saw those words in a book by Lawrence Langer, who was the first to study the Yale archive in *Holocaust Testimonies: The Ruins of Memory* (1991). That book did not quote these particular words, but a later book by Langer, *Admitting the Holocaust* (1995), does – in a chapter, interestingly enough, on Cynthia Ozick's 'The Shawl.'

In Pinter the original memory-milieu of the survivor's words is elided. No one could guess that 'Echo' (whom I have omitted from the quotation) is, in a sense, a real person, namely Pinter, whose mind has played back, almost verbatim, a description of the trauma of deportation. We pick up clues about the Holocaust context earlier in the play, but this final monologue clinches the matter. Yet what is remarkable here is less context than resonance: The Holocaust has invaded Rebecca's (and the dramatist's) consciousness to such an extent that no further historical specificity is needed – indeed, to be more explicit might limit the power and pathos of this short play.

We have no technical term I know of to describe the playwright's symbolic method, although Aharon Appelfeld too, in some novels, and Norman Manea in short stories, allows the setting of the action to be at once recognizable and unspecific. (The kind of denial depicted in Albert Camus's *The Plague*, whose context certainly includes the wartime persecution of the Jews in France, is conventionally, but effectively, allegorical.) However unique the contextualizing event, Pinter wishes to make the woman's narrative express a general aspect of the human condition. One is left wondering how often this occurs in literature – how often we fail to identify the elided circumstance. Perhaps this is what Aristotle meant, when he said that poetry is more philosophical than history. In Greek tragedy, moreover, with its moments of highly condensed dialogue, the framing legend is so well known that it does not have to be emphasized. A powerful abstraction, or simplification, takes over. In this sense, and this sense only, the Holocaust is on the way to becoming a legendary event.

In Pinter's case we can trace how the historical referent almost elides itself. The very resonance of the event both broadens it and makes it vanish – a pattern like waves from a pebble thrown into water. Key phrases have migrated from a videotaped testimony to a scholarly book, to a popular play, to an influential magazine's review of the play. *Ashes to Ashes*, however, is an unusually conscious case of memory envy. Holocaust imagery has been adapted rather than appropriated, and Rebecca's passion narrative suggests a sympathetic rather than total identification. Her repetition of the survivor's account is a self-redeeming, if non-consoling, reenactment.

Two concerns remain. At what point does diffusion become commodification and banalize, rather than universalize, a new representational genre (the videotestimony), or Holocaust memory itself? Will everything end up, not even in a scholarly book, or as the climax to an enigmatic and moving play, but as a series of conventionalized iconic episodes variously packaged? A second concern, more distinctly ethical, is Pinter's use of this incident. Imagery from the historical Holocaust is made to fuse with a very private and precarious mental condition. Some might characterize this as exploitation. Yet it may be, I have suggested, an inevitable and even appropriate development. The pathos of the testimony moment loses its specific context precisely because it arouses a widespread anxiety – here concerning the loss of a child and the traumatic repression of that memory. What others suffer, we should suffer.

Try to suffer, that is. The entire problematic of how we can feel for others –

and continue to feel for them – surfaces here. The pressure to respond with empathy (not an unlimited resource) is enormous, and it produces what has been called compassion fatigue and even boredom. But it could also incite anger and hate: first, perhaps, turned inward as a form of self-disgust (and leading to depression should we deem ourselves insufficiently responsive), then turned outward as a sadistic or callous action, and completing in this manner a vicious cycle. This cycle is inevitable if we over-identify, in the very name of morality, with the victims, or do not respect the difference between their suffering and our own. As Primo Levi and Charlotte Delbo (a French poet and survivor) have observed, even the words that seem to describe that suffering become false tokens when it comes to the Shoah. 'Hunger' and 'tomorrow' do not mean in everyday language what they meant in the camps.

At this point, art and especially literature disclose their truest reason. Art expands the sympathetic imagination while teaching the limits of sympathy. Such teaching hopes to bring the cognitive and the emotional into alignment. There is no formula, however, for aesthetic education of this kind: It must start early and continue beyond the university, perhaps for a lifetime. It is rarely prescriptive, and, although it may schematize itself as a set of rules (as a poetics or a hermeneutics), the type of thinking involved seems to import a structural moment of indeterminacy that escapes the brain's binary or digital wiring. A sort of unframed perception becomes possible, a disorientation that is not to be confused with scepticism or nihilism. Even the painter who titles his picture 'Six Unintelligible Figures' holds it together and creates a focus for thought.

Because to think suffering is different from thinking about suffering, it is not the absence of meaning that disturbs Maurice Blanchot, for example, but its presence: More precisely, what disturbs him is the temptation to foreclose 'the writing of disaster' by assigning meaning too quickly. 'Danger that the disaster take on meaning rather than body.' 'Keep watch over absent meaning.' 'Try to think with grief.'[12] Visual literacy is even further behind in recognizing this challenge than literary study. While Kracauer's axiom that the cinema 'aims at transforming the agitated witness into a conscious observer'[13] recognizes how important a human resource film can be, it understates the moral problematic: the guilt or shame accompanying sight and the vicissitudes of empathy.

Today the dominance of the video-visual has become a fact of life as clear as other global influences. It has a bearing on both morality and mentality. However difficult it is to disenchant the medium of TV, we must approach it as more than a source for entertainment or information. Above all, 'useless violence' (a phrase coined by Primo Levi to describe Nazi brutality), when routinely transmitted by TV in fantasy form or real-time reportage, should lead to intense self-reflection. The hyper-reality of the image in contemporary modes of cultural production not only makes critical thinking more difficult but at once incites and nullifies a healthy illusion: that reality could be an object of desire rather than an aversion to overcome.

Notes

1. Norman Manea, 'Blasphemy and Carneval' in *World Policy Journal*, Spring 1996.
2. Siegfried Kracauer, *Theory of Film: The Redemption of Physical Reality* (New York: Oxford University Press, 1960), 300.
3. Kracauer, *Theory of Film*, ix. Kracauer quotes here a journalist commenting on Louis Lumière's films.
4. Emily Dickinson, 'I heard as if I had no ear.' Poem 996 in *The Poems of Emily Dickinson*, Variorum Edition, ed. R. W. Franklin (Cambridge and London: The Belknap Press of Harvard University Press, 1998). First published in 1945.
5. Sarah Kofman, *Paroles Suffoquées* (Paris: Galilée, 1997), 16.
6. Terrence des Pres, *Praises and Dispraises: Poetry and Politics, the 20th Century* (New York: Viking, 1988).
7. Primo Levi, *The Drowned and the Saved*, tr. Raymond Rosenthal (New York: Summit Books, 1988).
8. Binjamin Wilkomirski, *Fragments: Memories of a Wartime Childhood*, tr. Carol Brown Janeway (New York: Schocken Books, 1996).
9. The tentativeness of my phrasing reflects the fact that the present chapter was written before most of the disclosures were brought together and augmented in Stefan Maechler's *The Wilkomirski Affair: A Study in Biographical Truth*, tr. John E. Woods (New York: Schocken Books, 2001).
10. Harold Pinter, *Ashes to Ashes* (London: Faber and Faber, 1996). The American edition was published in 1997 by Grove Press.
11. See Bessie K., Holocaust Testimony (HVT 205), Fortunoff Video Archive for Holocaust Testimonies, Yale University.
12. Blanchot, *The Writing of the Disaster*, tr. Ann Smock (Lincoln: Nebraska University Press, 1986), 41, 42, 145.
13. Kracauer, *Theory of Film*.

Chapter 33

Poetics after the Holocaust

It is not frivolous to ask for a rethinking of poetics after the Shoah. Although Aristotle's treatise is but a series of notes, one senses in the importance it assigns to tragedy a shift of representational modes obscure in origin yet involving a different balance of human and divine, of human agency and a Dionysian sensibility. It is this shift Nietzsche reconstructs in *The Birth of Tragedy*. Are we living through another shift of this kind, and is it related to the Shoah?

These questions could be considered premature, and they require in any case a new Aristotle. I can but offer sketchy notes of my own. Concerning the continuing relevance of tragedy as a genre, Isaac Deutscher expresses his conviction in 'The Jewish Tragedy and the Historian' that the passing of time will not lessen our sense of having been confronted by 'a huge and ominous mystery of the degeneration of the human character,' one to 'forever baffle and terrify mankind.' Yet Deutscher allows that 'a modern Aeschylus and Sophocles' might cope with it, 'on a level different from that of historical interpretation and explanation.'[1]

The odds against this rebirth of tragedy are formidable, however, unless an older, pre-Enlightenment attitude returns. Deutscher, resolutely atheistic, won't look in that direction; he covers himself against the imputation of a return to myth or religion by choosing two of the greatest of ancient artists, who somehow transcend the issue of religious belief. Yet a host of questions remain. Did Aeschylus and Sophocles owe their ability to produce tragedies – so powerful that we continue to read and perform them two and a half millennia later – to their art or to their myths? Can we even distinguish between their art and their religious beliefs? Further, if we manage to isolate what enabled them to represent catastrophe, is their method transferable to the Holocaust era? In brief, is it a new or an older type of tragic art we are seeking?

We cannot wait on mystery to resolve mystery. Even should genius arise, it is unlikely to yield the secret of its art. Moreover, the relation of art to audience, which made those ancient tragedies effective public testimony – a contract, as it were, with the collective memory – that relation has changed. The religious matrix, which embedded the Greek tragedies and gave them exposure, no longer prevails. And for any emerging art I do not discern a contemporary audience strong or constant enough to maintain a similar relation. For by pluralizing the curriculum and opening the canon, we have intensified the problem of consensus. Should a great work arise it could not be transmitted without a religious or para-religious reception.

Though I respect Deutscher and the way he has put the question, he is more radical about the limits of historical discourse than he is about art. The issue of whether tragedy can be an adequate interpretation of the events of the Shoah, or whether, to go beyond Deutscher, 'the worst returns to laughter' in some new, as yet unrealized, form closer to the grotesque[2] – these are by no means idle questions, yet they do not go to the heart of the matter. Beyond genre, I wish to suggest, the very rule of probability has suffered a shock, a rule that cannot be relinquished without giving up art's crucial link to verisimilitude: to a mimetic and narratable dimension.

What threatens the mimetic is, to put it bluntly, the infinity of evil glimpsed by our generation, perhaps beyond other generations. Though the Shoah proved finite, and the thousand-year Reich lasted but a dozen years, a limit was dissolved and an abyss reopened. How do we find a bridge over that abyss, a representation more firm than Apollonian form or neoclassical rules? Is there, for example, a 'plausible narrative representation' of that evil, in art or historical emplotment?[3] Should we turn to the leprous itch, the epidemic of figures, the disorderly excess of signifier over signified in Shakespeare's carnivalesque drama of errors, or to the opposite strictness of Greek hemistichs in dialogue, verging on the disclosure of unspeakable truth? Or is the mad, postmodern perspectivism of Syberberg the best we can do?

The trouble with infinity of any kind is that it dwarfs response and disables human agency. We feel compelled to demonize it, to divest the monster of human aspect and motivation, and create the stereotype of an evil empire. We romance ourselves into a psychically secure and ideologically upright posture, simplifying the representation of evil and the entire issue of mimesis. What is required, however, is a world that still has enough plausibility to represent what was almost destroyed: the trustworthiness of appearances, a consistency between the 'human form divine' and what goes on within it, shielded from the eye.

The hurt inflicted on appearances – on a (harmonious) correspondence between outer and inner – is so acute that it leads to a stutter in the representational faculties. That stutter in verbal form is akin to poetry like Paul Celan's, and in visual form it distorts or even divorces features that once were kind. When Wordsworth as a young man hears for the first time the 'voice of Woman utter blasphemy' (that is, a prostitute cursing), his reaction describes an ominous breach in the idea of the human, one that opens the possibility of deceptive look-alikes, and, since the human form is not radically affected, drives a wedge between outward appearance and inner reality. It is as if the baffled eyes, unable to read the soul from a physical surface, were forced to invent an anti-race or dark double:

I shuddered, for a barrier seemed at once
Thrown in, that from humanity divorced
Humanity, splitting the race of man
In twain, yet leaving the same outward form.
(1850 *Prelude*, 7.388–391)

This troubled, ambivalent moment could breed either a deep compassion or a demonization of the other race. If the sense of evil gets the upper hand, scapegoating becomes inevitable as a way of marking the evil, of making its hidden presence biological and photogenic. The correspondence between inside and outside is saved, but a group is ritually excluded from the human community to bear the stigma of what is evil and markedly inhuman.

The demonization of the Jews by the Nazis was a representation of this kind. Nazi propaganda seized on Wagner's characterization of the Jew as a 'plastic demon of decadence.' The demon is a shape-shifter, cold, vicious, unchangeable inside, yet on the outside able to mimic (assimilate) any national character or cultured facade. An entire subindustry invaded German education to aid a differentiation that would not have been necessary if Jews had the gross features which caricatured them. The notorious children's book *The Poisonous Mushroom* was based on this same need to identify the 'plastic demon' or deceptive look-alike. In short, the designation 'Jew' allowed a demonizing solution to the dilemma of distinguishing appearance from reality when an overpowering sense of the indistinguishable presence of evil rendered useless ordinary skills of telling good from evil, or what was trustworthy from what was treacherous. The SS became 'blade runners,' and turned into the very androids from which they thought they were saving mankind.

If I stress visual representations it is because they environ us, and because the critic's search must be to separate kitsch from an authentic imagination of evil in the wake of the Shoah. The proliferation in science fiction of a manichean war against uncanny robotic enemies that no longer wear uniforms but have the metamorphic power to infiltrate as look-alikes may express in new coloration a very ancient fear. The challenge to visual representation, as I have said, does not come in the first place from lack of technique – we are still in the cinematic age and rarely talk about the limits of film – but comes principally from a doubt about the ethics of a certain kind of mimesis, or super-mimesis. Just as the historical imagination often substitutes the violence of detail for the violence of violence, so the visual and cinematic imagination tends to save mimesis from a purely 'negative presentation' by grotesquing what it touches, or surfeiting our need for clear and distinct identities. Hesiod said that fear of the gods was alleviated by giving them distinct shapes; so too our fear of the evil in human beings is alleviated by marking them like Cain, though not for their protection. Lyotard and also Wallace Stevens would like to believe that art makes things a little harder to see, yet the present, popular exploitation of Holocaust themes suggests instead a repetition of the imaginative and ethical error that defamed the victims.

Notes

1. See Isaac Deutscher, 'The Jewish Tragedy and the Historian,' in *The Non-Jewish Jew and Other Essays*, ed. Tamara Deutscher (London: Oxford University Press, 1968).
2. See Terrence des Pres, 'Holocaust Laughter?' in *Writing and the Holocaust*, ed. Berel Lang (New York: Holmes and Meier, 1988).
3. The question in this form is most sharply posed by Saul Friedlander, especially in 'Historical Writing and the Holocaust' in *Writing and the Holocaust*, and 'The "Final Solution": Unease in Interpretation,' *History and Memory*, 1, no. 2 (Fall/Winter 1989).

Part VI

Coda

Chapter 34

Passion and Literary Engagement

Some time ago, I used as an epigraph for 'The Interpreter: A Self-Analysis' a quote from I. A. Richards's *Principles of Literary Criticism* of 1924: 'Critics have as yet hardly begun to ask themselves what they are doing or under what conditions they work.' I was protesting, in the semi-vigor of approaching middle-age, the status of criticism as a purely secondary, uncreative activity, with oppressive criteria of decorum that produced 'essays, called articles, merchandized in the depressed market place of academic periodicals, [conforming] strictly to the cool element of scholarly prose. They are sober, literate, literal, pointed. Leave behind all fantasy, you who read these pages.'[1]

My wish was to free up academic criticism, to acknowledge the passion that informs critical writing, to transgress in a formal way genteel boundaries, to merge critical and creative without abandoning the institutional and pedagogical discipline of literary commentary. Yet I did not want to return to a confusion of teaching with preaching, nor to 'live off authors like a pimp or cannibalize them with affection.' My aim was to unsettle a hierarchy in which imaginative literature was the act, and criticism the shadow. Ideally, both were to reflect a 'Heavenly City of Mutual Discourse.'

Even today I am not embarrassed by an outburst I called, after Freud, a 'Self-Analysis.' In the meantime, though, what literary critics do, and the conditions under which they work, have been affected by the increasing acceptance of two related perspectives. They are a questioning of the 'impartial spectator' theory of knowledge, mandating the hygienic detachment of scientific observer from object of observation,[2] and an understanding of Richards's 'conditions' in socioeconomic and political terms.[3]

'The social elements in intellectual phenomena,' Karl Mannheim declared, 'had not become visible to the thinkers of an individualistic epoch.' His sociology of knowledge exposes the 'social-situational roots of thought.' Politically oriented critique tears off disguises, unmasking 'unconscious motives which bind the group existence to its cultural aspirations and its theoretical arguments.'[4]

While currents, then, in both sociology and psychoanalysis have troubled the ideal of dispassionate scholarship, the repetitive emphasis on the subject position of authors, in terms that often devalue the subject, fosters a new simplification.

Do we need all those tedious demystifications by instant social thinkers who know where they are coming from, and pursue aesthetic or idealistic flaws in less enlightened writers? What of the individual's paradigm-breaking potential, the offending or inspiring excess of a sustained personal intervention?[5]

That the word 'passion' has entered the debate shows there is unfinished business. A certain vehemence, characteristic of passion, marks intellectual or ideological commitments, and compels public recognition. Yet the question of the relation between individual and collective remains unanswered. For Mannheim, the vehemence of intellectual strife is always at root political. (This itself seems to be a 'situated' reflection, if not a product, of life in the ill-fated Weimar Republic.) While Philip Fisher too describes how the vehemence of passion leads to discovery – the turmoil unlocks original trains of feeling and thought[6] – he sees, like Adam Smith, that 'social reciprocity' risks being upset not only by divisive political convictions but also by the dynamic of rage, fear, grief, wonder, and all such strongly emotional states characterized by self-absorption.[7]

'Genius,' another reactivated concept, suggests, like 'passion,' a creativity overriding for good or bad the determining conditions. A new astrology beams from the sky and mingles profanely, as in Harold Bloom's Genius book, with the kabbalistic sefirot.[8] In verbal works of art, of course, the creative bruises itself on a limit: that of language, which should achieve, in Erich Auerbach's phrase, a 'literary taking hold of reality' (die literarische Erfassung des Wirklichen).[9] Commentary, though shaped by different conventions than texts classified as literature,[10] also strives for a confirmation of the expressive power – whether mimetic or visionary – of words. Auerbach practices stylistics with style and demonstrates that philology does not have to be a dismal science.

Today, when an anthropology of everyday life[11] encourages memoirs, witness accounts, and a variety of first-person writings, a lively and inventive diction animates (sometimes hyper-animates) critical prose. The narcissism, however, often accompanying this animation confirms the truth of Oscar Wilde's dictum that literary criticism is the only civilized form of autobiography, because, Wilde said, it does not dwell on accidents but delineates 'passions of the soul.' The essay form, so important to major critics from the eighteenth century on, has never lost its role.[12] Criticism is not the place where language goes to die.

'Literary engagement' can be understood in two ways: as an engagement with literature, or an extra-literary engagement motivated by a passion for literature. I am risking not only the venial sin of tautology but also the cardinal sin of aesthetic ideology by asserting that the passion of the litterateur is for literature itself, and is comparable to that of the artist. This passion, which I cannot name further because it does not appear in any moral or psychological scheme, nevertheless suggests at least an additional direction of inquiry.

It points to love in Shelley's definition as a going out of our nature and an identification with a beauty not our own. Such outflow of the sympathetic imagination is rarely a voluntary affair, however. For it is provoked not only by the beautiful but also by strange and even aversive modes of being – those with an admixture of the dangerous, excessive, even repellent, and closer therefore to what aesthetics has characterized as sublime rather than beautiful. Compassion of this kind is itself a passion, as coercive as in Coetzee's novels where it engenders something between a sparagmos and a transfiguration of personal identity. Although we have turned the meaning of 'passion' toward activism, the word's history intimates also another aspect, almost the opposite.[13]

Consider the passion narrative, a perennial genre that focuses on persecution, torture, servitude, unjustly inflicted pain, cruel and inhuman punishment, devastating loss, catastrophic illness, madness, outrageous fortune. *Prometheus Bound*, the Book of Job, and Christ's Passion are exemplary. Exemplary also – and here I make a salto mortale into the modern period – are those amazing short stories by Freud and Breuer called *Studies in Hysteria*, whose literary implications Adam Phillips has teased out so eloquently.[14]

The contents of the passion narrative can also be less dire, as in Wordsworth's lyric: 'Strange fits of passion I have known.' This uneasy poem records an instance from the psychopathology of everyday life. It depicts a trance state that is a defence against suffering, specifically the anguish of mortality. Remove love's trance and you find death. In certain writers, like Rimbaud and Bruno Schulz, art itself becomes the passion story, pursuing a fickle, intimate, overwhelming mood of transcendent adventure, 'this shiver of fear, this sense of things beyond name whose first taste on the tip of the tongue exceeds all our capacity for wonder.'[15]

Maurice Blanchot links such amazement, with terror in it, to the shock of otherness itself. Writing becomes in response a 'passion anonyme,' an infinitely patient watch over pseudo-stabilizations of personal or group identity, including fascist types of egomania. Even after the Second World War, when philosophies of engagement gain a new political life, many writers continue to experience their work as a disengagement (Maurice Blanchot says 'désoeuvrement') instead of as a form of empowerment or cultural accrual ('oeuvre'). For what can guarantee that the writer's redirection of his pursuit is not premature, self-serving, or the effect of powerful propaganda forces? It is noteworthy, given Heidegger's political engagement only a few years after his inaugural lecture of 1929 as professor of philosophy at the University of Heidelberg, that the first sentences of that inaugural pose a version of the question we too are considering: what does it mean that scholarship ('Wissenschaft') has become our passion ('Leidenschaft')?

Blanchot, himself an angry young journalist of the extreme Right in the 1930s, changes course suddenly sometime after 1938. He allows for a personal and provisional swerve ('détournement') from writing to political action, but maintains the view that what happens between the writer and words – words as complex and insubordinate as fictional characters – is not an exercise in mastery. He insists that there is at best a deep sort of receptiveness, a 'non-pouvoir' close to what Keats may have meant by 'negative capability,' and which is described by certain religious traditions, not only the mystics, as a purgative emptying out of the self. Blanchot discovers in the process of writing a self without identity except through the other who 'escapes my power . . .'[16]

One would expect the passion narrative to disappear in a predominantly secular era. Far from it: such narratives have migrated to civic religion. Contemporary fiction and non-fiction are replete with them. (Mel Gibson's notorious *The Passion of the Christ* is an attempt to take back and outdo that displacement or expropriation.) This re-emergence of the passion narrative in modern civil society marks a shift. It signifies more than a resurgent focus on the victim, and more than a secular displacement of a religious form of imagination. The testimony paradigm, for example, so prevalent today, is a perplexed and often courageous grappling with injustice and defeat. Experiences dangerous even to try and recall become memorable by modifying their character in the process of being articulated. They enter a narrative searching for the victim's identity, or new identity, despite inherent trauma, disaggregation and disintegration.

The publication of suffering, however, increases the clash of activism and quietism. Tension between them leads to a moral impasse. However difficult it is to credit a wise passiveness, or the affliction that prefers to remain obscure, 'passion' retains its meaning of a suffering that drives and shapes human destiny. It is not the opposite of action but approaches the mysterious process whereby suffering, and even the meditation on suffering, exert a redemptive effect.

Even when the passion is love-passion it takes us beyond the pleasure principle. Hedonism cannot last when the so-called 'Enlightenment project' continues to be defeated by the persistence of aggressive drives and a politically inflicted misery. What remains is a forlorn hope: that bearing witness to suffering, by finding or fashioning testimonial narratives, will prevent untruth and injustice taking hold.

At present, the passion narrative has links to the everyday: to journalism, confession, talk-show, as well as exotic travelogue and ethnography. The narrator, moreover, may feel more like a witness, even a secret sharer who no longer occupies an emotionally safe position. Despite the growth of a society of the spectacle it is not always possible to maintain a pose of detachment. As in Levi-Strauss's *Tristes Tropiques*, or with more explicit pathos in Ruth Behar, a 'vulnerable observer' emerges. 'Anthropology,' writes Behar, '. . . is the most fascinating, bizarre, disturbing and necessary witnessing left to us . . .'[17]

Disturbing, in good part, because the basic enigma, one not yet brought entirely into focus, is passion's collective or 'cultural force.'[18] To employ the word 'creative' casually, as I did earlier in this talk, is to stress only the positive side of that force. The darker side, however, includes culture wars, increasingly global and inflamed by identity politics. They exhibit sinister modes of societal unification, including genocidal violence.

Perhaps, if passion leads to perception, having the courage to face what happened is an antidote to suffering. But should art try and 'compose' the victimized, lay their spectres to rest in the well-wrought urn of essay, poem, or novel? From the perspective also of the literary 'consumer,' the phenomenon Luc Boltanski has named 'souffrance à distance' – tele-páthy through the vicarious experience of books, TV, cinema or internet – elicits nervous, self-questioning narratives troubled by their striving for 'conceptual profit.'[19]

Clifford Geertz has remarked: 'We lack the language to articulate what takes place when we are in fact at work. There seems to be a genre missing.' Ruth Behar writes that her book, *The Vulnerable Observer*, is looking for that genre.[20] Literary criticism too, when seen in its interventionist as well as reflective aspect, in its relation to writing as disorienting as well as descriptive, could be a modality of that missing genre.

Notes

1. *The Fate of Reading and Other Essays* (Chicago: Chicago University Press, 1976), 3–19.
2. For how this issue of spectatorial detachment enters the more immediately influential public space of legal decision, see Dahlia Lithwick's op-ed, 'Personal Truths and Legal Fictions,' *New York Times*, December 17, 2002, A35. She posits 'two legal versions of what happened in the courtroom when Justice Clarence Thomas made a clearly personal history motivated remark on the issue of whether cross burning was protected speech: 'The first is that what Justice Thomas did is unforgivable; by highjacking the argument into the murk of personal experience, he did violence to the disinterested, lucid distance necessary for justice to be achieved. The second version is that he recognized, and his colleagues chose to respect, that some questions cannot be answered dispassionately, especially ones as fraught as, "Can symbols constitute threats?" In this version, personal narrative in appellate decision-making is ignored only at the peril of true justice.'
3. Derrida, in explicating Emmanuel Levinas, suggests a link between these two factors: 'The ancient clandestine friendship between light and power, the ancient complicity between theoretical objectivity and technico-political possession.' *Writing and Difference* (Chicago: Chicago University Press, 1978), 81.

4. Karl Mannheim, *Ideology and Utopia: An Introduction to the Sociology of Knowledge* (New York: Harcourt, Brace and Company, 1936), 35. The original core of the German book goes back to 1929.

5. 'A single man, a solitary man, sets himself face to face with an entire millennium and transforms that historical world.' E. R. Curtius, from his remarkable encomium on 'Dante and the Middle Ages,' in *European Literature and the Latin Middle Ages*, tr. Willard R. Trask (London: Routledge & Kegan Paul, 1953), 379.

6. Philip Fisher, *The Vehement Passions* (Princeton: Princeton University Press, 2002).

7. Adam Smith, *The Theory of Moral Sentiments* (1759), Sections I and II.

8. Even the notion of genius loci, while evoking geopolitical perspectives, respects native creative power that puts spirit of place on the map through personalities that embody it.

9. *Mimesis: The Representation of Reality in Western Literature* (Princeton: Princeton University Press, 1953). Original German edition, 1946. Auerbach's formulation is reminiscent of Dilthey's general methodological and humanistic principle summarized by Mannheim as 'das verstehende Erfassen des "ursprünglichen Lebenszusammenhanges".' See Mannheim, *Ideology and Utopia*, 40.

10. At least in the tradition descending in the West from Aristotle. Aggadic midrash, although exclusively centered on a sacred text and its legomena, is as much literature as it is literary commentary; while the linguistic imagination of the Kabbala creates from the very letters of the Hebrew Bible extraordinary mystical adventures, figures and spheres.

11. See, e.g., Richard G. Fox, ed. *Recapturing Anthropology: Working in the Present* (Santa Fe: School of American Research Press, 1991). The 'present,' for Fox, is an overdetermined word: it denotes not only a slice of time, like the present just past, but also the present of writing. The latter meaning connects it with the question of the 'work' we do and the conditions we work in: 'The notion of "working" no longer comes down simply to choosing a methodology and an analytic scheme; the action of "writing" is understood as much more than the mechanical process of "putting pen to paper" . . . These new understandings of "work" and "writing" have put anthropology's claims to authority under siege' (p. 2). For an astute analysis of sociological trends up to about 1970 see Edward Shils, *The Calling of Sociology and Other Essays: On the Pursuit of Learning* (Chicago: University of Chicago Press, 1980).

12. A passionate and well-informed, personal book on the essay is G. Douglas Atkins, *Estranging the Familiar: Toward a Revitalized Critical Writing* (Athens, GA: University of Georgia Press, 1992).

13. For the best short account of how the Christian Fathers modified the Stoic idea of passion, and how the union of passion and suffering enters the poetry of profane love, see Erich Auerbach on the 'gloria passionis' in *Literatursprache und Publikum in der lateinischen Spätantike und im Mittelalter* (Bern: Francke Verlag, 1958), 54–63. On the active turn in the semantic field of passio/passion 'Leiden/Leidenschaft'), see also Auerbach's 'Passio als Leidenschaft,' in *Gesammelte Aufsätze zur Romanischen Philologie* (Bern: Francke Verlag, 1967), 161–75.

14. Adam Phillips was one of the speakers in the 2002 Modern Language Association's Presidential Forum sessions, at which this paper was given.

15. From the opening of his story 'The Book,' in *Sanatorium under the Sign of the Hourglass*, quoted in Jersy Ficowski, *Regions of the Great Heresy: Bruno Schultz, a Biographical Portrait* (New York: Norton, 2002), 26–27. I have altered slightly the translation given there in the light of Celina Wieniewska's: see *Sanatorium under the Sign of the Hourglass* (London: Picador, 1980), 1.

16. *L'écriture du désastre* (Paris: Gallimard, 1980), 29–39. That theological thinking plays a part is suggested by reflections like the following: 'Retirement et non développement. Tel serait l'art, à la manière du Dieu d'Isaac Louria qui ne crée qu'en s'excluant.' (27) I leave aside the question of both Blanchot's and Emmanuel Levinas's pacifism: the pacifism that arose after World War 1, and contributed to a reluctance to engage Hitler, could not survive World War 2. The moral problem in the political sphere, then, is how to move toward a new ethic of non-violence.

17. Ruth Behar, *The Vulnerable Observer: Anthropology That Breaks Your Heart* (Boston: Beacon Press, 1996), 5.

18. The 'cultural force of emotions' is the subject of Renato Rosaldo, *Culture and Truth: The Remaking of Social Analysis* (Boston: Beacon Press, 1989). One of his chapters is 'After Objectivism.' Let me offer just two examples that illustrate the contemporary passion narrative in its reflective-modern (mediated by a secondary witness) form. One is J. M. Coetzee's *The Lives of Animals* (Princeton: Princeton University Press, 1999), in which the South African novelist uses a fictional lecture-within-a-formal-lecture format (the occasion was the annual Tanner lectures on Human Values at Princeton) in order to sensitize an academic audience toward its ethical indifference concerning animals. The other is Patricia Yaeger's 'Consuming Trauma; or, The Pleasures of Merely Circulating,' in *Journal x*, Vol. 1, # 2. Spring 1997, 225–51, which not only responds critically to the highly emotional issue of another researcher's account of lynchings and the possibility of finding meaning to black suicides in Mississippi jails but explicitly reflects on 'liberal academics' who 'reproduce for themselves and their students stories of trauma, structural violence, systematic injustice, slaughter, inequality.' 'We are obsessed,' she writes, 'with stories that must be passed on, that must not be passed over,' and cites 'the danger of commodification and the pleasures of academic melancholy' in 'those exquisite acts of mourning that create a conceptual profit.' Op. cit. 228.

19. Pat Yaeger's phrase, see above note 18. For Luc Boltanski, see his *Distant Suffering: Morality, Media, and Politics*, tr. Graham Burchell (Cambridge, UK: Cambridge University Press, 1999).

20. Behar, 9, referring to Geertz's *After the Fact: Two Countries, Four Decades, One Anthropologist* (Cambridge, MA: Harvard University Press, 1995), 44.

Index